SYSTEM
OF
CHRISTIAN ETHICS
BY
ADOLPH VON HARLESS

Published by Just and Sinner 2023 (2nd Edition)

Though the original text is in the public domain, regarding this updated edition, no part may be reproduced, stored, or transmitted in any form or by any means, electronic, mechanical, photocopying, recording, scanning, or otherwise without written permission from the publisher. Inquiries may be sent to Contact@justandsinner.org

Just and Sinner

www.JSPublishing.org

Ithaca, NY 14850

ISBN: 9780692248362

Original Publishing Info:

SYSTEM
OF
CHRISTIAN ETHICS
BY
DR. G. CHR. ADOLPH VON HARLESS
Translated from the German of the Sixth Enlarged Edition

BY THE
LATE REV. A. W. MORRISON;
AND REVISED BY THE
REV. WILLIAM FINDLAY, M.A.,
LARKHALL

EDINBURGH:
T. & T. CLARK, 38, GEORGE STREET
LONDON: HAMILTON AND CO. DUBLIN: JOHN ROBERTSON AND CO.
MDCCCLXVIII

CLARK'S
FOREIGN
THEOLOGICAL LIBRARY
FOURTH SERIES
VOL. XIX

Contents

NOTE 9
PREFACE TO THE FIRST EDITION 10
PREFACE TO THE SIXTH EDITION 13
INTRODUCTION 17

PART FIRST

THE BLESSING OF SALVATION 33

FIRST SECTION

THE LIFE OF MAN AND ITS RULES OF CONDUCT BEFORE THE MANIFESTATION OF CHRIST IN THE FLESH 34

CHAPTER I

THE NATURAL STATE OF HUMAN LIFE 35

CHAPTER II

THE POSITIVE LAW 128

SECOND SECTION

THE GOOD TIDINGS OF THE NEW COVENANT 171

PART SECOND

THE POSSESSION OF SALVATION 226

FIRST SECTION

THE ENTRANCE OF THE BLESSING OF SALVATION INTO THE SPIRITUAL LIFE OF THE INDIVIDUAL 227

SECOND SECTION

THE SPIRITUAL STRUGGLE OF THE INDIVIDUAL FOR THE POSSESSION OF SALVATION 276

THIRD SECTION

PERSONAL QUALIFICATION FOR PRESERVING THE POSSESSION OF SALVATION 358

PART THIRD

THE PRESERVATION OF SALVATION 390

NOTE

THE following Translation was left in a somewhat imperfect state by the late lamented Mr. Morrison. It has been subjected throughout to careful revision by Mr. Findlay, who is also solely responsible for the translation of the Prefaces, the Table of Contents, and the whole of § 29 (pp. 273–294). In order to compress the work within the necessary limits, a number of detailed quotations (principally from the Fathers and classical authors) have been omitted, but the references have been given.

October, 1868.

PREFACE TO THE FIRST EDITION

It is only with diffidence that I give publicity to the present attempt. This feeling would indeed be natural under all circumstances, in the treatment of a subject where one is exposed more immediately than elsewhere to the danger of falsely freeing or falsely binding Christian consciences. It is not, however, this consideration by which I feel myself embarrassed. I hope for the grace of the Lord, whom I serve in my church, and who has bestowed upon me His word and faith in the same, that He will bless this faith to me, at least so far as to preserve me from the teaching of errors which might become a snare to the souls redeemed by Him. It is not, however, to the contents, but rather to the form of that which I have attempted to give, that my anxiety relates.

And this anxiety is of a twofold kind. In the first place, it refers to the plan of the whole treatise. In science generally, but in theology from quite peculiar grounds, it appears to me a matter of doubtful propriety when a department of knowledge which is a common possession has not also a certain common form of treatment, so that one immediately perceives from the style of discussion whether what is new is meant merely to attempt a better establishment of an old knowledge of the truth. Where this mode of treatment is unnecessarily departed from, there arises not only the danger of ministering, even if involuntarily, to that craving after novelty which loves not what is true, but only what is new; but one also cuts asunder deliberately the threads of connection which bind to one another the different stages of culture and of knowledge, and whereby the possibility and ease of coming to an understanding free from mistake, as well as the consciousness of a common possession, is secured. And of what importance the latter circumstance is, one might readily become aware, if the misfortune should go on increasing in growing measure, that in matters of universal Christian knowledge every theologian should speak his own peculiar language. It must therefore in my case awaken suspicion, whether I am in the right in deviating in essential points from the mode of treatment which has become predominant in Protestant theology. It will thus perhaps surprise many to find, in a system of Christian Ethics, no trace at all of a so-called doctrine of duties (*Pflichtenlehre*). It ought, nevertheless, to be a matter of satisfaction to me, if I were conscious in all my alterations of being as much in the right as in this. Only I must be allowed, for the right of alteration in these and other cases, to point to the development of the book itself, instead of an explanation of this right in the Preface.

But for the clear and sufficient understanding of the nature and the design of a treatise, in which it is wished that these should be drawn from the treatise itself, a sketch which is to serve for lectures presents difficulties hard to be overcome. Much must be left over for oral explanation, if the book is not to take the place of the lectures themselves: the reader of the book, however, will then in many places feel the need of learning more than is to be found in the book itself. True, indeed, to meet the necessities of the reader, I have attempted to give the notes on the paragraphs more copiously than was my original design, and as much as possible in continuous connected development. It is, however, possible, that one may think too much has been given, another too little; or that, to express it more accurately, the corresponding proportion of explanation has not really been hit upon. In reference to these explanations, I must only make this additional remark, that the historical development of Ethics—the literature and all connected with it—has not been considered for this reason, because I intend, if God will, afterwards to give in a second volume a history of the development of Christian Ethics. Moreover, the printing in full of the separate Scripture testimonies, and that in the original text, will be approved of by everyone who approves of basing a system of Christian knowledge on the Scripture word, and who knows of what importance it is, even for the reading of such a book, but still more for lectures upon it, if one has immediately before his eyes the relation of the divine word to the exposition of the knowledge derived from it.

The second anxiety which I must still acknowledge, relates to the individual form of setting forth the subject. For the conviction presses itself upon me, that with us Germans, even those of the best tendency, systematic theology suffers from a certain affected superiority and abstract formulating of the thought, which stand in a not unsuspicious contrast with the divine depth and the fisherman-like simplicity of its apostolic origin. But in giving help here, I am conscious of a certain weakness. It is the tendency of the time, it is what remains of likings and occupations formerly cherished under which I labor, and in overcoming which I have not yet always quite succeeded in the scientific explanation of Christian knowledge.

With these confessions, I should like partly to prevent unjust censure, partly to secure a friendly discussion and correction of those points in which perhaps this attempt, against my will, is not destined to conduce to a fruitful study of Christian Ethics. In sentiment I joyfully attach myself to the earlier ethical writings of Schwartz—to the more recent ones of Beck and Sartorius. May that which is my own in the form of the scientific treatment serve the true interests of our Protestant theology! May God grant that the church of Jesus Christ may be profited by that which was written at least with the endeavor to serve her, and her alone!

MUGGENDORF, Jubilee Sunday, *17th April 1842.*

PREFACE TO THE SIXTH EDITION

TWO-AND-TWENTY years ago there appeared for the first time the Treatise which I now again, in a remodeled form, lay before the public. Once only, in the year 1849, was I able to bestow upon it a not very important improvement and enlargement. A tolerably changeful course of life brought me tasks which very often lay far from my inmost inclination. Thus, there was wanting to me that inward concentration of mind, as well as that outward leisure, which was indispensable for fundamentally transforming this attempt of earlier years. I cannot say even now, that I went about the remodeling under circumstances which appear to me desirable for such tasks. Whoever has been an academic teacher, will best realize what fulness of intellectual stimulus is irrecoverably and irreparably lost with the sacrifice of such a position. And a nature like mine, which has no peculiar satisfaction in book-writing, does not, by the mere amount of time which one perhaps finds for this purpose, gain the living impulse which the life of intellectual interchange, the perception of existing mental necessities, and the attempt at satisfying them in personal mutual intercourse, give and secure in ways unsought, and therefore only so much the more powerful. Yet I will not attribute to the unfavorable character of the circumstances anything in this remodeling which falls to be reckoned as personal defect. It appeared to me only a duty to regard neither the one nor the other, in order finally and once for all to improve in a more fundamental way a book which has found acceptance beyond its desert.

The outward framework I have left essentially unchanged. I have only endeavored to indicate better and more clearly than before, what I intended in laying down this framework, and what course of thought floated before my mind. Even in the form of the continuous exposition, I preferred thinking, as before, especially of students of theology as my readers. A complete change of this standpoint, which I contemplated in the year 1853, appeared to me, on more mature consideration, not advisable on external and internal grounds. On the other hand, I everywhere filled up those gaps which are wont involuntarily to remain when one, as was originally the case here, writes a book as a sketch for academic lectures, and thus having regard to further oral supplementary matter. Those parts in which the book has become essentially different, the reader who is inclined will find out for himself, if he should compare the present edition with the fourth of 1849, or the fifth of 1853 (second impression, 1860). Only in reference to one part of the book do I allow myself a short remark. When, *e.g.*, at that point where the relations of Christian conscience to the national and political community are discussed (see especially § 54), I appeal in many cases to J. Stahl, this is done for a twofold reason. In the first place, because in questions of law I do not wish to give to myself the arrogant appearance of self-derived authority, and also because much of that which appears to be correct I could not better say than Stahl has said it; but, in the second place, also because many circles of readers will not unwillingly hear from the mouth of Stahl, that which, if said by me, they might probably take very much amiss.

I owe very much stimulus to a friend quite unknown to me, whose comprehensive written observations on my Ethics, bearing the date of 17th May 1857, reached me from Paris. Even in points where I could not coincide with them, these observations have afforded me more instruction than all that I have seen elsewhere on my treatise. Everywhere subtle, clear, striking, these remarks give so much evidence of loving and thoroughly intelligent investigation, that I had a lively wish, for the sake of the author, that he might have published them as an example and specimen of a good review, instead of my being permitted, alone and in quietness, to enjoy his work and to make use of it for myself. That I have done the latter, my unknown friend will everywhere perceive, where I have not on other grounds changed the whole of my former plan. Where, however, in spite of the opposite considerations urged, I have adhered to my former opinion, he will have the opportunity now at least of reading more clearly, perhaps also more correctly, why I believed myself compelled to adhere to it. Whether and where these lines may meet my unknown friend, I know not. But if they meet his eye, I would be very much obliged to him if, for me at least, he would abandon his concealment, and permit me to know the name of one to whose censure I am more indebted than to the praise and censure of others.

Among the papers left behind by a celebrated German theologian, there is said to have been found a distich on another theologian, whose commendation closes with the censure:

"Yet—of system no trace."

In a certain sense, I should wish that this censure applied to my book also in this its altered shape. For I have a quarrel of my own with the theological "systems." It is with them often as with the systems of the investigators of nature. In nature as in revelation, God has His real system, which investigators may well follow after, but always with the modest suspicion whether also their formal system corresponds with that system. But if, perchance, they have beforehand adjusted for themselves their system like a pair of spectacles, through which they look at nature or revelation, the matter stands in very evil plight. For in that case the systems are in many respects only Procrustes' beds, in which men lay Jesus, and the form of His being which is incorporated in the word. For my part, I will be content if this treatise serves as a small index to those treasures of wisdom and knowledge which are presented by the Scripture testimony respecting Christ,—treasures whose life-giving power becomes here below a matter of experience only in first-fruits, and which, in representation corresponding to our knowledge, find only a feeble and very incomplete expression of what they really are, and what of their fulness they present for penetrating our whole being. I have now also, and still more frequently than before, gladly allowed my own exposition to be interrupted by quoting testimonies of Luther, because it was given to this man, as to few, to speak as a complete Christian and a complete man, and not as a school theologian.

I might close with those words which stand at the beginning of the Preface to the edition of 1849. But I prefer to be silent here respecting the present, and to "lift up mine eyes unto the hills, from whence cometh my help." For the tribulations of time will turn out to be preparers of the way for His advent. What remains unchangeable, is the throne of His kingdom and the scepter of His word. All man's work, on the other hand, will pass through the fire of that day. So also will this treatise. May all that is untenable therein be burnt up; but may that happen to me which stands written in 1 Cor. 3:15.

MUNICH, 5th February 1864.

INTRODUCTION

§ 1

WITH regard to the peculiarity of the development of his life, and to the aim of that life, the consciousness of the Christian rests on the certainty of that word of Christ, "I am the way, the truth, and the life: no man cometh unto the Father but by me" (John 14:6) (1). And in this consciousness the cognizance of the Christian is twofold: respecting Christ as the way, and respecting his own coming as a Christian by that way. And if he has a just appreciation of both, he perceives that the substance of his consciousness of the one side of this relation is not comprised in that of the other; and that the exposition of the manner and the extent in which Christ is the way, is and must be different from that whose object is to show how and to what extent here below we come to the Father by this way. For, first, we learn here on earth what is meant by coming to the Father through Christ, only in its beginning. And again, no light at all is thrown on the way by the understanding how we are to come; but our knowledge of the way gives us light as to our coming, not only as to its truth and vitality, but also as to its form and limitation on earth. Thirdly, Christ becomes what He is, not from the fact of our coming to Him; but He is the way, the truth, and the life, even should no one enter on that way. What Christ is to the world, He is in Himself; in other words, by His own objective relation to the Father and to the world, as well in its order as its disorder (2). Hence, that which Christ is to the world—that is to say, what the will of God in Christ is towards the world in its order as well as disorder, and the manner in which God by Christ desires to draw, and does draw, the world unto Himself (3)—must be in itself recognizable and capable of explanation. In that case, the immediate aim of the exposition resolves itself into a setting forth of the divine will, of the divine acts, and of the divine means whereby, in the midst of the order and disorder of the world, Christ is the way by which truth and life again return to the world, and, in fact, not only to the world of the present, but also to that of the future. But if the design is to show how and in what way the coming of men—that is, the Christian pilgrimage on earth—shapes itself amidst the order and disorder of the world, the immediate object of the exposition resolves itself into a statement of those human circumstances, struggles, and victories in which on earth the truth and the life in Christ take shape and form in Christians, both inwardly and outwardly (4). The connection between these two branches of knowledge and their exposition is as certain, as their difference in form and character is clear and justifiable. The first of them gives an answer to the question, What do you think of Christ? The second to the question, What do you think of the true character of a Christian upon earth? And both questions cannot be satisfied by one and the same answer. The first question and its answer touch immediately and primarily upon the knowledge of God and of His objective will in Christ towards the world; the second refers immediately and primarily to the Christian's knowledge of self, and that of the subjective condition of a Christian in this world (5). Each is supplemental to the other, but not identical therewith. The first is the business of that branch of knowledge which is called Dogmatics; while the consideration of the second is the task which we have set before ourselves.

(1) All human life reveals itself as one in process of becoming, which, starting from a certain fundamental life-principle which determines the man, is ever striving after a certain fixed purpose of life. The same holds good of that which is called the Christian life on earth. On the threshold of the investigation and setting forth of this life, it behooves us to find some universal and formal expression for that which constitutes the specific peculiarity of the Christian life-

consciousness from its commencement onwards, but not a material and exhaustive definition of it; for this must be reserved for a later part of our treatise. The universal characteristic of Christian consciousness must embrace two objects: that vital objective power which determines the Christian, and his own movement towards the highest aim of his life. Both these are comprehended in the declaration of Christ (John 14:6): as well the power that determines the life of the Christian, as our aim in that life which is to be striven after and rendered possible of attainment by its means. The Christian life-consciousness is the consciousness of a communion with God objectively secured through Christ, and to be subjectively sought after and obtained by us through Him. The declaration of its full reality is found in that other word of Christ: "I in them, and You (O Father) in me, that they may be made perfect in one" (John 17:23). Here, however, we are only standing on the threshold. And the saying of Christ above quoted, respecting that which, according to His will, is to regulate the consciousness of His own people, is at the same time fitted to make clear the nature and limits of the task we have undertaken in this treatise, and to distinguish it from others which are related to it.

(2) The idea of a Redeemer of the world is not formed from the relation of Christ to the world and to the human race, but from that of the Son to the Father, of Christ to God. The correlative of the Redeemer of the world is not the redeemed world, but the world which lies altogether in wickedness (1 John 5:19); it is not man united to God, but man hostile to God (Rom. 5:10). It is in contrast to this state of things that Christ is the Redeemer of the world (John 4:42): this He *is*, and does not *become* so only through a subsequent alteration of this state of things. The full conception of a Redeemer, and the full position of a Redeemer, is antecedent to the acts of redemption, and is their real ground not only in time, but before the foundation of the world. In the "beloved Son," by whom all things were made (John 1:3), all that is made is the object of redeeming love (1 John 4:10). In respect of Christ, the very reverse takes place of

that which we are accustomed to conceive and speak of in reference to men, when we call them in a relative sense redeemers in reference to this or that error, or this or that evil. These are and became what they are only by virtue of a work accomplished by them for mankind. Christ is what He is, irrespective even of this His peculiar efficacy. Christ is a Reconciler, whether we suffer ourselves to be reconciled through Him or not (Θεὸς ἦν ἐν Χριστῷ κόσμον καταλλάσσων ἑαυτῷ ... δεόμεθα ὑπὲρ Χριστοῦ, καταλλάγητε τῷ Θεῷ, 2 Cor. 5:19, 20). He is the Light of the world (John 8:12), whether the world remain in darkness or not. He is the propitiation for the world, inasmuch as He bears the sin of the world (John 1:29; comp. 1 John 2:2). The propitiation purposed in, and the redemption of the world which was accomplished by, Christ (John 3:17, 12:47), does not become actual merely by the fact that the whole world should be thereby actually saved. This indeed will only then be understood when we lay equally firm hold of this, that in the redemption of the world by Christ, the heaviest condemnation of the world is at the same time included (John 3:19, comp. 5:22).

(3) Comp. John 6:44 with 12:32.

(4) It is that which in the apostolic epistles is called "the race set before us" (Heb. 12:1); the running in the lists (1 Cor. 9:24); the following after if that we may apprehend that for which also we are apprehended of Christ Jesus (Phil. 3:12). It is the conflicts (1 Tim. 6:12) in the midst of which here below Christ is formed in us (Gal. 4:19), but in such a way that the end, the prize which the heavenly calling of God in Christ Jesus sets before us, still stands before us (Phil. 3:14); and our impression with respect to ourselves remains the same humble one as that of the Apostle Paul: "not as though I had already attained, either were already perfect" (Phil. 3:12). It is the full extent of that which, according to the testimony of Scripture, may and ought to become the actual religious and moral experience of the Christian in that domain of the life of the creature which belongs to this side of the grave; but also in its full limitation to this domain, and to the form of subjective

experience brought about and enlightened by the word of God. In reference to what should form the object of Christian ethics, I can only assent in all essential respects to what C. F. Jäger has stated in his *Fundamental Ideas of Christian Morality* (Stuttg. 1856), *Enleit.* § 4.

(5) At the basis of the inquiry lies the practical need of that self-examination which the Apostle Paul requires from Christians (2 Cor. 13:5).

§ 2

In the consciousness of the Christian, that the aim (l) set before us in Christ can only be attained in a manner of coming which corresponds both to the way and the aim, there exists a formal resemblance to that which is acknowledged by general human experience in the domain of created life. This formal resemblance consists in the notion of the normal movement of life, whose nature man is in a position to recognize in all that is living and created. What is normal depends on this, that the movement or development of the life proceeds in constant uniformity with the principle from which that life has originated, and in which, at the same time, lies always the final destination which forms the object of this development. Wherever this development is neither instinct nor an artificial direction, but the free course of rational beings, striving after an aim established for the whole of their life relations, and common to all, then this course of conduct is designated by the name of *morality*. This, which distinguishes morality from the isolated forms of life conceivable as mere habit, *i.e.* from custom, the free intelligent harmonizing of human life, in its essence as well as in its phenomena, with a supreme aim, regulating and embracing this life,—this general notion of morality is presupposed by Christianity, as the object of universal human recognition. And if Christian science may and will, for the theoretic exposition of the normal movement of Christian life, choose a name of universal validity, she has one of essential significancy for the nature of the thing when she speaks of Christian *ethics* (2).

(1) Let one compare the real and not abstract notion, τέλος, *aim = end*, in the declaration of Scripture concerning ζωὴ αἰώνιος as τὸ τέλος, Rom. 6:22, and concerning τὸ τέλος τῆς πίστεως, ὃ κομιζόμεθα, 1 Pet. 1:9. How the philosophical notion of an aim was regarded as an essential element of ethics, is shown by the history of ethics. Comp., for example, what Diogenes Laertius says on the division of the ethics of the later Stoics, ὁ περὶ τέλους τόπος, Diog. Laer. vii. 84, p. 415, ed. Meibom.

(2) Custom (ἦθος, *mos*) appeared to the human mind only gradually, not only as a contrast of form to formlessness, *i.e.* to *roughness*, but also as the standard which was destined to attain or had attained to universal ascendency under the point of view of the good. Comp. the connection of ἦθος and ἔθος, *soleo*, and ἔθω; and the equivalent designation of one and the same thing by ἦθος and τρόπος, as well as the connection between *mos* and *modus*; and similar modes of expression, as τρόπων ἤθη καὶ ἔθη in Plato (*Leg.* xii. p. 968 D). Furthermore, weigh the expressions χρηστὰ ἤθη, καλοὶ τρόποι, *boni mores*; finally, the connection of our word morality (*Sittlichkeit*) with the Greek καλοκἀγαθία, or with the Latin *honestas, sanctitas*. Hence the perplexity of Quintilian: "ἦθος, cujus nomine, ut ego quidem sentio, caret sermo Romanus, mores appellantur, atque inde pars quoque illa philosophiæ ἠθική, moralis, est dicta. Sed ipsam rei naturam spectanti mihi non tam mores significari videntur, quam *morum quædam proprietas*" (*Instit.* vi. 2). How closely, nevertheless, even in the Latin language, the notion of that which is "morally sanctioned," has become bound up with the word *mos*, may be seen from the proofs given in Dœderlein's *Synon.* Pt. v. p. 75. And not less so in German by the term *Sitte*, came to be understood the notion of an objectively established rule; compare *e.g.* the rendering commonly occurring in Luther's Bible of טַעַם, חֹק, חֻקָּה, עֵד, by this word. In its various meanings, this word embraces as much

that which is established by the determination of nature, as by free action and exercise, and applies not less to dispositions, customs, habits, and morality, than to right and arts or acquired skill (comp. Graff, *Althochd. Sprachschatz*, Bd. vi. S. 157 ff). The Scriptures of the New Testament use the word ἦθος only under the presumption of its general recognition as the word of a heathen poet, 1 Cor. 15:33. Even where there is a closer reference to the import of the word, the same assumption manifests itself, the same omission of any further explanation; comp. Phil. 4:8.

That which forms the most general preliminary supposition, without which morality is inconceivable, is the consciousness of an *aim*. In this consciousness, the mere natural impulse, the servile and absolutely dependent, is set aside by the recognition of the fact, that all dependence and determinativeness, so far from excluding personal freedom of action, arrives at its true acknowledgment only by the free fulfilment of the act. For the position that I exist for a definite end, presupposes an indissoluble unity between the two things: the dependence of my being, and the unconstrained movement of my actions as the solution of the problem of my existence. I hereby recognize not merely that I am what I am, but that I am to become something in which I am myself to take part. We assert this when we speak of an *aim* in life. Of course, morality as being the free accomplishment of an act, not to speak of true morality, is not established with the perception of such an end; though, indeed, a moral view of life as opposed, if not absolutely to one which is immoral, at least to that which is void of all morality, regarding it as a servile course of nature. See the striking discussions of Trendelenburg (*Log. Untersuchungen*, Bd. ii. S. 86 ff.; and his *Geschichte der Kategorienlehre*, S. 369–71).

§ 3

In addition to the formal resemblance before mentioned, there is also a material one, wherein that which is called

Christian moral consciousness touches upon the universal ethical consciousness of man. This rests as well on the identity of those faculties and endowments naturally belonging to man which are intended for the attainment of the aim of his life, as on the immutability of those moral conditions, those ordinances both of life and of the world, bestowed upon the creature and historically developed (1). To this concrete world of moral life-forces, that which proceeds from Christ holds the place neither of supplementary completion (quantitative difference) nor of antagonistic abrogation (qualitative diversity) (2). That power which proceeds from the Spirit of Christ is rather, on the one hand, the divine Yea and Amen, by which the moral consciousness of man is confirmed; and on the other, the full presence and efficacy in the hearts of His own (3), of Him who, as He is the Creator, so also is He the Reconciler and Sanctifier of the life of every creature. In this last relation, the Christian moral consciousness becomes at the same time a purification with respect to the different errors of humanity touching the nature of the highest aim of our life, its supreme guiding rule and normal development. But for this very reason, the various historically developed views and expositions of man's moral consciousness, as they have been formed independently of a vital connection with Christ, have no prescriptive significance for Christian ethics (4). The ethical relations in substance remain the same; but the spirit of renewal which pervades them will have itself represented from itself alone, and cannot, any more than new wine, be contained in old vessels, nor will it serve better than a piece of new cloth to mend an old garment. If in this manner we keep steadily in view both the resemblance and the difference, we shall find that Christian life as well as Christian ethics remain what they are. In both cases we have to do, not with a new creation of human life in its essential ethical relations, but rather with a representation of the natural condition of human life pervaded and enlightened by a renewing spiritual principle (5).

(1) It is certain that not only does the word of Christ appear to the natural man in the light of a new doctrine (Mark 1:27; comp. Acts 17:19), but that Christ Himself speaks of a new commandment (John 13:34), and calls His testament a new one (Matt. 26:28, etc.; comp. also Heb. 9:15), and that His apostles designate the Christian as a new creature (2 Cor. 5:17; Gal. 6:15), as a new man (Eph. 2:15, 4:24), and the Christian life as a new spiritual existence (Rom. 6:4, 7:6). But, irrespective of the relation between the old and the new divine covenant, this term "new" indicates only the opposition to an inveterate tendency,—a conversion in respect to the principle which dominates over man, independent of and antecedent to his fellowship with Christ; not a new creation in contrast with his original creation, not a new nature which was to abrogate the old *nature* of man, nor a new order of things which was to stand in opposition to that old natural order which was from the beginning appointed and willed by God. Christ, as the life-giving spirit, is called, in virtue of this very connection with the original nature of man, "the last Adam" (1 Cor. 15:45). And when the whole heart is full of the love of God, it thus becomes a new heart; but the heart itself—the soul—the disposition—which is full of this love, is not a new-created one, but the old and inborn one, just as certainly as the body and the members are so, which the new man devotes to God's service (Rom. 6:13, 12:1). What is new forms no contradiction to the old nature ("omnis natura in quantum natura est, bona est," says Augustine, *Enchirid.* ch. xiii.), but, if one may so speak, to the nature which has become hostile to nature. Were it not so, the apostle could neither reject that which is opposed to God as opposed to nature (Rom. 1:26), nor could he assert that nature teaches us what is due to God and what is becoming (1 Cor. 11:14), or that men do by nature the things contained in the law (Rom. 2:14), And the world which lies in wickedness is not so oppressed by disorder as to have become entirely void and destitute of God's regulating power. But rather, as it was in the very beginning placed in an order by God, by virtue of which it was both intended and able to guide us to God (Acts 17:26, 27;

Rom. 1:20), so also no sin of man was powerful enough entirely to destroy in the world that element by virtue of which it may, in so far as it is God's creation (1 Tim. 4:4), be recognized as good, and made use of by man. Nay, even those regulations and ordinances which one might, from misunderstanding of the divine will, be disposed to reject as being the work of man (1 Pet. 2:13), and not of God's appointment, New Testament Scripture shows us to have been permitted by the divine will, and teaches us to respect them even where the spirit that permeated their human framers was not the spirit of Christ (comp. with 1 Pet. 2:13 the passage in Rom. 13:1). So little is the spirit of Christ the destroyer, but rather the preserver and renewer, of the ancient and original order of nature.

(2) The vulgar rationalism occupies itself in such views of a supplementary completion, no matter whether it seeks to "augment" the natural moral consciousness by Christ, or to "uphold and throw light upon" it, or, in quite an inverse order, seeks to rectify by the light of nature that which is given to us by Christ. The other extreme is the mystical or pietistic view, which regards nature only as something opposed to God—as a disturbing and impeding element. Even Spener has greatly erred in this respect. See his treatise entitled *Nature and Grace; or, the difference between the works which spring from our natural faculty; and those which proceed from the gracious operations of the Holy Spirit*, etc., Frankf. 1687, and *Theolog. Meditats.* ii. 88, etc. etc., although in the last he also warns us against running into extremes in the application; comp., for example, iv. 567.

(3) Συνίετε τί τὸ θέλημα τοῦ Κυρίου, Eph. 5:17. The Christian consciousness of the will of the Lord is, however, not only a knowledge of a will of the Lord, whose injunctions impend over us, but one which lives in us, and which has bestowed on us its promises, in order that by these we might become partakers of the divine nature (2 Pet. 1:4). The communion with Christ works in us a pneumatic divine natural-ground of human life, which radically precedes all moral activity, as Peter further describes it in the same passage (ver. 5 ff.). But this is the

mystery of the same God, who has created all things (Eph. 3:9), and in truth by Christ and for Him (Col. 1:16), in such a way that the will of the Creator attains its perfect realization in the will of the Redeemer, and in the deed of redemption.

(4) By this introduction of entirely foreign forms as principles of ethical views of life, Christian ethics have at a very early period, especially from the time of the Alexandrian fathers onwards, been injured in a very perceptible degree. And yet even at the present day this wrong tendency is regarded as a genuine outflow of Christian spirit. In the *Wanderings of a Contemporary in the Domain of Ethics*, by Anton Rée, Hamburg 1857, 8, we have the production of one who stands on the ground of pantheistic humanism, and who has come to a rupture, as he alleges, with revelation and Christianity. What he asserts of the Christian view is partly so framed as if he had derived his sketches from the pattern of Platonizing and Aristotelian definitions of ethics to be found in Stobæus (*Ecl. mor.* ii. 7). They find or invent a caricature of Christianity, and pompously proclaim their quarrel with this as a quarrel with Christianity itself. They have no idea that Christianity is only humanism in its highest potency. "Ad hoc Deus noster factus est pater noster, ut quemadmodum ipse dignatus est consors fieri nostræ *humanitatis,* sic nos mereamar consortes fieri suæ *divinitatis,*" says Anselm.

(5) The old stands to the new life in Christ in the relation of elementary principles (στοιχεῖα, Gal. 4:3). The new is the fulfilment of these (πλήρωμα, Gal. 4:3; comp. Matt. 5:17). Where the fulfilment has come, there the beginnings, as such, cease. We cannot remain stationary at these beginnings (ἀπεθάνετε σὺν Χριστῷ ἀπὸ τῶν στοιχείων τοῦ κόσμου, Col. 2:20). On the other hand, these elements are not abrogated on their fulfilment, but matured in their perfection. What Christ says of the law of the old covenant—that He has not come to destroy the law, but to fulfil it (Matt. 5:17)—applies equally to that law whose work and efficacy, according to Paul, stands written in the hearts of the heathen (Rom. 2:14, 15). To the whole domain of moral life before Christ the new in Christ is

related, not as the abrogation, but as the fulfilment of it. From this relation alone we can perfectly understand how that aim which has been revealed to us in Christ corresponds to a longing desire (ἀποκαραδοκία, Rom. 8:19) of the whole creation. For the same reason, the formal conception of a supreme moral aim in life, of virtue and the like, comes not first to light in the world with Christ. They are all already, in their elementary state, in existence there, and are presupposed as existent. But the objective and subjective principle of their actual realization comes only with Christ into the world. What the words mean, "if there be any virtue, if there be any praise" (Phil. 4:8), is presupposed as what is universally self-understood. But when it is said that virtue is an offering which has its root in the power of faith (ἐπιχορηγήσατε ἐν τῇ πίστει ὑμῶν τὴν ἀρετήν, 2 Pet. 1:5), this can be understood only by him who knows the life-giving energy of Him whom faith apprehends (2 Pet. 1:3). In this sense also the expression holds good here, that what is old has passed away, and become new (2 Cor. 5:17).

§ 4

The manner in which that spiritual principle of renewal which proceeds from Christ pervades and ennobles the natural state of human life, finds on earth relatively its most complete expression only in the inner consciousness of the Christian (1). But it is impossible for us to obtain a true objective understanding thereof from the mere analysis of individual Christian experiences and conditions. For in such are found all those subjective limitations, not only as they occur in the individual and historical development of the life of the individual, but as they are involved in the different measure of the gifts of nature and of grace (2). The object of ethics is not an exposition of the Christian in his individual capacity (that would be the task of biography), but it has to do with that quality of the distinctively Christian ethical personality which remains the same in the midst of the most diversified individual forms. And this is not an abstract normal man or normal Christian, but it is that unvarying center which remains unchanged amidst the manifold differences of individuals,— the Ego, in which the God-man Christ lives (3). In this sense, the task of ethics is an anthropological one.

Man, however, is no isolated, solitary being. He is what he is in connection with the life of his species, which is carried on by those moral vital forces which operate in the order of nature and the world, and which at the same time modify the aim of human life. These are related to the central point, Christ in me, as concentric circles. This, however, is that very normal relation, as it was first restored by Christ in the Christian. Man would make the central point that which only appertained to the circumference; and this forms the tragedy of the world's history, which reappears in every human being. That which man gains in Christ the Deliverer, he will for this reason perfectly understand only so far as he comprehends the deliverance going on in his own person, not only in its personal, but also in its cosmical and world-historical significancy. For man is not a self-concentrated Ego, but the center of this world and its history. The concern of the Christian is the recognition not only of his own individual redemption, but of the redemption of the world, as his supreme personal good, and its possession and preservation as the highest aim of his life (4).

Hence, in order to arrive at a right understanding of this, we must first become acquainted with the natural state of human life and existence, as well as with those rules of life laid down independent of and before the manifestation of Christ, in their relation to the highest good of life given to us in our communion with Christ. In this way we obtain the preliminary conditions and preliminary steps of man's moral knowledge, in their innate relation to their fulfilment in the knowledge of Christ and communion with Him as the highest, nay, the only good which bringeth salvation. The next point is the knowledge of the internal process in which the communion with Christ realizes itself as a personal taking possession of the blessing of salvation, and the manner in which, from this point of possession, the personal capacity attains its knowledge of, and fitness for, the solution of the task of life. The third point concerns the understanding of the practical exercise of this capacity on the part of Christians for the purpose of preserving this possession of salvation, and of carrying out the object of the Christian life; and, in truth, this practical exercise in the unity of its essence as well as in all the manifold departments of its manifestation according to the relations of the Christian, to God, to himself, to his neighbor on earth, and to the divinely instituted forms of human society upon earth. The first point of the exposition deals with the knowledge of the objective principle given to us in Christ; the second, with that of the subjective principle of a Christian moral life as it has become operative in man. The third has respect to the knowledge of the internal connection of those manifestations and activities of the Christian life which flow from this principle in those relations of man's life upon earth which have been bestowed on him by nature, and which form part of his history. If this practical energy of life is called by the teleological name of "the keeping of salvation," it is so named for this reason, because the Christian looks upon all these present forms of his life-activity upon earth neither as a self-aim, nor as the perfect shape of an end of life already reached, but as the means for the attainment of an end which lies beyond the sphere of his earthly existence, and is present to him here only in its fundamental elements. And with respect to the principle of Christian life and Christian ethics, in its reality it is just Christ Himself who has taken possession of me; and for ethics the only question is to find an expression of the consciousness conformable to experience of the way in which I know myself regulated by Christ as the principle of my moral life, and in what form of my inner life I have Him as such. If I limit the expression for the relation in which Christ stands to me and to all men, to the person of Christ Himself, then I know and call Him our Savior, and that inner life in which I possess Him takes the shape of my healing and my salvation. If I connect as to form the exposition of Christian ethics with the form of the universal moral consciousness, which strove after the knowledge and notion of the good and the supreme Good, then do the terms "the blessing of salvation" (*Heilsgut*) and "the possession of salvation," as the objective and subjective principles of Christian life, express with reference to this universal consciousness at once the unity and the difference of Christian ethics. For the Christian finds not within himself the principle of a sound life, but in an objective power which brings him restoration. The beginning of this life he wins not by his own struggles after this good, but he obtains it as a gift of grace to be possessed, into whose fulness of life he enters (5).

(1) Ὁ ἔσω ἡμῶν ἄνθρωπος, 2 Cor. 4:16; ὁ κρυπτὸς τῆς καρδίας ἄνθρωπως 1 Pet. 3:4; τὸ πνεῦμα ζωὴ διὰ δικαιοσύνην, Rom. 8:10, and similar passages.

(2) The individual Christian element serves only for the understanding of the different members of the one whole, not for the understanding of the actual membership in the body of Christ. Compare, in reference to the first, Rom. 12:3, 4 ff., Eph. 4:7, 16.

(3) In all individual diversity of gifts, the permanent element, the true Christian characteristic, is, ζῶ δέ, οὐκέτι ἐγώ, ζῇ δὲ ἐν ἐμοὶ Χριστός, Gal. 2:20.

(4) The cardinal position of Christ is pointed out in the decree of God, ἀνακεφαλαιώσασθαι τὰ πάντα ἐν τῷ Χριστῷ, τὰ ἐν τοῖς οὐρανοῖς καὶ τὰ ἐπὶ τῆς γῆς, Eph. 1:10. To what extent this has its fulfilment at the end of time, does not properly belong to the experience of the Christian consciousness in this life. But, since everything that is future in the Christian has its fundamental beginning already here below, the limitation to the merely individual and personal moral wants of the Christian is not to be thought of without detriment to his moral relation to Christ.

(5) The knowledge of realities is, in my estimation, of greater importance than the needs of a formal logical system. We are willing to concede that it is possible perhaps to find a more scientific and satisfactory statement of the Christian

moral consciousness than the above scheme in its outline shows. But one thing is all-important to me. Luther says, "Seek yourself only in Christ, and not in yourself; so will you find yourself in Him for eternity." If this saying has its deepest import for Christian practice, it must also have the same for Christian science and knowledge. The meaning of it is this, that, as I actually come to a correct self-knowledge in Christ alone, so also a statement of Christian moral self-consciousness, conformable to that knowledge, must start not from the subject, but from the object, from Christ the Supreme Good of life. If the ethical science which preceded Christ began with the subject, *i.e.* man, it was therein relatively justified. It sought after the object; but that had not yet become perfectly revealed to it. The Word had not yet become flesh. In the same way, it was relatively right when it combined Ethics with Physics. The κόσμος was to it an objective reality, which concealed in the folds of its veil the God that dwelt above, and yet in the world. The veil is rent in twain. The light is there. In its splendor, we now for the first time understand ourselves and the world. It becomes not the children of the light, who walk in the day, again to tread the paths of night and of the morning twilight.

PART FIRST
THE BLESSING OF SALVATION

FIRST SECTION

THE LIFE OF MAN AND ITS RULES OF CONDUCT BEFORE THE MANIFESTATION OF CHRIST IN THE FLESH

CHAPTER I

THE NATURAL STATE OF HUMAN LIFE

§ 5. a. Self-consciousness

THE narrowest and most immediate sphere, in which the striving impulse of man is completed and presents itself to his consciousness, is the relation of man to himself (the human being as subject-object) (1). This striving impulse is there before he becomes fully conscious of it (2). It is there, inasmuch as man, from the first moment of his existence, not only is, but *wills* to be and to continue in being (3). In the child, the seeking for its nourishment is the first unconscious manifestation of that will which is inherent in man, and relates to his own existence. When his consciousness is developed, he recognizes this act of willing of his as the working of a natural principle or instinct which belongs to him, and which precedes and regulates this will. For man becomes aware that he existed before he willed, and exercised his will before he was conscious of so doing (4). In the difference of his willing, however, a difference in the ground of his nature reveals itself to his consciousness. For man feels himself moved not only to will that which relates to his body, and which serves for its preservation and welfare; but to will something which shows itself in its distinction from the form of bodily gratification, and the fulfilment of the ends of merely corporeal existence, as being not of bodily origin. This is the will, in the exercise of which man has for his object not only life and the maintenance of life, but also to *understand* the origin and purpose of that life. In the twofold nature of this impulse after life and after knowledge, as Tertullian, *de Animâ* 15, says, "Vis sapientalis et vitalis," man becomes conscious of a double natural basis of his will—a nature spiritual as well as corporeal (5).

In the face of this alternation and interchange of spiritual and bodily instincts, man at the same time perceives something permanent, which can and does deliberately act alternatively with respect to the different impulses; that is to say, at one time affirming, at another denying, sometimes with a view to self-gratification, sometimes to self-denial. This subjective center of his spiritual and corporeal nature, which remains permanent amid all the alternation and interchange of his impulses, man has discovered and asserted so soon as he learns to say "I," and is able not only to discriminate himself as an "Ego" from his natural constitution, but also, being determined by this natural constitution in his personal volition, is able to react upon and determine it. For the Ego perceives in the mixed bodily and spiritual basis of its nature, not only the power which immediately regulates its will and its perception, but at the same time also the object of that willing and perceiving Ego, and the domain subjected to its sovereignty (6). As man, however, recognizes this natural constitution as his own peculiar property, as that nature of his which either solicits his will or is solicited to activity by it, he knows his Ego to be the center both actively and passively of that vital movement which manifests itself both in impulse and will, and makes himself and his own gratification the aim of his life. Personal inclination or disinclination becomes to him the motive of willing or not willing, of doing or leaving undone. For the human being who is referred absolutely to self alone, or who refers everything to self, has in inclination or disinclination only the test of the attainment or non-attainment of self-gratification (7).

Supplement.—If this relation of man to himself is a normal one, it is quite impossible to conceive the attainment of this aim which is natural to man, or the fulfilment of the object of life, without self-gratification. But should this relation of the human being to himself comprehend the whole conditions of his life, or should it appear to him as the supreme object of existence, then self-gratification becomes to him the exclusive, or at least the highest, end of life. It is peculiar to the Christian consciousness, that it asserts the first and denies the second; that is to say, it rejects the second as an immoral and unchristian Egoism (8).

(1) Man strives after that which he loves. Self-love is presupposed as the natural basis by which man is enabled to understand the manner and measure of love for his neighbor also (comp. Lev. 19:18; Matt. 22:39; Rom. 13:9; Gal. 5:14; Eph. 5:29; Jas. 2:8). Self-preservation, self-support (ἑαυτὸν τηρεῖν), forms the object of that endeavor in which the human being actually carries out his most immediate relation. This actual existence, directed to itself as an object, not the mere consciousness of a condition, is the first form of manifestation of human life which is the object of ethics, because in it is mirrored the pursuit of an end of life. Man, as exercising will, is the subject of ethics; and this will, which is directed to the object of willing, and which affirms that object, and feels itself in harmony with it, is love.

(2) The primitive impulse of every human being is to will; and this, in the history of the development of every human being, is antecedent in point of time to knowing. The first is not that will which is brought about through consciousness, but my ethical consciousness is produced from what at first are unconscious acts of willing. It has been well remarked by one of the ancients, that the doctrine of the will, in its importance to the understanding of the soul, resembles what the doctrine of gravity is to the science of physics. See Claudian. Mamerc. *de statu animæ*, lib. ii. c. 5; see also Thorn. Aquin. *S. Th.* p. 1, qu. 20, art. 1.

(3) We are here discussing not the form of development of that willing which is brought about by consciousness and idea, but that primal and radical mode in which the reference of the human being to himself forms the fundamental type of the tendency of his impulses (ἐπιβολή, ὁρμὴ πρὸ ὁρμῆς, as the Stoics said). Man is not so organized, that his will is only first

directed to himself, it may be after a series of gradations, in the development of his consciousness, so that what is will might be perhaps only the product of a development. On the contrary, will is the substance of his being; and that self-directed impulse of the will, or willing tendency, is, to use the words of a physiologist (Joh. Müller, *Physiology*, ii. 539), "an activity conditioning the organization itself." Self-will (αὐτοθελής) precedes all reflex willing and perceptive action, and is the fundamental shape of the existence of the creature; and with it the first mentioned revelation of God in the Scriptures has to do (Gen. 2:16).

(4) As this self-will is antecedent to self-consciousness, and the latter is kindled into being by the actuality of the former, so also the difference between the will as an *actus* and the will as a *potentia*, presents itself to the awakened consciousness. I know that I am what I am by no effort of my own will; but that I, by means of being what I am, possess the power to will. That is to say, my self-existence is the potentiality of my will; not my will the potentiality of my self-existence. And since I do not recognize either myself or my will as my creator, I become conscious of a created causality of all my actual being independent of myself, which I distinguish as my proper nature from my willing self-existence, and regard as a natural instinct in contrast to my self-will. For this "self" is not a self conditioned by its own abstract will, but an organic composition and collective effect of different factors or forces, which are neither separately nor collectively products of my will. If this were not the case, I should also be in a position to organize myself according to my own will. This, however, I am unable to do. And the very perception of this will, conditioned by the natural constitution of my being, is of the last importance for the most profound questions of ethical science. And this, above all, in opposition to the fiction of a so-called purely "self-conditioned will." "And also for the ethical life which is in us," says F. Baader, "the law holds good, that self indeed hovers *over the nature* which produces it (*i.e.* supposing that this life is free, and in full enjoyment of its rights), but

could as little free itself *from this nature* as the flame from the smoke, or the plant from its root" (*Philos. Schriften*, Münster 1831, p. 173; and there also on the "spiritual *Selbstcombabisirung*" (?) which would be attempted in the tearing away of the will from the nature in which it is inherent). Here, however, we may immediately remark, that the empirical facts of our consciousness are, for more reasons than one, totally insufficient for a knowledge of that which, as effective and real *natural* constitution, limits our will. For, in the first place, our concrete consciousness never shapes itself out of a (so to say) universal and undiversified uniformity, but only out of the natural dispositions of the individual. In the second place, the natural impulses of the individual are never impulses of the purely natural abstract tendency of the individual by themselves, but at the same time reactionary workings of his ethical and historical development, as he forms himself both under the internal influence of his natural character, and under those of an external nature. Thirdly, and which is of the highest importance for Christian knowledge, man no longer experiences the influence of purely natural impulses, of purely natural instincts, but is subject to that of a *corrupt* nature, common indeed to all, however modified individually. Thus, from the so-called mere natural consciousness, no human being arrives only at a knowledge of that which is the true nature of man. But, nevertheless, the empirical consciousness of that which is corruption, furnishes him with the understanding of the difference between his own will and its natural ground. For what the apostle, out of the most profound and truest experience, says—"What I would, that I do not; but what I hate, that do I.... Now then it is no more I that do it, but sin that dwelleth in me. For the good that I would, I do not; but the evil which I would not, that I do" (Rom. 7:15, 17, 19; comp. Gal. 5:17),—this reveals to us man, the Christian determined in his actual conduct by something else than merely his own personal will. That is to say, it shows us the personal will in its tendency, whether to good or to evil, influenced and drawn aside by something which is not contained in the idea of that personal will. We must, however, be on our guard against naming, in the case mentioned by the apostle, that also which influences the will in the direction of what is evil without distinction—a natural principle, or the natural life; nor, indeed, are we to form at all from it the notion of a corrupted natural life, and of a life belonging to the person which has remained pure. But of this more afterwards. It will be sufficient here to draw attention to the ethical importance of that truth which Lotze has pertinently brought forward from a physiological and psychological point of view. He says: "The fact is not put prominently enough in view, that even in our inner life, our aims, the tendencies which we follow, and the means for their realization, do not in all cases depend on the freedom of our will, but that we likewise, in very important respects, find ourselves driven back upon a *natural quality* of our souls, from whose influence we can by no means free ourselves. In direct opposition to instinct, we are wont to imagine that *the Ego, free from all empirical determination*—this pure relation to self—forms *the original basis of our spiritual life*; and that all that is, on the contrary, determinately included *(Inhalt)*, by which this Ego separates itself from what is distinct from it, is an act proceeding from its own freedom. But our personality by no means consists only of that pure Ego, *but of an included substance*, to which this Ego belongs as the form of its existence. This substance, however, is one as entirely independent of ourselves, as that of instinct can ever be for the lower animals." Treatise on "Instinkt" in R. Wagner's *Handwörterbuch der Physiologie*, Braunschweig, 1844, p. 201 ff.

(5) It is a delusion to suppose that the impulse arising in us by which we desire and will, makes clear to us of itself—that is to say, purely as an impulse and irrespective of its object—the nature of the source from which it springs, as if we ourselves felt one impulse to be purely corporeal, or belonging to the body, and another purely to the soul, or spiritual. This delusion is also prejudicial to ethics, in as far as it conduces to the belief that it is of importance to know and to decide whether I desire and will by virtue of a bodily or a spiritual impulse. The main

point of ethics is not involved, so to speak, in understanding physiologically the genesis of the impulse and of the act of will, but in the weighing of the *aim* to which that impulse is directed, and in the testing of the relation in which I (not my body or my soul) stand to this or that impulse. *Whether I will, and what is the nature of that which I will*—on this will depend everything connected with the ethical estimate of those impulses, and of the willing. In fact, it is perfectly impossible, in the unity which exists in our organization, to arrive at a perception in that which impels us to will of body and spirit as two diverse but contiguous apparatuses for willing, of which the one is at rest, while the other is in activity. Luther very justly remarks: "I do not at all separate the flesh, the soul, the spirit, from each other; for the flesh may and can have no desire except through the soul and the spirit, by which it lives; but I understand by the spirit and the flesh the whole man, and chiefly the soul. Man is not two beings opposed to each other, but is like the dawn of the morning, which is neither night nor day" (*On the Epistle to the Gal., Works*, Hall. A. Th. ix. p. 314).

It remains, nevertheless, just as certain that, from the difference of *aim* after which our will strives, and, in truth, within the circle in which our endeavor refers merely to ourselves, and not to anything external to ourselves, there does also a different quality of our nature, out of which this impulse springs, present itself to our consciousness. For if man were an absolutely indivisible unity, any essential difference in the form of the gratification of his impulses would be perfectly inconceivable. But, in truth, an essential difference in the form of our self-gratification is an incontestable fact of our experience. The essential nature of the difference follows from this, that the forms and means of our self-gratification on one side of our existence are precisely those which exclude the forms and means of that gratification on the other. The hungry man is not satisfied with ideas, nor the inquiring man with food. On the one side of our existence, the form of gratification is purely material; on the other, as purely immaterial. Either this fact is something inconceivable, or the conception of it, which corresponds to the reality, essentially presupposes a duality in our nature. Only on the supposition that our nature is a union of something material and something immaterial, can be explained that twofold character of our desires, and of the difference in the form of their satisfaction. It must here also, however, be repeated that I do not perceive in the desire itself this two-sidedness of my nature, or become aware of it as a fact pertaining to my immediate consciousness. It is an afterconclusion drawn from the difference of aim, and the different forms and means of the gratification, to a difference of origin in my own nature. But this my nature is a *unio perfecta duarum naturarum*. No vital excitement of the one can be conceived without the participation of the other therein; no corporeal excitement without a spiritual one, nor a spiritual without a corporeal one. (See Tertull. *de resurr. carnis*, 14.) It is only in the object of the actual desire, and in the form and the means of its gratification, that we recognize a *preponderance* of relation to the one or to the other part of our natural existence. The desire itself is an excitement of my whole corporealspiritual nature. When I long for nourishment, I know that, viewed in a material light, this concerns the body (Matt. 6:31, comp. with 25), but in an immaterial one the spirit. (The spirit inquires, Ps. 77:7; the spirit perceives, 1 Cor. 2:11.) But it is the language of reflecting discrimination when I say, my body thirsts for water, my spirit for knowledge; while the language of concrete sensation declares itself alike in both cases in the words "I thirst."

Scripture also justifies us in naming this twofold ground of our nature spirit and body, or, still more correctly perhaps, flesh (σάρξ, Eph. 5:29). That individual existence depending on the organic unity of both is the "living soul." Comp. 1 Cor. 15:45 with Gen. 2:7. A life of the body, apart from this union with the spirit, does not exist (τὸ σῶμα χωρὶς πνεύματος νεκρόν, Jas. 2:26). A life of the soul resting on another basis than that of this mixed spiritual and corporeal one of nature, is just as little to be found on earth. Consistently with Scripture, we may call the spirit the basis of the bodily life; the mixed spiritual and corporeal life, the basis of the life of the soul in the present order of things. (See Irenæus, *adv. hæres.* v. 9, 1.) But here we must guard against the opinion that in the Scriptures the idea of πνεῦμα or ψυχή is merged in this or any other systematic scheme. Generally speaking, there is nothing correct but that in the Scripture the idea conveyed by πνεῦμα is more remote from individual-personal existence than that conveyed by ψυχή, and that it also conveys the notion of actual conscious bodily existence more remotely than ψυχή. But it would be no less erroneous to lay down the canon, that we should be justified from this, by the biblical use of πνεῦμα and ψυχή, to ascribe these meanings to these words without exception, as if πνεῦμα in some way corresponded more to the idea of a spiritual fundamental element in our nature—a fundamental element with regard to ψυχή; and that ψυχή, on the other hand, answered more to that of the relation of the personal existence of the individual to its mixed spiritual and corporeal natural life, and the like. There is in the Scriptures no arbitrariness at all in the use of the words πνεῦμα and ψυχή. But the connections in which they are employed are much less definite, and are rather expressions of a concrete feeling than the narrow and abstract framework of our ethical or psychological definitions. (If I had not long since been convinced of this, the treatise of my honored friend Delitzsch, *System of Biblical Psychology*, Leip. 1855 [Edin. T. & T. Clark, 1867], would only so much the more have convinced me of it. Irrespective of the fact that I cannot consent to the employment of foreign expository elements to explain the Scriptures, I am bound still further to assert, that if the system is really derived from the Scriptures, in place of being intruded on them, the systematic idea attached to a word must cover and explain its use and its connection in every passage. But I could not arrive at this by the mode adopted by Delitzsch, without here and there doing violence to Scripture.)

(6.) The ethical central point of the self-consciousness is the consciousness of myself as an Ego, which in its nature has not only its *potentia*, but its *potestas*, or better, its *dominatus*. The individual unfree natural disposition becomes a substratum and object of the personal will, distinguishing itself from its nature as the Ego, or free possession; that is to say, not a power by which I am possessed, but one which I possess. Not that we can conclude from this that its nature stands over against the Ego, as something neutral and impersonal. The nature which is organized to form a personality, may be distinguished as a personality in potency from that which is a person *actu*, without this nature becoming in its objective relation a neutral essence, cast adrift from personal existence. For the same thing which I can make the object of the action of my personal will, does not cease to be at the same time the power which conditions and forms the basis of the subjective life of the individual. This *my* spirit, *which I* recognize, to which in willing *I* refer myself, is no other than that *by means of which* I recognize *myself*, and in willing turn *to myself*. A personal Ego conceived of over against an impersonal spirit, would be an abstract phantom, without root and without substance, which would hover over a chaotic mass strange to me. Man's nature exists in the form of a personal Ego life, independent of which it does not exist at all. I have not body and soul, but I am body and soul. When, nevertheless, I distinguish my nature from my Ego, this is done not with relation to the Ego as existing, but to the knowing and willing Ego. For my nature in its totality is never the factor nor the object of the knowing and consciously willing Ego. It is always in isolated emotions or relations alone; and it is this or that affection, this or that tendency of the spirit or the body, in which I am conscious of being solicitous (μεριμνῶ) for that which belongs to the body or the soul. In every such act of my conscious personal will, in which I turn to my individual nature (ζητῶ τὸ ἐμαυτοῦ), there remains a whole series of real potencies and conditions of my mixed spiritual and corporeal nature, beyond the sphere of the activity of my conscious will. Thus the totality of my nature is at all times richer than the subject-matter of my actual, differentiating, conscious Ego (νοῦς in the sense of 1 Cor. 14:14, 15, 19). For that which I am according to my nature, and that which according to my nature is excited in me, I perceive and will not simultaneously, but successively and alternately. But this very circumstance, that I can make this or that relation of my natural life alternately the object of the activity of my personal will, forms the factor by which is developed the consciousness of the personal Ego, as the consciousness of one that rules (ἐξουσίαν ἔχων περὶ τοῦ ἰδίου θελήματος, the concrete act of willing, 1 Cor. 7:37). It is the consciousness, not of an absolute, but of a relative ruler, whereby, in relation to myself, I am conscious of the ability to do one thing, and to leave another undone,—to will one thing, and not to will another. Nay, the difference in the natural human constitution, as a unity of body and soul, appears as the primitive fundamental condition of man's united Ego-consciousness. Since I can exert my will in a twofold domain, which lies not without, but within me, I become aware, in the non-identity between the relations of my willing, of the identity of my Ego willing in these opposite directions, sometimes assenting, sometimes refusing. Whether the human Ego-consciousness develops itself only in the possibility of contra-position which exists in our human nature, is a question which can only be answered at a later stage.

(7) If the question is now asked, What is the end of our actual activity of will in the sphere of its action upon ourselves? we can call it nothing else but that self-gratification whose forms vary, but which is always consistent with itself in this, that it can never be accomplished without an actual relation of the man to the impulses of his mixed spiritual and corporeal nature. This actual relation is regulated by what man considers joy and pleasure (χαρὰν, ἡδονὴν ἡγεῖσθαι, mentioned as the presupposition of this relation, 2 Pet. 2:13; and as a motive of patience, Jas. 1:2). And the gratification will be felt as perfect, according to the degree in which it corresponds to that present desire which embraces the totality of the relations of the mixed spiritual and corporeal nature—the desire of the heart. Compare the excellent grouping of passages in Delitzsch, *bibl. Psychologie*, S. 203 ff. [pp. 292–296 of Clark's translation], on

the Scripture use of לֵב, καρδία. If in Scripture "the lusts of the heart" (comp. *e.g.* Rom. 1:24, Matt. 15:19) are named as the source of immoral self-gratification, it only refers to the possibility of an immoral, untrue, and consequently unnatural state of the heart, or state of the entire longing, loving personality of man, but by no means does away with the truth, that the perfect satisfaction (*delectatio*, not *oblectatio*) is the satisfaction of the heart, *i.e.* satisfaction of the individual personal relations of nature in their entirety. But the question, whether pleasure is something "sensuous," or whether there does not also exist a pleasure which is "not sensuous," and whether the one or the other is "moral," is in this alternative view a contradiction to the fact actually established, and a consequence of that crude Dualism, which equally rends asunder the organic and the moral unity of body and soul. For there exists indeed no moral *self*-gratification, which my whole self, in body and soul, hence corporeally as well as spiritually, would not feel; and one would only be justified in calling that immoral which in its *principle* would tend to destroy this mutual equality, and which, in the pursuit of purely spiritual or purely corporeal pleasure, would wrench it to a one-sidedness opposed to nature. See Eudorus in Stobæus, *Ecl.* ii. p. 64, p. 74 ed. Heer. Compare also the inquiry of the later Platonism.

That the proximate natural motive for the willing and acting of man is his own pleasure or displeasure, is a fact that did not escape even the Stoics. See Epictetus, *Diss.* ii. 22, 15 sqq. The school of Aristotle also says: πρῶτον μὲν ὀρεγέσθαι (τὸν ἄνθρωπον) τοῦ εἶναι· φύσει γὰρ οἰκειοῦσθαι πρὸς ἑαυτόν· διὸ καὶ προσηκόντως μὲν ἀσμενίζειν ἐν τοῖς κατὰ φύσιν, δυσχεραίνειν δὲ ἐπὶ τοῖς παρὰ φύσιν. And, in truth, that may hold good of those relations of the Ego which embrace body as well as soul. Stob. *Ecl. Mor.* ii. 7, p. 276 ed. Heeren, t. ii. If therefore Aristotle, in a passage in Stobæus (i. 1, p. 36), apparently taken from the last treatise, Περὶ Παθῶν, says, πάθος ἐστὶν ἄλογος ψυχῆς κίνησις πλεοναστικὴ ... κατὰ φαντασίαν ἡδέος ἢ λυπηροῦ, we can allow the ὄρεξις ἄλογος to rest as it is in the meantime; but the reference to ἡδύ and λυπηρόν is just. And when the Stoics, for example Zeno, designate the ἡδονή as ἀδιάφορον (Stob. i. 1, p. 91), yet Zeno himself cannot avoid defining the ἠθική as ἕξις προαιρετικὴ τοῦ καλοῦ περὶ ἡδονὰς καὶ λύπας (Stob. i. 1, p. 38). Nay, it is difficult to say how in that εὐδαιμονεῖν, which to the Stoic is the σκόπος, as the object of all endeavor, the τέλος, as the possession finally reached, the ἡδονὴ should not again appear (comp. Stob. i. 1, p. 136, etc.). Thus it will remain in the proposition of Aristotle: περὶ ἡδονῆς καὶ λύπης ἐστὶν ἡ ἠθικὴ ἀρετή. When he adds, διὰ μὲν γὰρ τὴν ἡδονὴν τὰ φαῦλα πράττομεν, διὰ δὲ τὴν λύπην τῶν καλῶν ἀπεχόμεθα, and points to ethics as assisting us to χαίρειν τε καὶ λυπεῖσθαι οἷς δεῖ, κ.τ.λ., he stumbles on the problem of ethics, how it comes to pass that pleasure inclines us to the bad, and displeasure makes us averse to what is good. If we concede these to be facts of experience, and yet stop, as was the prevailing case with the civilised nations before Christ, with the analysis of the empirical man, we shall have to explain, from the nature of man himself, this singular contradiction or dissension, in which the ἡδύ at one time is to lead to the κατὰ φύσιν, at another to the παρὰ φύσιν.

They then either halve man into body and soul, or halve the soul itself, and ascribe the pleasure-exciting πάθος to a μέρος ἄλογον τῆς ψυχῆς (comp. Stobæus on the Aristotelian school, *Ecl. Mor.* ii. 7, p. 244 ff), which is opposed to the rational part (comp. also the Stoics, Stob. *Ecl. Mor.* ii. 7, p. 166, with Diog. Laert. vii. 85, p. 416, ed. Meibom). If, therefore, one could not with the Stoics reject pleasure altogether as a motive (which, *e.g.*, Epictetus also does not: Ἡδονὴν οὐ πᾶσαν, ἀλλὰ τὴν ἐπὶ τῷ καλῷ αἱρεῖσθαι δεῖ), but identified perverted pleasure with corporeal impulse and corporeal pleasure, this comes very near to opposing a rational pleasure to sensual pleasure, as we know was done, *e.g.*, by the Socratic Aristippus (Diog. Laert. ii. 89, p. 132, ed. Meibom), or also by the Cynic Antisthenes (comp. H. Ritter, *Hist. of Philos.* part ii. pp. 120, 121). But here, if one stopped merely at the self-conscious Ego of man, and could not conceal from himself the fact that this Ego *in concreto* was just as much κατὰ φύσιν body and spirit, as the *individual* and personal shape of the mixed corporeal and spiritual natural life, then little was gained by this canon of "rational pleasure." On the one hand, it must have become difficult—and the dispute of the schools proves it—to lay down with certainty the just relation of corporeal and spiritual pleasure, to both of which they could scarcely deny the κατὰ φύσιν. And, on the other hand, it was no less a difficulty to set up the objective nature of the λογικόν as τὸ κριτικόν, without attributing to man a consciousness of a universal nature and of a universal reason, of which, however, the divergency of individual empirical experience appeared to show no trace. It is therefore no wonder if the Sophists, *e.g.* Protagoras, denied a universal ethical truth, and reduced everything to the individual standard. And from the point of view which regards man as placed for himself alone, it would be perhaps the most consistent course to make pleasure alone, as such, the standard of his conduct, as we find it in Democritus of the Atomic school, or in Epicurus. This reference to the history of man's different ethical views is only intended to make evident how, in point of fact, the most immediate sphere of the empirical self-consciousness—that is to say, the reference of the human will and action to the Ego—influenced the definition of ethical principles and rules. We meet everywhere here with that relation in which man as an Ego adapts himself to his natural constitution, and seeks his personal gratification in the actual fulfilling of its instincts. That the limitation of the end of life to the individual personal Ego is possible, is proved by its historical reality. And wherein their basis rests in no artificial system, but a natural one, becomes clear from the *immediate* source of human self-consciousness which we have pointed out above. The only question is, whether this is the sole factor which constitutes human self-consciousness. The further progress of our inquiry will deny its being so, and confirm the truth of the proposition that, even in reference to man, all that is termed the manifestation of life is not the result of the operation of *one* cause, but springs from the concurrence of many (comp. art. *Leben, Lebenskraft,* by Lotze, in R. Wagner's *Physiolog.*

Handwörterbuch). But in fact even the Stoics, for example, or the school of Aristotle, was very far from viewing the natural destiny of man as if it was solely organized for the purpose of placing man in reference to himself as an individual and personal Ego. It rested, however, just as much on a correct self-observation, when, within the circle of man's relation to himself, the motive of his willing and not willing was sought solely in the pleasure of self-gratification, or in the displeasure which stands opposed to it; and so in a certain degree this pathological subject was made the object of ethics (comp. *e.g.* the later Platonist, Philo of Larissa, in Stobæus, *Ecl. Mor.* ii. 7, p. 39 sq.).

(8) It does not require an appeal to the experience of a living Christian, but merely a glance at the words of revelation, with its promises of joy and peace, and with its assurance that on our part every life-activity of ours is only so far right and pleasing to God as we enter into it heart and soul (ἐκ καρδίας, Rom. 6:17; ἐκ ψυχῆς, Eph. 6:6, Col. 3:23), in order to know from this that the aim which the Christian sets before himself is at the same time pre-eminently and in the fullest sense of the word self-gratification, pleasure, joy, the delight of our heart (ἀγαλλιᾶσθε χαρᾷ ἀνεκλαλήτῳ καὶ δεδοξασμένῃ, 1 Pet. 1:8, the aim; χαίρετε, ch. 4:13, the present). What we found in the narrowest and lowest relation of human existence—the striving after joy and gratification of the heart—Scripture reveals to us not only as the intention of the divine testimony in God's universal dispensation in the earthly life of nature (ἐμπιπλῶν τροφῆς καὶ εὐφροσύνης τὰς καρδίας ἡμῶν, Acts 14:17), but at the same time as the will of God in the highest sphere—namely, in that of the redemption, sanctification, and glorification of man. The gospel is a message of joy (comp. Luke 2:10); peace and joy the fruit of the Holy Spirit, and the characteristic of the kingdom of God (Gal. 5:22, Rom. 14:17, etc.; comp. Augustine, *Conf* x. 22, 32). A philosophy or religion which has no room for the joy and pleasure of man's self-gratification, is as little conversant with the wants of man as with the will of God. We may here quote a very just remark of

Fr. Baader's (in his *Sätze aus der Bildungs- und Begründungslehre des Lebens*, No. 29), where he says: "By the word feeling, as well what is highest as what is lowest in the human heart is signified, according as we hereby intend its being affected by what is of a lower or higher nature, and consequently either something to which the heart is to elevate itself, or something above which it is to be elevated. The same holds good with regard to the words *pleasure* and *displeasure*; and hence we see what may be said of the endeavors of some philosophers, who would fain transform every emotion into knowledge (light), or *rob the heart of all pleasure* in religion— *that is to say, would fain place us in the very midst of sunshine, and have us to be frozen by the very concentration of its rays.*"

Not the less, however, is it firmly established, that by Christianity the reference of human life to self—the "living for self" (ἑαυτῷ ζῆν, 2 Cor. 5:15; comp. Rom. 14:7), the seeking for one's own (ζητεῖν τὸ ἑαυτοῦ, 1 Cor. 10:24; τὰ ἑαυτοῦ σκοπεῖν, Phil. 2:4), nay, even the Ego-life (ζῶ δὲ οὐκέτι ἐγώ, Gal. 2:20), i.e. the Ego considered as the center of human life—is opposed to the idea and essence of the true life. For the latter is comprised in the idea of self-denial (Matt. 16:24, Mark 8:34, Luke 9:23; comp. ἀποτάσσεσθαι πᾶσιν τοῖς ἑαυτοῦ ὑπάρχουσιν, Luke 14:33). And yet, on the other hand, that self-denial is not an annihilation of self, but a self-preservation; and he who hates his life in this world, preserves *the same* for life everlasting (John 12:25). What can the nature of that Ego be, which wills its own well-being *rightly* when it seeks *not* its own? which *loves* itself when it *hates* itself? which *finds* itself when it seeks not *itself?* which *saves* itself when it seeks not to save *itself*, loses its *life* when it seeks to save *its own* life, and saves its *life* when it *loses its own* life? (comp. Matt. 16:25, 10:39.) That can only be an Ego whose essence is not wholly comprised in the relations of the Ego-life and in the living for self, and which has for the constituent factor of its willing self-consciousness or of its self-conscious willing, from the very beginning, not only its so-called pure Ego, or the individual nature peculiar to it, but other factors besides.

§ 6. b. *Self-consciousness in its relation to the Consciousness of Nature and of the World*

It has already appeared in the relation of man to himself, that the self-consciousness of the Ego rests on an abstraction, by which man becomes conscious to himself of his Ego, as something which stands in contrast to the nature which belongs to it, and which is not comprised in the idea of the willing and knowing Ego. The same distinction leads beyond the sphere of man referred solely to himself, since he recognizes his own natural life as resting upon the basis of a universal life of nature, and his own individual and personal existence as the result of a life of the human race (1). This consciousness forms the other fundamental element of the individual and personal consciousness by the opposition of a collective existence independent of (that is to say, not assumed in) the Ego, in which that Ego finds itself placed, and from whose position standing over against it, it also arrives at the consciousness of self.

This collective existence man knows to be the result partly of human factors, partly of a factor which precedes all human existence. The word "world" designates both of these (2). In the one sense, it is the collective existence of the human race, with all the circumstances of its history, in which the Ego finds itself a part, and recognizes itself as only one among many others of its kind,—that is to say, as an individual of a species, the conditions and relations of whose existence are not all comprehended in that individual and personal life that has self for its object, but are also affected by a collective existence of the human race and its historically developed circumstances. In the other sense, the "world" signifies that earthly place of existence, which was anterior to the life of man, anterior to the development of man's history, anterior to the existence of the individual as of the race. In the last sense, man recognizes in the world, on the one hand, that universal and natural basis which absolutely conditions him here below, seeing that his own existence, as well as that of his race, is inconceivable without the supposition of the earth and its treasures. On the other hand, man perceives this universal nature which conditions his own existence as an object, which includes at the same time ends and aims of the actual energies of his life, since he is conscious of his own call to be sovereign over the earth, and of the appointment of her treasures for his service (3). In that other sense, however, in which the world designates a collective existence of relations supplied by nature, and historically developed, which belong to his race and its social fellowship, man feels himself indeed absolutely conditioned in the nature of his life, in so far as he enjoys his present existence under the supposition of its existing, and cannot become conscious of himself except in contrast to this totality of human existence. But the aims and objects of the life of the individual, and those of his actual vital energy, do not lie by an absolute necessity in the collective life of human society, inasmuch as this is not of itself the object of his consciousness of sovereignty; and he can seek his calling of sovereignty also in this, that he has the power of isolating himself by his conscious will from the world and the relations which belong to his race and to society (4).

But the relation of the willing, not the knowing man, forms here alone the object of ethical investigation. And in opposition to the self-consciousness the question presents itself, whether or not in the consciousness of that which is called, in a double sense of the word, world, a principle is given to us from which man, as exercising will, follows a different end from that of seeking the object of his life in individual and personal self-gratification. In appearance it is so, just because the world, as the universal, stands over against the separation of the individual and personal Ego; and hence that postulate may grow upon the will of man, which is called the surrendering of the Ego to the universal (5). More accurately defined, this, however, would be to declare that by virtue of man's consciousness of the world standing over against him, not self-gratification, but world-gratification, would appear as the purpose of his life. But since no one has hitherto said this, in the so-called surrender of self to the world or to the universal must exist an application peculiar to itself. This is explained by the twofold position assumed by the world under all circumstances, over against the willing man. For it appears to him either as identical with that which he, by virtue of his peculiar human nature, either general or individual, desires and wills, or it appears to him as not identical therewith. In the first case, man finds in that which constitutes the world the compensation of his own deficiency, an object of his longing, of his pleasure and of his love, and therefore seeks not the world, but self and its belongings in the world (6). In the second case, man sees in that which constitutes the world a limit and an impediment to his own efforts of will, to which he submits unwillingly and with dislike (7). If the Ego and the world were really the only two poles round which the willing man revolved, there would remain only a relation of variance, in which the world never really becomes the center of our activity, but only either a means or an impediment to our self-gratification. And however, amidst this discord, the Ego may seek to place itself, and what it may regard as its ethical medium, *from its own resources* it will attain merely to a seeming solution. The egoistic isolation of the Ego on itself, in order to maintain for itself a freedom from the restraints of the world, is as unjustifiable as it is delusive. Only relatively practicable, it is an imaginary denial, but not an overcoming of the restraints of the world. The converse to this, the pretended renunciation of one's self to the world, is equally unjustifiable and delusive, inasmuch as it can never be accomplished without self-gratification: the Ego crops up again in the midst of this apparent subordination of the Ego to the world. Human life, which on the one hand has only a consciousness of the Ego, on the other a consciousness of the world, remains a life which exists in ethical conflict with itself.

Supplement.—That, as the attainment of the end of life is self-gratification, so also it should have its sphere in going out from self and passing into the universal which stands over against it, is only natural. The world, no less than the Ego in its substance, has been established by a divine act, and has proceeded from God. Not the less, however, all theories (quite irrespective of the fact of the accidental corruption of the condition of the world) which make in this or that form the world the principle of the development of life, are in their consequence theories of an abnormal development of life, in appearance opposed to Egoism, but in fact either Egoism only under another form, or a violation of the rights and import of the morally free personality (8).

(1) No one becomes conscious *of his own* nature, without at the same time recognizing another which is *distinct from* that which belongs to him as an individual, and which is not that same nature which is common to the whole of the human race (φύσις ἀυθρωπίνη, Jas. 3:7). This consciousness is first of all brought about by our bodily existence, which in its destination for the earth (κατοικεῖν ἐπὶ παντὸς προσώπου τῆς γῆς, Acts 17:26; comp. παρεπίδημοι ἐπὶ τῆς γῆς, Heb. 11:13), and in its dependence on the earth and its productions (comp. Gen. 1:29, 9:3, and 1 Cor. 6:13, τὰ βρώματα τῇ κοιλίᾳ, καὶ ἡ κοιλία τοῖς βρώμασιν), points to a relation, by virtue of which our organism must bear in itself an essential connection with the earth, and consequently must presuppose the existence of the latter as the mother of our human nature (ἡμεῖς οἱ χοϊκοί, 1 Cor. 15:48). And as regards our personal existence, it is equally certain that, within the history of the present life of man, no one can recognize himself as man (ἄνθρωπος), without at the same time knowing himself to be one of the *children* of men (υἱὸς τῶν ἀνθρώπων, Eph. 3:5, Mark 3:28), and recognizing himself as an Ego over against the existence and life of a race which stands to my existence as an Ego, with its own peculiar human nature as a mother (ἐξ ἑνὸς αἵματος (?) πᾶν ἔθνος ἀνθρώπων, Acts 17:26; ὁ πρῶτος ἄνθρωπος ἐκ γῆς χοϊκός—φοροῦμεν τὴν εἰκόνα τοῦ χοϊκοῦ, 1 Cor. 15:47, 49).

(2) We are not here speaking of the world, in so far as it has a definite world-*position* or a definite totality of conditions; but we speak of it in the universality of the idea, according to which

the term embraces as well the totality of created beings, as also the community that has its existence as a fact of history on the earth—"the kingdoms of the world," the whole body of men, as well their communities as their individual members, which are opposed to the Ego. Everything which, and so far as it differs from the Ego, and possesses, independently of it as a creature, an independent existence, is a part of that totality which Scripture also calls the world. (In idea like γῆ, we find κόσμος, *e.g.* Matt. 4:8, 26:13, Mark 14:9, 16:15, Luke 12:30, 1 Tim. 6:7, etc. The earth, regarded as the complex of earthly possessions, is called κόσμος in Matt. 16:26, and in the parallel passages in Mark and Luke. Like γῆ, which is used alternatively for κόσμος (see Matt. 5:13, 14), κόσμος serves to designate the world of man (comp. Matt. 18:7, John 3:16, 17, 19, 12:19, etc.), or the earth as the abode of that world of man, *i.e.* comprising in one word the earth and the world of man, as, for example, in John 1:9, 10, 8:23, 16:28, 1 Cor. 5:10, 2 Pet. 2:5, 3:6, etc. etc.) It is of importance here to consider and hold fast to the language of Scripture, and for this reason, since Christian science has, following the guidance of that same Scripture, accustomed itself, in respect of the corruption which prevails in this same world (comp. 2 Pet. 1:4, 2:20; 1 John 5:19, 2:16, etc.), briefly to indicate by the term world its corrupt and ungodly condition. To distinguish this double use of the word is not only of importance for the right understanding of Scripture, but also for the ethical conduct of the Christian.

(3) The account of the creation given in Genesis (comp. especially 1:28–30 with 9:2) is also of no light importance for the ethical destination of man. In that which constitutes the earth, together with its animals and plants, man is to become conscious of his appointed dominion. That animate and inanimate nature by which man is surrounded is not only a power which conditions and supports the bodily existence of man, but forms also a domain allotted to him for the exercise of his authority.

(4) In the sphere of those relations which exist among men lies the possibility for man of not participating, so far at least

as he has actually to enter on them, and of withdrawing himself in this direction from all solicitude about that which constitutes the world (μεριμνᾶν τὰ τοῦ κόσμου, 1 Cor. 7:33, 34). It is necessary to mention this here, in order that we may not place on an absolute equality that kind of necessity which binds man to the earth, and those relations which unite him with human society.

(5) The postulate of the surrender of the Ego to the universal can only be laid down under suppositions, of which it must first be asked whether they are justifiable. In the first place, it must be assumed that this universal, as it stands over against us as the world in a double sense of the word, is in its true normal condition *(in statû integritatis)*. This Scripture denies, and the Christian along with it (ὁ κόσμος ὅλος ἐν τῷ πονηρῷ κεῖται, 1 John 5:19; τῇ ματαιότητι ἡ κτίσις ὑπετάγη—τῇ δουλείᾳ τῆς φθορᾶς, Rom. 8:20 ff.). Secondly, it would in this way be assumed that this universal, which is at present objective to us, is the form of existence in which the aims and destiny of the human Ego are to be comprised. This also is denied by Scripture, and by the Christian along with it (ὁ κόσμος παράγεται, 1 John 2:17; παράγει τὸ σχῆμα τοῦ κόσμου τούτου, 1 Cor. 7:31). Thirdly, it would also have to be assumed that the origin, essence, and purpose of the personal egoistic existence, and those of that universal which is the object of my perceptions, are identical, if I were able and wished to make that which is called the essence of the world the essential condition of the energy of my life, and of the fulfilment of the purpose of my existence. But the life of nature, as it presents itself to me in the state of the earth and of the ζῶα φυσικά (2 Pet. 2:12), is in all these respects unlike to man's natural life. I can, however, only regard as something humanly universal either human society, its real nature and the spirit animating it, or that common nature which belongs to all men. The life of human society is therefore a whole, which, as existing in family, people, state, etc., does indeed partly regulate my individual existence, and sets before me aims for the efforts of my life; but in its spirit, on the other hand, is just as much regulated by the

individual spiritual tendencies of those who belong to this whole, and dependent in what it chooses for its aim. I might thus often fall into the most critical conflict with that which springs from my truest and personal life, if I considered that which belongs to men (φρονεῖν τὰ τῶν ἀνθρώπων Matt. 16:23), and made the common spirit prevailing at any time the law and rule of my views. And as to what regards man's common nature (κοινὴ φύσις ἀνθρωπίνη), whose existence I may indeed assume, but whose substance, if I do not already possess it as part of my own, I can never by any means make so, men with their individual and personal nature are connected with that which belongs to humanity as a whole, not as mechanical portions of the same, which could not exist apart from the whole, or which would have the totality of this nature for the organic factor of their existence. We are rather organisms designed for particular functions, in whose variety alone the totality of man's natural powers appears. This organic knowledge, according to which we may compare individual men, in their relation to human nature as a whole, to *members* organized for special functions, stands in opposition to the error of that mechanical view, in which we make men to be, by their natural constitution, *parts* of a nature everywhere like itself, whose destiny was to be only the bearers, organs, and manifestations of this universal nature, which is common to all (comp. the survey of the view of the Stoic Schools in Diog. Laert. vii. 87, 88, 89; comp. also Epictet. *Dissert*, iv. 7, 6).

It is, moreover, worthy enough of remark, that, as among the Stoics, they did not venture to carry out in all their ethic force this pretended universal equality, and that natural aim common to all, without identifying the aims of nature, as such, with the divine will and intelligence (see Diog. Laert. *ibid.*). But this is impossible from the standpoint of Christian knowledge. For we know also of a wrathful will of God, which rules over nature and the human race, which suffered the nations to walk in their own ways (Acts 14:16), and which placed nature under the ban of vanity and transitoriness (see as before, Rom. 8:20), so that both the life of nature and the life of nations formed themselves by the divine will into a mirror of the need of salvation, but never by any means is in itself purely an expression of that order willed by God, much less a power of redemption which is to set us free.

(6) The world in the abstract, or in its purely sensuous aspect, is known indeed by the man who is void of a knowledge of God, but not by the Christian. The world to him is a concrete, in which not only man exercises his power, but also God. But to the Christian this divine agency also is not an abstract one above the world, and separated from it, but an agency in the world, and through the world. And since he does not divide, but only distinguishes the means of divine testimony from that God who testifies of Himself, the Christian recognizes the fact, that that which God in the world, and through the world, offers to man, is also a satisfying of his earthly needs,—an object of his desire, of his joy, of his pleasure. He recognizes the Θεὸς ἀγαθουργῶν in all the good things of the earthly life of nature, even though they are only destined for corporeal enjoyment, and the satisfying of corporeal wants (Acts 14:17; 1 Tim. 6:17). He sees in the κόσμος φυσικός not only the object of a pleasure, which is also known to the ἄλογα ζῶα φυσικά, but a means of satisfying higher spiritual knowledge (Rom. 1:20). And not less does he perceive in the various forms and relations of human society divinely hallowed benefits, and pleasing to God. But all this is under the supposition of a third factor in the human consciousness, of which he knows nothing, who knows only of the sensuous Ego and the world of sense.

(7) That the present natural state of the world, or its historical position as the world of human society, presents itself to us as merely the reality, satisfying our wants, is a fiction, which runs exactly counter to the facts of our experience. The Christian consciousness forms no exception to that of humanity in general; so that the Christian alone should feel what is meant when it is said, "In the world ye have tribulation" (John 16:33; comp. the πόλλαι θλίψεις, Acts 14:22, Rom. 8:35). This world, "in bondage to corruption," "under the dominion of death and sin" (Rom. 5:14, 17, 21), is in truth not

that "best world" of which the philosophers dream. And if the overcoming of the tribulation of the world is to be effected by that self-act of the spirit in "which we recognize the universal, which we falsely oppose to ourselves, as being something different, as an integral element of self," then, if an unreal phantom is not to result from this universal, with the highest good fortune, we arrive only at this, that we make ourselves the children of death, corruption, and sin, not, however, as Hegel says, that "the spirit, in the absolute certainty of itself, should become master over all facts and realities, and should be able to reject them or make them, as if they had not happened" (*Phenomenology*, p. 619). If the Stoics, without examination, took the reality for the truth, and laid down as a major premiss, τοῦ ἀνθρώπου ὄντος ζώου λογικοῦ θνητοῦ (in Stob. *Ecl.* ii. 7, p. 132), and maintained a rational law of change and dissolution (Epict. *Fragm.* in Stob. *Flor.* 108, 60; Collection, No. 134), it sounds very much like irony in the conclusion as there given. The apostle has another answer to the question of anguish: Ταλαίπωρος ἐγὼ ἄνθρωπος, τίς με ῥύσεται ἐκ τοῦ σώματος τοῦ θανάτυο τούτου; (Rom. 7:24). It is not from the finite in itself, not from the restraints of the world merely as such, that we would wish to withdraw ourselves, and yet are not so to do (comp. 1 Cor. 5:10 with John 17:15); but it is from something hostile to our nature, which has intruded itself also on that nature which surrounds us, and has no free-will (οὐχ ἑκοῦσα, Rom. 8:20), and which, in connection with the disorder of the human race, makes our life appear to us like a march through the wilderness, in which we are at one time disposed to play, at another to murmur, and yet must do neither (1 Cor. 10:7, 10), consoling ourselves with the thought that the time of *suffering* is short (ὀλίγον παθόντες, 1 Pet. 5:10; comp. Rom. 8:18). Such is the consciousness of the nature of this world that we derive from our experience, confirmed by the stamp of divine truth. Whence, then, is to come that "surrender of the Ego to the universal?"

(8) In what way the κόσμος was made the principle of a normal development of life, is shown by the ethical modes of

view of the most highly cultivated nations of the world before Christ, although nowhere strictly carried out, yet stamped in more or less decisive characters. Both forms of general life—the life of nature, or the historically developed life of nations—qualify the ethical modes of thought, and morals are brought into the closest connection either with physics or with politics. It is true we cannot say, that in the ethical view which prevailed, for instance, in classical antiquity, the κόσμος was, either in the one or the other aspect of its existence, raised in an exclusive sense to the highest standard of life. For in the more physical view, the political consideration also plays its part; and in the political there is a reference to the gods and the divine element, whose origin does not at all admit of explanation from either of the two previously considered spheres of consciousness. On this confused interpenetration of the spheres of law, morality, and religion, especially in the earliest theories of the Greeks, comp. *e.g.* Nägelsbach, *Die homerische Theologie*, p. 200 ff. The ethics of the Stoics is the most complete type of that view which is directed to nature. The *vita secundo defluens cursu* (εὐδαιμονία, εὔροια βίου) consists in the perception and giving way to the necessity of nature. Zeno's ὁμολογουμένως ζῆν, or what Cleanthes calls ὁμολογουμένως τῇ φύσει ζῆν, or, as Chrysippus more distinctly expresses himself, ζῆν κατ' ἐμπειρίαν τῶν φύσει συμβαινόντων (similarly Diogenes and Archidemus), is the sum of the normal conduct of life. The sum, consequently, of all abomination is, according to an Antoninus, ἀπόστημα καὶ οἷον φῦμα τοῦ κόσμου. Therefore also the counterpart, or rather the caricature, of the apostle's saying (Rom. 11:36), is the precatory exclamation of Stoic wisdom: ὦ φύσις ἐκ σοῦ πάντα, ἐν σοὶ πάντα, εἰς σὲ πάντα. Thus, according to Chrysippus also, all judgment respecting good and evil begins from Jove and universal nature. This nature, therefore—which, as the world, stands in contrast to the individual—assumes at once the place of God and of divine necessity; and to this nature the individual bears the same relation as the subordinate part does to the whole, as the soldier to the general (Epict. *Diss.* ii. 10, iii. 24,

34); and this alike whether we understand with Chrysippus by φύσις, τήν τε κοινὴν καὶ ἰδίως τὴν ἀνθρωπίνην, or with Cleanthes, τὴν κοινὴν μόνην (comp. Diog. Laert. vii. 87–89, and Stob. *Ecl.* ii. 7, p. 132 sq. ed. Heeren, t. 11). Over against the individual this whole stands as that which is necessary; and voluntarily to subordinate our freedom to this necessity is morality. The intrinsic contradictions of this mode of speaking are obvious. For if the *universal* alone is the authorized principle which is to regulate the "parts," then is the relation of parts something unjustified or delusive, and the universal alone has essential and permanent truth (as also the new Platonism affirms; see Procl. *in Tim.* lib. i. p. 14). And if the universal is the *necessary*, then either the free surrender to it must be a delusion (*faire bonne mine à mauvais jeu*), or this necessity is a delusion, since I can make it depend upon my own voluntary act. Finally, if the purpose of this surrender to the universal is to be *individual happiness*, then is this giving up of the Ego to the universal in every case a delusion, and self-gratification recurs again in the form of a yielding of self to the necessity of the universal.

But the view which prevailed in antiquity was one which saw in the nation, in the state and its laws, the embodiment of the universal necessity, or the rule of life before which the individual must surrender his own will; so especially with the Romans. But there, too, it was not properly the state and the idea of the state, but the practical *state interest*, whose maintenance appeared to be alike the duty and the interest of everyone. Virtue and morality were then properly the seeking and finding one's separate and individual interest in the interests of the state (see C. L. Roth, *de satiræ romanæ indole*, etc., Heilb. 1844; cf. Eundem, *zur Theorie and innern Geschichte der röm. Satire*, Stuttg. 1848, p. 26 ff.). The power which this idea exercised may be discerned in the fact that it was shared even by those who in another respect went beyond it. There is a saying recorded to this effect of Socrates himself: φημὶ γὰρ ἐγὼ τὸν νόμιμον δίκαιον εἶναι—νόμους δὲ πόλεως, ἔφη, γινώσκεις; With Aristotle the object of morals is not "abstract good, but human and political good—that which is practically useful, and can be carried out." Lastly, with Plato, who, to a degree unapproached by any other Greek philosopher, recognized and taught an absolute good, there nevertheless went forth, side by side with it, a representation of the universal, which in contrast with the special and individual was alone justifiable; and the position, that *that* state was the best in which πάσῃ μηχανῇ τὸ λεγόμενον ἴδιον πανταχόθεν ἐκ τοῦ βίου ἅπαν ἐξῄρηται, led him, to a conclusion in favor of a community of property, wives, and children. But independently of the immoral consequences which actually follow, or which may be conceived to follow, from this requirement, which insists upon an unconditional surrender of the special and all special property to the political whole and to the universal—*i.e.* demands that the right of the politically universal should be everything, while that of the individual should be nothing—here also the postulate goes to wreck on the fact that the general interests of political prosperity are certainly not striven after, except in the sense of at the same time gratifying the individual interests. Nay, even if, amid the greatest sacrifice in other respects, this satisfaction should take place only in such a way that a man should seek his own gratification in the repute of a good and patriotic citizen, then simply by this alone would the appearance of a surrender of one's own gratification for the universal good be destroyed; and of this pretended abandonment of one's own personal interest, that would hold true which one of the ancients remarked of the philosophers' renunciation of fame: "Philosophi etiam in libris, quos de contemnenda gloria scribunt, nomen suum inscribunt: in eo ipso, in quo prædicationem nobilitatemque despiciunt, prædicari de se ac nominari volunt" (Cic.). But the Christian, by virtue of revelation, knows himself placed in a relation to the κόσμος which resembles that in which he stands to himself. As, in reference to the latter, self-love is assumed as being natural, and yet φιλαυτία (2 Tim. 3:2) is rejected, so he also knows that he must not quit the world, and yet must not make the world the center of his affections (οἱ χρώμενοι τῷ κόσμῳ ὡς μὴ καταχρώμενοι, 1 Cor. 7:31). It is placed for him under the point of view of use and abuse, but not under that of his love. On the contrary, there is a beacon erected with the inscription: "Love not the world, neither the things that are in the world" (1 John 2:15); "the friendship of the world is enmity with God" (Jas. 4:4). Not that in the place of the right "use," *hatred of the world* should therefore be substituted. The key to this is to be found in the fact that the Christian regards the world as the object of God's love in Christ; of *redeeming* love, however (John 3:16, 17). And even with reference to this, there arise relations also in which we are led to a μισεῖν, which, like the μισεῖν τὴν ψυχὴν αὐτοῦ (John 12:25) even in the tenderest of human ties, as in μισεῖν πατέρα, μητέρα, καὶ τὴν γυναῖκα, etc. (Luke 14:26), has a force which not he who is entangled in the world, but the Christian, alone can understand.

§ 7. c. Self-consciousness in its relation to our Consciousness of God and to Conscience

In the relation of self-consciousness to our consciousness of the world, and the way in which man in the sphere both of the one and of the other learns to recognize the definite aims of his life, the facts that belong to the human moral consciousness are by no means exhausted. The proof of this is not to be looked for in that analysis of the individual empirical consciousness, which is more or less uncertain, and that from very different causes, but is found laid down in the history of the life of nations (1). There, in whatever direction we look, the fact meets us, that in the mirror of man's own nature, as in that of the world, he encounters a power which is higher than himself and the world,—a power which binds him and the world, which elevates him by this very restraint above himself as well as above the world, and holds out to him, as the aim of his life, a community, whose traces he finds in himself and the world, but whose aim, notwithstanding, lies above and beyond both himself and the world (2). Man hereby recognizes his own existence and that of the world not as being in itself an end, but as forms of existence through whose means there appears to him as the highest aim of his will also, to be, to live, and to move in Him who is the primeval source (ἀρχὴ τῶν ἀρχῶν), eternal and immutable, of the life of this transitory state of existence. Whether men did or did not discover the name, they called the unknown and the unnamed—God (3). In the consciousness of the reference of all creature life to God, man has found a rule of life, an aim of life, a principle of morality (whether it appears only in obscure conjecture or in clear knowledge), in which he *can* discover and gain that truth (ἀλήθεια, Rom. 1:25), whose possession is to free him from himself and the world, so that even in the darkest state of erroneous opinions a broken ray of this truth still sheds its light upon us (4). Man's consciousness of this higher relation which conditions the tendencies of his will, no matter how manifold the form in which it reveals itself to him, we name *conscience* (5).

(1) It may appear inconsistent, when it is asserted that we can appeal to the individual empirical knowledge of men in that which is called self-consciousness and consciousness of the world, but not in that which refers to our consciousness of God and conscience. Why not, if both are not less, as is alleged, facts of the human consciousness? To this we can reply, first of all, that in the first case the question is touching a consciousness which, in reference to its object—that is to say, man and the world—is necessary, because it is the result of the senses; but in reference to God and conscience it is not so. We cannot indeed conceive a human consciousness which should be absolutely without any inkling of God, and void of all whispering of conscience. As respects all purely spiritual facts, however, they do not operate on our consciousness in the manner of a necessity, so that we should not be able to close our spiritual eye more or less to their significance, and either avoid understanding them or obscure their meaning. What Paul says of the heathen, that their knowledge of God was not knowledge, but a perversion of knowledge (γνόντες τὸν Θεὸν

οὐχ ὡς Θεὸν ἐδόξασαν, κ.τ.λ., Rom. 2:21-23; for which reason he calls them ἄθεοι ἐν τῷ κόσμῳ, Eph. 2:12), may be said of conscience also. We may know it without hearing or understanding its dictates aright. Lastly, however—and this is not the least important point in the question before us—we must deny that, in reference to the genesis of man's consciousness of God, and the nature of his conscience in the case of man as appearing in history, and not as thought of in the abstract, it is merely man as existing entirely for himself and his consciousness that can and ought to be regarded as the factor. There are traditions of the history of the world and of nations whose bearing must in this question be duly considered, in order to avoid taking phenomena for pure developments of man's individual consciousness by itself, which are but reflections in the individual mind of a consciousness already developed, belonging to some fixed epoch, and prevailing over more general spheres. Above all, there needs no proof to show that where Christianity has become a power not only over minds which have actually embraced it, but over those also which it has touched only externally, the forms in which God and conscience are found as facts of consciousness cannot be explained by a purely developing process on the part of the individual. If we wish to trace out this latter, the testimonies are much more certain which are met with in the history of those nations which existed before the Christian era, and which were most developed in ethical respects, although even here it is difficult—nay, as it seems to me, impossible—to separate the facts of the individual from those of the national consciousness, and accurately to define that knowledge which man has derived entirely from himself.

(2) There is somewhat rhetorical and hyperbolical in the assertion, as is the way with Maximus Tyrius; but with regard to the *consensus gentium*, it is not absolutely untrue, when he says: Ἐν τοσούτῳ δὴ πολέμῳ καὶ στάσει καὶ διαφωνίᾳ ἕνα ἴδοις ἂν ἐν πάσῃ γῇ ὁμόφωνον νόμον καὶ λόγον, ὅτι θεὸς εἷς πάντων βασιλεὺς καὶ πατήρ, καὶ θεοὶ πολλοί, θεοῦ παῖδες, συνάρχοντες

θεοῦ. Τοῦτο καὶ ὁ Ἕλλην λέγει, καὶ ὁ βάρβαρος λέγει, καὶ ὁ ἠπειρώτης, καὶ ὁ θαλάττιος, καὶ οό σοφὸς, καὶ ὁ ἄσοφος, κ.τ.λ. Εἰ δὲ ἐξεγένοντο ἐν τῷ ξύμπαντι αἰῶνι δύο που καὶ τρεῖς, ἄθεον καὶ ταπεινὸν καὶ ἀναισθὲς γένος, καὶ πεπλανημένον μὲν τοῖς ὀφθαλμοῖς, ἐξηπατημένον δὲ ταῖς ἀκοαῖς, ἐκτετμημένον δὲ τὴν ψυχήν, ἄλογον καὶ ἄγονον καὶ ἄκαρπον, ὡς ἄθυμος λέων, ὡς βοῦς ἄκερως, ὡς ὄρνις ἄπτερος, καὶ παρὰ τούτυο ὅμως τοῦ γένους πεύσει τὸ θεῖον· ἴσασι γὰρ οὐχ ἑκόντες, καὶ λέγουσιν ἄκοντες· κἂν ἀφέλῃς αὐτοῦ τὸ ἀγαθὸν, ὡς Λεύκιππος· κἂν προσθῇς τὸ ὁμοπαθὲς, ὡς Δημόκριτος· κἂν ὑπαλλάζῃς τὴν φύσιν, ὡς Στράτων· κἂν δῷς τὴν ἡδονὴν, ὡς Ἐπίκουρος· κἂν μὴ εἶναι φῇς, ὡς Διαγόρας· κἂν ἀγνοεῖν τί φῇς, ὡς Πρωταγόρας (*Dissert.* xvii. 5). I have quoted this passage by way of example, for this additional reason, because it is correct even where it appears paradoxical. It is true that the consciousness of God comes, as it were, involuntarily to man; it is true that, even where it is perverted, it exists (for God is perverted in the perverted); it is true that it is there, where man denies God, and there, where he asserts that he knows not what God is. For if I deny God, I bear testimony that I know about Him; and if I did not know *that* He is, I could not assert that I do not know *what* He is—ἴσασι γὰρ οὐχ ἑκόντες, καὶ λέγουσιν ἄκοντες. And so Tertullian says: "Et tu tamen eum (Deum) nosti, dum odisti" (*De testim. animæ*, iii.).

In reference to the consciousness of a God, we must now further consider what testimony is given concerning its origin. On the one side stands the assertion, that this consciousness is not produced except by external means—namely, by reflection on that nature which stands over against us; on the other hand, we find it asserted that it is an internal consciousness immediately bestowed upon us. We must be on our guard against assuming the latter view in the way in which we find it laid down in the testimony of the ante-Christian world, without further examination, as a fact of the immediate empirical consciousness. It is in many and many an instance a conclusion resting upon suppositions which one cherishes respecting the nature of the human spirit. Whether these are correct, can only be tested in the light of revelation. In the meanwhile, we have merely to state the historical fact, that we meet with such assertions under very different suppositions, such as: ὁ θεὸς ἔνδον ἐστὶ, καὶ ὁ ὑμέτερος δαίμων ἐστί· θεὸν περιφέρεις, τάλας, καὶ ἀγνοεῖς (Epictet. *Diss.* i. 14, 14, ii. 8, 12); or as it occurs in that saying of the oracle: ψυχὴ ἡ μερόπων θεὸν ἄγξει πως ἐς ἑαυτὴν, οὐδὲν θνητὸν ἔχουσα, ὅλη θεόθεν μεμέθυσται· in short, the assertion of a σύμφυτος κατανόησις, of which, however, again it is also elsewhere said: Ἐνέφυσε γάρ τι ὁ θεὸς ζώπυρον τῷ τοῦ ἀνθρώπου γένει τῆς προσδοκίας τοῦ ἀγαθοῦ, ἀπέκρυψε δὲ αὐτοῦ τὴν εὕρεσιν (Max. Tyr. *Diss.* xxxv. 6). On the other hand, the latter says very decidedly in the passage before quoted (xvii. 5), of that knowledge of God which is derived from external sources: Τί ταῦτα, ὡραῖα, καὶ καλὰ, καὶ περίοδοι, καὶ μεταβολαὶ, καὶ κράσεις ἀέρων, καὶ ζώων γενέσεις; θεοῦ πάντα ἔργα ἡ ψυχὴ λέγει, καὶ τὸν τεχνίτην ποθεῖ, καὶ καταμαντεύεται τῆς τέχνης. If we begin with this last first, we find the apostolic testimony also confirming the fact that, by virtue of the rule which He exercises in that nature which surrounds us, God has at no time left Himself without witness (Acts 14:17); nay, that God has placed men upon this earth, and under their various arrangements, in order "that they should *seek* Him, if haply they might *feel after* (ψηλαφήσειαν) and *find* Him" (Acts 17:26, 27). And in the Epistle to the Romans it is distinctly brought forward as a fact, which shows the guilt of the God-estranged heathen world, that the invisible nature of God, *i.e.* His eternal *power* and *Godhead*, are seen and perceived from the creation of the world in the works of His hand (νοούμενα καθορᾶται, Rom. 1:20). From these testimonies we may conclude with certainty that the world of creation is a means of attaining to a knowledge of God appointed by Himself, not a means in the sense of necessitating this knowledge, but of soliciting us to it, or of a charm leading us to seek God and to find Him, and that as the beneficent Giver of earthly blessings (ἀγαθουργῶν, Acts 14:17), exalted above this transitory world, ruling it with an eternal power not derived from the world, but from Himself, and revealing Himself therein. There are the relations of a power and goodness exalted above, and yet manifesting themselves in the world, within which, (according to the statements above cited), man can and ought to arrive at a knowledge of God from objective nature, which only through his own fault he loses or does not attain. The means of this knowledge, however, cannot be understood without an understanding of the organ of that perception—(of that which νοῶν καθορᾷ). And to this refers that passage in the Acts (ch. 17:27, 28), where there is laid hold of a testimony of the Hellenic world to a relation in which we are to call man himself of a divine race (γένος ὑπάρχοντες τοῦ Θεοῦ), and may venture to say of him, that God is not far from every one of us, because, however unconsciously, "in Him we live, and move, and have our being;" so that even from being what we are, we are able to seek and to find the God who is near unto us. There is, like the bodily eye, *the light* of an eye (τὸ φῶς τὸ ἐν ἐμοί, Matt. 6:23) within us, which is organized for the knowledge of God, and is akin to God, but which can divest itself of its nature, lose its faculty of knowledge, and become blind and dark. Thus we may assert that that which brings about a consciousness of God is to be sought not only outside of man, but also within him. But accurately to determine these internal co-efficients has been always the most difficult of problems. See Anastas. Sinaita, *de hominis creatione*, etc., ed. Joh. Tarin, Appendix to Orig. *Philocalia*, Paris 1624, iv. p. 562.

(3) Compare that judgment of Plato, Θεὸν νοῆσαι μέν ἐστι χαλεπὸν, φράσαι δέ ἀδύνατον, ᾧ καὶ νοῆσαι δυνατόν, (Plat. *Tim.* p. 28, C), which is also cited as the Wisdom of Hermes (Justin. *Cohortatio ad Gentil.* 38). By the Chinese Laotse it is said: The essence which can be expressed is not the eternal essence; the name which can be named is not the eternal name; but this nameless one is the Author of heaven and of earth (compare similar statements in Tholuck, *Ssufismus*, pp. 201 ff., 203, 227).

(4) The uncertainty of that knowledge of God which is natural to man, is set forth in those verses of Xenophanes in *Sextus Empiricus* (p. 71). But at the root not only of this uncertainty, but even of error, of contradiction, of denial, there

lies γνωστὸν Θεοῦ, an ἀλήθεια from which man does not free himself, even when he struggles against it, and which shines forth out of this very struggle, although not as the light of life, yet as the fire of the judgment. And in all perverted piety there appears a course of action referring itself to God, in spite of the fact that man knows not God, and an ignorance of God in which, nevertheless, man will occupy himself with reference to God. Ἀγνοοῦντες εὐσεβοῦσι, καὶ εὐσεβοῦντες ἀγνοοῦσιν, may be said with reference to Acts 17:23, with regard to which passage John Gerhard correctly remarks: "Sic ergo in templis Atheniensium et reliquorum gentilium fuit *iniquitas* ET *veritas.*"

(5) If that consciousness, the object of which is the relations between something above nature and man, and conversely, is named conscience, it will be useful, first of all, to illustrate the use of this word in its formal authorization. It is correct—at least I have no recollection of the opposite—that this word, in the language of the world before Christ, as in that of the present day, is not identical with the idea of that consciousness of a God, at least not with that consciousness of a God which is developed out of the nature by which we are surrounded. It is a consciousness dwelling in man (συνείδησις as συναίσθησις), in which man is, as it were, present to himself in his ethical conduct, and an object of his own approbation or disapprobation. In this sense it stood for the most part in relation to the *virtues* and *vices of men*, and especially the latter, as Cicero expresses it: "Et virtutis et vitiorum, sine ullâ divinâ ratione grave ipsius conscientiæ pondus est, quo sublato jacent omnia." With striking truth does Juvenal describe the might of conscience in the well-known verses:

"Cur tamen hos tu
Evasisse putas, quos diri conscia facti
Mens habet attonitos, et surdo verbere cædit,
Occultum quatiens animo tortore flagellum?
Pœna autem vehemens ac multo sævior illis,
Quos et Cæditius gravis invenit aut Rhadamanthus,
Nocte dieque suum gestare in pectore testem.

> Has patitur pœnas *peccandi sola voluntas.*
> Nam scelus intra se taciturn qui cogitat ullum,
> *Facti crimen habet.* Cedo, si conata peregit?"
> JUV. *Sat.* xiii. 192–8, 208–10.

Compare, on the views of the Greeks, Nägelsbach, *die nachhomerische Theol. des griech. Volksglaubens*, vi. 11.

On the *other* hand, it cannot be denied that we must regard the fear of the wrath to come, and of the avenging justice of the gods, just as much as the working of conscience, as conversely the fear in this form is at the same time the effect of the traditional doctrine of the gods on the conscience. Comp. Nägelsbach, *homerische Theologie*, p. 200, and his *nachhomerische Theologie des griechischen Volksglaubens*, i. 17, 26. Enough, pre-Christian antiquity equally with us recognized conscience as a self-judgment, which man pronounces on himself. And the apostle attributes conscience (συνείδησις) to the heathen world also, in the same sense in which we employ the word (Rom. 2:15). Thus the testimony of the apostle finds its echo in the voice of the pre-Christian world, and conversely. And here it will not be superfluous to ask, whether here and in what follows we understand the word "conscience" in the same sense as the corresponding Greek word is used generally in the Scriptures of the New Testament. And, so far as the question is here with respect to a merely formal, so to speak, lexicographical investigation, it will not be difficult to characterize definitely the use of the word in Scripture. This use of the word differs from the sense of our German word (*Gewissen*) only in this, that the latter has a narrower and more exclusive sense than συνείδησις in the Scriptures of the New Testament. The original and general meaning of συνείδησις, consciousness, has been preserved. Συνείδησις ἁμαρτιῶν (Heb. 10:2), συνείδησις Θεοῦ (1 Pet. 2:19), is consciousness of sin, consciousness of God, and cannot here be translated by the word *Gewissen*. In all other passages συνείδησις is equivalent to *Gewissen*, conscience.

In what connections, then, do we meet with the word? (1.) Where the question is about a higher obligation than one merely human, of which man is conscious: ἀνάγκη ὑποτάσσεσθαι οὐ μόνον διὰ τὴν ὀργὴν, ἀλλὰ καὶ διὰ τὴν συνείδησιν (Rom. 13:5). Conscience is accordingly that consciousness which out of this conscious ground binds man (1 Cor. 11:25, 27, 28), which a man respects in another even at the time when in a given case he does not feel himself individually bound by it (1 Cor. 11:29). For just as in the ἀγνοοῦντες εὐσεβεῖν, the εὐσεβεῖν still remains a εὐσέβεια, so also the consciousness of something supposed to be, but not actually binding, yet remains conscience (Heb. 9:14), and is called merely a weak conscience, as being not yet freed from a supposed obligation, and not yet made strong in this freedom (1 Cor. 8:7, 10, 12). (2.) Conscience is that consciousness of man by virtue of which a feeling of approval of truth and sincerity is attributed to him. Conscience approves of that which is true. Therefore Paul says, τῇ φανερώσει τῆς ἀληθείας συνιστάντες πρὸς πᾶσαν συνείδησιν ἀνθρώπων ἐνώπιον τοῦ Θεοῦ, 2 Cor. 4:2; in a similar sense also, πεφανερῶσθαι ταῖς συνειδήσεσιν ὑμῶν, 2 Cor. 5:11. (3.) And just for this very reason, conscience is the *right* consciousness of the ethically right or wrong condition of man; and just in this way, always according to the nature of this condition and conduct, it is either an evil or a good, a pure or an impure conscience. As a *sincere* consciousness of pure conduct, the testimony of his *conscience* is to the apostle a cause of rejoicing (2 Cor. 1:12); and he knows the *sincerity* of his grief from the testimony of his conscience, which he, under the influence of the Holy Spirit, knows as doubly guaranteed against deception (συμμαρτυρούσης μοι τῆς συνειδήσεως ἐν Πνεύματι ἁγίῳ, Rom. 9:1). When we find in an exhortation, ἔχοντες τὸ μυστήριον τῆς πίστεως ἐν καθαρᾷ συνειδήσει (1 Tim. 3:9), there is hereby meant the pure and genuine consciousness, that the state of their disposition and of their conduct is not in opposition to the μυστήριον which they hold. When (1 Tim. 1:19) Timothy is exhorted to fight the good fight—ἔχων πίστιν καὶ ἀγαθὴν συνείδησιν—this is said with reference to the προφητεῖαι having application to him, with respect to whose contents he is to have faith, and in regard to whose application for him he is to have a good conscience in the knowledge of his καλὴ στρατεία. Thus the καλὴ συνείδησις, Heb. 13:18, rests on the consciousness of wishing to walk orderly in all things, and therefore on the consciousness of a good will; συνείδησις ἀγαθὴ, 1 Pet. 3:16, in contrast to the καταλαλία, rests on the consciousness of good conduct. Compare Acts 23:1, πάσῃ συνειδήσει ἀγαθῇ πεπολίτευμαι Θεῷ. (4.) Since, however, as is asserted in the last passage, man in his conduct knows himself as being placed not only in a certain relation to himself and his fellow-men, but also to God, his endeavors are directed ἀπρόσκοπον συνείδησιν ἔχειν πρὸς τὸν Θεὸν καὶ τοὺς ἀνθρώπους (Acts 23:1); and συνείδησις indicates precisely the "moral religious consciousness," the "knowledge of one's self in relation to God," as Delitzsch on Heb. 9:9 and 11:2 justly remarks. The true consciousness of a false relation of man's inner state to God is πονήρα συνείδησις (Heb. 10:22).

Conscience is therefore a δύναμις, a ἕξις, and an ἐνέργεια κριτική (comp. 1 Cor. 10:29), in opposition to κατὰ σάρκα κρίνειν (John 8:15). Conscience herein resembles the law of God (Rom. 2:14). But in this very similarity it is something different from νοῦς and καρδία, otherwise a pure heart and a good conscience could not be mentioned together (1 Tim. 1:5), and there were no speaking of a pollution *as well* of the mind (νοῦς) *as* of the conscience (Tit. 1:15). The polluted mind causes that those who Θεὸν ὁμολογοῦσιν εἰδέναι, ἔργοις ἀρνοῦνται, and the last brings it about that ἡ συνείδησις μεμίανται (Tit. 1:16; comp. 1 Tim. 4:2). The love which God requires is love out of a pure heart; and it is precisely when it is such, that it is also love out of a good conscience (1 Tim. 1:5). This relation, which depends on the existing state of the human mind and of the human heart, and which is consequently not that which conditions, but which is conditioned, remains everywhere, where we are required to conceive of man's character and conduct as the object of conscience. The qualities of these do not indeed determine the actual nature (*Actualität*) of their conscience, but the quality of its testimony. It is otherwise where the will of God is conceived to be the object of conscience. There the nature of conscience determines the quality of the consciousness and of the conduct of men. In this twofold position of conscience man knows himself to be equally the judge (ὁ κρίνων) and the judged (ὁ κριθείς).

But after all these investigations concerning the empirical shape of conscience as exhibited in Scripture, very little appears to me to have yet been done towards determining its true nature. For from this very source the further questions present themselves: How is it, then, that man should arrive at the consciousness of an obligation binding on him? How is it that the consciousness of a truth should belong to man, which forms the antithesis to the nothingness of his own mind, to the darkness of his understanding, and to the estrangement of his life from that life which is from God (comp. Eph. 4:18 with Rom. 1:21)? How, by virtue of this conscience, should it be possible for man, when in a perverted state of his being, to come to a correct knowledge of this perversion? How can man, by the force of his conscience, notwithstanding that he belongs to the ἄθεοι ἐν τῷ κόσμῳ, attain to this,—namely, the perception of a relation of himself not only to that self and to the world, but to God? No light is thrown in answer to these queries by all the passages of Scripture which have been quoted respecting the συνείδησις. Whether the assertion of the apostle in the second chapter of the Epistle to the Romans offers a solution of the question, we shall reserve for further inquiry. From it we have here only to draw attention to and mention the fact, that the internal processes which by virtue of conscience go on in man, and which are attributed to the heathen world sunk "in ignorance and hardness of heart" (Eph. 4:18), are characterized by the apostle, in direct contrast to an external and positive revelation of God, as a peculiarity of man's inborn nature (φύσει—ποιοῦσιν). The question which is connected with this is, for this reason, not so much what conscience may be, and how it may manifest itself, but rather *what kind of organization that of man's nature must be,* by virtue of which that which we call conscience must be attributed to it. For at this point we meet with a twofold character in the relations of man, which is quite distinct from the contrast of body and soul, of the Ego and the world, and which recalls the saying of that old writer, who said of the creation of man, "God created a being as it were of a mixed world, who is related to two worlds, the *heavenly* and the *earthly* world" (Anastas. Sinaita, *ibid.* p. 562). And the difficulty of the question, as it exists for men as men, is rightly brought before us by the same author, when he compares the soul of man to the incomprehensible God (ἀκατάληπτος Θεός), and says, "We know nothing at all concerning it, and believe in its existence solely from the activity it manifests in the body, as in reference to God we become convinced of His existence by virtue of His works as seen in the visible world" (Anastas. Sinaita, *ibid.* p. 570).

§ 8. *The Root and Essence of Conscience*

From whence conscience springs, and what is its nature, is not to be deduced from the form in which it appears in the reflex of our self-consciousness, and in which, in certain self-conscious movements of our spirit, it manifests itself (1). For that power of conscience which discloses and manifests itself in the reflex of our self-consciousness, is dependent on circumstances which do not belong to the nature of conscience in itself, but to that of man's condition (comp. Note (4) at § 7 and § 9). And here we have to consider, not the variety of its methods of outwardly manifesting itself, but that permanent element in the working of conscience which remains the same amidst all this variety, and which leads us to a knowledge of its real essence.

That which is presented to me under all circumstances, by means of the working of my conscience, is a power manifesting itself in my spirit, and which, proceeding from the spirit, takes possession of the whole man, whose manifestation I cannot summon forth by an exertion of my conscious will, but which involuntarily seizes me. In me thoughts arise, whose subject-matter I discover to be not only certain relations of myself to my own nature and to the world, but to something which is above me and the world. Whether these thoughts be peaceful or hostile, whether they be thoughts of accordance or of contradiction, yet the nature of their impression is ever such, that that which agrees with or even opposes me, is something in me, which nevertheless is not my Ego. And yet I know that these thoughts come not from without, but have their source within me, from the depths of my spirit.

This fact is an inexplicable one, if my spirit is so organized as only to bring about relations of myself to myself and to the world; or if the organization of my individual spirit and its origin is to be referred simply to that which is innate in me as a man, or acquired by education, or a product of that cultivation which I have acquired for myself, under the force of my own activity within, and of influences without. For that which I become aware of in my conscience, precedes, as in the case of the child, the process of education: it is something of which the cultivated as well as the uncultivated man is equally conscious, and brings something to my consciousness which I must call, not a product, but a factor of my consciousness, without being able to explain the nature of this factor, from the fact that I was begotten and born a man (2).

There is, to speak the matter out at once, something above man, and above created nature, of which man becomes conscious in the working of conscience, whether he himself recognizes it as such, and calls it so or not. The workings of the spirit in conscience do not, it is true, admit of being explained, as being themselves anything divine, and are in fact only the movements of the human spirit; but they involve something which I, when I reflect upon it, am unable to explain from the nature of the spirit, if the same is merely to be thought of as the natural ground of my individual personal life, innate in me as a man (3). I stand before myself as before a riddle, whose key is not to be found in the human self-consciousness, but is given to it by God in the word of revelation. From this word we gather a derivative relation of the human spirit, by virtue of which it is descended from God, and was placed in its creature-existence by God. This derivative relation is a permanent one, because it is divinely appointed, and can, it is true, to a considerable degree be darkened, but not absolutely abolished. And this derivative relation precedes the development of the intellectual self-consciousness: man's spirit does not place itself in relation to God, but God stands in relation to man's spirit. It is a bond of life and existence, in which the human and created existence of the spirit, by the fact of the creation of the spirit out of God, becomes indissolubly connected with God, and is not set aside through the human procreation of man, as a being compounded of soul and body, but is just simply perpetuated. For this reason the spirit of man's life is called at the same time "the candle of the Lord" (Prov. 20:27). And since the original root of the spirit's existence and life is God, even in the spirit itself is rooted that which forms a powerful impulse in the conscience, and brings to man's consciousness that he not only belongs to a human, but also to a divine race, and bears something in the essence of his spirit in himself, which has its origin not from man or his race, but from God (4). This is "that light in us" which aims at reflecting itself in the mirror of man's consciousness, in order that, by the reflection of what is above man, and supernatural or divine, the proper life of man should become awakened, should incline its efforts towards it, and find in this mutual relation its satisfaction and blessedness. No one could have a consciousness of the unconditioned *true* and *good*, if man's spirit had its existence totally independent of God. For God alone is the original and unconditioned true and good; and in a derivatory and limited manner, that only is so which can be conceived as His work or His working, and whose being exists in harmony with the ends appointed for it by God (5).

(1) What is wanted in the investigation touching the root and essence of conscience, cannot be better or more strikingly expressed than in the words of Thomas Aquinas (*Summa Theol.* p. II, qu. 3, art. 8): "Objectum intellectus est quod quid est, *i.e.* essentia rei, unde in tantum procedit perfectio intellectus, in quantum cognoscit essentiam alicujus rei. Si ergo intellectus

aliquis cognoscat essentiam alicujus *effectus*, per quam non possit cognosci essentia *causæ*, ut scilicet sciatur de causa quid est, non dicitur intellectus attingere ad causam simpliciter, quamvis per effectum cognoscere possit de causa *an sit*. Et ideo remanet naturaliter homini desiderium, cum cognoscit effectum, et scit eum habere causam, ut etiam sciat de causa, quid est, et illud desiderium est admirationis et causat inquisitionem." As a rule, however, in the doctrine of conscience, men have stopped at the *effect*. Thomas Aquinas himself, while treating, according to the *communis usus loquendi*, of conscience, distinguishes very acutely, that properly speaking conscience is not a *potentia*, but an *act*—an *actual application of knowledge to those things which we do* (*Summa Theol.* p. 1, qu. 79, art. 13). But then the further question arises, What kind of a "knowledge" is that which comes to be applied to the individual actions? This was called "synteresis," as being a "scientia quæ immediate versatur circa prima principia practica universalia," and conscience was derived from it: "est de universalibus." If, however, it must necessarily be admitted that this was properly one and the same knowledge, when resting on general principles, and when applied to particular cases, the same conclusion might be arrived at as by Duns Scotus (*Commentar. in* IV. *libb. sententiar.* lib. ii. dist. 39), of attributing to the "habitus proprius conclusions practicæ" the name of *conscience*. The main question, however, always remained,—namely, how the "intellectus naturalis" arrived at such "principia universalia" (the presentiment or the consciousness of a *bonum universale*). For in this way I properly know nothing, if I do as the older Protestant ethical writers did, and call conscience a "faculty of the mind," and an "operation of the human intellect," and assert, finally, "Conscientia est argumentatio hominis de actionibus suis ad legem relatis." That is, at most, to stop at the *communis usus loquendi*; and more narrowly examined, it is not even correct. The "argumentatio" is only *one* form in which conscience manifests itself, but not the form in which are comprised all its methods of manifesting itself. Why the "*actions* of man" merely should be regarded as the object of conscience, is not evident, since the *state* of man, or his *thoughts*, might just as well be so called. When Thomas Aquinas, in the *secundæ secunda*, as the subdivision of a whole, begins with the *notis actuum humanorum*, this is quite intelligible. But when later Catholic ethical writers still appeal to him, and begin their system with the chapter *de actionibus humanis* (as, for instance, Andr. Jos. Haehnlein, *Princip. Theol. mor.* Wirceb. 1855, I. P. Gury S. J. *Compend. Theol. mor.* edit. in Germania altera, Ratisb. 1857), it is perfectly incomprehensible. We shall never arrive at the proper signification of conscience, if we only keep in view its relation to human actions. And when the above-mentioned Protestant ethical writer designates, as the object of conscience, the "actiones *ad legem* relatæ," we must now further ask, How does the "intellectus naturalis" arrive at a "scientia legis?" What kind of a "law" is it? and is what I call a "law" actually the correct or comprehensive expression for that which presents itself to the human conscience as something which is placed above humanity? We ought not to rest satisfied with isolated manifestations, declarations, and workings of conscience, if we wish truly to understand what conscience really is.

(2) In the question concerning the root and essence of conscience, we view the latter only on one side of its relations or of its nature. It is not the consciousness in which the conditions, tendencies, or the deeds of a man's individual Ego come before him, but the consciousness in which something becomes present to him, which transcends the sphere of his Ego and the world, which does not correspond either to his individual circumstances and tendencies, or to the circumstances and tendencies of the world, but again and again contradicts them, and causes man, who fondly imagines himself to be the absolute lord of himself, to perceive that he is under the influence of a power which constrains him, and which, when he opposes it, strikes him down and crushes him. This is the sense in which certain of the ancients supposed conscience to be portrayed by the term "adversary" (ἀντίδικος)

with whom we are "in the way" (Matt. 5:25, 26). The question accordingly is, How comes it that man by nature (φύτει) should find within him a higher and directing power ruling over him?

Man is so organized physiologically, is the answer of modern physiology. All ideas of a higher system of the world, and of our relation to it, arise from perceptions of the senses. "The supposition of a so-called intellectual revelation, in so far as is meant thereby a particular way and a special kind of knowledge, rests only on a self-pleasing delusion" (so Spiess, *Physiologie des Nervensystems*, Braunsch. 1844, p. 345 ff.). How the same physiologist should come to speak of a "revelation of God in nature, and pre-eminently in history," is inconceivable. For neither the one nor the other is a perception of sense. But "conscience" (so the author says, p. 346) "is not a distinct power within us, by means of which we distinguish infallibly the good from the bad, and the beautiful from the ugly; it is, in short, nothing distinct from our ordinary empirical Ego, least of all an immediate voice of God in us; but it is our entire empirical Ego itself,—this association of series of ideas and of substances, as it has formed itself out of the two factors, *the innate physical organization* and the human *external influences brought into play by means of the senses* in process of time and with the co-operation of voluntary attention. *Whatever is in accord with this empirical Ego for the time being*, this appears to us, according as it has respect to a moral or an æsthetic object, to be right or beautiful, and conversely. It is for this reason that our views of what is right and beautiful vary so much," etc. Thus argues modern sensualism, in the garb of the ancient sophist Protagoras. But the assertion that conscience conforms itself to the empirical Ego for the time being, flies in the face of every fact, from the empirical knowledge of which we come to speak of a conscience. That conscience does *not* harmonize with the empirical Ego at any given time, but most frequently places itself in the way, as an antagonist to human thoughts and inclinations, is the most striking feature of that consciousness which we call conscience, and which I beg that physiology should explain. Does it lie in our physical organization and its sense-perceptions, upon which all our ideas are made to rest? Where, then, have I this sense-perception of a nature at strife with itself—of a *concordia discors naturæ meæ?* Or if the empirical Ego has for its factor not only the innate physical organization, but also the various external influences brought into play by means of the senses, what sort of a corrupt organization is it, which is never in a position to keep off from my body those "external influences brought into play by means of the senses," which disturb my harmony with my empirical Ego for the time being? Conscience is represented as punishing us "for an idea, a feeling, a desire, and a deed, which has obtained a temporary ascendency over us, in spite of the fact that it does not harmonize with our proper nature, with our empirical Ego." But if that empirical Ego for the time being is my own proper nature, and if conscience is the consciousness which accords with my empirical Ego for the time being, how then does it come to pass that my conscience should allow anything to obtain an ascendency over me which does not harmonize with my empirical Ego? How, moreover, does it come to punish me afterwards? Or if conscience knows, *i.e.* if I know by means of conscience, about my own proper nature, in contrast with my actual empirical Ego—a statement that physiology certainly neither could nor would make—then let some one show me, on physiological principles, by what sensuous perception man, by virtue of his conscience, arrives at the consciousness of his "*proper nature,*" as distinct from the empirical Ego for the time being. But, indeed, he who takes his stand on the physiology of the nervous system, and will not move from that position, would do better not to speak of conscience at all, nay, not even of morality. For that has not its origin in physiological processes which we can examine with the microscope, or measure out by millimetres.

But if, indeed, we might regard the spirit of man in the sense of the porch, as τοῦ Διὸς μέρος, τοῦ τὸν κόσμον διοικοῦντος ἀπόρροια, *divini spiritus pars ac veluti scintilla quædam*, the question would be easily answered; and we might say, in the words of Sextus Empiricus, which he used in justification of Xenophanes: τῷ ἐν ἑαυτῷ Θεῷ τὸν ἐκτὸς κατείληφεν. But the τοῦ γὰρ καὶ γένος ἐσμέν of Acts 17 has not this meaning. The Scriptures speak, indeed, of our becoming partakers of a divine nature (θείας φύσεως, 2 Pet. 1:4) through Christ; but they say nothing of our participating in it without Christ. The assertion "non est pars Dei anima" of Augustine (*Ep.* 28, *ad Hieronym.*) has a certain and incontestable ground in Scripture. If one should attribute the predicate θεῖος to the spirit or soul of man from the standpoint of Christian knowledge, then must we half affirm and half deny it, as the example of Isidorus of Pelusium may show. He says (*Epp.* iv. 124): θείαν μὲν ἡγούμεθα τὴν ψυχὴν εἶναι (οὐ μὴν τῆς θειοτάτης καὶ βασιλικωτάτης φύσεως ὁμοούσιον) καὶ ἀθάνατον (ἀλλ' οὐ τῆς ἀνάρχου καὶ ποιητικῆς καὶ ἀϊδίου μέρος). Εἰ γὰρ ἐκείνης τῆς ἀρρήτου ἦν μέρος, οὐκ ἂν ἥμαρτεν, οὐκ ἂν ἐκρίθη. Εἰ δὲ ταῦτα πάσχει, τῆς ἀνωτάτου οὐσίας ποίημα δικαίως ἂν πιστευθείη, οὐ μέρος, ἵνα μὴ ἑαυτὴν ἡ θεία φύσις κρίνουσα φωραθείη. The creation (ποίημα), although it is originated by God, is not to be considered as divine in its nature.

When the new Platonism, starting from entirely different premises than the facts of conscience, assigned to man two souls, and designated the one alone as capable of beholding God (θεοπτική), Jamblich, *de Myster.* viii. 6); when, in connection with the doctrine of the threefold, *i.e.* the vegetative, sensuous, and intellectual soul of the world (see Varro in Augustine's *Civ. Dei*, vii. 23), there is attributed to the human soul, as an efflux of this soul of the world, this last *pars animæ* as *animus*, and it is said: "hanc partem animæ mundi deum, in nobis autem genium vocari," such entirely heterogeneous views might, it is true, appear serviceable in explaining different phenomena or relations in the life of the human spirit, but could not be maintained either on the ground of Christian knowledge as warranted by Scripture, or upon that of rigid self-inspection. For the characteristic of self-consciousness is an indivisible totality (αὐτὸς ἐγώ); and my soul is well aware of a natural ground of its existence, which it employs according to the difference of the objects, as of an organ of twofold form, but never of a spirit in which it would not be itself—the soul that was recognising, and never of a body in which it would not be itself that was feeling corporeally. "Proinde et animum sive mens est, νοῦς apud Græcos, non aliud quid intelligimus, quam *suggestum animæ* et insitum et nativitatis proprium, quo agit, quo sapit, quem secum habens *ex semet ipsa* se commoveat in semet ipsa, atque ita moveri *videatur* ab illo tanquam substantia alia," etc. (Tertull. *de anima*, 12). "Præstruximus neque animam aliud quid esse, quam animæ suggestum et structum, neque spiritum extraneum quid, quam quod et ipsa per flatum (Gen. 2:7). Et nunc ad differentiam sensualium et intellectualium non aliud admittimus, quam *rerum diversitates*, corporalium et spiritualium, visibilium et invisibilium, publicatarum et arcanarum, quod illæ sensui, istæ intellectui attribuantur, *apud animam* tamen et istis et illis obsequio deputatis, *quæ* perinde per corpus corporalia sentit quemadmodum per animum incorporalia intelligit, salvo eo, ut etiam sentiat, dum intelligit" (*Ibid.* c. 18). This spiritual faculty of internal vision possessed by the soul is also what is meant by Claudianus Mamercus, when he says, "Huic (animæ) superpositus est non loco, sed vi ac potentia oculus quidam, qui sive spiritus, sive mens, sive intellectus unum atque idem est, etsi diverso nomine dicitur" (*de statu animæ*, i. 23),—not an *anima rationalis* alongside an *anima irrationalis*, nor an *anima animalis* alongside an *anima spiritualis*, wherein from of old the church was united alike against Gnostics and Manicheans, Eutychians and Apollinarists, as against that Pelagianism which still more immediately affected the questions of ethics. Comp. *e.g.* August, *lib. de duabus animis cont. Manich.* c. 14; *cont. Faustum*, vi. 8; *in Genes. ad litt.* x. 13; Gennad. Massil. *de ecclesiast. dogmat.* 10 and 15; Concil. Constantin. IV. (the eighth œcumenical), act. x. can. 10.

(3) But are we not, then, able to discriminate something in us, which we may contrast with the mere human creaturely element as something divine, and which we may perhaps

name, as does Chrysostom, the κριτήριον—φυσικὸν καὶ παρὰ τοῦ Θεοῦ ἡμῖν παρὰ τὴν ἀρχὴν ἐντεθέν or θεῖον καὶ παρὰ τοῦ θεοῦ ταῖς ἡμετέραις ἐνιδρυμένον ψυχαῖς (*in Ps.* 7 hom. 3, *in Jes.* vi. 2)? Here it is where a full understanding of Rom. 2:14, 15 appears unavoidably necessary. For only recently has it been repeated (by Delitzsch, *System der bibl. Psychologie*, p. 101 ff. [p. 163 ff. in Clark's translation]), that conscience is the "knowledge of a divine law which every man bears in his heart. Even the heathen have τὸ ἔργον τοῦ νόμου γραπτὸν ἐν ταῖς καρδίαις αὐτῶν, that is to say, the course of action by which the law of God is fulfilled: of what nature this is, stands written in ineffaceable characters in their hearts as an objective precept, as it stands for Israel on the tables of stone, and on the parchment of the Thora." If this word "written" is to be referred to a divine act, one naturally wishes to know more precisely how we are to think of it, how it is repeated in each individual, and the way in which it appertains to the organization of our nature, so that we do by nature (φύσει ποιοῦσιν, ver. 14) that which God has written in our hearts in ineffaceable characters. But the only statement afterwards made by Delitzsch (p. 103 ff. [p. 167 ff. of Clark's translation]) is this: "The powers of the spirit and of the soul themselves are, as it were, the decalogue of this Thora implanted in us by the Creator." This I do not understand. The *powers* of the spirit and of the soul are no objective *commandment*; and if the objective commandment is identical with the *powers* of our spirit and our soul, it is not a commandment within us, but at the same time a power of fulfilling it. Or if the powers of the spirit and the soul are, like the decalogue, of a legislative kind, I am at a loss to conceive how I ought to call this decalogue of the faculties of my spirit and my soul a "divine law." However, not only do I not rightly understand this exposition, but I understand the passage in the Epistle to the Romans in quite a different sense. In the first place, we must remark that it is not said of the heathen: Ἐνδείκνυνται τὸν νόμον γραπτὸν ἐν τ. καρδ. αὐτ.; also not, ἐνδείκ. τὸ ἔργον τοῦ νόμου γραπτοῦ ἐν κ.τ.λ.; but, ἐνδείκνυνται τὸ ἔργον τοῦ νόμου γραπτὸν ἐν τ. καρδ. αὐτῶν. Further, ἔργον in the context of our passage is anything but "the course of action by which the law of God is fulfilled." He who without positive law commits sin, is brought also without positive law to ruin—this is the thesis so far as concerns the heathen world; for the real point of the question is, not whether a law exists, or is heard, but whether it is carried out: that is the supplement, which establishes and justifies alike the ἀπολοῦνται as applying to the heathen, and the κριθήσονται as applying to the Jews. But in what way we are to conceive the ἀνόμως ἀπολοῦνται of the heathen, is shown and confirmed by that *self-judgment* which the heathen exercise on themselves, and according to which they also will at some future day be judged by God (ver. 16). Of this self-judgment vers. 14, 15 treat. What is meant by these words, that the heathen, without having a law (νόμον), do by nature the things of the positive law (τοῦ νόμου), is shown by the explanatory sentence, ver. 15 (οἵτινες). The positive law is the accuser and judge: accuser and judge are the heathen to themselves, in the testimony of their conscience and in the thoughts, which accuse or else excuse one another. The heathen, when they *by nature* do that which belongs to the positive law, without having a law, are a law *unto themselves*. And when their conscience bears testimony, and the thoughts accuse or else excuse one another, they show that the work of the positive law stands written in their hearts. The work of the positive law, however, is to accuse and judge. In their hearts they accuse and judge themselves—thereby showing, that what is the work of the positive law is engraven in their hearts. He who so understands the passage—and it seems to me it *must* be so understood—neither regards τὸ ἔργον τοῦ νόμου as that course of action by which the law is fulfilled, nor the γραπτὸν ἐν ταῖς καρδίαις as a commandment of law engraven on the human heart. The time and circumstances in which God will put His law into our mind, and write it in our hearts, belong to the fulfilling of the promise (comp. Jer. 31:33; Heb. 8:10). Of a decalogue engraven ineffaceably on the hearts of the heathen, no more trace is to be found in the passage of the Epistle to the Romans, than in the history of the heathen world, especially in what concerns the first table. Just as little does this passage in Romans serve to explain the origin and the nature of conscience. For now, for the first time, the question justly presents itself: How is it that the human heart, under the testimony of conscience, and the mutual accusing and excusing of its thoughts, comes to do that which belongs to the positive law, namely, to pronounce on itself a righteous judgment? Whence is that engraven on the heart, which is otherwise only a work of the positive divine law? How comes it that those, in whose hearts the law of God is *not written*, do *by nature* what belongs to the law, and are a law *unto themselves?* To all these questions the passage in Romans, when rightly understood, gives NO answer.

(4) The Confession of the Lutheran Church says: "Humana ratio seu naturalis *intellectus* hominis obscuram aliquam notitiæ illius scintillulam reliquam habet, quod sit Deus, et particulam aliquam legis tenet" (Rom. 1:19 ff.). We name the spirit, in so far as it is moral and religious consciousness, conscience. The faculty of human knowledge (τὸ πνεῦμα οἶδε, 1 Cor. 2:11) is the spirit. He who wishes to understand the nature of conscience, must first have understood that of the spirit. Everything, however, "quod factum et natum est," is understood not in the light of its existence, but in that of its origin. Man, consisting of body and soul, is now originated by procreation. But by procreation the substance of human *nature* is only so perpetuated, as in the beginning it came into being, not by human generation, but by divine creative act, and divine creative ordinance (see Claudian. Mamerc. i. 23). That corporeal nature which is perpetuated by bodily generation, never loses or falsifies its original source, by virtue of which God did not create it directly from Himself, but took it from the earth, made it by means of that earth which He Himself had first made. And the spirit, which is also perpetuated by generation, never loses or falsifies its original source, by virtue of which God, without any intermediate means, created the spirit from Himself, and made it the vital factor of the earthly body, and thus, by means of a bodily existence taken from a

creature condition, and a spiritual existence formed in the state of a creature, made man a living soul (Gen. 2:7; 1 Cor. 15). It holds good in a much more striking manner of the soul than of the body, *a Deo factus, a Deo datus*. The immediate character of its created origin from God, is that element which belongs especially to the spirit, "principale, divinum atque germanum, et proprie naturale." With this characteristic is the human spirit implanted in the life of the human race; and that spirit which is perpetuated and which enters into every individual existence never loses its peculiar essence,—namely, that of being in its first origin a creature substance, created most immediately from God. "Omnem autem hominis in utero serendi, struendi, fingendi paraturam *aliqua* utique *potestas divinæ voluntatis ministra modulator*, quamcunque illa rationem agitare sortita. Vis animæ, in qua naturalia peculia consita retinentur, *salvo substantiæ modulo, quo a primordio inflata est*, paulatim cum carne producitur" (Tertull. *de anima*, c. 37). The traces of this origin may indeed be obscured, but cannot be altogether blotted out. God stands in so marked a relation of creative Fatherhood to the human spirit, that even to the most degenerate child—that is, to the spirit in its greatest estrangement—the presentiment must still belong, Τοῦ γὰρ καὶ γένος ἐσμέν! It remains still, and manifests itself even in the fierce hate in which man praises the body alone, mocks at the soul, denies and blasphemes the nobility of a divine race, and takes pleasure in placing himself on a level with the brutes. "*Nosti dum odisti.*" And this presentiment remains so much the more, from the fact that even fallen man is, without being aware of it, supported by a nearness of God which preserves the bond of that primeval authorship of our spiritual life, although too often man does not in any way seek after it. It is to the human race, not to nature, to which it has been falsely transferred, that the saying applies: In God we live, and move, and have our being. And not because we live, etc. in God are we a divine race; but because we are a divine race do we live and move in God, "who is not far from any one of us,"— that is to say, God Himself supports the creature of His hand, places it not once only as "His work that man should be able to think, to speak, to act, and effect anything," but does not allow him to depart from that vital connection in which the consciousness, when he seeks after it, can be attained, that the thinking, speaking, acting, and working of the spirit rests on a power which springs not from a nature void of God, but from a God whom the Scriptures call the Father of spirits (Heb. 12:9). When I previously named the spirit as organized for the intercourse of God with us, and of us with God, and viewed it as an actual mutual relation, it was not my intention that a continuous speaking of God in us, and the like, should be thereby understood. It is a vital connection which man must first comprehend in presentiment, thought, or word, but could not do so without that connection. The last and deepest root of the spirit is the root of conscience: if the spirit were not and did not continue to be a spirit derived from God, it could neither comprehend, feel, nor conceive of God. This is asserted by one who was the first and most decided opponent of every sort of Creationism—of every heavenly, divine, transmundane origin of the human soul and human spirit. "Inest et bonum animæ illud principale, illud divinum atque germanum, et proprie naturale. Quod enim a Deo est, non tam exstinguitur, quam obumbratur. *Potest enim obumbrari, quia non est Deus, exstingui non potest, quia a Deo est*. Sic et divinitas animæ in præsagia erumpit *ex bono priori*, et conscientia Dei in testimonium prodit: Deus bonus est, Deus videt, et Deo commendo" (Tertull. *de animâ*, 41). "Mirum, si a Deo data homini, novit divinare? Tam mirum, si eum, a quo data est, novit. Etiam circumventa ab adversario, meminit *sui auctoris* et bonitatis et decreti ejus et exitus sui et adversarii ipsius. Sic mirum, si a Deo data, eadem canit, quæ Deus suis dedit nosse. Sed qui ejusmodi eruptiones animæ non putavit doctrinam esse *naturæ* congenitæ et ingenitæ *conscientiæ* tacita commissa: dicet potius, diventilatis in vulgus opinionibus, publicatarum literarum usum, jam et quasi vitium corroboratum taliter sermocinandi. Certe prior anima quam litera, et prior sermo quam liber, et prior sensus quam stilus, et prior homo ipse quam philosophus et poëta" (Id. *de testimon. animæ*, 5). When I, with the same eloquent witness, feel compelled to say, "(Deus animam) de suo efflatu ad similitudinem suæ *vivacitatis* animavit" (*de resurrec. carnis*, c. 9), by the similitude *vivacitatis* is meant just this: that as God has life in Himself, so the spiritual life of the soul springs originally from God, and, in truth, in a sense in which it can be asserted of no other creature; in such a way, however, that not the spirit indeed, but its individual form of existence, springs from man and the life of his race. By virtue of this relation, to which we may justly apply an expression of Jamblich's, already quoted by the Lutheran dogmatic divines, "συμπλοκὴ" Θεοῦ καὶ πνεύματος, or ψυχῆς, the last factor of the spirit that is cognizant of God or of conscience, is really God, not man. In this sense we are probably to understand what the abbot Jo. Raytu, in *S. Joannis Scholast. Climacem Scholia* (in the second half of the sixth century), intends when he says, "Conscientia est scintilla divini luminis in homine condito subseminata in primordio;" or when Petr. Cellensis, *lib. de conscientia* (twelfth century), called conscience a "creatrix imago in imagine creata." In the same sense I must still at the present day agree with Joh. Wessel, when he protests against the Aristotelian scholastic definition of conscience by *intellectus, conscientia, synteresis* (as it prevailed especially after it had been so developed by Thomas Aquinas, and is ever and anon brought forward in the compendiums of Catholic theologians—as, for example, in Gury, Hæhnlein, and others), and when he designates conscience according to its deepest root and its most peculiar essence: "Non animæ potentiam aut naturalem habitum animæ, sed magis inspiratum spiraculum vitæ divinitus et divinam turn voluntatis turn intelligentiæ assistentiam" (Jo. Wessel, *farrago rev. theol. de provident. Dei*, c. 11). The proposition would be false only if we were obliged to imagine the *naturalis animæ habitus* absolutely excluded. For precisely on the *naturalis animæ habitus* everything in the manifestation of conscience depends; and on it hinges, whether the natural man, ever according to the harmony or the discord of his spirit with the ultimate Origin of the existence and the life of the spirit, feels his conscience as approval and admonition, or as reproof and warning, or as judgment; and in the last named case finds by experience also that the natural man can carry about in the midst of his heart Him who is a consuming fire (Heb. 12:29). That man at least can never yet have felt the torment of conscience, who supposes that nothing is here at play but the spirit of man and his thoughts. For this reason, however, quite irrespective of the misunderstood passage in Romans, conscience is still far from being man's consciousness of a law within him. It has indeed also this form, but it is not totally comprised therein. And well for us it is that man's spirit has not been bound down as by a natural necessity to the stone of "that letter which kills." For on this very account, and from no other ground, can Luther say of conscience: "This same bride and queen shall remain of right unspotted and undefiled by the law, but be kept unmoved and pure for her right, her only and true Bridegroom, Christ." How would that be possible if man's conscience consisted of an indissoluble connection of the spirit with a law ineffaceably engraven on the spirit? See Anastasius Sinaita, *ibid.* p. 606 ff.

(5) Not, however, in the mere words, but in the nature of the thing itself, the idea and the consciousness of the unconditioned good coincides with that of God (good is in Gothic *gôds*, middle-high-German *guot*; God is in Gothic *Goth*, middle-high-German *Got*). The unconditioned good, however, presupposes the unconditioned true. For the true, when conceived of ontologically, and not noëtically, is the being consistent with self; and the good is in this self-consistency, the being self-sufficing. If I, therefore, *name* this the unconditioned good and true, I can only *derive* it from a consciousness of the unconditioned dwelling in me. For in the experience alike of my own state and of that of the whole world, I never find this self-consistent, self-sufficing being; nowhere do I perceive this absolute truth and absolute goodness, but everywhere only relative truth and relative goodness, in which a being which has fallen into discord with itself, and lacking contentment, has

only a share. If, in spite of this, I know of an unconditioned true and good, this consciousness cannot be a reflex either of my objective Ego or of the objective world, but must be a reflex of the unconditioned essence in my spirit itself. This is what Augustine named the "incommutabilis et vera veritatis æternitas infra mentem mutabilem" (*Conf.* vii. 17, 23). I know of this truth and goodness as of something placed above me, nay also as of something testifying against me, by which my changing and struggling Ego is supported, as by the Source of all life, and is attracted thereby as by a goal of its being. In this sense, what Simplicius says is right (*Comment. in Epict. Enchirid.* i. 1, p. 5), ταῦτα γάρ ἐστιν ἕν· καὶ ἀρχὴ, καὶ ἀγαθὸν, καὶ Θεός, and when he calls this one thing that οὗ πάντα ἐφίεται, οὗ πάντα ἀνατείνεται. And in comparison with the relative good it is the consciousness of a highest good, which under all circumstances is inherent in our thoughts of God. "Hoc omnes Deum consentiunt esse, quod ceteris rebus omnibus anteponunt" (Augustin, *de doctr. Christ.* c. 6). But considered in itself, the consciousness of God is the consciousness of the absolutely true and good. The ἀλήθεια is τὸ γνωστὸν τοῦ Θεοῦ (Rom. 1:18, 19). The good, the acceptable, and the perfect, is τὸ θέλημα τοῦ Θεοῦ (Rom. 12:2). The predicate good, Christ bids us give to none but God (τί με ἐρωτᾷς περὶ ἀγαθοῦ; Εἷς ἐστιν ὁ ἀγαθός, Matt. 19:17). And if there is anything good in a derived sense, it is so only so far as it manifests itself as a creature of God, as descending from above (κτίσμα Θεοῦ, ἄνωθεν καταβαῖνον, 1 Tim. 4:4; Jas. 1:17), and stands and has maintained itself in the same relation in which it was created for God (ἐξ αὐτοῦ καὶ δι' αὐτοῦ καὶ εἰς αὐτὸν τὰ πάντα, Rom. 11:36; comp. Col. 1:16). "Quia fecisti nos ad te, Domine, inquietum est cor nostrum, donec requiescat in te" (August. *Conf.* i. 1). "Ad ilium suspensa est anima nostra, a quo formata" Gregor. M. *moral*, xxvi. 16).

§ 9. β. *The Form of the Manifestation of Conscience*

The way in which conscience may manifest itself depends on other grounds than those which are given in the essence of it. The mere development of the human consciousness implies, that even in the case of a perfectly normal relation, conscience cannot possibly be reflected in like manner at the different stages of its development, or with the different kinds and degrees of the spiritual receptivity (1). And then in the personal Ego of the man, as well as in his position towards the world, there is implied a possibility that he may receive impulses from other sources than conscience,—that he may yield to this or that other element with one or other of the forces of his spiritual life, and indeed may make this other element the center of the movements of his personal life. Exactly according to the measure, therefore, in which this goes on, man's position with respect to conscience changes, and therewith the manifestation of the latter in the human consciousness. In itself, according to its essence, conscience, as the consciousness of God, would be beyond contradiction the inbeing of God as the True and the Good, around which, as their center, all the faculties of human nature would revolve in yearning love. It would be in its working on my self-consciousness, it is true, a consciousness of the dependence of my being and my will on a higher being and will; but there would be, as a bond of the communion of our nature with God, a consciousness of the unison of my will with the divine will standing above me (2). Such, however, it no longer is. The language of the world before Christ knows nothing of a conscience which brought to man's consciousness such a relation of God to us, and of us to God; and that which we still at the present day, in common with Scripture, call conscience, does not manifest itself to us as the consciousness of an undisturbed and perfect communion with God.

There even, in cases where our conscience approves of us, we feel this approval as one which holds good in this or that matter, which I think, will, or do, but not in our whole conduct. I *know*, by virtue of conscience, of a life in God; I know, however, by virtue of this same conscience, that my life is not merged in this life in God. Conscience holds before me the demand of God in a "thou shalt," which has not the significance of setting before me the divine will objectively, but rather of making clear the apostasy of my own will from the divine. It is predominantly in the form of accusation and self-judgment that conscience manifests itself in our experience; and in this, with reason, the ante-Christian world also found the chief import of conscience. This position of conscience, however, can only be explained by some superinduced but now habitual peculiarity of human nature, and not by the essence of conscience (3).

(1) We hold fast, in what follows, to the distinction which must be made between the objective reality which lies at the root of conscience, and the consciousness which springs from this root. It is essential to conscience, that it reveals in every form a dependence of the human spirit upon God, resting on a causal relation. But the form in which it manifests itself is accidental; that is to say, the way in which it makes itself felt in my self-consciousness, whether it be as a foreboding or as knowledge, whether it be as impulse or as remorse, whether it be as a yea or as a nay, and the like. Conscience is no formulated codex, but an informal, substantial relation of God to our spirit, and the converse. It is the same in the child as in the old man—the same in him who yields to it, as in him who resists it; but always according to the degree of the natural development or the ethical position attained by the individual, it manifests and reveals itself differently. Conscience is, as the fathers of the church justly remark, an ἄφυκτον, ἀδέκαστον, ἔχει ἔνδον ἕκαστος τὸ συνειδός, κἂν μὴ βούληται. It is, as Chrysostom says, a κρίσις τοῦ καλοῦ. But how "the voice of the crier" (καταβοῶν) makes itself felt in us, whether as a κατήγορον or as a παραμυθία, whether as ταραχή or as εὐφροσύνη, whether as *divinatio* or as *judicium*,—all this is independent of what conscience in its essence is.

(2) A real, substantial relation of dependence of the creaturely human spirit upon God—that is the essential fact

which, in the phenomena of conscience, presents itself to the consciousness of man. How that shaped itself in the primal man, we have naturally no facts of experience to enable us to decide. We can, however, define it according to that which the apostle allows to remain as a relation even of fallen man. It is the relation of God's nearness (Θεὸς οὐ μακρὰν ἀπὸ ἑνὸς ἑκάστου ὑπάρχων, Acts 17:27); which nearness the apostle defines, on the side of man, not as a task of approaching unto God, but as living, and moving, and having our being in God (17:28). By virtue of this *existing* relation God is near to us, and by virtue of the same *existing* relation we are and continue a divine race (γένος ὑπάρχοντες τοῦ Θεοῦ, 17:29). The natural and adequate expression of this relation, in the reflex of our consciousness, cannot be otherwise conceived, than that we are conscious of this relation as of one *actually existent*. For it is one that is, and has actually taken place in us as creatures, not simply one that *ought* to be, and which only exists in the will of God. When, therefore, one stopped at this or that form of the manifestation of conscience, and changed the relation of our spirit to God which conditions conscience into a *lex Dei* (as, for example, Origen has already done, *de Princip.* iii. p. 299, ed. Redepenn.), in this way the just view itself was lost sight of. Much more correctly says Tertullian: "Animæ a primordio conscientia Dei" (not *legis Dei*) "dos est." "Habet Deus testimonia *totum hoc quod sumus et in quo sumus*" (*adv. Marcion*, i. 10). And even in reference to Rom. 2, where the question is concerning the legal, that is to say, judging and judicial manifestation of this consciousness, he correctly varies the terms "lex naturalis" and "*natura legalis*" (*de coron. Milit.* c. 6), and says in another place (*adv. Marcion*, v. 13), "Is Deus judicabit, cujus sunt et ipsa lex" (namely, the law of Israel), "*et ipsa natura, quæ legis est instar ignorantibus legem.*" If, therefore, by virtue of our natural consciousness in conscience, a feeling or judgment takes possession of us, that we are indeed, through the relation of God to us and to our spirit, a divine race, and live, and move, and have our being in Him, but that in the movements of our spiritual tendency toward God we do not show ourselves to be a divine race, and do not live, and move, and have our being in Him, but that we *ought* to become or to be all this first, this is not the result of that spiritual relation of our essence in which we originally, according to the conscience-qualification of our spirit, stood to God, is not the manifestation corresponding to the nature of our spirit as conscience, but is the result of a depravation not originally belonging to conscience as such, but superinduced at a later period.

(3) It is quite in vain to attempt to explain the above stated manifestation of conscience from the nature of man, that is, the nature inborn in him, divinely implanted and divinely willed. If, according to the account of the creation in Genesis (ch. 2:16, 17), God took up His position *over against* man with His "thou shalt" and "thou shalt not," yet we cannot, it is self-evident, apply this to explain the original nature and contents of conscience. We can at most conclude therefrom, that God from the beginning wished that man should know that he was not left to his conscience alone. The testifying of the will of the *personal* God to man in words has indeed no other form. Conscience is, however, no personal testifying of the will of God, immanent in man. Man is not an incarnate God. But such would be the consequence, if we should choose to regard what is narrated in Gen. 2:16, 17 as simply the language or the form of manifestation of conscience.

But it may here be further said: The relation to God which has been implanted in the essence of the human spirit, by means of which we are a divine race, and live, and move, and have our being in Him, is, as a substantial relation of the conscious spirit, at the same time the object of my will. And since man's nature is not comprised entirely in this relation, I am thus able to turn away, according as I will, from this one relation of my nature, and to turn myself to another; for I am not *constrained* willingly to live, and move, and have my being in that which belongs to my spirit, by virtue of its relation to God. Over against this free disposition of man with respect to the tendency of his will stands his relation to God, which is given in conscience as obligation. This is quite correct, if in speaking of this free disposition I conceive of a possibility of an apostasy of my will from that which is my original and proper nature. For there can, out of the consciousness of my original and proper nature, arise in my very self the requisition by my own will to turn myself again to that from which I strayed, and to restore that which was my original nature. But even this is by no means the question. The question is, whether the proper and original relation of my spirit to God consists in a requisition of which I am conscious, and addressed to my will, so that either this relation is exhausted in a simple postulate of God to me, or is only real so far as man by his will performs this postulate. But what man *is*, as man of a divine race, that exists neither as a simple divine postulate; nor does man become such simply by his performance of this postulate. And it is more than a play upon words—it is a confusion of ideas—when I assert that what man is, that he also *ought* to be, in so far as this relation of existence is also one willed by God. For that "shall," by which I denote the will of God as the cause of anything existing, is distinct from that "shall" which is addressed to the will of man as a requisition to him to realize a relation. True, I may say that, from the relation in which I belong to a divine race, and live, and move, and have my being in God, under the supposition of an apostasy of my will from this relation, the requirement may present itself to me, that I should live, and move, and have my being in God. But in itself this relation is neither a divine postulate only, nor simply one fulfilled, and to be fulfilled by my human will.

From another point of view it may be also said, that certainly man in this relation is not actually such, but only becoming such. That which man, as man of a divine race, is at the termination of his process of development, presents itself to him during this development as a "shall," in the sense of a perfection not yet attained. But that can only be said with some show of reason when we attribute to the innate and inborn conscience a nature which it does not possess. As if the spirit in the conscience bore the stereotyped image of the ethically perfect man! Conscience is a ferment of ethical development, not a prototype of human ethical perfection. By the force of conscience nothing presents itself to my consciousness but a permanent relation of dependence of my spirit on God. If it mirrors itself in me as a relation of dependence in which I am to stand with my will, and if I understand again by this "shall" not merely this, that this relation is one willed by God, then is the obligation as a claim on my will or a demand on my spirit, which in its substance is will, now also conformably to its nature to will in God, only possible when I have endeavored to make myself, as to my will, independent of that which I am by the nature of my spirit. For a dependence in which my spirit stands by virtue of its own innate nature is never in itself a requisition to my will to place myself in such a dependence.

Most untenable of all was that opinion which appealed to the corporeal life of man, for which by the term sensualism a false notion was all at once substituted, and saw in it that side of existence which, as not being admitted into that union with God which belongs to the human spirit as conscience, had in conscience that opposition which works upon it "with a force of necessity." For if we do not start from the supposition of the extremest dualism, it is absolutely inconceivable how it should be the property of the divinely originated substratum of man's earthly existence, to have, as it were, an independent tendency, a principle of life, which should find itself in opposition to a no less divinely established principle—conscience.

When, therefore, it is asserted that, consistently with that which holy Scripture declares to us concerning this relation in which man by the nature of his spirit stands to God, we are unable to explain to ourselves from this original and innate relation the inward form in which conscience now manifests itself, yet the demanding and judicial position of conscience has not thereby lost its import for man's ethical development, but has rather only rightly attained it. Hereby is it at the same time the source of a just self-knowledge in our present state. Conscience, with its demanding "shall," does not portray to us a friendly light in whose glow we might disport ourselves (*verites lucens*, in the sense of Augustine), but it steps before us as a creditor before his debtor (*veritas redarguens*). It is a light that shineth in the darkness—not perverted by the darkness into a "shall," but by this "shall" asserting its form and authority against the darkness. For that which I might feel as a higher relation of my spiritual nature created in me, so as to love and cherish it with the same natural affection as I love, nourish, and cherish my own flesh, that I now feel as a power standing over me, with a strange and ever binding presence. Not, however, that conscience, whether the will of man be conceived of as in unison with God or in opposition to Him, explains to me the nature of the personal will of God, as of a will superior to man's will, in a series of requirements. Conscience is not such an interpreter of the personal will of God or of the divine law. For this, God has already before the fall adopted other means (Gen. 2:16, 17). But conscience really is the spirit of man, so shaped and organized that this higher relation, innate in the nature of the spirit—if I do not in my personal life allow myself to be carried along, swayed, and led by it in joy and love—comes upon me as a spiritual power of nature, of unsatisfied hunger, of disappointed longing, of violated shame, subdues me by its power, and makes me to perceive the perverted emancipation of my personal life from the most peculiar and permanent ground of my nature in the consciousness of unsatisfied higher requirements, and accusations not to be gainsaid, and sorrowful self-condemnation. True it is, that man knows not from himself what that peculiar nature is. *Sine ulla divina ratione*, said Cicero even of conscience for this reason. But, in truth, man experiences those inner ethical processes in which the thoughts accuse or else excuse one another, as facts not of his spirit as merely self-defined and appealing to itself, but of the spirit as bound by conscience to a higher ground of life: *animæ ad illum suspensæ, a quo formata*. Therefore are the facts of conscience also, in spite of their individually modified forms of manifestation, not thoughts originated and suggested in a purely individual way, but universal and universally valid truths. And to conscience also the words of Augustine are applicable: "Veritas tua nec mea est, nec illius aut illius, sed omnium nostrum quos ad ejus communionem publice vocas, terribiliter admonens nos, ut earn nolimus habere privatam, ne privemur ea. Nam quisquis id quod in omnibus ad fruendum proponis, sibi proprie vindicat, et quum vult esse quod omnium est, a communi propellitur ad sua, hoc est, a veritate ad mendacium" (Augustin. *Confess.* xii. 25, 34).

§ 10. γ. *The Testimony of Conscience respecting the Inclination to Evil*

When man, laid hold of by the power of conscience, sits in judgment on himself, he carries out this judgment both *in* the thoughts of his heart, and *on* the thoughts of his heart; that is to say, it is the inmost personality of the man which forms the subject (ὁ κρίνων) as well as the object (ὁ κριθείς) of the judicial activity of conscience, as we have to look at it as the self-performed act of the conscious man. Just as the spirit, considered as conscience ("*anima ad Deum suspensa*"), is the deepest and peculiar natural basis of man's ethical personality, in the same manner also the reflective activity of man's spirit, when set in action by conscience, has reference to the direction of the will in the personality of the man himself,—not to this or that which man, in distinction from his personality, may term nature, natural state, natural peculiarity, or natural life of man. That also which man in individual cases desires, thinks, wills, or does, is, it is true, the occasion and subordinate object,—not, however, the chief object of the reflective judgment of conscience. The chief object is the character of the personal tendency, or the state of man's heart (1).

This state of the heart never appears, however, in the light of conscience as identical with that goodness (καλόν) which we know of by virtue of conscience. Conscience is never a consciousness of a goodness of the heart, by virtue of which we might ourselves be immutably like that immutable goodness of which we know. In conscience we know at best only of a changeable state of our heart. It is for this reason that the world, independently of Christ, also has never known how to speak of a purely good conscience, but just as much, and still more, of an evil one. The apostle, however, names as the result of conscience in the self-consciousness of man only thoughts, which accuse or else excuse one another, and as the result of the same before God never speaks of our being void of blame, but of our being inexcusable before God. For our object, *i.e.* for the exposition of the premises of Christian ethics, it is therefore of no further importance to inquire in which way and to what degree the ethical life of man, which develops itself under the sway of natural conscience, shows elements of harmony along with elements of opposition to conscience. For the Christian this forms no part of his experience, and revelation furnishes nothing more explicit concerning it. But the history of the development of the nations, among whom we meet with a more cultivated perception of conscience, winds up with a universal condition, which they find objectionable according to the testimony of their conscience itself (2).

The principal point remains this, that man in his conscience is aware of a contradiction in which he, according to his personal tendency, stands in disunion with himself and the conscience of his spirit. And as in no case either Scripture or experience testifies that man is able in his conscience, or by virtue of it, to do away with this disunion, we must name this contradiction habitual, because though at times it may be made to cease, yet ever again it reappears, and is never eradicated. Furthermore, if such a relation is not conceivable without an inclination of man's personality perverted from that good of which we become aware in conscience, then shall we also find in conscience, with its ever-recurring demands and accusations, the testimony to a habitually evil personal inclination. But finally, if in conscience an impulse and capability were given to the spirit of man, to subordinate the individual and personal Ego with its relations to itself and the world to a higher aim of life, then the evil inclination can only consist in this, in seeking in the individual Ego, and its relations to itself and the world, the highest aim of life, and in wishing to make this predominantly or exclusively the center of human life and endeavor (3).

This is the evil inclination as testified to by conscience, and it makes no essential difference which side or relation of the Ego-life or world-life may form this central point. For every inclination to displace, to subvert, or to subordinate to other ends, that relation of the highest end of life of which man, by the agency of conscience, has an inborn perception, must be called hostile to conscience, and consequently hostile to God, or evil (4). Since conscience, in accordance with its nature, offers to man the possibility of acquiring a knowledge of this, it shows itself in this its conceivable effect on man, as a preparatory school in which he may learn what Christ requires of him,—namely, to hate his own soul, or himself (5).

(1) The position and import of conscience, as a preparatory teacher, will only be justly estimated in the same measure as we accurately observe and fix down in their mutual relations alike *that which* it presents objectively to us in reference to ourselves, and *the way in which* it brings this objectively before our consciousness when under the operation of conscience. As to what regards the last, we must, in the first place, keep steadily in view, that the relations of the existence and life of our spirit are just as organically formed in our spirit as impulse, instinct, and the like, as in our body. Conscience is a predisposition of our spirit, which no man can by an effort of his own will summon up in himself, or acquire by practice or by learning, and the like. It is an inborn impulse of our spirit— a power and faculty of its action; and as a natural quality and natural faculty of our spirit, it is at once an object and a potency of the self-conscious, self-active personality. Conscience, therefore, when it determines us, works in no other way than this, that we by virtue of this faculty stand in the relation to ourselves of determining ourselves. That is to say, the critical ethical power (which is innate in our conscience) reveals itself in us always as self-criticism, first of all in the sense, that in

thoughts, which have flowed out of our spirit, we place ourselves in a sifting relation to ourselves. Here, however, the thoughts, as they form themselves in us as reminiscences of the workings of conscience, and can be summoned up and imagined by ourselves by the imaginative power of memory, must be carefully distinguished from those thoughts which are the immediate reflex of the working of conscience in our self-consciousness, the first and truest prototype of all human ethical judgment. The characteristic feature of the thoughts of conscience is this, that they are thoughts which arise without the intervention of any process of thinking, not thoughts derived from other thoughts (συλλογισμοί), but thoughts (λογισμοί, comp. Rom. 2:15) which are the most immediate impress of a personal spiritual sensation, and bear the stamp, not of a derived certainty, but of an immediate self-conviction. So indeed must it be, provided conscience be not a relation of ourselves to God effected by the operation of our own thoughts, not a formula of our conduct toward God with which our spirit is impregnated, but a simple natural determination of the human spirit (which constitutes the person), by virtue of which the spirit, in its original relation as a spirit derived from God, forms the natural ground of human personality. For that which precedes all discursive thinking, as an *immediately* given relation of the spirit, is also primarily discovered and felt, not through reflections, but through *immediate* consciousness, as a fact of experience. And that which is a natural determination of the spirit, which conditions and supports the *personality*, is felt as a relation of the *person* in the inmost recesses of the personality. For this reason Scripture calls that which is excited in us by means of conscience, and which we do by means of conscience, a something written on the heart (Rom. 2:15). And the working of conscience is just for this reason a working of the heart, the judgment of conscience, the judgment of the heart (ἡ καρδία καταγινώσκει, 1 John 3:20), because the working of conscience lays hold of the totality of our personal life, and makes its force actually felt from that center of the personality in which feeling and knowledge and all capabilities and powers of the personal life form an undivided unity.

Not less is the object to which the working of conscience is directed, and to which the right investigation of conscience applies, the personal state of man's heart. When the apostle says, "I know nothing by myself" (1 Cor. 4:4), he points in what follows in the clearest manner to that which is here the question, since he speaks of that God who in His own time will make manifest the counsels of the heart (τὰς βουλὰς τῶν καρδιῶν, ver. 5). And this very thing denotes that direction of the conscience which corresponds to its nature. The criticism of a false moral reflection upon ourselves keeps clinging to individual expressions of our tendency of heart. It criticizes this or that lust, this or that deed, and never reaches to the knowledge which Christ reveals to us in the words: "Out of the heart proceed evil thoughts, murders, adulteries, fornications, thefts, false witness, blasphemies" (Matt. 15:19). On the contrary, we stop at the several spheres of relation of human life in which the corrupt state of the heart reveals itself, and hold the domain of this manifestation as the root of all corruption. Thus we bring as a charge against human nature, or ascribe entirely to external circumstances and relations, what is the fault and aberration of the heart and of the personal tendency, and even perhaps in this way find an excuse for "the heart." And yet the expression for the varying forms of corrupt lusts, as to their root, is concentrated in the word "lusts of the heart" (ἐπιθυμίαι τῶν καρδιῶν Rom. 1:24), "lusts of men" (ἀνθρώπων ἐπιθυμίαι, 1 Pet. 4:2), as the mark of the lust of the individual and personal man concentrated on himself, in opposition to his impulse toward God, or to the divine will standing over against him.

(2) On the testimony of conscience against man, and on the inexcusableness of man before God, compare the already cited passage Rom. 2:15 with 1:20. The whole result, even in reference to those of whom it is said that they know the testimony of conscience, and are by nature a law unto themselves, comes to

this, that all are under the dominion of sin (πάντας ὑφ' ἁμαρτίαν εἶναι, Rom. 3:9).

When it is said, that in the word of revelation we have no more precise testimony as to the way and as to the degree in which the ethical life of man, which develops itself under the natural conscience, exhibits elements of agreement as well as of discord with conscience, our chief object thereby was to guard against the false application of Rom. 7 to this question. The connection of the statements there laid down by the apostle has again very recently been made the subject of a comprehensive and circumspect exposition by Delitzsch (*System of Biblical Psychology*, pp. 320–340 [pp. 433–459 of Clark's translation]). When he there justly says, that "there is no section of the Bible which affords a deeper insight into the inner state of the *regenerate* man than Rom. 7 in connection with ch. 8," it follows simply from this, that we are wrong to apply the declaration of the apostle as a characteristic of man under the influence of his inner conscience. Since, however, the above-cited section of Romans must hereafter be brought under discussion, this is not the place to go more deeply into it. Only it may be as well to repeat what follows, in order to bring it to remembrance. We must guard against identifying those facts of experience which *we* observe in ourselves and others, and which we call workings of conscience, with those which we may perhaps find in the pre-Christian world as testimonies of conscience (*vid.* § 7, note (4)). Let a man only represent to himself the involuntary results of the hearing of the divine word, and of the receiving of Christian baptism, and so forth. We should accurately analyze, too, the testimony of the pre-Christian world, in order to avoid stamping the traditions of the schools of philosophy and of religious doctrines and the like, without further inquiry, as testimonies of conscience (*vid.* § 7, note (4)). However, as to what concerns the testimony of the pre-Christian world against itself, compare afterwards at § 12. Only in reference to these it must be borne in mind, that they are isolated voices, and that we can by no means assert that the pre-Christian world had, by virtue of conscience, a just and universal perception that their whole condition was blamable. That it is just as little to the purpose to imagine, as the result of conscience, a *consciousness* of righteousness before God, to say nothing of a *being* righteous before God, will, as being superfluous, scarcely need to be explained more exactly. No one surely will again appeal in earnest to the history of Cornelius (Acts 10). Even if the fact were not to be dwelt upon, that this man appears to have been affected by the revelation that had been given to Israel, and to have forsaken the worship of the gods (vers. 2, 22, 33), this at any rate would be a rare instance of righteousness, as it required for its perfection the baptism of the forgiveness of sins. But if we here read, that this man felt himself impelled to pray to God, and to the exercise of benevolence towards the people of Israel, and that the state of his heart was well-pleasing to God, and appeared to the apostle to be such that he judged him worthy of baptism, it does not follow from this, that we are to call this state of mind righteousness before God, nor this disposition of mind the effect of conscience, in such a sense as we attribute conscience even to the heathen unaffected by the word of God. The whole history, surely, is related to us, merely in order that we should learn how the Apostle Peter received the knowledge, that not only from Israel, but also from the heathen world, some were attracted to the kingdom of grace in Christ, and that God did not regard the person, that is to say, his position in this or that people, but only the heart, that felt itself moved to prayer, and to the fear of God, and to the performance of works of righteousness. We might be justified in calling the last a working of conscience, if the history did not attribute to Cornelius a knowledge of the God of Israel, in a way which did not spring from conscience.

(3) When we say that in his conscience man becomes conscious of a perverted tendency of his *personality*, this is just that essential point in which the present natural condition of man differs from that opposition and dissension of which, according to the apostle (Rom. 7), the Christian also is conscious. It is the Ego become selfish in its propensity to live

for itself, to seek its own, to strive after its own, and, indeed, determined to this by the lusts of the human *heart*. Man seeks *his own selfish ends*. In the words of the New Testament, therefore, the expression *their own* desire—*their own* lusts—suffices perfectly to indicate the perversity of this propensity (κατὰ τὰς ἰδίας ἐπιθυμίας, 2 Tim. 4:3, 2 Pet. 3:2, Jude 16, 18; comp. § 5, note (8) at the end). This state of personal aim determined by an habitual propensity, or the selfish man, as perverted from that higher tendency which is innate in his spirit (πνεῦμα), we might with the apostle also call the "natural" man (ψυχικός), although indeed this word, in the passages bearing upon this subject, indicates primarily the apostasy of the selfish man from the Spirit of God (comp. 1 Cor. 2:14, Jude 19, ψυχικοὶ, πνεῦμα μὴ ἔχοντες; or as predicate of a wisdom proceeding from man's own spirit, side by side with ἐπίγειος and δαιμονιώδης, σοφία ψυχική, Jas. 3:14). For the "natural" man is just ὁ φιλῶν τὴν ψυχὴν αὐτοῦ ἐν τῷ κόσμῳ τούτῳ in opposition to ὁ μισῶν (John 12:25). Only this perversion of personal selfish propensity and tendency is again not to be derived from an abstract, non-existing, pure Ego of man (comp. § 5, note (4)), but from that Ego which, being under the influence of man's own corrupt nature as well as of a corrupt state of the world, follows not the higher impulse of the spirit, but seeks its self-gratification in the corruption and vanity of this transitory existence. But neither the corrupt nature, which is man's own (σάρξ), nor the corrupt world standing over against it (πᾶν τὸ ἐν τῷ κόσμῳ, ἡ ἐπιθυμία τῆς σαρκός, καὶ ἡ ἐπιθυμία τῶν ὀφθαλμῶν καὶ ἡ ἀλαζονεία τοῦ βίου, 1 John 2:16), would suffice in itself to drive man to a dissension with his better knowledge, if he did not at the same time know both as the object of his *own* inclination (Jas. 1:14)—as the coveted means of his selfish gratification, perverted from the higher impulse of the spirit. This is what conscience testifies to man, since it accuses simply *ourselves*, not *something* in us, or on us, or outside of us, and reveals to us that our Ego, our heart, our personality, lies in discord with itself; while the thoughts of our conscience, springing from our *heart*, sit in judgment on the lusts of our *heart*, and hold up before us the fact that our *hearts*—that is, we ourselves, in our personal propensity—are following a tendency of whose corruption we have nevertheless an equally personal conviction in our conscience. Such is the tenor according to Scripture of the declaration of conscience, when man knows nothing but himself and his conscience. It is a testimony to the deepest *personal* disunion, which in its inmost significance man himself, without the aid of revelation, is unable to understand, and which in this its deepest import will first be made clear at a future day (Rom. 2:16). So much for those who long to return to the pure state of man under the guidance of his conscience, and who understand neither what they say nor what they wish for.

(4) When Scripture at one time speaks of worldly lusts (κοσμικαὶ ἐπιθυμίαι, Tit. 2:12), and at another of fleshly lusts (σαρκικαὶ ἐπιθυμίαι, 1 Pet. 1:14), these are but appellations of one and the same selfish propensity, according to the domain in which this propensity is indigenous, and out of which it takes its impulses (ἐν τῷ κόσμῳ καὶ ἐκ τοῦ κόσμου, 1 John 2:16; so also ἐν τῇ σαρκὶ καὶ ἐκ τῆς σαρκός). For the lust of the flesh as well as the lust of the world becomes *my* lust only by this means, that my personal propensity meets it, and my Ego becomes a fleshly (or carnal, ἐγὼ σάρκινος, Rom. 7:14) or a worldly Ego. The Ego, to which all dominion in obedience to the higher impulse of the spirit is unpalatable, seeks its gratification in that sweet slavery (δουλεύειν ἐπιθυμίαις καὶ ἡδοναῖς ποικίλαις Tit. 3:3), in which the higher element (τὰ ἄνω, Col. 3:1, 2) subjects itself to the lower (τὰ κάτω, John 8:23), in order to escape the bitter contest in a self-pleasing and fallacious peace. Conscience disturbs the fallacious peace, without being able to restore the true peace. The heart, which has fallen into discord with itself, cannot do this. Beyond this limit conscience cannot reach (*vid.* § 11). But what is of importance in the testimony of conscience, is not the perception of the manifold character of those relations or attractions into which our personal propensity enters, not the perception of the individual cases in which we are conscious of

this in our own actual life; but this, that neither those various allurements nor those individual cases would have been possible, if "out of the heart" wicked thoughts did not proceed, and if by virtue of this state of the heart the *life* had not become, instead of ζῆν ἐν Θεῷ, a ζῆν ἐν τούτοις δι' ἃ ἔρχεται ἡ ὀργὴ τοῦ Θεοῦ. A *life* of corruption precedes all corrupt *conduct;* all corruption of the tendency of our life rests upon a corruption in the tendency of our heart. That is the declaration of the heart's testimony in conscience against the lusts and thoughts of the heart. And for this reason the apostle also declares in so pointed and striking a manner of the condition of man before his conversion through Christ, and of his walking in sin: ἐν οἷς περιεπατήσατέ ποτε, ὅτε ἐζῆτε ἐν τουτοῖς (Col. 3:7).

In what sense conscience of itself brings about in man a consciousness of an *evil* propensity of heart, cannot be so easily determined. If we are unable to attribute to conscience alone a *distinct* consciousness of God, or a consciousness of the *explicit* will of God; if its manifestation in us resolves itself into that which the apostle says, that the thoughts among each other accuse each other, etc., it would be advisable to remain satisfied with the fact, that conscience in itself brings about for man the consciousness of an evil propensity dwelling in him in the form of an *internal discord*, which robs man's heart of peace. For that in which wickedness properly consists— namely, hostility to the living God—supposes an antecedent consciousness of God, as factor or factors of which I nowhere find conscience alone named in Scripture. The potency of this perception lies indeed in the organization of the human spirit. Where, however, it is *actually* present, there Scripture everywhere points to other factors besides, which exist outside of man. And this also must be brought prominently forward in order not to overrate the importance of conscience.

(5) It is indisputable that traces of such a working of conscience are to be found in the history of nations. "Quis enim," says Seneca, "non in hoc magnitudinem ingenii sui concitavit, *detestatus* consensum humani generis tendentis ad vitia?" And to the testimony of the poets respecting that sin in

which all are involved, he adds: "Fugiendum ergo, et in se redeundum est, *imo etiam a se recedendum*" (*Natur. quæst.* iv. præf.). The *displicentia sui*, which the same author calls *effectus vitii* (*de tranquill. an.* 2), is, on the other hand, nothing else but the working of that conscience, which Seneca is equally well aware of. Yet, according to the history of the world before Christ, the energy of conscience expires in manifold conceits concerning the manner in which it lies in man's nature (πεφυκότες ἁμαρτάνειν) to sin; and conscience shows itself indeed as a thorn against a state of perfect lethargy, but nowhere as a life-giving light. So much is the nature of man organized with the tendency to find his peace and salvation in nothing that belongs to *his* nature in its highest relations. Compare, moreover on the testimony of conscience to the all-prevailing propensity to sin, according to the Greeks, in Nägelsbach (*Die nachhomerische Theologie des griech. Volksglaubens*, vi. 3 ff.).

§ 11. δ. *The Testimony of Conscience to the Powerlessness of the Will*

If, from the analysis of conscience, and its manifestation in man, a conclusion results as to the character of the personal tendency of the heart of man, as testified by conscience, there follows thence naturally the further question: Whether man, so far as nothing else is to be regarded than his inclination and conscience, possesses the power, by his will and its freedom, of breaking this ban. Here it must be premised, that we must distinguish the will as a substance from the will as an act (*actus, motus*). For our question, the will as substance of the spirit does not come into consideration; that is to say, in the sense in which the existing man is necessarily a walling, knowing, sensitive being, and the like. We have to do rather with the self-determining will, or the impulse of the will *per accidens*, turning towards this or that object or end, with will in the concrete. Of the last the fact holds good, that the will in its actual nature is not free in the way that it should be able to will independently of the quality of the human Ego (§ 5); not free in the sense, as if with its freedom, as such, a disposition of the will for this or that end, an ethical quality of the will were supposed; but that with the freedom of the will nothing is to be asserted, except that the willing man, in his concrete willing directed to a definite object, is limited by nothing but his own proper inclination. For where the inclination ceases to be the determining reason of the act of willing, there enters a compulsory force; but forced will is no longer free-will (1). In opposition to this compulsion, conscience itself testifies to the freedom of the human will, since it reckons to man's account whatever it testifies to, and equally whether it attests that his willing is directed to what is bad or to what is good.

The question consequently is not, whether conscience testifies to man that he has a free will. This indeed is testified by it under all circumstances (2). Rather is this the question: Whether conscience bears testimony to this, that the will of man, not because it is free, but because it is a power, by which man can make himself the object of his willing energy, renders him capable of overcoming the selfish direction of his heart's desires, and gives him the power to change the latter to a conformity with that which he perceives by his conscience to be good and true.

We might now conceive this possible in the same way as it lies in the power of man to overcome propensities which are rooted in the domain of the body, through the exercise of a will directed to the body, in a system of corporeal asceticism, and finally to make acceptable to himself that to which before every inclination was averse. But here at the same time it must certainly be supposed, that with the same determination of nature by which a sphere of the bodily life is entirely subjected to the exercise of the power of the spirit, so now also the spirit should be submitted to the same power exercised by the will. But in this the question still remains unsolved: In what, then, the power of the will lies, if not in the substance of the will itself. Enough, however—we may imagine things of this kind; and such things have been imagined. It has been conceived, after the analogy of the relation in which the willing spirit stands to a part of the bodily life, that another relation may exist, in which the willing spirit stands to itself; and an unlimited power over the ethical tendency of the spirit has been at a cheap rate theoretically attributed to the will in the abstract.

Whether this, however, is correct, must be decided not by theory, but by those life-experiences which are testified of everywhere by conscience. If this testimony is true, it is at the same time a witness against all theories which attribute to man's will the power of overcoming the selfish tendency of the heart, in such a way that man, by his own inclination alone, wills that which his conscience holds before him as a requisition. For conscience knows just as little of such a conformity of the actual human will with conscience, as of a conformity of the inclination of the heart, which conditions the free-will, with the dictates of conscience. The testimony of conscience contradicts also that other falsity, with which man deceives himself, and supposes that one is conscious in one's self, partly of a discord, partly of a conformity of the will with conscience. The moral personality does not permit itself to be thus divided, and conscience does not allow itself to be imposed on. A will which is only half good is simply not a good will; and in the particular impulses of will struggling with each other, no power of the will over the evil inclination, but a weakness thereof, no freedom to be able to will what is good unconditionally, but a want of freedom in this very respect, a latent bondage, comes to light. The testimony of conscience consoles no man on account of his half goodness, but it shows to all men that they are not good (3). And in the light of conscience, (I mean, in the inner discontent and want of peace,) this also appears as a delusion, when man dreams of demonstrating and strengthening the power of his good will in this way, that contrary to his own inclination, and thus properly against his will, he gives to his external actions that form in which they carry on their face the appearance of good, or of that which is indicated as good by conscience. For these have only the form and shape (μόρφωσις), not the essence and the reality, of good actions. On the contrary, this mere external show of good actions, which does not correspond to the inclination of the heart, shows only the want of a good will, and the powerlessness of the will to break the perverted inclination of the heart. For that which, in the domain of morals or in the testimony of the willing personality and of the undivided man, is not done from the ground of the heart and with the whole soul (compare § 5, note (8)), is not good, nor the object of the approval of conscience (4).

We can perhaps, it is true, call it in individual cases a working of conscience, in the sense that man, alarmed by his conscience, gives to his actions the appearance and form of being the fruit of a conscientious inclination of the heart. That this will is better than that depraved will wherein man wills and does the very contrary to that which conscience holds up to him, is not to be denied. But that which is better than depraved is not yet on that account good, and least of all proof of a free good will. It is an endeavor to constrain one's self to that which one has no inclination to will, in such a form that one gives to the outward action the appearance of a will filled with and conditioned by the desire of good. In this procedure is shown, it is true, the power of the will over the external behavior of man, but not a power of the will over the proper tendencies of man's heart. By such actions man may indeed deceive his fellow-men, but not his own conscience. Conscience in the heart brings a charge rather against the heart, that that heart is not in what man does. So long, however, as this happens (and conscience follows us in this manner our whole life through), so long does it remain absurd and an internal contradiction, to speak of a free will directed towards what is good, while its own inclination is averse from it.

In order to know whether my will is powerful enough to crush the selfish inclination of my heart, it is of no moment to investigate whether I do and can do that which bears on its face the form of goodness, but whether I, out of a good and willing heart, will and do that which of itself is good, and remains good also in my willing; that is to say, whether I, in willing and doing what is good, seek not *myself*, but that good which the voice of conscience admonishes me of, in opposition to the selfish tendency of my own heart. Conscience says, No. And here conscience denies to man the power of overcoming the selfish dictates of the heart. The reason is very simple. That which is to subdue *me*, must be more powerful than I. This, however, I cannot find in myself, nor in that which is mine own; I can only find it out of myself, and above myself, in Him to whom I belong. And towards this the voice of my conscience draws me (5).

Opposed to this stands the desire of the will to free itself from the dictates of conscience, the displeasure at the feeling of knowing one's self bound by conscience, the hankering of the Ego to find its pleasure in that which is not approved by conscience, and the inability of the human will to give to man "a new heart." All this is attested to us as a fact of experience by conscience itself.

(1) The question which arises from the selfish inclination of man testified of by conscience, is this: whether we ought to regard this inclination as a natural necessity in the sense that man suffers it involuntarily, perhaps like the sensations of corporeal want in hunger, thirst, and the like. No explanation of this can be given without first getting for one's self beforehand a clear idea of that which we call inclination, will, and free-will. A part of what has reference to this has already been discussed in § 5. But here, above all things, it must be borne in mind that the analogy of corporeal instincts was only brought forward for the purpose of illustrating a false conception. For, in point of fact, not the slightest analogy in this case exists with that which is called selfish desire. It is no natural determination, if we understand by nature the original and divinely established organization of man. It is not connected with the natural difference of our nature as consisting of body and soul, nor with the different natural relations of our Ego to this its twofold natural constitution. The selfish inclination shows itself not in this or in that, but in all

the relations of the Ego to its nature, and to the world which stands over against the Ego. Nothing, however, that man has in himself as his nature, or over against himself as the world or the earthly nature, is the point from which the selfish inclination develops itself and has its home. It has its root and its throne in the inmost recesses of the individual personality, whose nature is an object of experience to every man, and, at the same time, an object of the accusation of conscience in the case of those who are willing to listen to conscience.

As to what regards the will in itself, or the assertion that man is a being that wills, this lies in the organization of his spirit, constitutes its essence, without which we cannot conceive of the spirit at all, and the question cannot be of an inclination to will or not to will. It is a natural necessity of the human spirit to know and to will, or to set objectively before itself and to strive. But it is not so with that knowledge which is consciously directed to a definite object, and as little is it so with the actual will when consciously turned to a definite end. This willing, when it is actual and free willing, is not to be conceived of without inclination, whether its exercise may be directed to an acquisition in knowledge or to the taking part in an action. This has long ago been recognized and expressed. In reference to the substance of the spirit as knowing and willing, Claudian. Mamerc. remarks (*de statu animæ*, lib. i. c. 24) under the heading, "Quod non est aliud anima, aliud memoria, cogitatio vel voluntas, cum hæc eadem una sit anima," as follows: "*Quod* enim cogitat, accidens ejus (animæ) est; substantia vero quæ cogitat. *Hoc equidem de voluntate agnoscas.* Nam sicut tota anima cogitatio est, ita *anima tota voluntas est,*" etc. In this sense Jo. Damascenus distinguishes (ἔκδοσις τῆς ὀρθοδοξ. πίστ. lib. ii. c. 22, p. 189, ed. Lequien) θέλησις and βούλησις, and says: Θέλησις μὲν γάρ ἐστιν αὐτὴ ἡ ἁπλῆ δύναμις τοῦ θέλειν· βούλησις δὲ ἡ περί τι θέλησις. The first is *voluntas,* the second *motus voluntatis* in the sense of Thomas Aquinas. And of the latter, the same author says, "Ipse motus voluntatis est inclinatio quædam in aliquid, et ideo sicut dicitur aliquid naturale, quia est secundum inclinationem naturæ, ita aliquid dicitur voluntarium, quia est secundum inclinationem voluntatis" (*Summa theol.* Th. i. qu. 82, art. 1). This is the disposition to will (ἡ προθυμία τοῦ θέλειν, 2 Cor. 8:11), and forms the opposite to the conception of a *necessitas coactionis*. "Hæc coactionis necessitas," says Thomas Aquinas, "omnino repugnat voluntati. Nam hoc dicimus esse violentum, quod est contra inclinationem rei." And what has been taught in relation to this from the beginning is briefly indicated by Jo. Bonaventura (*breviloq.* lib. ii. cap. 9) in the words, "Hoc est de natura voluntatis, ut nultatenus possit cogi;" and the Lutheran dogmatic theologian Gerhard mentions, as the harmonious acknowledgment of Christendom, that "libertas a coactione, quâ fit, ut non possit voluntas cogi ad faciendum aliquid contra suam inclinationem." It is this negative judgment which we, in reference to the inclination to will this or that, wish first to keep in view. But what, then, is meant by inclination of will? Shall we be able to take our stand merely upon pure will? It does not indeed belong to the substance of the will to be determined by this or that inclination, that is to say, by the impulse of liking in any certain direction. Furthermore, there exists no abstract self-determined will. The will is dependent on the quality of the Ego; and the Ego is, by the nature of its spirit, at the same moment knowing and willing. Of a self-conscious inclination we cannot speak at all, without we keep in view the totality of the man, as knowing and willing at the same time. When the will, directed to some determinate object, with the possible conception of several objects higher or lower, which is given in the natural circumstances of the man himself, was called choice, and the power of choosing was spoken of, one looked for this rightly, not in the *voluntas* alone, but in the *liberum arbitrium*. What has been said about this subject may be briefly comprised in the words of Hildebert of Tours (*tract. Theol.* c. 29): "Liberum arbitrium consistit in duabus, scilicet in voluntate et ratione. Liberum namque dicitur quantum ad voluntatem, arbitrium quantum ad rationem." Compare, in earlier times, Pet. Lombard. *Summa dist.* 24, c. 3e, and subsequently Thomas Aquinas, *Summa theol.*

p. ii. qu. 1, art. 1. I would wish certainly to use, in place of *ratio*, in order that we should not exclusively think of *ratiocinatio*, rather the term *intellects*; but with this reservation, (which I shall immediately explain more fully,) will that inclination also, as it is called up by the movement of the will towards anything, rest just as much on a discriminating consciousness, (which in this sense we may call a *ratio collativa*,) as on a yearning will, which does not yet partake of a consciousness of an end, and thus both in common upon an *appetitus intellectivus*. For will, conceived purely as will, is blind, purposeless will. The will which strives after a purpose and an object is conscious will. In knowledge man realizes that which he can, in the exercise of will, lay hold of as a purpose and object of his will. Whether this object which is present to his knowledge becomes really also the object of the will, depends upon the relation in which the object which is present as an end stands to that which fundamentally moves the will as a motive—to the loving desire of the man. For this there exists only one form, namely this, that the foresaid object is present to the consciousness of the man as something good (*bonum*), and its attainment as happiness (*beatitudo*), no matter whether this consciousness wears the form of imagination, of reflection, and the like. The proposition remains true under all circumstances: *Voluntas in nihil potest tendere nisi sub ratione boni*.

Let us now apply this to the selfish tendency. Its natural basis lies first of all in the experience, by virtue of which the individual spirit knows its will as individual self-will; then further in this, that it knows the relation of the will to the individual Ego, as one of the relations of this will. As in knowledge man is objectively present to himself, so by virtue of this knowledge the Ego can become objectively present to the will. It becomes the object of desire, since to man this his individual existence, its preservation and satisfaction in the attainment of those ends as they lie in the sphere of the Ego-life, appear as something good, and as happiness. Thus far the perverted inclination of the will, which is opposed to nature, is not yet supposed. This comes rather with that experience, by virtue of which the individual man becomes aware that those relations of the Ego (which belong no less to his nature) to a universal existence standing outside of himself, and to a higher nature which is placed above him, include in them ends whose pursuit is impossible for the Ego without the discipline of subordination. In this discipline the good is not felt to be the sweet. Man wills, however, that what is sweet should be the good. Thus the position of the Ego becomes self-perverted in the exaltation of the Ego over everything which is called non-Ego; and that which we name selfish desire, is not, in fact, an affection which we suffer, but a continually recurring, actual contraposition of our Ego against all the relations of our nature, which do not promise advantage to the individual Ego, and are not comprised in its gratification. The selfish direction is an *actus personæ*, not an *affectio naturæ, contra naturam*. It is a tendency, because these acts of the refractory Ego habitually recur, wherever in the relations of our nature something presents itself to us as an end, which can only be reached by the subordination of the Ego. The selfish tendency is consequently no mere calamity *arising from a* corruption of our nature, but is the factor which continually corrupts that nature. For we selfish men not merely suffer from a corruption of our nature, but are, as such, also the actual corrupters of our nature. This is proved by conscience, which accuses of crime the man who lives for himself.

A question of quite another sort is this: Whence, then, does the universal ascendency of this propensity arise? Why is it found existing in all men without exception? and on what grounds does that which conscience testifies to the individual, as a testimony which recurs to all, point to a propensity lording it over the human race? It is quite impossible to answer this question from the experience of the individual. It extends far beyond this domain, and far into the history of the human race, concerning which we have no empirical consciousness, and no solution derived from conscience. What Scripture testifies (especially Rom. 5) is unintelligible only to those who represent to themselves the first man as the first human individual; while he is that one in whom the human species has its origin and its historical development, in such a sense that in him is fashioned beforehand the type of the later species. But this innate type would not be in all its corruption our corruption, if we did not ourselves, by our own perverted personal propensity (*nostro arbitrio*), show our esteem for what is corrupt, and make it the object of our desire.

(2) In this sense the older divines of our church said: "Liberum et voluntarium sunt synonym a, ac voluntatem non liberam dicere, est perinde ac si quis dicere velit calidum absque calore." Just so Anselm: "Quis ergo potest voluntatem dicere non esse liberam ... si nulla tentatio potest illam, nisi volentem, avertere a rectitudine ad peccatum, *i.e.* ad volendum, quod non debet?" (*De lib. arb.* c. 5.)

(3) Ὦ πῶς πονηρόν ἐστιν ἀνθρώπων φύσις τὸ σύνολον, says that maxim recognized by the pre-Christian conscience. Suppose even it were permitted, which I cannot allow to hold good in this form, to regard the description in Rom. 7 as applying to man in his present condition, or to say, according to the testimonies of the world before Christ, that man in his conscience has not only a perception of what is good, but also an inclination to act according thereto,—nay even, partly performed that which conscience requires of him,—I would simply ask, in opposition to this, whether a man ever quieted the qualms of his conscience in this way, when it made itself heard in him? That which is said in reference to the law of God, that he who will keep it, and fails in any one particular, is guilty of breaking the whole (Jas. 2:10), applies also in reference to the true goodness of the moral personality. When I just only in one respect will that which is not good, and by this will do that which is evil, there is thereby given simply the proof of a ruined moral personality. Much less still in such manifestations does the isolated act merely come in question, as if perhaps we could conclude from the one act that man possessed in himself the freedom to will and to do what is good, and from the other that he had the freedom to will and to do what is evil. I will allow the misapplied term freedom to stand here, although in its

proper sense it means unhindered power, unhindered ability. But when I assert of one and the same person that he wills and does what is good, and he wills and does what is evil, this personality has in no respect an unbroken freedom, an unimpeded ability, an unlimited power; but there is revealed in the man a power of attraction to the good, and a power of attraction to the evil; and as to his own personality, he stands between the two, powerless and incapable of deciding unconditionally for the one or for the other. He appears not as the "lord of his own will," but stands on the one hand under the dominion of his conscience, like a slave who fears for himself, and under the dominion of sin, as a slave who loves this master. When Christ our Lord says, "Verily, verily, I say unto you, Whoever *commits* sin is the *servant* of sin" (John 8:34); when, according to the apostle, even the conscience of the Christian is still conscious of being relatively sold under sin (πεπραμένον εἶναι, Rom. 7:14), it is thus not only a foregone conclusion as to the condition of man outside of the fellowship with "the Lord who makes free," but at the same time a fact attested by man to his conscience, that the will of man shows itself in the conduct of man as not free to will in the way God would have it. For God wills not that man should serve two masters, or should will in opposite directions; and in the long run, man cannot do so without falling into a love for the one, and into hatred against the other (Matt. 6:24).

(4) It holds good in the most general application what Paul says in reference to a definite relation: εἰ γὰρ ἑκὼν τοῦτο πράσσω, μισθὸν ἔχω, 1 Cor. 9:17; or when Peter requires of others that what they have to do they should do cheerfully and willingly, not as of constraint (μὴ ἀναγκαστῶς, ἀλλ' ἑκουσίως, 1 Pet. 5:2).

(5) Anselm of Canterbury says (*de concordant. præscient. Dei cet. cum lib. arbitr.* quæst. iii. c. 3): "Dubium non est, quia voluntas non vult recte, nisi quia recta *est*. Sicut namque non est acutus visus, quia videt acute, sed ideo videt acute, quia acutus est: ita voluntas non est recta, quia vult recte, sed recte vult, quoniam recta *est.*—Dico, nullam eam (volunt.) posse

velle rectitudinem, si non habet rectitudinem qua illam velit." If, indeed, freedom of the will were identical with goodness of the will, then all would be well. "Semper est autem in nobis voluntas libera, sed non semper est bona. Aut enim a justitia libera est, quando servit peccato, et tunc est mala; aut a peccato libera est, quando servit justitiæ, et tunc est bona."—August. *de grat. et lib. arb.* c. 15. The chief point is however this, that man from the beginning was organized to seek the fountain of all goodness, and the goodness of the will also, not in himself, but in God. From this fountain the will, becoming selfish, has become estranged, and flies from the channel of conscience as a well of bitterness.

§ 12. ε. *The Darkening of the Consciousness in regard to Conscience*

If conscience were a table of laws engraven on the heart of man, which by a natural necessity mirrored its full contents uniformly in the human consciousness, we might, in accordance with what we have as yet explained, conceive the state of men to be only such, that we had to presuppose in all men the permanent consciousness of an internal ethical discord, which man is incapable of overcoming by the effort of his will. But this is not the case. Another danger lies near at hand, which again, it is true, *must* not of necessity occur to every individual, but which not only may occur to individuals, and actually does so, but even, according to Scripture and experience, becomes the distinctive character of the condition of whole peoples.

There is given in the constitution of man, who by his nature is a knowing and willing being, this element, that the mental perception comes to be reflected in full form in the individual, and to have a permanence in the subjective consciousness, only in the same proportion in which man turns himself with his will to what he perceives, and preserves the recollection of that of which he has become conscious. This holds good of the mental perception in general, so far as it has something else for its basis than the impressions of the senses, which operate by a natural necessity on the body. It holds good especially of everything which springs up in me out of the nature of my spirit (which unconsciously to me is full of matter, and which builds up my consciousness), in order to win form and consistence in my subjective personal consciousness. It comes to no shape, to say nothing of a permanent hold, if I have no desire to hold fast the unformed thoughts which present themselves, to give them full shape, and to impress them upon my mind in durable recollection.

Quite in a peculiar manner this applies to conscience and its perceptions. For from its organization, it is destined to bring before our consciousness our inmost being, in relations which concern the whole spiritual man, and can only be understood in their full extent in the same measure in which man not only is willing to perceive, but is ready to follow, the movement of the spirit in a comprehensive examination of conscience. And in order that we may take our stand by that which we by virtue of conscience perceive to be above ourselves, our conscience exhibits to us the image of our spiritual ethical condition. If we desire to forget this image, then will this forgetfulness come to pass even much more easily than in the case of that man who, having seen his natural face in a glass, straightway forgot what manner of man he was (Jas. 1:24). Now since the image, as we behold it in the conscience, is an ill-favored, disagreeable, and to us an unwelcome one, there lies near at hand not the desire to recollect it, but that of forgetting it—not the inclination to meet, but that of fleeing from, conscience. In the same measure, therefore, in which we yield to that, and in which our selfish heart fights shy of allowing itself to be punished by the spirit of conscience, the sensitiveness of the soul decreases; as also its capability, by meditating on the testimony given by conscience, and by yielding to its warnings, to examine itself and its condition, and to lay them to heart. Nay, this can proceed to the extreme of a loss of sensibility and of consciousness by this means, that the desires of the heart, with its thoughts and its will, sink entirely into that which does not belong to conscience. For then in appearance the opposition of conscience to our evil inclination ceases, while the proper condition of the heart is one of apathy and callousness (1).

Against this danger no irresistible barrier is conceivable, which is given in the nature of man himself (2). Out of the natural position of man under the working of conscience only a twofold kind of need could arise: First, a certainty, relieved from the vacillations and disturbances of the human consciousness, concerning the nature of that higher will affecting man; secondly, a solution of that discord in which man finds himself according to the testimony of his conscience. In what manner the Christian consciousness knows both, is to be set forth in what follows. And first of all, we must show, how and in what manner the Christian arrives at a consciousness of a divine law, which, in spite of all its connection with the essence of conscience, is not human conscience.

(1) The whole spiritual nature of man is so constituted, that in its development it is just as much conditioned by an inner law of its being, as by the free, personal self-activity of man. The personality of man is just as much receptivity as spontaneity. The soul becomes aware of that which belongs to the spirit, only in the same proportion in which it, which *has* a spiritual hearing, *affords* that hearing. And the last depends on that "heavy weight" of inclination or aversion which belongs to the soul. Continuous inclination for what is perverted, perverts and corrupts even that faculty of hearing of the soul. Those relations which the human spirit has in conscience are, as divinely established, unsubvertible. But the soul, the heart's faculty of hearing, is subvertible. For its preservation is a matter of human fostering. It is destroyed, as respects conscience and all natural knowledge of God, through the conceit of self-wisdom (φάσκοντες εἶναι σοφοί, Rom. 1:22; σοφία ἐπίγειος, ψυχική, Jas. 3:15; σοφία σαρκική, 2 Cor. 1:12; ἡ σοφία τοῦ κόσμου, 1 Cor. 1:20, 3:19; σοφία ἀνθρώπων, 1 Cor. 2:5; ἀνθρωπίνη σοφία, 1 Cor. 2:13; οὐκ ἔγνω ὁ κόσμος διὰ τῆς σοφίας τὸν Θεόν, 1 Cor 1:21; εἴ τις δοκεῖ σοφὸς εἶναι ἐν ὑμῖν ἐν τῷ αἰῶνι τούτῳ, μωρὸς γενέσθω, ἵνα γένηται σοφός, 1 Cor. 3:18). Self-wisdom is

that love of man for himself, in which it is repugnant to him to recognize as his highest end of life, and happiness of life, anything else than that which man sets before him in the inclinations and thoughts of his own heart. In self-wisdom man places in himself the end of life, and seeks the means of its attainment, in opposition to the monition and warning of conscience, exclusively in himself. Self-wisdom is the negation of all higher wisdom, for the reception of which, however, the spirit of man itself is organized: it is the negation of God, as of Him who alone is wise (Rom. 16:27, Jude 25); the negation of the wisdom which comes from above (Jas. 3:15); the negation of conscience which wishes to exalt the consciousness of man above the limits of the Ego, and which convicts the Ego, while persevering in its egotism by the antagonism of its thoughts, of folly. With this self-wisdom the heart becomes foolish (Rom. 1:21); with it commences the darkening of the consciousness with respect to conscience, which, by various stages and degrees, finally leads to that hardening of the heart which the Apostle Paul describes as the prevailing condition of nations (Eph. 4:17–19).

This last-cited passage points, when compared with Rom. 1:18, 21, 28, to the phenomena and internal process of this darkening, in a manner which is also applicable to the position of man in relation to his conscience, and deserves a more narrow examination. For the history of the heathen world is a type of that of the natural heart of man, when it enters upon that process by which the man hardens himself against the voice of his higher and better consciousness. The heart is not by nature callous, nay, not even in the present corrupt condition of the human race. It is not devoid of higher aspirations, nor does it want the capability of following them out. The process of darkening begins with the keeping down of a truth which dwells in man, and which presents itself to his consciousness,—a keeping down by unrighteousness, or by an act of injustice which one does to this truth (κατέχειν ἐν ἀδικίᾳ, Rom. 1:18). We esteem this truth *undeserving of being kept fast hold of in our knowledge* (οὐ δοκιμάζουσίν ἔχειν ἐν ἐπιγνώσει,

Rom. 1:28, the *æstimatio* of the *arbitrium*), and accordingly our own mind becomes *worthless* (νοῦς ἀδόκιμος, Rom. 1:28). And why do we reckon this knowledge of no value? Because it lowers the worth of man in his own eyes, destroys the self-glory and the self-importance of his self-wisdom; and we wish to be rid of that "higher element" to which alone all glorifying and all thanks are applicable. And yet it is this higher element of which our spirit admonishes us in conscience as the alone real, so that, torn away from its connection with that, everything else that exists is valueless and unreal. In the avoidance of this, which alone is real, our thoughts fall away to what is shadowy (ματαιούμεθα ἐν τοῖς διαλογισμοῖς ἡμῶν, Rom. 1:21): they become vain, nugatory, foolish; and our mind itself is vain, nugatory, and foolish (ματαιότης τοῦ νοός, Eph. 4:17; comp. on the word μάταιον of the Greeks the excellent remarks in Nägelsbach, *Nachhomer. Theol.* vi. 2, p. 321 ff.). This holds good of the mind, the disposition, as the tendency of the knowing and willing soul (νοῦς as in Rom. 1:28, 12:2, etc.). The state which is there represented is, on the side of knowledge, a darkening (ἐσκοτισμένοι τῇ διανοίᾳ ὄντες, Eph. 4:18), seeing that the spiritual eye of the soul is closed to the perception of that higher truth. It is, however, also at the same time an internal estrangement from the life which proceeds from God (ἀπηλλοτριωμένοι τῆς ζωῆς τοῦ Θεοῦ, *ibid.*), since the desire of the will turns away from those vital bonds which knit the soul to God. For this state is not that of an internal ignorance (ἄγνοια), so that the truth might not yet at all have presented itself to the consciousness, or only as in forgetfulness might have again become obliterated from it, but a hardening of the receptive personality (πώρωσις τῆς καρδίας), in which one has become callous to the sting in his heart (ἀπηλγηκώς), apathetic, and thus yields himself with his eyes open to the lusts of his heart. Blindness of the spiritual eye goes hand in hand with this hardening of the heart; compare the prophetic word in John 12:40, Matt. 13:14, 15. What is most shocking in this state is this, that, taken subjectively, it becomes a certain truth, when such a man asserts he feels no trace of conscience.

The ancient world knew well this very condition, and Epictetus calls it moral petrifaction (ἀπολίθωσις). But he knows not the central point from which it proceeds. And the difference of degree which he draws between the ἀπολίθωσις τοῦ νοητικοῦ as the less, and the ἀπολίθωσις τοῦ προτρεπτικοῦ as the greater, is so far untenable, as they mutually condition each other. To a certain extent, however, he perceives this himself, since in the latter case he calls the soul a ψυχὴ ἀπονεκρουμένη, and describes such a state in the words: ἐκτέτμηται τὸ αἰδῆμον αὐτοῦ καὶ ἐντρεπτικόν, καὶ τὸ λογικὸν οὐκ ἀποτέτμηται ἀλλ' ἀποτεθηρίωται.

(2) As already remarked, this hardening of the heart was, according to the apostle, the state which characterized the prevailing tendency of the whole of the then heathen world. The nations had followed *their own* ways (Acts 14:16). They were those of man's self-choosing, and the hardening of the heart was their result. History with its testimonies confirms the words of the apostle. In the face of this twofold witness, it is absurd to talk of the possibility of conceiving that any other result could have followed, so far as men were concerned. But it is only right that that which characterizes the whole condition of the fallen heathen world should not necessarily be conceived as that of every individual in this assemblage of nations. Exceptions are to be made of all those who were able to recognize and to deplore this universal corruption. And the testimonies of such are not wanting in the history of the ancient world. The same apostle attributes even to the heathen a natural capacity of sitting in judgment upon themselves, and by this doing that which belongs to the positive law of God. This formed a barrier against the entire hardening of the heart; not, however, one that could not be broken through. And this barrier was still less a power of making free. It did not remove that inner discord which conscience reveals.

The natural man, however, is never a self-dependent, isolated person. He is a member of a family, of a people; and in all these relations he is not only a child of nature, but also a child of history, who in the course of his moral life is not merely left to himself, but is conditioned by historically established and firmly settled common forms and rules of human life. In this relation, again, it is not to be denied that, among the nations who walked in their own ways, an element is found in the laws made by the state, as well as in the religious traditions, which may be called an embodiment of conscience, and exists as an objective barrier against the subjective degeneracy (comp. *e.g.* as to what regards the laws of the state, Nägelsbach, *Nachhom. Theol.* v. 53). In all these forms, however, an element of truth appears mixed with elements of falsehood; and in the objective external forms of the moral consciousness are stamped in their own manner the same dissension and antagonism which we meet with in the subject—in man himself, as we have to think of him in his present condition, when he finds himself thrown back on nothing save on his conscience. Last of all, the whole barrier which men erected in their laws and worship against moral degeneracy, crumbles down in the hands of those very parties for whom it ought to hold good (comp. sec. viii. in Nägelsbach, *l.c.*).

Finally, it is not to be denied that, in opposition to other sides of the common forms and rules of ethical life, as the heathen world before Christ had developed them, there reacted a spirit which, though in effect a spirit destructive of heathen religion and morals, was yet in its essence also partly a spirit awakened by conscience,—a spirit of longing, of wrestling, and conflict to break the barrier which their walking in their own ways had brought upon the races of men. Of this the greater part will only be known in that day to which also the apostle points forward the heathen world (Rom. 2:16). A not unimportant element, however, is obvious in the manifestations which the world before Christ called love of wisdom (φιλοσοφία). What, however, could it be which moved a Tertullian to appeal for his testimony against paganism much rather to the simple, untaught consciousness of the soul, as he supposes it to exist among the heathen of his own day, than to the "educated" mind? (see *De testim. an.* i.) The reason why Tertullian did so was simply this, that his clear and sober judgment could not soar to the giddy height of the Christian Alexandrian and Platonizing fathers of the church, so as to discern in the development of the Hellenic philosophy a schoolmaster to lead to Christ, or to forget, in the partial connection with the correct knowledge of divine truth, the difference of principle, the human self-formed conceits of the philosophical schools. The philosopher could, like Cicero, bear testimony to the universal depravity which surrounded man from youth up (*Tuscul.* iii. 1); but philosophy was incapable of arresting the ever increasing stream of licentiousness. Philosophy was obliged to confess that we, while our spirit is sick, pronounce judgment upon ourselves ("animus de se ipse tum judicat, quum id ipsum, quo judicatur, ægrotet"); but just as strongly, at the same time, that the medicine which she offered found no acceptance ("animi medicina nec tam desiderata, antequam inventa, nec tam culta, posteaquam cognita, nec tam multis grata et probata, pluribus etiam suspecta et invisa," *Tusc.* iii. 1), nay, that the philosophers did not even apply it to themselves (*ibid.* ii. 4). The ideal man of philosophy was even by its own testimony nowhere to be found (see Cic. *ibid.* ii. 22). The Stoic discovered no marked example anywhere, nay, not even one lying merely within the criteria of a Stoic practically applying his own precepts (Epictet. *Diss.* ii. 19, 24 ff.). But perhaps it may be said, Was not this ideally conceived man, this conception of a perfect philosopher, a means of sharpening the conscience? By no manner of means. The effect of the whole Grecian philosophy was to weaken the conscience, owing to its ignorance of the source and magnitude of the evil, owing to its delusion concerning the means of eradicating it, owing to its affectation of a height of perfection which stands in opposition not only to the facts of our corrupt nature, but to the fundamental conditions which belong to true human nature. Where this was not done, they turned that which was actually existing into what was naturally and divinely justifiable. They knew not God, in whose mirror alone man can arrive at correct self-knowledge. How, then, would philosophy have been able to render conscience more healthfully acute, not to speak of its being able to deliver us from that discord of which conscience convinces us?

CHAPTER II

THE POSITIVE LAW

§ 13. *The Existence, the Nature, and the Import of the Positive Law*

THE inkling or the postulate of a divine law, standing above man, and ethically determining and regulating his will, may be described as a working of conscience (1). But the actual existence of such, in its full manifestation before the eyes of man, is not given in conscience. Such a self-explication of the divine will touching the whole relations of human life, is found neither in man nor in the natural organization peculiar to him, nor in that of universal nature, standing over against him, as the latter is antecedent to the existence of man, and the supporter of it. Such a self-explication of the divine will, should it be actually present, can only come within the sphere of the historical existence of man as a historical act on God's part. Out of this sphere it has no existence; for it is not a fact common to the experience of all men. This should follow as the result of our previous investigations.

The question is therefore this, how the Christian consciousness comes to the knowledge of such a positive divine law. For the Christian consciousness, it is its vital connection with Christ which is the guarantee to the Christian of the existence of an historical divine law in the law given to the people of Israel, and which unfolds to him as well the unity as the diversity of what he has in the law, and what he has in Christ (2). As, however, the law, already before the appearance of Christ, was calculated to be recognized by man as a divine one, so now also the recognition of its divine origin lies not only in the declaration of the incarnate One, that it proceeds from God, but at the same time in the position which *this* law occupies in respect to the requirements of the soul, as awakened by conscience, and seeking for *salvation*. For this law alone shows itself as part of a historical and in itself united education of the human race; and its divinity is recognized in the essential connection of this fact with the preceding, as with the following historical manifestation of one and the same God, whose incarnation is the completion and key of the whole revelation (3). The significance, however, of the declaration of God, promulgated historically, and embodied in words, touching the nature of His will, as He wishes to have it fulfilled by men, is twofold. For the undarkened conscience the law has the import of explaining, that the human knowledge of which conscience is the medium has its essential position only in this, that it is conscious of being at the same time also conformable to a divine will, which exists over and external to the spirit of man. For the darkened conscience, however, the significance of the law consists in its being a declaration of the divine will, independent of human vacillation and obscuration, applicable to all, and available for all, whose intelligibility is by no means taken away by the darkening of conscience (4).

(1) From the doctrine of conscience the reason becomes evident why the existence of a law, or of legal determination, is in general of no importance for ethics, unless a law exists in fact, whose existence can be derived neither from the Ego-life nor the world-life, nor from conscience. Only when such a law is found, which has proceeded from the same causality, from which there accrues to conscience in its original nature the import of an unconditioned rule of man's life, can it form a subject of consideration for ethics. The necessity of a divine sanction for human legislation was therefore felt also by the heathen world. That ancient proposition of Heraclitus, τρέφονται γὰρ πάντες οἱ ἀνθρώπινοι νόμοι ὑπὸ ἑνὸς τοῦ θείου, may in this sense also serve as proof. Nay more, the enlightened and mature (*alternde*) wisdom of the times of Cicero knew not how to find a firmer basis for human legislation than the order of the world proceeding from the gods, in which ordaining power man takes part, as possessing reason in common with God; so that out of this alone, not from the laws historically

existing and the like, the truth of the "lex," of the "jus *per se* expetendum et colendum*,"* was to be derived. Comp. *De Legg.* i. 7 with 15, 16, and other passages, especially ii. 4, where it is said: "Legem neque hominum ingeniis excogitatam, nec scitum aliquod esse populorum, sed æternum quiddam, quod universum mundum regeret, imperandi prohibendique sapientia. Ita principem legem illam et ultimam mentem esse dicebant, omnia ratione aut cogentis aut vetantis dei, ex qua illa lex, quam dii humano generi dederunt, recte est laudata." But that *lex vera et princeps,* that *ratio summi Jovis* has, however, no manifestation for the heathen world, but just again in the *recta ratio* of the lawgiver, of the philosopher. The restoration of the true law, therefore, is for man, abandoned merely to himself, a problem whose solution, it was imagined, might possibly be found in that fiction, which they framed for themselves concerning the nature of the *mens,* of the *ratio hominis.*—But in the creative instinct of word-forming in the German language, all unconscious as it is, there are likewise shadowed forth the various factors of this idea. That which lies before time, as well as that which is historically valid, as coming from ancient times, is right and law (*Recht und Gesetz*). This is expressed by the old high-German *ewa,* root *ew,* kindred in stem with *ævum,* αἰών. Comp. von Raumer, *althochd. Spr.* pp. 329, 330.

(2) The commandment of the Old Testament is, according to Christ's word, the commandment of God (Θεὸς ἐντείλατο, Matt. 15:4; comp. τὸ ῥηθὲν ὑμῖν ὑπὸ τοῦ Θεοῦ, Matt. 22:31). And just for this reason it cannot be broken; comp. Matt. 5:17. Comp. νόμος Κυρίου, Luke 2:23 ff., 39; νόμος τοῦ Θεοῦ, Rom. 7:25, 8:7. The will of God in the form of the law, that is to say, of commands and prohibitions affecting men, forms at the same time the contrast to that which was brought to pass through Christ. Ὁ νόμος διὰ Μωϋσέως ἐδόθη, ἡ χάρις καὶ ἡ ἀλήθεια διὰ Ἰησοῦ Χριστοῦ ἐγένετο, John 1:17. This is said in that passage, to make plain in what sense the disciples of the Lord had received out of His *fulness,* and in truth, *grace for grace.* The fulness of divine truth was not yet suited to the previous

revelation. By Moses God gave the law, the sum of *requirements* which the true God makes upon men. From this requirement man receives nothing but an indebtedness of performance. But from the fulness of Christ he was to receive. For by Him came into the world the grace of that God who gives exceeding abundantly (πλοῦτος τῆς χάριτος), and herewith, the whole undivided truth of God, the necessity for which the law awakens and confirms. Compare afterwards, § 17.

(3) As Christ confirmed the divine character of the law and of the whole Old Testament revelation, so also ought, according to His words, the Scriptures of the Old Testament, in their turn, divinely to accredit His mission and divinity. Εἰ γὰρ ἐπιστεύετε Μωϋσῇ, ἐπιστεύετε ἂν ἐμοί, περὶ γὰρ ἐμοῦ ἔγραψεν, John 5:46; comp. with 5:39. Ὅτι δεῖ πληρωθῆναι πάντα τὰ γεγραμμένα ἐν τῷ νόμῳ Μωϋσέως καὶ προφήταις καὶ ψαλμοῖς περὶ ἐμοῦ, Luke 24:44. Here also it is the essential connection of the historical manifestations of God upon which this mutual attestation rests; and for this very reason, therefore, it was only Jesus Christ who could remove the veil from the words of the Old Testament which rests upon them (2 Cor. 3:13, 16).

To the Christian consciousness, therefore, comes first of all, through its genetic connection with Christ and the relation of Christ to the words of the Old Testament covenant, the knowledge of a law which has proceeded from God, and has been promulgated at a fixed historical period. Not, however, in the manner of an external acknowledgment, in which, as it were, we only repeat after Christ what *He* has said concerning the law of Israel, but in the way of an inward satisfying of a moral and religious want. In order to understand this, we must not, however, stop at the law of Israel as such, at the law isolated from its real connection, but must take a comprehensive view of it in the historical-organic position in which it actually stands. That is the inseparable connection of the law with the prophecy and promise of Israel. In this twofold position Moses himself appears in the New Testament: comp. John 5:46, Luke 24:27, Acts 7:37, 26:22, with John 1:17, Rom. 5:14, etc.—For such a revelation, not for the revelation of a divine law *per se*, longs the conscience-awakened man. And he who, impelled by such longing, becomes aware of the true position occupied by the law of Israel, then learns from the bottom of his heart to say with Christ, "Salvation is of the Jews" (John 4:22; comp. Rom. 11:17, 24). He who does not know this from living experience, possesses no perfect Christian consciousness.

Two things, namely, man must become aware of through the conscience,—a relation of God to him, and a relation of himself to God. The first, so far as it becomes known to us in conscience, is a permanent requisition on the part of God; the second, a permanent shortcoming on the part of man. Such a state of things cannot be what God wills. The communion of God with us cannot have for its object merely to reveal and to establish the defect of our communion with Him; and if He brings before us in our conscience this communion with Him as the object of our life, this cannot be for the mere purpose of letting us conceive that the frustration of our life's object should be the only thing which God will bestow upon us by the fact of this testimony of our conscience. Conscience certainly impelled even the heathen world to fear, to a yearning for change, and to prayers to their gods. The God who in our conscience makes a demand upon us, will therefore reveal to us our false relation to Him, which has become historically fixed and now natural, as something which He will not have so, but which we so have and so wish to have. If God, however, wishes that man should abandon this false relation so historically fixed, then is it inconceivable that this His will should be made known to us by Himself only in the form of a requisition. That is to say, in other words: if this communion with God is to appear to us as an attainable end of life, then must this communion be equally that of a God who makes demands, as of one who imparts (*i.e.* the needed grace). That this relation, however, of God to the human race is as old as the history of this race, is declared to us by one history alone,— that of Israel, which at no time and in no place knows of law except in connection with promise—nay, resting on the ground of previous blessing and promise. And Israel is the bearer of this relation in such a way, that even, according to the express terms of the revelation peculiar to this people, it should avail not alone for the people of Israel, but for all nations of the earth. This is the Christian-ethical and inwardly necessary recognition of the historically revealed law, as it develops itself on the basis of the fact of conscience, taken in connection with the history of the salvation of the human race in Christ.

(4) The first import of the commandment appearing in words, and of the declarations of God given in words (Gen. 2:16 ff.), is this, that man should recognize the law of his spirit and his natural inclinations not as an autonomy of *his own* spirit and *his own* nature, but as ordained by God, and as the effects of the will of a personal God standing over him. Man's conscience was intended to be a depository of divine command and prohibition. But man struck out of his recollection these divine words, and his inclinations turned towards that which God did not wish. And this took place in those human beings whose species and nature were destined, as root of the race, to set forth the nature and kind of the whole stem throughout all its branches and ramifications out of themselves as out of a root. And thus it was, that that aversion to call to mind that which belongs to God, became the nature of the human race. Conscience itself becomes a thorn to man against which he kicks, a voice which he wills not to hear, or would wish to drown. Nothing is of greater importance, as opposed to this tendency of the race, than a law proceeding from God, not latent in the human spirit, but a law of the divine will expressed in words.

When, therefore, in spite of this, we shall not in what follows enter upon the contents of this law in its whole extent, this will be chiefly from the reason, that what is peculiar to the moral consciousness of the Christian is given not in the law, but in Christ the end and object of the law (τέλος γὰρ νόμου Χριστός, Rom. 10:4). The analysis of the law of Israel, together with the whole position of Israel, belongs to the preparatory teaching of the divine acts, not to the characteristic of the existence and life of the Christian, which root themselves in Christ. Therefore that element of the law of Israel which conditions for all time the moral consciousness of Christians, is to be derived and understood not so much immediately from the law of Israel, as from Christ the fulfiller of the law, as it is also objectively present to the Christian in Christ and in communion with Him.

If, consequently, in what follows, the question is of a position under a law of God, the position indicated by God to Israel is not hereby intended. For Israel was placed under law *and* promise. But it is a position which Israel attempted arbitrarily to assume; and thus, while seeking after a *law* of righteousness, they failed to attain to the law of God in its true signification (or, according to the other reading, to a law of *righteousness*, which would have produced righteousness), Rom. 9:31. And because throughout all times the temptation crept upon Christendom even to place itself under law, we shall only have to point out in what follows, what would be the import of that will of God revealing itself in the form of a law, and making requisitions from man, and how far its effect reaches, if we should have to think of man *merely* as placed under a law of God, as we, however, have not so to think either of the children of Israel, much less of Christians. And the firmer the conviction of the Christian that God is a lawgiver and judge, the more deeply he feels what is the nature of the law that "worketh wrath," so much the more clearly and definitely must this his consciousness stand up before him, that he may know why he shudders at any attempt again to seek in Christ either a law or the law, instead of "grace and truth."

True it is, indeed, that conscience and law are not stages of development which the man has left behind him when he stands as a Christian in the faith. And this so much the less, the less, as we shall show hereafter, the actual condition of the Christian is comprised in that life which is born of faith. So far, however, as he lives in faith, not only are conscience and law not *against* him, but he does not even stand *under* his conscience and law, and law and conscience are not *above* him, but both live *in* him, and he lives *in* both, but not by virtue either of conscience or of the law. That in which the Christian finds peace and freedom, is derived neither from *his own* conscience nor from the divine *law*.

True it is, however, that in the Scriptures that principle of a new life in which the Christian stands, whether we call it Christ, or the spirit of life, or freedom, or faith, is also called a law (ὁ νόμος τοῦ Χριστοῦ, Gal. 6:2; ὁ νόμος τοῦ πνεύματος τῆς ζωῆς ἐν Χριστῷ Ἰησοῦ Rom. 8:2; νόμος τέλειος τῆς ἐλευθερίας, Jas. 1:25; νόμος ἐλευθερίας, ch. 2:12; νόμος πίστεως, Rom. 3:27). And not only is that, which remains the task even of the Christian, in general called keeping the commandments of God (τήρησις ἐντολῶν Θεοῦ, 1 Cor. 7:19), but that specially which Christ gave and left behind Him is time after time called a commandment, or commandments, and indeed a new commandment (καινὴ ἐντολή, John 13:34, 1 John 2:8; comp. generally the whole of this epistle). And thus just here will be the proper place to investigate the reason why, when we are speaking of a divine law, the law of Christ also, the commandment of Christ, the law of the Spirit, or the law of faith, and so forth, are not drawn into the circle of inquiry. The question is indeed not settled in this way, by our asserting, perhaps, in reference to those expressions of a νόμος Χριστοῦ, and so forth, that this is only a figurative mode of speaking, arising out of a comparison with another νόμος mentioned at the same time (as in Rom. 8:2, 3:27; Jas. 2:12), so that we could speak there of a law only in a certain sense, and by way of comparison, or relatively and not literally. For this mode of expression occurs also where no parallel is drawn with another law (Gal. 6:2; Jas. 1:25). And the Christian knows and feels in his inmost man, that this is rightly and truly meant. But from our own language, we are convinced that the word law (*Gesetz*) does not always mean the same thing, that is to say, that we thereby do not always understand a requisition made to man from without. When the apostle (Rom. 7:23, 25) speaks of "a law of sin," by this is meant that internal necessity which belongs to the nature of sin, by which, where it has its hold, it regularly works that of which the apostle had before made mention. The law of faith (Rom. 3:27) is not a law which demands faith, but a law which belongs to the nature of faith, by which regularly and necessarily all boasting on man's part is excluded. The law of the spirit of life in Christ Jesus (Rom. 8:2) is that power indwelling in the spirit of life by an internal necessity, by virtue of which this spirit of life effects that freedom which is there spoken of. That which James (ch. 1:25) calls the perfect law of liberty, is nothing else than that New Testament word of truth before mentioned by him (ver. 18), by which we Christians are regenerated (ἀπεκύησε). Its perfectness consists just in this, that it is not merely the norm of free moral activity, but is the power thereof; that it does not demand, but produces this freedom. If we wish to be judged by this law of liberty (ch. 2:12), then have we so much the more necessity to inquire whether we have fulfilled the positive law of God, the more the power of fulfilling the law which is awakened in us by the word of truth surpasses the demand for the fulfilling of the law (compare Wiesinger on both passages). Finally, Paul (Gal. 6:2) calls the mutual bearing of each other's burdens the fulfilling of the law of Christ. Who he is who can fulfil it, was previously stated—those who do not stand under the law, but who, led by the Spirit of God (ch. 5:18), live in the Spirit and walk in the Spirit (ch. 5:25), and are therefore called spiritual men (πνευματικοί, ch. 6:1). These fulfil the law of Christ in the mutual bearing of each other's burdens. It is not an isolated command of Christ that is named or intended, but the law of Christ. Ought we to explain the expression "law" of Christ from an "antithesis" of Christ with the law of the old covenant, of which we find no trace in the immediate context? Or if a definite commandment of Christ were meant, as *e.g.* John 13:34, why is it called here τὸν νόμον, not τὴν ἐντολήν? Is it for this reason, perhaps, because that commandment of love is the whole law? But Christ regards not one, but two commandments, as including the whole law and the prophets (Matt. 22:40); and the mutual bearing of burdens is the fulfilling of only one side of that love which Christ requires, not the fulfilment of the commandment in its entirety. I imagine, however, that I take quite a correct view of the words of Paul, when I here think of Christ as the bearer of our burdens, and understand by the law of Christ that law embodied for us in Christ for the bearing of our mutual burdens. For this is certain, that the unattained majesty of the fulness of love and of the long-suffering of Christ stands over against us Christians *instar legis:* only that Christ the Lord is not merely the embodied law, nor the embodiment of the fulfilment of the law which has been realized in Him, but the Lord who, as He places before us His nature as the law of our nature, so also He pours forth in the Holy Ghost the law and the virtue of His nature, by whom we must be led, in order to fulfil the law of Christ. Christ the bearer of our burdens is not merely the law which regulates our conduct by a demand, but also, at the same time, an embodied type of the way in which the Spirit of Christ works in us, and makes us able to follow Christ. And just because I *must* keep both things unchangeably in view in my thoughts of Christ, Christ falls not under that idea of the law, in which I *cannot* think of both, but *must* think only of the one that the law *requires,* but *does not bestow.*

Similarly the case stands also with the commandments, or the new commandment of Christ. That this is a charge, a command in the true sense of the word, there can be no doubt (comp. John 15:17). But as the commandment of love it is not at all new, but something primeval. That in which this commandment is new, is not to be sought either in its being in a new form of commandment, or in its having a wider range or a higher degree of love, or even in this, that perhaps the command demands from us a love like the love of Christ. Rather does the novelty, not of the commandment, but of the love demanded, consist in this, that this love in its *source* rests upon the love of Christ, that is to say, springs up in us out of the love of Christ towards us, and presupposes that state of things which is equally true in Christ and in Christians, that the darkness is past, and that the true light now shineth (1 John 2:8). That we should hold fast to that love which has been kindled in us by the light of Christ's love streaming into our hearts—this is the new element in the commandment of love, as it springs from Christ. "A new commandment give I unto you," says Christ, "that ye love one another; as," or "since (καθώς) I have loved you, that ye love one another" (John 13:34; comp. 15:12, and καθώς, 17:2). He who believes in Christ is born of God, and loves Him who has begotten him, as well as him who is begotten of God (1 John 5:1; comp. 1 Pet. 1:22, 23). And since in this commandment of love, as in all Christ's commandments, I cannot stop at the commandment in order to derive from the commandment of Christ the fulfilling of that commandment, what Christ commands does not therefore fall under the notion of the law, which merely makes demands on us; and in truth as certainly so, as that Christ in His essential aspect is not the requirer of a life in God, but the giver of this life (ζωὴν διδοὺς τῷ κόσμῳ, John 6:33).

What the true character is of that hankering to place the Christian life, as to its principle, under law and commandment, is shown by the history of ethics. We will briefly sketch merely its leading features, in a glance at its beginnings. Quite gently it makes its appearance in the apostolic fathers in the *Shepherd* of Hermas, in the second book. The life of the Christian is based on *mandata*. Faith also is a *mandatum*. With these commandments, of which the Christian is to suppose that he can obey them all, the Christian arrives only, so to say, at a common everyday Christianity. When, on the other hand, he adds to these something more which Christ has not enjoined— as, for example, special fasts (lib. iii. similit. v.)—then he gains especial honor and merit before God. All this, indeed, man does not do of himself, but "the man who has the Lord in his heart." But yet it is just man's own doing, the fulfilling of the commandment, the going beyond what is commanded, which is the ground of justification, nay, of especial honor before God.

To Hermas we must join in the third century Clement of Alexandria. In a certain way, however, after the manner of the Stoics and Neo-Platonists, he reverses this relation. The sum of the commands of Christ, and of the course of action corresponding to these commands, is only a preparatory training for the higher Christian perfection. Christ Himself is our Schoolmaster (*Pædag.* i. 7). The difference between the new and old covenant consists merely in the nature of the commandments. There the commandment of fear; here that of love for the Lord (!). Thus to him the law of Moses becomes a χάρις παλαιά; the law of Christ is distinguished by the mildness of the λόγος, by that alternation of praise and blame, of exhortation and prohibition, which is suited to the constitution of man. Faith is obedience. Obedience rests on commands. The obedience shown in our manner of acting is guided by the system of the commandments of the Lord. At the head of these commandments stands the proposition: "And as ye would that men should do to you, do ye also to them likewise" (Luke 6:31). This might also be expressed in the propositions: "Thou shalt love the Lord your God, etc., and your neighbor as yourself" (Luke 10:25–28). But in this the Schoolmaster gives only teaching for children and food for children, and prepares for the reception of the knowledge of wisdom (*Strom*, vi. 1). To this knowledge the Decalogue ceases to be ten moral precepts; it is the symbol of the φυσικὴ δημιουργία (*Strom*, vi. 15). The goal of this higher knowledge is Gnostic holiness (i. 7). It consists in a contemplative union with God, by virtue of which he who possesses this knowledge, himself in a certain sense a God, acts like a God in a state of perfectly passionless existence (*Strom.* ii. 19, iv. 23, vii. 5). "If we say that we have no sin, we deceive ourselves, and the truth is not in us," does not stand written in this codex of Gnostic perfection.

It is otherwise with those who in other respects represent the church system. They know nothing of this height of perfection; but they separate works from the vital ground of grace received, place them side by side with this grace as a fulfilling the commandments of Christ, and characterize them as means of again obtaining the grace which has been lost through after offences. On this rests the doctrine of penance. What Origen had taught in this respect (comp. *e.g. contra Cels.* iii. 71), and what he meant when he calls good works the perfecting of justification (*Comment, in Ep. ad Rom.* iv. 6), reappears in Cyprian (*De opere et Eleemosynis*, shortly after the commencement). The whole of this *salutaris operatio* is not a living energy springing from the nature of faith, but the effect of a knowledge in which the believer knows that God and Christ command this or that, and that this commandment is truth. For this Christ gives to that man who is saved by grace a *law* (*De op. et Eleemos.* p. 237, ed. Paris). Thus, therefore, it is said of him who is active in deeds: "Operatur ideo quia credit, *quia scit vera esse*, quæ prædicta sunt verbis Dei, nee scripturam sanctam posse mentiri, arbores infructuosas, *i.e.* steriles homines excidi cet." (*l.c.* p. 239). That the believer knows this is quite true. But the terror arising from this knowledge is neither the substance of his faith nor the power of that love to God in Christ, from which the vital energy of the Christian life springs. And still more suspiciously is it said in another passage: "Præclara et divina res ... salutaris operatio, *solatium grande* credentium, *securitatis nostræ salubre præsidium, munimentum spei, tutela fidei, medela peccati, res posita in potestate* FACIENTIS."

If the peculiar principle of the Christian's life had not gradually been lost to view, the appearance of such a book as that of Ambrosius, *de officiis*, that transfer of Cicero's book to the domain of Christian life, would have been utterly inconceivable.

This downward path was crossed by Augustine in a way that forms an epoch. This is not the place for entering into an exposition of this. I will only cite three passages: "Non ... sumus sub lege bonum quidem jubente sed non dante; sed sumus sub gratiâ, quæ id quod lex jubet faciens nos amare, potest liberis imperare" (*De Continent*, c. 3). "Quia lex per literam jubet, non per spiritum juvat, quicunque sic audit literam legis, ut ei sufficere videatur, cognovisse quid jubeat aut prohibeat, quo id se arbitrii sui virtute impleturum esse confidat, nec fide confugiat adjuvandus ad spiritum vivificantem, ne reum factum litera occidat, is perfecto zelum Dei habet sed non secundum scientiam" (*Ep.* 186, c. 3). "In quantum quisque spiritu dicitur, non est sub lege, quia in quantum condelectatur legi Dei non est sub legis timore, quia timor tormentum habet, non delectationem" (*De nat. et grat.* c. 57).

This evangelical principle laid down by Augustine traverses and combines itself in the further development of theology through the course of the middle ages, in the most diverse manner, with the legal type, with the mystic contemplation, and with formal definitions, which are borrowed from the ethical systems of philosophy of the pre-Christian world. I would refer, for this development and this complication, to the sketch given in *my* Encyclopedia. The true knowledge had become at the end of the middle ages a rarity, until, after some precursors like Joh. Wessel and others, the evangelical principle again burst forth in the Reformation. And yet at the end of the eighteenth century, one who calls himself a Protestant theologian, in reference to the complaint of Luther, that "many great and excellent men did not know how rightly to preach Moses, but wished to make a Moses of Christ, a lawbook of the gospel, and works out of the word," in sober earnest made this declaration, *"On these principles no true Christian morality could exist"* (see my Encyclopedia, p. 241).

§ 14. *The Working of the Law on the Human Consciousness*

a. *The Knowledge of the Law*

If, first of all, we look altogether away from the nature of the divine law, and contemplate it only in its form as a system of divine commands and prohibitions, in order to ask ourselves the question, What man hereby becomes conscious of, then something becomes manifest therein which is partly analogous, and partly distinct from the working of the conscience in the present state of mankind. The working of the law is analogous in this, that I, by virtue of the law, *acquire the knowledge* of a higher determination for my will, without gaining in the law, and by the law the identity of the inclination and direction of my will with the law (1). The working of the law is distinct in this, that by virtue of this law I can on no account view this higher determination of my will as an autonomy of my nature or of my Ego, but I recognize it as a rule outside of me, established by God. And in this the law brings to light a latent relation of the human conscience. The nature, however, of the law of Israel is not an interpreter of the nature which belongs to the universal human conscience, although in so many points the testimony of the human conscience, which has made itself heard in history, accords with the nature of the law. For the essential design of the law of Israel is not to promulgate the contents of the human conscience, but the thoughts of God respecting Israel and the whole human race, in preparatory connection with the redemption of that race (*vid.* § 13).

The points, then, in which the nature of conscience comes in contact with that of the law, are the relations of man to himself and to other men. For an *adequate* knowledge of God is, according to the evidence of Scripture and the experience of history, not a result of the testimony of conscience (2). But even in those points the knowledge which is the result of the divine law, is not precisely similar to that consciousness which is conditioned by the spirit of conscience. For that which, according to the law of development of the human spirit, comes to man's knowledge subjectively and successively in his conscience, presents itself objectively in the law with its commands all at once, and is present to him in its full extent. And that which, in accordance with the corruption of man, may become dark and uncertain in relation to his conscience, the same presents itself to him in the law clearly and unambiguously (3).

Before everything, however, the relation to the living, personal, self-testifying God is that element wherein the knowledge which is brought about by the law, has, in comparison with the conscience, its characteristic trait. This, not the formal conception of the law as such, it is, by which the power of self-judgment given in the conscience arrives at its standard, the requiring and judging will of God (4). And in the same knowledge by means of the law, which, as the requisition of God to man lying under the dominion of sin, does not subdue the evil tendency, but only gives occasion to sin to break forth in all kinds of lusts, there is produced in man a consciousness of sin as it really is,—namely, a rebellion against God's holy will (5). In this way the law unveils the true nature of the moral position, which has not yet been revealed to man by his conscience, of which he has an inkling in conscience, but knows not with perfect clearness.

(1) Whether under the term "law" we choose to think of that "primordialis lex data Adæ et Evæ in paradiso quasi matrix omnium præceptorum Dei," or of all the later manifestations of the requiring divine will up to the final revelation of the law by Moses, it always is, and continues to be, a declaration addressed to man from without, by which he is instructed in what God requires of him. The nature of this declaration as a law is absolutely comprised in its requisitions; so that this "docere legem, erudire" proceeding from God, as Tertullian rightly calls it (*Adv. Judæ.* 2), has this only for its result, that man learns the requisitions of the will of God. For if man, in connection with this his knowledge of the law, knew also something besides, *e.g.* that he willed that which the law required of him, or that in actual fact he discharged the requirements of the law, then would he know that he *could* will, or do so, not in reality from the law. For in the law, as such, we have no revelation of the divine will to bestow on us the power to fulfil its requisitions. If, consequently, I knew of such a power, and if, at the same time, I knew not of the revelation of a divine will granting to me such a power, then I could derive such power from man's own resources alone. To endeavor to derive it from the law, would be exactly as if I should wish to make out of a demand for payment the proof of my ability to do so. By virtue of the divine law considered in itself, I *know* only of a divine requisition, and nothing more. God teaches (comp. Deut. 4:1, etc.), and causes Israel to know His judgments (comp. Ps. 147:20). Here we find the capacity for a complete knowledge of the requirements of the divine will, but

not the least trace of any necessity given of imagining that, by virtue of the law, the law should also be one with the inclination of the heart, and so the vital impulse and center of our free vital movements. The Old Testament revelation speaks indeed of a nearness of the law, by virtue of which it is in our heart as well as in our mouth (Deut. 30:14). But all this is under a supposition, which can by no means be regarded as the result of the position of man given him under the law as law,— namely, under the supposition of his turning, not to the law, but to *Jehovah the Lord* (comp. the תָּשׁוּב, vers. 8 and 10, in opposition to אִם־יִפְנֶה לְבָבְךָ, ver. 17). To attempt to derive this free act of the heart from the law, would be just as unreasonable as to say, I will, *because* I ought, and to assert, that this was a genuine, free, and perfect will of the heart. Compare with this passage of Deuteronomy, the significant application of this passage by the apostle, Rom. 10:6 ff. Our Christian consciousness is filled with the testimony of the apostle to the fact that the law is not there to *give* to man life and righteousness. Speaking of the final revelation of the law to Israel, written on the tables of stone, he calls the law the letter (γράμμα), which *kills* (2 Cor. 3:6); and the ministry of the law a ministry of death (2 Cor. 3:7), a ministration of condemnation (2 Cor. 3:9). Opposed to this παλαιότης γράμματος stands the word of the new covenant, the fulfilment of the old promises in the word, as καινότης πνεύματος (Rom. 7:6). "If there had been a law given which could have given life, verily righteousness should have been by the law" (Gal. 3:21). But this is not the case.

(2) Compare, on the relation of conscience to the consciousness of a God, § 10, note (4) at the end. It is not by this to be denied, that "man's reason or natural intelligence has a glimmering spark of the knowledge that a God exists" (*Form. Conc.* ii. 2, 9), or "that the heathen have in some degree a knowledge of God from natural law" (*ibid.* v. 22). The "quod sit Deus" we have before discussed. Is there, however, a testimony of conscience as to these questions, *quid sit* and *quid velit Deus*?

We find, according to the history of the heathen world in reference to the *quid sit*, that it is nowhere of such a nature as to correspond to God's revelation of Himself in His word. And in respect to the *quid velit*, we find only a relative approximation ("humana ratio naturaliter intelligit *aliquo modo* legem," Apol. iv. 7; "*particulam* aliquam legis tenet," Form. Conc. ii. 2, 9), and indeed in reference to the relations in which man stands to himself and other men. But even there not in the form of the knowledge of a divine will in regard to man, but of a mutual human standard, by which the will of the individual is limited. "Ab altero expectes," says Seneca, "alteri quod feceris." Compare what Diogenes Laertius relates of Aristotle (v. 21): Ἐρωτηθεὶς πῶς ἂν τοῖς φίλοις προσφεροίμεθα; ἔφη· ὡς ἂν εὐξαίμεθα αὐτοὺς ἡμῖν προσφέρεσθαι. This has been compared to the words of Christ: Πάντα οὖν ὅσα ἂν θέλητε ἵνα ποιῶσιν ὑμῖν οἱ ἄνθρωποι, οὕτως καὶ ὑμεῖς ποιεῖτε αὐτοῖς· οὗτος γάρ ἐστιν ὁ νόμος καὶ οἱ προφῆται, Matt. 7:12; comp. Luke 6:31. Formally, these expressions are perfectly alike. They assert that we ought to have the same standard for ourselves and for others, and that the good we desire for ourselves we ought to show towards others. But the expressions acquire quite a different meaning according to the supposition of what we conceive to be that good which we wish for ourselves. For, according to this supposition alone, this equal standard obtains a moral or immoral character, and one pleasing or displeasing to God. Nay, the true standard of that which man has to wish for himself, he finds at no time in himself or his own inclination, but in the will of God. Under the supposition that man has such an objective standard for the good, this equal standard, according to which he does to others that which he wishes to receive from them, is the simplest guide. But never without this supposition. To such a leading proposition is the discourse of Christ joined. When the question is of the love which tolerates an association with the unholy neither with carping censure nor with profanation of what is holy, and the power of which one obtains by prayer, we may go on to say, "*Therefore*, all things whatsoever ye would that men should do to you, do ye even so to them." And just so we find the word in Luke, after an exhortation to a self-denying, long-suffering love, at all times ready to be shown even towards our enemy. This love fixes the standard for that which is morally good. By this alone is to be determined what we should wish for ourselves from others, and what we should voluntarily do towards them. Isolated from such connection, the proposition that from the measure of our own wishes we ought to measure and to satisfy those of others, is not at all a moral precept. And yet, after the example of Clement of Alexandria, it has been endeavored to make this the leading proposition of the moral precepts of the Lord, or to trace herein the identity of the natural requirement of conscience with the principle of Christian morality. The law of God, however, does in nowise begin with the relation of man to man, but with that of man to the revealed and personal God.

(3) The law of God in Israel is not the product of a development-process in the people of Israel, in which they had gradually become conscious to themselves of what is right and good in the relation, whether of man to man, or of man to God. On the contrary, God testifies His will in gradual revelation, in opposition to the spirit predominating amongst the people. The law is not implanted in the people by God as a spiritual principle, whose development He might have left to them; but it places the totality of the relations of human life in this people, through the manifoldness of the commandments of the law (ὁ νόμος τῶν ἐντολῶν, Eph. 2:15), under the rule of the divine requiring will. It is not left to the vacillation and investigation of human knowledge, and nothing is handed over to the doubtful settling of man; but it stands, (which could not be said either of conscience or of any human law,) incontestably before us as the "holy law," and its commands as "holy, just, and good" (Rom. 7:12). And thus it stands before even the apostle of Jesus Christ.

(4) The dissension, as it makes its appearance by means of conscience, is, in the form in which it shows itself, an internal one. There are λογισμοὶ μεταξὺ ἀλλήλων κατηγοροῦντες ἢ καὶ

ἀπολογούμενοι, Rom. 2:15. It is otherwise with the force of the law. The law is the word of revelation: *"I am the Lord your God"* (Deut. 4:5, 30, etc.). In and by these words God is *Judge* upon earth. The blaze of the lightning which accompanied this revelation is the visible sign of that power of judgment belonging to the word, which, as the word, inherently announces to the creature-life the presence of God as Judge (comp. Ps. 1:1–4, 58:11, 82:1, 7:12). And not only on Sinai, but from paradise onwards, the self-testifying of God among the people of Israel produces the consciousness of God as a Judge (Gen. 3:8 ff., 16:5, 18:25; comp. afterwards Eccles. 12:14, Isa. 66:15, 16).

(5) The effect of the law in reference to the knowledge of evil can be no other than this, that we should now recognize that evil is not altogether comprised in the wrong done to a better knowledge dwelling in us, but is also an offence against the person of the holy judging God, standing over against the Ego. What Nägelsbach (*hom. Theol.* p. 268, Anm.) says, that the word "sin" is not adapted to express the idea of the ἁμαρτήματα of the Homeric man, might in a certain sense apply to the whole of that self-judgment which was extraneous to Christianity, and to the law of that holy God who had been historically manifested. The element is wanting which consists of the personal guilt which at the same time supervenes in the offence against a present and holy God, as it is unconsciously expressed in our word "sin" (*Sünde, sunta, sons; peccatum* and *culpa* at the same time). To do evil in the presence of a revealed God, is to "sin against God" (חָטָא לֵאלֹהִים, Gen. 39:9; comp. 13:13, 20:6). And this also not merely as the form of the consciousness developing itself under the law, but in consequence of express declaration, "Whosoever hath sinned *against me*, him will I blot out of my book" (אֲשֶׁר חָטָא־לִי, Ex. 32:33),—a repetition of that which was spoken to our first parents, and suspended over them, Gen. 3:8 ff. Hence also the confession, "We have sinned against Thee" (Deut. 1:41). With the law begins the consciousness of being *debtors* (*reus,*

ὑπόδικος). (Οἴδαμεν δὲ ὅτι ὅσα ὁ νόμος λέγει, τοῖς ἐν τῷ νόμῳ λαλεῖ, ἵνα ... ὑπόδικος γένηται πᾶς ὁ κόσμος τῷ Θεῷ, Rom. 3:19). For the φρόνημα τῆς σαρκός shows itself as ἔχθρα εἰς Θεόν, Rom. 8:7. And against this ἔχθρα—ὁ νόμος ὀργὴν (*scil.* Θεοῦ) κατεργάζεται, Rom. 4:15. In this mutual relation the discord which necessarily exists between holiness and unholiness reaches its acme, and at the same time is fully revealed: sin has showed itself in its true nature, as a separation between man and God, for whose removal a third element—an *atonement* is required; comp. Ex. 32:30. Hence John's definition of what he calls sin: πᾶς ὁ ποιῶν τὴν ἁμαρτίαν καὶ τὴν ἀνομίαν ποιθῖ, καὶ ἡ ἁμαρτία ἐστὶν ἡ ἀνομία, 1 John 3:4. Ἀνομία stands here, not in the general sense of what is contrary to law and ordinance (as *e.g.* in Matt. 13:41, etc.), but in the special sense of what is directed against *God's* law. And in this light, sin in the children *of God* shows itself as what is in its inmost nature opposed to their position. Comp. v. 1 and 9. With the law the true nature of evil becomes first manifest. Οὗ γὰρ οὐκ ἔστι νόμος, οὐδὲ παράβασις (Rom. 4:15). Along with the testimony which God bears to Himself in the law, sin becomes conscious transgression of the known will of God. Not that sin first became sin when the law was given. It has been in its nature present from the beginning onwards. But before the law divine justice silently, (*i.e.* without a distinct testimony placed before the eyes of all,) executed in the case of the human race its judgment on sin (ἐβασίλευσεν ὁ θάνατος, Rom. 5:14). In and with the law, however, sin is formally and solemnly imputed (ἐλλογεῖται, Rom. 5:13) as what it really is. In this act of ἐλλογεῖσθαι, the relation of sin to what is good is manifested as the discord between two personalities, the person of God and the person of man, to all those who hear the law: in this ἐλλογεῖσθαι *appears* at the same time in its whole extent the judicial majesty of God. But the law brings about the recognition of sin not merely in this way, that it calls sin sin, not merely so, as the apostle says, διὰ νόμου ἐπίγνωσις ἁμαρτίας, Rom. 3:20. Rather does the apostle at Rom. 7:7–13 explain himself respecting the import which the law has for his inner life as well as for every individual man. And this very position of the law it is which enables us at the same time to recognize why freedom from sin is not to be obtained from the law. We give to the apostolic thoughts, as we think we are bound to look at them, their general expression. Through the law alone we, as self-acquired experience, derive a perception of the true nature of sin. For, on the one hand, I know not what it is to covet, unless the law speaks to me, and says, "Thou shalt not covet." In this way only do I rightly *understand* coveting as an offence against the will of God which is over me. And, on the other hand, sin, that perversity which kicks against everything which prevents man from giving way to his own impulses, takes occasion from that very command not to covet, to excite and set in motion within me all kinds of evil desires. And hereby alone I learn by experience rightly the nature and power of sin. For without the law, sin is dead. True, it is there; but for my consciousness it is as a lifeless body, which moves not, and whose stirring I cannot trace. And before the law comes to us, we find in the life of all of us a section of that life in which we live unmoved by the law, whose cleaving sword has not yet smitten our consciousness, and summoned us forth to the decisive contest. But when the command, that we must not allow ourselves to covet, comes forth before our souls, in such a decisive hour sin revives in us: it wrests this very commandment into an occasion for deceiving me, inasmuch as it excites me to lust by the very prohibition of it, and at the same time slays me by the commandment, which declares that he who lusts against God's command has fallen under the power of death. Thus I die, and the commandment destined for life is by me found to be the bearer of death. This, however, does not destroy the holiness of the law, nor the holiness, righteousness, and goodness of the commandment. It in no way proves that it is that which is good which brought about my death. Rather is it sin that has brought death upon me. But the object is, that sin should be manifest to me as that which, through what is good, works my death, in order that by the commandment the exceeding sinfulness of sin should be presented to me in living reality.

This is the testimony of the apostle against those who are of opinion that they possess, in their knowledge of the law, the power to fulfil that law. How otherwise could the same apostle call the law the power of sin (1 Cor. 15:56; comp. Rom. 5:20)? The law forces out the disease that is spreading under the skin. Such is its task. But healing it does not bring.

To the exposition given of the apostolical declaration I only add a few more remarks. It appears to me, that we are not justified in concluding, from the passage in the Epistle to the Romans, that the working of the law and its commands, under all circumstances, is this, that sin arouses by it desires contrary to the law. The apostle does not use the present tense, nor does he characterize the relation as a constant one, and always remaining identical. He speaks only of an experience through which he has passed, from which he has concluded how it stands in respect to the law with sin and evil desire. This, however, is the experience, that when the law comes into conflict with sin within us, the law in itself does not become master over our evil desires, but only greatly inflames them. It is the old experience: *nitimur in vetitum*. But then we are not so constituted, that the sin which dwells in us has actually and simultaneously, at all points of our life's relations, evil desires opposed to God; nor is the nature of the law such, that it actually and simultaneously presents itself before our soul with all its commands. It is rather isolated critical moments in which such a conflict between law and sin arises. And if nothing stands before our souls but command and prohibition, then in such cases, at all times, we become aware that our evil desires are more powerful than the prohibition, and are, in truth, first stirred up thoroughly by the prohibition. And this disposition of our heart is the decisive point for the question, whether then the holy law, the holy, just, and good commandment, makes us holy, just, and good men. The answer to this is, and remains, a most decided No.

§ 15. b. Legal Obedience

With what has hitherto been discussed is associated the question, whether the law as a requisition of the divine will addressed to man, inasmuch as it does not as requisition include in itself the bestowing of any power for its fulfilment, becomes of no importance for the Christian consciousness, and remains a requisition to which no response of any kind at all can be made on the part of man. If this last is denied (1), and it is notwithstanding asserted that the law of God requires something of man which cannot be performed by man in the power of the law, and that what man, placed under this divine requisition, may perform is not fulfilling of the law in a true sense, then it is to be shown that notwithstanding the object of the divine law is attained in both cases.

By virtue of the law I become conscious that the will of the personal and holy God over me can only arrive at its just accomplishment out of a sanctified will in man. The more definitely, however, law and conscience reveal to me my own unholiness, so much the more decidedly does the law drive me from the requisition of holiness to that revelation of the divine will, by virtue of which God will begin with this, that He sanctifies me. If this desire takes possession of us, then is the purpose of the law attained (2).

In the separate commandments, the requiring God holds up to me that which it is my *duty* to do, and what is *right* before Him, in the manifold relations of the life of man; and the task of my life stands before my soul as energy in every direction in the performance of a dutiful *obedience*. But so long as that which is right before God, and which is my duty, stands before me as debtor as the requisition of God the creditor, and so long as I feel this obedience to be not the fruit of a willing heart, but only perform it at the command of this requisition; so long is my obedience the obedience of a servant, who has reason not to rejoice at his position, but to be ashamed of it. Hence springs up the longing after freedom, not after a freedom from right, duty, and obedience, but after that freedom which, instead of being bound by a law from without, is bound by a law of its own inner essence: so that we, sanctified for communion with God, should have in all the relations of our life that which is right before God as the inclination of our own hearts, our duty as an instinctive impulse of our love, and our obedience as the lordship over those servants of righteousness, in which we have not to strive to pay God our creditor that which we have not of ourselves, but to offer to God the bestower that which He has given to us men. Where this desire is awakened in every relation of my life, there is the design of the law as that of a schoolmaster unto the promises of God accomplished in me. Where this does not occur, there the design of the law remains, not by the fault of the law, but by my own fault, unattained, inasmuch as I obstinately adhere to the law; which, however, was not destined, and therefore also has not the power to renew my heart, and in this renewal to make me capable of a true obedience. For this is the obedience of a heart sanctified to God, and sanctified by God (3).

So long, therefore, as an unsanctified heart stands over against the law, no true fulfilling of the law takes place. For it fails, above all, in obedience to the chief commandment, namely, to love God with the whole heart, and with the whole soul, and with the whole mind. And if I merely recognize the law as the holy, just, and good will of God, without, however, yielding lovingly to this will with all my heart, it comes only to the forsaking of acts for which the heart lusteth, or to the performance of the law with half a heart, but never to a union of the moral personality with the requiring will of God, but to a mere conformity of my action with that which the law prescribes as the form of man's course of action, which corresponds to the commandment (4). This, in contrast to a course of thinking and acting opposed to the law, we may call thinking and acting in accordance with the law; or we may call it, as being practice, and a facility and readiness acquired by practice, legal virtue, but never nor in any wise genuine fulfilment of the law (5). For where the principal commandment remains unfulfilled, there a perfect fulfilment of the law is never reached. But whoever would derive life from the law, must do that which belongs to the law, not this or that commandment out of the law, but the whole law, and that, moreover, in the spirit and in the power of that love, which the law requires indeed, but does not give. He who is not aware, in reference to the law of God, that by his obedience he does not fulfil that law, that man, with all this pretended keeping of the commandments, has not as yet in true obedience executed on himself the sentence of the law (6).

(1) When it is denied that man can *in any way at all* meet the requirements made by God in the law, we may realize to ourselves the instance of that young man to whom Christ quoted the commandments, "Thou shalt not kill, you shalt not commit adultery," and the rest; to which the former replies, "All these things have I kept" (Matt. 19:18–20). As little as the Lord expressed any doubt of the truth of this answer, so little will we also throw doubt upon it. As to the one point, whether he really had loved his neighbor as himself, we will here pass that over. The keeping of the other commandments, however, in the sense of actually refraining from what is forbidden in them, we concede: we can confirm it from our own experience or from our knowledge of others, and may call it a keeping of the law in a certain sense. But in a certain sense only. In the first place for this reason, because the keeping of individual commandments does not involve the conclusion as to the keeping of the whole law. Secondly, because along with the non-commission of the forbidden deed, it is not yet asserted also that we do not allow ourselves to lust against the law. Thirdly, because we must first ask, whether then such keeping of individual commandments flowed from that love to God as the law requires it, or from other motives (*e.g.* Matt. 23:5, πάντα δὲ τὰ ἔργα αὐτῶν ποιοῦσι πρὸς τὸ θεαθῆναι τοῖς ἀνθρώποις). First let this question be answered before we make a panegyrical epitaph out of the whited sepulcher of a pretended fulfilling of the law. If the Apostle Paul, as over against the boasters, designates himself κατὰ δικαιοσύνην ἐν νόμῳ

γενόμενος ἄμεμπτος (Phil. 3:6), this was just as true a plea before a human tribunal, as he knew it to be untrue before the judgment-seat of God. This kind of blamelessness did not prevent him at an earlier period from being a Pharisee and a persecutor of the church of God.

(2) It is radically false to say that the law of the old covenant stopped with the deed, instead of entering upon the intention; that it looked at the work, but not at the heart. Such distorted views could enter the mind of ancient and modern Pharisees only. Whoever wishes to understand the difference between the law and the gospel, let him take into view 1 Pet. 1:15, 16, and 5:2. In ver. 16 the Old Testament commandment is repeated: "Ye shall be holy, for I am holy" (*vid.* Lev. 19:2, 11:44, 20:7, 26). The words of the Old Testament have not indeed the sense, that man ought to be holy because God, by virtue of His nature, is that which is called holy. Luther justly remarks on Ps. 22, that even in reference to God, "a thing is called holy that is separated." But God speaks not as He who was separated from Israel, but as He who had entered into fellowship with Israel, when He says they should be holy because He is holy. He is the God of the covenant which He has made with Israel. Israel has entered into a relation with God, in which they are enabled to take part in that which belongs to God. God is holy as a light in which there is no darkness (1 John 1:5), as an essence distinct from all that is not like to this essence. In a derivative way, that man is holy who separates himself from all that is not conformable to God. In the command, however, "Ye shall be holy," God does not establish this communion of man with God, but under the supposition of this communion He makes the requisition. And such a supposition belonged to Israel also. It rested, however, not upon the law, but upon the covenant of promise. And in the time of the fulfilment, therefore, a beginning is not made with the requisition to be holy, but reference is made to a ἁγιασμὸς Πνεύματος (1 Pet. 1:2), to a reception of man into that communion with God, brought about by the Spirit of God, in which those are regenerate (1:3) according to God's great mercy to whom the requisition is

made, conformably to the Holy One who has called them to be also holy as He is holy. But he who appeals to the law alone may consider whether indeed that which he boasts of in himself as a fulfilling of the law, is really the result and working of that holiness required by God, of that holy keeping of its essence which separates itself from all unholiness. If not, then is all this alleged keeping of the divine commands not a fulfilling of the law. And if man sees this clearly, then can the working of the law on his consciousness only be such, that he turns from the God who demands of him this holiness, to the same God who says, "I am the Lord who sanctifies you" (Lev. 20:8). "Turn you me, and I shall be turned" (Jer. 31:18); "Heal me, O Lord, and I shall be healed" (Jer. 17:14). That is then the prayer which takes the place of the boasting of pretended holiness. And where it does so, there is fulfilled the design of that requisition, "Ye shall be holy."

(3) The commandments contain that which Paul calls πᾶν θέλημα τοῦ Θεοῦ, Col. 4:12 (comp. § 14, at note (3)). They exhibit to us all the relations of man's life, arranged in an order which is grounded not on the will of man, but on the will of God, which, however, attains its realization by the will of man subjecting itself to this ordinance of God. Now the substantial relation in which man finds himself through the law with its commands—namely, that relation of indebted obedience in which man is determined, or ought to consider himself determined, by that which is just before God (δίκαιον ἐνώπιον τοῦ Θεοῦ, Acts 4:19), and which, for this very reason, is a higher obligation binding on him—this substantial relation, presaged by conscience, declared by the law, corresponds to relations which were already laid down at the creation of man, and which were not first realized with the law, and do not cease with the gospel. There exists no stranger mistake than the opinion, that we strike out the idea of divine right and human duty—consequently, that of objectively and subjectively conditioned obedience—from the consciousness of the Christian, by asserting that in principle it is not the righteousness fixed by the law, or the duty prescribed in the

law, that stands before the Christian, and conditions his obedience. On the contrary, hereby is only said, that the Christian in far higher potency knows what is meant by right, duty, and obedience. But the Christian consciousness, in its peculiar principle, is never to be derived from the general human idea of right and duty, as it can be built up out of premises which have no connection with the communion of the spirit with Christ. It is no abstract idea of right and duty, or one to be separated from this relation to Christ, if it is to have any value for Christian ethics. The same holds good of the relation of the Christian to that which he recognizes as divine law. This latter does not exist for him apart from the connection of the law, as well as of the Christian himself, with Christ. What is right before God—what is man's duty—is revealed to the Christian in Christ. This and nothing else is the "dignity" of that conception of duty as recognized by the Christian. But the relation of the Christian to Christ is not exhausted in that idea of requirements which have become objectively present to the Christian in Christ. This is only *one* side of the relation, and indeed not that which *in principle* determines this relation. On the contrary, we must hold fast the fact, that in Christ it is not the law, even were it the so-called most perfect law, which has been given us. If this is and remains an incontrovertible truth, it remains just as necessary to keep steadily in view that the Christian's consciousness of right, duty, and obedience is brought about in the Christian, as to its principle, not in the manner that should lead us to suppose that all was effected in us by a divine law. Only that which is laid down in the law is not abolished, but fulfilled in Christ. How it is so, is hereafter to be shown.

Here I would wish, in anticipation, to bring forward only what follows. Even in the Christian, the objective rule of the divine law is not changed into a mere subjectively-inherent conformity of his nature to the law. The antecedent conversion, by the renewal of his mind, in the Christian is intended to serve just this end, that he should perceive more and more fully the objective will of God, and herein that which is just before God (comp. Rom. 12:2; Eph. 5:17). From the acting of Christ towards men is derived a duty (ὀφείλομεν) of Christians to others (Rom. 15:1–3): the active proof of the love of God in Christ exhibits to us, by way of pattern, a duty which we Christians have on our part also to discharge (1 John 3:16, 4:11). The whole course of Christian conduct, over against the revelation of the will of the grace of God in the gospel, is called obedience (ὑπακούειν τῷ εὐαγγελίῳ, Rom. 10:16, in opposition to 2 Thess. 1:8, 3:14), obedience to the truth (1 Pet. 2:22), obedience to Christ (2 Cor. 10:5). Christians as Christians are called children of obedience (τέκνα ὑπακοῆς, 1 Pet. 1:14); their position as δουλεύειν τῷ Χριστῷ is obedience (Rom. 16:18, 19); and Christians are δοῦλοι ὑπακοῆς εἰς δικαιοσύνην (Rom. 6:16, 17). For even their faith, in its ethical relation to God's will in Christ, is obedience (ὑπακοὴ πίστεως, Rom. 1:5, 16:26); an obedience to the faith (ὑπακούειν τῇ πίστει, Acts 6:7). All this, however, which is expressed in the passages cited, would be understood in the most one-sided way, and just in this way fundamentally misunderstood, if the attempt were made to take, as the exponent of this Christian consciousness and conduct, something which essentially resolved itself into the idea of a divine law (comp. § 13, at note (4)).

If, however, we return from this digression to that which may be viewed as a course of conduct conformable to the commandments, we find this nowhere passing beyond that idea of ἔργα νόμου, to which is unconditionally denied the possibility of justifying man before God (Rom. 3:20; Gal. 2:16). When, therefore, it is elsewhere asserted that the doers of the law are justified before God (Rom. 2:13; Gal. 3:12), these works of the law must be wanting in something which we should have to attribute to them, if they actually were the fulfilling of that which the law requires. This, however, is nothing else than the want of a pure undivided heart—of a personality penetrated with the holiness of God. There the works are dead (ἔργα νεκρά, Heb. 6:1, 9:14); they spring not out of a heart regenerated unto life, but only serve to veil the dead heart. Nay, what is worse, man makes from them a temptation to himself to establish his own righteousness before God (Rom. 10:3), as if the law were given to produce righteousness, instead of the knowledge of sin (Rom. 3:20).

(4) It has been thought necessary to combat the idea, that from the law as such nothing further is derived than a conformity of action with it. This action, it has been alleged, is, in truth, only the result of a frame of mind consonant to the law. An inward harmony with the law must thus precede such action conformable to the law. But here the question at the very first presents itself, What do we understand by law? and, What do we term conformity of disposition? That I do not fulfil the law when I keep and have kept this or that commandment, which enjoins or forbids this or that action, needs no repetition. The law, moreover, is not a collection of commandments to be added up, but the detailed exposition of that many-sided course of action in life which is well-pleasing to God, and which flows from a supreme postulate. The supreme postulate is that of the holy frame of mind, whose character is perfect love of God and of our neighbor. And this postulate is addressed to human hearts that are void of this love, and no iota of the law mentions as presupposed by this postulate, or as a result of the law, our hearts being filled with this love. If I, therefore, do not attribute something to myself which I do not in reality possess, there remains to me, in every single keeping of a commandment, only the consciousness of the want of conformity of my state of mind with that supreme postulate of the law. But if I suppose that I possess that which this supreme postulate of the law requires (the supposition also being conceded as just), then would this inference be surreptitiously drawn, that I imagined I had to thank the demand of the law for this frame of mind. For, as before said, the law demands, but gives not. But if it is supposed that we have a testimony to the conformity of the mind with God's law in expressions of the Apostle Paul—such as those in which he says, "I consent unto the law that it is good," "I delight in the law of God after the inward man" (Rom. 7:16, 22),—this, upon closer examination, proves to be a delusion. I will, first of all,

altogether waive the consideration that in those words the apostle is portraying how he as a Christian, in the light of a true self-knowledge, feels with respect to the law. It might be conceded that at least a recognition of the law as being good, and that a delight therein, might be found in man, as we have to think of him apart from communion with Christ. But is that, then, a conformity of mind, of heart, of the whole undivided man, where an intellectual perception of some one excellence is forced from me, against the grain of my own inclination, where I am compelled to say, "I know indeed that this or that is good, but I will have none of it?" or where at most it is said, "I do it, it is true, because it is commanded, but in reality against my will?" And what, then, does he declare, who confesses he has done this or that for this reason only, because the law required it? Does he not just in this way confess the discordance of his own proper will with that of the Lawgiver? Or does not all the world know that, if this were not the state of the case, the confession would run: I have not done this because I was commanded, but out of my very heart, with deepest love, with freest inclination? "For this reason," says Luther, "there is as much sin as there is unwillingness (*noluntas*), difficulty, repugnance; and then, on the other hand, as much merit as there is will, freedom, cheerfulness."

(5) In the above proposition it is only meant, in the first place, to be maintained that, although the law declares the whole world as fallen under sin (Rom. 3:19), it does not follow from this, that we should have to regard man's relation to the law of God as an unconditional rebellion against that law. We not only concede that individual cases of internal acquiescence and external obedience to the commands of the law are to be admitted, but that also a continued practice (ἄσκησις) is conceivable, in which the individual is capable of conforming his course of conduct to the commands of the law. We grant this, with the exception of the supreme postulates of the law, in which the question turns not upon our actions, but upon the frame of mind which lies at the root of all our actions. If, therefore, from this it certainly follows, that this conformity, as

we have pointed out, is not a fulfilling of the law, it is, however, of importance to distinguish this conduct from that which carries with it the declared form of opposition to the law. For thus only can be explained the possibility of that colossal self-delusion, by which men come to this, that they desire to establish a righteousness of their own, and consider themselves as doers and fulfillers of the divine law. If in due obedience they executed the law on themselves, then would they judge themselves in order that they might not be judged (1 Cor. 11:31, 32). Thus, with the conceit of having fulfilled the law and of the righteousness of the law, there comes upon men the being full (κεκορεσμένον εἶναι, 1 Cor. 4:8), and the thinking themselves rich (1 Cor. 4:8; Rev. 3:17), the very opposite of that which the law is intended to work, namely, poverty of spirit and hunger and thirst after righteousness (Matt. 5:3, 6). For he who places himself exclusively under the law, supposes that he has his righteousness in this, that *he* has fulfilled the requirements of the law, and knows nothing of the reception of a grace which excludes all boasting (1 Cor. 4:7; Rom. 3:27). He knows not the inefficiency of the law which rests on the nature of man (τὸ ἀδύνατον τοῦ νόμου, Rom. 8:3), the fleshly enmity to God which belongs to man, by virtue of which he *cannot* obey the law (Rom. 8:7). For this reason, that supposed ability of fulfilling the law, and everything which, as contrasted with the violation of the law, wishes to be called legal virtue, and as such, wishes to boast of itself, is burdened with such internal falsity, and is condemned by the law of God itself. Not to the law, but to Himself, does Christ point and say, "Without *me* ye can do *nothing*" (John 15:5). And His apostle says, "It is God who worketh in you both to will and to do of His good pleasure" (Phil. 2:13). That, however, is the voice of the promising, not the requiring God.

When, in the above paragraph, we used the word virtue, our intention was not to do so as if this idea had its force only in the sphere of the law. On whatever is called virtue, the Christian's thoughts also are to be steadily fixed (Phil. 4:8). But this word, which in the Greek and Latin tongues in its strict and proper sense proclaims what belongs to manly power, along with the glory that naturally belongs to it, comes to shame by the law of God. In this law we perceive how it stands with man's virtue. If, however, in what follows we do not place in contrast with that virtue which we have designated "legal virtue," a doctrine of gospel virtue, or at all make the idea of virtue the basis of Christian ethics, the reason of this is very simple. For if we take the word in the general sense of an ability to fulfil the end of life, without an understanding of the divinely appointed end of life, and the means ordained by God for the attainment of this ability, no use can be made of the bare word virtue. What is most preposterous, is the giving to this formal idea a signification from premises which belong to the ancient pre-Christian civilized world. Not even from the law of God, to say nothing of such premises, do I know what I have to consider as an ability of attaining the object of life (well-pleasing to God, and actually to be attributed to man). This unfolds itself to the Christian merely from his knowledge of Christ as the τέλος νόμου (Rom. 10:4), and of His powers, gifts, and grace. If a play upon words might be allowed here, I might say, he alone who knows the virtues (1 Pet. 2:9, LXX. for תְּהִלָּה, Isa. 43:21; comp. 2 Pet 1:3), that is to say, the sum of the glorious powers of Him who has called us out of darkness into His marvelous light, understands how rightly to think of human and Christian virtue, and what is to be said touching its object, source, and extent.

(6) In place of all further inquiry, compare Luther, *Sermon on Gal.* iv. 1–8, *on Christmas Day: On the People of the Law and of Grace.* There it is said of one who still walks in the works done under the law, and is its slave: "The law is his tutor and governor, and he walks thereunder as under the hand of a stranger. And it is given to him, in the first place, that he may remain at home and be brought up, that he may refrain from evil works externally from fear of punishment, that he may not become too wild, and risk all he has, that he may not estrange himself entirely from God and His blessedness, as do those who, as a matter of course, abandon themselves to sin. In the

second place, that he may learn to know himself, and may arrive at understanding, may see how unwilling he is to be under the law, and performs no work as a willing child but all like a constrained slave; that thereby he may learn in what he is wanting—namely, in a new, free, willing spirit, which the law and its works are unable to give him; nay, the more he works, the more unwilling and the more averse he becomes to work, from the want of such a spirit. When, therefore, he finds this in himself, he perceives how he merely keeps the law externally by his works, but inwardly in his heart is an enemy to it, and opposed to it with his displeased and unwilling heart. Thus is he certainly without intermission inwardly a sinner against the law, and externally a saint according to the law, *i.e.* a veritable Cain and a great hypocrite; and it becomes plain to him that his works are works of the law, but his heart is a heart of sin. For the heart is opposed to the law in its inclination, and is surely inclined to sin, and the hand alone is bound to the law. Therefore St. Paul has well named such works "works of the law." For the law forces them out, and nothing more falls to it but the works. But the law will have the heart also, and will have its injunctions willingly performed, that we should not alone say works of the law, but also hearts of the law; not alone the hand of the law, but also the will, mind, and all the powers of the law, as is said in Ps. 1. 'Blessed is the man whose delight is in the law of the Lord.' Such a disposition the law indeed requires, but does not give; and as nature cannot bestow this of itself, so the law presses upon them, and condemns them to hell for disobedience to God's commandments. Then, in such a case, there is anguish and a miserable conscience, and yet no help" (this is Cain's race). Then, however, it is said, "But those who are the future Abels, they learn by the law respecting themselves, what unwilling hearts they have for the law, fall from their presumption, let go their hands and feet, and are reduced to nothing in their own eyes by this knowledge. Then comes, however, the gospel; then God gives grace to the humble, who receive His testament and believe. And together with and in their faith they receive the Holy Spirit, who gives them a new heart, which brings with it delight in the law and hatred to sin, and does willingly and cheerfully that which is good. *Then are there no more works of the law, but there is a heart of the law.*"

§ 16. c. Fear

If it stands thus with the nature of the law, and with the obedience which may be conceived to arise out of it, the man who places himself under the law alone must continue in a threefold manner the slave of *fear* (1). He places himself *under* the law, with fear of the law; for he finds in himself nothing of a love to God with all his heart and with all his mind, or of a fear of God in undivided love to Him (2). Further, he does what the law requires either from a dread of its threatenings or from a fear of losing the reward of such doing; and this is the fear of a servile mind (3). And finally, since by the law as such this alone is declared to man, "Cursed is everyone that continues not in all things which are written in the book of the law to do them;" and notwithstanding from the law itself we become conscious that we neither fulfil the whole law, nor do that which we do in obedience to isolated commandments of the law in the spirit required by the law, therefore the man who places himself under the law alone remains a slave to the fear of the threatened judgment of death and the wrath of God, knows that when called to a reckoning he has nothing to say in his defense, and obtains no peace at the thought of God's judgment (4).

And this it is that God purposes in His law, in order that we should seek our rest in that God who is not merely the God of the law (5). Should we desire, however, to find our rest in the law, and in *our* obedience thereto, then this fear comes upon us as a just punishment,—not that fear which is the beginning of wisdom, but that restless fear which is the end of hope and the commencement of despair. This, however, is the fruit of our guilt, that we do not allow ourselves to be guided by the law of

God to Him to whom the law, as our "schoolmaster," is intended to bring us (6).

(1) An observation, professedly derived from history, has been opposed to what may be immediately concluded from the nature of the case; and it has been asserted that to the saints of the old covenant, right and law, instead of being objects of fear, were objects of the most intense joy. But here, as well in general and on the whole as in reference to individual testimonies, it has been overlooked that nothing at all can be said of a position of the Old Testament saint with respect to the law thus in the abstract. The law is to Israel the revelation of *his* God. But God is not *his* God through the law, but by virtue of the promise. The first revelation of God to Israel coincides with the promise, and the fuller revelation of the promise is older than the full manifestation of the law. Then God reveals Himself in actual fulfilment as the Savior of the apparently lost people. Finally, first as Lawgiver in the wilderness. And even this revelation is to the Israelites a manifestation of the glory of *their* God. But in this very consciousness the *Promiser* and the *Lawgiver* coincide; and the praise of this God is not the praise of the law, but the praise of that gracious God rich in promises, who reveals Himself *also* in the law. The justice of this remark is confirmed by means of the very passages cited to prove the contrary, namely Ps. 19:8, 9, 111:3, and 9. For, as everywhere else, those passages also can only be rightly understood in connection with the whole text,—the praise of the law in unison with the hope and the prayer for forgiveness of sin (Ps. 19:13), in unison also with the praise of the certain promised redemption (Ps. 111:9). And so the whole 119th Psalm is on the one hand praise of the law, and on the other prayer and hope that the Lord will make good His promise of help and assistance to those praising Him. This confidence, however, is not the effect of the law. The law, considered by itself, completely excludes a confidence of such a kind. Consequently, because the Old Testament *revelation* has promise *and* law, the result thereof is not fear in our sense, but

a fear which essentially includes in it trust. This is the beautiful acknowledgment of the 115th Psalm: יִרְאֵי יְהֹוָה בִּטְחוּ בַיהֹוָה (Ps. 115:11). It is the fear which is due to the holy majesty of God, without which no humility, no true piety exists; so that those who would wish to know *nothing* of fear have no inkling of genuine piety. Only the sheerest misunderstanding has endeavored to find *this* fear in the well-known passage, 1 John 4:18, where it is said, "Perfect love casts out fear." This, however, is that fear which κόλασιν ἔχει, as it is said even in the same passage. What, therefore, has this fear to do with that reverential fear which is full of confidence? That love which has not φόβον Θεοῦ is from the wicked one; and this is testified by the revelation of the new covenant plainly enough (2 Cor. 7:1, ταύτας οὖν ἔχοντες ἐπαγγελίας καθαρίσωμεν ἑαυτοὺς ... ἐν φόβῳ Θεοῦ; 1 Pet. 1:17, εἰπατέρα ἐπικαλεῖσθε τὸν ἀπροσωπολήπτως κρίνοντα ... ἐν φόβῳ τὸν τῆς παροικίας ὑμῶν χρόνον ἀναστράφητε: comp. Phil. 2:12, 13). Therefore, under all circumstances, fear remains the beginning (*principium*, not *initium*) of *that* wisdom which makes wise unto salvation (Ps. 111:10; Prov. 9:10); while a wisdom which imagines itself relieved from *this* fear is the wisdom of diabolical pride. In the relation, however, which we were obliged to point out as mere legal obedience, and therefore the opposite to the fulfilling of the law, there is naturally no question concerning this kind of fear.

When it is asserted above, that fear necessarily comes upon the man who *places* himself under the law alone, two points are hereby intended to be made prominent. First, namely this, that such an effect is not the *final* end of the law intended by God, in so far as God has appointed the law not for itself alone, but in connection with the promise; while it is the act of man, and not of God, this disregard of the promise, and placing one's self under the law alone. Secondly, it is intended by this statement to be brought into view, that the terrors of the law only come upon those who, in this their perverted position, do not entirely free themselves from the law of God, but still allow themselves to remain under its influence. For it is perfectly just what Luther says, that "men stand to the law in a threefold position. *The first are those who hazard everything, and boldly act in opposition to it in a free course of life; and to these it is just the same as if there were no law.* The second class are those who restrain themselves from this wild life, and live a respectable life, who thus subject themselves outwardly to its discipline, but inwardly are enemies to their taskmaster: all their performance arises out of a fear of death and hell. Consequently, they keep the law outwardly only; nay, the law keeps them outwardly, but inwardly they do not keep it, and are not even kept by it. (The third class are those who keep it both inwardly and outwardly. These are the tables of Moses written within and without by the finger of God itself.)"

(2) The diversity of the position of a Christian man, in respect to standing under the law, is pointed out by the apostle (Rom. 8:15) in the words, οὐ γὰρ ἐλάβετε πνεῦμα δουλείας πάλιν εἰς φόβον. comp. 2 Tim. 1:7, οὐ γὰρ ἔδωκεν ἡμῖν ὁ Θεὸς πνεῦμα δειλίας, ἀλλὰ δυνάμεως καὶ ἀγάπης καὶ σωφρονισμοῦ. What kind of fear this is, and in what it differs from that fear of God which becomes the children of God, all this belongs to those rudiments of Christian knowledge, as they are to be found in the earliest of Luther's sermons. It is the fear of the evil, dismayed conscience which the law alarms, but cannot pacify. It is that terror of God which is to be distinguished from the fear of God. And this terror is just the fruit of a love not directed to God, while the fear of God is the fruit of love to God. Comp. Luther's *Sermon on the Fear of God* (in the year 1515; *Works*, pt. xii. p. 2188): "The terror one has of God is one thing, and the fear of God is another. The latter is the fruit of love, but terror the ground and source of hatred. Man, therefore, should not be in terror of God, but should fear Him, in order that he may not hate Him who ought to be loved. Therefore this fear of God will be better understood as that reverential fear which we have towards those whom we love, honor, esteem, and whom we fear to offend. But this is impossible to one who loves aught else but God; for since he strives after this love, and trusts himself to it, in this way he necessarily falls into terror when such a thing is taken away from him which he loves" (Sermon

of 1516). Servile fear "loves something else than God, and therefore fears God, since it gives God fear without love, and the creature love without fear." Luther therefore remarks on 1 John 4:18: "Some have fear and terror: to those love is wanting. Others have fear without terror: in these is love perfect." On Rom. 8:15, however, he says: "Those who have or know nothing more than the law, these can never possibly attain to this, that they should have a just, heartfelt confidence and comfort in God, although they may do much and exercise themselves with great zeal in the law. For when it flashes before their eyes in its true light, then they see what it requires of them, and how far they still are from fulfilling it, and it reveals to them God's wrath; and thus there is nothing but mere terror, dread, and fleeing from God, under which they must finally perish, if help is not brought them by the gospel. This is what the apostle here calls a slavish spirit, which only terrifies and makes us flee from God."

(3) He who places himself under the law goes to the work as to a drudgery, for the sake of fear and of reward. (Τῷ ἐργαζομένῳ ὁ μισθὸς οὐ λογίζεται κατὰ χάριν, ἀλλὰ κατ' ὀφείλημα, Rom. 4:4; ζυγῷ δουλείας ἐνέχεται, Gal. 5:1.) "We must, however, remark that no one likes to fulfil the law, *except he be free from the law, and no longer under it*. For this reason we must here again mention the discourse of Paul, where he speaks of the being under the law—that we may know who is and who is not under the law. All those, then, who do good works because that is so commanded, out of fear of punishment or the desire of reward, these are under the law— must be pious and do good, yet unwillingly. Therefore is the law their lord and driver, but they are its slaves and prisoners. For were there not the law urging them, and the punishment or the reward, but were every one allowed his own free discretion, that he might do what he wished without the fear of punishment or hope of reward, then would he do what was evil, and leave undone what was good, if beforehand temptation and motive allured him. But now that the law, with its threatening and promise, lies in his way, he refrains from

evil, and does what is good, not from love of the good and hatred of the evil, but from fear of punishment or looking for reward. Therefore they are under the law, and constrained by it like bondmen: these are the saints of Cain's race" (Luther's *Sermon on the People of the Law and the People of Grace*). "The prison is the law in which our conscience is incarcerated, and with aversion we are under it. For no one does freely what is good when bidden by the law, nor leaves the evil undone when the law forbids; but from fear of the penalty one must do it, or he does it for the sake of the reward. This fear or the threatening, and the reward or the hope of it, are the two chains which hold us in bonds under the law" (*ibid.*).

(4) The law of God itself breaks in pieces the chain of self-conceit and self-righteousness, when we would have our "recompense." The law is the handwriting which bears witness against us (Col. 2:14); it works the wrath of God (Rom. 4:15). It pronounces its curse against every man who does not keep the whole law, against all who range themselves under the law and desire to obtain righteousness by their fulfilling of the law. "The law therefore is also a light which shines forth, making visible and manifest, not the grace of God, and not that righteousness by which we may obtain everlasting life and blessedness; but sin, our frailty, death, God's wrath and judgment—*this is the true and proper work of the law, with which it is to rest satisfied, and go no further*" (Luther, *Table Talk*, chap. xii.). "Whatever brings before us sin, or wrath, or death, that exercises and performs the office of the law, *whether it is done in the Old or New Testament*. Law and conviction of sin, or manifestation of wrath, are expressions which mean the same thing, and may be used one for the other. Since, however, there is nothing else but the law to show us whence sin and death come upon us, it is abundantly manifest that the law is *very necessary and useful to us*" (Luther, *Second Disputation against the Antinomians*). Nay, in the highest degree necessary and useful against all self-justification. For our proud heart requires the goad all our life long to alarm it, in order that man may learn to despair of himself. The terror and alarm which arise from the law rests

not on a misunderstanding, but on a right knowledge of the law. "For the law, *when it is rightly understood*, dismays us, and causes despair; when, however, it is not rightly understood, *it makes us hypocrites*" (Luther, *Table Talk*, chap. xii.).

(5) That was already understood by the pious of the Old Testament. In their case, along with the fear of God's righteous judgment, prayer and hope in a gracious and forgiving God were quite common, because they knew the God who had given the law and the promise. And so, on the other hand, even in the times of the fulfilling of the promise in the New Covenant, the law remains in its rights and use, in order that it may alarm us at our state, and drive us to Him who knows how to wound us by His law, to excite pain in us, and through the word of His grace to heal our pain and wounds. "In such a way does the law resemble a driver who drives the hungry to Christ, that He may fill them with His good things. And this, then, is the true office and work of the law, that it should accuse, humble, kill, and plunge us into hell, and take from us everything, that there may be nothing whatever which we might have to comfort us. And finally, this is done by the law for this end, that we may be made by faith righteous and loving, exalted, led to heaven, and may attain everlasting life and blessedness" (Luther, *Exposition of the Epistle to the Galatians*, iii. 23).

(6) If the law works that fear which the Apology in our Confession calls servile fear, because it is "without faith," and on this account works "only wrath and despair," this lies so far in the law, as it does not in itself bestow on us the comfort of faith, nor is it intended to bestow it; but it does not lie in the God of the law, since He at no time placed man under law alone. It is man's own fault, who neither understands nor uses the law rightly. For if he understood the law, or rather the God who has given the law, he would know that the same God who in the law threatens death, does not wish the death of the sinner. If he knows it not, it is not God's fault, but man's, who will place himself under the law, while the dominion of sin is powerless only over him who stands not under the law (ἁμαρτία γὰρ ὑμῶν οὐ κυριεύσει· οὐ γάρ ἐστε ὑπὸ νόμον, ἀλλὰ

ὑπὸ χάριν, Rom. 6:14; comp. Gal. 5:18). For in this, as Luther says in one of the earliest of his sermons, "the law is the best thing, since it points out the evil, and teaches us to recognize our own wretchedness, and thus urges us to seek for the good. For the beginning of our cure is the knowledge of our malady, and the fear of the Lord is the beginning of wisdom; but the law puts us in fear, in order that man may be humbled, while he sees that he does not keep the law, and consequently incurs the judgment of God." He who does not recognize this result of the law as the "best thing," may, however, expose himself to the curse which is attached to a misuse of the law. Nothing is and remains under all circumstances the import of the law but its being the παιδαγωγὸς εἰς Χριστόν (Gal. 3:23, 24), if man has not yet found Christ, or stands in danger lest he should use the freedom in Christ as a cloak for his wickedness. The law for ever remains the goad which impels us to flee away from that law to God in Christ, the Fulfiller of the law, the Mediator of the forgiveness of sins.

SECOND SECTION

THE GOOD TIDINGS OF THE NEW COVENANT

§ 17. *The Existence, the Essence, and the Import of the Gospel*

THE reconciliation of that discord between God and man, of whose existence both our conscience and the law of God convince us, is not nor can be regarded as a fact of the natural human consciousness. For although the yearning for it rests not only on the subjective feeling of man's want and misery, but also on the objective position of all preparatory revelation, yet the consciousness of its accomplishment does not run parallel with the traces of this yearning in history (1). And least of all can man conceive the idea of bringing about this reconciliation out of himself without obliterating the truth of what is attested by conscience and the law (2). For since the law bears witness that the discord in its ultimate ground is conditioned by that wrath of God which rests on the unholy man, so a certainty that this wrath is turned aside can never possibly let itself be conceived as a fact proceeding from man. Therefore, as the gospel bears witness to itself as to our knowledge and consciousness, as the revelation of a mystery hitherto hidden from the world, and as something only promulgated in the fulness of time, and hereby excludes the idea that our consciousness of this reconciliation, like conscience, is something innate in the human spirit, so also it repudiates all human agency and authorship in such redemption, since it derives that which neither conscience nor the law of God can bestow exclusively from an *act* of God in Christ (3). And the verification, that this act proceeds from the same God who in conscience and law sits in judgment upon us, as it has been given historically in the historical connection of the gospel with all the preparatory revelations that God has made to us of Himself from the beginning of days, so does it lie for our moral consciousness just in this, that the deliverance from God's wrath which has been accomplished in Christ is declared and offered to us in a way which, far from destroying the testimony of the law and conscience, only confirms it (4). This confirmation may be traced in this, that the word which proclaims to us, for Christ's sake alone, the forgiveness of sins, is presented to us as the security for whose sake alone also we are to consider ourselves as freed from the wrath of God. For although herewith the will of God in Christ towards us does not attain its accomplishment without a moral procedure on our part towards this word, yet does the same word testify to us that God bestows upon us that grace *in the way of promise* (not on account of this our moral procedure, but for the sake of Christ alone), by virtue of which we are delivered from the divine wrath (5). For His own sake, God in Christ rescues the world from the divine wrath. And to the universality of the judicial word of God in the law corresponds the universality of the grace-offering word, not only in its being designed to be preached to all the world, but in its subject-matter, as having respect to the grace of God in Christ, available for the whole world (6). The realization, however, of this gracious will in the midst of a world still exposed to the wrath of God, corresponds to the universal relations of that self-consciousness and world-consciousness, (ordained for us as creatures,) in this respect also, that it is announced and offered to us in the form of a kingdom, and of a fellow-participation in a kingdom, which here below is destined, as a kingdom of grace, to be an all-dominating and pervading power of human society, until in its future perfection as a kingdom of glory, in the full purity and glorification of the whole man, both body and soul, and of the whole world, as well of heaven as of earth, it manifests itself as the perfected will of God towards His creatures, and the perfect contrast to this present world placed under the curse of sin and the ban of transitoriness (7).

What influence on the moral consciousness of men God intended to produce by means of this gospel, and how this is specifically distinguished from that working of the law, which on the one side lies in the divine purpose of the law itself, and on the other is the fault of man, by his placing himself purely under the law, and seeking his justification in a fulfilling of the law,—all this is first to be investigated before the question is answered, how man comes, and when he has come, to receive in his inner man the gospel as the principle of a new moral life, and to carry this principle in him.

(1) There exists a common saying, according to which the yearning of man after deliverance bears already in itself the guarantee of its accomplishment. But in as far as this yearning is only a creature excitement on man's part, it is a proof of the need, not the promise of a possession. The history of the heathen world bears testimony to this. Where this yearning, however, is supported by a conviction of its accomplishment, there it rests on promises of God. This is proved by the history of Israel (comp. § 16 at note (1), and Jer. 17:13, 50:7; Ps. 130:8). But where the question is about the entire fulness of the deliverance, there the words of the old covenant point beyond themselves to a new covenant (Jer. 31:31 ff.; Heb. 8:8 ff.).

(2) The sum of all the yearning excited in us by conscience and the law is comprised in the knowledge that no man can effect his own redemption. To the question, Τίς ἄρα δύναται σωθῆναι, the answer of Christ holds good universally and unconditionally: Παρὰ ἀνθρώποις τοῦτο ἀδύνατόν ἐστιν, παρὰ δὲ Θεῷ πάντα δυνατά, Matt. 19:25, 26.

(3) As to how the possibility of man's being saved lay with God, all preparatory revelation was intended to excite man to ask. The full revelation and disclosure, however, is expressly testified to be the announcement of a mystery hitherto hidden and withheld from the world (Rom. 16:25; Eph. 1:9; Col. 1:26; 1 Cor. 2:7–10). To give the explanation of this economy of God in the history of salvation, is the sphere of dogmatics. In this place, our business with it is merely to press this as an ethical determination of the Christian consciousness, that it has the root of saving knowledge only in that which before the advent

of Christ was hidden from all the world, and which is given and revealed in Him alone, and indeed as the last, conclusive, and ever-enduring revelation, after which no further, least of all a different, revelation of salvation is to be looked for (Heb. 1:1, 2). Ἰδοὺ νῦν καιρὸς εὐπροσδεκτὸς, ἰδοὺ νῦν ἡμέρα σωτηρίας, 2 Cor. 6:2. Now holds good, πεπλήρωται ὁ καιρός, Mark 1:15. Now is πλήρωμα τοῦ χρόνου, Gal. 4:4; πλήρωμα τῶν καιρῶν, Eph. 1:10 (comp. Tit. 1:3, 1 Pet. 1:20, Χριστὸς φανερωθεὶς ἐπ' ἐσχάτου τῶν χρόνων).

But the testimony to this divine deliverance of man's race from the wrath of God has this for its characteristic sign, that it declares to us an act of God in Christ as that in which once for all this deliverance is concluded. Τὰ δὲ πάντα ἐκ τοῦ Θεοῦ τοῦ καταλλάξαντος ἡμᾶς ἑαυτῷ διὰ Ἰησοῦ Χριστοῦ· ὡς ὅτι Θεὸς ἦν ἐν Χριστῷ κόσμον καταλλάσσων ἑαυτῷ, 2 Cor. 5:18, 19. The facts of the death and resurrection of Christ were those by whose testimony (comp. Acts 1:22, 2:24, 32, 3:15, etc.) the apostles conquered the world. The fact of the death of Christ is that which is named as the consummation of the reconciliation, *"when we were still enemies"* (Rom. 5:10). No reconciliation and redemption of the world accomplished by Christ could at all be spoken of, if it were not effected by an act of Christ, and by that alone. By virtue of this is Christ (ὁ δοὺς ἑαυτὸν ἀντίλυτρον ὑπὲρ πάντων, 1 Tim. 2:6; Εἷς ὑπὲρ πάντων ἀπέθανεν, 2 Cor. 5:14) truly the Redeemer of the world (ἀληθῶς ὁ σωτὴρ τοῦ κοσμοῦ, John 4:42), the propitiation for the whole world (ἱλασμὸς περὶ ὅλου τοῦ κόσμου, 1 John 2:2), the deliverer from the wrath of God (ὁ ῥυόμενος ἀπὸ τῆς ὀργῆς τῆς ἐρχομένης, 1 Thess. 1:10; comp. with Rom. 5:9). And that which is offered to us by God as our justification, is nothing else but justification in the blood of Christ (Rom. 5:9), and absolutely identical with forgiveness of sins: 2 Cor. 5:19, Θεὸς ἦν ἐν Χριστῷ κόσμον καταλλάσσων ἑαυτῷ, μὴ λογιζόμενος αὐτοῖς τὰ παραπτώματα; Eph. 1:7; Col. 1:14, τὴν ἀπολύτρωσιν, τὴν ἄφεσιν τῶν ἁμαρτιῶν. As also Christ says of Himself, τὸ αἷμά μου τὸ περὶ πολλῶν ἐκχυνόμενον εἰς ἄφεσιν ἁμαρτιῶν. Matt. 26:28. Therefore ἄφεσις ἁμαρτιῶν is the comprehensive expression for the salvation which has been offered and is still being offered to us (Luke 24:47; Acts 2:38, 5:31, 10:43, 13:38, 26:18). For the imputed righteousness consists only in the non-imputation of sin (ᾧ Θεὸς οὐ μὴ λογίσηται ἁμαρτίαν, Rom. 4:7, 8). As being freely justified (δικαιούμενος δωρεάν, Rom. 3:24), the Christian is to feel and know himself. Such is he, and remains such only if God for Christ's sake alone declares the sinner righteous. "Since we all, as being born in sin and enemies to God, have deserved nothing less than eternal wrath and damnation, so that *all that we are and can do* is condemned, and no help or counsel can be found for our state—for sin is too grievous for any creature to abolish, and the wrath so great that no one could still or appease it;—therefore must another man step into our place, namely Jesus Christ, God and man, and by His suffering and death must do enough to expiate and atone for sin. That is the cost laid out for that end and expended upon us, through which sin and God's wrath are extinguished and taken away, the Father reconciled and made our friend" (Luther).

(4) That Christ, with that which He is and brings, did not come to destroy the law, He himself says (Matt. 5:17). And the apostle shows more in detail how he, by his preaching of righteousness in Christ, casts no dishonor upon the law, but in truth only establishes it (Rom. 3:31). How this is done, can scarcely be more tersely expressed than in the words of Luther: "The gospel is a narrative of God's glory and honor, in order that God alone may be praised. Such preaching, however, of the honor of God brings along with it the preaching of our shame; for God's honor and our honor cannot lie together in the same bed." Precisely in the specific difference of the gospel from the law lies the essential confirmation of the law and of the judgment of condemnation against us which is to be derived from it. This confirmation disappears only in the same measure in which the specific difference is obliterated, weakened, or destroyed. For in this case, contrive it as we may, our justification before God comes to depend upon a relation which takes up the ground of a requisition fulfilled by us. We

may qualify this act of *our* fulfilment as we will, by representing it as an internal operation of grace, that is to say, the grace of God in us: the fact, however, remains always the same, that we wish to let pass, as adequate to the holy will of God respecting His creatures, a something of our own, and belonging to us, of which we do not certainly wish to affirm that it is achieved entirely without our co-operation. Or if we call it inadequate, and consequently not truly a fulfilment of the divine will, but something which God of His grace allows to hold good as adequate, then in this manner we come not only to a perfect elimination of the requisition made to us in the law, and of the divine sentence of condemnation to be derived from it, but we hereby destroy all moral truth of our own self-knowledge. Both are only preserved by this means, that we hold fast as the ground of our righteousness before God, not a work to be carried out by God through our own instrumentality, much less one to be attributed to ourselves, but a work accomplished by Christ the God-man. That is the revelation of grace, by virtue of which man depends for his justification and righteousness before God in no conceivable manner of any kind on his own work and doing, but absolutely on the work and doing of Christ. While in this way everything which is termed law and man's fulfilling of the law is excluded from justification and our consciousness of it, it is just hereby that what the law truly is in itself, and in respect to us, is alone properly confirmed. That which, in reference to the revelation of God to men made in the word, specifically belongs to Moses, viz. the law, the same is unconditionally excluded from that which specifically belongs to Christ, viz. grace and the truth which makes free; just in order that what saves us from wrath should be grace, and grace alone, and all salvation should come to us by virtue of promise only, and not by virtue of law: comp. John 1:17, ὁ νόμος διὰ Μωϋσέως ἐδόθη· ἡ χάρις καὶ ἡ ἀλήθεια διὰ Ἰησοῦ Χριστοῦ ἐγένετο; Gal. 3:18, εἰ γὰρ ἐκ νόμου ἡ κληρονομία, οὐκέτι ἐξ ἐπαγγελίας. "The law is that which lays down what man is to do; the gospel reveals whence man is to obtain it. For it is quite a different thing to know what we ought to possess, and to know whence we may procure it. As if, when I place myself in the hands of the physicians, there is one branch of the art to say where the disease lies, and another to say what course we are to take to get quit of it. So is it here also. The law discovers our disease, and the gospel supplies the remedy" (Luther).

As the idea of that righteousness which is imputed to us for Christ's sake essentially confirms the judgment of the law of God against us, so does it also form the most important ethical element for the consciousness of man when delivered from the wrath of God by means of the gospel. It is purely absurd to reproach this idea with its being "externally juristic." Possibly we may represent the work of Christ, for the sake of which God reckons the sinner righteous, in so one-sided a way as to make this reproach applicable. Possibly also we may, with the doctrine of imputed righteousness, omit and tacitly pass over what belongs to the complete picture of the operations of God in Christ which act upon us. Nothing, however, of all this need take place, and everything be said which belongs to the perfect conception of that restored communion of God with men, and of men with God, which is effected through Christ, not only in Christ, but in man; and yet the idea of imputed, that is to say, of righteousness referred by God to men freely and purely of grace, remains inviolable. It is the palladium of true self-knowledge, of the right understanding of the law, of true self-judgment and self-condemnation. Under shelter thereof alone, everything that God works at the same time within us, pours out upon us and brings into being as a new life, remains preserved pure and unpolluted from the poison of self-admiration, self-exaltation, self-justification. It remains true in all ways, and for the whole of this earthly life, not only for its beginning, but also up to the end, that Christ came to call not the righteous, but sinners to repentance, and to save such (Matt. 9:13; 1 Tim. 1:15). And he who does not understand the contradiction of sinful saints and sanctified sinners—whose solution lies alone in the idea of imputed righteousness—is as yet ignorant of the whole gospel in general.

(5) Hitherto, in the first place, the question was of the *act* of God in Christ, in which the reconciliation, redemption, and deliverance of the world from the divine wrath was accomplished. Now there comes also under our consideration the *word* in which this act is offered to us for our acceptance. And the more a mode of view which is alien to the gospel placed this act in the background, or set it aside, in order to give a value to the word only as doctrine,—that is to say, not as an announcement of the facts of redemption, but as a setting forth of new propositions (laws, maxims, rules of life, and the like),—so much the more must we guard against the other extreme, by which we are wont to undervalue the import of the circumstance, that the redemptive act of God in Christ is offered to us in the word for our acceptance. Rather is the question just as much concerning the knowledge, what import for the ethical consciousness of the Christian the offer of the redemption in the word may have both in general and in special connection with the justification of the sinner.

In the first place, then, and in general, the objectivity of that vital power which determines the Christian, nowhere presents itself to us more plainly than in the fact that the Christian finds himself pointed away from his own thoughts to thoughts of God, which are comprised in words which claim for themselves eternal duration and force, and whose abiding appropriation and keeping is made the condition of an abiding communion with Christ. He who speaks this word, and at the same time asserts such things of this His own word, is Christ Himself. By His words He removes what He is, wills, and does, even before the last is accomplished, from the interpretation of human thoughts. And to regard the words of the Son of man as the outpouring of human thoughts, is what He Himself forbids, since He denies that He says what He does say of Himself (John 14:10, τὰ ῥήματα, ἃ ἐγὼ ὑμῖν λαλῶ, ἀπ' ἐμαυτοῦ οὐ λαλῶ; comp. 12:49), but characterizes His word as the word of His heavenly Father (John 14:24, 17:6, 14:17). The declarations of God to Israel of old through human organs, in many parts and divers manners, reached their climax in the speaking of God to us by

His Son (Heb. 1:1). As the final historical revelation of God taking place in time, in comparison with which no other has any value, even though an angel should come from heaven to preach another gospel (Gal. 1:7, 8), this word is exempted from that passing away which is the lot both of heaven and earth, and never passes away (Matt. 24:35: Mark 13:31; Luke 21:23; 1 Pet. 1:23, 25, τὸ δὲ ῥῆμα Κυρίου μένει εἰς τὸν αἰῶνα· τοῦτο δέ ἐστιν τὸ ῥῆμα τὸ εὐαγγελισθὲν εἰς ὑμᾶς). In this word of the good tidings (ὁ λόγος τοῦ εὐαγγελίου, Acts 15:7), as we have before said, is the mystery of salvation, which was hidden from former generations (Rom. 16:25; Eph. 3:5, 9; Col. 1:26), made known not as something absolutely new, but just as the word of the "new covenant," which is founded on the blood of Christ (Matt. 26:28, and the parallel texts), and which is the fulfilling of the promises made in the Old Testament (Jer. 31:31; comp. on the idea, as appearing in the history of salvation, conveyed by the word ברית, διαθήκη, Delitzsch on Heb. 7:22, pp. 302, 303), and the disclosure of that which is hidden in the revelation of the Old Testament (comp. with 2 Cor. 3:15, 16, passages such as Luke 24:27, etc.). It is that word (λόγος) which comprises the eternal thoughts of God, and their development and accomplishment in the history of salvation; that declaration of God (ῥῆμα τοῦ Θεοῦ) which, spoken to the world, brings near and is the medium of our salvation,—without the hearing, understanding, reception, and keeping of which there is salvation indeed present for us in Christ, but it is not truly our own portion, one of which we are self-conscious, freed and purified from selfish lusts as well as from our own thoughts. And this word is offered to us not merely in order that we may by it rightly understand the work and history of Christ, which in themselves might be misunderstood or misinterpreted, but in order that with the first disciples of Christ we might hold it fast, that we might be *pure for the word's sake* which Christ has spoken to us (John 15:3). Hence the expressions, holding fast to Christ, holding fast to the word which has been spoken to us, resting ourselves upon nothing but the word for whose sake we are pure, and with the blessed confession that Christ is the Son of the living God (Matt. 16:16, 17) associating unmixed and inseparate that other, that He, Christ, has the words of eternal life (John 6:68, 69). As the incarnate Word is the salvation of the whole human race, He will be so to the individual only in His word, which He brings and offers for our acceptance. Without His word, Christ is not our salvation: He is so only in, with, and through His word.

For, as the condition of true discipleship, Christ names the abiding in His word (ἐὰν ὑμεῖς μείνητε ἐν τῷ λόγῳ τῷ ἐμῷ, John 8:31); as conversely we abide in Him, if His words abide in us (ἐὰν μείνητε ἐν ἐμοὶ καὶ τὰ ῥήματά μου ἐν ὑμῖν μείνῃ, John 15:7). He who does not receive the words which have proceeded from Christ, has already his judge in the word of the Father, which Christ proclaims; and this word will also judge him at the last day (John 12:48). Where this word takes no hold (χωρεῖ, John 8:37) in the inner man, there abides open or hidden enmity to Christ; and conversely, the communion of life with Christ abides only there where His word is kept (τηρεῖ), as Christ keeps the word of His Father (comp. John 8:51, 55). For not without reason are both things—the word of the historical testimonies to Christ (οἱ λόγοι), and Christ Himself—placed in juxtaposition, where it is said that Christ hereafter will be ashamed of him who here below is ashamed of Christ and of His words (Mark 8:38; Luke 9:26). That Christ whom we, as it were, portray to ourselves according to our own ideas, we might perhaps be loth to feel ashamed of, as being the work of our own imagination. But what is implied is the not being ashamed of that Christ as He represents Himself to us in His own words: it is the finding spirit and life in the words which have been declared to us by Christ, and which in this their historical form are spirit and life (John 6:61). Therefore, just as certainly as Christ has brought salvation to us, not by a certain doctrine, but in His person and His work of redemption, so certain is it that both are not only for us a riddle without a key, and a closed book with seals that cannot be broken, but they are also for us not present and not effective for our salvation, and are to be in no wise and by no means appropriated by us, except by that which Christ Himself calls His doctrine (διδαχή), which, as He says, is not His,—that is, as a man, in which light they looked upon Him,—but His heavenly Father's, who sent Him, the Only-begotten (John 7:16, 17). Nay, the ethical position which we have to take in regard to Christ, depends most essentially on the offer of salvation *through the word*, and has its decisive test in that which is called the doctrine, or the word of God and of Christ, and in the way in which we act toward the doctrine of this word. For he who abides in the doctrine (ὁ μένων ἐν τῇ διδαχῇ, 2 John 9), says John, hath the Son and the Father: he who will know whether he hath the Son and the Father, let him make the attempt by the historically promulgated and given word, whether he can, without corrupting and dealing deceitfully (καπηλεύειν, δολοῦν, 2 Cor. 2:17, 4:2) with that word, confirm his possession by it. As the certain knowledge of the will of that God who makes demands in His law is given to us by the embodiment of this will in human language, even so by the same embodiment in word we have certain knowledge with respect to the salvation-bringing, divine will in Christ.

Where, however, we are to find this word, on this point Christ Himself refers us to appointed bearers and messengers of His word. We have not merely that command to the apostles who were chosen by Him personally, which makes the teaching of that which the Lord has confided to themselves a duty (Matt. 28:20), but we have also the prayer of Christ, in which, at His departure, He prays for those who, through the word of His chosen messengers (διὰ τοῦ λόγου αὐτῶν), should believe on Him (John 17:20). So completely by Christ's prayer and command are the word of Christ and that of His disciples combined together in one, that a distinction is impossible; and thus surely also the word of the disciple has always for its basis and presupposition the word of Christ Himself. True, indeed, the word, the doctrine which the word hands down, and the instruction which bases itself upon this doctrine, branch out from each other (λόγος, διδαχή, διδασκαλία, comp. Tit. 1:9 with Rom. 6:17: so, side by side with the λόγοι τοῦ Κυρίου ἡμῶν Ἰησ.

Χρ., the κατ' εὐσέβειαν διδασκαλία, 1 Tim. 6:1; or with λόγος, the διδασκαλία 1 Tim. 5:17; the καλὴ διδασκαλία with λόγοι τῆς πίστεως, 1 Tim. 4:6; the ὑγιαινούσῃ διδασκαλία with the εὐαγγέλιον τῆς δόξης τοῦ μακαρίου Θεοῦ, 1 Tim. 1:10, 11: comp. διδασκαλία by itself, 2 Tim. 4:3, Tit. 1:9, 2:7, 10). But all this is organically interwoven; and as we, by Christ's will, are to have and obtain His word in the word of His disciples, so do the messengers of Christ receive it without any error with thanks to God, when one receives *their* word as God's word (παραλαβόντες λόγον ἀκοῆς παρ' ἡμῶν τοῦ Θεοῦ, ἐδέξασθε οὐ λόγον ἀνθρώπων, ἀλλὰ (καθώς ἐστιν ἀληθῶς) λόγον Θεοῦ, 1 Thess. 2:13), and know that not human wisdom, but the Spirit of God, has taught them to speak what they speak (1 Cor. 2:13). He, therefore, who will take his stand on Christ's will, must take his stand without distinction on the word of Christ and the doctrine of His messengers: he alone stands under the curse who seeks any other gospel (Gal. 1:8, 9). But for the ethical determination of our own conduct one mode of judging alone is of value, in order to ascertain whether this gospel be really God's word. This mode of judging is traced out for us in the word of Christ: "If any one will *do* the will of Him that sent me, the same shall know whether my doctrine is of God, or whether I speak of myself" (John 7:17). That will of God of which Christ speaks, is just that which was preached by Christ Himself, and delivered to His apostles, to be afterwards preached by them. Wherein the doing of this will consists, is hereafter to be described. Enough that we are pointed by Christ to the way of experience and the test of experience; as the earthly physician can return no answer to the sick man to the critical question, whether the physic will help him, but that he should take the medicine. This holds good beyond all comparison of the final revelation of God, the revelation of the grace of God in Christ, which bears no proportion to any other which we may call a revelation of God, as it is the highest and all-overtopping summit, and in reference to its working is intended to bestow upon man a something, a life of which, independent of the working of grace in the word, he has no inkling, and which, before it was revealed and inwardly experienced by men by means of revelation, had never entered into the heart of man (comp. 1 Cor. 2:9). For the divine power of a word of such position and influence there exists no proof but that of experience, when we subject ourselves and our thinking to the word, and permit that word to have its effect upon us.

But just exactly in this circumstance, that the grace of God in Christ offers itself to man in the word, in that mixed spiritual and corporeal form of divine thinking and willing, whose contact with the spirit of man cannot possibly be conceived without a process of our own thinking and willing, consenting or not consenting thereto, do we find the proof that this salvation is not presented to man as a power not to be grasped and not to be comprehended, unconsciously transforming us, and entirely removed from man's own conduct; but as a good whose influence cannot possibly be imagined without a corresponding ethical position and activity, affecting the knowing and willing of the whole man, and following up the end of life held out to us by God in Christ. Since the Spirit of God presents Himself to me in the word, just in this circumstance I become at the same time aware that no forcible seizure is intended against which I could not defend myself, but an offer which, from the nature of its instrumental means, can only be designed for freest, conscious, spiritually accomplished acceptance. Thus Christ Himself testifies. He attributes to His word no power without adoption by the understanding (ἀκούειν καὶ συνιέναι, Matt. 13:19, 23), without voluntary acting out (ἀκούειν καὶ ποιεῖν, Luke 8:21; comp. Matt. 12:50, Mark 3:35), and without constant keeping and holding fast in an honest and good heart (comp. Luke 11:28 with 8:15).

The form, however, which is specifically peculiar to the word of the gospel, whether we here think of the preparatory or the final revelation of the God of grace, also determines essentially the manner of the working on man which proceeds from this word, as well as the nature of that conduct on the part of man which corresponds to this working. And the specific form of the whole gospel is *promise*—promise which God for His own sake, determined by Himself, and dependent on nothing but the will of His grace, gives in the word, and causes to be preached. The last period of the world is the *reign of grace* (ἡ χάρις βασιλεύει, Rom. 5:21). And where grace reigns in the word, there also can it only reign in the word of promise. For as certainly as grace has nothing to do with law and requisitions of law, so certainly can the word of that grace which thus gives be no other word than a word of promise. And indeed of that promise which is peculiar to grace in this respect, that it also grounds the *fulfilment* of the promise entirely on God's grace. "For," as Luther says, "the promises of the law are those which, if I may so say, let themselves down to our works; the promises of grace, however, stand not upon such works, but absolutely on God's goodness and grace that He wills thus to do." Hence in Scripture χάρις and ἐπαγγελία form an indissoluble unity (Rom. 4:16). For to this end is Christ the Mediator of the New Covenant, that we may receive the *promise* of the eternal inheritance (Heb. 9:15). The *promise* of life which is in Christ Jesus is the word of the New Covenant (2 Tim. 1:1; comp. 1 John 2:25), as also the difference between the gospel of the Old Covenant (the διαθῆκαι τῆς ἐπαγγελίας, Eph. 2:12; comp. Rom. 9:4) and that of the New Covenant rests alone on the transcendently greater glory of its promise (ἡ διαθήκη ἐπὶ κρείττοσιν ἐπαγγελίαις νενομοθέτηται, Heb. 8:6; comp. the entire eleventh chapter of this epistle). That these very great and precious promises are given to us (τὰ μέγιστα καὶ τίμια ἡμῖν ἐπαγγέλματα δεδώρηται, 2 Pet. 1:4; ταύτας ἔχοντες τὰς ἐπαγγελίας, 2 Cor. 7:1)—this fact establishes the position of a Christian man; and if he calls himself a son and heir, he is to know no other title for this except that of the promise alone, purely of grace (ἐπαγγελίας τέκνα, Gal. 4:28; κατ᾽ ἐπαγγελίαν κληρονόμοι, Gal. 3:29; τὰ τέκνα τῆς ἐπαγγελίας λογίζεται εἰς σπέρμα, Rom. 4:16). That, and how God *for His own sake* blots out our transgressions, and remembers our sins no more (Isa. 43:25)—this is the substance of the word of promise given in the New Testament, which fulfils the promise given in the Old.

But not only does this characterize the word of the gospel, that it is promise, but that it has the promise of possessing through itself—that is to say, through Christ, whose word it is—the power of working salvation. In this sense the ῥήματα of Christ are πνεῦμα and ζωή (John 6:63); and the word of promise of the New Covenant stands opposed as καινότης πνεύματος to the παλαιότης γράμματος, *i.e.* of the law (Rom. 7:6). For this reason—that is to say, by virtue of the connection of this word with the effectual working of the Lord who is that Word—it is called a λόγος ζῶν and ἐνεργής (Heb. 4:12). It is compared to the rain which falls upon the earth (Heb. 6:7), and has the promise that it shall not "return void" (Isa. 55:12). Nay, more still: it is the imperishable seed of which we Christians are born (comp. 1 Pet. 1:23 with Jas. 1:18). For the gospel, the word of the cross of Christ, is in itself a power (δύναμις) unto salvation (Rom. 1:16; 1 Cor. 1:18; Jas. 1:18).

(6) That is the word which is appointed to go out into all the world, and to be preached to all nations (Matt. 28:19; Mark 13:10; Luke 24:47). But this just by virtue of the universal gracious will of God in Christ towards all flesh. For grace is ἡ χάρις τοῦ Θεοῦ σωτήριος πᾶσιν ἀνθρώποις. 2:11; and our God is ὁ σωτὴρ ἡμῶν Θεός (comp. σωτὴρ πάντων ἀνθρώπων, 1 Tim. 4:10) ὃς πάντας ἀνθρώπους θέλει σωθῆναι καὶ εἰς ἐπίγνωσιν ἀληθείας ἐλθεῖν, 1 Tim. 2:3, 4. Therefore is φιλανθρωπία attributed to God (Phil. 3:4); on which Luther remarks: "God loves not the person, but the nature; and is not called gracious to the person, but to the race, in order that His honor may remain entire, and that no one may boast of his worthiness, that no one may be terrified at his unworthiness, but that one as well as another may comfort himself with the undeserved grace, which He in so friendly a way and so universally offers and bestows."

(7) In accordance with this, its world-embracing relation, the gospel of the grace of God in Christ is also called the gospel of the kingdom (εὐαγγέλιον τῆς βασιλείας, Matt. 4:23, 9:35, 24:14; Mark 1:14, etc.). But in reference to the existence of this kingdom, distinctions are, at the same time, to be steadily kept

in view. For the kingdom is one thing, as it already is present and existing in and with Christ, by virtue of the sovereignty hidden in Him. In this relation it not only will be, but is already. In Him to whom all power is given in heaven and in earth, both heaven and earth are already comprised in one (Matt. 28:18; Eph. 1:10; Col. 1:20). And in this relation Luther says very justly: "The kingdom of God is not preparing, but is prepared; but the children of the kingdom are being prepared, and do not prepare the kingdom." Just as much, on the other hand, however, this kingdom already existing in Christ is one which is growing upon earth from beginnings like a grain of mustard seed, and spreading itself (Matt. 13:31, and parallel passages). In this sense the kingdom, which is already come, is the subject of the prayer that it may come (Matt. 6:10). And this coming kingdom has again a double relation, according as it is to be regarded in its present form upon earth, or in the state of its future perfection (βασιλεία τῆς χάριτος, and βασιλεία τῆς δόξης, βασιλεία καὶ δόξα 1 Thess. 2:12; ἡ βασιλεία ἡ ἐπουράνιος, 2 Tim. 4:18). In all these relations it is the subject of the evangelical preaching.

This element of the gospel comes here so far under our consideration, as it has the power of itself of working determinately on the Christian moral consciousness. Here there is, first of all, the knowledge that the power which has and will have dominion in this kingdom upon earth, is just no other, and is meant to be no other, than the grace of God in Christ. "The gospel or kingdom of God is such a state or government in which there is simply forgiveness of sins. Forgiveness of sins are not more than two words, wherein the whole kingdom of Christ consists" (Luther: comp. the passage, Rom. 5:21, ἵνα ἡ χάρις βασιλεύσῃ, quoted towards the end of note (5)). In this sense Christ will have His kingdom and the righteousness which belongs to it sought (Matt. 6:33), for it is the kingdom of the Lord who remits debts (Matt. 18:23, 32)—the kingdom where not compensatory righteousness, but free goodness and grace prevail (Matt. 20:1–16). The righteous, who have their portion in it, are for this very reason those who, in the name of Jesus Christ, and in the communion of the Spirit of God, are justified (1 Cor. 6:11). And from the same ground that which (inside this kingdom) comes within the circle of its subjects to spiritual dominion, is called righteousness, and peace, and joy in the Holy Ghost (Rom. 14:17).

The universal relation of that reign of grace which prevails in the kingdom of Christ has its outward expression also in this, that this kingdom, by the will of Christ, is one embracing all nations. As in this fact, that this kingdom is taken from Israel (Matt. 21:43), there is at the same time accomplished a judgment, so its transfer to all nations (comp. with Matt. 21 the passages Matt. 8:11, Luke 13:29) is equally a fulfilment of the promises which were given to Israel (Ps. 72:11, 86:9; Isa. 55:5; Jer. 4:2; Hag. 2:8, etc.). That Christ will fulfil the purpose of grace to Israel, as well as to the nations of the heathen world, He declares in the prophecy of *one* Shepherd and *one* flock (John 10:16); and His apostle sees already the dawning of its fulfilment (Eph. 2:19; Rom. 10:18), and hopes for its still more glorious fulfilment (Rom. 11:11, 25 ff., 32). That gracious will of God, which from the beginning of days held good for the whole race of man, and which was deposited with Israel by way of promise only as in a place of security, comes in the message of the kingdom to its manifestation and realization. The miracle of tongues on the first Whitsuntide is the salvation-proclaiming symbol of the final fulfilment of God's great purpose of a kingdom. And the fellowship of this kingdom is in itself one independent of all national limitation.

Thus, consequently, the domain on which the kingdom of grace here below reaches, and is to reach its manifestation and realization, is the world, that is to say, the entire human race dwelling upon this earth. But the instruments of its dominion are not worldly. The kingdom is not of this world, that is to say, not founded on earthly power and might (John 18:36); but the means of dominion is the scattering of the word of the Lord (Matt. 13:37 ff.), and those who receive this word are members of the kingdom. To this kingdom belong the simplicity and the humility of a child (Matt. 18:3); and no one attains to it unless through a new birth from God (John 3:3, 5, 6). In so far, this kingdom, and he who belongs thereto, are indeed in the world, but separate from the world, and yet not less for the world and for the service of this world. For it is the kingdom of ministering love, which has in the ministry of the love of Christ its source and its standard (Matt. 20:25-28),—the kingdom in which, from Christ's sin-forgiving compassion, sin-forgiving love is to be learnt (Matt. 18:23 ff.),—a kingdom whose members, for this very reason, must not quit the world, nor pray to God that He should take them out of the world (John 17:15), but rather that God should make them fit for that end for which they are appointed, namely, to be the light and the salt of the world (Matt. 5:14-16; Phil. 2:15). Therefore, so certainly as the godless and unrighteous have no abiding portion in this kingdom (1 Cor. 6:9 ff.; Gal. 5:19 ff.), so certain is it, that, according to the nature of this kingdom, the boundaries thereof are not so firmly closed, that in its domain wicked men also (πονηροί, Matt. 22:10; ζιζάνια, Matt. 13:38; σαπρά, Matt. 13:48) should not be found, to whom, without anticipating the judgment of the final separation (Matt. 13:29), just as much as to the frail and weak, and to those in need of many kinds, internal and external, suffering under much affliction, conflict, and struggle (Matt. 10:34-36; Acts 14:22), the instructing, helping and supporting, reproving and correcting love of Christ, which also alleviates want and misery, is to be shown (νουθετεῖτε τοὺς ἀτάκτους, παραμυθεῖσθε τοὺς ὀλιγοψύχους, ἀντέχεσθε τῶν ἀσθενῶν, μακροθυμεῖτε πρὸς πάντας, 1 Thess. 5:14; comp. Matt. 25:31-46, etc.). For in this kingdom it concerns us that the gifts we receive from grace should gain interest (Luke 19:11 ff.); and that we should serve, not rule, in the same same way that Christ came not to be ministered unto, but to minister (Matt. 20:25-28). With these relations of the kingdom the Christian forsakes all selfish enjoyment of his justification before God, and of his peace with Him, in order to show in all the relations of life, of which he considers none in themselves to be unclean (οὐδὲν κοινὸν δι' αὑτοῦ, Rom. 14:14), his mastery in Christ (πάντα μοι ἔξεστιν, ἀλλ' οὐκ ἐγὼ ἐξουσιασθήσομαι ὑπό τινος, 1 Cor. 6:12) in right use (οἱ χρώμενοι τὸν κόσμον ὡς μὴ καταχρώμενοι, 1 Cor. 7:31); and in their sanctification through God's word and prayer (1 Tim. 4:5), to make them serviceable for the purposes of the kingdom of Christ.

But this kingdom is perfected only with the second coming of the Lord (Matt. 25; 2 Thess. 1:7 ff., etc.). Then only is all sorrow with the dominion of death destroyed (1 Cor. 13:13; Rev. 21:4); and those who have been raised from the dead for perfect blessedness, will have as their abode a new heaven and a new earth, wherein dwelleth righteousness (2 Pet. 3:13; Rev. 21:1). This time of universal restoration (Acts 3:21) is the goal of all promise, and the conclusion of that kingdom of grace which prepares for this end. And with this promise which marks the end, whose riches can only here be hinted at (comp. § 20), the Christian becomes conscious of this, that his calling in this world, and for this world, is nothing but a preparatory step; and that if in this world alone we had hope in Christ, we should be of all men the most miserable (1 Cor. 15:19). On the contrary, this also belongs to the triumph of the cross of Christ, which reigns in the kingdom of grace, that through the same the world is crucified to me, and I to the world (Gal. 6:14); and all thought and endeavor are comprised in the word, "We have here no continuing city, but we seek one to come" (Heb. 13:14; comp. Rom. 8:18–23).

§ 18. *The Working of the Gospel on the Human Consciousness*

a. Evangelical Faith

Since in the gospel, on account of that fulfilling of the law which was accomplished in Christ, grace and forgiveness of sins are held out to us in the word in the way of promise, an ethical procedure is hereby called forth on man's part (that is to say, one which has its root in his will), in which he takes his stand for his justification before God entirely and alone on this grace, which has been given him by God in Christ, and made over to him in the word of promise (1). This procedure of his is, however, conformably to its origin, justly appreciated in a moral point of view, and kept pure, only in the same proportion as man recognizes and holds firmly to its possibility and reality as an effect proceeding from the word of God's grace, and which makes him free for such self-action, and seeks the appropriation of the grace offered to him in the word of promise in no act which is prejudicial to or altogether sets aside the gift of grace proceeding from God, as a gift freely offered to us, and that purely for Christ's sake (2). This renunciation on our part of everything in us which might be conceived as a ground of God's grace, is the ethical continued characteristic of that appropriation of the word of promise which is called by Scripture justifying faith (3). Since man perceives from the working of conscience and the law, that he has nothing in himself which could justify him before God, he is enabled by the working of the gospel-word to grasp in faith that gracious relation of God in Christ, which his eye cannot see, and which far transcends his inner knowledge and experience, but which is guaranteed to him in the word of promise, and to receive it in confident assurance of the all-powerful efficacy of God in Christ as also availing for him (4). And here presents itself a change of the whole relation in which man would have to stand, if law only prevailed, since by means of the gospel he is not only to learn, but also to be rendered capable of appropriating to himself, the justification and forgiveness of sins, the whole communion of peace with God (which he in vain struggles for as the end and effect of *his* fulfilment of the law), as the beginning and permanent foundation of a new life in God, by virtue of the grace made over to him for Christ's sake in the way of promise, in a faith which he himself recognizes not as the result of his own work and deserving, but as the gift and bestowal of God (5).

(1) We have already, at an earlier stage in our investigations of the workings of the law (§ 15, note (3)), alluded in anticipation to the fact that the gospel also, when it exercises its influence and attains its purpose, cannot be conceived

without there being on the part of man an obedience (ὑπακοή, not merely ἀκοή) corresponding to its specific nature. This obedience, as regards its nature generally, has this in common with every relation of moral government, that it is a subjection of our own *will* to a higher one. Indeed, every ethical determination involves the will, and every submission to ethical guidance is rooted in the will of man (comp. § 5, p. 17). If we had so to think of the effect proceeding from the gospel as that it did not solicit the co-operation of the will of man, or if that which the gospel bestows did not, under all circumstances, presuppose for its reception an inclination rooted in the will of man in favor of its acceptance, we should not have to deal with this relation in an ethical treatise at all. But now, as often happens with respect to Scripture truths, men have allowed themselves to be enticed from the apparent formal opposition of the one side of the truth to the other, to throw the one overboard, in order to hold fast by the other. Giving the name of an *act* to our reception of the gospel has been avoided, because on the other side it is called a gift—as if a gift in its actual existence could take effect otherwise than in the form of an energy excited in the will. Thus, also, the reception corresponding to His word of salvation is undoubtedly required by Christ as an act well pleasing to God. To the question of the Jews, Τί ποιῶμεν, ἵνα ἐργαζώμεθα τὰ ἔργα τοῦ Θεοῦ; He answers, Τοῦτό ἐστιν τὸ ἔργον τοῦ Θεοῦ, ἵνα πιστεύσητε εἰς ὃν ἀπέστειλεν ἐκεῖνος (John 6:28, 29). And how this is to be understood, Luther has not hesitated to point out in the sharpest and most pregnant manner: "Here God will so have it, that this shall be called His work and true service—that you shouldst believe on Christ. He speaks consequently of *the work that we are to perform,*—namely, to believe. For that is to be the right *conduct, work, life,* and *merit* wherewith God will be honored and be served. Without faith God accepts of nothing as a service done to Him." And then, for the first time, he goes on and says with a reference to vers. 44 and 65: "Whence, however, faith comes (for no one has faith of himself), that does Christ afterwards teach. For faith is a divine work which God requires of us, but which He Himself also must bestow on us; for of ourselves we cannot believe." Now the tenor of this discourse of Christ is also that of our investigation. The import, however, of that knowledge placed at the commencement, that the gospel requires a voluntary operation of our own as the form of its reception, depends upon this, that where this reception does *not* take place, even when the gospel is heard, listened to, and understood, the deficiency lies in our *not having so willed*. This it is with which Christ upbraids Jerusalem in that οὐκ ἠθελήσατε (Matt. 23:37). In the same sense He makes the citizens of the city in the parable say, Οὐ θέλομεν τοῦτον βασιλεῦσαι ἐφ' ἡμᾶς, Luke 19:14, comp. 27. (See also John 5:40, οὐ θέλετε ἐλθεῖν πρός μέ; and comp. Stephen with that accusation of his, ὑμεῖς ἀεὶ τῷ πνεύματι τῷ ἁγίῳ ἀντιπίπτετε, Acts 7:51; οὐ πάντες ὑπήκουσαν τῷ εὐαγγελίῳ, Rom. 10:16; Israel a λαὸς ἀπειθῶν καὶ ἀντιλέγων, Rom. 10:21.) And the reason why our selfish will must be broken, when we come, and have come, to a reception of the gospel, lies just in this, that we must take the "shame" to ourselves, when God in His gospel gives the "honor" to Himself alone; that we prefer having honor amongst men than with God (John 5:44, 12:43); that it is repugnant to us to judge ourselves, that we may not be judged (1 Cor. 11:31); that it grieves us to have nothing hut what we have received (1 Cor. 4:7); and that with the reception of the gospel all self-glorification is at an end (Rom. 3:27).

(2) He who receives the grace of God in Christ, has only then truly received it, when he at the same time holds fast the fact that he has to thank this grace alone that he has received it. It stands but ill with the πεπιστευκὼς εἰς τὴν χάριν, if he does not at the same time esteem himself as a πεπιστευκὼς διὰ τῆς χάριτος (Acts 18:27). If we are saved by grace through faith, yet is all this God's gift (Eph. 2:8). It is God who assigns the measure of faith (Rom. 12:3); or what sense otherwise would there be in the cry of supplication, "Lord, I believe; help you mine unbelief?" (Mark 9:24.) In the same discourse in which Christ requires faith as our "work," He says: "No one can come

to me, unless the Father, who hath sent me, draw him. No one can come to me, unless it be given to him of the Father" (John 6:44, 65); or, as He elsewhere says (John 15:5): "Without me, or apart from me, ye can do nothing." When it is said that faith comes by preaching, and preaching by God's word (Rom. 10:17), it is not meant as if by the preaching of the word we had only the outward occasion which led to that acceptance by man which is there named faith. On the contrary, the preaching of the divine word is the divine means by which faith comes as a divine operation. For faith is numbered among the gifts of the Spirit of God (1 Cor. 12:9). Nay, nothing is more strongly incumbent on us than to distinguish the human faith, or human opinion that we have faith, from that faith which is divine, and which is worked in us by God. "They think nothing else," says Luther, "than that faith is a thing which rests in their own power, to have or not to have, as any other natural work. Therefore, when a thought springs up in their heart which speaks on this wise, "Verily the doctrine is true, and I believe that it is so,' they imagine immediately that they possess faith. And when they see and feel in themselves that no change has taken place, and they remain as before in their old ways, then it occurs to them that faith is not enough: there must be something more, and something greater. Lo! then they fall, therefore, and exclaim and say, 'Ah! faith does not do alone.' These are they whom Jude in his epistle, ver. 8, calls dreamers, who deceive themselves with their own dream. For what else is such a thought of theirs, to which they give the name of faith, than a mere dream and a semblance of faith, which they of their own power, without the grace of God, have produced in their hearts? They become thereafter more wicked than they were before. But the true faith, of which we speak, cannot be built up out of our own thoughts; but it is purely God's work in us, without any co-operation of ours. Therefore, is it also a powerful, active, restless, busy thing, which immediately renews the man, makes him a new creature, and leads him into an entirely new mode of conduct and behaviour." All this, however, just because it is *God*, and not man, of whom it is said: τῇ πίστει καθαρίσας τὰς καρδίας αὐτῶν (Acts 15:9).

This reception of the gospel, then, which is brought about by God, may be called by any name we please; but *one* thing must always remain essential to it—that it never claims, in contradiction to that which it has to receive as grace, the wish to pass current as something which *deserves* grace for its own sake. Certainly, Christ denies this very claim with respect to the perfect fulfilling of the law, in the case that such should be thought possible. One has only done what he was bound to do, and remains an unprofitable servant (δοῦλος ἀχρεῖος), even when he has performed all he has been commanded (Luke 17:10). How much more does this apply to the offer of grace! Its reception really takes place, and what we receive remains uninjured, only in the same degree as it is received as a χαρισθέν, *i.e.* as a freely bestowed reward, which is not a reward in the sense of a recompense due to us, and which we have a right to, but is reckoned rather of grace, and not of obligation or of debt (οὐ κατ' ὀφείλημα λογίζεται, Rom. 4:4, 5). No matter that this reception, as an actual subjective laying hold of, in distinction from the antecedent being laid hold of, which precedes and conditions our laying hold (Phil. 3:12), bears the form of an act or a work: this act or this work does not, however, come into the reckoning; and in this sense also the words in Rom. 11:6 apply: εἰ δὲ χάριτι, οὐκέτι ἐξ ἔργων, ἐπεὶ ἡ χάρις οὐκέτι γίνεται χάρις. Here it rather comes to the oft-repeated simile of the beggar, to whom the gift of grace is not a merited reward, because he reaches out his hand to receive the same.

(3) While the objective ground of our justification before God is grace, and nothing but grace, which is offered to us in the word in the way of promise, there also is named, as the subjective ground or the subjective means of our justification, faith (that is to say, the true and real faith, not the self-imagined and false), and nothing but faith, for which the promise of the righteousness which avails before God exists, and by which that promise is laid hold of. That it is so, and

cannot be otherwise, is grounded just on this, that the gospel is the promise of a gift of grace, in words of God which pronounce an acquittal; and not the requisition of a duty to be performed, in words of God which are commands. Just as it is inconceivable to imagine that he has received the law who "believes" that God gives him this or that command, equally inconceivable is it also to think that he has received the gospel who "does" that which it is declared in the gospel that God alone does, and gives the power and the will to do. Law stands in no connection with faith (ὁ νόμος οὐκ ἔστιν ἐκ πίστεως, *non nexa est e fide*, Gal. 3:12), and the gospel in just as little with doing (τῷ δὲ μὴ ἐργαζομένῳ, πιστεύοντι δὲ ἐπὶ τὸν δικαιοῦντα τὸν ἀσεβῆ, λογίζεται ἡ πίστις αὐτοῦ εἰς δικαιοσύνην, Rom. 4:5). But if we wish to speak of a course of action corresponding to the gospel, *i.e.* to the word of promise, which offers the grace which freely justifies, nothing else could be mentioned than the ἔργον τῆς πίστεως above described,—the act of faith in which man renounces all claim to self-righteousness, and in faith permits the righteousness which avails before God to be bestowed upon him by God. But all other work which is not faith would remain excluded, as the ideas νόμος τῶν ἔργων and νόμος πίστεως mutually exclude each other (Rom. 3:27). It is a perfectly inseparable connection, an absolutely necessary mutual relation, which binds together πίστις, χάρις, and ἐπαγγελία. Διὰ τοῦτο ἐκ πίστεως, ἵνα κατὰ χάριν, εἰς τὸ εἶναι βεβαίαν τὴν ἐπαγγελίαν, (Rom. 4:16). When, in any one point of this triad, anything is put out of place, the whole falls to the ground. To be found in Christ, means not to have a self-righteousness springing out of the law, but that which comes from faith in Christ, the righteousness which comes from God on the ground of faith (Phil, 3:9). The rock on which Israel split, and on which all pseudo-Christianity also splits, is the establishing a righteousness of their own, derived from the law, in opposition to the knowledge: τέλος γὰρ νόμου Χριστὸς εἰς δικαιοσύνην παντὶ τῷ πιστεύοντι (Rom. 10:3, 4). If a man will have righteousness, οὐκ ἐκ πίστεως, ἀλλ᾽ ὡς ἐξ ἔργων, then will he be dashed in pieces on the stone of stumbling, which is meant to be for us a rock of salvation (Rom. 9:32, 33). For this reason the whole conception of that revelation, to which the revelation of the law stood in the relation of a preparatory education, is comprised in the revelation of faith (εἰς τὴν μέλλουσαν πίστιν ἀποκαλυφθῆναι) Gal. 3:23); as in the same sense Paul testified to the Jews in Antioch: ἀπὸ πάντων ὧν οὐκ ἠδυνήθητε ἐν νόμῳ Μωϊσέως δικαιωθῆναι, ἐν τούτῳ πᾶς ὁ πιστεύων δικαιοῦται, (Acts 13:39). Therefore the *design* of faith in Jesus is to be justified by means of this faith in Jesus, and not by works of the law (εἰς Χριστὸν Ἰησοῦν ἐπιστεύσαμεν, ἵνα δικαιωθῶμεν ἐκ πίστεως Ἰησοῦ καὶ μὴ ἐξ ἔργων νόμου. Gal. 2:16). This is that righteousness of faith (δικαιοσύνη πίστεως, κ.τ.λ., Rom. 4:11, 13, 9:30, 10:6; Phil. 3:9; Heb. 11:7), in which faith, which in itself is not righteousness, is counted for righteousness (λογίζεται εἰς δικαιοσύνην, Rom. 4:5), in order that man should be justified by grace alone (δικαιωθεὶς τῇ χάριτι, *sc.* τοῦ Χριστοῦ, Tit. 3:7), and all that is called work of the law should remain excluded from justification (Rom. 3:28, λογιζόμεθα γὰρ δικαιοῦσθαι πίστει ἄνθρωπον χωρὶς ἔργων νόμου). The last passage, it is well known, is the one in which Luther interpolated in his translation the word "alone." It is more than a prejudice when the ancient opposers of the apostle's doctrine of salvation, even to this day, are not weary of complaining of this addition as an intentional falsification. Intentional it certainly was, but in a just appreciation of the sense. Luther has himself repeatedly explained this. It will suffice to quote the one passage in the famous letter to Wenceslaus Link, of the date 1530: "True it is, these four letters '*sola*' are not to be found in the text. But do you not see, that notwithstanding it contains the meaning of the text? and if we wish to express this sense clearly and forcibly in German, the word assuredly belongs to it. For I intended to speak German, not Latin or Greek; for I had undertaken to speak German in my interpretation. But this is the nature of our German tongue, that if we are speaking of two things, of which *the one is admitted* and *the other denied*, we use the word '*solum*' (*allein*) next to the word *not* (*nicht*) or *no* (*kein*)." Enough; thus much is clear as sunshine, that if I propose the alternative, whether we are justified on the ground of works or of faith, and strike out works, nothing remains but faith alone. And since the apostle often enough in his epistles speaks of the same subject always in the same sense, we need only to compare the other passages, in order to be convinced that Luther has quite rightly interpreted the sense of Rom. 3:28.

The real ground of offence, also, does not at all lie in the word "only," but in this, that it is not understood what it is that the Apostle Paul calls faith. As soon as I substitute for this faith a false and unapostolic idea, justification by faith becomes a perversion. Nay, I must, in the face of this self-devised, perverted, and falsified faith, alter my whole manner of speaking, if I wish to bring him who so deceives himself to a perception of that in which he errs. The proof for this is supplied by the Epistle of James. When some theologians, because *they* had to differ from Paul and James, supposed that James differs from Paul touching justification by faith, this was a strange transference of their own intention to James. The writer of this epistle had to do with people, no matter whether apostates from Christianity or still far from it, whose pretended faith was not far removed from the faith of devils, who believe and tremble (Jas. 2:19). Only their faith was worse in this respect, that in place of trembling, they prided themselves on the fact that they believed "*in the one God*"—a faith which, indeed, in itself has nothing to do with justifying faith. Such people as these Paul had nowhere to deal with in his epistles; and therefore never had he the same occasion to speak to his readers in the same terms as James had to his. He says, indeed, apparently the very contrary of that which Paul says, namely, Ὁρᾶτε, ὅτι ἐξ ἔργων δικαιοῦται ἄνθρωπος, καὶ οὐκ ἐκ πίστεως μόνον (Jas. 2:24). And in addition to this, with an appeal to the same example of Abraham to which Paul appeals (Rom. 4; Gal. 3:6, 8), with the limitation, however, that Paul does not mention *the act of believing obedience* in the offering of Isaac, because *it was not at all necessary for his object*. Now, let any one imagine that it was related in Scripture that the faith of

Abraham was reckoned to him for righteousness, although he refused to offer up Isaac for a sacrifice. We immediately feel that this is perfectly inconceivable; for by his refusal of faith's obedience, or in refusing this act of faith, the fact would have been immediately revealed that Abraham had no faith. What further follows from this? That a difference exists between works and works, but that faith never exists without some *specific* ἔργον πίστεως (comp. 1 Thess. 1:3, τὸ ἔργον τῆς πιστέως, along with ὁ κόπος τῆς ἀγάπης). This may be very different, according as the faith of the believer is put to the test. But when it comes to "Show me your faith" (δεῖξόν μοι τὴν πίστιν σου, Jas. 2:18), then can I only show it by this or that act which happens to be the specific manifestation of faith corresponding to the given circumstances. Rahab might have offered up I know not how many sons, and Abraham have received spies after spies— that would have been neither for the one nor the other that act of faith by which God had put them to the test. Still less does the specific act of faith require to be any particular external work. Faith has every day works to do by which it inwardly overcomes unbelief, weakness of faith, lusting after self-justification, or attacks of despair; and where such specific operations of faith do not exist, there, in short, a justifying faith is not present. When, therefore, any one comes to me and says much about his faith, and yet I see nothing of that which either under all circumstances, or in the given and special circumstances, ought to be looked for, not as this or that self-pleasing work of fulfilling the law, but the one thing *which is the entirely special and immediate operation of the energy of faith*, then I say to him: By a faith which wishes to be a mere faith, without that activity of faith which is inherent in true faith, you art not justified. As, for example, if thou, like the devils, believest in God and tremblest, instead of letting your Lord Jesus become master over such trembling. Such are the works which James means; and both of the instances cited by him out of the Scriptures of the Old Testament show this in the clearest manner. It is precisely the same which Paul preaches, for he knows of no πίστις without ὑπακοὴ πίστεως. We require not, however, in any way to explain James by Paul, but only to understand James from himself, and from the opposition which he alone, but Paul nowhere, has to contend against, to get at his manner of speaking; and thus we shall soon give over harassing ourselves with a supposed contradiction between Paul and James without any necessity. The whole perversity consists in this, that we conceive that faith which Paul requires, to be the same as that dead faith which James contends against, or also *vice versa*, and that we do not consider the distinction which exists between the idea conveyed by ἔργα in James and by ἔργα in Paul. For that which Paul understands by ἔργα is either the works of the fulfilling *of the law* attempted without justifying faith, or, on the other hand, those works which flow out of a justifying faith—works of *love* towards God and our neighbor—operations of faith in a wider and derived manner, but not the operation of faith or the act of faith—the work of faith in the narrowest and most specific sense of the terms.

(4) In order rightly to understand the nature of justifying faith, we must consider that the frame of mind in which faith comes to the man who has attained a perfect consciousness of himself has not the gospel alone for its factor. This fact the church has well brought forward in its Confession, when it names the preaching of faith a preaching for the "*alarmed conscience.*" Hence the inseparable connection between repentance and faith, turning from and turning to, conversion of heart *from* sin and *to* holiness (μετανοήσατε καὶ ἐπιστρέψατε εἰς τὸ ἐξαλειφθῆναι ὑμῶν τὰς ἁμαρτίας, Acts 3:19; μετανοεῖν καὶ ἐπιστρέφειν ἐπὶ τὸν Θεόν, *ibid.* 26:20; μετανοεῖτε καὶ πιστεύετε ἐν τῷ εὐαγγελίῳ, Mark 1:15; ἡ εἰς Θεὸν μετάνοια καὶ πίστις ἡ εἰς τὸν Κύριον ἡμῶν Ἰησοῦν Acts 20:21; ἡ κατὰ Θεὸν λύπη μετάνοιαν εἰς σωτηρίαν ἀμεταμέλητον ἐργάζεται, 2 Cor. 7:10). It is the drawing of the Father, who strikes in the conscience and by the law, in order to prepare the soul for faith in the Son. Thus true faith is not arrived at without the most definite moral self-knowledge (ἐπίγνωσις ἁμαρτίας, Rom. 3:20). And for this reason "Christ and His work appertain only to those who are in

a state of alarm; the law, the threatenings, terrors, and so forth, only to those who fancy themselves secure" (Luther).

As now, on this side, faith is the fruit of a very clear and definite knowledge, so does it, on the other side, include in itself a knowledge not less definite. There is nothing more perverse than in the usual manner of speech to speak so of faith, as if that faith which Scripture preaches stood opposed to knowledge and perception, and excluded both. On the contrary, this faith is perfectly inconceivable without knowing and perceiving. Οἶδα γὰρ ᾧ πεπίστευκα, 2 Tim. 1:12; πεπιστεύκαμεν καὶ ἐγνώκαμεν, ὅτι σὺ εἶ ὁ ἅγιος τοῦ Θεοῦ, John 6:69; πιστεύετε, ἵνα γνῶτε καὶ γινώσκητε, ὅτι ἐν ἐμοὶ ὁ πατήρ, John 10:38 (comp. 1 John 4:16, 1 Tim. 4:3, etc.). Wherefore Luther does not scruple to compare faith to the dialectic art, and says, "It is nothing else than wisdom and prudence; it dictates, distinguishes, teaches, and is science and knowledge." For it bears in itself the γνῶσις Ἰησοῦ Χριστοῦ (Phil. 3:8, comp. 2 Pet. 3:18), in whom are hid all the treasures of wisdom and knowledge (Col. 2:3); and the end of all growth of believers is unity of the faith *and* the knowledge of the Son of God (Eph. 4:13; comp. πληροφορία τῆς συνέσεως, εἰς ἐπίγνωσιν τοῦ μυστηρίου τοῦ Θεοῦ, Χριστοῦ, Col. 2:2; comp. 1 Cor. 1:5, ἐπλουτίσθητε ... ἐν πάσῃ γνώσει). Nay, so inseparable are faith and knowledge, that where the position of the Christian is the theme, and where we might expect the mention of faith, the same is designated by a *knowledge* of grace and truth (ἠκούσατε καὶ ἐπέγνωτε τὴν χάριν τοῦ Θεοῦ ἐν ἀληθείᾳ, Col. 1:6; Θεὸς, ὃς πάντας ἀνθρώπους θέλει σωθῆναι καὶ εἰς ἐπίγνωσιν ἀληθείας ἐλθεῖν, 1 Tim. 2:4; μετάνοια εἰς ἐπίγνωσιν ἀληθείας, 2 Tim. 2:25). The divine power has bestowed on us all that pertains to life and godliness: διὰ τῆς ἐπιγνώσεως τοῦ καλέσαντος ἡμᾶς, 2 Pet. 1:3, comp. 8, 2:20. Only the knowledge of this truth bears the same character which the truth itself has. It is the truth which serves unto godliness (ἡ ἀλήθεια ἡ κατ' εὐσέβειαν, Tit. 1:1), the truth which announces the great mystery of godliness (1 Tim. 3:16), given for life and for godliness (2 Pet. 1:3), destined for a knowledge whose object is moral deliverance through the truth (γνώσεσθε τὴν ἀλήθειαν καὶ ἡ ἀλήθεια ἐλευθερώσει ὑμᾶς, John 6:32),—truth for the sanctification of our souls (τάς ψυχὰς ἡγνικότες ἐν τῇ ὑπακοῇ τῆς ἀληθείας, 1 Pet. 1:22); in a word, a truth which is intended to make wise unto salvation (σοφίσαι εἰς σωτηρίαν, 2 Tim. 3:15) in that Christ, who has been made of God unto us wisdom, and righteousness, and sanctification, and redemption (1 Cor. 1:30). Thus this knowledge, which is of faith, has nothing in common with that gnosis which is puffed up and puffeth up, which knoweth nothing as it ought to know, because it allows itself to think that it has known (1 Cor. 8:1, 2). It has nothing in common with those learned discourses of human wisdom (1 Cor. 2:13), with that earthly, sensual, devilish wisdom (Jas. 3:15), which cometh not from above, is full of bitter envy and strife, destitute of all meekness of wisdom (πραΰτης σοφίας), full of false boasting, and of lying against the truth,—a wisdom of this world, because it is a wisdom far from the mind of Christ (νοῦς Χριστοῦ, 1 Cor. 2:16),—a wisdom not born of the Spirit of God, but of the spirit of this world, which shuns nothing more than the words of the apostle: "If any man among you seems to himself to be wise in this world, let him become a fool, that he may be wise: for the wisdom of this world is foolishness with God" (1 Cor. 3:18, 19). To all this, the knowledge which cometh by faith is the very opposite. This is knowledge which makes us to be filled with the fruit of righteousness which comes through Jesus Christ (Phil. 1:9-11), not knowledge for the sake of knowledge.

It is also a knowledge not fully adequate, but *belonging to the economy of salvation,*—a knowledge which does not lead us beyond the limits of faith to sight, but to a confirmation of faith without sight,—a knowledge that lies far more in a *distinctive* perception of the opposition between good and bad, falsehood and truth (δοκιμάζειν τὰ διαφέροντα, Phil. 1:10), than in exhausting, because never indeed to be exhausted (γνῶναι τὴν ὑπερβάλλουσαν τῆς γνώσεως ἀγάπην τοῦ Χριστοῦ, Eph. 3:10), knowledge of its divine subject-matter itself. The completely certain and sufficient knowledge (which needs nothing supplementary) of the nothingness of all other pretended ways of salvation, is the ground from which faith comes to knowledge: "Neither is there salvation in any other; for there is none other name given among men by which we are to be saved, than the name of Jesus Christ" (Acts 4:12). But before the depth of the riches of the wisdom and knowledge of God, this very knowledge of faith stands still, as before an un searchable fulness. And the modesty, truth, and purity of faith rest exactly in the consciousness of, and in the keeping within the limits of, its knowledge. The consciousness of the state of salvation and grace in this world *must* consist in this, in walking not by sight, but by faith (2 Cor. 5:7). "Now we see (in the word) through a glass, darkly; but then face to face: now I know in part; but then shall I know even as also I am known" (1 Cor. 13:12). "Now it doth not yet appear what we shall be; but when it shall appear, then shall we see God as He is" (1 John 3:2). Now all knowledge is concentrated in that which God in Christ is *for us*.

But this knowledge I have in the word, and from the word. And the transcendent ethical power of faith consists in this, that I pass out of myself, and beyond myself, and, contrary to all feeling and experience of life, hold fast to what is declared and promised to me in the word. There is much unnecessary talk carried on about feelings of faith and experiences of faith. But whatever may be true therein, still that faith would be utterly unsound which should have no other guarantee of its certainty than the feelings and experiences of man, instead of that word which cannot deceive. "Feeling is against faith; faith against feeling" (Luther). "Faith is *not* experience, although we often also experience that which we believe; but yet faith must always be put *before* experience" (*id.*). "Faith looks (merely) to the word or to the promise, *i.e.* to the truth" (*id.*). Nay, so much does faith renounce everything that is of man, that no true believer wishes to be justified *for the sake of* his faith, but exclusively for the sake of the grace of God in Christ which is promised in the word. "Faith, if it is genuine, is of this sort, that it does not rely upon itself, upon its faith, but holds itself to Christ, and betakes itself to His righteousness, lets the same be its guard and protection, just as the chicken trusts not to its own life and running, but shelters itself under the body and wings of the hen" (Luther).

Thus, under all circumstances, it remains correct that faith is a confidence in that which one hopes for, and an evidence of things not seen (Heb. 11:1). And much more than to understand what ὑπόστασις and ἔλεγχος mean in this passage, is it incumbent on us that we should hold fast the ἐλπιζομένων and the οὐ βλεπομένων, in order that our faith may never lean upon what is present and visible, but may ground itself on the comfortable promise alone, which lifts us above the present and makes us confident of the future. But this is the nature of this justifying faith: Εἰ ἐχθροὶ ὄντες κατηλλάγημεν τῷ Θεῷ διὰ τοῦ θανάτου τοῦ υἱοῦ αὐτοῦ, πολλῷ μᾶλλον καταλλαγέντες σωθησόμεθα ἐν τῇ ζωῇ αὐτοῦ. Οὐ μόνον δὲ, ἀλλὰ καὶ καυχώμενοι ἐν τῷ Θεῷ διὰ τοῦ Κυρίου ἡμῶν Ἰησοῦ Χριστοῦ, δι' οὗ τὴν καταλλαγὴν ἐλάβομεν (Rom. 5:10, 11). These are the great acts of salvation of God in Christ, *in their value for us*. Not belief of the facts merely is a justifying faith, but to believe that not for the sake of my faith, but for the sake of these acts, God in Christ is gracious to me, and forgives my sins. That Christ is what He declares Himself to be, the Son of God, the Sent of the Father, who is one with the Father, and so forth,—all this belongs also to faith, and is, equally with His death and resurrection, defined in Scripture as the object of faith. But to believe, or to hold as true, that all this is and took place as it is detailed, *i.e.* the so-called historical faith, is not justifying faith. The latter rather looks to that which God, in the person of Jesus, has wished to be to me and to do for me, what He is for me and what He has done for me, and promises to me as the effect of all these acts in the word of promise. And thus Christ comes to us this very day in His word, and asks, Πιστεύετε, ὅτι δύναμαι τοῦτο ποιῆσαι; And faith answers Yes to this question, and commits itself with all the powers of the soul to the gracious promise of the Lord: κατὰ τὴν πίστιν ὑμῶν γενηθήτω ὑμῖν, ἀφέωνταί σου αἱ ἁμαρτίαι. For thus says Luther, with reference to John 3:16: "Faith is, and means, not a mere abstract idea of God, that He was born of the Virgin, suffered, was crucified, rose again, ascended into heaven, but such a heart as comprehends in itself and embraces the Son of God, according to the tenor of these words, and holds for a certainty that God has given up His only-begotten Son *for us*, and has so loved us that we, for His sake, shall not be lost, but have everlasting life." Or, as he says in another place: "Believing in Christ is not believing that Christ is a person who is God and man—*for that would help no one in any way*; but that this very person is Christ—that is, that He *for our sakes* has come forth from God," etc.

But when the Christian in faith ventures to call Christ *his* Lord, *his* Savior and Redeemer, and to comfort himself with that grace and forgiveness which the same Lord promises by the gospel to the believer; then, on the other hand, the same word strengthens him, and powerfully hinders him from esteeming this as presumption. For thus testifies the apostle: "No one can call Christ Lord except by the Holy Ghost" (1 Cor. 12:3). And thus to the believer his faith becomes neither boasting before God, nor dread of presumption, but simply a testimony that God has actually had pity on him, and has given him the Holy Ghost, by whose power he can call Christ his Lord. And also the word of the Lord, πάντα δυνατὰ τῷ πιστεύοντι (Mark 9:23), is received in faith by the believer; not indeed because he believes in the omnipotence of his faith, but in the power of that God who has given him the promise (Rom 4:21), and because he knows that all the promises of God in Christ are yea, and therefore also through Him amen, to the glory of God by us (2 Cor. 1:20). For thus speaks the man who is truly justified by faith: "*Faith makes Christ ours, and His love makes us His*" (Luther).

(5) Because it is Christ's love alone which makes us to be His, and permits us to esteem ourselves so—not our faith, not our love, not our obedience, not our works—and we have the certainty of this nowhere except in His word and by His word, which promises us grace and forgiveness of sins, and directs us to seek herein our justification, herewith an ethical relation

presents itself which runs directly counter to all human imagination of righteousness before God, and which, previous to the revelation of God in Jesus Christ, had never entered into the heart and mind of man. For there God begins the work, and not man, and bestows on us as a free gift what man otherwise conceived to himself as the object and end of his works and ways, and for which he vainly strove. And not this merely. It is not only a treasure which was presented to us at the beginning that we perhaps should imagine, that we might afterwards console ourselves with its possession on account of our good conduct; but the same treasure becomes a two-edged sword, which cuts asunder all conceit of a conduct satisfactory to God, confirms the law's sentence of judgment, and hews down at the same time all assaults of conscience and despair, since it is required from us always and every day to comfort ourselves purely with the grace which God has given us in Christ, in order that in it alone we should have and hold the ground and foundation of our justification before God. And God has known far better than human self-conceit and human wisdom can imagine, wherefore and how greatly we need such comfort, of which only the self-secure servants of sin or the proud Pharisees wish to know nothing. But he who with the apostle learns the complaining cry even of the redeemed, "O wretched man that I am!" (Rom 7:24), he knows what he has in this comfort. Not only for the beginning of a new life do I need, above all things, a conscience free from the accusations and the judgment of the law, but also for the continuance and perfection thereof, in order that my conscience may remain free equally from the thunderbolt of judgment, as from dead works (Heb. 9:14) and the pollution of self-righteousness. There is at stake peace and joy of conscience, which no one can restore, no one preserve, no one place in safety against assault, and keep accessible under all circumstances, except God alone, who holds out to us in His word of grace forgiveness of sins and justification for Christ's sake. That is "the sun which daily rises in the heavens, and not only chases away the past night, but ever pursues its course, and lights up the whole day. Although it comes into darkness and is enveloped in thick clouds, nay, although a man may shut out its light from himself with closed doors and windows, yet does it remain the same sun, and breaks forth again, that we may continually look upon it again" (Luther). For "Christ commands to preach the gospel in His name, and therein is proclaimed grace and remission of all sins, and how He has for us fulfilled the law: thus the heart is freed from the ban of its own conscience, and obtains grace, which makes the heart and the inner man free and joyful, willing and glad to perform and to undergo all things. And thus is the man released not from the law that he should do nothing, but from the cheerless and burdened conscience which he has from the law, and which makes him an enemy to the law, which threatens him with death and hell; and now he has a good conscience in submission to Christ, and is faithful to the law, and never does he dread death and hell, and does freely and cheerfully what before he did unwillingly" (*idem*).

§ 19. b. Evangelical Love

Out of the faith, which takes what no man is able to give, is born the love, which gives what no man can give of himself. For it only gives back that which faith has received from God, viz. a joyous and cheerful heart for the service of God and man. Therefore it is faith which makes us free for love, not love which makes us free for faith. For the heart-constraining love of God comes not upon me, if I do not believe that God in Christ first loved me before I loved Him (1). And just as love and faith are inseparable, so certain is it that we must first come to faith before we come to true love. For only the love which is born of faith can prove its truthfulness in this, that in such love it does not seek its own, least of all does it seek a righteousness of such love before God. Rather it knows well, that it is nothing in comparison with that love with which God has loved us in Christ, and has given up His only-begotten Son for us, and cannot do otherwise than love God in return who has so loved the world (2). And because it proceeds from faith, such responding love is a fruit not of the natural, but of the purified heart, delivered from the wrath of God and justified. In this heart dwells through faith the word of the living God, which announces and promises such love of God; and because this word is spirit and life, it works in the heart that love to God which is a fruit of the Spirit of God, yea, is the same love with which the Father loveth the Son, so that by such love we are in God, who is love (3). But since God in His love loves not only the beloved Son, but in Him loves the whole world, and has loved it, so the love which is wrought by God through faith embraces in God the whole world, just as the love of God in Christ avails not only for those who are in Christ, but for such also as are still afar off from Him. And thus the love which flows from God in Christ, produces first the brotherly love to all who are born of God, and in that the love to all men, for all of whom the Lord Jesus Christ has died (4). Thus out of faith there arises that love which by its nature is a fulfilling of the law. For it stands entirely in the freedom of a heart, freed not indeed from the fear of God, but certainly from terror at the idea of God, and fulfils the highest law of the love of God and of one's neighbor just in this, that it springs not out of a command of love, but out of the stream of the love of God towards us and towards all men, poured forth into our hearts by means of faith (5). Herein it is at the same time the leaven of all true sanctification, in which we sanctify ourselves for the service of God and our neighbor, and is the mother of good works, whose father is faith, and in the performance of which true Christian virtue specifically discriminates itself from everything which is called legal obedience and works of the law (6).

(1) Here, where we begin to speak of the relation of faith to love, and of both to hope, it may be remarked in the outset, that this threefold working of the gospel is undoubtedly an organic, and in itself united whole; and yet that it is not well to incorporate in a certain measure the parts or several relations of this united whole, instead of distinguishing them from one another in the most definite manner. Into this mistake I myself

have previously fallen. By wishing to avoid a mechanical juxtaposition, I fell into a false complication of them. For although this threefold effect springs from the one united root of the evangelical word of promise, yet in their inner origin and existence the one is conditioned by the other, has distinct relations, manifests itself in distinct forms and functions, and has distinct reflex influences on its own disposition and its own natural conduct, whether internal or external. Since I do not arrive at faith through love and hope, but by faith arrive at love and hope; believing, therefore, is also something different from loving, and loving something different from hoping, and hoping something different both from believing and loving. I arrive at faith when, by the working of conscience, the law, and the gospel, I have first lost faith in myself; at love only then, when I have first won faith in God's love in Christ; and at hope only in this way, that by faith I have become certain of an inheritance which here below is worth the continual aspiration of my love, and is by divine appointment to become its object. And the relations also, as well as the forms and functions, in which faith, love, and hope are exercised and have their actual existence, are distinct. Faith hangs on the word of promise, love on that God who gives, hope on the promised inheritance. Faith receives and has, love gives, hope waits. Faith makes the heart firm, love makes it soft, hope expands it. Faith holds fast to what it has received, love gives up what it has received, hope triumphs over what is wanting. Faith capacitates us for dominion over this world, love for ministering to this world, hope for renunciation of this world. Faith rests on that wherein it has for this present time full sufficiency; love acts and finds employment in that in which it can never satisfy itself; hope loses itself in that which lifts it above all the sufficiency and insufficiency of this world. Faith is the confidence in what one hopes for; love the proof of this—that one has faith; hope the taking possession, before we have reached the goal, of that which we have learned by faith to love and to yearn after. Faith is what it ceases to be in sight; hope is what it ceases to be in full possession; love is that which it never ceases to be, for God is love.

After this preliminary remark, we must yet add one thing more to what is contained in the paragraph, that it is self-evident that this idea of "love" has nothing at all to do with that which is so named in the domain of natural life (as, for example, the natural love of self which is spoken of in Eph. 5:29), but with that love alone which the gospel requires and at the same time bestows.

In the kingdom of grace holds good that universal and fundamental law, that we have nothing which we have not received (1 Cor. 4:7), and that no one has first given anything to God, and has had it recompensed to him (τίς προέδωκεν αὐτῷ, καὶ ἀνταποδοθήσεται αὐτῷ, Rom. 11:35), but the reverse. And it specially holds good, that we must first have received grace (δέξασθαι τὴν χάριν, 2 Cor. 6:1), in order to show ourselves servants of God in unfeigned love (συνιστῶντες ἑαυτοὺς ὡς Θεοῦ διάκονοι· ... ἐν ἀγάπῃ ἀνυποκρίτῳ ibid. vers. 4, 6). Then, as to how grace is received, namely through faith, that has already been spoken of. But if the reception of grace renders us capable of the service of love, faith must first exist, and then alone comes love on the scene. We cannot infer the contrary from the fact that it is said of those who are lost, "They had not received the love of the truth" (2 Thess. 2:10), and hence conclude that love must first be there, before we receive the truth in faith. For when I say what is wanting to any one, it is very unreasonable to conclude that he comes to this want by the very thing which is wanting to him. And as our whole inborn shortcoming is this, that we love the lie rather than the truth, so are we all by nature wanting in genuine love to God and our neighbor. And again, as to what specially concerns love to God, even in the eyes of God the effective ground of the want of perfect love is the well-founded terror of God's wrath. Our love, however, does not overcome this wrath, but God turns away the wrath in His love. Of this He convinces me in His word; and only when I have appropriated this to myself in confident faith, does my heart become free for that love of God which is exempt from the pain and punishment of fear (1 John 4:18; comp. § 16, at note (1)). Nay, love consists in this, *not that we have loved God*, but that He has loved us, and sent His Son to be the propitiation for our sins (1 John 4:10). He, therefore, who believes that God has so loved him, his heart becomes free for that love, in which he now truly serves the living God (δουλεύειν, λατρεύειν, 1 Thess. 1:9, Heb. 9:14). At a perfect love, however, we cannot arrive, if it has not before been received by faith that God has such love for us. My love does not cause me to believe; but my faith causes me to love. And that, moreover, not in such a way that it lies in the abstract nature of faith that it is inseparable from love. I may have faith so as to remove mountains, and yet may be without this love (1 Cor. 13:2). Sin can divide the tie which by God's gracious will unites faith and love, and sin can falsify faith. But if my faith is the right faith, and in truth fixes itself only on the word of the love of God in Christ to me, then must it produce of itself the love which, according to God's gracious will, forms an indissoluble unity with faith (ἀγάπη μετὰ πίστεως, Eph. 6:23; πίστις καὶ ἀγάπη ἡ ἐν Χριστῷ Ἰησοῦ, 1 Tim. 1:14, 2 Tim. 1:13). For in Christ Jesus that faith alone avails which worketh by love (Gal. 5:6). And although in that passage this is spoken of love to one's neighbor (ver. 14), we may reasonably transfer it also to the relationship Godward. This same passage, however, shows that faith is the power of love, not love the power of faith; that faith is active and powerful to work by love, not love active and powerful to work by faith. "Therefore Paul does not say that love is active, but that faith is active—that faith puts in exercise and makes love active, and not that love does so with faith" (Luther). Nay, it would be the same thing as to overturn the whole gospel, if we wished to teach that we could love God before we believed in Him, or that we could in any way by *our* love bring about our having in Him a gracious God. "As if we were obliged to begin by loving Him! It is certain, however, that He begins by loving us (1 John 4:10). Nay, if He were not to begin, then should we never be able to love Him. For no one can love Him, except he who believes that he was first loved by Him, and that he has in

Him a gracious God; otherwise the heart flees before Him, and is secretly hostile to Him as One who wishes to plunge us into hell" (Luther). And he who really knows what love is, and speaks of love not as a dreamer or as an idle talker, that man knows also most certainly that he must first have God Himself before he will have love. For "love is a living essence in the divine nature which burns there, full of all that is good. Love does and practices the very same works which God Himself does. He who has love must also have God Himself, and be full of Him" (Luther). God, however, dwells in the heart by faith.

(2) In that 13th chapter of the first Epistle to the Corinthians, in which Paul praises love, he also describes its characteristics. And although there also the question is not so much of love to God as of love to our neighbor, these criteria of true love remain the same in their relation to God as in that towards our neighbor. For when this love is true, it is just our love to God which shows itself in our love to our neighbor, just as the love which is born in the Christian is a reflex operation of that love with which God in Christ has loved the world (ἐάν τις εἴπῃ, ὅτι ἀγαπῶ τὸν Θεόν, καὶ τὸν ἀδελφὸν αὐτοῦ μισεῖ, ψεύστης ἐστίν· ὁ γὰρ μὴ ἀγαπῶν τὸν ἀδελφὸν αὐτοῦ ὃν ἑώρακεν, τὸν Θεόν, ὃν οὐχ ἑώρακεν, πῶς δύναται ἀγαπᾶν; 1 John 4:20). Of love, however, Paul says, "Love vaunts not itself, is not puffed up, seeks not its own" (vers. 4, 5). Now we ask, Whence cometh this? If there ever has appeared in the world anything which is boastful, puffed up, seeking and claiming its own—that is to say, honor, glory, and righteousness—it is that which the world calls love. Nay, the apostle's glorying over the humility of love has been converted into an article of pride. How is this possible? Just because the world does not know what love is, and is not acquainted with that love which the apostle praises. That, however, is the love which is born from faith in God—a love overcome and kindled by the love of God. This love does not say, Behold how great a love we have, that we are called God's children! but, Behold how great a love the Father has shown to us, that we are called the children of God! (1 John 3:1.) As a drop compared to the ocean—as a small spark to the

world-embracing fire—such is our love compared to the love of God. And the more certainly we know that we derive our righteousness from our faith in that God who has manifested *His* love in this, that Christ died for us while we were yet sinners (Rom. 5:8), so much the more remote are we from the presumptuous dream of wishing to derive our righteousness before God from our love. Nay, this is the very peculiarity of love, whether it is love to God or love to our neighbor, that it can never do enough, and always feels itself a debtor. For this reason we cannot speak of our love in comparison with God's love in Christ, in any other way than as a debt which cannot be discharged. And it has only this meaning for us, that as it is the fruit, so is it the manifestation and proof of our faith. "For faith is certainly not there where love is not; but the contrary shows itself, and follows. And although the works of love do not make us righteous and blessed, yet are they to follow as fruits and true tokens of faith" (Luther).

(3) Not that we of ourselves should love and have love, but that the love of God should dwell in us—that is the design of the revelation of God in Christ. Nothing more wonderful and more glorious can be conceived, than that which Christ (in John) mentions as the purpose of His declaring the name of the Father—namely, that the love with which the Father has loved Christ may be in us, and Christ in us (John 17:26; comp. 13:34, 35). And when Paul says that the love of God is shed abroad in our hearts by the Holy Ghost which is given unto us, he means that same love by virtue of which Christ, when we were yet without strength, died for the ungodly (Rom. 5:5, 6). The power of this love is to become our own portion in faith: in this love we are to abide, after our stony heart has been softened by it through the working of the Holy Ghost. "As the Father hath loved me," says Christ, "so have I loved you: continue ye in my love" (John 15:9). And because God gives the spirit of love (πνεῦμα ἀγάπης, 2 Tim. 1:7), therefore we ought and are enabled to walk in love, as Christ also hath loved us (Eph. 5:2). "For love is of God; and every one that loveth is born of God, and knows God. He that loves not, knows not God; for God is

love" (1 John 4:7, 8). Hence, not he who knows God, but he who loves God, the same is known of Him (εἰ δέ τις ἀγαπᾷ τὸν Θεὸν, οὗτος ἔγνωσται ὑπ' αὐτοῦ, 1 Cor. 8:3). And because that which is truly love is like in nature to God, and, even in the shape in which it takes possession of our heart upon earth, belongs to the things which never perish (οὐδέποτε πίπτει, 1 Cor. 13:8), therefore it is greater than faith and hope, which only here below remain in equal importance, and endures forever. Faith has only to do with God in our hearts in this life; but love has to do with God and the whole world to eternity. Faith justifies by the word, and brings love. "But both the word" (that is to say, the word in its outer form and testimony) "and faith cease; and righteousness and love, which are attained by means of them, remain eternally, just as a building, which is completed by means of scaffolding, remains after the scaffolding is removed" (Luther). But our attaining to such a love is God's work alone; and only that love which adoringly recognizes this, is love by which God truly dwells in us. "God has overshadowed us with His own nature, and has poured out Himself upon us, with all that He has and can do for us—upon us who were sinners, unworthy, enemies, and servants of the devil; so that He can do no more for us, and can give us no more. He therefore who considers such divine flame of love, which fills heaven and earth, and yet is not contained thereby, and does not allow himself to be won to love,—such an one will in truth never, through law or command, doctrine, driving, or compulsion, become pious, and arrive at this love" (Luther). "Briefly, love must first be in the heart, otherwise nothing comes of a man's keeping the law. First, therefore, show how one may get the love; then afterwards will he be able to execute the law. Christ wills not that we should keep His word with the hand, as the laws of men are kept; but with the heart, with cheerfulness and love. But what gives this cheerfulness and love? The Holy Ghost gives this love, and none other but He" (Luther).

(4) "Faith makes us masters, love makes us servants" (Luther). "Faith receives, love gives; faith brings man to God,

love brings him to man; through faith he allows himself to receive God's kindness, through love he does good to men; he draws good from above through faith, and bestows good below by love" (*idem*). "For where so strong a confidence exists, that you doubt not that God is your Father, it must certainly follow, however weak the faith may be, that it break forth with the mouth, with our acts, and with the hand, and care for our neighbor with teaching and help" (*idem*). And, "When your heart is fixed in faith, so that you know that your God has thus shown Himself to thee so compassionate and kind, without your deserving, and purely gratuitously, when you were still His enemy and a child of the everlasting curse: when you believe this, then canst you not fail to show yourself the same to your neighbor also; and all this from love to God, and kindness to your neighbor. Therefore see that you make no difference between friend and foe, worthy and unworthy" (*idem*). Nay, if the heart is thus established in faith (βεβαιούμενος τῇ πίστει, Col. 2:7, Heb. 13:9), and grounded and rooted in love to Christ (Eph. 3:18), then will the service of our love be a service of God, and the poor love of sinful men will be a course of acting like unto God's. For "we are children of God through faith, which makes us heirs of all divine benefits; but through love are we gods (Ps. 82:6), which makes us do good to our neighbors" (Luther).

As it is of the most essential importance to the birth of this love, that it springs from faith in the love which God has *to us* (ἐγνώκαμεν καὶ πεπιστεύκαμεν τὴν ἀγάπην ἣν ἔχει ὁ Θεὸς ἐν ἡμῖν, 1 John 4:16), and that we love because He has first loved us (1 John 4:19), so it is of no less importance, that by virtue of this love, if we abide in it, God abides in us (ὁ μένων ἐν τῇ ἀγάπῃ ἐν τῷ Θεῷ μένει καὶ ὁ Θεὸς 'ν αὐτῷ, 1 John 4:16), who so loved *the world* that He gave His only-begotten Son (John 3:16); and we therefore are to become imitators of this God, and to walk in love, as Christ has loved us (Eph. 5:1, 2), since as He is, so are we also in this world (1 John 4:17). Hereby is that self-seeking of love broken down, where we only love those who love us; and that command to love our enemies (Matt. 5:41–48), which as a command was not at first expressed even by Christ, comes to its true fulfilment in the spirit of Christ, and through the power of Christ. And just as certainly as the impulse of God-born love at first draws us only to those who with us are born of God (1 John 5:1, πᾶς ὁ πιστεύων, ὅτι Ἰησοῦς ἐστὶν ὁ Χριστός, ἐκ τοῦ Θεοῦ γεγέννηται, καὶ πᾶς ὁ ἀγάπων τὸν γεννήσαντα, ἀγαπᾷ καὶ τὸν γεγεννημένον ἐξ αὐτοῦ), so certain is it that this love has yet only this, for its true criterion, that it extends beyond these limits, to bring peace in Christ to the far off as well as to the near (Eph. 2:17; οἱ εἰς μακράν, Acts 2:39; φιγαδελφία and ἀγάπη, 2 Pet. 1:7), and not to remain by the sheep of the fold alone (John 10:16), but, in and with the love of Christ, to embrace the whole world. For not where love, but where misery is, there the love of the Samaritan (Luke 10:25 ff.) finds the neighbor whom it has to serve, just as God in Christ has not accepted our offered love, but has had compassion on the misery of our loveless condition.

(5) As Christ characterizes the love of God and our neighbor as the highest command, and the sum of the law (Matt. 22:37–40; comp. Mark 12:28 ff., Luke 10:25 ff.), so also does His apostle call the love which flows from the love of God to us (Rom. 5:5), and which is poured into our heart by the Spirit of God, the fulfilling of the law (Rom. 13:10; comp. the νόμος βασιλικός, Jas. 2:8). But we must mark well that it is only this. For herein is it the fulfilling of the *law* of love, that this fulfilling takes place in the *free* impulse of the *love* which is born of the Holy Ghost. This holds good just as much of the love to God as of the love to one's neighbor. That we call God Abba, Father! is the working of the Spirit of the Son, whom God sends into the hearts of those who, being justified by faith, have become children of God (Rom. 8:15). And from the same Spirit of the Son alone comes also the true love of one's neighbor. Those, however, who are moved by the Spirit of God, stand not under the law (Gal. 5:18), but fulfil the law in freedom. For where the Spirit of the Lord is, there is freedom (2 Cor. 3:17). Called to this freedom by the word of the gospel and the power of the Holy Ghost, we can and ought to serve one another in love (διὰ τῆς

ἀγάπης δουλεύειν ἀλλήλοις, Gal. 5:13). And only in reference to the power of love rendered possible after the measure of the love of Christ to us, and flowing out of it, is the command which proceeds from Christ a new one, which was not in existence before (καινὴ ἐντολή, John 13:34, 1 John 2:8). For this commandment rests on the preliminary overcoming of the darkness by the light (1 John 2:8), and applies to the God-given power of the new birth, of the new man (εἴ τις ἐν Χριστῷ, καινὴ κτίσις, 2 Cor. 5:17, Gal. 6:15, Eph. 4:24, etc.; comp. above, § 13, at note (4)).

But if, in the Scriptures of the New Testament, this love is called a fulfilling of the law, it is so called in the sense that hereby is expressed what love effects without its needing the law. For "if one has love, no law is necessary: if he has it not, no law is sufficient" (Luther). But that any one so lives in love, that he fulfils the law of love, is nowhere asserted. We remain only in debt to love, as towards God, so towards every man (μηδενὶ μηδὲν ὀφείλετε, εἰ μὴ τὸ ἀλλήλους ἀγαπᾶν, Rom. 13:8). But when it is said that love covers a multitude of sins, this is meant, in the one passage (1 Pet. 4:8, ἀγάπη καλύπτει πλῆθος ἁμαρτιῶν), in the sense that brotherly love, by forgiving, covers a multitude of sins; and in the other (Jas. 5:20, καλύψει πλῆθος ἁμαρτιῶν, in which it is spoken of the conversion of the sinner by the saving effort of brotherly love, the sense is, what effect such saving act will have for the sinner—namely, the forgiveness of sins. And when, in a third passage (Luke 7:47), the extent of the forgiveness of sins appears to be made dependent on the greatness of the love, it is sufficient to refer to the conclusion of the narrative, where Christ says, "Thy faith hath saved thee" (ver. 50). Rather is the greatness of thankful love in that very passage set before us as the fruit of the forgiveness of sins previously received in accordance with the greatness of that forgiveness (ᾧ δὲ ὀλίγον ἀφίεται, ὀλίγον ἀγαπᾷ, ver. 47, comp. with vers. 41, 42), and opposed to the coldness of self-righteous pharisaism.

(6) Πάντα ὑμῶν ἐν ἀγάπῃ γινέσθω, 1 Cor. 16:13. What we wish to be done we present daily to God in the prayer, "*Thy will be*

done on earth, as it is in heaven." How that is done and has to be done by us, follows hence of itself; thus, namely, that *His* will should be *our* will. But His will respecting us, as has been said, is comprised in the commandment of love to God and to our neighbor. If this will is *in us*, then it is so only in the love which flows out of the whole heart. How we come to this love through faith, has before been shown. What takes place in us by virtue of this love, is a union of love, and therefore a free union of our will with God's will. In it alone is perfected true sanctification, which consists in the union of our will with God's will. Out of this alone proceed good works, which are the fulfilling of the divine law out of a heart by faith made free in love and to love. Grace, faith, love, freedom, good works—such is the indissoluble chain, outside which no work is good; while within the same every work is good, because it springs from the God of love, who makes us ready in every good work to do His will, and works in us that which is well-pleasing in His sight, through Jesus Christ (Heb. 13:21). But the element in which every good work—that is to say, all true fulfilling of the law, or fulfilling of the divine will—is perfected, is and remains love. "There must first be love: thereafter perform your works, and thus will they be pleasing to God; for all works of the law are directed to this point, that one should thereby show the love of God which he has in his heart" (Luther). "*All* the commandments require love; for all the commandments, if they are obeyed without love—that is, without an *easy, ready, cheerful*, and *well-disposed will*—remain unfulfilled, although the external" ("dead," Heb. 9:14) "works are done, since there remains in that case a disinclined, that is, a sinful will" (Luther). The word from Prov. 22:9 which Paul quotes (2 Cor. 9:7), holds good of each and every relation: "God loves a cheerful (ἱλαρόν, טוֹב־עַיִן) giver."

Our sanctification is a participation, an appropriation of the divine holiness (μεταλαμβάνειν τῆς ἁγιότητος τοῦ Θεοῦ, Heb. 12:10). This God, however, as the Holy One, stands opposed to our selfish nature just in His absolute love. And for this very reason, also, no sanctification proceeding from God is conceivable otherwise than as a sanctification in love. Who will imagine to himself, as being without love, that sanctification without which, as the Scripture says, no man shall see that God who is love? (comp. Heb. 12:14.) But while through faith we become free to the love of *God*, we become by the same love servants of God, and of all that is conformable to the divine will (ὡς ἐλεύθεροι καὶ μὴ ὡς ἐπικάλυμμα ἔχοντες τῆς κακίας τὴν ἐλευθερίαν, ἀλλ' ὡς δοῦλοι Θεοῦ, 1 Pet. 2:16; ἐλευθερωθέντες ἀπὸ τῆς ἁμαρτίας, ἐδουλώθητε τῇ δικαιοσύνῃ, Rom. 6:18; ἀκάλεσεν ἡμᾶς ὁ Θεὸς ... ἐν ἁγιασμῷ, 1 Thess. 4:7). And since the operation of this love springs from the call of grace, and the gift of the grace of God, all the works in which faith worketh by love are just as much an operation of God as they are a free act at the same time (αὐτοῦ—Θεοῦ—γάρ ἐσμεν ποίημα, κτισθέντες ἐν Χριστῷ Ἰησοῦ ἐπὶ ἔργοις ἀγαθοῖς, Eph. 2:10; ἔδωκεν—Ἰ. Χρ.— ἑαυτὸν ὑπὲρ ἡμῶν, ἵνα λυτρώσηται ἡμᾶς ἀπὸ πάσης ἀνομίας, καὶ καθαρίσῃ ἑαυτῷ λαὸν περιούσιον, ζηλωτὴν καλῶν ἔργων, Tit. 2:14; κατανοῶμεν ἀλλήλους εἰς παροξυσμὸν ἀγάπης καὶ καλῶν ἔργων, Heb. 10:24; comp. on the relation of χάρις to the ἔργα ἀγαθά, 2 Cor. 9:8). In the practice of these good works consists the specific character of that Christian virtue which, springing from faith, exercises itself in love. Compare afterwards §§ 30 ff.

§ 20. c. *Evangelical Hope*

What man needs here below for his mastery over the accusations of conscience and of the law—what he needs for the assurance of his justification by grace before God,—that is given him in the word of promise, and that he has in faith. What he requires for the service of God and of his neighbor, that he receives in the divine spirit of love, which springs from the love of the grace-promising God. But that which extends beyond this world, and lifts man above this world, is presented to him in the promise of benefits which, destined for future possession in another world, are here below benefits of hope, and remain the object of hope. The comprehensive expression for them, in contrast with the future judgment which awaits those who obey not and believe not the gospel, is the complete redemption of believers (comp. § 17 and the concluding note) (1). In as far as this hope is identical with the goal, given in Christ and recognizable, of our own perfection, with the divine promise of its actual future possession, with that which is guaranteed to us of future glory in Him who calls us and the word of our calling, the hope of the gospel means nothing else than the good itself which we look forward to in hope (2). In as far, however, as this good is given us in the way of promise, to the end that an inner tendency corresponding to it should become the power of our earthly life, that hope which is rooted in the grace of God in Christ, and wrought in us by the Holy Ghost, designates the disposition which is proper and becoming to the Christian upon earth (3). Its certainty rests entirely on the truthfulness and infallibility of the God who promises; on which account, without faith there is no hope (4). Its goal, on the contrary, it has purely in the heavenly perfection of the kingdom of God; hence hope has not the same sphere as that in which faith rests (5). But since hope waits for that of which faith has already laid the foundation, it is only the understood expression and the consciously apprehended working of that relation in which the earthly already stands to the heavenly; and the present already embraces in itself the future; and he who hopes, already possesses the beginning and foundation of that whose accomplishment he is waiting for (6). On the peace and joy which faith has, rests the perfect self-assurance of hope; and on the glorious aim of that hope which is realized in Christ, and presented to us in the way of promise, rests that onward striving which is peculiar to the believer—that heavenly frame of mind which looks forwards and upwards (7).

(1) Hope has this in common with faith, that it looks towards invisible things (ὁ γὰρ βλέπει τις, τί καὶ ἐλπίζει; ὃ οὐ βλέπομεν ἐλπίζομεν, Rom. 8:24, 25). But it is distinguished from faith by this, that the latter seizes on something invisible, whose saving efficacy is destined for the present, while in the

latter case the saving operation is reserved for the future. But again, the two-sided relation is not this, that both run parallel with each other,—the one directed to something invisible, which is destined to bring about a present benefit, while the object of the other is future good. On the contrary, faith and hope are interwoven with each other, and indeed in such a way that it is not hope that supports and upholds faith, but faith that does so for hope. For faith fastens on the root from which both the present and the future salvation come—that is, the word of promise of the living God; but hope embraces the crown which is held out for it there in the life everlasting, but which is also objective to us only in the word of promise. Hope, therefore, has not immediate access to the future benefits, but only by means of faith, which, in its laying hold of the word of promise, is a confidence in that which we hope for (Heb. 11:1). For which reason faith also resembles the watchman under whose protection we are shut in for the salvation which is ready to be revealed in the last time (οἱ ἐν δυνάμει Θεοῦ φρουρούμενοι διὰ πίστεως, εἰς σωτηρίαν ἑτοίμην ἀποκαλυφθῆναι ἐν καιρῷ ἐσχάτῳ, 1 Pet. 1:5), so that we are capable of hoping perfectly for the grace presented to us in the revelation of Jesus Christ (τελείως ἐλπίσατε ἐπὶ τὴν φερομένην χάριν ἐν ἀποκαλύψει Ἰησοῦ Χριστοῦ, 1 Pet. 1:13). And just in this way the words of faith (οἱ λόγοι τῆς πίστεως) are the promises of the present and the future life, from which springs hope in the living God, who is the Savior of all men, but especially of *believers* (1 Tim. 4:6, 8, 10).

When, on the other hand, it is said of love, that it hopes all things (1 Cor. 13:7), as it is also said there of it that it believes all things, this is said not in reference to God, but to men, of whom that love of one's neighbor which is born of God never despairs. Well, however, may it be said, on the other hand, that the future salvation for which man hopes, is at the same time also loved at present: for hope is yearning love; and yearning, God-taught love, is in itself God-justified hope. And for this reason, then, the hope and appearing of the glory of the great God and our Savior Jesus Christ (Tit. 2:13) lie at the heart of those only, and has any value for such only as here below have *loved* this appearing (ἠγαπηκόσιν τὴν ἐπιφάνειαν αὐτοῦ, 2 Tim. 4:8).

That, however, which the Christian hopes for, is called by the same name which that bears which he already possesses—redemption, salvation (or blessedness), righteousness, adoption, everlasting life. All this, however, in the form of future perfection and glory (δόξα). What deep, internal significance this may have, is hereafter to be told. Here we have only to remark, that over against the present day of salvation (νῦν ἡμέρα σωτηρίας, see § 17, note (3)) there stands another and coming day of salvation and redemption (ἡμάρα ἀπολυτρώσεως, Eph. 4:30; ἡ ἡμέρα τοῦ Κυρίου ἡμῶν Ἰ. Χριστοῦ, 1 Cor. 1:8; Phil. 1:6, 10, etc.; μέλλουσα δόξα ἀποκαλυφθῆναι, Rom. 8:18), which stands in the same relation to the first as the completion to the beginning, as the finishing of a building to its foundation, as the full "revelation of what is now concealed, and is the specific object of Christian hope. That which unconditionally is already perfected and received here in faith, that is the atonement and justification (δικαιωθέντες ἐκ πίστεως ... νῦν τὴν καταλλαγὴν ἐλάβομεν, Rom. 5:1, 11). The full deliverance from evil, however, for which we pray, is the object of hope, because of future fulfilment. This hope of faith forms the opposite of that which awaits those who have not obeyed the gospel (2 Thess. 1:8; Rom. 2:8, etc.).

(2) That the Scriptures speak of hope in a double sense of the word, is well known. "The word 'hope' is used in Scripture in a twofold manner. In the first place, it means that great courage which in all temptation remains firm, and looks forward to victory and final blessedness. In the second place, it means this victory and final blessedness itself, which the hope and courage of the heart look forward to, and are to obtain" (Luther). That this is so, is of no slight importance to ethics. Hope is hereby removed entirely from the domain of what is merely subjective. It rests on objective grounds. When an ancient author says, "Spem metus sequitur, nec miror ista sic ire; utrumque *pendentis animi* est, utrumque futuri expectatione solliciti ... *spes incerti boni nomen est*" (Senec. *epp.*

v. 10), then is this from the standpoint of the natural heart psychologically quite correct. But the heart of the Christian, with its subjective hope, is established on the basis of an objective hope. This is given in Christ's deeds of victory, whose victory, resurrection, glorification, is to become our victory and our portion; and this is guaranteed to us in the word of promise connected therewith, which promises us such final victory through the power of Christ. For this reason Jesus Himself is called our hope (Ἰησοῦς ἡ ἐλπὶς ἡμῶν, 1 Tim. 1:1: Χριστὸς ἡ ἐλπὶς τῆς δόξης, Col. 1:27; see also Tit. 2:13). And thus also the expressions, the hope of the gospel, the hope of the calling of God, the glory of the hope, indicate not the subjective hope which is awakened in us, but that objective good of hope which is the basis of, and produces our hope, that our deliverance is offered to us only in the way of hope, and of the hoped-for good (ἡ ἐλπὶς τοῦ εὐαγγελίου, Col. 1:23; ἡ ἐλπὶς τῆς κλήσεως τοῦ Θεοῦ, Eph. 1:18, 4:4; ἡ ἐλπὶς ἡ ἀποκειμένη ὑμῖν ἐν τοῖς οὐρανοῖς, ἣν προηκούσατε ἐν τῷ λόγῳ τῆς ἀληθείας τοῦ εὐαγγελίου, Col. 1:5; καύχημα τῆς ἐλπίδος Heb. 3:6; τῇ γὰρ ἐλπίδι ἐσώθημεν, Rom. 8:24; ἵνα δικαιωθέντες τῇ ἐκείνου χάριτι, κληρονόμοι γενηθῶμεν κατ' ἐλπίδα ζωῆς αἰωνίου, Tit. 3:7). In the same objective sense is the hope of Israel spoken of (Acts 28:20; the ἐλπὶς τῆς εἰς τοὺς πατέρας ἡμῶν ἐπαγγελίας γενομένης, Acts 26:6).

(3) That which characterizes the subjective hope which is peculiar to the Christian is just this, that it is not of human origin, and does not pursue earthly aims. It is effected by the consolation of the Scriptures (διὰ τῆς παρακλήσεως τῶν γραφῶν, Rom. 15:4); it comes from the God of hope, in the power of the Holy Ghost (Rom. 15:13); it has its origin in Jesus Christ and God our Father, who has loved us, and who gives us everlasting consolation and good hope through grace (2 Thess. 2:16); it is a living hope, through the resurrection of Jesus Christ from the dead (1 Pet. 1:3; comp. 1:21), and is entirely directed to the salvation which is to come (ἐλπὶς σωτηρίας, 1 Thess. 5:8; see also Heb. 9:28; Rom. 8:23).

(4) The unwavering profession of our hope rests on the truth and trustworthiness of Him who has promised (πιστὸς ὁ ἐπαγγειλάμενος=ὁμολογία τῆς ἐλπίδος ἀκλιβής, Heb. 10:23). From that God who lieth not (ἀψευδὴς Θεός, Tit. 1:2), for whom it is impossible to lie (ἀδύνατος ψεύσασθαι Θεός, Heb. 6:18), springs the hope which lies before us of everlasting life: therefore is the Christian's hope so certain and assured (πληροφορία τῆς ἐλπίδος, Heb. 6:11; comp. τῇ ἐλπίδι χαίροντες Rom. 12:12). Hope just as little as faith has its assurance in itself, in things which belong to the inner conditions of man's nature: not because it hopes does it infer the certainty of the fulfilment of its hopes, but because the God of hope who promises cannot deceive it. Hence also arises its inseparable oneness with faith. Nowhere is this more distinctly expressed than in the prayer for blessing of the Apostle Paul (Rom. 15:13) "The God of hope fill us with all joy and peace in believing, that we may abound in hope, through the power of the Holy Ghost."

(5) Faith attaches itself to the word of Christ: "I *have* overcome the world" (John 16:33). And thus this faith is the victory which *has* already overcome the world (1 John 5:4). Thus by faith we enter into rest (Heb. 4:3, comp. 5:10). But the longing-glance which hope casts after us is first directed on ourselves, on our circumstances, our struggles, our misery, and our remoteness from the goal set before us. To the sufferings of this present time, to the straitened circumstances of beginning, to the pain of longing, in which we lift up our head for full deliverance, the hope given us by God forms the counterpoise (comp. Rom. 8:18–25). It is the impelling but gentle goad which will not let us rest in false security. For since we know that we are now indeed the children of God, but it hath not yet appeared what we shall be, and we direct our glances of hope to that goal, when we shall see God as He is, this same hope impels us to a continual self-purification (ἁγνίζειν ἑαυτόν, even as God is pure (1 John 3:2, 3). And because such a work in us is supported by hope, that abiding patience enters our hearts, which God will give and bring about just through His word of promise, rich in hope as it is (ἡ

ὑπομονὴ τῆς ἐλπίδος τοῦ Κυρίου Ἰ. Χρ., 1 Thess. 1:3; ὁ Θεὸς τῆς ὑπομονῆς, Rom. 15:5; ἡ ὑπομονὴ τοῦ Χριστοῦ, 2 Thess. 3:5; δι' ὑπομονῆς ἀπεκδεχόμεθα, Rom. 8:25). The oil for the limbs of the wrestler is faith; the oil for his wounds is hope.

(6) Nothing is more perverted than the opinion, that hope, because it is directed to something future, stands out of all connection with the present. It stands certainly in indissoluble connection with that which faith here below already possesses. But just because that which man possesses in faith has a double side, of which the one corresponds to the relation of grace in this present world, the other to that of the glory which is to come, one and the same name serves both for the designation of that which man by faith already has here below, and for the designation of that which he is only looking forward to in hope. For to him only who hath shall be given (Matt. 13:12, 25:29; Luke 8:18). And so much is all future good the development of that which has already been received here below, that we can neither rightly possess what we have received, nor rightly hope for the future, without understanding and justly appreciating both in their mutual relation to each other. All false over-estimation or under-estimation, all false exaggeration or depreciation, is connected with the displacement of the limits of both these sides, or with the misapprehension of their mutual relation. What we have in us of God's power, is the earnest of the Spirit (ἀπαρχὴ Πνεύματος, Rom. 8:23). What we are by faith—namely, God's children—has not yet so appeared as we shall be (1 John 3:2). We have eternal life, but it is hid with Christ in God (Col. 3:3, 4). We are accounted righteous by grace; but the righteousness where there is no more sin is not yet our portion ("If we say that we have no sin, we deceive ourselves," etc., 1 John 1:8). We are saved and redeemed; and yet we are still to be saved and redeemed (σωθησόμεθα, Rom. 5:9, 10). We have justification, but not yet a justification which brings perfect life (δικαίωσις ζωῆς, Rom. 5:18). For this reason we wait in hope for the adoption (Rom. 8:23); for eternal life (ἐλπὶς ζωῆς αἰωνίου, Tit. 3:7); for righteousness (ἡμεῖς ἐκ πίστεως ἐλπίδα δικαιοσύνης ἀπεκδεχόμεθα, Gal. 5:5); for

redemption (Χριστὸν ἀπεκδεχόμενοι εἰς σωτηρίαν, Heb. 9:28). All this, however, because the gift which is given us here below is not intended to be, nor can be, given us in such a manner as to exclude the self-conquest and the self-victory, in which, by virtue of this gift, we are to become ripe for perfection. It is for training that we endure (εἰς παιδείαν ὑπομένετε, Heb. 12:7). To him that thirsts does the Lord give of the fountain of the water of life without price, but only he who conquers will be heir (Rev. 21:7). But the confidence of hope is this, that we shall be more than conquerors through Him that loved us, and that nothing—neither things present nor things to come—is able to separate us from the love of God which is in Christ Jesus our Lord (Rom. 8:37–39).

(7) Compare the passage, Rom. 15:13, before quoted in note (4), at the conclusion. The place where our hope rests is not an earthly, but a heavenly one (ἡ ἐλπὶς ἡ ἀποκειμένη ἐν τοῖς οὐρανοῖς, Col. 1:5; κληρονομία ... τετηρημένη ἐν οὐρανοῖς, 1 Pet. 1:4). Hence the striving of the Christian is a striving after things above (τὰ ἄνω ζητεῖν, φρονεῖν. Col. 3:1, 2; a contrast to τὰ ἐπὶ τῆς γῆς). But the mystery of the ethical power which lies herein is declared by the apostle, when he says that he *forgets those things which are behind, and reaches forth unto those things which are before,*—that he presses towards the mark for the prize of the heavenly calling of God in Christ Jesus (Phil. 3:14).

PART SECOND
THE POSSESSION OF SALVATION

FIRST SECTION

THE ENTRANCE OF THE BLESSING OF SALVATION INTO THE SPIRITUAL LIFE OF THE INDIVIDUAL

§ 21. *The Principle of Christian Life and Christian Ethics*

WE have shown, in the first part of this work, that the gospel, as being the vital power of faith, hope, and love, is our salvation, and in what manner it is so. How man attains to the possession of this blessing of salvation, in such a way that his life may effectively become faith, love, and hope, is the question we have next to answer. When previously (at the end of note (5), § 17) we specified, as the essential peculiarity of the gospel word of promise, that, in virtue of its connection with Christ Himself, the Dispenser of life (ζωὴν διδοὺς τῷ κόσμῳ), the power dwelt in it of bestowing such a life, in this word the objective means alone, and not the actual commencement of such a life, is indicated. And if we have pointed out faith as its subjective reception on our part, answering to this word of promise (§ 18), in the mere fact of our laying hold of it there has not yet been mentioned that working of God, the Giver of the word, which renders us capable of so doing. For the Scripture certifies that a work or operation of God is antecedent to any such reception of it by us in faith, qualifying us for it (§ 18, note (2)). This work of God in us is the origin and groundwork of the Christian life—the source of its power to believe, to love, and to hope. And since by this divine agency God effects in us the commencement of a new life, it is called a birth from God, and in distinction from the first birth of the flesh, regeneration. And since nothing which we can regard as specifically a movement of a Christian life can exist previous to this regeneration, all exposition of Christian life, as laid down by ethics, must begin with *regeneration*.

(1) In the testimony furnished us by Scripture concerning the new birth, we find a new confirmation of what we had at an earlier stage to deduce from the nature of the law and the gospel. It is a corroboration of the judicial sentence of the law; for, according to this, we find that man has nothing of himself and in himself by which he is enabled to begin living a life in God. And it is for this reason that Luther also, with reference to the commencement of Christ's discourse with Nicodemus, remarks: "In order to discourage such vain boasting, Christ begins at once *by rejecting him, both works and person.*" And the doctrine of regeneration is also a confirmation of what we derive in another way from the gospel. For since God, contrary to all human ideas, by His gracious gift of righteousness before Him, bestows on us beforehand that which we are wont otherwise to regard as the fruit and object of our own conduct (comp. § 18, note (5)); so He begins by living in us, and giving us as our own the power of His new-creating and transforming activity, in order that we may be enabled to live our life in Him. This fact must be definitely apprehended and expressed before I will speak of any working of life, by virtue of which I have my life in God. "For birth is the beginning of the whole life and of the whole man, who works not for this, that he may be born, but is first born to the end, that he may work" (Luther). "He who belongs to the kingdom of God and heaven must first have come into existence, before he begins to do works pleasing unto God" (*idem*).

With respect, however, to the idea of this birth, we must first keep steadfastly in view the fact that it is referred solely to God. It is a γεννᾶσθαι ἐκ Θεοῦ (John 1:13; 1 John 2:29, 3:9, 4:7, 5:1, 18); more clearly defined, ἐκ τοῦ Πνεύματος (John 3:8). The word is named as the means (ἀναγεγεννημένοι διὰ λογοῦ ζῶντος Θεοῦ καὶ μένοντος, 1 Pet. 1:23; ὃς ἀπεκύησεν ἡμᾶς λόγῳ ἀληθείας, Jas. 1:18), and baptism in like manner (ἐξ ὕδατος καὶ Πνεύματος, John 3:5; διὰ λουτροῦ παλιγγενεσίας καὶ ἀνακαινώσεως Πνεύματος ἁγίου, Tit. 3:5). The ἄνωθεν (comp. the δεύτερον of Nicodemus, John 3:4) points out, like the ἀνά and πάλιν, the position of this birth in relation to the first birth into the natural life, as beginning over again from the commencement, a second birth. The first, as the birth of the flesh, forms the contrast to the birth of the Spirit (τὸ γεγεννημένον ἐκ τῆς σαρκός, John 3:6). The new birth from God is a creative act—a κτίζειν; and its immediate result affects the spiritual life of the whole man, inasmuch as he is thereby made partaker of a new vital energy—a new principle of life—which is able to guide the ethical tendency of his nature in conformity with the will of God (κατὰ Θεόν), because it is from God (ἐκ Θεοῦ). For this reason the regenerate one is called a new creature—a new man (καινὴ κτίσις, 2 Cor. 5:17, Gal. 6:15; ὁ καινὸς ἄνθρωπος ὁ κατὰ Θεὸν κτισθείς, Eph. 4:24; ὁ νέος, ὁ ἀνακαινούμενος, κ.τ.λ., ὅπου πάντα καὶ ἐν πᾶσιν Χριστός, Col. 3:10). And what is new is characterized as being absolutely new also in the fact of its being contrasted with our former condition as life with death (ὡς ἐκ νεκρῶν ζῶντες, Rom. 6:13). And in this new vital principle is involved also the final and complete mastery over the death of the body, inasmuch as the resurrection of the body to a life of blessedness is to be accomplished by God through the Spirit which dwelleth in us (διὰ τοῦ ἐνοικοῦντος αὐτοῦ πνεύματος ἐν ὑμῖν, Cod. Sinait. Rom. 8:11). Moreover, this new power, so far as it concerns only the life produced in man, or the new *man*, resembles the natural birth also in this, that, just as man passes from the newborn child to the perfect man, so it has its stages of development. Such expressions, however, as ἀρτιγέννητα βρέφη (1 Pet. 2:2), νήπιοι (1 Cor. 3:1; Heb. 5:13; Eph. 4:14), by no means denote the evolution of the new vital principle in itself, but obstacles to our progress and improvement, which have their root in the weakness of the flesh and the opposition of the old man. Nay, the whole growth of which Scripture speaks is connected not only with the creature existence, and the process of development which goes on in the receptive man, but just as much also with that power which death holds in our old nature, which can only be gradually overcome by this new vital energy. This new principle of life is, however, in regeneration as incontestably present, wholly and indivisibly, as by the operation of the Holy Spirit not the half, but the whole Christ lives, works, and operates in him who is regenerate. There will then occur no difficulty in personally adopting this doctrine of regeneration in a manner not only intelligible, but consonant to experience, if we sufficiently separate the first creative act from its after results, and do not wrongly divide what is created from Him who is constantly creating, the operation from Him who is constantly operating, the birth from Him who is constantly begetting, and regard ourselves in the light of a product divorced from its producing cause, like a world perchance that, loosed from its Maker's hands, continues to maintain an independent existence. It is called, indeed, an accomplished act—a birth—like everything which has its beginning in time. That, however, which in this case has taken its beginning, is not merely a newly-originated spiritual life in men, but a spiritual communion of the living and everlasting God with us, which we can in no possible way destroy, unless by virtue of offences on account of which God is resolved to cause it to cease. Regeneration is consequently the commencement of that communion of God with us, by which He in Christ illumines us by the Holy Spirit with the light of life (φωτίζειν ζωήν, 2 Tim. 1:10), and creates in us a new thing which was not before in us. For the Beginner and Perfecter of the good work in us is God (ὁ ἐναρξάμενος ἐν ὑμῖν ἔργου ἀγαθὸν, ἐπιτελέσει ἄχρι ἡμέρας Ἰ. Χρ., Phil. 1:6), and all gifts and operations in us are manifestations of the present and acting God (1 Cor. 12:4-6), whose Spirit dwells within us (ἐνοικεῖ, 2 Tim. 1:4, Rom. 8:11). Hence it is purely impossible to separate the operation from Him who operates, the κτίσις from the κτίζων, the γέννημα or the γέννησις from the γεννῶν. And if we keep steadily in view the fact, that there must be the perfect communion of the regenerating God with us, even when the new life only commences in us, then there vanishes also the altogether untenable supposition of a regeneration only half accomplished—of a man half regenerate, and half not—as we should have to view the opposition between the old and the new man, if in our conception of regeneration we should only have regard to what takes place internally *in* man. But the idea of regeneration is not exhausted in that of a finished operation internally wrought on us and the complex state of our natural condition. Rather is it the commencement within us of an essential relation between us and the regenerating God. This relation, when once it has begun, is not half, but fully and entirely present: the bond of our union with the God who regenerates us is by that same God restored; and with the commencement of this bond of union, regeneration within the limits assigned to it upon earth is complete. For this very thing belongs to the nature of regeneration, that it does not all at once and mechanically transform the whole man, but that it transplants us into a perfect communion on the part of God with us, who comes to meet us with the fulness of His grace, in order that we may thereby obtain the power for a gradual transformation. But wherefore and to what extent does this belong to the *nature* of regeneration? This can only be clearly and distinctly answered in proportion as we discriminate between the idea of regeneration and that of its after-results (comp. *Form. Conc.* S. D. p. 613), and view it in its strictest and narrowest sense as an act and work of God in us, by virtue of which He bestows on our inner man, with the indwelling of His Holy Spirit, that which is to become the power of life and the commencement of *our* life in Him, by which we are once for all rescued from death and made alive, and indeed in such a manner that that which is bestowed upon us by God's grace in our regeneration as the vital power destined to have dominion over us, is recognized by us at the same time as an entirely new life, notwithstanding that we still feel in us the death of the old man. But how is it, then, that we are made alive by God, in spite of the fact that our life was not and is not a life in God? The Apostle Paul explains it (Col. 2:13): God has made us alive with Christ, *since He has of His grace freely forgiven us all our sins* (συνεζωοποίησεν σὺν αὐτῷ, χαρισάμενος ἡμῖν πάντα τὰ παραπτώματα). And inasmuch as this God, who in Christ forgives us our sins, enters into communion with us in the power of the Holy Ghost, we are saved from wrath and born again into a new life, whose power triumphs in us over sin and death, and whose continuance and certainty rest not in the life bestowed upon us, but in the continuance of the unchangeable truth of the merciful and gracious God: "Faithful is He that calleth us, who also will do it" (1 Thess. 5:24).

Of the act of God in itself and as such, by which, through the operation of the Holy Spirit, He enters into communion with us, and effects in us the groundwork and beginning of a new life, we are never conscious, but only in its results, which are at the same time impulses of our own life actuated by the Holy Ghost. The divine operation in itself by which we are regenerated, at whatever period of our existence it may be conceived as taking place, is and remains to our spiritual apprehension an unapproachable and hidden mystery, and is effected as unconsciously to ourselves as our procreation and birth in the natural life. Thus also in the domain of the spiritual life procreation and birth have already taken place, when our consciousness of the same first arises. So much the more is it of extreme importance that God has established the guarantee for the new birth which He accomplishes in us, not merely in the facts of our consciousness, but, above all, in His word and sacrament. He who receives this pledge has perfect certainty; but he who relies upon the facts of his consciousness alone, has at least in them a certainty not altogether free from doubt. It is nevertheless these facts of our own conscious life-impulses which, along with the guarantee which God has placed in His word and sacrament, must afterwards occupy our attention so much the more, since that gracious dawn of a new life which God works in us is hidden from us. "For," says Luther in a passage of which regeneration is the subject, "the grace of God is indeed a great, a mighty, and an active thing, not lying dormant in the soul, as a painted board bears its color, as the preachers of dreams represent. No, it is not thus. *It* supports, it leads, it impels, it draws, it changes, it effects everything in the man, and makes itself truly felt and realized. *It is hidden, but its works are not hidden; and where it exists, it shows itself in words and deeds*, just as the fruit and leaves of a tree manifest its species and nature."

The fact we have wished to establish in the foregoing is this, that the rise of a new life in the individual is in its origin purely an act of God, which the Holy Ghost accomplishes in our spirit, though not in our consciousness, in order that it may present itself to that consciousness as an act accomplished by God, and may be accepted by us with conscious will. We become new creatures not by any act of our own, but by God's act. If we consciously accept this gift of a new life, which is the indwelling of the Holy Spirit of the God who forgives us our sins, and willingly and consciously enter into it, it is not by this means that this indwelling is first made complete, but thereby it only attains the object for which it was accomplished by God. Just as we have the natural life complete by means of our birth, and do not first make it so by our consciousness of it, so also we have by that birth from God our new life complete, which is a living and working of God within us, and do not first make it so by the fact of our becoming conscious of it. In our conscious possession, and the conscious entrance of our will into the potencies of the one life as well as of the other, we only fulfil the design for which both the natural and spiritual life were bestowed upon us. We obtain by this conscious entrance of the will on the life thus given, in the one case as in the other (so far, that is to say, as we understand by the natural life, not the corruption which cleaves to it, but what God has willed and given it to be), not the life itself, but only *the blessing of this life* intended by God. The life itself, however, is by the divine operation present before our conscious participation. And since this indwelling of God by the Holy Spirit may also become for us a consuming fire (καὶ γὰρ ὁ Θεὸς ἡμῶν πῦρ καταναλίσκον, Heb. 12:29), that is to say, a curse instead of a blessing, if we consciously and willingly withdraw from it;—for this reason, and not in order first to make the idea of this new divine birth complete, which it is already in itself, is it of such importance here also not to stop at that which God alone effects, but forthwith to take into view that which as its consequence takes place, and must take place, in our own conscious and willing nature, if that which God has accomplished is to acquire a *blessed* permanence in us.

An example will more distinctly explain this. When, for instance, it is said that we become regenerate by faith, or that regeneration comes by faith, I could only assent to this with a reservation; but, on the other hand, I can without any reservation admit that we become and are regenerated *to* faith. For faith is as certainly already a fruit of this life born of God, as it is our own act by the working of the Holy Ghost. He, however, who has become a partaker of the Holy Ghost, has already that life from God, and does not first receive it through faith. When I, therefore, say that I become regenerated through faith, by this at least cannot be intended the origin of the life born of God, but only a means for the transplanting of that divine life (bestowed upon us in God's communion with us) into the conscious and willing life of our own souls. Or, in other words, God, who, according to His gracious will (βουληθείς, Jas. 1:18), has His life, working, and doing in me through the Holy Spirit, becomes to me in my own person a life *of blessedness* through faith. The Confession of our church marks with equal emphasis both these points. It says, "Spiritus Sanctus operatur fidem," or "fides est opus Spiritus Sancti;" and on the other hand, "Fides affert," or "accipit Spiritum Sanctum." Hence it follows that I do not receive by faith that Holy Ghost who produces faith, but conversely, that I must first be a partaker of the Holy Ghost before I can believe. Even so must that mode of action of the Holy Spirit, in which by means of faith He works and operates in me, consist in something else than in producing and bringing about faith. Moreover, this further working belongs not to the beginning, not to the birth of our life from God. Rather might I say, faith is the beginning of *my* life in God. If I wish to speak of my *conscious* life in God, then can I justly so speak; but not so, if I wish to indicate the beginning of that life—that is, of the creative energy of *God in us*, which produces faith. For faith itself is only the effect and product of this life and operation of God within, which regenerates us. First must a regeneration on the part of God have taken place in us, before we are able to believe, and in order to our being able to do so. And this I call the primal and fundamental regeneration, by virtue of which God begins a new thing in us, and not we in Him. And this new thing is *the gracious presence of God the Holy Ghost in us*. Before this we can conceive of nothing which can be called a life from God; and after it, nothing which does not presuppose this inward change in our relation to God. The entrance of this communion of God the Holy Spirit into our inner man is the hour of our birth into a new life, the regenerating starting-point and groundwork of a life where God works and acts in us; and all regeneration to faith, to love, to hope, and everything which may be called Christian life, where we live in God, is only the further result of that σπέρμα Θεοῦ implanted in us, with whose presence the regeneration from God begins. We do not yet ask here, how the man must be constituted in whom that regeneration which proceeds from God alone has reached its end and purpose. The question is rather only this: In what, then, does this new creation, this new work of God in us consist, by virtue of which we also are enabled to begin to live a new life of faith, etc., in God? He who will answer this question rightly has nothing else to name than the entrance of the energy of God the Holy Ghost into us, when the life of estrangement from God disappears, and that of nearness to God, and the presence of God in us, commences. This regenerating presence of God is everywhere to be thought of where we have a word of promise from God to this effect, that His Holy Spirit will dwell and work in a man.

§ 22. a. The Working of the Spirit of Regeneration on the Spirit of Man, and on the Personal Consciousness

Along with the operation of the Holy Spirit in our spirit, there begins, in contrast with our natural condition, a new relation and procedure of God toward us, in the shape of a real vital energy, in consequence of which a new course of conduct toward God on our part also is rendered possible. Inasmuch as the spiritual basis of our life becomes a partaker of the divine nature, there dwells within ourselves a divine ground for the determination of our conscious personal conduct (1). The connecting point for this fundamental working of God in and upon us, is the human spirit originally organized in its conscience for the reception of this agency of the Divine Spirit (§ 8). The new relation into which we enter by the operation of the Holy Spirit, is a communion of life with that Christ who died and rose again for us, in order that He might Himself become in us a power enabling us to give up our old life unto death, and to rise to a new life. By virtue of this bond of communion, in which we are joined to God in Christ by the Holy Ghost, we are no longer under wrath, but under grace; no longer under the dominion of the law which brings death, but under that of the Spirit which giveth life. And this is accomplished in us, without any co-operation on our part, at baptism, wherein we at the same time receive the divinely-appointed means, and the divinely-appointed pledge that such things can be effected and are effected in us by God (2). But all that is effected and accomplished in us has for its object to form the permanent ground of a growing and conscious creaturely life. And this can only become obvious to our consciousness in a double form: as grace to one who is conscious of deserved wrath; as the receiving of a good conscience by one who is conscious of an evil one; as an internal quickening of the law of God in our hearts, while we are conscious of the unfruitfulness of the external letter thereof; as a peaceful and joyful resurrection through the power of the God who forgives our sins, while we are conscious of that state of death into which the old man had fallen; as sorrow in joy, and as joy in sorrow. These are the pains of that divine birth, on whose dark background alone we become aware of and understand the peace- and joy-bringing power of the same birth. For that Christ who desires by the Holy Spirit to take up His abode in us, and to make us like Himself, is no other than He who has passed through death unto life, through suffering unto glory (3).

(1) What we have wished to assert in the above proposition is not to be found expressly taught in the passage, 2 Pet. 1:4; but it may be deduced from it and other testimonies of Scripture, and is consistent with a just knowledge of our own nature. In this passage of his second epistle, Peter mentions participation in the divine nature (ἵνα γένησθε θείας κοινωνοὶ φύσεως) as the aim of the promises given to us. And this takes place only when that which God Himself is, has become the normal ground of our own nature. This, however, is the case when that which we name the gift of God is not resolved into any quality of our creature nature produced in us by God, but is the communion of God Himself with us. And this view we have steadily adhered to in the former paragraph: "Spiritus Sanctus non est separatus a donis suis, sed in templo illo, quod donis suis exornat, etiam ipse habitat" (Joh. Gerhard). It is the Father and the Son who, in the communion of the Holy Ghost, take up their abode with us (John 14:23). The true significance of such a communion we see revealed to us in the incarnate glorified Son. "In Christo enim," says Athanasius, "natura nostra facta est consors divinæ." And in the same way another: "Quantum quisque habet Christi formitatis sive cum Christo conformitatis, tantum habet veræ Christianitatis" (compare Joh. Gerhard on 2 Pet. 1). If, therefore, we wish to characterize that which belongs to a divine nature in such a way as in one word to indicate what we may conceive as purely the fundamental destination and purely the aim of our own life, we might venture to say with Scripture, that it includes everything which is called good. Luther wrestles with language in his endeavor to exhaust all that is contained in that assertion of the Apostle Peter. "This," says he, "is such a saying, that its like is not to be found either in the New or the Old Testament, although to unbelievers it is a light thing that we should have communion with the divine nature itself. What, however, is the nature of God? It is eternal truth, righteousness, wisdom; eternal life,

peace, joy, and pleasure, and whatever we can call good. He, therefore, who is made a partaker of the divine nature, has the whole of this falling to his lot, that he lives eternally, and has everlasting peace, happiness, and joy, and is clean, pure, just, and all-powerful against the devil, sin, and death." In which words Luther evidently takes for granted what the apostle himself afterwards asserts, that all this which God has given would remain in us, if we remain in Him, and flee from that which is contrary to Him. If, however, that which may be truly called the regenerating communion of God with us, can take place in us, then must it enter into the spiritual basis of our natural life and being, no matter whether I regard the hearing of the word, or the taking of the sacrament of the new birth, as the means. What some one said, "Christianity must become natural to us," is to be taken in a much more exact sense than he himself meant it. If the way varies always according to the nature of the means, the end, the intended result, the true life-giving and regenerating communion of God, is reached in one and the same hidden fountain of all the creaturely and spiritual impulses of our life. What is to spring up from that inward source must have become in the unconscious depths of our spirit a creative and impelling power; in other words, this which is laid hold of in our consciousness is to be the genuine fruit of a sound root, the actual property of our nature, the homogeneous, evermore manifest working of that power which rules us in the inmost depths of our existence. If not, then that which is laid hold of in my consciousness remains something foreign to me, something indeed that I have apprehended, but which has not apprehended me. Then is it a mere external apprehending, but not a being apprehended inwardly. If, however, this last takes place, it shows itself not in the form of a conscious action of mine, but as something conditioning that conscious action. It makes itself felt as a power which comes upon me, and seizes upon my spirit, not as a power which I consciously, and in the way of self-determination, impart to myself. My own action in this domain is only that of consenting, of receiving into the form of what is self-perceived and self-chosen, and not an action self-derived and self-determining. If it is not so, then does the word heard cease to be a faith-producing power, and receives its power only from faith and through faith. Faith, however, is not a condition of the power of the word, but only the condition of the continuance of the blessed and saving operation of this power. There remains, under all circumstances, an act of God which lays hold of and quickens our spirit, *i.e.* the unconscious root of our conscious existence,—an act of God whence all true, living, life-giving, thinking, willing, and doing of our consciousness proceeds. And only thus it remains true in reference also to the word, that God has regenerated me through His word, and not I myself through my faith. He who is actually a believer knows that right well from his own experience. For true faith is never and in no case obtained, except in consequence of a spiritual quickening not springing from myself, nay, which stands opposed to my natural knowledge and will, which presents itself to my consciousness as an overpowering force, and to which, as a truth and actuality coming not from myself but from God, I say in faith, Yea and amen. And the fact remains quite the same, whether I regard this operation of God as effected either through the word heard, or through the sacrament received. This, however, has nothing in common with the so-called efficacy *ex opere operato*, inasmuch as the *blessing*-bestowing permanence of this work and working of God in all those whom He has laid hold of, and who are capable of a conscious faith, is made to depend on the presence and permanence of that faith.

If I had to define to myself clearly the distinction which marks that communion of the regenerating Spirit of God with us, as it is to be conceived of when effected by the hearing and reception of the word in faith, in the case of those who have not yet been received with us by baptism into the full communion of Jesus, I should only be able to express it as follows. In this case, we are never to expect that the efficacy of the Holy Spirit, when it commences, is at once present in all its fulness. For though Christ indeed, in all His fulness, stands over against me in His life-giving word, yet the full measure of His presence and efficacy is given only in proportion to the faith in which I appropriate the word to myself. Not that in itself the life-giving efficacy of God in the word was first rendered possible by my faith. On the contrary, it is the working of the word when unbelief is overcome in me, and faith is born. But in reference to its pervading my whole nature, the greater or less degree of the power it displays, whereby the commencement of the communion of the Holy Spirit through the hearing of the word is accompanied in us, is conditioned by the greater or less intensity with which I consciously turn to that word. For the conscious will of the natural man is of such a nature, that it closes as with bolts the approach to the inner man against that working of the Holy Spirit which comes upon him from without through the word; so that only in proportion as these bolts one after another give way, does the efficacy of God the Spirit penetrate deeper and deeper into our inner man. The true and precise central working of the Spirit of God upon the spiritual ground of our nature is, when the question turns upon the commencement of its agency through the medium of hearing the word, the successive result of a series of conducive spiritual events in proportion to the measure in which, when aroused and rendered capable by the word in conscious action, I unlock my inner man in faith to that word. It is otherwise with the sacrament of regeneration. There that fulness of God's fellowship with us, as it is appointed for us in this life, is bestowed as a free gift. The fountain of life sinks into our inmost man; and this full entrance of the fellowship of God with us is conditioned, not by the measure of our faith, but purely by the will of God touching His sacrament. Out of the spiritual groundwork of my being there spring up then, through God's agency, the waters which are destined to fructify my personal consciousness unto eternal life. Not that I have to obtain by means of a struggle a measure of God's fellowship proportioned to the measure of my own faith; but by God's will this fellowship has fully taken place, and only the degree of its blessing depends on that of my faith, and my faith can only guard against the conversion of that blessing into a curse. And here we have to repeat what we formerly had to say on this point (§ 21, note (1); § 18, note (5)) touching the exceeding glory of the grace of God in Christ, viz. that it prevents us in all things, and freely bestows upon us for the beginning and ground of our life in God, the full measure of that which God in Christ is for us.

(2) If Christian ethics is an exposition of the life which, as produced by God, is realized in Christendom and in a Christian man, it can take no other starting-point than baptism. Christ affirms baptism to be the condition of entrance into the kingdom of heaven (John 3); and baptism is the means entrusted to the church by which, among all nations, men are to be made disciples of Christ (Matt. 28:19). Our next task, therefore, for the end we have in view, will be to declare more precisely the way in which by baptism the commencement of a new life is brought about. That which takes place in baptism, Christ affirms to be something effected by the Spirit, and the man born of water and the Spirit to be one born of the Spirit (John 3:6, 8). And if in the command of Christ baptism is made to bear an equally prominent relation to the Father, the Son, and the Holy Ghost (Matt. 28), it is so done just for this reason, because the Holy Spirit, who by means of baptism begins His work in man, is both of the Father and of the Son (John 14:26, 15:26, 16:7; τὸ Πνεῦμα τοῦ Θεοῦ, τοῦ Κυρίου, Ἰησοῦ Χριστοῦ, τοῦ υἱοῦ; Rom. 8:9; 2 Cor. 3:17; Phil. 1:19; Gal. 4:6, etc.); and because that which He bestows He takes from what belongs to the Son; but what the Son has, the Father has just as much (John 16:14, 15). That, however, which begins in a man in and by means of baptism, is the gracious presence and the activity of God the Holy Ghost. And this is never to be softened down into a mere operation of the Spirit taking place on our spirit. Rather is it just God the Holy Ghost Himself who makes the relation of the Son to the Father actually vital within us; seeing that He it is who, as the Spirit of truth, of grace, and of life (John 14:17, 15:26, 16:13; Heb. 10:29; Rom. 8:2), in our hearts cries to God, Abba, Father (Gal. 4:6), and hereby renders possible to us a similar

appeal to God (Rom. 8:15), and confirms by His testimony that we are the children of God (Rom. 8:16), and Himself with supplication maketh intercession for us (Rom. 8:26). Wherefore also all ungodly conduct on the part of the Christian is termed, in the truest sense of the word, a grieving of the Holy Spirit (Eph. 4:30). The way, however, in which this presence of the Holy Ghost in us, and that especially in baptism, aims at bringing about our communion with Christ, may be briefly characterized as a fellowship of death and of life with Christ. We are buried with Him by baptism into His death for the resurrection of life (Rom. 6:4, 5; Col. 2:12), transplanted into the fellowship of His sufferings, conformed unto His death, in order to feel inwardly the power of His resurrection (Phil. 3:10). And since in such a manner, by virtue of the presence of the Holy Ghost, that Christ, who died and rose again for us, lives in and is present with us, therefore we who are baptized have "put on" Christ (Gal. 3:27), are made dead to the law (Rom. 7:4), appointed by God not unto wrath, but to obtain salvation (1 Thess. 5:9), are heirs of the grace of life (1 Pet. 3:7), washed clean from our sins (Acts 12:16), freed from an evil conscience (Heb. 10:22, 23), (since baptism secures to us that which we desire with God, viz. a good conscience (1 Pet. 3:21)), and now for the first time, by the aid of the indwelling Spirit, bear in our hearts the law of God, together with God's sin-forgiving mercy (Heb. 8:10, 12), and are freed from the body of flesh (Col. 2:11, 12), since the body is dead indeed because of sin, but the spirit is life because of righteousness (Rom. 8:10). In such a way is baptism the washing of regeneration and renewing of the Holy Ghost (Tit. 3:5). Our life is hid with Christ in God (Col. 3:3); but it is just a life of Christ in us, who, as having died and risen again as the Fulfiller of the law and the Deliverer from the curse of the law, is for us and makes intercession for us with God. And this indwelling of the Holy Spirit bears the shape of firstfruits—that is to say, of that by which a beginning is made (ἀπαρχή, Rom. 8:23)—but is at the same time a guarantee, an earnest of future complete redemption given in our hearts (δοὺς τὸν ἀρραβῶνα τοῦ Πνεύματος ἐν ταῖς καρδίαις ἡμῶν, 2

Cor. 1:22, 5:5; Eph. 1:14). The outward and sensuous man, who is given over to the doom of transitoriness, bears no trace of this; but the inward man, the hidden man of the heart—the "heart," the central point of the human personality—is the place where it desires to become effectual (comp. Eph. 3:16; 2 Cor. 4:16; 1 Pet. 3:4). And this dawn of light in our heart is compared to the *creative* fiat of God, who caused the light to shine forth out of darkness (2 Cor. 4:6). The work of the Holy Ghost, however, only then retains this creative character when all our life in Christ is preceded by a living presence of Christ in us through the Holy Ghost, as a result of which our life can no longer be a living to ourselves (ζῶ δὲ, οὐκέτι ἐγώ, ζῇ δὲ ἐν ἐμοὶ Χριστός, Gal. 2:20), but may become a life for Him who died and rose again for us (2 Cor. 5:15; comp. § 5, at the end of note (8)).

In all that takes place in baptism there is supposed not an acting of ours, but an acting and an internal, real, and effective relation of Christ, of which he becomes a partaker, whom Christ desires to make a sharer of the same according to His will ratified in His word and sacrament. A convert like Paul requires the same, and receives it at his desire (Acts 22:16), just as much and in the same way as it is bestowed upon the little children who cannot as yet desire it, but who are brought to the Lord by those who know what Christ desires to be and to become to the child also, as to every one who is born of the flesh (comp. respecting Matt. 19:13 ff., and the parallel passage, von Hofmann, *Schriftbeweis*, ii. 2, p. 197, 2d edition). That all flesh stands in need of baptism, and that the promise of Christ concerning His baptism is valid for all flesh, forms the ground on which rests the certainty of that faith in which infants are brought for baptism, and not a command or law enjoining infant baptism. "Baptism is free, and is not demanded or made compulsory, like circumcision. Therefore also it was not to be fettered and restricted to times, ages, places, and other externals, because it is quite free in itself" (Luther). Here, however (John 3), stands a plain declaration which applies universally to all, and is a *divine ordinance*. "Therefore it behoves us not willingly to despise or postpone it, for this would be wilfully to despise and neglect the ordinance of God" (*idem*). It is he alone who should wish to baptize only on faith, who would baptize on a "peradventure" (Luther), because he does not know the heart. He, however, who on God's ordinance and promise brings the child for baptism, he baptizes rightly. For he whom the Lord Jesus Christ takes in His arms, that one reposes there, whether sleeping or waking, whether man or child, hid in Him; and before all anxiety whether I may receive him, this must be my principal concern, to know whether He receives and has received me. And hence there exists no greater seal (*obsignatio*) of all subsequent faith than baptism, by which the Lord Jesus Christ owned me, and freely gave me His fellowship even before *I* was able to desire it. That a great part of those who at the present day call themselves believers know so little of this, is a circumstance which makes, to my eyes, the Christianity of many so lame and slothful, so little courageous against death, and confident of victory. But he alone can cradle himself in false security, who, aroused to a perfect self-consciousness, desires to attain the *blessing* of baptism without faith, and forgets the warning words against a wicked, unbelieving heart (βλέπετε, μήποτε ἔσται ἔν τινι ὑμῶν καρδία πονηρὰ ἀπιστίας, ἐν τῷ ἀποστῆναι ἀπὸ Θεοῦ ζῶντος, Heb. 3:12).

(3) It lies in the nature of that relation in which Christ gives Himself to us in the fellowship of the Holy Spirit to become ours, that it can only become known to our consciousness in the form of an opposition overcome by Christ, and continually to be overcome by us in Him. Our heart ought not to be troubled, and will not be afraid, if Christ leaves us peace, and gives us His peace, not as the world gives (John 14:27). He who in Christ is not at peace, has in Him at the very same time one whom John the Seer reports as saying, "All whom I love, I rebuke and chasten" (Rev. 3:19). And hence a change of mind never takes place or continues without a godly abiding sorrow preceding it (ἡ κατὰ Θεὸν λύπη, 2 Cor. 7:10). Since, then, we have our life in Christ as a life out of death, as a continual death and resurrection, how shall I comprehend the riches of Christ

without a consciousness of my own poverty, and His comfort, unless I feel also the smart of my own sorrow? How shall I be satisfied through Him, without a hunger and thirst after righteousness? (Matt. 5:3, 4, 6.) How shall I seek His righteousness without the knowledge of my unrighteousness, and His forgiveness of sins without a consciousness of my sins? How shall I seek the strength of His life without the feeling of the death that is in me; and His acquittal of me from judgment, and the dominion of the law, without the feeling of the goad and condemnation of the law, and His grace without the feeling of the wrath of God upon me? Nay, in the death of Christ, the wrath of God, and that tender compassion which swallows up that wrath, are so far concentrated, that, when this Christ becomes alive in me, His life can only be experienced by me as a fire which consumes my old nature, and as a light which, with a new life rescued from God's wrath, illumines my darkness. There is no life with Christ without a dying with Him, no partaking of His dominion without sharing His endurance, no partaking of His glory without participation in His sufferings (2 Tim. 2:11, 12; Rom. 8:17).

There is, nevertheless, no description of the phenomena of that form of life and consciousness which developes itself out of the spirit of regeneration in itself. The divine pedagogy has not only bound up from the beginning that offer of salvation as it has to be made by the community of believers in Christ in baptism, with the teaching of what Christ has enjoined (Matt. 28:16); but the work and working of the Spirit are just this, to put us in mind of all that Christ has said (John 14:26). Therefore, if you wishest to find yourself in Christ, then hast you to seek and to find yourself not in the incomprehensible spirit of your regeneration, but in Christ's word. If you findest yourself and your life in this word, then hast you indeed to thank for it the same Holy Spirit, who for the conscious life of your soul has and desires to have His work in the word and by the word, and by this alone. But if you lose yourself and your life, then dost you lose it because you wish to seek and to find it purely in the Spirit, and independent of the word, that is to say, of God's discipline. By the word it will be shown whether the spirit within thee is the Spirit of God, who has sealed the word, and says to the word, Yea and amen (comp. § 17, at note (5)). And all phenomena connected with the faithful believer, who is born of God and arrived at a consciousness thereof, will always be concentrated in the blessed confession: "Lord, to whom shall we go? you hast the words of eternal life. And we have believed, and known, that you art the Holy One of God" (John 6:68, 69).

§ 23. b. The Appropriation of the Spirit of Regeneration in our Conversion

It belongs to the original organization of the human spirit, that every impulse thereof, no matter whence its source, that arises in the individual who has reached the maturity of his creature life, is and continues its own actual personal property, only so far as that by which we feel ourselves spiritually determined, is and continues to be at the same time willed by ourselves (comp. § 5). It is consonant, therefore, to the will of God the Creator and Redeemer, that what He bestows upon us by the working of the regenerating Spirit—that is to say, the property assigned to us—should be appropriated by the conscious individual, and should be voluntarily embraced by him. So much the more so for this reason, that the working of the regenerating Spirit has for its object to subdue the selfish will, and to awake in us a life in which we no longer wish to live unto ourselves. Freedom to this end—that is, the power and the actual inclination thus to will—springs from a working of the Spirit of God upon our spiritual nature, by virtue of which God Himself renders it possible for us, in Him and through Him, to be able to will that which is of God (1). So far, therefore, as this willing on our part has for its ground a causality which we must attribute not to ourselves, but to God who prevents us [with His grace], such willing is not the work of man, but of God. So far, on the other hand, as the work of God in us attains the object at which it aims only by a voluntary, self-appropriating, but still self-abjuring action of the individual, this operation of God, when it has thus reached its object, is perfected by an inward deed and an inward acting on the part of man. It is only where that inclination of the heart, (never to be separated from God's active working,) exists, voluntarily to enter upon that which the God who has thus made Himself ours causes us spiritually to experience, that the design and end of the regenerating Spirit is attained in the conscious man (2). But this agency of God's Holy Spirit upon our spirit, as a result of which our hearts are disposed voluntarily to apply themselves to this work of God within us, is not to be termed a general, or virtually an indefinable one. On the contrary, God's Holy Spirit causes us to realize a something quite distinct, which as a passive experience precedes all inward acting of our wills, and which works in us that disposition of heart which determines our will in conformity with that of God. We are to regard as the working of that God who is alike holy, and a God reconciled and graciously disposed to us in Christ, on the one hand our anguish of conscience, and on the other our yearning after peace with God, which inclines us to lay hold of that which God in Christ is for us and has done for us (3). This twofold passive experience worked in us by God is the ground, which determines us voluntarily to desire what God in Christ holds out to us in His word as our highest good. And it is the actual disposition of the human will springing from this, which we call, as well at its commencement as in its permanent existence, man's conversion (4).

(1) So far as what we have here said has reference at the same time to the understanding of our own spiritual organization, we refer back to what has been discussed in § 5, note (4), § 8, note (4), and § 11, note (1). The chief point, however, in connection with ethics, which we must keep steadily in view, consists, on the one hand, in the fact that our life in Christ can in no wise begin without a fundamental and actual relation of God in Christ to our spirit,—a relation whose substantial nature is withdrawn from our consciousness, but

whose effective energy is guaranteed to us in the word of promise, and its sacramental effect upon us; and that, on the other hand, the continuance of this actual relation of God to us becomes a blessing only when it is presented to our consciousness in a series of effects, whose common characteristic is, that we become aware of them as impulses of our own will, the causality of which we are unable to find in ourselves and our own nature, but in God alone, as the real ground of the deliverance of our life from the compulsion of our natural proclivities. And herein is perfected, in the sense of our restoration, a state of mutual relation between God and man, for which the spiritual nature of man was from the very beginning organized. This *restitutio in integrum*, however, takes place under those modifications which are determined, on the one hand by the now corrupt tendency of man's nature, on the other hand by the peculiarity of that act of redemption in which God again turns to man, and, by a bond of communion proceeding from Himself, and which has a delivering and redeeming power, unites Himself with man. For that which is primitive in regeneration is a new and actual relation of God to man; and on such relations of the real ground of our existence to our spirit rests altogether all so-called power of man, which is purely and truly spiritual, and which specifically belongs to him. And if I call this power freedom, I da so also for this reason, because "that which we justly designate with the name of the freedom of the human spirit, lies exclusively in the mutual relation between God and man,—not, however, in the creature as such, conceived of as separate and void of this actual relation." That which is able to take us out of the domain of the purely earthly tendency of our nature, is to be sought for, not in nature by itself, but in God, the Creator and Preserver of nature. That, however, which by virtue of this mutual relation appears in our nature as so-called qualities, consists only of functions which arise within us, as the result of that mutual relation between the Creator and the creature which we have to regard as uninterruptedly at work. And that which presents itself to our consciousness is not the substantial relation in itself, but it is rather the effects, phenomena, results, workings of the mutual relation of two quantities, God and our spirit, which form the real ground of our existence. But wherever these effects have really penetrated into the inmost life of our spirit, there they reveal themselves to us as solicitations of our will, as that in which man has the true actuality of his organization. Such, as we have already seen, is the nature of that relation of God to the human spirit, whose phenomena we comprise under the name of conscience,—phenomena also, that we were only able to explain by an actual relation of God to the spiritual groundwork of our existence. That which constitutes its peculiarity, however, depends at the same time upon that position which God Himself assumes in this relation, since He turns Himself against our selfishness only in such a way as to make us sensible of the antagonism of His nature and will to our depraved nature and will. Herein lies the reason why, in those relations which are supposed in conscience in themselves, there lies no power of being able, in that God who testifies against us, to will in conformity with His will. The new relation, however, into which God in Christ through the Holy Ghost enters with us, is of a purely opposite nature. It is that relation in which God turns to us, because He in Christ is for us, and with us. If this relation is to become one full of effect in us, and one that shall stimulate our will, this can only be accomplished by the taking place of an actual mutual relation between God and the spiritual basis of our nature. For just as little as there exists an abstractly conceived will of man, which as such might subsist or become a reality, isolated from man's natural spiritual basis, so little is there a supposed abstract causality of the Holy Spirit, which might call forth an effect of the will, if the Holy Spirit of God had not first in some other way entered into a relation of communion and attraction with the basis of our own spiritual nature. Only that this attraction does not solicit our will without the instrumentality of another operation, which stands in the relation of the negative pole to the positive. For if this entrance of God within us is to become an effectual determining ground for our willing, then is it impossible to conceive this to take place without our feeling ourselves at the same time impelled to go out from and to turn from ourselves unto God. For God enters not into the new relation with the human spirit, as we must conceive it to have been according to its original organization, but as it is in its actual condition, swayed and corrupted by selfish desires. And it is in the breaking down of these selfish tendencies, that the operation of that Holy Spirit who enters into fellowship with us first negatively reveals itself. And this rupture with our selfish desire is, moreover, only accomplished in such a way that we ourselves become to ourselves an object of that aversion which the Scripture terms a hating of one's self,—a hate by which we gain ourselves, since we strive to seek and to find ourselves not in ourselves, but in God. Only this is no longer a seeking which takes place while we are still far from God, nor a finding in which we by our seeking establish and effect a fellowship with God. Both are rather an irresistible working of that fellowship of God with us which has already begun, which shines as a light into our darkness, reveals to us the darkness of our selfish nature, and makes us deserving of hatred in our own eyes. And from this hatred, the energy of God, who in His grace does not disdain to let His light shine into our darkness, becomes our own energy, by which we turn against ourselves; and thus, in that abnegation of self and our own selfish nature, the possible basis of which can by no means be thought of as in our own nature, but only as proceeding from God and His working on us, we become participators of the only true freedom. For then alone, when we divest ourselves of *self*-will, the will becomes free for the enjoyment of that freedom which is essentially freedom, because it is not of ourselves, but of God. But this is accomplished within us only in such a way, that what we term the effect of God's Spirit becomes in us an affection which tears us off from ourselves, and thus inclines and enables us to will not that which is of ourselves, but that which is of God. This is the sense in which Luther bids us distinguish between *self*-will and *free*-will. "We never rightly name or understand free-will, unless it be adorned with the grace of God, without which we should rather term it *self*-will than *free*-will."

Freedom, according to Scripture, only exists where the Spirit of the Lord is (2 Cor. 3:17). And just when delivered through Christ from his selfish nature, does the man who is so delivered by Christ actually become the servant of Christ (ἀπελεύθερος Κυρίου = δοῦλος Χριστοῦ, 1 Cor. 7:22). And in this relation he experiences what true freedom is. For only when the Son makes us free are we truly free (John 8:36). It is a *law* of the Spirit of life that makes us free in Christ Jesus from the law of sin and death (Rom. 8:2). For it is a relation equally consistent with law, that is to say, established in the nature of the case, that man abandoned to himself, and taking himself as his only standard, neither has nor can have the true life, which exists not in the relation of man to himself, but to God. Where, however, the Spirit of freedom from God enters, there is His first business to direct Himself in the way of winnowing and judging against that spirit of bondage to selfishness. And just to this purpose also is the instrument of the Spirit, the word of God, applied, which presents itself as a discerner (κριτικός) of the thoughts and intents of the heart, powerful and sharper than any two-edged sword (Heb. 4:12). For he who is to be born of God unto life, the same must first be given over to the bitter pangs of death. And where the love of God to us and our love to God is to enter into us, there must first our selfish love to ourselves be buried. For, as Christ says, "He that loves his life shall lose it: and he that hates his life in this world, shall keep it unto life eternal" (John 12:25). To arrive, however, at such a hatred, man must first have become conscious of something else than that life of his which stands related merely to this world. The relation of the living God to his soul must first have dawned on man as the experience of a good, whose result is that he shrinks in horror from clinging to his life, to his Ego, for itself as an object worthy of his love.

(2) If we wish to represent to ourselves the relation of that which is effected by God's regenerating Spirit, to that which by

virtue of His operation arises within us, we have something analogous in all that takes places in the willing and conscious spirit, by the force of a natural creaturely endowment (talent). There also an effect is antecedent to all conscious willing, which proceeds from an effective combination of those real elements, as they form the basis of our individual existence and our individual organization, calling forth effects which first form the contents and object of our conscious will. Without such antecedents, will and consciousness are absolutely void. It lies within our own power to allow this or that effect to pass, by an act of will either consenting to it or rejecting it. But the possibility of this willing adoption lies not in the will itself as will, but purely in the effect, which springs from the combination of those real elements of our individual existence which are beyond the reach of our consciousness. If we name this a natural gift or natural endowment, this term is not quite suitable, inasmuch as the gift is not a fixed product, but a constant process of the substance of our organization in its state of action and reaction. At all events, there is something which we can neither make nor bestow upon ourselves by our own will, and which we must possess beforehand, ere there can be a procedure of our will corresponding to it. Under all circumstances, however, this individual determination of nature, which is not produced by our own will, is the only real ground of the possibility of a productive act of the will corresponding to it. Hence we possess, by virtue of the so-called natural endowment, in an effect which is independent of our will, but which takes place antecedently in our spiritual life, the possibility of effecting something by our will, which rises from the form of a natural tendency to that of a something willed by ourselves. If now we wish to designate that which takes place independently of our will within us a *passive* state, and to distinguish the operation of willing which it renders possible and conditions as inner *action*, then the assertion would run thus, that in general, without something passive as well as something active, no perfect result follows. But the very notion of this passivity itself presupposes some actual energy within us, which we avoid naming action in that specific sense alone in which our action is to us that which has for its immediate causality our will when excited by something, or struggling after something. And so that which we name *passivity* is not an absence of excitement, but only the designation of our subjective relation to some causal excitement, which is distinguished from the conscious excitement of our will as a *motus primus* from the *motus secundus*. So far the analogy, as it presents itself in the phenomena of the natural life. Now it is in the same sense only we are able also to say, that man stands as passive in his relation to the operation of the regenerating Spirit of God in him. By this, however, nothing more is affirmed, than that the causality of that excitement, as it here takes place in the spirit of man, is to be sought not in man, but in God alone. The operation itself is, however, a stirring of the spirit of the creature by God. And where this stirring attains its end and purpose, there it comes to that second movement which is conditioned by the first, that I—namely, by my own act—turn myself willingly to that which, independently of my will, has presented itself to my consciousness as a solicitation of my will.

(3) The effect produced in my spirit by the Spirit of God, as it becomes a solicitation of my will and desire, resembles the truth of that actual relation which has been revealed in Christ. The Holy Spirit takes of the things that are Christ's. Now Christ is actually our Peace, and the Prince of peace, that is to say, the Reconciler of the rupture between God and man. But He is so not as the denier, but as the affirmer of this rupture. He does not so deliver us from the accusations of conscience and the judgment of the law, that He should deny their truth and righteousness; but He affirms both, since He vicariously allows the sentence of the law to take effect in His own person, and perfects the triumph of God's mercy over the righteous judgment. Such He desires by the working of the Holy Ghost to make known to our inner experience. And thus, from Christ the Prince of peace, something arises in us which does not in any way resemble peace. And the point of connection which is

organized in the creature for this energy of Christ in us, is just the human conscience. And thus the work of peace resembles in one aspect a work of destruction, for it is the destruction of the slothful and false peace of conscience. It is a solicitation to the hunger after grace, in a keener feeling of the anguish of conscience. And above the despair, which such anguish in itself would bring with it, the Lord lifts us only by allowing really to happen in us that which He testifies to us in His word,—namely, that in our groaning after complete deliverance, the Holy Spirit Himself intercedes for us before God with groanings that cannot be uttered (Rom. 8:26); as also already in the Old Testament this is the comfortable certainty, that God does not despise the broken and contrite heart (Ps. 51:19; comp. Isa. 57:15). And also it is certainly not the case, that such groaning forms merely the beginning, but ceases with the full possession of grace in this world. On the contrary, here below it forms the dark but permanent background of the bright peace in Christ (Rom. 8:23; comp. 2 Cor. 5:4, Rom. 7:24). Wherever, in opposition to this, a false feeling of supposed riches and of a need of nothing will make its appearance, this is destined to be destroyed by a recognition of the fact, of how wretched, miserable, poor, blind, and naked we are (Rev. 3:18). This is the call with which Christ stands at the door and knocks: if any one listens to this voice, and opens the door, Christ enters and sups with him, and he with Christ (Rev. 3:20). This opening of the door on the part of man I call his conversion (ἐπιστροφή, Acts 15:3).

(4) In the same sense Luther also employs the word conversion. "What is conversion?" he asks, in the *Exposition of the Prophet Hosea*. "Nothing else than obedience to the gospel, which reproves the world because of sin, righteousness, and judgment." It is the same use of the word which older dogmatists designated *conversio intransitiva*, and distinguished from the *conversio transitiva* as the fundamental operation of God in us: "Intransitive accepta conversio significat actum voluntatis immanentem et reciprocum, quo peccator seipsum convertere denominatur. Conversio

intransitiva est terminus et effectus conversionis transitivæ estque ipsa pœnitentia, qua peccator per vires, a gratia convertente collatas et passive receptas, seipsum convertere dicitur.... De conversione intransitiva notari merentur verba Petri Act. 3:19: Agite pœnitentiam, et convertite vos (καὶ ἐπιστρέψατε), ut deleantur peccata vestra. Quam ob rem peccator, pœnitentiam agendo, se convertit viribus non nativis, sed dativis" (Hollaz, *exam. theol.* pp. 853, 854). It is correct that the Scripture word which corresponds to our term serves also to designate the converting energy of God upon us (comp. with Jer. 31:18 the passage 1 Pet. 2:25, where ἐπεστράφητε will have perhaps a passive signification). Quite as often, however, the converse also is to be found (comp. Isa. 6:10 with Matt. 15:13; John 12:40 with 2 Cor. 3:16, 1 Thess. 1:9). If, therefore, we use the word exclusively in the latter sense, we do so for this reason, that otherwise, in our conception, regeneration and conversion coincide, and it becomes difficult to keep properly distinct and separate, for the object of understanding it, that which is indeed essentially bound together, but is not one and the same in the form of its inner process. This was also the ground why the earlier divines, as Buddeus and Pfaff, after the example of Quenstedt (*Syst. theol.* T. ii. p. 705), König (*Theol. posit.* P. iii. § 451), distinguished conversion in the narrower sense of the word from regeneration, and indeed attributed the latter to the baptized infant; not, however, the former. And it appears to me they were fully justified in so doing. For by this means alone we can keep a stedfast hold of that which, in reference to the inward process of conversion, is of such infinite practical importance,—namely, that in this it is not a question of a relation of God to us, which once for all has really taken place, and has at its entrance a complete existence, but of a procedure on man's part, which has its course, its definite stadia, its beginning and its progress—in short, has its vicissitudes, which are to be explained not from the nature and attributes of the God who works in us, but from the nature of man, and the relation in which he stands to that operation of God. That is also the signification of that assertion of Chemnitz, the importance of which Thomasius has justly brought forward with prominence (*Person and Work of Christ*, iii. 1, p. 417): "Conversio non est talis mutatio, quae uno momento statim omnibus suis partibus absolvitur et perficitur, sed habet sua initia, suos progressus, quibus *in magna infirmitate* perficitur." (Comp. Joh. Gerhard, *locc. th.* T. v. p. 204.) In regeneration I fix my gaze stedfastly on the great power of God; in conversion, on man's great weakness. And with respect to the "course" of conversion above hinted at, it may, in contrast to an earlier state of my conscious soul-life which is conceivable, occur as a definite and decisive act taking place but once. If, however, it has once decidedly happened, yet here below it moves on only as a continual turning from and turning to.

§ 24. c. *The Nature and Permanence of Conversion, and the Criteria of the Converted Man which result therefrom*

Our experience of the force with which God can break the heart, and rebuke us by means of our conscience, is the first impulse towards conversion, which removes the internal obstacle to our reception of grace. Where, however, conversion itself has taken place, there this passive sorrow (λύπη) has led to a change of mind, and a mental revolution (μετάνοια), in which we our own selves alike forsake that within us which constitutes the bitter root of such a sorrow, and turn to the God who stills and lays to rest the sorrow of the soul and the anguish of conscience (1). For the work of the Holy Spirit in our hearts consists in this, that He testifies to the truth of the twofold word, and quickens it in us,—the twofold word which, as the word of one and the same God, condemns us in the law, and in the gospel rescues us from this condemnation, in such a manner that we become recipients of grace only in the proportion in which we judge ourselves rightly. To this relation of the regenerating Spirit of God to us, in which the working of the law and the gospel coincide in *one* "mathematical" point, the nature of conversion must be equivalent (2). We do not yet ask what further conditions and activities must follow, where conversion has actually taken place. Rather is this alone the question: How and where conversion has so taken place, that we willingly permit the working of that which the regenerating Spirit of God works in us. We gather this just from the way and manner in which the one and the same Spirit of regeneration in us operates as a convincing and also as a comforting Spirit (3). Such is the relation, namely, in which the Holy Spirit as the Spirit of God stands to us, whose wrath is so swallowed up in grace that He delivers the sinner unto death, not to leave him in death, but in order by this very death to make him alive. And since we become conscious of this in an undivided way, the passive sorrow of our conscience also undergoes a change. For the change of heart, if it in this point of view may be named genuine repentance, consists in this, that I, in so suffering from the stings of conscience, have also become willing to let myself be rebuked and condemned, and to acknowledge the justice of this rebuke and of this condemnation with my whole heart. Otherwise I do not become free of the lie and a partaker of the truth, in which I give honor to the God who judges rightly (4). But this readiness is not attained by the perception of the rebuke and the merited judgment by itself, but through a contemporaneous consciousness and belief of the consoling design with which God's regenerating Spirit causes me to feel the conviction of the judgment I have deserved. For the consolation of which I am made certain by the Holy Ghost is this, that in such rebuke God desires not the death of the sinner, but that he should turn and live. This, however, is not the case in a conversion in which I perhaps imagine that, on account of my repentance, I shall become a recipient of grace, or be justified before God. For in repentance I recognize only the justice of the judgment I have merited, and willingly allow myself to be judged, because in the very midst of this judgment I at the same time, and out of the same source, but through other means, experience consolation. That, however, is the consolation of which the Holy Ghost makes me certain,— namely, that for Christ's sake, in whom judgment is swallowed up in grace, God makes over to me forgiveness of sins in His word of promise. If I receive this grace, which serves only to confirm God's judgment impending over me and all flesh; that is to say, if I cheerfully consent to this, that God accepts me a sinner, not on account of my repentance, but for Christ's sake,—then has my conversion fully taken place. Such willing acceptance comes to pass, however, only in faith (§ 18). For in repentance, in so far as it only feels the anguish of the conscience and the brokenness of the heart, there is accomplished in me only the operation of God the Holy Spirit as confirming the truth of the law. In faith, however, which makes the alarmed soul willing to kiss the rod, to submit to judgment, and nevertheless to comfort itself with grace, the agency of the Holy Spirit, as confirming the truth of the gospel, reaches its consummation. Both these effects must be indissolubly united in one, if salvation is really to be the result. For if I surrender my own will to the *whole* will of God, as expressed in the law and the gospel, I can make this surrender only in faith and repentance. Hence we can name nothing else but faith and repentance as the essential marks of that conversion, in which the law and the gospel coincide in *one* saving result. Repentance impels me to that faith which appropriates salvation, and faith conditions the saving character of repentance, and makes me confident of the same. For in faith alone, and not in repentance, I receive the power of life; but I do not arrive at faith without repentance, by which I perceive my need of grace, and the necessity of an appropriation of the same in faith.

(5) The relation in which the Spirit of regeneration stands to me is not this, however, that God extirpates the old man, in order by an act of creation to put a complete new man in his place; but God desires, by the gracious presence and operation of the Holy Spirit, to bestow upon me the real possibility of overcoming the death of the old man, and, in spite of sin which still cleaves to me, of appropriating the grace of forgiveness of sins, and the free gift of righteousness before God. This relation of God to me is here below a permanent one; and just because it is to endure for the whole of this life, at no stage of my life is

any other form of appropriation of this saving relation of God to me conceivable, than that in which I in my conversion for the first time enter upon it. If, therefore, this surrender to God's gracious will, which takes place once for all in our conversion, becomes permanent, we can have no other mark of a converted man than the permanence of that penitent faith, nor other criterion for the decision of the question whether or not he is in that condition in which he may confidently comfort himself with the grace of God in Christ as being sure to him (6).

(1) Compare on this point § 18, at the commencement of note (4). The signification of the Scripture word μετάνοια, "change of mind," is a wider one than that of the German word *Busse* (repentance) in its original sense. For it serves equally to denote the turning away from what is opposed to God (μετανοεῖν ἀπὸ τῆς κακίας, Acts 8:22; μετάνοια ἀπὸ νεκρῶν ἔργων, Heb. 6:1; ἐκ τῶν ἔργων τῆς πορνείας, Rev. 2:21: comp. ch. 9:20, 16:17, = ἀποστρέφειν ἀπὸ τῶν πονηρῶν, Acts 3:26), as the turning to God (ἡ εἰς Θεὸν μετάνοια, Acts 20:21, = ἐπιστρέφεσθαι εἰς Θεόν). But just because the word embraces both relations, it serves to indicate at one time the one aspect, at another the other by itself (ἐν σάκκῳ καὶ σποδῷ μετανοεῖν, Matt. 11:21; μετανοεῖν καὶ ἐπιστρέφειν, Acts 3:19, 26:20; μετανοεῖν ἐπὶ τῇ ἀκαθαρσίᾳ, κ.τ.λ., 2 Cor. 12:21: compare this with the passage above cited, Acts 20:21), where, for example, according to the idea conveyed in the word, the change brought about by repentance does not yet express the conversion effected by faith. In the nature of the thing itself, however, the true signification is always given only where these two elements coincide. And in this sense alone we here employ it. In both points of view, however, in μετάνοια, μετανοεῖν, "change of mind," it is indicated by the word itself that this process is to be regarded as having its seat in the conscious, individual and personal spirit-life, in the disposition directed to a determinate end, that is to say, capable of impelling itself in an actual direction of the will. For the word νοῦς, like our German *Sinn* and *Gesinnung*, serves to denote the mind of man

somehow or other ethically directed. Thus the conduct of the heathen is characterized as ματαιότης τοῦ νοός, Eph. 4:17; ἀδόκιμος νοῦς, ποιεῖν τὰ μὴ καθήκοντα, Rom. 1:28. On the other hand, the fellowship with Christ has its expression and its realization in the unity of the same mind (νοῦς) and the same judgment (γνώμη), 1 Cor. 1:9, 10. And in cases where (in things not to be decided by ethics) there arises difference of opinion, there it becomes incumbent on us at least to attain in our own mind (ἐν τῷ ἰδίῳ νοΐ) a clear and full conviction of that which therein it is ethically lawful to desire (πληροφορείσθω, Rom. 14:5, comp. 6). The root of everything which shapes itself in the mind, lies of course in (so to say) an affection of the spirit (πνεῦμα). An ethical result, however, is reached only in the form of a definite, individual and personal tendency of mind. This is meant, when it is said that he who has become a partaker of the Holy Spirit, the πνευματικός, has the mind of Christ (νοῦν Χριστοῦ, 1 Cor. 2:16), or when it is said that we need a renewal in the spirit of our mind (ἀνανεοῦσθαι τῷ πνεύματι τοῦ νοὸς ὑμῶν, Eph. 4:23), that is to say, in our spirit, as it is the impelling and determining power of the conscious tendency of our mind. And just because in the νοῦς the rule of our spirit in its ethical determination comes to light, νοῦς may be precisely used for πνεῦμα in the ethical relation in which the spirit stands (comp. Rom. 7:23, 25). If νοῦς, however, serves to denote that in which it differs from πνεῦμα, and has its own characteristic peculiarity, it everywhere signifies that which has entered into our conscious intelligence and the conscious tendency of our will. This is not a mere "formal and complementary notion" with respect to πνεῦμα (G. v. Zezschwitz, *Profane Greek and Biblical Forms of Speech*, p. 73), but an entirely concrete name for real psychological processes. And in this sense I assert, that that which takes place in regeneration is accomplished in the spirit (πνεῦμα) of man; and that which takes place in conversion (ἐπιστροφή = μετάνοια) is accomplished in his mind or disposition (νοῦς) as a conscious, individual and personal tendency of the will. From a similar relation, that passage is to be explained where sorrow (λύπη) is distinguished from that repentance which is not to be repented of (μετάνοια ἀμεταμέλητος), and the first is declared to be that which leads to the second (2 Cor. 7:10). This "godly" sorrow lays hold of the spirit, not the flesh, and makes the mind meet for wholesome repentance. Just in the same way also, conversely, we may conceive of processes in the spirit in which the νοῦς remains unfruitful (comp. that statement, τὸ πνεῦμά μου προσεύχεται, ὁ δὲ νοῦς μου ἄκαρπός ἐστιν, 1 Cor. 14:14): for where the process perfected in the spirit has had a fruitful working in the individual and personal existence, there is it brought to light in the νοῦς of man, and makes him able to enter with his full consciousness into that which moves in his spirit. In brief, that which is called πνεύματι ἄγεσθαι must come to an ἀνακαίνωσις τοῦ νοός (Rom. 12:2).

This is not an idle and merely theoretical distinction, but of the greatest practical importance. There are not a few who, in the domain of the spirit, never in their life pass beyond what I call temporary affections of the spirit. By these I understand not beginnings beyond which we may pass in our progress, but rather radical elementary conditions, which do not produce the fruit for which they were bestowed, if we do not concentrate ourselves upon them with our conscious will. For then we stop at the fitful change, but never reach conversion. And with such fitful changes, of which experience supplies instances enough, we then console ourselves, and regard them as conversion.

(2) Since the regenerating Spirit, in the essential peculiarity of His nature, is called a Spirit of grace and life, of peace and joy, and so forth, one has often been tempted to overlook the means by which, as such, He manifests His activity, and has torn asunder the totality of the relations in which God stands to us by His Holy Spirit, and regarded it in the light of a partial and fragmentary work. Just as if the law ceased to have force where the gospel has its work; God's holy indignation against sin had none, where His grace prevails; judgment had none, where the forgiveness of sins rescues us from its sentence. Thus we come to imagine that the entrance of conversion is the

restoration of a condition in which nothing but peace and joy exist, and, as in the future glory, there is neither sorrow nor crying any more. And yet the Confession of our church already justly says, that the Holy Ghost fulfils both offices: He kills, and makes alive; He leads into hell, and brings us out again;— which office is not only to comfort, but also to reprove, as it stands written: When the Holy Ghost is come, He will reprove the world (and in this is the old Adam also included) of sin, of righteousness, and of judgment (*Form. Conc.* P. xi. Sol. Decl. p. 642). In practice, says Luther, the law and the gospel are "more closely associated than any mathematical point" (on Gal. 3). And so is it also with the "practice" of the Holy Ghost. And just for this reason, because it is the office of the Holy Ghost to bring to life in us that which the gospel is in its relative position to the law. This is, however, even while it delivers us from the curse and judgment of the law, a confirmation of the law (see § 17, note (4)).

(3) For what I have asserted above, I refer neither to the ἐλέγχειν (John 16:8), nor to the signification of the word Παράκλητος, as Christ names the Holy Ghost in John's Gospel. To the first passage, which in the following verses is extremely difficult to understand, I do not appeal; for this reason, because the question there is of a reproving, convincing position of the Spirit (appropriated to the disciples) as He stands towards the unbelieving world, which, as far as I can see, has nothing in common with conversion, of which we are treating. He, the Holy Ghost, whom Christ sends to His disciples (John 16:7), will in reproving convince the world (ἐλέγχειν περί τινος, Jude 15, John 8:46); and sin, righteousness, and judgment will be the object of this conviction by the Holy Ghost. For the children of the world believe not in Christ; therefore in Christ's stead the Spirit of God will convince them by reproof of what sin is. Christ goes to the Father, and His disciples behold Him no more; therefore in His place will the Spirit of God convince the world by reproof of what righteousness is. The prince of this world, moreover, was then already judged; and therefore in Christ's stead will the witness of the Holy Spirit be only a

reproving witness of condemnation, and that against the world (similarly also, if I rightly understand him, v. Hofmann, *Schriftbeweis*, 2d ed. ii. 2, p. 19). If this, therefore, is really the sense of the passage, then it speaks of something else than that which I understand as the reproving office of the Holy Ghost, as that is accomplished in conversion. In like manner, it is not my opinion that Παράκλητος in the true idea of the word signifies Comforter. At least the import of that παράκλησις which is ascribed by Christ to the Holy Ghost after the departure of the Son will not be exhausted in the notion of comforting; as, besides, the same John does not employ the word everywhere in such a sense. For, speaking of Christ, he uses it to denote that position which Christ, as being the propitiation for our sins, assumes with the Father as our Advocate (1 John 2:1). And in the Gospel, indeed, it also serves to denote a position of the Holy Ghost which is similar to that of Christ (ἄλλον Παράκλητον, John 14:16); but the likeness is immediately indicated by this, that as Christ is the Truth (John 14:6), so the Spirit is the Spirit of truth (14:17), whose business it is to teach them everything, to bring to their recollection everything which Christ has told them (14:26), to testify of Christ (15:26), to lead them into *all* the truth (16:13). If such is the task of that παράκλησις which is attributed to the Holy Ghost, it is certainly not exhausted in the narrower sense of comfort. "One who speaks to us," in the same intensive sense in which this signifies more than a "teacher," is the Holy Ghost. His speaking (παράκλησις) is, like to that of Christ, and to the use of the word παράκλησις, as much admonition as comforting; and, in truth, just because it leads into *all* the truth. That is the truth which, as much in reference to man as to God, testifies of that which is true in both aspects. And this testimony is the testimony of the whole truth, both as an attestation of the judgment (John 8:16) and of the grace which is in Christ Jesus. Hence the office of the Holy Ghost is, at the same time, an office of reproof and one of comfort.

(4) If the truth is in us, and it is only so by the Spirit of truth, then the first thing is, that we acknowledge and confess our sin.

"If we say that we have no sin, we deceive ourselves, and the truth is not in us. If we say that we have not sinned, we make God a liar, and His word is not in us" (1 John 1:8, 10). Therefore, when by the operation of the Holy Ghost His word is to be made alive in us, it must be that word which reveals to us our sin—accuses, judges, and condemns our sin. That, however, is the word of the law (see § 14, note (5)). And because this word is appointed by God's will to be the schoolmaster unto Christ (see § 16, note (6)), no operation of the Holy Ghost upon us is conceivable without its bringing to our inner experience, as a preparatory aim, this crushing power of the law. It is brought to our experience not in a general anguish of conscience, but in the definite consciousness of sinfulness and guilt before God (§ 14, note (5); Ps. 51:6, comp. Delitzsch on the passage). And when this is presented to his consciousness in a just manner, the man is not only bowed under the burden of such guilt, but he bows himself under it, and justifies God in His condemnation of himself. This willingness to bow down characterizes the true repentance of the converted man; but this willingness springs not exactly from the law, which by the working of the Holy Ghost has been made alive in the heart, but from the contemporaneous inward confirmation of the evangelical word, that in heaven there is more joy over one sinner who repenteth, than over ninety and nine just persons, who need no repentance (Luke 15:7). The course of conversion resembles that of the prodigal son to his father. "I have sinned against Heaven, and before thee, and am no more worthy to be called your son"—that is the confession (Luke 15:18). But then the prodigal son arises and goes to his father. The way to the Father, however, is pointed out only by the Holy Ghost by means of the gospel of Christ. The cutting sword of the law would neither point out nor open up this way. On the contrary, the end of that way, which he goes who knows nothing but the stings of conscience, is shown to us in the repentance of Judas (Matt. 27:3, 5). This repentance exhausts itself in that sorrow which the world also knows; but this sorrow worketh death (2 Cor. 7:10). If sorrow is to work life, then must yet another factor be contemporaneously in operation. This, however, is not the law which bringeth death, but the life-giving gospel (comp. § 17).

But the deeper the lie of self-righteousness and the reluctance to judge ourselves are rooted in us, so much the more earnestly must we go to work with repentance. And this earnestness consists in this, that we do not measure by the standard of human and self-conceived ideas that which is called sin and guilt, but let it be revealed by the word of the divine law. That, however, which is thus revealed to us, is not, as it were, a mere reluctance to be subject to the law of God, but that hidden enmity to God (§ 15, note (5)) which poisons our natural and individual life, and which without God's working on us is irremediable. "True repentance," says Luther, "does not consist in such thoughts as are our own and self-devised, which the monks call *contritio* and *attritio*, whole or half repentance; but is seen where conscience begins really to bite and torment thee, and your heart is terrified in earnest at God's wrath and judgment, not only on account of open and notorious sins, but on account of those very strong and root sins,—when you see and feel that mere unbelief, contempt of God, and disobedience towards Him, and, as St. Paul (Rom. 8:7) says, enmity against God, stick fast in your flesh and blood, and stir in thee with all kinds of evil concupiscence and desires, etc., by which you hast drawn God's wrath upon thee, and deserved that you shouldest be eternally cast out from His presence and be consumed in hell-fire. That, consequently, repentance goes not to work *piecemeal in regard to particular deeds* which you hast openly committed against the ten commandments (where, however, stops the dream and conceit of the hypocritical penitence of the monks, who imagine to themselves a distinction among their works, and notwithstanding find something good in themselves), but deals with *the whole person, with all its life and character, yea, with the entire nature*, and shows to thee that you lie under God's wrath, and art condemned to hell. Otherwise the word repentance sounds also still *too juristic*, as we are wont in worldly matters to speak of sin and repentance as of a work which one has done, and afterwards taken another view of and wished that he had not done it. Such repentance and earnest horror proceed *not from man's own intention or thought*, but must be effected in man *by God's word*, which denounces God's wrath and strikes the heart, so that it begins to tremble and to shake, and knows not where it is to rest. For human reason is by itself incapable of seeing and understanding such a things that all which is within human powers and faculties is under God's wrath, and is already condemned to hell at His bar. Hence such things must be preached and proclaimed, if people are to be guided and brought to true repentance, that they may become aware of their sin and of God's wrath, and so *first of all permit themselves to be thrown under God's wrath and condemnation by the word*, in order that on the other hand also they may, by that other preaching of the forgiveness of sin, be helped to right comfort, to divine grace, and their own salvation. Otherwise would man never at all be able to discover his own misery and wretchedness, and to sigh after grace; still less would he learn how he is to pass from God's wrath and condemnation to grace and forgiveness of sins."

(5) The more necessary it is to cling to the fact that this wholesome repentance, as it forms the criterion of conversion, springs out of a willing heart; so much the more impossible is it to regard this as the work of the Holy Ghost, unless here the law becoming a living power, and the gospel becoming such also, coincide in the same point. The willing state of the heart, however, is a postulate absolutely necessary. With perfect justice Luther says: "Every one ought to search his heart whether he thoroughly, *from the desire of a willing heart*, hates sin; and when he does not find it so, *he should only despise his own repentance*, and first fall down and pray his Lord, and get others to pray for him, that he may obtain a true and genuine repentance, and then reflect on his sins. It is indeed a rare thing, and a *high attainment of grace*, this repentant heart, and is not to be prepared by thoughts of sin and hell, but is to be poured into us by the Holy Ghost alone." Now I would ask every

one who has had individual experience, every one who knows human nature and human souls, whether he thinks that from anguish of heart and the stings of conscience of themselves proceed the willing heart and the inclination to submit one's self to it, and "thoroughly" to hate sin and one's self. What has the fetter in common with freedom, torment with joy, anguish with delight? What this bowing under the punishment of sin with the being lifted above it? Truly not through anguish do I become free from anguish, not from the curse of sin by the experience of this curse, nor from the divine wrath by feeling the same. On the contrary, if a pause is made here, sin only entangles me ever deeper, for it strikes a defenseless and unarmed creature into its toils. Nothing, therefore, is more dangerous to the soul than the mere yielding one's self to the anguish and smart of repentance, and therewith supposing that freedom from guilt and sin will come with and from the bonds of sorrow. That would be a tearing asunder piecemeal of the work and design of the Holy Ghost, a mistaking of the subordinate means for the chief business, the preparation for the object aimed at, the discipline for the deliverance itself, and a putting of the law as the power of redemption in the place of the gospel. "But *through such repentance and suffering we are not yet freed from sin*; but it is needful for that, that we believe the gospel, and comfort ourselves with that which is promised us *in the gospel* and *in baptism*. For forgiveness of sins rests on Christ *alone*" (Luther). If the Holy Ghost, therefore, is working in us, it is right that first He should drive into our conscience the goad of the law. With this, however, He begins; and he who allows this alone to happen to him, stops in the midst of the work, and deprives himself of the whole. Nay, he withdraws himself precisely from that which the Spirit desires to bestow out of the fulness of Christ. That is the righteousness in Christ, in the delight and love of which repentance first becomes perfect and saving. Of this the bull of that ecclesiastical court of justice knew nothing, which condemned the following proposition of Luther's as a heresy: "The repentance which is prepared by inquiry after, consideration, and hatred of his sins, when a sinner reflects with bitterness of heart on his life,—thinks upon the greatness, number, and filthiness of his sins, and, besides, thinks upon the loss of eternal happiness, and the gain of eternal damnation,—this makes a hypocrite and a greater sinner." Speaking against the condemnation of this proposition, Luther says: "Just as out of the beautiful rose the spider sucks poison to its own detriment, out of which the good little bee sucks honey unhurt, so this miserable 'generation of vipers' (as Christ calls them) have treated my sermon on repentance, in which I have taught that repentance should spring from a love of and pleasure in righteousness, as they themselves also write and teach, and yet do not understand. And where this love does not exist, there remains a hatred of righteousness. Where that remains, there repentance is feigned and false, and makes only hypocrites, nay, greater sinners; and for this reason, that it arises not from a love of righteousness, but is such repentance as was that of Judas." For, much as the proposition may be misunderstood, that repentance flows from a love of and pleasure in righteousness, so true is it that the willing reception of the deep sufferings of repentance nowhere appears, where the heart is not inflamed by the contemplation of that treasure which God offers to the penitent sinner in the gospel. For this reason it is, also, that this repentance alone is the work of the Holy Ghost, and the commencement of true conversion, in which the heart is at the same time kindled to a faith in Christ. Where, however, this is the case, there, according to the contents and nature of the gospel (§ 17), is that conceit also annihilated, that our penitence should be anything meritorious before God, and that we, on account of our penitence, should be pleasing unto God. and obtain righteousness before Him. This is a conception so full of internal contradiction, that it is difficult to imagine how it can ever cleave to a soul which has once experienced what the pangs of repentance really are. For this is nothing but the feeling, consciousness, and perception of our extreme offensiveness to God. How, then, is such a perception in itself to work pleasure on the side of God, or in us a consciousness of our well-pleasingness to the holy and living God? All true knowledge of God and all just self-knowledge must have been at the same time destroyed, ere any one pretended to feel himself in his repentance, and because of that repentance, in a state of favor with and pleasing unto God. For this would right properly be called wishing to make a glory of our shame. Nay, that such shame does not inwardly consume us (unless we make out of our pride a heart-petrifying preservative), is caused by God's grace alone, which we lay hold of, not in the despair of repentance, but in that faith which annihilates at once doubt and despair. And this faith is of such a nature, that it excludes all idea of any meritoriousness of faith (§ 18, note (2)); to say nothing of the notion, that it stamps the anguish of regret at our own worthlessness as having any degree of worth or meritoriousness. For all repentance is the consciousness of not being righteous before God. Wherefore it is the greatest folly to call repentance a beginning of justification, or even to bring it in any way into juxtaposition with justification or a consciousness of the same. For justification is the silencing of our despair. How, then, can despair in me be the means of stilling my despair, whether at its beginning or at its end? If repentance in me resembles the burning sand of the desert, which excites the torment of thirst, shall I then say, the sand quenches my thirst, or that to thirst is to drink? If in the wilderness I find not the spring of water, which is not exactly burning sand, but spring water, then does the desert remain a desert, and the thirsty one pines away. His thirst produces no water, and the fever in him still less a quenching of his thirst. As little does repentance produce justification before God;—to pass over in perfect silence the fact, that no man can be found on earth who could say that he has a repentance which sufficiently corresponds to the divine judgment. For if "the man should say that he has truly repented, then would he be driven to self-presumption, and to the impossible work of knowing all his sins and wickedness. Nay, since all the saints have still something evil and sinful in them, it is impossible that any one should have repentance which would satisfy God's judgment, but all of them exclaim with David (Ps. 143:2), 'Lord, enter not into judgment with your servant: for in your sight shall no man living be justified.' If no one is found justified, how then shall he be found to have repented, if repentance is a beginning of justification?" For this reason it remains certain at the outset, that a sinner who has nothing but repentance, stands only under God's wrath, and in the consciousness of the same. When he is delivered from this, it is by the grace of God in Christ alone, which is appropriated for one's self not in repentance, but in faith. Since, however, it is not faith but repentance alone which shatters the security of the sinner, faith, therefore, is not inwardly attained without repentance. And because repentance does not attain to assurance of the forgiveness of sins, the sinner has his life not from repentance, but from faith alone. Since, however, faith has nothing in and about man to hold up before God, on account of which God should be gracious to the sinner, and absolve him from sin and guilt,—has nothing but Christ alone, the Propitiator and Intercessor,—therefore we know that we find favor and are justified before God *in* penitent faith, not, however, *for the sake of* our penitent faith. If this permeates our consciousness, then are we freed from ourselves, and converted to Christ; only in this sense are repentance and faith the mark of conversion, and of a state of favor with God.

(6) If the question is raised, what we must conceive to ourselves as marks of one who is converted, which witness to the man himself the permanent state of his conversion, we must first rightly lay down the sense in which this question is put. It is rightly put, partly under the right presupposition of that which is called regeneration, partly under the right limitation of that which here below is called the state of grace of the converted. In regeneration an effective relation of God the Holy Ghost to our spirit has commenced, by virtue of which we are able to turn away from our own selfish nature, and to turn to that which Christ is to us. In the conscious and willing entering upon this relation is conversion achieved. Now, we do not inquire, what are the conceivable results of this relation,

proceeding from God and entered into by us; but within what limits here below that which may be truly called a state of grace becomes our portion. This excludes the state of future glory, that is to say, the state of that likeness to God which will be the inheritance of that perfection which belongs to the next world (ὅμοιοι αὐτῷ ἐσόμεθα, 1 John 3:2). This unlikeness has no reference to that in our nature which is still hostile to God, but to everything which as God's working has been received by us into a willing consciousness, and has become our own endeavor, will, and doing. All this is outside the relation of likeness to God; and for this reason, nothing of all that which may be called the inwardly appropriated working of the Spirit of God in us, can be mentioned as anything which in its present state would be an adequate object of divine complacency. But just because it is so with him, not merely at first, but up to the end, the position of a Christian is one under grace, and indeed purely unmerited grace. For, with the exception of that perfect grace which is in Christ and for Christ's sake, everything which belongs to our life, even in the very highest degree of development on earth, is in the state of imperfection. We never cease in the light of truth to be an object of dissatisfaction to ourselves; nay, the brighter this light becomes in us, so much the more clearly do we see the depths of that darkness which is still within us. Now, it is of course certain, and guaranteed to us in the promises of the gospel, that by the penitent and believing reception of the same, not only does a fulness of good things fall to our lot, the future possession of which is the object of our hope (comp. § 20), but that already at present there enters into our hearts a fulness of impulses of spiritual and God-born love (comp. § 19), which are not at all comprised in the conception of repentance and faith. The spiritual man, and that which he is and possesses, are not exhaustively described by the designation of a penitent and believing man. But he is to be described by no other criterion when I wish to express the condition under which alone he stands in the spirit of truth and in the state of grace. For he slides from the truth and falls into the meshes of falsehood in the same measure, as he views the spiritual life which he has in himself as his righteousness before God. Then certainly he makes out of that which is unlike God, and which as yet is polluted with sin, a something which resembles God and is pure before God. And he falls away from grace in the same measure, as he regards the spiritual life which dwells in him as an inherent righteousness, and just in this way will have it that the grace which for Christ's sake pronounces him righteous is no longer grace, but an inner contradiction, that is to say, a grace which recognizes a righteousness which dwells in man. For grace which recognizes a righteousness before God inherently belonging to man, is just no longer grace. And the man who desires such a thing stands not in grace, but in self-deception, self-delusion, self-conceit, and the pride of that affectation, in which he wishes to be as God, or that God should be as he is. Not, however, on the proud, but on the humble, does God bestow His grace,—not on him who is something, but on him who is nothing in his own eyes. And to attain to this, costs certainly no affectation, but only a small spark of that self-knowledge which is kindled by God's Spirit through His word. Never does a feeling of consummate silliness steal upon me so much as when I desire, in the emotions of my spiritual, God-born, and God-bestowed life, to pass for something in the eyes of God. Nothing, on the contrary, humbles me so much in the dust as the fact, that in spite of my unfaithfulness, God, for Christ's sake, not for my own, does not forsake the work of His hands, and ever and ever again breaks through the death of my old nature with the gracious power of His life. Of all this, however, I see and discover absolutely nothing, if I do not judge myself daily in repentance, and comfort myself daily in faith, in which faith I lay hold not of my own righteousness, but of that righteousness which God, for Christ's sake, bestows upon me in the way of promise. He therefore who, when converted, desires to remain in the state of grace, in which grace God merely for Christ's sake alone accounts us righteous, can do so only by continual repentance and constant faith. He then is the man of God, who thinks no higher of himself than as of a lost lamb, which feels itself saved, not because it follows its Lord, but because the good Shepherd follows it, and takes it in His arms, and bears it to the eternal home. And only thus is our whole life a continual exercise of that which was given to us in baptism (§ 21, note (1)).

The knowledge that he is in a state of grace, in whom penitence and faith have a permanent place, guards against more than one error to which precisely the domain of the Christian life is liable. Only, this statement with respect to the continuance of repentance and faith must itself first be rightly understood. The chief stress lies upon the connection, that is to say, the simultaneity, of these two dispositions and emotions of the soul. Nothing have we more to guard against than a repentance which is without faith, and a faith which is without repentance. And the surest, nay, the only way to guard against this, is by turning ourselves directly in spirit to the divine act of salvation, from which we derive the assurance of the forgiveness of sins and the justification of the sinner before God. That is the cross of our Lord Jesus Christ,—the fact that Christ could only by the ransom-price of His blood redeem the world and me from God's wrath. For if our redemption was possible only at such a price, who can reflect upon this and lay it to heart, without at the same time trembling at the heinousness of sin, and the earnestness of God's wrath against the human race? He however who sees on the same cross wrath swallowed up in grace, cannot perceive this without recognizing in repentance the wrath that he has merited, in order to receive grace in faith, and so to overcome this wrath. On which account also the Confession of our church says (*Form. Conc.* P. 1, Epit. v. 9, 10): "Accordingly, although the preaching of the sufferings and death of Christ the Son of God is an earnest and fearful preaching and proclamation of God's wrath, in order that thereby the people, having been first led rightly to the law, after the veil of Moses is removed for them, may first rightly understand how great a thing it is that God requires from us in the law, of which we are able to keep no tittle, and hence are to seek all our righteousness in Christ; yet, so long as all this (namely, the sufferings and death of Christ) proclaims God's wrath and alarms man, it is not yet the true preaching of the gospel, but Moses and the preaching of the law; and hence, a work strange to Christ ('alienum opus Christi'), by means of which He comes ('*per* quod accedit') to His own office, that is, to preach grace, to comfort and make alive, which is properly the preaching of the gospel." And just for this reason, the way to experience in our heart by faith this, Christ's "own" office, is this, that we should permit the "strange" work of Christ to take effect on our own hearts in repentance. This is the reason why we have to guard so strictly against a repentance without faith, and a faith without repentance.

With regard, however, to the lasting character of repentance and faith, what is hereby meant is, that these two must be constantly together if the sinner wishes to comfort himself with the grace of God. It is not, however, meant that this continuance is to be taken in the sense of an equality of measure, in which I become as much conscious of my repentance as of my faith. For, in the first place, it is a different thing *to have* repentance and faith, and *to become aware of* repentance and faith in their reflex influence on the consciousness. Upon this, however, depends that which we on purely subjective grounds call a measure of the one or the other. But no weight whatever is to be laid on this subjective decision. Nay, if I arbitrarily require in my self-examination an equal measure of repentance and faith, then in the time of temptation I fall into the greatest danger that in the anguish of my repentance I should become perplexed as to my faith, and that in the time of quickening, in the confidence and joy of faith I should doubt of my repentance. It avails nothing whatever, in the second place, to prop one's self up on a measure of inward consciousness of repentance and faith, if I do not wish to let myself be led astray, so as to build my confidence toward God in repentance on my repentance, and in faith on my faith, so far as I am conscious of both. But my confidence must rest wholly and entirely upon that God who in His word chastises and comforts me. And before this God no repentance and no faith are so weak and so small, that if we bewail it before Him, He will not have compassion on our weakness; and no repentance and no faith are so strong and great, that God will not reject both, if we wish to place them on a level with the greatness of His compassion. It comes therefore simply to this,—that never without repentance before the face of the holy God should I seek in faith the countenance of the gracious God, in order to comfort myself with that grace which He for Christ's sake promises me.

The importance of the knowledge of this consists herein, that I may guard myself against the mistake of considering repentance and faith as a something which might here below ever be done away with, so that I might perhaps reach beyond the one by means of the other, or might reach, as it were, some higher point beyond both by means of some other third thing. A passing beyond repentance would be possible only to him who leads himself astray, and by a denial of his sin makes God a liar. A passing beyond faith would be possible only to him who puts the truth of the gospel to shame, and denies that here below no man has favor and righteousness before God, except by virtue of the promise in which God offers us grace for Christ's sake. By either denial we should fall from a state of grace; if we remain therein, it is by virtue of that twofold truth, only in faith and repentance that we can remain in this state.

In this sense the *Smalcald Articles* say (P. iii. Art. iii. 20): *"This penitence abides with the Christian to the end of his life;"* for it keeps quarrelling with indwelling sin through his entire life: as St. Paul testifies (Rom. 7) that he wages war with the law of his members, etc., and that not by his own strength, but through the gift of the Holy Ghost which follows on the forgiveness of sins. This same gift purifies and cleanses away day by day the rest of our sins, and labours to make the man thoroughly pure and holy. (Compare also what has been before said, § 18, note (5).)

SECOND SECTION

THE SPIRITUAL STRUGGLE OF THE INDIVIDUAL FOR THE POSSESSION OF SALVATION

§ 25. *The Activity of the Converted Man in the Work of his own Renewal*

CERTAIN as it is that out of a true justifying faith love is born (§ 19, note (6)), it is equally certain that in him who is truly converted and delivered by the grace of God, along with the power for the free fulfilling of the law, which he possesses in that very love which is born of God, and devoted to God, the struggle must arise to keep himself from all things which the same Spirit of grace rebukes and condemns in him. And in that lively hope to which he is born again in faith (§ 20), he has before his eyes that aim of future perfection which he, provided that he has laid hold of it in love and hope, can pursue only by self-effort. For the free gift of righteousness before God is bestowed on us for the purpose of a resurrection to a new life (1). And the regenerating fellowship of God the Holy Ghost, which God has entered into with our spirit, has for its object our own entrance into this communion with the holy God, by virtue of which we are called in the sanctification of the Spirit to self-sanctification (2). And the truer it is that the blessing of the forgiveness of sins and of justification before God can only become our blessed possession in repentant faith, so much the less can we conceive the permanence of this possession without a turning away of our mind (νοῦς) from that of which we repent, and the entrance of our mind upon what is of God and in itself well-pleasing to Him (3). For persistence in sin, and seeking of God's grace in repentance and faith, mutually exclude each other (4). Rather is this the mark of the sinner when converted to God and justified by His grace, that he, on the ground of having received such grace, strives after that righteousness which consists in a conformity with the nature and will of God and with the mind (νοῦς) of Christ (5). And this is not a something which the converted and faith-justified sinner adds to that which God does and has done for him; but it is that wherein he employs that which God does and has done for him as a power of life for working on himself. And since God has entered into a relation of gracious fellowship with the sinner, which is new to the latter, and which did not proceed from himself, his self-sanctification is not a manifestation or preservation of a holiness dwelling in his own nature, but a self-renovation, in which he sets to work in himself the renovating power of that relation of grace into which God in Christ has entered with him by the Holy Ghost (6). This, however, takes place when we sanctify Christ, who by virtue of regeneration dwells in our hearts by faith, and make Him the center of all our thoughts, desires, and actions, and in these keep a right state of heart toward Him, permitting no pleasure or affection to sway us which would be antagonistic to our love for or pleasure in Him, and forsaking everything which might disturb the peace and joy of a good conscience in Him, and which might convert the blessed knowledge of His grace and truth into a witness against ourselves (7). In our knowing and willing to live more and more in Christ, not for the purpose of knowing about Him, but of becoming like Him—that is the struggle of our renewed state (8). And this is a work which, here below, is constantly to be carried on, but is never completed; it is the fruit, but not the ground of our justification in God's sight,—the practical demonstration of our regeneration and conversion, if they are to bear fruit unto ourselves; and of such a practical demonstration we are first rendered capable by our regeneration and conversion (9).

(1) Compare § 22, note (2), on the relation established along with baptism. Life is the result of justification (δικαίωσις ζωῆς, Rom. 5:18); and this not merely in reference to the hope of eternal life (ἵνα ἡ χάρις βασιλεύσῃ διὰ δικαιοσύνης εἰς ζωὴν

αἰώνιον, Rom. 5:21; comp. χάρις ζωῆς, 1 Pet. 3:7), but also in relation to the present condition of our spiritual existence (εἰ μὲν Χριστὸς ἐν ὑμῖν, τὸ μὲν σῶμα νεκρὸν δι᾽ ἁμαρτίαν, τὸ δὲ πνεῦμα ζωὴ διὰ δικαιοσύνην, Rom. 8:10). That we should live through Him, was the object of Christ's mission (1 John 4:9). And this life has just this form, that henceforth we no longer live unto ourselves, but unto Him who died and rose again for us (2 Cor. 5:15). He who has entered into the fellowship of the death and life of Christ must consider himself as dead unto sin, but alive unto God in Christ Jesus (Rom. 6:11). For that of which he has become a partaker is the promise of the life which is in Christ Jesus (2 Tim. 1:1), the word of life (Phil. 2:16), whose power he has felt. Through this the Holy Ghost has His work in him. But if he lives in the Spirit, it concerns him also to walk in the Spirit (Gal. 5:25).

(2) The life of Christians begins with a sanctification proceeding from the Spirit of God (ἁγιασμὸς πνεύματος, 1 Pet. 1:2), in which, from the very fact that the Holy Ghost enters into fellowship with them, and makes them His own in grace, they are placed in a region of life in which they cannot continue without their striving, with all the strength imparted to them, after a conformity of their own conduct with that God who has called them (κατὰ τὸν καλέσαντα ὑμᾶς ἅγιον καὶ αὐτοὶ ἅγιοι ἐν πάσῃ ἀναστροφῇ γενήθητε, διότι γέγραπται· Ἅγιοι ἔσεσθε, ὅτι ἐγὼ ἅγιος, 1 Pet. 1:15, 16). This self-sanctification, however, consists in nothing else but this: in making the God whose absolute love has rescued us from our own selfish nature, in the reciprocal love which He has wrought in us, the present and future determining principle of our own creature conduct, desires, and thoughts (comp. § 19, note (3)). The deeper, however, the consciousness of the perfectly undeserved character of that love with which God has first loved us, so much the more inseparable from our reciprocal love is the fear of forfeiting by any unholiness of conduct this "goodness" of God, and so much the more earnest is our striving to perfect holiness in the fear of God (ταύτας οὖν ἔχοντες ἐπαγγελίας, καθαρίσωμεν ἑαυτοὺς ... ἐπιτελοῦντες ἁγιωσύνην ἐν φόβῳ

Θεοῦ, 2 Cor. 7:1; μὴ ὑψηλοφρόνει, ἀλλὰ φοβοῦ, Rom. 11:20, comp. 22, Heb. 4:1, and § 16, note (1)).

(3) If, by the truth which has laid hold of our *spirit*, our *souls* have really become pure in obedience to the truth (ἡγνικότες τὰς ψυχὰς ἐν τῇ ὑπακοῇ τῆς ἀληθείας, 1 Pet. 1:22), in that case only does the exhortation rightly find a place, to transform ourselves by the renewing of our *mind* (μεταμορφοῦσθαι τῇ ἀνακαινώσει τοῦ νοός), in order to prove what that will of God may be, which is good, and acceptable, and perfect (Rom. 12:2). For, to stand fast perfect, and with full certainty, in all the will of God—that is the aim of Christianity (Col. 4:12). And that which inwardly impels him who has become conscious of the difference between the life in Christ and the life which is outside of Him to renounce his old conduct, is shame at the fruit, which grew for him out of that conduct (ἐφ᾽ οἷς νῦν ἐπαισχύνεσθε, Rom. 6:21).

(4) With reference to baptism, the apostle excludes persistence in sin as something inconceivable. "How shall we, that are dead to sin, live any longer therein?" (Rom. 6:2 ff.) In that victory of Christ over the deadly power of sin, which is made ours in baptism, lies the whole possibility of a conduct on our part in conformity to God. But the blessed permanence of this gift is itself again conditioned by the right appropriation of it on our part, which it renders possible. Where baptism has not produced penitent faith, there also it loses its power to bless. It is not possible for us by baptism only, when unaccompanied by repentance and faith, to abstain from sin and to arrive at holiness. If we desire to know whether the grace given us in baptism is working in us, what is more necessary than to try whether we stand firm in faith? (ἑαυτοὺς πειράζετε, εἰ ἐστὲ ἐν τῇ πίστει, 2 Cor. 13:13; γρηγορεῖτε, στήκετε ἐν τῇ πίστει, 1 Cor. 16:13.) And on the ground of the divine gift of grace proceeds the exhortation to employ all diligence, and to display our virtue in our *faith* (2 Pet. 1:5), by which faith the blessed result of the means of grace and the power of a self-proving ability are equally conditioned.

(5) Ὁ ποιῶν τὴν δικαιοσύνην δίκαιός ἐστιν, καθὼς ἐκεῖνος δίκαιός ἐστιν, 1 John 3:7. That we, having escaped from sins, should live unto righteousness, was the object for which Christ died on the cross (1 Pet. 2:24); since the freedom from sin effected for us by Christ involves in itself an equally binding obligation on His servant to righteousness, because an obligation to God, in which we are to have our fruit unto holiness (Rom. 6:18, 22). In such a manner is Christ formed within us (μορφοῦται ἐν ἡμῖν, Gal. 4:19), who in the days of His flesh sought not His own will, but the will of Him who sent Him (John 5:30). In like form our aim also is, to live the rest of our time in the flesh no longer to the lusts of men, but to the will of God (1 Pet. 4:2). For he who doeth the will of God abides for ever (1 John 2:17).

(6) We must carefully distinguish that which in the Scriptures is characterized as the working of the fellowship of grace, as it appears in regeneration, from that conduct of our own which the same Scripture exhorts us to follow, on the ground of that relation of grace bestowed upon us, especially as both are often denoted by the same terms. It is just one and the same relation of grace, whose powerful working is bestowed upon us as a gift, and by which we are to show ourselves as powerful over ourselves. It is a *result* of this relation of grace, if we have put off the old man, and have put on the new; which is just nothing else but that putting on of Christ as it takes place in baptism (Χριστὸν ἐνεδύσασθε, Gal. 3:27; comp. with Col. 3:10, Eph. 4:22, 24). We *become* clothed with the strength of Christ, which makes us free from our old nature, in that fellowship into which Christ Himself enters with us. But the conduct which corresponds to this, therefore, bears no other name than the putting on of Christ (ἐνδύσασθε τὸν κύριον Ἰ. Χριστὸν καὶ τῆς σαρκὸς πρόνοιαν μὴ ποιεῖσθε εἰς ἐπιθυμίαν, Rom. 13:14). The further working which accompanies the relation of Christ to us in grace, when once established, is that continual being renewed in the spirit of our mind or disposition (ἀνανεοῦσθαι τῷ πνεύματι τοῦ νοός, Eph. 4:23), to which, as conduct in a similar sense, the transforming

ourselves in the renewing of our mind corresponds (μεταμορφοῦσθαι τῇ ἀνακαινώσει τοῦ νοός, Rom. 12:2). The new man *has been* created in righteousness and holiness of truth (Eph. 4:24); *is being* renewed unto knowledge after the image of Him that created him (Col. 3:10), and indeed day by day in the inward man (2 Cor. 4:16); and purifies *himself* (ἁγνίζει ἑαυτόν, 1 John 3:3; καθαρίζει ἑαυτόν, 2 Cor. 7:1). He who neglects it, neglects not something which he might have been directed to do by his own strength, or in his own way, but despises God, who gives unto us His Holy Spirit (ἐκάλεσεν ἡμᾶς ὁ Θεὸς ... ἐν ἁγιασμῷ. Τοιγαροῦν ὁ ἀθετῶν—ἀθετεῖ τὸν Θεὸν τὸν διδόντα τὸ πνεῦμα αὐτοῦ τὸ ἅγιον εἰς ὑμᾶς, 1 Thess. 4:7, 8).

(7) Christ's fellowship with us is effected by the Holy Ghost. For the self-agency which is to preserve this fellowship we have the most characteristic expression: to sanctify Christ in our hearts (κύριον τὸν Χριστὸν ἁγιάσατε ἐν ταῖς καρδίαις ὑμῶν, 1 Pet. 3:15). For this comprehends the sanctifying of Christ, who has taken up His abode in us, and the sanctifying of our own hearts, in one expression. And this takes place when we allow that Christ, who has given Himself to us to make ours as the only true and essential ground of life and of all our individual existence and nature, to be and to remain what He is, and when we strive against everything which tends to displace Christ from this central position to us, and us from our position to Him. "He in us, and we in Him;"—His love, our all-mastering love. For our heart is where our treasure is, and our treasure where our heart is (Matt. 6:21). "To have God in our heart is to depend continually on Him; abandoning one's self to Him, to trust Him, to have pleasure, love, and joy in Him, to have Him continually in our thoughts. Heart, therefore, signifies great and forcible love" (Luther). He, therefore, to whom Christ's love to us is the sanctuary of his heart, sanctifies his heart, since he allows no pleasure, love, or joy to arise which would militate against this sanctuary of his heart, and cheat him of its blessing. The deceitful lusts (Eph. 4:22) are, however, "our own lusts" (αἱ ἰδίαι ἐπιθυμίαι, 2 Tim. 4:3; αἱ ἡμῶν ἑαυτῶν ἐπιθυμίαι, Jude 18),—those which spring up out of our own selfish heart, and which

covet only the satisfaction of this our heart, estranged as it is from God and turned to the creature (ἐπιθυμίαι τῶν καρδιῶν, Rom. 1:24; ἐπιθυμία τῆς ψυχῆς, Rev. 18:14; ἐπιθυμία τῆς σαρκός, 1 John 2:16; τῶν ὀφθαλμῶν, *ibid.*; ἐπιθυμία τοῦ κόσμου, 1 John 2:17; κοσμικαὶ ἐπιθυμίαι, Tit. 2:12; ἡ ἐν τῷ κόσμῳ ἐν ἐπιθυμίᾳ φθορά, 2 Pet. 1:4. Comp. the heart as the spring of all these lusts, Matt. 15:19, Luke 6:45, and the seat of all obduracy and resistance to what is divine, Matt. 13:15, 15:8, Acts 28:27, Rom. 2:5, etc., and § 5, note (8)). What we wish to avert when we struggle against these lusts, is the condemnation of our own hearts and the loss of cheerfulness (παῤῥησία) before God (1 John 3:21). This, however, is fundamentally nothing else than the desire to prevent Christ from becoming in our hearts a Judge to condemn us, and from taking away the peace and the joy which is the peculiar work of the Holy Spirit (Gal. 5:22; Rom. 14:17; 1 Thess. 1:6). As little as we can bestow upon ourselves this peace, so little is everything that is called self-renewing a maintenance and development proceeding from ourselves of those powers, which are purely those of our Lord Jesus Christ, and not our own. The renewing, as it is accomplished by us with the powers bestowed on us by Christ, is rather a constant conflict with all that which aims at exalting itself in us against Christ; and in this is a preservation of faith and a good conscience (ἵνα στρατεύῃ τὴν καλὴν στρατείαν, ἔχων πίστιν καὶ ἀγαθὴν συνείδησιν, 1 Tim. 1:18). The weapons which are mighty through God are given us to cast down strongholds, since we cast down (not only in others, but above all in ourselves) devices (λογισμούς), and every high thing which exalteth itself against the knowledge of God, and bring into captivity every rising thought (πᾶν νοήμα) to the obedience of Christ (2 Cor. 10:5; comp. καρδίαι and νοήματα, Phil. 4:7, and as a contrast the corruption of the νοήματα ἀπὸ τῆς ἁπλότητος τῆς εἰς τὸν Χριστόν, that is to say, in the estrangement from the undivided and sole direction to Christ, 2 Cor. 11:3). In the conflict against the opposition which rises in us to Christ, and obedience to Christ, we find the work of our self-renewing; and in the apprehensible and perceptible weakening and discomfiture of these thoughts which are opposed to Christ, we possess the testimony to our progress, not in the inapprehensible and, by our hands, intangible growth (wisely removed from self-contemplation and self-reflection) of the spiritual, new man, born of God, and to be commended to the power of His grace only. We should like, however, to feel and perceive this latter as plainly, sensibly, and as much after the manner of the earthly man as we do the former,—that is to say, that against which we are struggling, and have continually to struggle. By wrongly desiring this, and making it both the object and standard of our self-renewal, we go astray, and fall into that which has been justly called "the false Christianity of feeling." For not only is it the case that we thereby are easily apt artificially to produce and force ourselves into feelings which at last destroy the truth and purity of our self-knowledge, but we also desire to build our peace with God, in the midst of the struggle of self-renewal, on our own feelings of peace, instead of on the infallibility of God's words of promise. Or do such understand those words of the song, "I am, however, your loved child, in spite of devil, world, and all sin?" On the contrary, the *new* man *sighs* with the whole creation after complete redemption (Rom. 8:23, comp. § 23, note (3)); the *old* man, on the other hand, would fain *dispense with such sighing*, and would at once have in feeling that which he ought to possess in faith only. It is for this reason that Luther, from his own experience, warns us so earnestly against this error. "This is the high art and power of faith, that it sees things unseen, and *sees not that which yet it feels*, nay, represses and subdues this, just as *unbelief only sees what it feels, and desires to rest upon nothing which it cannot feel.*" "No such righteousness, holiness, life, and blessedness are seen and felt as those of which Scripture certainly speaks, and which faith must lay hold of." "This point in the gospel is the most important and most worthy of observation, that we must give the honor unto God, that He is good and gracious, although He may assume another aspect in regard to us, and declare Himself otherwise, and all ideas and all feelings tend otherwise.

For thereby is feeling killed, and the old man perishes, in order that faith only in God's goodness and no feeling should remain in us." The peace of God, however, surpasses all our understanding (ἡ εἰρήνη τοῦ Θεοῦ ἡ ὑπερέχουσα πάντα νοῦν, Phil. 4:7).

For this reason, also, the state of the case is not such that the powers of the new man, the impulses of the divinely born life, as they present themselves or have presented themselves to our consciousness, should be placed before us only as a material at our disposal, with which we had to work out our self-renewal. True it is, no self-renewal is conceivable without the efforts of the new man. The new man, however, is not precisely one who subsists by himself, but, like the branch on the vine (John 15), one who without Christ can do nothing (χωρὶς ἐμοῦ οὐ δύνασθε ποιεῖν οὐδέν, John 15:5). The question, therefore, is not, what the new man, with all that he is and has—if we may in general, and thus in himself think of him—can and ought to do for self-renewing, but how he can maintain himself in Christ's fellowship, and establish himself more and more deeply and firmly therein; for without Christ he can do nothing. Hence it is incumbent to seek Christ where we may find Him, to embrace and to lay hold of Him wherever He is really to be grasped. But He is not to be in His secret presence in our hearts, but in His open presence in His word. When our Lord prays for His own, "Father, sanctify them in your truth," He adds thereto, "Thy word is truth" (John 17:17). All redeeming power which has a real existence is comprised in this word, and is to be imparted to us by means of this word (comp. § 17, note (4)). If we, sanctified and regenerated by the word, desire to sanctify ourselves, then must this word be sanctified and revolved over and over again in our hearts. If the apostle exhorts us to mutual strengthening, "Let the word of Christ dwell among you richly" (Col. 3:16), in like manner, no other way, no other means, and no other exhortation avails for our own self-renewal than this, "Let this word of Christ dwell in you richly." A Christian, even if he were ever so far advanced, who forsakes this way, and, in the struggle after self-renewal, attempts the work merely with that which he bears in himself, such an one returns (provided the spirit of complete self-deception does not ensnare him), under the most favorable circumstances, back again to the condition of the natural man, and has nothing else but thoughts which accuse or else excuse one another (Rom. 2:15). To bring our thoughts into captivity to the obedience of Christ, the word, and nothing but the word, is given us. Nay, when the fulness of the living apostolic word still lived in the Christian communities, then the apostle referred to the Scriptures of the Old Testament, and better understood the method of training: of the Holy Ghost than that pseudo-spirituality which emancipates itself from the word, since he wrote: "For whatsoever things were written aforetime were written for our learning (διδασκαλίαν), that we through patience and comfort of the Scriptures (τῶν γραφῶν) might have hope" (Rom. 15:4). And in the same dependence on the word, as a means of self-renewal, lies also a further confirmation, that we are not referred to the real or supposed measure of our renewal as the power of self-renewal, much less that our sanctification should be only the manifestation of an inward holiness,—that is to say, a conformity of our whole nature with God, attributable to ourselves; but that for this we stand in need of a power which, as given in the word, God points out most evidently as one which does not absolutely belong to or reside in ourselves. He, therefore, who strives to maintain a good conscience in his self-renewal, let him take heed that, not only in reference to the object, *i.e.* what he proposes to himself as a good conscience, but also with regard to the way and the means of renewal, the word should not bear witness against him.

(8) Comp. § 18, note (4), on the knowledge which belongs to faith. The object of our future perfection is that we shall be like God (ὅμοιοι αὐτῷ ἐσόμεθα, 1 John 3:2). More accurately defined, it is a being transformed into the image of Christ (2 Cor. 3:18). Towards this, which is the goal, must all preparatory self-renewing strive, otherwise it deserves not the name of renewal.

(9) "The new inner man in us is not perfected in an hour, but is to become stronger from day to day. A Christian must, therefore, not be slothful, nor allow himself to imagine that he possesses all that is necessary, but must grow and increase ... But where it happens that I have heard of faith, ten commandments, baptism, and sacrament, but go away, feel secure, and suppose I understand it all, and need neither to *learn* anything further, nor to *practice*, nor to *combat*, then I do nothing else than deceive myself with a false presumption, for there can be no earnestness or true faith there" (Luther). With the earnestness of self-renewal, consequently, all presumptuous and pretended faith is dissipated. Not less, however, is every delusion of self-righteousness—that is to say, of an indwelling conformity of our whole nature to God—destroyed; and that which we previously stated concerning the constant necessity of a state of repentant faith is only confirmed if we wish to remain in the state of grace which alone justifies (§ 24, note (6)). It appears, in fact, scarcely credible that we should entertain the idea of regarding ourselves as righteous before God, on account of our self-renewal and self-sanctification; for nowhere is it easier than in this point to detect by one's own experience the want of a perfection conformable to God. But here one error produces another. He who is too high-minded to allow himself to be absolved of God by grace alone, and for Christ's sake, makes, in the first place, of the faith in which he embraces the promise of justifying grace, a *ground* of his justification before God. And if he then reflects that this would be too poor a title to God's approbation and our justification before Him, he adds something thereto, and finds the ground in this, that in such faith he renews, sanctifies, and purifies himself. But if he does not regard this addition with the eye of a Pharisee, he must be fain to confess that the plea of his justification before God on this ground would be still more pitiful than that of faith, the supposed ground of this justification. At least one might more easily indulge in the dream of the conceivableness of a perfectly correspondent faith, than of a perfectly correspondent

holiness. He, however, who in earnest would wish to make out of holiness a ground of our justification and righteousness before God, must say, "Cursed is every man who is not holy as God is holy." This would be spoken according to the earnestness and truth of divine righteousness in God's law, but not according to the truth and grace of the gospel. He who stands by this does not allow the *first* falsehood to grow up, that we are justified before God *on account of* our faith (§ 18, notes (2) and (3), and § 24, note (5)). Hence also he does not reach the *second* falsehood,—namely, that we are justified before God by faith on this account, that we sanctify ourselves by means of this faith. He will rather adhere to the whole truth, that no one here below is accounted just before God except for Christ's sake in His word of promise. To wish to be justified on account of his holiness, would be to trample this word beneath his feet. If he desires, however, to cling to this word of promise, I know not how he could do so with this holiness. In no other manner but in faith only can he lay hold thereof (§ 18, note (3)). If, however, he has in faith embraced the promise of justification by grace alone, then does he attain to cheerfulness of conscience, and joyful love, and a willing heart,—in short, to all that is requisite for the true fulfilling of the law. Such a man of God is furthest from afterwards making out of this his fulfilling of the law an idol, by which he allows himself to be justified. But he practises it because he cannot help it; and in it he has the further verification and proof of his faith,—not, however, the reason for which he feels himself justified before God by faith.

On this account, he who does not wish to deceive himself touching the efficacy, the truth, and the blessing of all self-renewal and self-sanctification, must absolutely expunge them from the chapter of righteousness before God. "For our *life* consists in that inward *holiness, which is the word, or the blessing which is made over to us,* and consists not in our works. Hence we ought to make a right distinction,—namely, that there is one *holiness of works,* and another *of the word, or of faith.* The latter overcomes the devil and makes me a child of

God, which is not effected by the holiness of the flesh or of works, even of the ten commandments, wherein we do not even comprehend this holiness, for we have only in some measure a beginning of it" (Luther).

§ 26. a. The Form of Renewal as a Struggle on the part of the Converted Man

It is manifest, from what has hitherto been said concerning regeneration and conversion, that our renewal is only conceivable in the form of a struggle, in which he who is born of God and converted to God strives to maintain in its integrity the fellowship of God the Holy Ghost, which has been bestowed upon him as the power destined to exercise over him a dominion which is to set him free, in opposition to the rebellion of his old nature (1). And this struggle has this in common with his former condition, that it is a contradiction which makes itself known in the man himself (2). What is new and specifically peculiar to this struggle consists, however, as much in the power with which the contest is carried on, and in the relation of the regenerate and converted man to this power, as in that form of inward resistance hereby conditioned, and of the peculiar consciousness of the regenerate convert concerning the nature of this contradiction and its ultimate causes. For in the regenerate and converted man, by the operation of the Holy Ghost upon his spirit, his own individual mind (νοῦς) is turned to the renewing Spirit of God, and the heart freed from the bondage of sin (3). That nature, on the contrary, which belongs to man individually and generally, which comes to him by his birth in the flesh, and constitutes in the inseparable junction of body and spirit the nature of fallen man, is still subject to all those affections which have their origin in the relation of this nature to the corruption of his race and that of the world, and which seek again to entangle the human Ego, whom the drawings of grace have set free. Against this corrupt nature, the Ego of the new man, made free by the fellowship of the Holy Ghost, is engaged in perpetual warfare

(4). And at the same time the converted man, by being transplanted into the kingdom of Christ, becomes first fully conscious that the opposition he has to contend against is not peculiar to his own individual existence, much less still has in him its origin; but that over against the kingdom of Christ is set a kingdom of the devil, and that his own struggle is only part of a world-struggle, of a struggle with Christ against world-corrupting powers, superior and external to human nature. From this last point of view alone is a full insight into the import of this struggle to be gained, to which the Christian is called in Christ and with Christ (5).

(1) The result of regeneration is not this, that sin should cease to exist, but that its power is broken and its curse removed from us. Besides, a knowledge of sin and repentance thereof are in the strictest sense a mark of the converted man (§ 24, note (4)). That which is incompatible with such a state of grace is merely the *dominion* of sin (ἁμαρτία ὑμῶν οὐ κυριεύσει· οὐ γάρ ἄστε ὑπὸ νόμον, ἀλλὰ ὑπὸ χάριν, Rom. 6:14). For those who receive the abundance of grace and the gift of righteousness, these shall live and *reign* through Jesus Christ (ἐν ζωῇ βασιλεύσουσιν, Rom. 5:17). On this ground we are admonished: Let not sin reign in your mortal bodies, that ye should *obey* its lusts (Rom. 6:12, where Cod. Sinait. also reads αὐτοῦ instead of αὐτῇ).

(2) The perversity which is incompatible with the knowledge of a Christian, is the seeking the origin of his struggle purely outside of and not within himself, that is to say, in that nature which belongs peculiarly to him as a fallen man. To the question, "From whence come wars and fighting among you?" James replies, "Come they not hence, even of your lusts that war in your members?"—that is to say, war not among each other, but in order to possess what one has not, and what he might perhaps obtain, to consume in lusts (Jas. 4:1, 2, 3). And even so all internal conflict has its rise in the fact that the desire of the flesh goes contrary to the Spirit of God, and the desire of the Spirit contrary to the flesh (Gal. 5:17). Considered in itself,

and in accordance with our own inner experience, this stands in the relation of a mutual opposition, and has a tendency to prevent the doing of that which we desire to do, either in the one or the other direction. And this conflict in which the two forces are in equilibrium can only be put a stop to in this way, by those who are led by the Spirit also walking in the Spirit (Gal. 5:18, 16, comp. 5:25), that is to say, that we should not merely adopt a passive course with one as with the other potency, but that we should allow only the one to influence us as a determining ground of our conduct, in order by means thereof to crucify by our own efforts the flesh, with the affections and lusts thereof (Gal. 5:24). For even the blessed fruits of the Spirit have no permanence, if the power of the Spirit does not become the instrumental means of our own acting in opposing the flesh, *i.e.* where in the case of the ἐν πάσῃ δυνάμει δυναμούμενοι, it does not reach the περιπατῆσαι ἀξίως τοῦ Κυρίου (Col. 1:11). If then, in this way, even in the regenerate and converted man, a conflict of opposing forces makes itself felt in the domain of his inward experience, yet is this experience essentially distinct from that which presents itself to the unconverted and natural man, and which was before discussed (§ 10, note (3)). For the regenerate and converted man discovers in this opposing power an obstruction to his personal tendency, which is supported by God's Holy Spirit, but not an overpowering might which overmasters this good tendency and enslaves his heart.

(3) Comp. § 23, note (1). Within the fellowship of the Holy Ghost with us, in which relation the man who is born of God or who is regenerate is placed (comp. § 21), sinning is inconceivable. In such a relation no man stands of himself; but rather the condition of man in itself brings with it this alone, that we cannot look upon him otherwise than as a sinner. The possibility of conceiving, on the other hand, that in the idea and essence of regeneration and of the regenerate man in itself, the possibility of sinning should find a place, is what John contends against (1 John 3:9), in opposition to the erroneous idea, that any one could remain in Christ, in whom there is no

sin, and yet commit sin (πᾶς ὁ ἐν αὐτῷ μένων οὐχ ἁμαρτάνει, ver. 6),—as if rather such an one would not practise righteousness, in order to be righteous, even as He is righteous (ver. 7). In this connection, against this false doctrine, and not as an answer to the question whether a Christian is a man without sin (which he has already before expressly denied, 1:8 and 2:1), John says, "Whosoever is born of God does not commit sin, for the seed of God remains in him; and he cannot sin, because he is born of God." By this it is not denied that a man may fall from that of which he has become a partaker in regeneration; but it is indeed denied that one who desists from the practice of righteousness, and lives in sin, may dare to look upon himself as a regenerate person, who abides in Christ. The comfort, however, contained in the words of the apostle is this, that he who is born of God, in the fellowship of the Holy Ghost, which as a seed of divine life abides in him, has really a power which otherwise no man possesses, viz. the power of being able not to sin, the potentiality of sinlessness. He who in faith can lay hold of this power, wages quite a different conflict from his who dreams of being able to combat sin by his own strength alone.

(4) The necessity of regeneration is pointed out by Christ Himself in John, in these words: "That which is born of the flesh is flesh" (John 3:5). What is of this nature cannot enter into the kingdom of heaven. Related to this, though not in the same sense, is the expression of the apostle, that flesh and blood cannot inherit the kingdom of God (1 Cor. 15:50); for there is only meant that the corruptible cannot inherit incorruptibility. Both, however, coincide in this, that that which is subject to death is at the same time subject to sin and guilt—that, in short, man is viewed as σάρξ. For in σάρξ, that is, in his nature as he receives it at the birth of the body, is established that connection with his species by reason of which his mixed spiritual and corporeal organization—this indissolubly united natural basis of his soul's life—is degenerate (§ 5, note (5), p. 22). Far from the truth as it would be to identify that which is called flesh with the body and bodily existence, it were equally

wrong to separate this nature from its corporeal connection with the race, and to attribute it entirely to the soul, which has no existence except in connection with the life of the body. But since the nature of mixed *spiritual-corporeal* existence is brought about by corporeal birth, the degeneration of this nature likewise can only come to light both in the affections which attach themselves to the spiritual and soul portion, and those which belong to the corporeal and the sensuous. And in regard to this twofold tendency, the basis of these affections is, as our inborn and degenerate nature, called the flesh. How little by this we are warranted in asserting that this degeneration may perhaps only affect the body and not reach the spirit, becomes as clear as day, where the difference is distinctly expressed, and that self-purification which is incumbent on the Christian is expressly called a purifying from all pollution of flesh and spirit (ἀπὸ παντὸς μολυσμοῦ σαρκὸς καὶ πνεύματος, 2 Cor. 7:1). But since all this has for its source an inborn and corrupt basis in our nature, the most diverse errors of a corporeal and sensuous kind, as well as those belonging to the soul and spirit, are called in one and the same line works of the flesh (Gal. 5:19). Nay, in the same degree in which we may say of the regenerate and converted man, that his spirit is life because of righteousness, but his body dead or exposed to death (νεκρόν, Rom. 8:10); in the same degree the apostle bids us direct our weapons against this body of death (Rom. 7:24), this body of sin (Rom. 6:6), and know that our old man was crucified with Christ for this very purpose, that the body of sin should be rendered powerless (καταργηθῇ), that we should no longer be the slaves of sin (τοῦ μηκέτι δουλεύειν τῇ ἁμαρτίᾳ), that sin should no longer reign in our mortal (θνητῷ) body, to be obedient to the lusts thereof (6:12), but that we should yield our members as instruments of righteousness to serve God (6:13), by mortifying (νεκροῦν. Col. 3:5) these members which are upon the earth, and in which the different lusts are excited, and giving the deeds of the body up to death (θανατοῦν τὰς πράξεις τοῦ σώματος, Rom. 8:13). This entire mode of expression would lose all signification, if it were not meant that precisely in this corporeal nature of man sin developed itself. But this, again, is not so to be understood as if sin existed in man because he possesses a body, but because by reason of *this* body (τὸ σῶμα τῆς σαρκός, Col. 2:1), through a corporeal medium, he stands in a generic connection with his race, in which his nature is subjected to the flesh and the affections of a mixed corporeal-spiritual kind, which are in hostility to God. And these, therefore, become affections of his personality, pass over to his thoughts (the θελήματα τῆς σαρκός become θελήματα τῶν διανοιῶν, Eph. 2:3), and the φρόνημα τῆς σαρκός (Rom. 8:5) becomes a φρονεῖν τὰ τῆς σαρκός (Rom. 8:4). And just to prevent this result the struggle of the Christian is directed. For this purpose, spiritual and individual freedom has been won by him through the fellowship of the Holy Ghost, which is called, in reference to this, its effect in setting us free—a putting off of the body of the flesh (comp. § 22, note (2)).

This putting off of the body of the flesh is a deliverance from its predominating and enslaving power, but not an annihilation of the same. For even the Christian has the σάρξ, the flesh, still in him, not merely as the mortal flesh (θνητὴ σάρξ, 2 Cor. 4:11) in which he lives (ὃ δὲ νῦν ζῶ ἐν σαρκί, Gal. 2:20; ὁ ἐπίλοιπος ἐν σαρκὶ χρόνος, 1 Pet. 4:2), but also that flesh in which sin dwells (Rom. 7:17, 18; comp. ἐν σαρκὶ περιπατοῦντες οὐ κατὰ σάρκα στρατευόμεθα, 2 Cor. 10:3). But that "being in the flesh" is one thing, when it denotes those who as yet know nothing of Christ (ὅτε ἦμεν ἐν τῇ σαρκί, Rom. 7:5), or who have again relapsed into the old nature (οἱ ἐν σαρκὶ ὄντες, Θεῷ ἀρέσαι οὐ δύνανται, Rom 8:8); and another thing, when the same is to be spoken of the Christian. He is σάρκινος (Rom. 7:14), but not σαρκικός. And of him, notwithstanding, it may be said that he is in the spirit and not in the flesh (Rom. 8:9), because, although *in* the flesh, he is not *according to* the flesh, nor lives or walks *after* the flesh (κατὰ σάρκα εἶναι, ζῆν, περιπατεῖν, Rom. 8:5, 12, 13, 4), and desires not nor directs his mind (φρονεῖ, Rom. 8:5) to that after which the mind (φρόνημα) of the flesh goes. He feels himself rather, in his new state of life, under obligation to the spirit, and not to the flesh, in order to live after the flesh (ὀφειλέται ἐσμὲν, οὐ τῇ σαρκὶ, τοῦ κατὰ σάρκα ζῆν, Rom. 8:12).

How greatly, notwithstanding, this inner strife is to the Christian an object of the bitterest experience, is shown by the Apostle Paul, when the cry of woe, "O wretched man that I am! who shall deliver me from the body of this death?" is blent with the thanksgiving, "I thank God, through Jesus Christ our Lord" (Rom. 7:24, 25). That the apostle is here (ver. 14 ff.) speaking of the nature of the Christian's experience is manifest from the context, and I shall not again have to prove it, after the recent and excellent investigations of Hofmann (*Schriftbeweis*. 2d ed. i. p. 551 ff.), Delitzsch (*Bibl. Psychol.* p. 433 ff. [Clark's translation]), and others. Every Christian can find the best proof of it in his own self-knowledge and self-experience. But it is as little the case that the experience of the Christian is exhausted in the perception of this inward strife, as that the apostle stops at this mere exclamation of wretchedness, or at the consideration of his inward state, without going on to that grateful and joyful upward glance to Christ, and the means of triumph which he already has in Him (8:1 ff.). That, however, which the apostle declares in the seventh chapter of the Epistle to the Romans, has for us in this place, first of all, only the import of proving by this exclamation how much in the Christian, even if he limits himself to that which he can consider as his internal state by itself and irrespectively of the power of Christ, the consciousness of his strife differs from that which is in appearance analogous in the experience of the natural man in himself (πᾶν ἁμάρτημα μάχημα περιέχει, Epict. *diss.* ii. 26). The apostle, however, acts under the influence of a twofold limitation, and indeed as certainly as his glance in his cry of woe is directed to something other than in his thanksgiving. In the first he has in his eye that which he is in himself (αὐτὸς ἐγώ, 7:25), and irrespectively of that of which he is certain in Christ (8:1 ff.). And even in such a light does he view himself in the keen and judicial exercise of self-examination, occasioned by the context and conditioned by the nature of the case, as he feels himself to stand over against the law and in the light of the law. That, therefore, which he in this relation, when regarding himself in himself alone (*i.e.* purely in the state of his inner man), is able to say of himself, is, if we begin from the closing point of his declarations concerning himself, in reference to God's will and law the following: He knows himself in his own mind to be the servant of the law of God (τῷ μὲν νοΐ δουλεύω νόμῳ Θεοῦ, ver. 25). This, however, not in a slavish sense. He has in his inner man, or in the inmost recess of his nature, his joy in the law of God (συνήδομαι τῷ νόμῳ τοῦ Θεοῦ κατὰ τὸν ἔσω ἄνθρωπον, ver. 22). He wills that which is good, and desires not that which is opposed to this (vers. 19, 20). If he comes to the doing of this opposite, he does that which he hates (ver. 15). Thence he concludes that he is enslaved by sin as by some alien power, when he knows not (οὐ γινώσκαι, ver. 15, the expression for being alien) what he does, just because that which he desires to do he does not perform, but does that which he hates (ver. 16). And so he is no more able to say that *he* or his Ego effects it, when he does that which he desires not to do, but it is the sin which dwells in him that does so (ver. 17). This "in him," however, is not his "Ego," but his "flesh," in which dwells nothing good (ver. 18). And thus over against the law, which has become a law of his individual mind, or a power prevailing in him (ὁ νόμος τοῦ νοός, ver. 23), there stands another law, another determining power, which wars against this in his members, and takes him captive to the law of sin which is in his members (ver. 23), that is, to that law by which, when he desires to do good, evil is present with him (ver. 21). Thus the apostle judges his own inner state, when he looks only upon that which he finds in himself, and asks of himself, What would become of him, if he had nothing but the law of God. But he gives thanks to God when, turning away from himself, he regards that which he has not in himself, but in Christ. And to this very expression of thanks he comes after, and because he has fully concluded his judgment on that which he is in the mere condition of his inner constitution and after his flesh.

We need only compare that which the apostle here says of himself, with that which he in another place describes as the condition of men without Christ, to perceive that one and the same person could not intend to portray an image of the natural man in such colors. For where in the inmost heart of man, in his individual mind, instead of enmity against God, there has entered in assent, joy, delight in obedience to His law, there the inner man precisely is already removed from the dominion of the flesh (Rom. 8:7, τὸ γὰρ φρόνημα τῆς σαρκός, ἔχθρα εἰς Θεόν· τῷ γὰρ νόμῳ τοῦ Θεοῦ οὐχ ὑποτάσσεται, οὐδὲ γὰρ δύναται). And this is possible neither to the natural strength of man nor to the law of God, but to God's grace only. This it is which puts God's laws into our mind, and writes them on our hearts (Heb. 8:10; comp. § 22, note (2)). But he who knows Christ, knows at the same time that not even his personal acquiescence in the law makes him free, but the law of the Spirit of life, which *has* delivered him in Christ Jesus from the law of sin and of death (Rom. 8:1 ff.). To this the Christian ever and anon mounts up from his own frames, and lives in the full assurance that everything which is born of God overcomes the world; and that not from the contemplation of our own frames, but from our *faith*, arises the victory which has overcome the world (1 John 5:4). For in faith he embraces Christ daily, our only Redeemer. That is, to speak according to the course of thought of this epistle, the Christian daily goes over from the seventh to the eighth chapter of the Epistle to the Romans.

(5) The tempter who overcame the first man, was overcome by the second Adam (Matt. 4). The works of him who, from the beginning of history onwards, was a murderer (John 8:44), Christ has come to destroy (1 John 3:8). The perfect victory over him has already been achieved by the death of Christ upon the cross (Col. 2:15; comp. Heb. 2:14); but those who are in Christ have no less to undergo the conflict with Satan, and to overcome him through Christ (Eph. 6:12, comp. 1 Pet. 5:8; Jas. 4:7; Eph. 2:2, etc.). For their conversion is in itself a conversion from the power of Satan unto God (Acts 26:18; comp. in

opposition to this, 2 Cor. 4:4). And in faith in Christ the Victor, the victory is already gained over the wicked one, and over the world, the domain of the power of the wicked one (1 John 2:13, 14, 5:4, 5; comp. John 16:11). At this point also commences the struggle of the Christian, in the victory of Christ which is made his, and in the consciousness of a power to conquer. This is the essential point for the inward and genuine disposition of the Christian. What import this recognition of the ultimate basis of all evil and wickedness in the world, of which every leaf of the New Testament speaks, may have for the inner development of our struggles conformably to experience, will hereafter be discussed. It is of the highest importance for the understanding of the historical development of the world and its kingdoms, and our own relation to the cosmical signification of this struggle. We are called in Christ and with Him to overcome the monstrous offence of a creaturely apostasy,—not, however, belonging to this world, although affecting its history and that of the human race. It involves in itself that enigma of the world's history which for us is only half solved. At the same time, however, there is revealed to us herein both the depth of our need of redemption and the ground of our capability of redemption. We are not the contrivers of the fall of Satan, but the perverted, and therefore redeemable. And if we conquer, our conquest is quite distinct from one over our own flesh. It is a share in the final victory of Christ, in which He will establish the kingdom of His glory in triumph over all the powers of darkness (1 Cor. 15:24).

§ 27. b. *The Struggle as the Acceptance of a divinely appointed Probation*

The struggle of the converted man conduces to the end for which we become partakers of the spirit of regeneration (§ 26),—namely, to his education for freedom, for a voluntary, self-active mastery over evil, and for a free embracing of the grace of Christ which alone is able to make us free (1). This our freedom we are to experience here below, not as our own strength, but as the power of the grace of God in Christ; and for this reason it will be at the same time accompanied by a consciousness and conviction of our own helplessness (2). God removes us, therefore, neither from the sinful flesh, which at the same time convinces us of our weakness, nor from the world, amidst whose affliction and misery we become conscious just of the infirmity of the flesh, in order that we may learn from faith alone in the power of Christ to overcome the world, and at the same time, in the compassionate mercy of Christ, like Him to subdue the evil external to us with good, and to practice mercy towards all men, even as we ourselves have experienced nothing but mercy (3). This relation, however, in which we are called upon to struggle against the sin that is within and without us, and the sufferings of this present time which spring from it, serves for the trial or probation of our faith, so long as we feel it as a suffering in and with Christ, to which we continually oppose, not a barren hope of final triumph, but the power of the received grace of the promise in patience and joy (4).

(1) In and with that freedom which is born of God, we are at the same time subjected to a trial of that freedom. That is to say, the dominion of Christ in our hearts must show itself as a self-mastery, through Him, over all which is not of Christ. We have to take a share in His victory over us by subduing ourselves. This exercise of dominion constitutes our royal priesthood (βασίλειον ἱεράτευμα, 1 Pet. 2:9). And inasmuch as we are assured by faith, not through ourselves, but through Him who loved us (Rom. 8:37), of more than conquering every hostile power, that which afflicts us becomes an object of our triumph in faith. This, however, only on the supposition that we preserve inviolate our freedom as service to Christ (ὁ ἐλεύθερος κληθεὶς δοῦλός ἐστιν Χριστοῦ, 1 Cor. 7:22). And this takes place in our casting off the bondage of the flesh, nay, every occasion of fleshly lust (ἐπ' ἐλευθερίᾳ ἐκλήθητε·—μόνον μὴ τὴν ἐλευθερίαν scil. τρέπετε or μετατίθεσθε εἰς ἀφορμὴν τῇ σαρκί, Gal. 5:13; ὡς ἐλεύθεροι, καὶ μὴ ὡς ἐπικάλυμμα ἔχοντες

τῆς κακίας τὴν ἐλευθερίαν, ἀλλ' ὡς δοῦλοι Θεοῦ, 1 Pet. 2:16). But inasmuch as, according to this, the freedom of the Christian has to approve itself, he is also not taken away from that in which it has to approve itself. Nay, the relation in which Christ became and is our help and our Redeemer, corresponds exactly, and in the manner peculiar to it, to that in which we are to become aware of our own need of help, and are to receive His help. He was to resemble His brethren in all points, sin only excepted (χωρὶς ἁμαρτίας, Heb. 4:15), "in order that He might become a merciful and faithful high priest before God; for in that He Himself hath suffered, being tempted, He is able to succour them that are tempted" (Heb. 2:17, 18). To help such as (not without sin) are tempted, is the office of Christ. And on this very ground He did not withdraw Himself from the temptation inconceivably greater of sinless and guiltless suffering, in order that out of such a depth He might be able to sympathize with the depth of our misery. Hence also as πειραζόμενοι only do we realize what Christ is for us.

(2) The relation in which we are exposed to a constant conflict, does not make it necessary that it should always exist in the form of a struggle against that hostile antagonism in which the flesh opposes itself to the will of God. It is, however, an inevitable consequence of our carnal nature, that we should feel ourselves, both with respect to the will of God and to the sufferings of this present time, burdened with a weakness which renders difficult for us the accomplishment of the one and the endurance of the other. But neither is this anything which is to lead us astray. For as, in respect to the fulfilment of the divine will, we are referred not to our own strength, but to Him who works in us both to will and to do, and who is the Beginner and Finisher of the good work (Phil. 2:13, 1:6); so also, with respect to every guiltless suffering, whatever it may be, and although our weakness in the endurance of it is not blameless, there holds good what the apostle reports as addressed to himself, "My grace is sufficient for thee; for strength is made perfect in weakness" (2 Cor. 12:9); and that

which he himself also, in the acceptance of this saying, might and could say, "When I am weak, then am I strong" (ver. 10).

(3) The school into which we are thus brought, corresponds also to our Christian calling in the world. On the one hand, the declaration of Christ applies to all His disciples, that He prays to the Father, not that He should take them out of the world, but that He should keep them from the evil; just as, on the other hand, does that statement of His, that as the Father has sent Him into the world, so also He has sent His own into the world (John 17:15, 18). And it is in accordance with the object of this sending, that, as being strong, they should bear the infirmities of the weak, and should not please themselves (Rom. 15:1). Everything, in short, which is meant hereby, or in the requisition to a mutual bearing of each other's burdens, and so to fulfil the law of Christ (Gal. 6:1, 2; comp. § 13, p. 126 ff.), or to the receiving of one another, as Christ also hath received us (Rom. 15:7),—all this no one understands or is capable of carrying out who in his own case knows nothing of burdens and infirmities, nor measures thereby what is implied when it is said that Christ notwithstanding has received him. As it is only in our personal struggles that we acquire, by reason of use, senses exercised to discern good and evil (Heb. 5:14), so also it is from the sufferings of our own conflict alone that we learn sympathy with the suffering members (1 Cor. 12:26); and only by our conformity to our High Priest, who was in all points tempted like as we are (Heb. 4:15), do we learn what moves to compassion in the mind of Christ, and is called compassion in His spirit.

(4) We must begin first of all with the distinction which exists between trial as such and temptation. This distinction we meet, *e.g.* placed in the clearest light in the Epistle of James. One and the same word there serves to denote things in their nature distinct. At one time it signifies something which assails us from without (ὅταν πειρασμοῖς περιπέσητε ποικίλοις, Jas. 1:2); at another, something emerging from within (springing forth from the ἰδία ἐπιθυμία, 1:14). Forasmuch as, in regard to the latter, all causality on the part of God is denied (God cannot

be tempted with evil, and in this sense in His own person He tempts no one, ver. 13), it lies in the nature of the antithesis to regard the former as proceeding from God. And since in this epistle the writer is going not upon general possibilities, but upon concrete relations, it is also easy to express what is here intended. It is the antithesis of poor and rich (vers. 9, 10), this disparity which is the result of God's providence, every such disparity with the temptation peculiar to it, there consisting in depression, here in elevation, and both to be overcome only if there arrives in the one case a consciousness of exaltation, and in the other of abasement,—a consciousness which each can and is destined to attain by his portion in Christ, so soon as he reflects that Christ, in His compassion for the sinner, regards neither the lowly condition of the poor nor the high estate of the rich. If, however, the relation in which he stands becomes a temptation to evil to the one party as well as to the other, he must attribute this not to God, but to his own perverted desires. In this example we become aware how something ethically neutral—in this case the greater or less amount of worldly possession—becomes a source of ethical temptation, through a position which does not belong to the objective relation in itself, but which the subject takes with regard to it. The means, however, by which this last is brought about, lies in an effect which has its rise in the objective relation, which involuntarily calls forth a certain disposition on the part of the subject,—in the one instance a sense of adversity, in the other one of prosperity, in the positions which they occupy in this present life. This involuntary result is also one divinely appointed. Not, however, for itself, but for a divinely appointed ultimate aim; namely, in order to this, that in these mutually opposite states of mind the power of Christ might be proved in a manner equally opposite: here, in lifting up above depression,—that is to say, in disregarding the absence of worldly wealth in comparison with the greatness of the spiritual possession; there, in the subduing of pleasure,—that is, in the disregarding of transitory prosperity as compared with the greatness of the everlasting possession. Where this possession is the delight of the heart, there in neither case do arise perverted desires. Where, however, such is not the case, then both earthly possession and the want of it, although not in themselves evil, become an occasion to a desire tempting to evil, through that involuntary working upon us which in itself also is not evil, but only then turns to evil when we allow it to obtain the mastery over us, instead of making it the means leading alike to our elevation and our humiliation, according as we measure our earthly good, from the feeling of its deficiency or of its superfluity, by the standard of that other good which we owe to Christ. Compared with our happiness in Christ, riches are not happiness, nor poverty unhappiness. What, therefore, God desires in permitting a condition accompanied by various and involuntary effects, is not temptation to evil (the πειράζεσθαι, ver. 14), but probation (τὸ δοκίμιον, ver. 2),—the trial of our freedom, whether we have become free enough in Christ to allow the involuntary effect of riches as well as of poverty to conduce to a just appreciation on our part of the good which we possess in Christ, and which makes us equally free, though in a different manner, from the attack both of riches and poverty.

The first Epistle of Peter exhibits to us another domain of probation. There also it is a question of manifold temptations (πειρασμοί, 1 Pet. 1:6). As he, however, attributes to them the exclusive effect of heaviness (λυπηθέντες), we find ourselves on a more limited area than with James. And if that of which the apostle is thinking is to be gathered from the epistle itself, these manifold temptations are pointed out to us in ch. 4:12 ff., and how they are associated with the reproach which we undergo in Christ's name and for Christ's sake (εἰ ὀνειδίζεσθε ἐν ὀνόματι Χριστοῦ, 4:14). Hence it follows in what specific sense the apostle characterizes their sufferings as a partaking of the sufferings of Christ (4:13). The undiscretionary or involuntary effect which may become a temptation, is the divinely appointed sorrow which such reproach is to cause us. But it would become a temptation leading to evil only, if we wished to estimate the temporary and transient sorrow (ὀλίγον ἄρτι, εἰ δέον ἐστίν, λυπηθέντες, 1 Pet. 1:6) higher than that everlasting heritage of glory which is prepared for those who love Christ (1:4, 7-9), and preferred the honor which is from men to that which is of God. When God thus permits the sorrow-bringing hatred of the world to arise and to fall upon us, it is according to His design just only a probation of our faith (τὸ δοκίμιον τῆς πίστεως, 1:7), whether we have become free in Him to subordinate the pain of such experience to the joy over the possession in Christ, and allow even this sorrow to turn to the occasion of clinging all the more closely to that unspeakable joy transformed into glory (δεδοξασμένῃ) which is the hope of our future in Christ (1 Pet. 1:8, 9). It is in the same sense that Paul bids us overcome the sufferings of this present time, with the thought that they are not worthy to be compared with the glory which shall be revealed in us (Rom. 8:18). And the same sufferings which Peter calls a fellowship of the sufferings of Christ, Paul names in the same sense sufferings of Christ which abound in us (2 Cor. 1:5), fellowship of His sufferings (Phil. 3:10), afflictions of Christ, which are continued in our sufferings, and are to attain their full measure in us (Col. 1:24), just because the disciple is not above his Master, the position of the disciple resembles that of his Master, and therefore, like His, our task is a task of suffering, wherein we suffer from the same enmity from which Christ also suffered (Matt. 10:24; John 15:18, 20). These are all divinely appointed relations, whose sorrow and suffering are to serve for our probation, and whose purifying virtue, like a fiery furnace (1 Pet. 4:12), we do not perceive in such a manner that what causes us pain might and ought in itself to become joy, but that we overcome the sorrow with the joyful thought either of standing in the service of Christ under such sorrow (Col. 1:24), or of possessing in it a means of confirmation (Jas. 1:2, 12, μακάριος ὁ ἀνὴρ ὃς ὑπομένει πειρασμόν), or of arming ourselves against such sorrow by a glance at the unchangeable joy of the future glory (1 Pet. 1:6, καιρὸς ἔσχατος, ἐν ᾧ ἀγαλλιᾶσθε; 4:13, χαίρειν ἐν τῇ ἀποκαλύψει τῆς δόξης). Here also, however, the source of temptation does not lie in that which happens to us through others in itself, but in our own capacity for suffering, which again is connected with the weakness of our flesh (ἀσθενεία τῆς σαρκός).

We are therefore justified also in asking the question, In what sense and to what extent that weakness of the flesh, which leads us to an inward antagonism between the flesh and the spirit, is and remains a divinely appointed probation. That this state is divinely willed is unquestionable, since, although not introduced by God, it is nevertheless not absolutely removed by Him in regeneration. It is left as something that we must continually strive to overcome in the power of God. In this respect it stands in the category of a pedagogical ordinance of corrective grace belonging to this present world. The carnal will, when it obtains the *mastery* over that which is the will of the Spirit, becomes a movement which withdraws itself from this ordinance. But this takes place only when our personal will enters into the carnal will, and when the temptation becomes what we personally will, because we find pleasure in being tempted (comp. Luther in the *Larger Catechism* on Petition VII. of the Lord's Prayer). So long as that which inwardly tempts us remains for us a grief and suffering, in which we yearn after deliverance from temptation (Rom. 7:24), and pray to God not to lead us into temptation, and that we may avoid it (Matt. 6:13, 26:41; Luke 22:40, 46), so long also does this antagonism of the flesh remain in us a probation; for the carnal will does not become our own personal desire. Only when we wish to free ourselves from temptation common to man (πειρασμὸς ἀνθρώπινος, 1 Cor. 10:13), look upon it as something foreign, which has not been ordained for our salvation (1 Pet. 4:12; 1 Thess. 3:4), or when we yield ourselves to temptation, the anxiety enters lest Satan tempt us (1 Cor. 7:5; 1 Thess. 3:5). Otherwise the promise stands fast to the Christian in faith, that God is able to deliver the godly out of temptation (2 Pet. 2:9), and that He is faithful, and will not let us be tempted above our strength, but will with the temptation also make a way of escape, that we may be able to bear it (1 Cor. 10:13). This faith, which embraces the foundation of the promise of our hope of final victory, is the mother of that enduring patience in which we have to undergo trial, and to inherit the promise (Heb. 10:35, 36). But patience is no barren state of expectancy; but it has and is to have its *perfect* work by asking in faith for the strength it needs, and with that strength which God bestows making resistance to temptation (comp. Jas. 1:4–6). He who goes to meet temptation as a self-probation divinely ordained, gains, in the knowledge of this, joy in the midst of its assaults; and in whatever shape it may present itself, whether it comes upon us from without, or springs up from the conflict in our own bosom, it is still probation, so long as our "heart" does not allow itself to lust after that which tempts us in opposition to our will.

It will be difficult to decide in a hundred practical cases of self-examination, which merely measures the forms of the internal process, where probation ends and temptation begins. Much more, however, depends upon the position and the disposition in which we meet every individual case, than upon our decision as to the individual case. And here the chief point appears to me to be this, that the Christian should guard himself against false terrors. He is to keep in view not so much that which happens to him as that for which according to God's will such a thing happens to him. This, however, is the self-probation and trial of faith, in which the promised assurance of effectual divine help is to stand nearer to the Christian than aught beside.

§ 28. *c. The Struggle as a Warding off of Ungodly Temptations*

In the same element in which there is given here below the opportunity for the confirmation or the divinely appointed trial of our faith, the ungodly temptation to renounce that faith may also develop itself (1). Temptation presents itself so soon as something belonging to the creature, *i.e.* any relation we may think of as proper to man's creaturely existence, and arising therefrom (whether it be given in the relations of man to himself, or to what is external to him), becomes the object of selfish desire or our own lust, in the sense that we adopt, as a standard of that which we may venture to desire for ourselves, our own lust, and raise this in an apparent equality above our love to God, above the will of God concerning us, and above our obedience to this will. For in the heart which desires to divide itself between opposing desire and love, love to God is already overcome (2). Hence, in regard to that which becomes a temptation to us, we have to consider not so much the object with which the temptation is associated, as rather the state of the heart itself, in order to test against what we have to guard ourselves as offering temptation to us (3). On the energy and constancy of the resistance which our heart wages by the power of God's Holy Spirit, which it derives from faith in His promises, it depends whether the temptation becomes momentary or permanent, and one that gains the mastery; and in proportion as the temptation assumes the form of lust, propensity, or passion, the danger of the temptation increases (4). The more, however, the increasing danger of the temptation lies not so much in the object of our selfish desire (whether real or imaginary) as in the state of our heart relative to the object which excites our desire, so much the more intimately is the guarding against the entrance of the temptation, and the conquest of it when it has entered in, connected with that self-examination and self-knowledge by which we are not only on our guard against that which God has expressly forbidden us to desire, but also are circumspect as to the manner in which we either wish for or enjoy that which God has permitted us to wish for and enjoy, in order to oppose in both directions every commencement of that lust which enslaves us, and which threatens to be prejudicial to our freedom and lordship in Christ over all things (5). In order to proceed surely here, we must neither palliate the selfish lusting of the heart with the unobjectionableness of the object in itself, nor deceive ourselves with a pretended unobjectionable state of the heart concerning what is objectionable in the object which we desire: we must neither wish to be sure of our heart while we expose ourselves to the charm of things which have a temptation for us; nor must we wish, by mere outward abstinence from things which have a temptation for us, to reach that which is to be reached by fighting with the heart (6). And since we take equally into view ourselves in regard to the state of our heart, as well as the objective nature of the task of our lives, which has become ours in Christ, it is incumbent on us to judge what we have to flee as temptation to ungodliness, as much by the standard given by the divine word respecting us as by the subjective experience of our own personal condition,—not so as to apply individual standards to what ought to be objectively condemned, but rather so as to adapt the individual nature of our resistance to the individual form of the temptation; looking, however, for the victory in the proper use of the universal means of grace, according to the rule of the divine word, and not in our own self-devised means and methods (7).

(1) We are here speaking not of temptation as it presents itself to the natural, but to the regenerate and converted man. The possibility of temptation lies without doubt in the same relations which he as man partakes with other men. Since, however, he has by faith become partaker of a power of resistance which the natural man does not possess, in him the temptation also takes the form of a conflict which in that manner is unknown to the natural man. And this is a conflict not merely between evil propensity and better will, but between that love to God which is born of faith, and the awakening of a love which draws him away from this power which has been bestowed on him by faith. And the wider the life-relations in which the Christian stands by the power of faith, so much greater also is the manifoldness of the conceivable temptations which are calculated to assail his faith. And as he must rest assured of this fact, that he possesses in faith the power to overcome; so also must he cling to the conviction, that every temptation has for him the grave significance of an enticement to a renunciation of his faith. Thus alone can he keep steadily in view both what he possesses

in his faith, and what significance his being tempted has for him. The object of his faith is not merely the reception of justifying grace before God, but also to fulfil in the power of God all the will of God respecting himself. And temptation occurs to him not merely to induce him to think, will, and act contrary to the will of God, but to force him from that state of possession in which he is enabled by God's grace to think, to will, and to act conformably to the divine will. And whereas a false mode of thinking and speaking understands by renunciation of faith that only which is directed against our faith, so far as that comprises what *God* in Christ is for us and has done for us, we must bear steadily in mind that renunciation of faith no less takes place where we allow ourselves to be tempted to enter with personal affection and pleasure on any one thing which stands in opposition to that which *we* ought to be and to do in God through Christ. That which in him who is not a Christian may be termed a violation of natural affection, of human law, and of the divine will as far as he can know it—as, for example, the neglect of a proper provision for his own—is named in Scripture, when it happens in the case of a Christian, a renunciation of the faith (τὴν πίστιν ἤρνηται. 1 Tim. 5:8). And this just from the inseparable connection in which faith stands with love, the fulfiller of the law (§ 19).

It is, however, not one and the same position which we take up as Christians in the power of faith and of the love (which is born of faith) towards God, towards ourselves, and towards other men. We have previously seen in what sense faith makes us masters, and love servants (§ 19, note (4)). Hence we may say that everything has for us the nature of temptation, which leads us into danger of injuring or destroying either the power of our mastery in Christ, or our power for faithful service in the same Christ. By this standard we may try what is a temptation to us. And from this point of view we cannot continue seeking the essence of temptation in those relations only which in themselves appear objectionable before God; but it is the totality of all creature relations, as we may regard them in involuntary reflex influence upon ourselves, as exciting either pleasure or pain, and as they hereby form a means of trial for the confirmation of our faith, to which may cling the temptation to a denial of our faith.

(2) Where that temptation to evil which is not divinely ordained trial has entered in, James tells us in his epistle (1:14). It takes place when any one is drawn away and enticed by his own desires. We have no intention in this place of entering into an explanation of the several occasions from which such desires arise. The perverted tendency which had taken possession of those to whom the epistle was addressed, is held up to them afterwards in express terms as a love of the world (φιλία τοῦ κόσμου, ch. 4.); and their own conscience must have told them with how good reason that was said of them which stands here in the first chapter. Here, however, it stands at the same time as a *universal* truth not applicable to them alone; and, indeed, for the purpose of making them sensible of the difference between such temptation to evil and those divinely ordained trials under which those who love God are to prove themselves, in order to receive the crown of life. For the natural course of that temptation to evil which, whenever it occurs, commences with the allurement of our own desires, is quite different. In this case, if man permits himself to be enticed and drawn away, instead of offering resistance, he is thus led by his own covetous instinct. It does not remain mere desiring: the desire, with which the will of man has united, conceives and brings forth sin; but sin, when it has come to ripeness (ἀποτελεσθεῖσα), brings forth death (ver. 16, in opposition to ζωή, ver. 12). And the fact that, where man permits himself to be drawn away and allured, that temptation has occurred which in its nature has sin for its fruit, may serve for a mark of distinction from that trial which is ordained by God. The impulse and allurement of his own desire belong exclusively to man, and are never of God; and no divinely appointed trial is so constituted as, according to its nature, to have sin as its fruit. Such only occurs when our own desire draws and entices us to consider the element of our temptation which we ought to

reject as something worthy of being desired. The commencement of sin is that permitting ourselves to be enticed and drawn away. A sinful root alone produces sin for its fruit. And this lies not only in the nature of the thing, and remains therefore unsaid, but lies also in the context, since this kind of temptation is said to be ungodly, and springing purely out of the nature of man. Thus it suffices to name the nature of the fruit, in order to arrive at a certain conclusion about the nature of the root. The sinful desire is followed by the act of sin. This itself, however, has, in its reflex influence on man, a definite course, in which it tends to a definite goal. And this goal is the subjection of man to the lordship of sin. And its fruit stands in diametrical contrast to that which constitutes the object of divinely appointed trial; for the fruit thereof is death, in place of the crown of life. Herein is revealed the whole extent of that danger, which is imminent where man allows himself to be drawn away and enticed by his own desire.

The short declaration of this passage serves this practical purpose. It suffices for this, without there being required in this place any further explanation touching the exciting causes of this desire, the relation of the sinful prompting of our nature to the yielding of the individual will thereto, the difference between the sin thence arising and the sinful beginning, and the genesis of the death-bringing ripeness of sin. Even the idea of our own (ἰδία) lust is sufficient to mark it as sinful, in its opposition to that which comes from God. For man has already fallen from his relations to God and his communion with Him, when he makes *his own* lust the measure of what is worthy of his desire, and allows himself to be guided thereby (comp. § 25, note (7)). This is always a relapse into that living for self (ἑαυτῷ ζῆν) instead of living to Christ. The various forms of selfish desire, as they are bound up with its manifold objects, are not here taken into consideration in fixing the characteristic of that which remains under all circumstances ungodly temptation. For where man lusts to seek for his own, there he desires that which is not of God, and is tempted in a way which is not from God. Within what life-relations he does this, however, is, considered abstractly, quite immaterial. For in all departments of life it behooves us to serve one master, and not two; and in all life-relations it is impossible so to divide our affection, as to desire and love equally that which belongs to the creature and that which belongs to God (Matt. 6:24; Luke 16:13); and in every department of life we have lost the standard of lawful desire, if we follow only the impulse of *our own* lust.

From what has been said may be deduced the universal canon, under what supposition those divinely appointed trials, which have their beginning not in our own desires which spring up within, may become for us a temptation to evil. Under all circumstances, it so happens that the involuntary working proceeding from them to us becomes to us the object of a desire in which we do not subordinate this effect to its higher aims and designs settled in the divine scheme of training, but only view it as deserving our desire in proportion as it corresponds with our own peculiar views. And this is equally true whether the relations in which we find ourselves placed without our own co-operation, excite in us pleasure or pain. For in the one case as in the other, this effect is not intended to subserve that which is pleasing to ourselves, but that which is profitable for us in our relations to God in Christ (comp. § 27, note (3)).

(3) If we make that involuntary working (whether as producing pleasure or pain), which is destined to serve higher ends, in selfish mode the object of our own desire, we convert that working of divine trial and proof which was appointed for a blessing, through our own fault, into a curse and a temptation to evil. And that not merely that object which excites pleasure, but even that which causes pain, can become the object of such a selfish desire, which is disconnected from the divine will with respect to us, is taught to every one by observation, whether of himself or of others. For even there, where the element of temptation presents itself in the sufferings of the present time, and ends its final destructive working with despair, in which the joyful communion of grace is abandoned, even there the temptation to evil commences by our making the indulgence

of our sorrow a desire of the heart, to which the heart becomes more prone than to the delight in God's comforting promises. This suicidal pleasure in affliction often accompanies the most severe actual sufferings, but changes the blessings that belong to that suffering into a curse, and the disciplinary virtue of the inward sorrows into a ban, which finally with overpowering might enchains the soul and destroys the good that appertains to the fellowship of grace. And all this arises when, with self-indulgent sinking down into that which, according to God's will, is merely a means of trial for higher and divine ends, we elevate the means to a selfish end, separate the temporal experience from the divine will, and place the indulgence of momentary feelings above the clinging fast to God's purposes of training, and, by yielding to temporal and creaturely dispositions, deprive ourselves of that power which we have and hold only by faith in God's gracious will, which is not visible or tangible, but guaranteed to us in the word of promise. Whether, now, this takes place from our cherishing this temporal affliction as a kind of enjoyment, or (which is more frequent) from our coveting that only which brings with it a spiritual or bodily state of self-satisfaction, and in the gratification of this selfish desire resisting and murmuring at those sufferings ordained by God,—in both cases the real element of temptation does not lie in that which happens to us from without, but in that inner proneness to wish to determine by the standard of our own self-will, and not by that of God's will in respect to us, what is worthy of our desire, and to cling to it.

In this sense I said that, in order to guard against the approach of temptation to evil, we must steadily keep in view not so much things, *i.e.* real relations of ourselves, to which we attribute a power to tempt; but the state of our heart, on which alone it depends whether the involuntary sorrow- and pleasure-giving excitement which springs from those relations becomes an occasion of selfish, and consequently of evil concupiscence. We are not justified in so dividing these relations, as if those only which have a tendency to produce pleasure were capable of being associated with temptation to evil. Neither can we so venture to divide or distinguish them, as to consider the relations which give rise to the sensation of pleasure or pain in a corporeal and sensuous point of view, as more dangerous in themselves than those within which the same may occur to the spirit and the soul. In itself it cannot be done; we cannot do it even for the inner life of the natural man who stands aloof from Christianity; still less can we do it in the case of the regenerate and converted man, of whom Christian ethics must treat. And if we admit it to stand as a fact of experience, confirmed by history and Scripture, that the greatest danger of temptation to selfish desire opposed to God's will and ordinance threatens the natural man from the side of excitement of corporeal and sensuous pleasure or pain, this can just as little be admitted as being exclusively the fact. History and Scripture point quite as much on this side to aberrations upon the purely spiritual domain, in the false conceit of wisdom, and the like. And just as little is it possible to determine beforehand, on an abstract scheme of the position of a Christian man, whether the one or the other side of his creature-relations may bring him into more or less danger of temptation. Scripture and experience are equally against it. He who has read the apostolic letters knows that there was enough of occasion for both, for warning alike against a relapse into carnal conduct, and against the voluntary humility of spiritual error (Col. 2:18). Least of all is it practicable to make a distinction in the nature of spiritual and corporeal relations, of such a kind as to call one sphere, with its temptations to selfish desires which pervert God's will and ordinances, more dangerous for the Christian than the other. For, in the first place, it is false, and associated with a spiritualistic view of the world, to look upon relations of the earthly life of the body in themselves as something ethically lower and further removed from the divine will with respect to man and the Christian, than the relations of our soul-life and spirit-life. Here there has been formed out of the organic subordination, in which that which is of the body ministers to the ends of the spiritual life of the soul, a false ethical estimate of their respective value. Body and soul, regarded in themselves, are vessels organized by God to the end that, in the inseparable and mutual relation of both spheres of life here below, man should live to God; and hence man stands no further from God when by his selfish lusts he disorganizes the body, than when he does the same to his spirit. Again, it is quite as false to suppose, that corrupt spiritual desires estrange us less from God, because spirit is more allied to God, who is a spirit; but that corrupt bodily and sensual desires remove us further from God, because that which is corporeal is more unlike to God, who is not body, but spirit. For man is not a spirit in the same sense that God is; and in that creaturely sense in which we call our spirit the image of God, the body is so also. He who sins either in the one or the other commits sin, neither more nor less, against that God to whom both man's body and spirit belong. And if it is asserted that corporeal and sensual desire enslaves us more than desire of the soul and the spirit, and that therefore the Christian must guard more strictly against the first than against the second, this is neither true in itself, nor is it equally applicable to the state of every Christian. It is not true in itself, because the pretended "more" of enslaving power rests on a confusion, in which, from the perception of the extension of an evil, we draw a conclusion respecting its greater intensity. For what we really perceive is this only, that with the majority of men the tendency to allow themselves to become enslaved by their corporeal and sensual desires is *more perceptible* than their bondage to perverted desires in the domain of the spirit. I say *more perceptible*; but even hence a certain conclusion touching the extent of this evil is not at all allowable, much less respecting the excess of its intensity or the power exercised by it. For, in the first place, this alone is a matter of certainty, that the corruption which is manifested in the bodily and sensual lusts is, from the nature of the case, *more discernible*, and therefore more exposed to observation. That, however, which is in itself not certain, is the notion that such a bondage proves nothing but the preponderating force of bodily and sensual desire. Does not the question now first arise, whether such a force was not the *result* of a spiritual apostasy from spiritual and divine relations—of some selfish aberration in the domain of the spirit? Not from any preponderance of bodily and sensual desire does the apostle (Rom. 1:21) deduce the spiritual apostasy of the heathen world from God; but, on the contrary, from that very apostasy he deduces their abandonment to the bodily and sensual lusts. A tendency of their thoughts to vain imaginings, and a darkening of their hearts in spiritual matters, preceded, according to the apostle, that bondage to the mastery of bodily and sensual desires. How, then, can it be pretended that these desires are in themselves more dangerous and enslaving than a selfish corruption of our spiritual life in reference to its spiritual and divine relations? And how are we justified in establishing such a proposition for Christians in particular, as a truth of universal application? It may be said that with the Christian, who has experienced in his spirit the full power of redeeming grace, while yet he lives in the body of this death, temptation within the sphere of his corporeal relations, we may presume, lies nearer to him than in the domain of the spirit. But not even is this presumption generally suitable and applicable to all occasions. There exists no absolute equality of the Christian state from which, without any reference to individually inherited predispositions and individual (natural as well as spiritual) life-development and life-history, we could draw the conclusion, that for him the being tempted and permitting himself to be tempted in one sphere of his life, lay nearer and was more dangerous to him than in the other. What may be said with the utmost confidence is this one thing alone, that the Christian can oppose in comfort, and with the certainty of victory, all temptations, whether in the spiritual or the bodily sphere of his nature, only in proportion as he does not allow the personal and spiritual state of his heart toward God in Christ to be perverted. The direct assault on this position lies in temptations of a spiritual nature—weakness of faith, unbelief, vanity, high-mindedness, and the like. The indirect assault comes with temptations of a bodily and sensual nature, as in the desire of excess, unchastity, and so forth. Which of these is in itself the more dangerous cannot be determined, in the first place, because there is no necessity in the nature of these several temptations that they should tarry in their own peculiar domain, without passing over into that of the other in the course of their development—from the sphere of the bodily and sensual to that of the spiritual and of the soul, and conversely. Again, the direct attack upon the central position of a Christian may in itself be called more dangerous, because it is immediately prejudicial to the root; but, on the other hand, less so, because its antagonism to that salvation of which the Christian has become cognizant is more open: while we may call the temptations of a bodily and sensual nature less dangerous, because they do not directly undermine the chief stronghold of the Christian; and, on the other hand, more so, because they may indirectly, and consequently more secretly, injure and undermine the spiritual stronghold of the Christian. But the real occasion of either of these dangers exists absolutely nowhere in the nature of the temptation in itself, but is conditioned by the conduct of the Christian with respect to it. And if I might assume from the nature of the regenerate and converted man, that it must have become easier for him to subject his spirit to discipline than his body; and again, that, from the nature of the body, it must be easier to bridle it simply by bodily habitude than to bridle the spirit by spiritual wrestling and struggles,—yet all such universal assumptions have not a universal value or truth. And all this, because there exist no universal rules for the historical development of the individual Christian, or for his conflicts with temptation; because the confines of bodily and spiritual temptation in their course cannot be kept invariably asunder; and because, if a temptation to evil has occurred, I do not thereby recognize whether it proceeds in this or in that sphere of life, but whether in the one or the other sphere of life, be it a relation that excites pain or one that excites pleasure, it becomes, or has become, for me an object of my own selfish concupiscence, by virtue whereof I am induced to place the standard of what is admissible in the satisfaction of this selfish desire, apart from that ordinance of God's will which is recognizable and recognized by me. True it is, I can feel and declare out of my own individual experience whether the temptations of the one or the other domain of my life are the more perilous *for me;* but I cannot convert this into a universal rule, not even for myself, much less for others, or for all Christians. It does not even apply to myself, since the experience based on past facts does not entitle me to draw from it an unconditionally available conclusion for the future of my earthly life. The opinion, on the contrary, that temptation threatens us only on this or that side, may become at last a notion which exposes me, unwarned and defenseless, to temptations from new quarters. All this forms the ground why, in order to guard against temptation to evil, and to decide whether temptation to evil is stirring in us, we ought above all things to direct our eyes to that attitude of our heart which we take up with respect to painful or pleasurable emotions, whether corporeal or spiritual, as they are conceivable in the manifold relations of our mixed spiritual and corporeal existence and life, and affect us involuntarily, because naturally.

(4) On this state of the heart, and not on the various kinds or sources of involuntary pain- or pleasure-giving emotion, it depends whether this is to become a temptation to evil, and whether it is to bring us into a greater or less degree of danger of bondage. How this state of the heart is constituted in the regenerate and converted man, and for what course of conduct it equally qualifies and binds him, on the strength of the freedom bestowed upon him by grace, has been before discussed (see § 25, especially notes (4) and (5)). The position in which the regenerate and converted man is placed by the working of God in Christ, is that of *freedom* in Christ, in contrast to the *dominion* of sin over him (§ 26. note (1)). His state is not that of the enslaved natural man. Wherefore also no temptation presents itself to him as possessing in itself the power to enslave him. It obtains this power only in the measure

in which the Christian offers no resistance (ἀντίστητε τῷ διαβόλῳ, καὶ φεύξεται ἀφ' ὑμῶν Jas. 4:7). The resistance, however, and the capability of resistance, lie in this, that we should in *faith* oppose to that *feeling* of pain or pleasure, which has a tendency to take our minds captive, the power of Christ and of His word, by virtue of which He is willing to aid us against all feeling, and to gain in us the victory over feeling. For just as this faith in us ceases to be the center of our life, and we bear in us the desire to yield to our feeling a mastery over our faith, that bondage commences in which the impulses of our effort and aim lie beyond those relations within which Christ is willing to remain with us and in us as Overcomer and Conqueror. For His will it is, that we should cling to Him in faith against all feeling of our natural desires, as to the Lord who overcomes all our feeling, and hereby either turn it into the paths of that order of nature sanctioned by Him, or mortify it where it is directed against this order. But just as we make our feelings the law of our conduct, our heart falls away from that command over our nature which is given us in Christ; and our Ego, thus forfeiting this command which we possess in Christ, relapses into the bonds of our natural and corrupt life, which, in itself enslaved, involves more and more our selfish desire in emotional appetite (πάθος ἐπιθυμίας, 1 Thess. 4:5), in sin-producing passions (παθήματα τῶν ἁμαρτιῶν, Rom. 7:5); and, as the *materia peccans*, sin, which works every kind of concupiscence (Rom. 7:8), gradually regains mastery in us. This relapse into old ways is, however, not merely the result of a process of natural necessity, but at the same time the consequence of judicial abandonment, whereby the Lord turns away from those who sell themselves to their personal feeling, instead of opposing themselves to all feeling, in faith on their merciful Redeemer. Therefore here also I abide by this opinion, that, in the struggle against temptation to evil, the chief point is not to investigate what kind of painful or pleasurable feeling excites our selfish desire, but to prove ourselves, whether in each moment of such excitement we betake ourselves in faith for refuge to our Lord and Savior, who forgives our sins and delivers us, and by His help mortify the power of those feelings which enslave us. For only by faith in His grace, which overcomes sin (ἁμαρτία ὑμῶν οὐ κυριεύσει· οὐ γάρ ἐστε ὑπὸ νόμον, ἀλλὰ ὑπὸ χάριν, Rom. 6:14), do we become master over all sinful temptations, and are enabled to make that calling of ours and election sure (2 Pet. 1:10), whose strength lies in this, that in full assurance of that divine power we set ourselves against our feeling—that power which, in the very midst of our conflict with sin, has bestowed upon us all things that pertain to life and godliness (2 Pet. 1:3).

That confidence, moreover, which enables us perseveringly and energetically to resist the rising of a temptation to evil, I would describe in the words of Luther, when he says: "It matters not that a man feels evil desires, provided only that he strives against them. For this reason such a one must not judge by his feelings, as if he were therefore lost; but must wrestle with the remainder of sin, which he feels, all the days of his life, and must allow the Holy Spirit to work in him, and must sigh without intermission that he may become free from sin. Such a sighing never ceases with the believer, and reaches deeper than can be expressed (Rom. 8:26). But he has a precious Hearer—namely, the Holy Ghost Himself—who feels that yearning deeply, and also comforts such consciences with divine consolation. Thus must there always be a mixture, so that we feel both the Holy Ghost and our own imperfection; for it must always be with us as with a sick man who is under the hands of the physician, yet in order to be cured by him. Let no one therefore think thus: This man has the Holy Spirit; therefore he must be quite strong, and do only meritorious works, and have no infirmities. Nay, it is not so; for it cannot come to that, while we live in the flesh upon earth, that we should be without weakness and defect: therefore the holy apostles themselves also often lament over their conflict and sorrow. And thus the Holy Spirit is indeed hidden from themselves according to their feeling, except that He *strengthens and sustains them in their conflict through the word and faith.*"

(5) It is of importance for our conduct toward ourselves, for the regulation of our daily life, to ascertain and to keep in view the relation within which we feel ourselves tempted by ungodly desires. But here the point is, not the quality of the original cause of the temptation in itself, nor the diagnosis of the passive emotion we undergo, but this, that we test ourselves, whether our state, both with regard to the things which supply the allurement of temptation, and to the emotion excited in us thereby, is regulated conformably to our faith. The mere self-examination of our conditions, as distinguished from this, and of those relations which regulate and call them forth, does not lead to the right goal. For herein is wanting that ὄμμα πνευματικόν, that eye of faith, which, although at moments obscured, has yet learned and is capable of testing and of determining man's inward state by the light of the word. That which Paul demands under special and definite circumstances, and for a particular object, that we should examine ourselves whether we be in the faith, that we should prove our own selves, in order to know ourselves as those in whom Christ dwells (2 Cor. 13:5), holds good universally as a means of protection, and remains the principal task in all those manifold temptations in which He who was tempted in all respects like ourselves, yet without sin, wills to show forth by us and in us the power of His rich and sin-subduing grace. But whether we stand in the faith, is not to be learned from such considerations as these, whether or not we feel and experience temptations to sin, and of what sort they are, still less from the circumstance that we are in no wise aware of this or that, or perhaps of any kind of temptations; least of all from our supposing, by aid of means which lie outside of Christ's fellowship with us, and of our fellowship with Him, to obtain the mastery over our temptations to evil, but from the fact that at the very first rise of tempting thoughts we oppose the same with the confidence that the Lord knows how to deliver us from temptation (2 Pet. 1:9), that we are more than conquerors through Him that loved us (Rom. 8:37), and that this our faith is the victory that overcomes the world (1 John 5:4). No kind of analysis of

ourselves and of our frames strengthens us for this certainty, but only the believing grasp wherewith, in spite of them, we lay hold of that power of our Lord (assured to us in the midst of temptation and in the word of promise) which overcomes the world.

On the other hand, for a just and successful practical manifestation of our faith, for that effective concentration of its power which is required by the nature of the temptation (the μὴ εἰς ἀέρα δέρειν, 1 Cor. 9:26), for that which consistently with faith we have to do and to *leave undone* in temptation (the ἐγκράτεια of faith; comp. 2 Pet. 1:6 with 1 Cor. 9:25), it is of great importance clearly to ascertain the individual nature and root of the temptation springing up in us. Only this again must be so accomplished, that, in order justly to estimate the commencement of temptation, and effectually to resist it when it has commenced, we should look for the enticement to evil not so much in the concrete world of things that surround us, as in that selfish perversion of the mind by which we convert the order of their relations to us into disorder. We regard that which in the last instance is of God, as something which in the first and last instance is our own, and subject to our own voluntary disposition, and then attribute the perverted propensity with which we attach ourselves to our relations with external things to the things themselves, while its root rests in our perverted position with respect to these things. In other words, we make the human depravity which prevails in this world, the world in which evil predominates, identical with the world of divinely constituted relations, in which the evil nature that lies in man exercises its destructive lust. From this error and confusion we must first be free in that self-knowledge and a knowledge of the world which belong to faith, in order that we may oppose a proper resistance to evil temptations. The earth is the *Lord's*, and the fulness thereof (1 Cor. 10:26). Nothing is in itself impure (Rom. 14:14). "Unto the pure all things are pure; but unto them that are defiled and unbelieving is nothing pure, but even their mind and conscience is defiled" (Tit. 1:15). True indeed, there is no creaturely goodness which is also unobjectionable, in the sense that anything creaturely possesses in itself an absolute goodness and perfection, when separated from God and that order and object of its being which have been established for it in this relation. But as a creature *of God*, and received in this light with thanksgiving, everything is good, and nothing to be refused; for in this relation it has its sanctification in itself, and is also subjectively sanctified by us through our prayer, which brings God's word before Himself (1 Tim. 4:4, 5). But if we strip the creature of this its relation to God, and ourselves (in our position with respect to the creature) of our relation to God, then do the so-called *pura naturalia* become *impura*, and take the shape of a world of temptations, not by their own nature, but through the depraved nature of our selfishness, in which we place nature out of its relation to God, and God out of His relation to nature, and place ourselves, *i.e.* our Ego isolated from God, over against a godless nature and a God isolated from nature, as a *spiritus rector*, and hence fall into bondage. And not less do those who, as they say, desire to keep their relation to God pure, fall under this curse and righteous judgment—since they tread under foot the created nature in them and outside of them, as something severed from its connection with God—than do those others who, as it were, tread God under foot, while they concede to creaturely nature, severed from God and His will, a kind of divine and sovereign right to its impulses over us. For there is no will of God in us and over us which is not at the same time a will of God which extends to the totality of all those actual conditioning elements of our existence which support us, and to all those relations therein implied of ourselves to God as well as to the world, to spirit as well as to body, to ourselves as well as to the fulness of things external, to the end of a harmonious superiority and inferiority. Where man isolates himself from this organically composed, divinely established reciprocal relation, and by his selfish choice subordinates the higher to the lower, or breaks the chain of those relations which are appointed for our training and the practical manifestation of our faith, and only permits to separate and isolated members a power of influence, making of these objects of exclusive partiality and nurture,—there this disorder which we thus introduce continues to produce new and inordinate desires,—inordinate, because turned against that comprehensive order, by whose instrumentality the Christ-restored man has practically to manifest his dominion over every domain of life, as a power of life and not of death, as a power of sanctification and glorification, not as one of unsanctification and destruction. Wherever any one withdraws himself from this task, placing individual relations within which this task is to be performed by us, whether it be in selfish aversion and rejection, or in selfish partiality and fondness, out of connection with that calling of Christians to dominion and to holiness,—there those relations of life, though in themselves divinely appointed, become to us a constant leaven of ungodly temptations. And all this because there arises in us a self-pleasing desire, either not to rest at all in those divinely established relations, or not so to rest in them as we have been appointed for them and they for us by God, and as they have been organically arranged for the totality of our life relations.

Thus, in order to avoid temptation, and to resist it when it has entered into us, the chief motto must not be this: This or that is in itself impure; but rather this: "All things are ours; but we are Christ's" (1 Cor. 3:22, 23); "All things are lawful for me; but I will not be brought under the power of any" (1 Cor. 6:12). And this holds good universally of all created things, and of their divinely established relations to us, as exciting pain or pleasure. Whether we remain their master in Christ, and make them, through the instrumental service of their working on us, serve as an exercise of our dominion over the whole domain of life, is really what it comes to, and is that to which we must look. When in all these relations Christ in us abides the Lord over all things, there is temptation overcome. And wherever and in whatever way anything tempts us to weaken this dominion, there there exists a temptation to evil, which comes not out of the things, but out of ourselves. The chief point always is, to keep the faith, and with it the obedience of the heart in faith (τηρεῖν τὴν πίστιν, 2 Tim. 4:7). The domain of life, however, in which temptation of our faith presents itself, conditions only the secondary form of our resistance, and of our self-struggle in faith. The primary point is, that our resistance should be made in the strength of faith; but in the second rank it is of importance that the form of resistance should also be adapted to the form of temptation, and that the subjection of the body (ὑπωπιάζειν τὸ σῶμα καὶ δουλαγωγεῖν, 1 Cor. 9:27), as well as the bringing into captivity of every thought and imagination which exalteth itself against obedience to Christ (2 Cor. 10:5), should be present where the nearest form of the temptation, or its nearest relation, demands either the one or the other. For the aim of our preservation embraces us wholly—spirit, soul, and body (1 Thess. 5:23). And whatever the aims and objects of our inclination and love may be, which are external to us, there is no naturally sanctified love of such a nature, that the sanctification of our hearts in Christ does not demand the subordination of this love to our love of Christ. Wherefore the requisition that applied to the Levites in the Old Testament (Deut. 23:9) is to be held sacred by all Christians, as the vital law of their heart—to love nothing, not even father and mother, beyond, that is more than, Christ (Matt. 10:37). Yea, rather does it concern us in every possession, in all sorrow and joy, in all gain and use, to elevate the heart in Christ above all this, and so to secure ourselves from the danger of abuse. (Comp. 1 Cor. 7:29–31, τὸ λοιπόν ἐστιν, ἵνα καὶ οἱ ἔχοντες γυναῖκας ὡς μὴ ἔχοντες ὦσι, καὶ οἱ κλαίοντες ὡς μὴ κλαίοντες, καὶ οἱ χαίροντες ὡς μὴ χαίροντες, καὶ οἱ ἀγοράζοντες ὡς μὴ κατέχοντες, καὶ οἱ χρώμενοι τὸν κόσμον ὡς μὴ καταχρώμενοι.)

(6) The recognition of the infallible certainty of a struggle with temptation, is the best weapon against the highly dangerous spiritual state of false security in the Christian. It stands in direct opposition to the prayer which our Lord has charged us with, "Lead us not into temptation." And as this delusion rests on a misapprehension alike of the proper state of the soul of one who is converted and regenerate, and of the

way in which even that which is in itself unobjectionable may become for us an occasion of objectionable desire, so it also entices us to a false line of conduct, both towards ourselves and towards those external things which constitute the sphere of life which supports our earthly existence. The Christian is in a false state of security if he is ignorant of the sin which so easily besets us (εὐπερίστατος ἁμαρτία, Heb. 12:1), and in the willingness of his spirit forgets the weakness of his flesh (Matt. 26:41). To him rather must the words ever be applicable: "Let him that thinks he stands, take heed lest he fall" (1 Cor. 10:12). For in the opposition between the old and new man the danger impends over the Christian of a divided soul (δίψυχον εἶναι, Jas. 1:8, 4:8). And we can only avoid this danger by a constant purifying of the heart (ἁγνίσατε καρδίας. Jas. 4:8). For the evil comes not from without into us, but from within, out of the heart (comp. Matt. 15:19 with vers. 18 and 11). In general, therefore, it is to be called wrong to suppose that we ought to place the precept, "Touch not, taste not, handle not" (Col. 2:21), either in place of, or before and above the purification of the heart. But, on the other hand, since the heart of the Christian even needs a constant purification, the statement, "To the pure all things are pure," does not become an opiate to the Christian, but rather a goad to his conscience. For precisely on that account he is careful over himself, that not even that which is in itself unobjectionable should become to him, in an objectionable state of mind, the source of a defiling pleasure. And this so much the more, the more decidedly he knows how delicate the relation of the Christian is to Christ, and that the slightest leaven of impurity tends to trouble and corrupt the whole of that relation (in the same way that he who offends the law in one point is guilty of all; Jas. 2:10). And since, when a perverted propensity and direction of heart has once established itself, abstinence cannot be practised in us without at the same time abstaining from those things which exercise a charm over us, which acts perversely upon our perverted nature, although it is in itself not opposed to God; therefore an honest purification of heart must have, as its result, abstinence even from such things as have a creaturely power of attraction, which threatens to injure the perfect power of those relations of ours which are above the creature, even if we here took into consideration nothing else but the fact that our delight in things temporal must not stand higher than our delight in things eternal. For in this case it serves for no excuse, that that transitory delight is in itself truly blameless.

(7) That is blameless which is in nowise prejudicial to us in the solution of our life's problem as appointed by Christ; while that is more than all else to be desired which avails for this solution, and furthers it either directly or indirectly. This problem of our life is pointed out to us in the word, and comprises not only our personal and individual relations to God in Christ, but also the totality of our relations to the world which Christ has come to redeem, as well as to those who have become participators of the same redemption as ourselves. For this reason, we have first of all not merely to deduce and to decide from ourselves and the state of our own personal and individual experiences, that which, as furthering us in all these relations of life, we have to oppose to what is a source of temptation for us; but we must herein be guided by the standard of the divine will as laid down in the word. It is this sure objective standard alone which guards against the false subjectivism of our judgment concerning that which we have to avoid as a source of temptation. On the other hand, however, we have to do no less with a question of accurate self-knowledge in reference to our own individual and personal nature and character, in order to guard against and subdue, in true watchfulness and abstinence, those temptations which lie nearest to us, which might injure and disturb the right solution of our life's problem, in our position alike towards God and ourselves, and towards the world and the brethren. And here, along with that maxim, "All things are lawful for me" (1 Cor. 10:23), this other also applies, "but all things are not expedient; all things are lawful for me, but all things edify not" (*ibid.;* comp. 1 Cor. 10:33). For that power over all things which I possess in virtue of my freedom by faith in Christ, becomes

itself a temptation to me, if I allow myself to be led away by it, to free myself from that bounden duty of love to my neighbor, and allow my freedom to become to him a stumbling-block of temptation. Even to the Christian, regenerate and converted "Ego," apply, as a caution against temptation, the words, "Let no man seek his own, but every man what belongs to another" (1 Cor. 10:24). In so far as this comprises at the same time a positive testimony of the Christian character in its outward relations, it will be reserved for after discussion. To this place it only so far belongs as was necessary to point out how little the standard of that which, as a source of temptation for *ourselves*, and for the position in which we stand to Christ (when viewed as limited to *ourselves*). suffices to determine what we have to put away from us, as being a temptation hostile to the task of the Christian's life.

The struggle against *all* temptation is, however, erroneous and fruitless in proportion as the Christian desires to carry on the warfare with other weapons than those which have been given him by Christ, as a means of self-renewal (comp. § 25, note (7)). The state which forms the distinction between Christianity and heathenism is thus characterized in Scripture, that "God suffered men to walk in their own ways" (Acts 14:16). Hence nothing is of more importance than that the Christian, in the struggle ordained for him, should shun all ways of his own, all ways of merely human commandment and teaching (Col. 2:22). The armor of God, in which we become victorious, is that alone which the Apostle Paul describes (Eph. 6:13–18). And the chief pieces of it are the shield of faith and the sword of the Spirit—the word of God. With these the might of Satan is to be overcome, of which the apostle there expressly declares that against it, and not so much against flesh and blood, lies the warfare of a Christian.

Touching the universal importance of this knowledge to the Christian, comp. § 26, note (5). The question which might here immediately arise is this: Whether it is important to the Christian, and in what sense, in that warding off of temptation to ungodliness which is incumbent upon him, to become conscious in the individual instances of the satanic origination of such temptation; or in this way perhaps to distinguish individual temptations as satanic, from others whose origin we seek in our own heart, in the condition of our natural state, or in the form of a corrupt state of the world around us. In this inquiry, it will be necessary to bear in mind at the outset what follows. This in the first place, that in *every* temptation to ungodliness the Christian has the firm assurance that it is connected with him who opposed Christ as tempter, and whom Christ, for us and for our advantage, has overcome. We cannot distinguish in their *origin* satanic from non-satanic temptations, but must remain convinced in *every* temptation with whom, in our struggle against it, we have in the last instance (so far as the creature is concerned) to do. For all that is opposed to God belongs to the rule and sovereignty of the tempter. By the knowledge, therefore, that it is in one case our own carnal incontinence (1 Cor. 7:5; comp. 1 Tim. 5:11–13), or in another case the world's hatred, and the oppressions and sorrows which arise from it (1 Thess. 3:3), or in a third case the lusts which come from our own selfish love of the world (Jas. 4:1 ff.), that prepare temptation for us, there is not excluded that other knowledge, that in all this the tempter has at the same time his work (1 Cor. 7:5; 1 Tim. 5:15; 1 Thess. 3:5; Jas. 4:7). Just as little is the parable of Christ, of the way in which in different souls the word of God is dishonored, so to be understood as if at one time the destructive influence came from Satan (Matt. 13:19; Mark 4:15; Luke 8:12); at another time from persecution for the word's sake (Matt. 13:21; Mark 4:17; Luke 8:13), or from the cares and pleasures of this life, and the deceitfulness of riches (Matt. 13:22; Mark 4:19; Luke 8:14). For as even in the first of the instances set forth in the parable, not only Satan is taken into consideration, but the heart also (there likened to a hard-trodden road), which is only so far moved by the word as its sound reaches the ear without the word being opened in the heart to the understanding; so also the mention of the immediate (εὐθύς, Mark 4:15) entrance of the satanic power serves only to portray the state of those in whom, through the hardness of their own heart, the dominion of Satan is still entirely unbroken, so that there is not yet any special need, by other painful or pleasurable enticements or assaults, to detach the heart from the word. But where, as in the other two instances, the word has begun to cleave to the heart, and just in this way a beginning is made in breaking the power of that dominion, then it happens that by means of other enticements, *i.e.* if I may so say, in roundabout ways, Satan endeavors to reestablish his half-broken sway. For those who become children of the evil one, or, in the words of the other parable, tares among the wheat, become so by the influence of the enemy of Christ (Matt. 13:38, 39), without hereby excluding those intermediate instruments by which Satan again seeks to acquire power over those who had begun to free themselves from his ascendancy. From all this it follows, that it is not permissible for us to be unwilling to trace a display of the power of the tempter, in the case in which we are able to perceive and name the instrumental means of our temptation, existing in our own state or in the conditions of the world which stands over against us, or to wish to call those temptations alone satanic for which we suppose ourselves unable to find or to detect any point of contact either with ourselves or our relations to the external world. For (and this is the other consideration) we cannot speak at all of any satanic temptation to ungodliness as having actually taken place, except the heart in its own desire has consented to enter on that which, in its ungodly tendency, reveals itself as appertaining to the kingdom of the tempter (see above, note (2)). Only this, again, is not to be understood, either as if the consciousness of our own selfish, ungodly propensity excluded the perception of the influence of the tempter and its importance, or as if the seduction of Satan to ungodliness is only present *to* us, when an actual selfish and ungodly desire is already formed *within* us. This last supposition is false for this very reason, that the tempter has a domain not only in the actual ungodly lusts of men, but in the whole state of man's nature, as well as in that of the world, so far as this has fallen a prey to unnatural corruption,—a domain which in itself is exposed to the wrath and judgment of God, but which is appointed by God to be experienced even by the Christian as an object of the divine wrath and judgment, not in order that he may continue under this wrath, but in order, through his experience of it, that he may ever again and again flee to God's grace, and let himself be satisfied with this grace alone. The whole of this domain, which we have to distinguish from actual sin, as an evil resulting from the divine wrath on account of original sin, and which meets us in the weakness, destructibility, and frailty of all the conditions of created nature, is in itself not one willed by God, although brought to pass by His wrath; but now a domain received into the economy of the divine scheme of salvation, within which an agency of the tempter is both conceivable and real. And indeed this takes place in such a way, that the tempter—who, not of his own power, not to speak of his own right, but by the decree, will, and permission of God, is allowed to become in the sphere of existence thus subject to the divine wrath, the executor of divine visitations and judgments (comp. 1 Cor. 5:5, 1 Tim. 1:20; and, in another way, Rev. 2:10)—at the same time has for his object falsely to mirror forth to the human imagination, as an absolute judgment, that effect of the wrath of God which, in His designs, is intended to lead to a laying hold of grace. Thus the apostle saw in the bodily sufferings which fell to his lot a result of the power of Satan decreed by God, the triumph over which was already consummated in this, that he understood them to be a means of corrective discipline against spiritual exaltation, and gave himself up to repose on the (to him) certain grace of his Lord (2 Cor. 12:7–9). In the same sense, the divinely decreed sentence of death is elsewhere named a domain subjected to the power of Satan (ὁ διάβολος ὁ τὸ κράτος ἔχων τοῦ θανάτου. Heb. 2:14) not as if the devil absolutely decreed death, but because death, as the final accomplishment of that corrupting power of the tempter which allures to sin, takes place, where the looking to Christ, the Subduer of the prince of death, has not taken away the power of Satan, and hereby brought about also the deliverance from the bondage of the fear of death. If we reflect on all this, we shall, in the first place, not everywhere so speak of the agency of Satan as if it stood apart from divine government; but we shall distinguish the place where Satan, against his own will, must become the executor of God's visitations, which he intends to serve for corruption, while in God's purposes they are to serve for probation, for "sifting the wheat" (Luke 22:31; comp. the passages already quoted, 1 Cor. 5:5, 1 Tim. 1:20). For the decree as well as the fear and terror of death, the decree as well as the fear and terror of suffering, become an effect of Satan's power answering to his designs there alone, where the tempter gains room to pervert the immediate, and at the same time divinely appointed, disciplinary feeling of such decrees into a slavish terror contrary to God's word, by which we abandon faith in God's triumphing grace. Again, we shall not so speak of any power of Satan to tempt to ungodliness, as if such could take place, where our own heart had not at the same time given way to the evil desire of rather believing the lies of Satan than God's word and God's truth. For it avails not to accuse and condemn Satan, but ourselves, if we wish to endure temptation, and to abide in the sin-forgiving fellowship of Christ. Finally, we shall not venture to divest this or that temptation of its final connection with the tempter, and, on the contrary, to characterize others as exclusively satanic, but only to describe that shape in which a temptation has openly assumed a *satanic shape*. Such is that temptation in which, by reason of being and becoming tempted, we come to this, to allow the word of Christ to be torn from our hearts—that word by whose instrumentality He desires to be just with those who acknowledge to Him their temptation and liability to be tempted, provided they ask, at the same time, exclusively after His thoughts and His intentions revealed to them in His word, and not after the thoughts and designs of the devil, in order to acquire and to keep in these thoughts of comfort and promise power against all temptation of Satan, of our own hearts, of the flesh, and the world. This conflict between the lies of Satan and

God's word and truth is, according to the nature of the case, only experienced by those in whom the word has taken root; and its possession has to undergo the fiery ordeal of the high spiritual assaults, of which just as naturally those know nothing whose heart is estranged from the word of God, and lies in unconscious bondage to its own lusts. Hence the predominant renunciation of Satan, whose existence, mode of action, and power reveal themselves to those alone who are truly in Christ, and have learnt in Him to resist and overcome the tempter. For the perfect light alone reveals the whole depth of the darkness, and becomes master over the evil in subduing its deepest root, while at the same time in Christ we recognize the foe as one already judged and overcome by Him—one who has no more part in those who are in Christ and abide in Him. What it is, however, amidst and in spite of all satanic assaults, to be and to abide in Christ, of this Luther has borne testimony in innumerable passages, of which I will here only bring forward one, in which he makes the following application of the words of the fifty-first Psalm, "Against Thee, Thee only, have I sinned:"—"If Satan, by the law, harasses and torments the conscience, as it stands in the Revelation of St. John (12:10) that he day and night accuses the saints before the face of God, then is it time, and highly needful, that we should meet him with this verse, and thus address him: What do my sins concern thee, Satan? I have not sinned against thee surely, but against my God. I am not your sinner: what right, therefore, hast you over me? If, therefore, I have sinned and committed what is truly and indeed sinful (for Satan is wont sometimes to terrify us with pretended and fictitious sins), on which account you blame and accuse me, yet have I not sinned against you, but against my God, who is long-suffering and compassionate; not against the law, not against conscience, not even against men and angels, but only against my God. But the Lord my God is no devil, no cruel one, no tyrant, nor executioner, as you are, who does nothing but terrify us men, and threaten us with death and hell-fire. But to those sinners who feel their misery and covet His grace, God is compassionate, kind, just, and gracious. Against such a God, not against a tyrant and murderer as you art, have I sinned. Therefore, O cruel one, you hast no right over me, neither to claim nor to accuse me; but God, who is kind and gracious, He has right and cause against me. But He has given promise to me, and to all those who confess their sin, that He will forgive us our sin, and show us grace and mercy in Christ. With those only is He wroth, and threatens to punish them, who will not acknowledge their sin and uncleanness, and will not allow Him to be justified in His words, in which He adjudges us all to be sinners."

Such an application of the divine words is the way to resist and to overcome even the greatest and most perilous assault, not with our own thoughts or in self-chosen ways, but with the armor of God.

§ 29. d. The Import of the Struggle as Self-preservation against Fall and Apostasy

The full earnestness and the entire meaning of the struggle against temptation, ordained for the Christian, lies in the knowledge that that blessing of grace and salvation assigned to him in regeneration and appropriated by him in conversion, is one that may be lost (1). And indeed, in the case of the Christian, this knowledge attaches itself to his possession of salvation in such a way, that he knows of a peculiar danger of abuse of the same, along with which the commencement of that apostasy may begin which deprives him irrecoverably of grace. The abuse consists in this, that we turn away the grace and freedom received from being actively employed alike in the lordship and in the service which are in Christ, and that we wish to make this grace and freedom serve for the purpose as well as for the palliation of self-seeking enjoyment. Without this perversion, the more or less conscious kind of which determines not the nature, but the degree of the offence, a regenerate and converted Christian could not fall away from that "steadfastness" of which he has become a partaker through grace (2). And just in the knowledge of this possible perversion there at the same time remains with him that salutary fear of God, in which he has to work out his own salvation, and wherein he possesses the corrective against false security. Only where the Christian divests himself of this fear does the temptation with its lust gain power over him, so that he forgets to make active use of the grace and freedom bestowed upon him, neglects the bridling of his old nature, and thus falls back into the same (3). The relapse occurs where the consent of the will to the enticement of the desire takes place, so that one "does the will" thereof—an act which is sin, it matters not whether this act be an inner one performed in thought, or one consisting in an outward work, *i.e.* a work which embraces the soul, and at the same time the members of the body as instruments (4). This relapse does not involve in it the loss of grace, if two things are held fast: first, the incompatibility of such sinning with the position of a child of God; but at the same time also the certainty, sealed by promise, of our being able to rise again, in Christ and through Christ, from such sin in repentance and faith. The first knowledge keeps us in a state of receptivity for the inward correction and chastisement, in which the Holy Ghost judges our sin; the second protects us from that despair, in which we pervert the salutary chastisement into a supposed token of reprobation (5). But in proportion as we become steeled against the one as well as the other knowledge, turn ourselves against the goad of repentance as well as against the comfort of faith, and allow the mastery to that sin which is incompatible with both, the danger of apostasy threatens. Apostasy has actually taken place when the initiatory fleeing from the corrective as well as comforting grace degenerates into conscious and persevering blasphemy. Not as if this sin alone led finally to judgment. For judgment is threatened against all those who suppose themselves able to have and to keep grace without actively employing the grace possessed in corresponding ways, and in such active employment fulfilling the will of their God. But that sin of apostasy alone is threatened with this, that whosoever falls into it, no more on earth will find a way of repentance (6). And because, in the case of those who are regenerate and converted, this can only come about in a gradual development of the lordship of sin, and no one is able to determine beforehand when the ripeness for such fruit of corruption takes place, so much the more does the Christian know that he has to protect himself against every fall as a possible commencement of apostasy into corruption (7).

(1) There is within the compass of Christian ethics no point which so much needs to be considered with "fear and trembling," and to be guarded on every side, as that which lies before us. For in none is the delicate and sacred boundary-line so easily injured, which protects the joyousness of believing confidence in the grace of God, on the one hand against despondency, and on the other against presumption. Least of all in this case does a mere theorizing drawing of inferences suffice, without the actual knowledge and experience of the struggles and temptations which move a Christian heart.

In order to destroy the dream of a possession of grace which cannot be lost, and of an unconditional continuance in the same promised to the individual, there needs, along with the recollection of what has been explained in earlier paragraphs as to the relation of regeneration, conversion, and renewal, only a glance at the admonitions and warnings laid down in New Testament Scripture. They not merely hold up before us possibilities and actualities of wandering from the truth (πλανᾶσθαι ἀπὸ τῆς ἀληθείας, Luke 5:19), of making shipwreck of the faith (1 Tim. 1:19), of apostasy from the living God (Heb. 3:12), and of falling into ungodliness of every sort (comp. 1 Cor. 11:5–12, and other passages); but they also require positive activity in order to make our calling and election sure (2 Pet. 1:10), and speak of a faithfulness even unto death (Rev. 2:10), and of a holding fast of the beginning of our confidence even unto the end, as the condition under which alone we are at liberty really to regard ourselves as fellow-partakers or fellow-heirs of Christ (Heb. 3:14). Certainly the prediction of an impending general apostasy (ἀποστασία) forms the dark background to the prophecies which refer to the kingdom of Christ and its history (comp. Matt. 24:11 ff., 24; 2 Thess. 2:3 ff.; 1 Tim. 4:1; 1 John 2:18; 2 Pet. 3:3; Jude 18).

(2) The process by which, in the case of a Christian who is converted and a partaker of the new birth, actual antichristian conduct is arrived at, is a different one from the way in which temptation acquires the mastery over the natural man. True, indeed, the latter is not without God to such a degree that there should come into consideration merely his creaturely corrupt nature, and not also that creaturely relation in which he stands to God by means of the spirit of his conscience. But in quite a different way has he who is regenerate through God's word and sacrament, and converted, acquired a power of withstanding temptation, and a capacity of obeying God's will, by virtue of which it is not possible to conceive of his succumbing to temptation without a simultaneous or antecedent turning away from that which has become his in regeneration and conversion. Now this turning away may enter in and make its appearance in very different forms, just according to the manifoldness of the objects for which the fellowship of the regenerating power of the Holy Ghost is bestowed on a Christian. But a radical injury done to the gracious relationship in which God stands to the Christian, and the Christian to God, will precede all these forms. And the common characteristic feature of this injury can be no other (according to the root of sinful conduct in man) than that he desires to possess, to use, and to *mis*apply in selfish ways, the grace and freedom bestowed upon him for destroying selfish conduct (comp. as contrast to this, § 28, note (1), and § 19, note (4)). The possibility of this result lies in the way in which the Christian also, along with the possession of the blessings of grace, is subjected to a test of his freedom (§ 27, note (1)). This freedom, however, is just as much the possession of a definite ability (δύνασθαι). rooting itself in the grace of Christ alone, as a corresponding active employment (ποιεῖν) of this possession (in opposition to ἀργὸν, ἄκαρπον εἶναι, 2 Pet. 1:8). And the test consists, on the one hand, in this, whether I seek this my ability

only in Christ (χωρὶς ἐμοῦ οὐ δύνασθε ποιεῖν οὐδέν, John 15:5), and then also hold fast the full power of this ability in faith (πάντα ἰσχύω ἐν τῷ ἐνδυναμοῦντί με, Phil. 4:13; πάντα δυνατὰ τῷ πιστεύοντι, Mark 9:23); but, on the other hand, in this, whether I keep all my doing in conformity with Christ's doing, *i.e.* do nothing which I cannot do in the name of Christ, as representing Him and His will working in me, and regulating my willing and acting (πᾶν ὅτι ἐὰν ποιῶμεν ἐν λόγῳ ἢ ἐν ἔργῳ, πάντα ἐν ὀνόματι Ἰ. Χρ. ποιεῖν, Col. 3:17). Where I neglect the first, I fall away from the way of grace, on which Christ wishes to go along with me, and to fit me for right acting, and fall into ways of my own (as *e.g.* is meant in that τῆς χάριτος ἐξεπέσατε, Gal. 5:4, if a man will seek by the way of the law what the gospel bestows and gives). And if I do not hold fast the second in faith, instead of that courage which Christ wishes to give me, I fall either into the presumption of self-made courage (that ὑψηλοφρονεῖν in contrast with φοβεῖσθαι, Rom. 11:20, where one strikes out the ἐν τῷ ἐνδυναμοῦντί με, and says, ἐγὼ πάντα ἰσχύω), or into the despondency of pusillanimity (ὀλιγόψυχον, ὀλιγόπιστον εἶναι, 1 Thess. 5:14, Matt. 8:26). And where, finally, I throw to the winds the third—the placing of all my acting under the name and the rule of Christ—there I fall with my acting into that lawlessness which is nothing better, if one desire to serve God after rules of his own (ἐθελοθρησκεία, Col. 2:23), than if one adorns with the name of grace and freedom the lawless, selfish tendency of life, makes liberty a cloak of maliciousness (1 Pet. 2:16) and an occasion for the flesh (Gal. 5:13), and turns the grace of our God into lasciviousness (Jude 4). But whatever form, in the case of the individual, in its further course wandering from the truth may assume, it can certainly occur in no form, as regards the regenerate and converted man, without some injury being first inflicted on his fundamental relation to Christ, in consequence of which that is possible which in the second Epistle of Peter is so expressively called falling away from one's own steadfastness (ἐκπίπτειν τοῦ ἰδίου στηριγμοῦ, 2 Pet. 3:17).

When I said in former editions, that the common characteristic of every fall in the case of the regenerate and converted man is a sinning against better knowledge and conscience, in a certain sense this is to be maintained even still. Only not in such a way that at every moment of every fall, the fall is a denial of a distinct better knowledge and conscience. It is applicable only so far as in him who is regenerate and converted, the ignorance respecting the gracious and saving will of God is broken up; and a violation of this will cannot take place without the darkening of a better knowledge (ἡ σκοτία ἐτύφλωσε τοὺς ὀφθαλμοὺς αὐτοῦ, 1 John 2:11). But this darkening can just as well begin at the knowledge of the root of all Christian right conduct, in such a way that, in consequence of this fault, in individual cases of temptation a clear individual knowledge respecting the special form of right conduct is not objectively present to the Christian; as it is also possible that the Christian, as regards all general knowledge of the divine will, is wanting in that exercise of the senses which is necessary for distinguishing good and evil in the individual case. And if the latter is a facility to be acquired by exercise (αἰσθητήρια διὰ τὴν ἕξιν γεγυμνασμένα. Heb. 5:14), then in that case, where this facility is not present, we are not forthwith everywhere to take into consideration an antecedent blameworthiness, but also a want of that ripeness which is attached to the natural stages of human development. All this is to be borne in mind, in order that, quite apart from the natural human development from childhood to manhood, in regard to spiritual birth also, there may not be expected from the very beginning that perfection to which even in Christ we must first grow up and be trained (Eph. 4:13, 14). Nay, the very supposition of some kind of perfection already reached, is to be reckoned among the most dangerous enticements to a fall, and hinders alike the acknowledgment that in many things we all offend (Jas. 3:17), as it makes us blind to our need of the daily petition that God would grant us eyes enlightened (Eph. 1:18; comp. Rev. 3:17). For there comes in addition that other peculiarity of the deceitfulness of sin, that it makes us as it were blind (τυφλὸς μυωπάζων), whereby, according to the striking expression, a forgetfulness comes over us (λήθην λαμβάνειν τοῦ καθαρισμοῦ τῶν πάλαι ἡμῶν ἁμαρτημάτων, 2 Pet. 1:9) of what we ought to do; which forgetfulness disappears, perhaps immediately after the fall, but cannot be called excusable on this account, because, in the form in which it gains power over us, it cannot be called the denial of a present and better knowledge and conscience. And therefore also a Christian may pray for forgiveness for faults concealed from him with the hope of being heard; not on this account, however, because they are concealed from him, but because he regards himself rightly as being bound to pray for forgiveness for those faults concealed from him, inasmuch as he knows of no sin at all excusable in itself, but is acquainted only with degrees of greater guilt and desert of punishment, when the servant who knows his lord's will, and has it present before him, does it not (Luke 12:47, 48). When the apostle speaks of a mercy extended to him who was before a blasphemer, persecutor, and injurious, and explains the extending of this mercy to him in this way, that he did these former things ignorantly in unbelief, he thus as much confesses his guilt in this unbelief, as by his pointing to grace and mercy he wishes to bring forward and to praise the (in contrast with his guilt) marvelous procedure of Christ towards him, "the chief of sinners" (1 Tim. 1:14, 15); while the ignorance connected with his unbelief serves to explain the mercy that has been extended to him only so far as the apostle's conduct was no obduracy and hardening against an enlightenment and awakening to faith, in which he had formerly participated. As also, on the other hand, he says in the days of his apostolic office: I am *conscious* of nothing; but herein am I *not* justified (1 Cor. 4:4).

(3) This same fundamental element of Christian knowledge, that without Christ we can do nothing, includes in it this other knowledge, that we are able to protect ourselves against falling, not with that which *we* are or have become in Christ, but only in maintaining the constant connection of that nature which has become ours in Christ, with that God who

works in us to will and to do (Phil. 2:13). Such working of God in us takes place according to His gracious will (ὑπὲρ τῆς εὐδοκίας). But just because it is so, faith in this gracious will has at the same time, as its salutary attendant, that fear and trembling with which we work out our salvation; *because* everything here depends on this working of God in us, and nothing on that which we perhaps might ourselves be able to do and to perform of ourselves, and separated from this working of God in us (Phil. 2:12, 13). For this same God is that God who, without respect of persons, judges according to every man's work (1 Pet. 1:17); and without thinking thereon, there is no reaching in the fear of God that holiness which lies at the goal (2 Cor. 7:1); yea, no experience of the *comforting* consolation of the Holy Ghost, without walking in the *fear* of the Lord (comp. Acts 9:31; and concerning the nature and import of this fear, as compared with legal fear, above § 25, note (2), and § 16, note (1)). Yea, the same Epistle to the Hebrews, which in the loftiest strains celebrates the power and joyousness of faith, holds up before the reader the alarming word: "It is a fearful thing to fall into the hands of the living God" (Heb. 10:31). Certainly, the Apostle Paul directs those already often-quoted words, "Be not high-minded, but fear" (Rom. 11:20), to those who stand by faith, and who look on those others who were righteously excluded from the fellowship of God's people by reason of their unbelief, without reflecting thereanent that the same thing will happen to them if they continue not in that goodness of God of which they have become partakers (ἐὰν ἐπιμείνῃς τῇ χρηστότητι· ἐπεὶ καὶ σὺ ἐκκοπήσῃ, Rom. 11:22). And thus, inasmuch as the Christian, along with the goodness of his God, holds up before himself at the same time the entire earnestness of His judgments, he has in this fear of the Lord the defensive weapon against that forgetfulness of the mere hearer of the word (ἀκροατὴς ἐπιλησμονῆς), who does not think on this, that if he is really absorbed in the gospel as the perfect law of liberty, and continues therein, he recognizes it just as a binding rule of free activity, which is not satisfied if the hearer is not also a doer (ποιητὴς ἔργου), a fulfiller of that rule, and one who actively makes use of that freedom (Jas. 1:25).

(4) Respecting the way in which we come to fall into sin, we have already before (§ 28, note (2)) spoken in general with reference to Jas. 1:15. Here we have only to complete what was there said, in so far as we have to deal not merely with the falling into sin alone, but with the knowledge of when and how such a fall leads to corruption, to the judgment of death. It is that sin which bringeth forth death that is there spoken of. It bringeth it forth as infallibly as the desire, when rendered fruitful by the consent of the will, bringeth forth sin. What we are to understand by sin in the first member of the sentence (τίκτει ἁμαρτίαν), is placed beyond doubt by the context. It is the act of sin which is infallibly reached, so soon as one has consented to the desire; and it depends only on the nature of the desire and its object, whether this act shall be an inward and spiritual, or an external one, at the same time accomplished with the organs of the body. In the second member of the sentence, where the death-bringing fruit of sin is spoken of, the character of sin is defined by the addition, "when it has reached its goal, its maturity" (ἀποτελεσθεῖσα). By this addition, the idea of sin in the second member of the sentence is distinguished from that in the first. But a growth in that sin which has manifested itself as sin in act, takes place only in that sin which has acquired the mastery, has robbed man of his freedom in Christ, and has thrown him again into the chains of slavery. It lies in its nature, that it infallibly bringeth forth death, according to the righteous judgment of God. What is here deserving of special remark is therefore this, that not some particular kind of sin, but sin in general, when it has gained this character, is designated as death-bringing. That the individual act of sin in itself infallibly bringeth death, is asserted neither here nor elsewhere. But everything depends on this, that we do not allow sin to reach that maturity.

(5) As to how the Christian has to conduct himself, in order that in his case sin may not reach such maturity, a reference to the first Epistle of John might suffice. There, close beside one

another, stand the apparently mutually exclusive antitheses, by holding fast to both of which unitedly, and by that alone, the Christian is able to protect himself against the over-exuberant corrupting power of sin. The first point is the consciousness of the violent contradiction in which the committing of sin stands with our divine sonship in Christ. To have communion with that God who is light, and to walk in darkness, are absolutely incompatible (1 John 1:6). "Whosoever is born of God doth not commit sin" (3:9, 5:18); "He that commits sin is of the devil." So says John. Just as he lieth who walketh in darkness, and saith that he stands in fellowship with God, so not less does that man lie, who wishes to walk in the light, without acknowledging that he needs the blood of Jesus the Son of God to cleanse him from all sin (1:7). We lie if we say that we have no sin: if we say that we have not sinned, we make God a liar (1:8, 10); and have no blessing from our walking in the light, if we confess not our sins, in reliance on the faithfulness and righteousness of Him who forgives us our sins for Christ's sake, and cleanses us from all unrighteousness (1:9). In this twofold knowledge alone lies the power of acknowledging thoroughly the greatness of our guilt, and yet again rising from our fall by a look to Christ. Only there is then no rising up, where, along with the light estimate of our sin, there at the same time enters the contempt of the grace of Christ,—where confession of sin, and confession to the sin-forgiving Savior, alike die away.

But if this twofold disposition remains, then also we do not withdraw ourselves from that twofold operation of the Holy Ghost of which we had to make mention at an earlier stage, when speaking of conversion (§ 24, notes (2) and (3)), and whose chastisement and consolation bring about the permanence of repentance and faith (§ 24, note (6)). We preserve the childlike spirit, which discerns in punishment the chastisement of a father; and even in the manifestation of wrath, learn to feel that love which would fain, by means of chastisement, protect from the judgment (ὃν γὰρ ἀγαπᾷ Κύριος παιδεύει, μαστιγοῖ δὲ πάντα υἱὸν ὃν παραδέχεται· εἰ παιδείαν ὑπομένετε, κ.τ.λ., Heb. 12:6–8; κρινόμενοι ὑπὸ Κυρίου παιδευόμεθα, ἵνα μὴ σὺν τῷ κόσμῳ κατακριθῶμεν, 1 Cor. 11:32). Where, however, we wish to know nothing of deserved judgment—where we accept the confession that in many things we all offend as an indifferent truth—where, along with the sorrow because of sin, the need of comfort disappears,—there we gradually harden ourselves against both things—against the chastisement as against the comfort of the Holy Ghost—and the last state becomes worse than the first: the condition of the Christian who has apostatized from Christ, and fallen into the slavery of sin, becomes worse than the condition of the natural man (see especially 2 Pet. 2:20, 21). For all continuance in sin, every slavery of sin, it matters not of what sort the sin may be, gradually destroys the capacity for repentance, and along with that the capacity and the inclination to raise one's self up by faith in Christ's power and grace, and to break asunder the chains of slavery. "For of whom a man is overcome, of the same is he brought in bondage" (2 Pet. 2:19; comp. Rom. 6:16, οὐκ οἴδατε, ὅτι ᾧ παριστάνετε ἑαυτοὺς δούλους εἰς ὑπακοήν, δοῦλοί ἐστε ᾧ ὑπακούετε, ἤτοι ἁμαρτίας εἰς θάνατον ἢ ὑπακοῆς εἰς δικαιοσύνην;).

(6) After what has been said, I cannot hold it as correct when one designates some individual and isolated act of sin, or a special description of the slavery of sin, as that falling away with which one has unconditionally deprived himself of grace. For if there is an act in which one finally rends asunder the bond between him and the grace of God in Christ, then such an act is reached only in consequence of a mastery of sin, which has arrived at that maturity of which it will not be possible to assert, that in its beginnings, and in the further stages of its course, it must of necessity bear that character which marks out the act of final and complete rupture. And if we have found that relapse into the slavery of sin, and the (herewith associated) absence of all corresponding Christian activity of life in general, deprives one of grace, just as little will one be able to assert that this condition always, and in all cases, must have those marks which perhaps characterize the actual fact of the decisive rupture with Christ. It would be a very false

security, if any one, in thinking of God's judgment, wished to comfort himself with this, that he could not perceive in the state of his soul those marks which are perhaps alleged to be those of "the sin against the Holy Ghost." Of such marks we certainly find no trace, *e.g.* in those who, according to Christ's words, fall victims to the last judgment (Matt. 7:22). Their saying "Lord, Lord," their acts of prophesying, of casting out devils in His name, help them nothing, because they are at the same time simply ἐργαζόμενοι τὴν ἀνομίαν, *i.e.* such as in their own person and their whole conduct toward God *do* not the will of Christ's heavenly Father (ver. 21; comp. with ver. 24). And just so in the words of Christ, at Matt. 25:41-46, nothing presents itself to us as a mark of those who are rejected in the judgment, but that there was wanting in their case every practical proof of love towards the disciples of Christ. Now, even if in the last passage, according to the connection of the whole, it is not so much the characteristics of those who are rejected, as the importance of the disciples and messengers of Christ, and our conduct towards these, for the judgment upon the world, that is intended to be brought forward; and if one is thus reminded of the passage Matt. 10:40-42, and if at the same time in the passage Matt. 25 the lacking practical manifestation of love to those messengers of Christ who are experiencing the oppression and the enmity of the world, serves to make visible the want of love to the Sender of these messengers, lightly esteemed and persecuted by the world as He was; yet this passage also belongs to that series of others (such as Matt. 7:16-27; Rom. 2:5-10; 2 Cor. 5:10), by comparison with which it is impossible, in the case of all Christians without distinction who act in unchristian ways, to hold the approach of the final judgment exclusively and alone as the result of a specific offence, common to all alike. Certainly in Scripture the slavery of sin is of the most diverse kind, which falls under the collective idea of ἀδικία, ἀπείθεια, and the like, and which threatens with the divine judgment (1 Cor. 6:9, 10; Gal. 5:19-21; Eph. 5:5; Rev. 22:15).

There are, nevertheless, statements of New Testament Scripture which come to be considered, and which speak of a specific offence, for which forgiveness dare not be expected. These are the passages: Heb. 6:4-6, 10:26; comp. with Matt. 12:31, 32; Mark 3:28, 29; Luke 12:10; 1 John 5:16. The expositions of these passages—as in more recent times von Oettingen in his treatise *de peccato in Spir. Sct. cet.* 1856, von Hofmann in his *Schriftbeweis*, Delitzsch in his *Commentar zum Hebräerbriefe*, have furnished them—compel me, although these parties do not in all points coincide with each other, to acknowledge that at least as correct which they brought forward against my earlier treatment of these passages. How far I am able otherwise to agree with them, will appear from the discussion, now about to be renewed, of the passages quoted.

The two passages of the Epistle to the Hebrews come first of all to be considered, for this reason, because they speak in the most definite way merely of a fall and apostasy in such a way as is possible only in the case of Christians, and is assumed in the epistle itself as conceivable, or as having actually taken place. Besides, the two passages are completely intelligible, and explicable from themselves and their immediate context; while the other passages partly receive their light from the Epistle to the Hebrews, partly, however, must first be investigated with respect to the question whether and how far their being brought into parallel connection with the statements of the Epistle to the Hebrews is correct. In this place, however, I can only bring forward that which has impressed my mind as an undoubted result for the ethical meaning and consideration of those passages.

Under what circumstances the author of the Epistle to the Hebrews arrives at his warnings, may be mentioned merely in passing. It is the apprehension of a falling back into the synagogue, and into Jewish, antichristian conduct, under which he generally writes. For this apprehension the writer has facts in his eye, and mentions also (10:25) one such, viz. the forsaking of the Christian assembly, as the manner of some was. This outward fact is, however, to him only a symptom of a conceivable disposition and state of mind far worse still, of which he had already before come to speak (6:3–8). There the expression of apprehension and warning interrupts an attempt already begun, by means of introducing his readers into the depths of Old Testament statements, facts, and types, to bring about their reception of the glory of the New Testament, and thus to fortify them. He wishes with them to rise to the perfection of Christian knowledge, and will do so in their case by means of His word, *"so far as God permits it."* But that which he thinks of as a hindrance to this permission—nay, what he lays down as an impossibility not to be overcome—is introduced by him with the words (6:4), "For it is impossible." The impossibility of his word producing fruit is then given him, when a fall, and in consequence thereof a state [of the individual], has occurred, which (vers. 4–7) he portrays, and finally compares to the state of the ground which brings forth thorns and thistles, and therefore is rejected and nigh unto cursing, whose end is to be burned (6:8). That he hopes this has not yet taken place in the case of his readers, he asserts in ver. 9 ff. Now it is undoubtedly certain that the writer of the epistle conceives to himself this fall as the falling back of such as have fully experienced the power of the gospel. For he designates them as those who have been once (ἅπαξ), through a fundamental act of God, enlightened, and herewith have tasted, *i.e.* livingly experienced, the heavenly gift—the blessing of grace in Christ—and have become partakers of the Holy Ghost, and have tasted the goodness of the divine word—the good divine word of promise—and herewith the powers of the world to come. Nevertheless the writer imagines to himself such as having possibly fallen away (παραπεσόντας), for whom renewal unto repentance (μετάνοια) is impossible. A turning-point, not a state, is doubtless indicated by this παραπεσόντας. But what serves as the characteristic of this turning-point, is indicated by a course of conduct in which the apostasy manifests itself. And this is called crucifying for one's self the Son of God afresh, *i.e.* for one's self making away with the Son of God, and that upon the cross, as Israel once did, and setting Him forth as an object of mockery to others (παραδειγματίζοντας). It is therefore not said in this passage, that there is a state in which renewal unto repentance is impossible, but that there is an apostasy in which such a renewal is not conceivable, because it manifests itself in a course of conduct which is the most direct hostility to Christ. Quite similar is the statement in ch. 10:26 ff. With a glance at the approaching day of judgment he has censured the custom of some—that of withdrawing themselves from the Christian assembly. Immediately on this there follows, with the words ἑκουσίως γὰρ ἁμαρτανόντων ἡμῶν, a statement as to how and under what presuppositions such acting is delivered over to judgment. Because a habit, not a single act, was spoken of, it is said ἑκουσίως ἁμαρτανόντων ἡμῶν: "If we sin willfully, deliberately, after that we have received the knowledge of the truth, there remains no more sacrifice for sins, but a certain fearful looking for of judgment," etc. The writer of the epistle sees in the deliberate avoidance of the church assembly (which served the purpose of a means of grace) not a negligence, but the outward token of a complete rupture with Christ. For after he had pointed to the punishment which was decreed in the law for him who broke the law of Moses, he proceeds: "Of how much sorer punishment, suppose ye, shall he be thought worthy, who hath trodden under foot the Son of God, and hath counted the blood of the covenant, wherewith he was sanctified, an unholy thing, and hath done despite unto the Spirit of grace?" In this way (καταπατήσας, ἡγησάμενος, ἐνυβρίσας) is the matter represented, because the writer looks upon the outward sinful acting (ἁμαρτανόντων) as the token of an inwardly accomplished, actual, and complete rupture with the truth formerly known. In the first passage the inward act of apostasy (with παραπεσόντας) stands in the foreground, and is afterwards described outwardly by the tokens of the state of mind therewith introduced, and of the course of acting resulting therefrom (παραδειγματίζοντας); but here an outward sinful acting is first mentioned, and it is afterwards said from what sort of a rupture inwardly accomplished this is to be derived, and on this account infallibly handed over to judgment. For such a rupture has a much more fearful meaning than the violation (ἀθετήσας) of the law of Moses, for which the punishment of bodily death was appointed.

From the epistle itself, then, it is first of all clear, that its author has not in view to describe the process of the development of sin, as it takes place and must take place in a Christian man, in case he is righteously handed over to the divine judgment. He is not treating of sin in general, and its progressive unfolding; but he has quite definite, historical occasions to hold up before his readers the apprehension of a quite specific offence, in respect to which renewal unto repentance is impossible. The fact that this danger, in the case of his readers, bore the shape of a relapse into antichristian, Jewish ways, will not become the occasion to any half intelligent man to assume the possibility of such an apostasy only then, when it wears the form of relapse into Judaism. The nature of the breach is to be determined by those marks whereby it is described in ch. 10, and whereby it leads, according to ch. 6, to an inward and outward course of conduct whose characteristic mark in reality is applicable not merely to such as incline to Judaism. The breach stands there as an outbreak and culmination of the deepest hostility towards Christ; and its greatness and fearfulness consist in this, that it is apostasy from the essence of Christianity, as livingly known and thoroughly experienced. The truth in its generally applicable form is therefore this, that in the case of those really regenerate and converted an apostasy may occur, in consequence of which an inward and outward course of acting takes place which directly closes up the way to grace, because it is ripened hostility toward Christ, contempt and blasphemy of grace. We cannot speak of an act of apostasy or rupture except in connection with the existing disposition and conduct, considered as a whole, in which the breach already consummated manifests and carries itself forward; and we cannot speak of a collective disposition and conduct which brings on the judgment, except in connection with a breach or apostasy in which enmity against Christ has reached the ripeness of inward outbreak, and which is the ground and commencement of the continued antichristian disposition and conduct. Thus the matter appears to me to stand in opposition to those who lay the whole stress either upon the act of apostasy, or upon its actually existing consequences and manifestations. For at the mere act of apostasy in itself we can the less stop, the less such an act in its very nature is conceivable (in the case of those regenerate and converted) as occurring immediately, *i.e.* without a series of departures from the truth and the life in Christ bringing it about as means. Nowhere has an after life and conduct corresponding to the nature of regeneration and conversion taken place where apostasy from Christ is reached; and never does the love to God produced by His love in Christ, transform itself all at once by an inward act into enmity and blasphemy. But even upon the existing antichristian conduct in itself we cannot lay the stress alone, because such a course is not arrived at by the regenerate and converted man without an initiatory turning-point, in which he has rent asunder the bond of love and communion with Christ. One must first *have* inwardly trodden under foot the Son of God, counted the blood of the new covenant an unholy thing, and done despite to the Spirit of grace, before he arrives at this—the crucifying of Christ afresh for himself, and making Him an object of mockery for others. It is only from this last point alone that a certain conclusion is possible, whether I have actually in myself consummated the act of apostasy; while no description of an act of apostasy in itself helps me to ascertain with certainty whether I have fallen irrecoverably from the state of grace, and am lost before God.

With all the fearfulness of the warning laid down in the Epistle to the Hebrews, yet the words at the same time contain the inestimable benefit of scaring away that dark spectre of an act not rightly comprehensible—to be explained, and actually explained, sometimes in one way, sometimes in another,—an act with which one is alleged to have forfeited irrecoverably the grace of God in Christ. For here all is light, clear and self-intelligible. We have not to do with an isolated act, incomprehensible in its connection with the whole state of the Christian man in his entirety, indistinct in its characteristics, but with an act of rupture which is an outbreak of a ripened hostile disposition towards Christ, whose preparatory beginnings I am able to watch over, to overcome in continual repentance and faith, while I can protect myself from the imagination that I have fallen into it by watchfulness over the symptoms which are here in the epistle mentioned by name as characteristic marks of the actual conduct in the given case of apostasy. For, that apostasy has actually taken place, is indicated by this, and this alone, that for myself I crucify Christ afresh, and set Him forth to others as an object of mockery. For such, and for such alone, remains the whole fearfulness of the warning against irrecoverable loss of grace. And indeed for them as a mirror of self-judgment; for no one as a sword of infallible judgment with respect to others. In this sense also, the passage from the Old Testament, quoted in the Epistle to the Hebrews, is applicable: "Vengeance belongs to me, I will recompense;" and, "The Lord shall judge His people" (10:30). For we have to judge ourselves, not others. And this so much the more certainly in this case, where we are at the same time reminded of that other word, "The Lord knows them that are His." The fearful judgment of unpardonable apostasy takes place only in the case of those who have come to know the power of the gospel in its whole extent by their own experience. The symptoms of enmity against Christ, which we may perceive in others, do not suffice to determine whether such an one has with conscious aversion renounced the knowledge of the truth which has become his. Saul also was a blasphemer and persecutor, and one who in actual fact showed himself a reviler, and that not without the guilt of an unbelief in which he had turned away from the preparatory light of the Old Testament word, as well as from the message of the disciples of Jesus. And yet mercy was extended to him, and from being a Saul he became Paul. Then, certainly, he first tasted the good word and the powers of the world to come, and remained afterwards faithful (2 Tim. 4:7, 8). But among those who bear the name of Christians, there are also parties innumerable who have not yet penetrated to such "tasting," because they have not turned to the grace of their regeneration, and often enough blaspheme what they do not know. And in this case we have not to judge, but to pray, "Father, forgive them; for they know not what they do" (Luke 23:34). But for us who believe must the possibility of unpardonable apostasy, with its whole fearful earnestness, be constantly preserved undiminished; only that we may judge ourselves not according to self-discovered signs, but according to the signs which are laid down in the word.

That there is a reviling of Christ which is pardonable, is attested elsewhere also. This is done in those words of Christ where the reviling of the Son of man is contrasted with the blasphemy against the Holy Ghost, and only the latter (whether in contrast with that, or in general with every blasphemy) is called unpardonable. This last statement of itself leads us back again to the Epistle to the Hebrews. Respecting the reviling of the Son of man, so much only requires to be said as serves for confirmation of what has been brought forward a little ago. The blasphemy of the Pharisees, that Christ cast out devils only in the power of Beelzebub, the prince of the devils, was the occasion of Christ's making His declaration (Matt. 12:24; Mark 3:22). But only in Matthew is the statement found, that that man will be forgiven who may say a word against the Son of man (Matt. 12:32); while the same statement is found in Luke (12:10) out of connection with that deed of Christ and with the blasphemy of the Pharisees following upon it. What is thus said is not to be shown from the context of Matthew and that of Luke without narrower investigation. That in Matthew the mention of that speaking against Christ appears to be *occasioned* by the blasphemy of the Pharisees, is of course to be recognized. But that in these words of Christ the blasphemy of the Pharisees itself *is meant*, is not to be supposed. The blasphemy of the Pharisees has not two sides: one against the Son of man, the other against the Holy Ghost; the one pardonable, the other unpardonable. Rather is the blasphemy wholly and indivisibly directed against the Holy Spirit of God, in whose power Christ performed His deeds; and the blasphemy of the Pharisees, whole and entire, directed in this form against the Son of man, is called unpardonable. In this way it is understood by Mark also, when he adds (3:30), by way of explanation, "Because they said, He hath an unclean spirit." This statement is meant when the Pharisees' blasphemy, as being blasphemy against the Holy Ghost effectually working in Christ, is declared to be unpardonable. In what sense, and why, is to be afterwards discussed. The question which first of all arises is this: How is it, nevertheless, that the blasphemy on the part of the Pharisees, recorded by Matthew, can serve Christ as an occasion to speak in general of a word spoken against the Son of man, which, in contrast with the pharisaic blasphemy, is designated as pardonable? If we stop at what is furnished by the context in Matthew in answer to this question, I am able to refer only to one point as explanatory. The Pharisees blaspheme works of Christ as satanic, which they look upon in the case of their own as done in the power of God. Since in this way their own children will become judges of them and their blasphemy (Matt. 12:27), their own children themselves must give judicial testimony that this blasphemy, following upon these deeds, and happening in this way, is a deliberate one against the better knowledge of the blasphemers, and thus uttered with the denial of a known truth. But this is an unpardonable blasphemy. If, however, on the other hand, a word may be thought of as directed against the Son of man, which is pardonable, then must it be distinguished from that blasphemy in this respect, that it is not denial and blasphemy of the Christ as known by the blasphemer. And in the position in which the Son of man stood to Israel, and Israel to the Son of man, Christ might well have occasion to intimate that He does not so look upon every word directed against the Son of man as He does upon the blasphemy of the Pharisees. For the latter bore the character of denial and of obduracy against a truth otherwise known by the blasphemers themselves. To something similar that word of Christ in Luke (ch. 12) points, which is directed not against the Pharisees, but to the disciples, only that here the index to a correct apprehension [of the passage] does not lie so plain before us as is the case in Matthew. But the right view is quite evident from the relations of discipleship in which those addressed stand to the Lord. From this point of view Christ refers them at the end of His discourse, in order to their strengthening against the impending oppressions of the world, to the assistance of the Holy Ghost (ch. 12:12). As standing in the relation of discipleship, He strengthens them with the reference to this, that He, the Lord, will one day confess those who confess Him before men, before the angels of God, and warns them with the words that His deniers before men will be denied before the angels of God (12:8, 9). When, therefore, Christ proceeds in His discourse to say, "And whosoever shall speak a word against the Son of man, it shall be forgiven him; but unto him that hath blasphemed (βλασφημήσαντι) against the Holy Ghost it shall not be forgiven" (12:10),—then also can this word, capable of being forgiven, directed against the Son of man, only then escape being blasphemy against the Holy Ghost, when it proceeds from those who have nothing before them but the Son of man, and to whom the Holy Ghost has not yet opened up in living experience and knowledge the question, "What think ye of Christ? whose son is he?" But to the disciples, denial and blasphemy of the Son would be denial and blasphemy of the Holy Ghost, through whose working they had learnt this: "Thou art the Christ, the Son of the living God." Thus, therefore, only then is a word directed against the Son of man pardonable, when it was concealed from the speaker what Christ was. But if he knows the Lord, whom no one in truth can call Lord except by the Holy Ghost (1 Cor. 12:3), then is every word directed by him against this Lord, and blaspheming Him, blasphemy against the Holy Ghost, to whom he owes that knowledge which he renounces in blasphemy.

And in this way we are naturally brought nearer to the knowledge of what the sin against the Holy Ghost is. We should very badly understand the way in which it is contrasted with the speaking against the Son of man, if we supposed we were able to measure the greatness of this guilt in this way, that the one time it referred to the Holy Ghost, the other time only to the Son of man. The sin against the Holy Ghost is an offence against Christ, and not against the Holy Ghost (conceived of outside of His relation to Christ). It can be committed by such as do not yet stand in fellowship with Christ, as well as by disciples of Christ. But even by the former not in such a way that they in a certain measure, as it were ignorantly, fall into this sin; but only in such a way that they, like the Pharisees, against better knowledge, blaspheme as satanic what belongs to *God* in Christ, or, as would be possible in the case of disciples of Christ, in such a way that they, against the knowledge of Christ wrought in them by the Holy Ghost, fall into denial and blasphemy of their Lord. With the former it is obduracy, and indeed obduracy rising up to the pitch of blasphemy against a preparatory knowledge; with the others obduracy, and indeed obduracy rising up to the pitch of blasphemy against a full knowledge, wrought by God's Holy Spirit, of what Christ is. From this last point, what is said in the Gospels respecting the sin against the Holy Ghost coincides with what stands in the Epistle to the Hebrews. And we have and need, as marks of the way in which the sin against the Holy Ghost can be committed by disciples of Christ, to say and to place nothing else from our own experience than what stands in the Epistle to the Hebrews. Everything that was said before in reference to the passages of Hebrews respecting the inconceivability of such a sin, without an intermediate, gradual estrangement from the truth, applies also here. But where the estrangement from the truth has reached this highest stage of blaspheming and blasphemous enmity, there is its outbreak, as being not an isolated act by itself, but a proof of that state of soul which, in conscious opposition, bars itself against the fountain of salvation,—the deed of one who, as it is expressed in Mark (3:29), will be guilty of everlasting transgression (ἔνοχος ἔσται αἰωνίου ἁμαρτήματος); or, as it is said in Matthew (12:32), a deed which will not be forgiven him, neither in this world, nor in the world to come. For in this act there comes to light a ripeness of wicked obduracy, which, as conscious blasphemy, excludes from grace, alike whether we stood, by virtue of God's preparatory revelation, on the threshold of being able to lay hold of grace, and then by denial of the preparatory knowledge blasphemously push it from us; or whether we had been already introduced into the sanctuary of grace, from which, through denial of the truth fully known, we fall away.

According to every estimate, the same sin floated before the mind of the Apostle John also, when he writes in his first epistle (5:15), that one ought to pray for forgiveness on behalf of a brother, if he sees him commit a sin which is not unto death, and then proceeds: "There is a sin unto death: I do not say that he shall pray for it." For these words are found in connection with the mention of the fact, that whosoever hath the Son, hath life; and whosoever hath not the Son, hath not life. But whoever believes on, hath the Son. Whoever believeth not on Him, that man hath not received the testimony which God hath given for His Son. But the testimony consists in the everlasting life which God hath given us, and this life is in His Son (*vide* 5:10–12). Thus will the sin which tends to the brother's death be precisely this, that, in contradiction with his own life-experience which he has of this testimony of God, he turns away from the Son and denies Him. And here, then, that other word of John applies, "He that believeth not is condemned already;" and, "He that believeth not the Son shall not see life: but the wrath of God abides on him" (John 3:18, 36). Certainly at the time of writing his first epistle, already in the present there stand before the eyes of the Apostle John antichristian manifestations. What occasions difficulty in reference to the passage in John is much less the question what John looks upon as such death-bringing sin, than how and when the intercession is to be regulated in accordance with it, *i.e.* in the given circumstances to be omitted. For we shall not be able to say, as I formerly supposed, that we cannot make this sin, considered in itself, an object of prayer for forgiveness; but we can pray for the sinner, that he may turn from this sin. For between such prayer and God there stands for me, like a partition-wall, the knowledge that God cannot forgive the sin of apostasy from Christ, the well-spring of salvation, to him who knowingly and wilfully has renounced this Lord. But of false fondness this very John, who has been called not without reason the preacher of love, will least of all know anything. For he preaches, as scarcely any other does, the holy love of Christians. But it will always be only with fear and trembling that we shall be able to omit the prayer—with fear and trembling, lest I contemptuously lift up myself, or lest I pronounce too hasty a judgment on my brother. He who does not omit the prayer with deepest pain, will not have the omission conducing to his salvation. Only he dare not endanger his own soul by looking perhaps upon the sin of apostasy as not exposed to the judgment, while God has judged it in His word. But one thing will he be able to do with a good conscience, nay, be under obligation to do it, viz. to call upon God, that He may preserve him from false judgment respecting his brother; and if he should too hastily omit to pray for him, that He, according to the riches of His compassion, will not allow to be recompensed to that brother the offence which he himself commits through his own fault, and what he without proper ground omits to perform.

But as respects the application of all these fearful warnings to ourselves, and to our own soul's state, for the purpose of conscientious investigation, here precisely we must repeatedly refer to what was formerly (§ 28, note (5), towards the end) said respecting that satanic poisoning which makes itself felt by us just upon the domain of the revelation of the wrath of God. For that man must yet have little experience as to the state of tempted souls, who does not know how frequently one meets there with a satanic perversity of anguish lest the sin against the Holy Ghost has been committed. How watchfully in these cases we must look not merely to the soul's state, but also to the bodily state of the tempted; how carefully we have to trace and to distinguish thoroughly what is perhaps not at all a struggle of conscience, but an after-working of perverted doctrines and views of others, and the like—to all this we can here only call attention in passing. But where we have really to do with a purely spiritual struggle, which has sprung up from the innermost depths of one's proper self, there let one above all see to it whether the struggling one, as well as he who gives advice, keeps himself within the rule of the certain divine word, instead of befooling either others or himself with his own thoughts, it being all the same whether he wishes to comfort or to rebuke with such thoughts. For nowhere does the dealing with our own thoughts, the want of conscientious investigation, pondering, keeping of the word (of the word, however, as a whole, not in a fragmentary, piecemeal way), revenge itself more fearfully than at the time of severest and strongest temptations. Everything, on the other hand, depends on this, that one early and lovingly enters into that faith which attaches itself merely to the certain word of promise (comp. § 18, especially note (4)), and is mighty in this, that it believes against feeling (comp. § 25, note (7)). This faith alone is strong enough to pillow itself against the strongest temptation upon the apostolic word, and to ask, "If God be for us, who can be against us?" (Rom. 8:31–34.)

(7) The spiritual house into which the Christian enters bears also the inscription: "Let everyone that names the name of Christ depart from iniquity" (2 Tim. 2:19). This word is not kept by that man who guards himself only against this or that specific offence, instead of renouncing iniquity in general. For everything depends on this, that our minds are not corrupted and moved away from simple, undivided surrender to Christ (2 Cor. 11:3). Where this simple and undivided surrender is corrupted in any one point, there no one can say what issue of corruption this beginning may reach. Therefore "he that is begotten of God keeps himself, and that wicked one touches him not."

THIRD SECTION

PERSONAL QUALIFICATION FOR PRESERVING THE POSSESSION OF SALVATION

§ 30. Christian Virtue as Fidelity

CHRISTTAN virtue is that personal qualification which verifies itself struggle previously described (1). As its objective distinction from mere legal virtue consists in this, that it commences with that freedom to be good which is the gift of gospel grace (see § 23), so its subjective distinction and its formal character are of such a nature, that it is equally *fidelity* in its pursuit of an end not yet attained, and preservation of a received blessing, by virtue of which fidelity is actively engaged in the attainment of that end (2). From the character of the received gift, which Christian virtue preserves in faithfulness, will result as well the subjective motive and the objective standard, the subjective means of preservation and the subjective fundamental power of virtue, as well as the extent of the same in its self-manifestation (see § 31–35).

(1) The new life is a conflict. There is a twofold conceivable issue of its development. Now, if the question arises as to what may condition this issue, and what may protect us against a fall, then the chief ethical element lies in this, to emphasize the personal qualification and activity of the regenerate. That this rests on divine gift and grace, and can only be conceived of in continual connection therewith, we are taught by what we know of the essence of regeneration. But just on this account it is doubly important to bring into prominence the other aspect of this personal qualification and activity, even in the name of that capacity and attestation which solves the problem of sanctification and renewal in the strength of the Spirit of God.

Hence the significance of the name, Christian virtue. It declares that Christian virtue has its formal aspect—namely, the character of personal ability and practical manifestation—quite in common with man's general conception of virtue (see § 15). This also it partakes with this general notion of virtue, that it can only be conceived of as the reflex influence of continuous practice and self-realization. It is the fruit of the γυμνάζειν ἑαυτὸν πρὸς εὐσέβειαν (1 Tim. 4:7), and has its realization in the γυμνάζειν ἑαυτὸν πρὸς εὐσέβειαν (1 Tim. 1:18). For one has only διὰ τὴν ἕξιν τὰ αἰσθητήρια γεγυμνασμένα πρὸς διάκρισιν καλοῦ τε καὶ κακοῦ (Heb. 5:14), as on the other side the true practical realization of what has been received is only conceivable under the form of personal diligence. Πᾶσαν σπουδὴν παρεισενέγκαντες ἐπιχορηγήσατε ἐν τῇ πίστει ἡμῶν τὴν ἀπετὴν, κ.τ.λ., 2 Pet. 1:5.

(2) The characteristic form of Christian virtue rests on the foundation of the Christian life. This is a personal, gracious fellowship with God, spiritually received. (In Stoicism and kindred systems it is the indwelling God, the higher spiritual nature of the divine Ego, whom as being a son of Zeus man must seek to please, in order to conquer in the struggle with the φαντασίαι; Epict. *Diss.* ii. 18, 19.) In the blessing received lie the seeds of all the blessings of eternity. The problem is the preservation of this imparted good. The only conceivable qualification and action for the solution of this problem is personal *fidelity* (Rev. 2:10, γίνου πιστὸς ἄχρι θανάτου). What is true of the teachers, holds good in its way of all Christians: ὧδε λοιπὸν ζητεῖται ἐν τοῖς οἰκονόμοις ἵνα πιστός τις εὑρεθῇ (1 Cor. 4:2). Compare our Lord's parable of the servants and the received talents (Matt. 25:14 ff.). Moreover, the peculiar nature of this fidelity is determined by the peculiarity of the blessing of salvation. It is not fidelity to a duty coming upon us from without—to a precept, rule, maxim, or the like, but fidelity to an inwardly working principle of life—personal fidelity to that personal fellowship with God which has been brought about by the Holy Ghost. It is the fidelity of a child born again of God (of the δοῦλος ἀγαθὸς καὶ πιστός as of the υἱὸς πιστός), who in his

whole consciousness and acting will be determined by nothing but by the power of the gift of grace promised in the word, and which has been sealed to him by the working of the Holy Spirit, and which is there called regeneration, sonship, power of life drawn from the spring of imperishable life (Rom. 8:14–17; Gal. 4:6; 2 Cor. 1:21, 22; Eph. 1:13, 14). A violation of this fidelity is consequently nothing less than a grieving of the Holy Spirit, with whom the regenerate one is sealed unto the day of redemption (Eph. 4:30, λυπεῖν τὸ Πνεῦμα τὸ ἅγιον τοῦ Θεοῦ, ἐν ᾧ ἐσφραγίσθητε εἰς ἡμέραν ἀπολυτρώσεως; comp. § 22, note (2)). That this preservation of the gift received is at the same time an endeavor and striving after an end not yet attained, is involved in the (already explained) nature of the blessing received, and its position relative to the nature of the old man and the general development of the world (comp. § 20, note (5), and § 25).

§ 31. a. The Subjective Motive of Christian Fidelity—Gratitude

Christian virtue, as self-realization in fidelity, can be found and be permanent only where the impulse corresponding to it is present and maintained (1). But if the fidelity of the Christian is due to a received blessing, and if this blessing is the foundation of his new life, then the disposition which corresponds to this relation, in which at the same time is given the impulse to faithful self-activity, can be none other than that of *gratitude*. As a breach of fidelity on the part of the redeemed man makes itself pre-eminently felt as crying ingratitude, and even restrains the resistance of the old man by the sense of a duty of gratitude, so is this gratitude on the other side, to him who is born of the Spirit of God, not an outward duty, but, so far as it really lives in him, the characteristic reflex working on that subjective disposition with which man recognizes as a free gift of grace that divine communion worked in his heart by God's preventing love. This tone of mind, which alone corresponds to the essential relation of the divine and human fellowship of love, gives and also keeps up the right inclination and the right strength to maintain this communion in fidelity (2).

(1) There can be no free personal activity of the will without impulse of our nature. Herein consists one's own inclination, and with it are bound up our personal freedom and its variously determined resolve (comp. § 5). So also, in the regenerate man, no active realization of personal qualification is conceivable without a divine impulse incorporated with his nature (comp. § 22). If I now ask, What impels the Christian to remain faithful to that God who has qualified him in grace, by the fellowship of the Holy Spirit with his spirit renewing his spiritual nature, for the realization of every Christian virtue? this can be only designated a frame of mind which is the concentrated expression of the relation in which the receiver stands to the giver, and by virtue of which the former feels himself also constantly impelled to preserve this relation inviolate. For all the workings of the Holy Ghost, such as faith, love, and hope, in which the Christian possesses the strength to fulfil the will of God in every particular, point out indeed the divinely purposed and divinely worked shape of the Christian frame of mind, but not the disposition or the real subjective motive which urges me, in a manner consistent with the entirety of my relation to God the Giver, to cleave faithfully to all that has been bestowed upon me by God's grace, in faith, hope, and love. Nay, faith, love, and hope become themselves weak and degenerate, when they do not possess as a common characteristic trait, and are not fostered in, that tone of mind in which one holds and maintains them as gifts of grace. And this tone of mind, as the immediate reflex of our consciousness of having nothing but what has been received (1 Cor. 4:7), is no other than that of a constant sense of thankfulness and gratitude. And if previously (§ 19, note (5)) we have recognized in that love alone, which is worked in us by the Spirit of God, the fulfiller of the law; so a perseverance in this love, and a faithful practical realization corresponding to it, in a manner conformable to the Christian character, are then only attained,

when thankfulness and gratitude are and remain the predominant tone of mind, impelling us to serve God truly in love. For not through fidelity do I attain to gratitude; but through gratitude and thankfulness, as a constant sense of gratefulness for the blessing received, do I arrive at a free, affectionate Christian fidelity, answering to the relation in which God stands to me, and I to Him.

(2) Without the presence of this fundamental disposition of gratitude, there can be no question of a fidelity which would correspond to the nature of the Christian. For by virtue of the relation in which the redeemed man can discover that which now constitutes the most essential peculiarity of his nature, in his having become through grace a partaker of the divine nature, no feeling or tone of mind can be thought of as being that which is natural, newly inborn, and growing up with the Christian, so much as that of gratitude. And this not only in reference to the spiritual blessing of salvation already received, but also in reference to the whole further guidance of life, internal as well as external, up to that day of the future; since the Christian knows that, by his communion with Christ, he has entered into a life which in all its relations is governed throughout by grace. And to this also there corresponds only a grateful frame of mind, pervading the Christian everywhere and in every relation. This gratitude is a free no less than a binding motive for personal fidelity. For, in addition to its natural root in the Christian heart, the gratitude of the redeemed is the feeling and consciousness of a restored liberty. But this liberty is at the same time essentially a dependence on God; and in gratitude this dependence has the character of that which it really is, viz. free, loving obligation. This obligation is of the greatest importance, when contrasted with the element of no-obligation which still dwells in the nature of the old man. In gratitude the Christian has a motive for fidelity, in consequence of which, with love and pleasure, the new man, born again to liberty, binds the resisting nature of the old man in fetters.

But even in the natural man, revolt from God is supposed in and with ingratitude (Rom. 1:21). How could gracious communion with God be otherwise perfectly maintained, except in and through gratitude alone? It is in its nature not an act, but a constant frame of mind. Εὐχαριστοῦντες πάντοτε ὑπὲρ πάντων ἐν ὀνόματι τοῦ Κυρίου ἡμῶν Ἰησοῦ Χριστοῦ τῷ Θεῷ καὶ πατρί, Eph. 5:20. Πάντοτε χαίρετε, ἀδιαλείπτως προσεύχεσθε, ἐν παντὶ εὐχαριστεῖτε· τοῦτο γὰρ θέλημα Θεοῦ ἐν Χριστῷ Ἰησοῦ εἰς ὑμᾶς, 1 Thess. 5:16–18. It produces the most intimate and tenderest phenomena of the life in God, in the utterance and maintenance of prayer. Τῇ προσευχῇ προσκαρτερεῖτε γρηγοροῦντες ἐν αὐτῇ ἐν εὐχαριστίᾳ, Col. 4:2. Compare § 33. As it is given in and with our transplanting into the communion of grace by faith, so does the overflowing gratitude for this glorious gift itself react upon our strengthening in the faith. Ὡς οὖν παρελάβετε τὸν Χριστὸν Ἰησοῦν τὸν Κύριον, ἐν αὐτῷ περιπατεῖτε, ἐρριζωμένοι, καὶ ἐποικοδομούμενοι ἐν αὐτῷ καὶ βεβαιούμενοι τῇ πίστει, καθὼς ἐδιδάχθητε, περισσεύοντες ἐν εὐχαριστίᾳ, Col. 2:6 f.

§ 32. b. *The Objective Standard of Christian Virtue, or Christ's Example and Word in relation to the Law*

In the inwardly working principle of life, the maintenance of which the virtue of Christian fidelity strives after, lies also the necessity by virtue of which thankful fidelity, in its practical realization, knows itself to be bound to an outward rule, which is at the same time equally intrinsic to it (1). For the Spirit of regeneration, who will gloriously transform us into Christ's image step by step, refers Christians, even with the inward workings of this new birth, at the same time to the exemplar of Christ, as it lies before us in word and deed, and points out the perfection which is according to His will, and ought to be striven after by us (2). In this exemplar, in which Christ at the same time manifests Himself as the fulfiller of the law, the law also retains its binding character for the redeemed; but the fidelity, in which I comply with the will of God in the law, consists in this, that I undertake the fulfilment of the law, the schoolmaster to bring us to Christ, in the power of Christ, and look for the standard of my right fulfilling of the law not in the law itself, but in the example of Christ the fulfiller of the law. For the law, apart from Christ, holds good only for the unredeemed; to the redeemed, however, the law in Christ is, and remains, the standard of their fidelity (3).

(1) Jesus Christ, the fulfiller of the law (see § 17, note (4); § 18, note (1)), proves Himself as such just in this, that He does not abrogate the essential significance which the law possesses as the manifestation of the personal will of God, but fulfils it in His own person, with a view to a permanent reflex influence on His redeemed (comp. § 13, note (4)). And the manner in which the Holy Ghost perfects in the regenerate themselves the work of the law, has been previously discussed (see § 24, note (2)). The life which from Christ is kindled in His followers, is a life which, by virtue of its principle, brings to inward accomplishment that will of God which rules over us both in the law and the gospel. Only the creature in whom God the Holy Ghost dwells, should know and keep clear in his consciousness, that this inward event is not an immanent state of his own being, a principle inherent in it, but a gift of grace, dependent on the gracious will of God with respect to the creature, regulated not by the measure of evolution in the new spiritual life of the creature, but by the law of a divine will standing over the creature, and in it first of all gradually realizing itself. The relation of Christ to His own is of such a nature, that the head of the serpent is being trodden clown, who is seeking to seduce man to a false equality with God, as if he bore in himself alone and in his new spiritual life the law of normal development. Therefore the new life makes its appearance not by any means solely in the form of an inward spiritual working, of which as a divine fact a man would become conscious absolutely only through inward testimony. Rather is that which is operated by God held up at the same time also before the Christian as that which is willed by God;

and Christ leaves behind Him not only His Spirit, but also His ἐντολαί, by virtue of which that which the Spirit of God works is also placed before our eyes as God's requisition addressed to us. 1 John 3:23, Αὕτη ἐστὶν ἡ ἐντολὴ αὐτοῦ, ἵνα πιστεύσωμεν τῷ ὀνόματι τοῦ υἱοῦ αὐτοῦ; John 15:12, Αὕτη ἐστὶν ἡ ἐντολὴ ἡ ἐμὴ, ἵνα ἀγαπᾶτε ἀλλήλους, κ.τ.λ. (comp. 13:14); Ἐὰν τὰς ἐντολάς μου τηρήσητε, μενεῖτε ἐν τῇ ἀγάπῃ μου· καθὼς ἐγὼ τὰς ἐντολὰς τοῦ πατρός μου τετήπηκα, καὶ μένω αὐτοῦ ἐν τῇ ἀγάπῃ (15:10, comp. 14:15); 1 John 3:24, Καὶ ὁ τηρῶν τὰς ἐντολὰς αὐτοῦ, ἐν αὐτῷ μένει, καὶ αὐτὸς ἐν αὐτῷ· γινώσκομεν ὅτι μένει ἐν ἡμῖν, ἐκ τοῦ Πνεύματος οὗ ἡμῖν ἔδωκεν (comp. 5:21). So, too, the ἁγιασμός is brought before us not merely as operated in us by God, but also as commanded by Him: 1 Thess. 4:3, τοῦτο γάρ ἐστι θέλημα τοῦ Θεοῦ ὁ ἁγιασμὸς ὑμῶν. Therefore, also it is the definition of all enlightenment, that those who are led by the Spirit (Πνεύματι ἀγόμενοι, Rom. 8:14) recognize the working of the Spirit as that which is God's will, and in the will of God the true working of the Spirit. Rom. 12:2, Μεταμορφοῦσθε τῇ ἀνακαινώσει τοῦ νοὸς ὑμῶν, εἰς τὸ δοκιμάζειν ὑμᾶς τί τὸ θέλημα τοῦ Θεοῦ τὸ ἀγαθὸν καὶ εὐάρεστον καὶ τέλειον; Eph. 5:17, Μὴ γίνεσθε ἄφρονες, ἀλλὰ συνιέντες τί τὸ θέλημα τοῦ Κυρίου.

(2) The will of God is to the Christian that which has been fulfilled in Jesus Christ. The God-man, Jesus Christ, is the personal manifestation of God who wills, and of man who fulfils. The shape of this fulfilling is made public both in word and deed. In this shape it is the will of Christ to become living, through the operation of the Holy Ghost, in those that are His; that is, so to pervade their mind and their life, that they should become like to the mind and life of Christ. (Rom. 8:29, Προώρισε συμμόρφους τῆς εἰκόνος τοῦ υἱοῦ αὐτοῦ, εἰς τὸ εἶναι αὐτὸν πρωτότοκον ἐν πολλοῖς ἀδελφοῖς.) But as Christ, through the operation of the Holy Spirit, lives in those who are His (Gal. 2:20), so is it also His will to remain objectively before them; and their lasting consciousness is to consist in this, that they should walk after His example. 1 John 2:6, Ὁ λέγων ἐν αὐτῷ μένειν, ὀφείλει, καθὼς ἐκεῖνος περιεπάτησε, καὶ αὐτὸς οὕτως περιπατεῖν; 1 Pet. 2:21, Ὅτι καὶ Χριστὸς ἔπαθεν ὑπὲρ ὑμῶν, ὑμῖν

ὑπολιμπάνων ὑπογραμμὸν, ἵνα ἐπακολουθήσητε τοῖς ἴχνεσιν αὐτοῦ; John 13:15, Ὑπόδειγμα γὰρ ἔδωκα ὑμῖν, ἵνα, καθὼς ἐγὼ ἐποίησα ὑμῖν, καὶ ὑμεῖς ποιῆτε. Not in himself, but in the possession of grace, in the contemplation and imitation of Christ, is the Christian here below to be blessed and holy. Even the last stage of blessedness consists in this, that God is the God of the redeemed one, and that he, the redeemed, is His son (Rev. 21:7). Not to be in one's self God, nor to have in one's self full sufficiency, is the final consummation, but to see God face to face (1 Cor. 13:12), and over against one's self to know God as He is in Himself (1 John 3:2). So also the training and preparation consist in this, that God *in* the redeemed brings the objective God, that the law *in* their hearts brings the *objective law* and the *personal will of God*,—to ever clearer consciousness, to ever increasing distinctness of apprehension and understanding.

(3) Christ being the objective standard of Christian life, in Him the law is at the same time the standard. He is in no respect a destroyer, but a fulfiller; He gives to the word the spirit and the reality of life, to the letter of the law its full force, to its pedagogic power of training its full and perfect fulfilment. He establishes no rule different from or higher than the law of God, but He reveals only the inmost nature and the highest aims of this same law. And this equally in reference to the law of conscience as to the revealed will of God in the law and the prophets of Israel (Matt. 5:17). Τέλος γὰρ νόμου Χριστός, Rom. 10:14; (Ὁ νόμος) σκιὰ τῶν μελλόντων, τὸ δὲ σῶμα Χριστοῦ, Col. 2:17; σκιὰν ἔχων ὁ νόμος τῶν μελλόντων ἀγαθῶν, οὐκ αὐτὴν τὴν εἰκόνα τῶν πραγμάτων, Heb. 10:1, comp. 8:5. On which account Paul could with right say: Νόμον οὖν καταργοῦμεν διὰ τῆς πίστεως; Μὴ γένοιτο· ἀλλὰ νόμον ἱστῶμεν, Rom. 3:31. But should it be asked what law is here meant, then we must answer with Christ: The law revealed concerning Israel, such as in Christ the fulfiller of the law it is perpetually for the human race the divine requisition and fulfilment. This, however, is the law, as it is at once law *and* prophecy. For the law is the written, abiding prophecy, at once the denunciation of curse and the

setting forth of salvation; but prophecy is the oral, ever newly unfolded law, the continual attestation and new development of threats of punishment and promises of salvation. Just as little as the separation of law and prophecy avails, so little does that of *leges particulares et universales*. Here nothing is so particular that it has not at the same time a universal reference, and nothing so universal that it is not at the same time joined on to something particular (*e.g.* the decalogue, the law of the Sabbath; comp. Deut. 5:15). These are elements which mutually permeate each other, and do not stand isolated alongside of each other. The same holds good of the separation into *leges morales, cærimoniales, forenses*. It is an arbitrary division, useful for an index to the Old Testament, but perplexing as a designation of the essence of the legislation of the Old Testament, still more unsuitable for the definition of the Old Testament revelation in its relation to Christ, the fulfiller of the law. Rather is the Old Testament revelation, alike in its requirements and its promises, as well an exhibition of the preparatory deeds of God and of man's preparatory state, as an exhibition beforehand alike of God's perfect revelation, and of the perfect state of the human family. So far as the contents relate to the goal of God's revelation, so far are the form of preparation and the pre-exhibition at the same time abrogated in the fulfilment through Jesus Christ. So far as the contents refer to the shape of the life of man, there in and with Christ the state of preparation has retired before the fulfilment, and the perfect shape of the inner man has been realized. In this position of Christ, and along with this in the limitation resulting therefrom, the law in Christ, afterwards as before, continued to be at once a requiring and a fulfilled standard. What it is in Christ, that is it also in those in whom Christ truly lives—no more a mere outward requirement, but an internal requirement and fulfilment at the same time. For everything that is a fruit of the Holy Spirit [has this to be said of it]: κατὰ τῶν τοιούτων οὐκ ἔστι νόμος, Gal. 5:22, 23. But this fruit of the Spirit is only attained when the law is approached not outside of Christ, but in Christ, and when it is our will to fulfil the same not through the power of the law, but through the power of Christ. For to those who act otherwise apply the apparently paradoxical assertions of Luther: "After that Christ is come and revealed, the laws of ceremonies have become injurious and deadly sinful; nay, moreover, all other laws besides are so too; even the ten commandments are quite deadly, if Christ is not added to them. Besides, in the conscience of a Christian believer should no law rule or dominate, but only the law of the Spirit who makes alive, through which law of the Spirit we are free and set loose from the law of the letter and of death, from its works and the sins which it excites. Not in such a way that the law in itself is evil, but that it cannot help and serve us in reaching the righteousness which avails before God" (Luther, *Table Talk*). For, so far as Christians are truly Christ's, they are in and with Christ, through the Holy Ghost, ἔννομοι—law and fulfilment alike. So far, however, as in them lives the old nature in which Christ does not live, or which is not yet put to death by Him, even in Christ the law, afterwards as well as before, stands over against His followers in the form of requisition and judgment (comp. § 26, note (3), on Rom. 7). But in any case, there is no law for the regenerate, that continues to exist in and by itself, but merely the law in and with Christ, in and with the voice of the Holy Spirit. "Lex hoc loco unam tantum rem significat, immutabilem videlicet voluntatem Dei, secundum quam homines omnes vitæ suæ rationes instituere debeant. *Spiritus* sunt duo officio—consolandi et arguendi ... evangelii et legis."—*Form Conc.* p. 721.

The truth, that solely the law in Christ is the standard of Christian virtue, stands at the same time also opposed to the untruth, that the perfection of Christian virtue rests on the fulfilment of the so-called *consilia evangelica*. For that would be as much as to say that the perfection of the Christian consisted not in the existence of absolute goodness, but merely of relative goodness. Whatever occurs in Scripture of the so-called *consilia*, is a form either of absolute right conduct, or of what is consistently required under the supposition of certain individual, local, temporal circumstances: as, for example, the counsel of Christ to give away one's possessions under the supposition of slavery to mammon; or that of Paul, to remain unmarried in consideration of the calamities of the times, under the supposition of no existing necessity (of the non-existing πυροῦσθαι). Matt. 19:21; 1 Cor. 7:7–9, 26, 35. Wonderful it is, how the terms of the stoical school, *officia media et perfecta* (κατορθώματα μέσα καὶ τέλεια), find in the phraseology of the church fathers a perfectly reverse application. Τέλειον is the ἀεὶ καθῆκον, μέσον τὸ οὐκ ἀεὶ (οἷον τὸ γαμεῖν). "Christ in the whole gospel has only given one counsel, viz. the chastity which any man who has grace may keep even in the least element. But they have made twelve out of it, and go about doing what they will with the gospel. With this view have they divided and broken up the world; measured and regulated their life by the counsels, and the laity by the commandments: they assert their life as higher than the commands of God. In this way the life and faith of the common Christian have become, as it were, stale sour beer. Every one has had his eyes opened, despises the commandments, runs after the counsels" (Luther). Modern Romanists understand the difference as of "common virtue and moral virtuosity" (Hirscher),—as if special virtuousness were anything else than a special gift, which only then continues to be virtue when it is not taken out of the region of general virtue just by this, that it plumes itself on being something higher and more meritorious.

§ 33. c. *The Subjective Proof and Maintenance of Christian Fidelity in Watchfulness and Prayer*

When the grateful fidelity of the Christian recognizes it as the problem of the Christian life to hold fast to the principle and rule of life which was imparted in grace to the regenerate man by the word and Spirit of Christ, then there also results from the same blessing of grace the peculiarity of that subjective proof and maintenance, by which alone Christian fidelity is in a position to solve the problem. For if the objective means of the new life are those blessings of grace dispensed to him in Christ's word and sacraments, which overcome in the divine strength the resistance of the old nature, so will the thankful fidelity maintain itself and remain fitted to solve its problem in the same measure alone in which the Christian prepares himself to abandon self, and to seek the strength of his fidelity only in that which is bestowed upon him by God (1). But this subjective preparation, in which the Christian is able as well to guard against the enticement of his old nature as to preserve himself in communion with that God who gives, and thus to solve the problem of his life, consists in *watchfulness* and *prayer*, or in the inward practice of that *humility* in which a man steadily turns away purely and without reserve from all that is his own and of self, to the strength of grace given him in Christ. This watchfulness in a life of prayer it is alone which corresponds to the character of the regenerate and converted man in the position in which he stands to God, to whom he owes both his new birth and his conversion,—corresponds as being the practical realization of a grateful fidelity, which is ever returning to its fountainhead (2).

(1) The fellowship of the Spirit is a fellowship in order to liberty, in order to free self-action. Even when the Father draws in the spirit of the conscience by the excitement of divine spiritual inclination of the heart (John 6:44, 65), He draws the heart in order I that in its right tone it may attain to a free resolve. With this call to freedom, the means established by Christ for the maintenance of the communion of grace presuppose at all times, for their blessed efficacy, also the right tone of mind, and the spiritual activity corresponding thereto. Where the question is, therefore, of the maintenance of the right relation and conduct towards Christ and His salvation, it is absolutely impossible to speak merely of the objective means of grace as the sole means of such maintenance. As in the unregenerate they can furnish the means of his new birth, as they are constantly able to invigorate the regenerate with new powers of life, so they require in him who has been transplanted into the kingdom of liberty also the right spiritual disposition, and the corresponding activity of life, in order to

be effective. But, again, we must not speak of this right disposition either as faith, love, or the like. These are already important, positive workings of the means of grace. Here the point is exclusively about the disposition and the spiritual activity in which the regenerate and converted man is able to keep up his receptivity for new strengthening of faith, love, and hope, which is constantly to be derived from the means of grace. Such a disposition is also distinctly presupposed by the objective means of grace for maintaining the fellowship of grace, viz. the word of holy Scripture and the sacrament of the Lord's Supper. Of those who are Christ's, the word expects that, when its voice is heard, the hearers should not harden their hearts through the deceitfulness of sin (Heb. 3:7, 13–15); and the word of Scripture has not only a promise, but also an element of correction, opposed to the selfish tendency of the heart, and it exercises the divinely appointed influence for the right disposition of the heart (πρὸς διδασκαλίαν, πρὸς ἔλεγχον, πρὸς ἐπανόρθωσιν, πρὸς παιδείαν τὴν ἐν δικαιοσύνῃ, 2 Tim. 3:16). And in the same way, to the promise of grace by the sacrament is joined the requirement of a preceding strict self-examination (1 Cor. 11:28).

(2) Whoever wishes to continue to be a partaker of the grace of the new creation, in which, as in the creation of the world, God creates something out of nothing, must bring to the means of grace the true and sincere conviction of his nothingness, strip himself of all his own honor, and seek only that honor which cometh from God. Τὰ μὴ ὄντα ἐξελέξατο ὁ Θεός, ἵνα τὰ ὄντα καταργήσῃ, 1 Cor. 1:28; Πῶς δύνασθε ὑμεῖς πιστεῦσαι, δόξαν παρὰ ἀλλήλων λαμβάνοντες, καὶ τὴν δόξαν τὴν παρὰ τοῦ μόνου Θεοῦ οὐ ζητεῖτε; John 5:44. This conviction, at the same time, implied in the true thankfulness in which one thanks God *alone* for His whole salvation, as a state in which man feels in himself, is called *spiritual poverty* (πτωχὸς τῷ πνεύματι, Matt. 5:3), and as he feels before God, *humility* (ὁ Θεὸς ὑπερηφάνοις ἀντιτάσσεται, ταπεινοῖς δὲ δίδωσιν χάριν, Jas. 4:6). In reference to true Christian humility, we may here well recall the following words: "By this, above all else, one may

know the pure from the impure. They who are pure *humble* their souls, and recognize and confess their impurity; absolutely and entirely, they know nothing of their innocence and purity. On the contrary, the impure will know nothing of their impurity, but imagine and pride themselves in a purity with which, however, they rather make themselves impure, and defile themselves" (Luther). Compare the same elsewhere: "Christ (Matt. 11:29) joins the phrase 'of heart' to lowliness. For He saw in His church hypocrites, whom He greatly hates, and who get the predominance by no other semblance of virtue so much as by that of humility. And the world also is deceived by nothing so much as by pretended humility: hanging the head, humble words, bowing the back, looking sad, and being singular—that does it. To be mild and lowly of heart—that does it not. And yet under these masks the haughtiest pride rages, as the examples of all ages demonstrate."

He, however, who has been saved by grace recognizes himself in himself, not merely as nothing, but, contrasted with God the alone good, as also vile. Accordingly there is involved, at the same time, in the consciousness of spiritual poverty, this, *not to trust one's self*; and in the humility of faith, on the other hand, *to trust everything to God alone*. Now the inward self-behavior corresponding to the former side is that of steadfast *watchfulness*; and that corresponding to the second, a *life* of steadfast *prayer*. Scripture brings both together before us in close connection, and gives as a reason the danger of temptation, as it exists in ourselves, and proceeds from the devil. Comp. Matt. 26:41, Γρηγορεῖτε καὶ προσεύχεσθε, ἵνα μὴ εἰσέλθητε εἰς πειρασμόν· τὸ μὲν πνεῦμα πρόθυμον, ἡ δὲ σὰρξ ἀσθενής. Mark 13:37, ἃ δὲ ὑμῖν λέγω, πᾶσι λέγω· γρηγορεῖτε (comp. Rev. 16:15). 1 Thess. 5:6-8, Ἄρα οὖν μὴ καθεύδωμεν, ὡς καὶ οἱ λοιποί, ἀλλὰ γρηγορῶμεν καὶ νήφωμεν. Οἱ γὰρ καθεύδοντες νυκτὸς καθεύδουσι· καὶ οἱ μεθυσκόμενοι, νυκτὸς μεθύουσιν. Ἡμεῖς δὲ ἡμέρας ὄντες, νήφωμεν. Col. 4:2, Τῇ προσευχῇ προσκαρτερεῖτε, γρηγοροῦντες ἐν αὐτῇ ἐν εὐχαριστίᾳ. 1 Pet. 5:8, Νήψατε, γρηγορήσατε· ὁ ἀντίδικος ὑμῶν διάβολος, ὡς λέων ὠρυόμενος περιπατεῖ, κ.τ.λ. This union of watchfulness over one's self and communion with God in prayer forms the opposite to all false "absorption in God" *(Eingottung),* self-forgetfulness and self-abnegation of spiritual intoxication. In like manner, however, do the riches of the life of prayer form the opposite of false poverty, of self-tormenting or self-sufficient watchfulness. The import of prayer, however, is not merely the making known of one's individual wants (οἶδε γὰρ ὁ πατὴρ ὑμῶν ὧν χρείαν ἔχετε, πρὸ τοῦ ὑμᾶς αἰτῆσαι αὐτόν, Matt. 6:8). And yet an abiding prayerful disposition and prayerful state of the heart is required. Luke 18:1, πάντοτε προσεύχεσθε καὶ μὴ ἐκκακεῖν; 1 Thess. 5:17, ἀδιαλείπτως προσεύχεσθε. Prayer is rather the real substantial expression of the relation of a child, of personal communion with God through grace in love, and therefore the emanation and operation of the Spirit, who abides in the redeemed of Jesus Christ (Rom. 8:16; Gal. 4:6). And as it is an operation of the Spirit, so the word teaches us to look also on prayer as the will and requisition of God, without our fulfilment of which He does not dispense to us the blessings of His grace. Matt. 7:8, πᾶς γὰρ ὁ αἰτῶν λαμβάνει, καὶ ὁ ζητῶν εὑρίσκει, καὶ τῷ κρούοντι ἀνοιγήσεται; comp. Jas. 4:2, οὐκ ἔχετε διὰ τὸ μὴ αἰτεῖσθαι ὑμᾶς. For only with His children does God keep up His fatherly communion. Prayerful hearts, however, are true children's hearts. In prayer, too, the communion of sons is maintained against every entanglement in the sophistries of pantheistic, fatalistic, and atheistic falsehood (causal-nexus, moral order of the world, and the like). But the true prayer of the regenerate man is the prayer in the name of Jesus Christ, as through Him he has access to the Father (John 14:13, 15:16, 16:23, 24). In this prayer lies alike the consciousness of the justification of the suppliant as to his person, and of the prayer in its substance. It is the prayer of the believer who doubts not of the power of his God. Jas. 1:6, 7, Αἰτείτω ἐν πίστει, μηδὲν διακρινόμενος· ὁ γὰρ διακρινόμενος ἔοικε κλύδωνι θαλάσσης ἀνεμιζομένῳ καὶ ῥιπιζομένῳ. Μὴ γὰρ οἰέσθω ὁ ἄνθρωπος ἐκεῖνος, ὅτι λήψεταί τι παρὰ τοῦ Κυρίου. It is also the prayer of him who is acquainted with the will of his Lord, and knows wherefore and how he may and ought to pray.

1 John 5:14, 15, Καὶ αὕτη ἐστὶν ἡ παρρησία ἣν ἔχομεν πρὸς αὐτὸν, ὅτι ἐάν τι αἰτώμεθα κατὰ τὸ θέλημα αὐτοῦ, ἀκούει ἡμῶν· καὶ ἐὰν οἴδαμεν ὅτι ἀκούει ἡμῶν, ὃ ἂν αἰτώμεθα, οἴδαμεν ὅτι ἔχομεν τὰ αἰτήματα ἃ ᾐτήκαμεν παρ' αὐτοῦ. Comp. on the other hand, Jas. 4:3, Αἰτεῖτε, καὶ οὐ λαμβάνετε, διότι κακῶς αἰτεῖσθε, ἵνα ἐν ταῖς ἡδοναῖς ὑμῶν δαπανήσητε. A type for the substance of our prayer is the prayer of our Lord (Matt. 6); a type of the absolutely hearable prayer is (Luke 11:13) the prayer for grace, and the gifts of grace; a type for the prayer that will be relatively heard, and is to be uttered with restriction, is Matt. 26:39 (comp. Matt. 6:33, 34), the pattern of the praying Redeemer. The prayer comprised in words has its force as the clearing up of an undefined feeling, as an incentive against slothfulness in prayer, and above all, as the presentation of divine words to God Himself. Otherwise the mere human words have no importance. "A true prayer asks not at all for many words, but makes only much sighing; and no words follow this but what are merely faint sounds." "Oral prayer, however, is not to be dispensed with, but is necessary in order to kindle and purify the inward prayer of the heart" (Luther).

This life of prayer forms the profoundest and most decisive contrast between the Christian character and ancient or modern heathenish illumination. Self-examination and self-observation are praised by the Stoics in the words of the poet: Μηδ' ὕπνον μαλακοῖσιν ἐπ' ὄμμασι προσδέξεσθαι Πρὶν τῶν ἡμερινῶν ἔργων λογίσασθαι ἕκαστα, κ.τ.λ. But the life of prayer and thanksgiving is unknown to these Stoics (Epict. *Diss.* iii. 10). What the ancients have told us of the prayers of Socrates, the conceited later writers thus put into shape: εὔχετο μὲν τοῖς θεοῖς, ἐλάμβανε δὲ παρ' ἑαυτοῦ, συνεπινευόντων ἐκείνων, ἀρετὴν ψυχῆς, καὶ ἡσυχίαν βίου, καὶ ζωὴν ἄμεμπτον, καὶ εὔελπιν θάνατον, τὰ θαυμαστὰ δῶρα, τὰ θεοῖς δοτά (Max. Tyr. εἰ δεῖ εὔχεσθαι, *Diss.* 11). What the same author there argues, that an unworthy person receives nothing although he prays, whereas a worthy one does receive although he prays not, is, as the style of testing of that vulgar wisdom now again current, not without interest.

"Be on your guard against that Turkish, Epicurean faith, since some say, What shall I do? What is the use of prayer? What avails too much care? It is provided; so it must be. Yes, true it is; what is provided comes to pass: but I am not commanded, but rather forbidden, to know what is provided. I am bidden that I should be certain what to do" (Luther, *Vermahnung zum Gebet wider die Türken vom J.* 1541). "Thou must learn to call (upon Him), and not sit there by yourself, or lie on the bench, droop and shake your head, bite and devour yourself with your thoughts, and be full of care and anxiety how to get yourself free, and look to nothing else but how badly things may be going with thee, what woe may be upon thee, how wretched a man you mayest be. But up, you lazy knave; fall on your knees, and with hands and eyes uplifted to heaven, and repeating a hymn or a paternoster, lay with weeping your need before God, declare your sorrow and invoke His aid. To pray, to declare your needs, and to lift up your hands, are the most acceptable sacrifices unto God. He desires it; His will is to have it so, that you should lay before Him your needs, and not that you should leave them lying on yourself, and crawl along with them, tease and torment yourself, so as out of one misfortune to make two, nay ten, and a hundred others. It is His will that you should be too weak to bear and overcome such need, in order that you should learn to become strong in Him, and that He should be praised in thee through His strength. See, there are people who call themselves *Christians*, but who are nothing else than gossips and chatterers, who spout forth much about faith and the Spirit, but understand not what it is, or what they themselves say." (*Exposition of the* 118*th Psalm*, comp. the glorious passages there, and *Exposition of* 120*th Psalm.*)

§ 34. *d. The Subjective Foundation and Strength of Christian Fidelity, or the Union of the inward Working of Grace and inward Self-activity in Christian Conscientiousness*

In that thankfulness which has the impulse of continual watching and prayer, are given the personal disposition and spiritual activity which render him that is born of the Spirit of grace qualified in faithfulness to solve the problem of Christian virtue according to the rule of Christ. This personal disposition and activity must rest on a fundamental personal relation and personal conduct, in which the Christian no less has the power of such disposition and activity as a gift, than he keeps it as a possession, or in which the power and the act of fidelity coincide (1). This fundamental personal relation and personal conduct, which are at the same time an operation of grace and self-activity, constitute Christian *conscientiousness*. The Christian conscience is that real communion with God originally given in the conscience, restored and destined to be perfected by the imparted grace of the Holy Spirit, in which God continually attests His faithfulness to the redeemed (comp. § 22). In this conscientiousness the principle of divine life and its communication of strength become coincident with our act of personal adherence to this principle, or with the personal fidelity of the redeemed (2). As this principle bears in itself the ends and means of the practical realization of the new life, so there is involved in the exclusive adherence to it the power of purity and simplicity no less than that of wisdom and prudence; and herein Christian conscientiousness has in itself both the essence and form of its own practical realization (3). Inasmuch, then, as this conscientious disposition precedes all acting, accompanies it, and in the consummation of that which has been conscientiously begun has its own satisfaction, it thus preserves for the Christian the feeling of a good conscience, thus forming the contrast to that evil conscience which is indeed also a manifestation of conscience, but at the same time a testimony to a want of conscientiousness.

(1) That the strength of this fidelity must, from the nature of regeneration and conversion, be carried back in the last resort to a fundamental relation, bearing equally the character of personal faculty and of divine endowment, was felt at an

early date by men who were nevertheless unable to express this feeling clearly; and also that in its ultimate origin there was involved a union of endowment and of personal self-effort, was long ago expressed, although in no very sufficient way. "Virtus duplicem habet comparationem," says, for example, Peraldus, "unam ad id, a quo est, scil. ad Dei liberalitatem, cujus donum est, et sic dicitur gratia; aliam comparationem habet virtus ad id, quod ab ea est scil. ad opus scil. suum, et sic vocatur virtus." The truth herein contained is this, that all the power of fidelity can in its ultimate ground rest only on the one principle of the new life. This is the Holy Spirit of regeneration united with the spirit of conscience in the heart. But the operation of this Spirit, as the ground of personal fitness and activity, can no longer be absolutely regarded in the light of an endowment, but in that of a personal potentiality which has been developed into *habit*. In this form it does not lose its essential character of an endowment, but it ceases to be an endowment of the divine and spiritual ground of our nature which the Spirit of regeneration has worked in man, but has passed from thence into the center of his conscious personal volition (comp. § 23). And then is that which the Spirit has effected in truth something θεανθρώπινον, alike *donum* and *virtus*, alike *infusum* and *inhærens*, the. Working of the Spirit of God renewing and endowing the human nature, and equally the property and attribute of the personal spirit of man. This fundamental force of fidelity, in which God does not cease in the least to work everything in His people, and is nevertheless the last root of a faculty most personal in its nature, do we find in this sense in Christian conscientiousness.

(2) A specific character of Christian conscientiousness is this, a desire of adhering to and preserving that which constitutes the essence of baptismal grace and baptismal efficacy (comp. § 22, note (2)). It is deliverance from an evil conscience. The manner in which the Spirit of God, from the commencement of His communion with man in the sacrament of the new birth, works and will work this deliverance of the conscience according to His word, supplies a standard for the

conduct of Christian conscientiousness. For this reason, all that was previously stated (§ 22) concerning the efficacy of the Holy Spirit, is likewise characteristic of the conduct of Christian conscientiousness, and requires no special confirmation. For this conscientiousness consists just in this, that we strive to have and to maintain our life in no other way than just as Christ gives it by the Holy Spirit. We surrender, therefore, our doing and working to be determined conformably to the doing and working of the Spirit of God in us; we put off the old man, and put on the new, which after God is created in righteousness and holiness of truth (Eph. 4:22–24); we renounce the dead works which proceed not from the life in God (Heb. 6:1), since we surrender ourselves to the fellowship of death and life with Christ, of which He through the Holy Ghost will make us partakers, and we seek after deliverance from the curse of the law and the wrath of God, peace of conscience, and communion of the heart with the will of God in the law—in Christ alone, at the same time devoting the life imparted to the spirit in righteousness through grace to the mortifying of the flesh, and of the life of the flesh (comp. § 22, note (2)). This is called holding the mystery of the faith in a pure conscience (1 Tim. 3:9), or holding faith *and* a good conscience (1 Tim. 1:19). And from this center we attain first to that perfect preservation of a good conscience throughout the whole periphery of our earthly existence, to that universal conscientiousness which the Apostle Paul elsewhere also acknowledges to have been his earnest endeavor to obtain (1 Tim. 1:3; Acts 23:1), and in which he continued to exercise himself (αὐτὸς ἀσκῶ, ἀπρόσκοπον συνείδησιν ἔχειν πρὸς τὸν Θεὸν καὶ τοὺς ἀνθρώπους διὰ παντός, Acts 24:16).

(3) It is involved in the essence of the Christian conscience, *i.e.* in the unity of the conscience with the Holy Spirit of grace, that in it there are given alike a divine knowledge and a divine power of life. Conscientiousness, therefore, comprises in itself not merely the capacity of moral judgment, or some one aspect of Christian perfection, but the potentiality of perfection in the whole life. In the personal adherence to the *one divine* principle

of life, the effluence of this relation can be only alike purity and simplicity; in other words, ungodly *impurity of conduct* and ungodly *contrariety of motive* (of purpose and tendency) remain excluded from all those doings which proceed from the spirit of Christian conscientiousness. Purity and singleness of heart mutually condition each other as objective conduct and subjective motive. 2 Cor. 1:12, Ἡ γὰρ καύχησις ἡμῶν αὕτη ἐστὶ, τὸ μαρτύριον τῆς συνειδήσεως ἡμῶν, ὅτι ἐν ἁπλότητι καὶ εἰλικρινείᾳ Θεοῦ ἀνεστράφημεν ἐν τῷ κόσμῳ. (Another reading is ἁγιότητι.) Whatever is ἐκ Θεοῦ is ἐξ εἰλικρινείας (see 2 Cor. 2:17). On the other hand, whatever is directed to *one* aim, without any side view, that is ἁπλοῦς. It is ἡ ἁπλότης ἡ εἰς Χριστόν (2 Cor. 11:3). The eye is ἁπλοῦς when it does not squint (comp. Matt. 6:22, 24). And so also the only true obedience is that ἐν ἁπλότητι τῆς καρδίας (Eph. 6:5; Col. 3:22). *This* purity and singleness of heart is in itself *wisdom* and *prudence*; for that principle of the divine life on which conscientiousness depends in pure simplicity, has in itself the end of its existence as well as the means of carrying out what it desires. But wisdom is knowledge of aim, and life consistent with that aim; prudence, knowledge of the means, and life in accordance with those means (σοφός, *sapiens*, φρόνιμος, *prudens*; comp. also σοφία and γνῶσις, Rom. 11:33). And in this relation is carried out what Christ in another point of view testifies as His will and requisition: Γίνεσθε φρόνιμοι ὡς οἱ ὄφεις, καὶ ἀκέραιοι ὡς αἱ περιστεραί (Matt. 10:16). In and with the fellowship with Christ there is bestowed the possession of wisdom: Ἐπιρίσσευσεν εἰς ἡμᾶς ἐν πάσῃ σοφίᾳ καὶ φρονήσει (Eph. 1:8). That it may increase and diminish, but may ever again be obtained by prayer, is shown in Jas. 1:5 (comp. with 3:15). Finally, that this wisdom is in itself life and the power of life, is abundantly confirmed by other passages; such as Jas. 3:13, Τίς σοφὸς καὶ ἐπιστήμων ἐν ὑμῖν; δειξάτω ἐκ τῆς καλῆς ἀναστροφῆς τὰ ἔργα αὐτοῦ ἐν πραΰτητι σοφίας; ver. 17, Ἡ δὲ ἄνωθεν σοφία πρῶτον μὲν ἁγνή ἐστιν, ἔπειτα εἰρηνική, ἐπιεικής, εὐπειθής, μεστὴ ἐλέους καὶ καρπῶν ἀγαθῶν, ἀδιάκριτος, ἀνυπόκριτος. For it is the wisdom which proceeds from the fellowship with that

Christ, ὃς ἐγενήθη σοφία ἡμῖν ἀπὸ Θεοῦ, δικαιοσύνη τε καὶ ἁγιασμὸς καὶ ἀπολύτρωσις (1 Cor. 1:30).

(4) The usual doctrinal definition of an antecedent, accompanying, and following conscience, supposes only the formal diversity of that reflex influence on the personal consciousness which proceeds from conscience, or of the moral judgments in their relation to action. So far as this doctrinal definition rests upon a confounding of the manifestation of conscience with its nature, it is to be rejected; and as a mere formal definition of the moral judgment, it is unimportant. What is essentially important is this, that where the Christian conscience is what it is intended to be—a union of the Spirit of God with the personality of man—consequently where it is really present as conscientiousness,—there it is continually an "antecedent, accompanying, and following conscience;" in other words, a permanent communion of God with our personal consciousness. Where such is not the case, there conscience itself testifies to man its instability and vacillation: the consciousness of the wrathful Spirit of God in the conscience is the evil conscience.

§ 35. e. The Sphere and Extent of Christian Fidelity

The extent of that domain in which the thankful, conscientious fidelity of the Christian has actively to manifest itself, consistently with the law of liberty in Christ, is traced out in the sum of all those relations which constitute the natural basis of human existence and consciousness, and to imbue which with His own Spirit was the object of Christ's own coming into the world, and in which the Christian has to put to the test against trials as well as temptations that power of dominion, as of service, which has been bestowed upon him (1). And inasmuch as the whole domain of earthly and created things and relations is thus incorporated in the divine plan of the world's redemption, therefore the conscientiousness of Christian fidelity consists just in this, in withdrawing none of these relations from the true sphere of its manifestation, and in not abusing the distinction between higher and lower relations in such a way as, while displaying fidelity in the greatest of these, to take no account of fidelity in the least, but in our allowing that distinction to conduce only to this purpose—to the true maintenance of a just ordering of the higher and lower relations and manifestations of life, subjecting all of them, however, alike to the center-point of fidelity to Christ.

(1) I may here not only refer back to what has been said in § 5 and 6 about the natural form of human existence, as it forms the basis of ethical relation, and in § 17 (comp. especially note (7), about the gospel and about the idea of the kingdom of God); but even those paragraphs (§ 27 and 28) which treat of the ordained conflict under trials and against temptations, show us how manifold are the relations in which the Christian is to abide here below according to God's will, in order to verify in all of them his Christian fidelity. And it is necessary to mention this, because a false view of our Christian relations, and a no less perverted confounding of the corrupt state of the world, designated by the term "world," with the world of created things ordained by God (comp. against that, § 6), lead to a narrowing of the sphere of activity of our Christian fidelity, which in an ethical point of view is in the highest degree pernicious. We sever, if I may so say, the fidelity of our Lord as well as our own from a whole series of the relations of our life, in order to conceive of it as concentrated in that one which is necessary, in such a way as prevents us from improving the talent entrusted to us in all domains of life, and leads us arbitrarily to contract the riches of divine bounty, as well as the full measure of the task of our earthly life. What not without cause strikes those who do not yet know Christ as a something barbarous in Christianity, is, when viewed in its proper light, a denial of the all-sidedness of those relations of life in which the Christian in Christ finds the sphere of his dominion, and the field for the exercise of the duty of loving service. For to this domain belongs everything in the earthly life of the creature

that the Christian is permitted to regard as a gift and providential arrangement of his God, in and with which he is destined, nay, bound in duty, to serve his God and seek His honor.

(2) In a certain aspect also the parable of Christ in Matt. 25:14 ff., Luke 19:11 ff., applies here. For if, in their more immediate reference, those talents which the lord, on departing, entrusted to his servants in definite and diverse shares and quantities for their management, must certainly be regarded as the collective sum of those blessings which belong specifically to the kingdom of grace (χαρίσματα); yet, on the other hand, it is equally certain that these very things are the workings of the Holy Spirit, in which, at the same time, gifts of nature appear sanctified, transfigured, and ennobled, and that that domain which is Christ's (τὰ ὑπάρχοντα αὐτοῦ, Matt. 25:14), in its comprehensive relation cannot really be limited merely to that which we in the narrower sense of the word call gifts of grace, in order to exclude from it that which He as the Lord of nature, Lord of history, Lord of the universe, has, works, and brings about in the most various of this life's earthly blessings, in order also to appoint His servants as stewards thereof. Hence, when the Apostle Paul wishes to point out that which a Christian ought to strive after in genuine fidelity of Christian life, he chooses the most comprehensive expressions, and says: "Whatsoever things are true, whatsoever things are honest, whatsoever things are just, whatsoever things are pure, whatsoever things are lovely, whatsoever things are of good report; if there be any virtue, if there be any praise, think on these things," in order to do them (Phil. 4:8; comp. πράσσειν, ver. 9). A glance at the twelfth and thirteenth chapters of the Epistle to the Romans, or an examination of all the so-called hortatory portions of the apostolical letters, will bear witness to this, what a manifold variety of earthly vocations and of earthly duties to be performed by us the apostles include in the sphere of the fulfilment of Christian fidelity. Nay, the very way in which ordinary modes of thought exclude a series of so-called purely natural aims and activities of life as profane from

what is sacred or what is sanctified, and so to be considered from its relation to God, is foreign to the Christian. Not in any such separation and condemning as profane does the fidelity of a Christian manifest itself to his Lord, who is Lord of all things, and who will have all things subjected to the sphere of His sovereignty, but by his placing all those things in relation to Christ, and regarding all as objects in which Christian fidelity is to display itself. Rejoicing with them that do rejoice, and weeping with them that weep (Rom. 12:15), eating and drinking (1 Cor. 10:31), yea, everything which we do in word or in deed, is to be done in the name of Jesus Christ (Col. 3:17). This is Christian fidelity.

This does not exclude the fact that striving after the kingdom of God (ζητεῖν τὴν βασιλείαν τοῦ Θεοῦ, Matt. 6:33), the care for that which is the Lord's (μεριμνᾶν τὰ τοῦ Κυρίου, 1 Cor. 7:32), remains in a specific sense the first and the highest object, and that we are fully to maintain that of which the apostle thus writes: "Think on the things above, not on things on the earth" (Col. 3). But just on the earth and in the things of the earth, to think of that which is above, to secure and to maintain for all earthly things their relation to things above, and not to pervert by exclusion their subordination to the highest end,—that is the task of the Christian's fidelity, who knows the transitory nature of this world to be destined not for annihilation, but for lasting glorification on a new earth and under a new heaven (comp. § 17, note (7), towards the end).

§ 36. f. *The Right Knowledge of Christian Fidelity, and the Errors of a seeming Conscientiousness*

That knowledge of the essence, extent, and the mutual relations in which the applications of Christian fidelity stand to each other, which is to be derived from the word of God, forms the contrast and antidote to that which is called a weak, doubting, and erring conscience. That is an error of conscience so far, when by conscience is meant that consciousness of man in which he feels himself bound by some obligation standing over him; while the error consists in this, that in the given instance there is no such obligation objectively (that is, according to God's word and will) binding on the conscience of the Christian (1). In this error we either fail to discriminate the higher and lower position of blessings, and of the fidelity which is to be shown them (2); or we mistake between conscientious conduct and the objective relation, and represent the entering or not entering upon relations which in themselves are quite neutral to the Christian conscience as a matter of conscience, whereas only the personal bearing in them or to them is a matter of conscientiousness (3). The distinctive expression for this error is, to *make* one's self a conscience beforehand. The obligation which we voluntarily assume in this error has all the danger of a temptation to look upon the subjective obligation as an absolute rule, and out of the weakness of error to fall into obduracy against the truth (4). The danger of this temptation is met only by means of a right insight into the true nature of that Christian fidelity born of faith, which, even in cases of a weak and erring conscience, seeks for the right standard of conduct both towards one's self and others not in one's own conceptions, but only in those rules of right behaviour which are laid down for its guidance in the divine word.

(1) Here we must refer back, above all, to what has been already stated (§ 7, note (5), pp. 46–48) concerning conscience, and in regard to a weak conscience. Since hereafter we shall have to take into consideration certain passages of Scripture which partly confirm by examples what is here to be discussed, and partly serve as a substratum for general conclusions, it will not be superfluous to make some remarks beforehand touching these passages, especially as in earlier editions I took a different view of them from what I do at present. The passage in Rom. 14, for instance, appears to me to apply here only in a more remote sense; and what is there meant by ἀσθενεῖν τῇ πίστει (14:1), appears not to be identical with that which in 1 Cor. 8:7 is called συνείδησις ἀσθενής. Those referred to in the Epistle to the Romans were weak in the Christian faith, in the sense of

their not seeking in this faith alone the power of their sanctification. In firm and confident conviction (that is, in πίστις in the sense it bears in vers. 22, 23) they were by no means weak. On the contrary, they had such a conviction in reference to the advisableness of abstaining from certain kinds of food, of their keeping holy certain days in preference to others. And this was done not at all from a sense of legal obligation, or in any other manner directly opposed to the Christian faith, as it happened in the case of the Galatians and Colossians; but they did it voluntarily, in accordance with notions and opinions (διαλογισμοί) about that which they considered as advisable for themselves. And hence the apostle also says, that they were not to be received to "disputations about opinions, carpings at opinions" (μὴ εἰς διακρίσεις διαλογισμῶν, 14:1), since these opinions may well be allowed to rest on their own merits, provided only one does not, on account of opinions for or against, sit in judgment on a brother who thinks differently. But the apostle does not keep out of sight that in such opinions a weakness in the faith is revealed. In the Epistle of Paul to the Corinthians, this weakness of the conscience consists in a customary conception (τῇ συνηθείᾳ, 8:7) of a falsely conceived reality of heathen idols, and the relation they would stand in to them by a partaking of the meats offered. By virtue of this idea, they considered themselves bound in conscience unconditionally to abstain from such participation. (To what extent such an idea was justifiable, is stated afterwards, 10:20, 21.) This weakness of conscience was the result of a want of the knowledge that the idol as such is nothing in the world—no God nor Lord for those who cleave to the one God the Father, and the one Lord Jesus Christ. But what was justifiable in this weak conscience was this, that they felt themselves bound in conscience not to enter into any relation to idols, even when they thought erroneously respecting the nature and possibility of such a relation. And the apostle for this reason wishes to have this weak conscience spared, and not injured.

The general conclusion to be drawn from these two examples may be laid down in the following manner: First, That which one considers advisable for one's self as a means for promoting sanctification in a way not hostile to the faith, even if not consistent with the full strength of the same, ought not to be a matter of contention, where such a course of conduct is not imposed upon others as a law, or the opposite course made the rule for sitting in judgment upon them. Secondly, Where a certain line of conduct, not conformable to the correct knowledge of faith, arises from a desire of conscientiously avoiding everything which is inconsistent with the position and duty of believers, there we are bound to spare this weakness of conscience which arises from defective knowledge, and to honor the conscientiousness even where it errs in its motives.

An opposite line of behavior towards errors of conscience can only then be justifiable, when such weakness and error manifest themselves in open contradiction to the faith and the self-activity that belong to it.

(2) To this head belong what was formerly designated as collisions of duties. They are the fruit of a false equalization of duties, or more correctly of the relations of life, in which the Christian has, by virtue of his natural and historical existence, as well as by virtue of his regeneration from God, to exercise himself by placing in juxtaposition, or in one line, things which (properly understood) stand to each other in the relation of superiority and inferiority, and which have to be viewed and judged not abstractly, but with an impartial subjection of all these relations to the highest relation of the Christian life to Christ. This will be discussed hereafter.

(3) To this category belongs the strife about the so-called *adiaphora* (indifferent things). When one looks at the relations of life in themselves, there present themselves, no doubt, not a few which may be called *adiaphora*, that is, which in themselves are not the expression and manifestation of any Christian moral element. But placed in reference to any particular person, they naturally and immediately lose the

character of indifferent things, because the persons between whom and such things the relation exists, and on whom they exert an influence, cannot be thought of as neutral, *i.e.* outside of all ethical relation. Always according to the state of the person, this relation, indifferent in itself, ceases to be (in an ethical point of view) a thing indifferent, whether the person who has entered into any relation with it may be viewed therein either as active or passive. The personal relation therefore in such cases decides, be it the relation to his own personality or to that of others. If here scruples of conscience arise, by virtue of which the man then naturally judges always only relatively, *i.e.* in reference to personal states, such a judgment is a working of conscientiousness. If, however, apart from all personal states, the ethical element of what is allowable or not allowable is attributed to the relation itself, then the error begins. Comp. on the whole question as analogous, Rom. 14:13–15:2. The voluminous, and on both sides unrefreshing literature respecting pleasures as things indifferent, called forth by the controversies in the time of Spener, may be seen in Walch, *Einl. in die Rel. Streit. der luth. Kirche*, Pt. v. pp. 821–841. Spener certainly makes a distinction between "the thing in itself," and the way "in which it is carried on in these days." But in connection therewith, he places, without further qualification, dancing, for instance, "among the carnal pleasures from which a true Christian abstains" (*Letzte theol. Bedenk* i. 305); and the mode of speaking adopted from him—"The Christian even there, where he is enjoying bodily pleasure, has his eye to God's goodness, and delight in His creatures" *(ibid.)*—is, if it is not a kind of scruple whether a Christian may enjoy corporeally in order to enjoy corporeally, in any case in its form a very unfortunate paraphrase of the words of the apostle: "Every creature of God is good, and nothing to be refused, if it be received with thanksgiving" (1 Tim. 4:4).

(4) Two things here present themselves for more careful consideration. First, in what sense, in the case of a Christian, we can speak of an error, by which he binds himself, and may

consider himself bound; and next, to what limit this may go, without becoming obduracy against the truth. Of the first, nothing certain can be said, if we are not in a position to distinguish accurately between error and untruth, and sharply to define the domain in which an error is possible, which is accompanied by a relative truth. An error of this latter kind is inconceivable, where the question turns upon the inner core of Christianity, *i.e.* of the way in which we have to procure our righteousness before God. The way and manner in which this is attained in faith, is absolutely regulated by the revelation in Christ; and every departure therefrom falls under the judgment of a self-chosen service of God (the ἐθελοθρησκεία). And in a no less absolutely binding manner are those means laid down, by which we have to work out positively, and indeed in a manner under all circumstances alike, our renewal and sanctification. They result immediately from the nature of genuine Christian faith; and no departure from them could be thought of without injury to that faith itself. But the case is different in the province of things which are to us objects of temptation (see § 28), in which rules of conduct absolutely binding are neither given nor conceivable, because here, according to the individual and personal tendency and temperament, something may be an object of temptation to one, and not so to another. Here an error of a double nature is possible: in such a way, namely, that we should deceive ourselves concerning the true character and source of the charm of what is tempting, as well as concerning the adequate means of resistance; and also in such a way that we should make available the true knowledge of both in face of the erring one, in a way in which we keep in view ourselves alone, and not the weak conscience of others, and thus make what is right for ourselves a stumbling-block and a vexation for our brother (ἐν ᾧ ὁ ἀδελφός σου προσκόπτει, Rom. 14:21; comp. vers. 13, 15, 16, 20, 1 Cor. 8:9; τύπτειν, "to wound," τὴν συνείδησιν ἀσθενοῦσαν, 1 Cor. 8:12). The last ought unconditionally not to be done. Nay, it is called a sinning against Christ (ἁμαρτάνειν εἰς Χριστόν, 1 Cor. 8:12) when one offends the weak conscience of a brother, for whom Christ died, and thus walks not according to love (Rom. 14:15). In regard, however, to the first-named error, in every case where the error itself is repudiated, this must be acknowledged, that even in this weak conscience is displayed a conscientiousness which has striven to keep aloof from what might possibly tempt, and from temptation. In this no one is to be made out mistaken. For without doubt such an one, with the views he holds, cannot enter into anything which presents to him the appearance of temptation, without doing violence to his conscience. One cannot and dare not do or leave undone anything within *these* limits, with respect to which he has not the strong confidence (πίστιν, Rom. 14:22, 23) that he may do it or let it alone. "Happy is he that condemns not himself in that which he allows." But he that doubts when he does anything is condemned, because he does it not out of strong conviction. For all that does not flow out of strong conviction is in *this domain* sin (Rom. 14:22, 23).

This subjective sense of duty, however, ceases to be consistent with the truth, as soon as one makes what is subjectively justifiable a rule of objective right, and a standard of universal obligation, by which he judges others, or measures the propriety of their conduct. For that would be not less than that judging of the weak on the part of the strong—an acting against truth and against love; and conscientiousness towards one's self would become a want of it in regard to others.

PART THIRD

THE PRESERVATION OF SALVATION

OR,

THE CONCRETE MANIFESTATION OF CHRISTIAN VIRTUE IN THE FUNDAMENTAL RELATIONS OF HUMAN LIFE

§ 37. *Christian Piety as the Mother of all the Virtues*

To the Christian it is natural to recognize in the one blessing of salvation and its possession the *highest relation* of all earthly existence. With this recognition begins the Christian frame of mind; and only where this remains its leading characteristic, is to be found that virtue or fitness of disposition in which the Christian is in a position to regard the preservation of salvation as the problem of his life, and to labour at its solution (1). Thus Christian virtue has only *one* ultimate and highest relation, without which no virtue is virtue, and in which all other virtues lie as in their germ. This virtue of all virtues is, however Christian piety (2).

(1) What is meant by the preservation of salvation, and in what sense it comprises a multitude of Christian virtues, comes out clearly from the following testimonies of Scripture: Heb. 3:12–14; comp. with 2 Pet. 1:8–10. In the latter passage, after the unfolding of faith (πίστις) into many kinds of virtue is mentioned in ver. 5 ff., it goes on to say: Ταῦτα γὰρ ὑμῖν ὑπάρχοντα, καὶ πλεονάζοντα, οὐκ ἀργοὺς οὐδὲ ἀκάρπους καθίστησιν εἰς τὴν τοῦ Κυρίου ἡμῶν Ἰησοῦ Χριστοῦ ἐπίγνωσιν· ᾧ γὰρ μὴ πάρεστι ταῦτα, τυφλός ἐστι, μυωπάζων, λήθην λαβὼν τοῦ καθαρισμοῦ τῶν πάλαι αὐτοῦ ἁμαρτιῶν. Διὸ μᾶλλον,

ἀδελφοί, σπουδάσατε βεβαίαν ὑμῶν τὴν κλῆσιν καὶ ἐκλογὴν ποιεῖσθαι. Ταῦτα γὰρ ποιοῦντες οὐ μὴ πταίσητέ ποτε.

(2) What presents itself to the Christian consciousness at the head of all blessings, the participation of salvation in Christ, is again mirrored forth in the apostle's confession (Phil. 3:8 ff.). The apostle has mentioned before his position in Israel, his blamelessness in the eyes of men, "as touching the righteousness which is in the law." And yet the things which were gain to him, for Christ's sake he has counted loss (for they kept him far from Christ). Nay, rather does he count all that he has before mentioned even now again for loss, for the sake of the surpassing glory of the knowledge of his Lord Jesus Christ, for whose sake he forfeited all this, and holds it continually as dung, in order that he may win Christ, and be found in Him, as one who has *his* righteousness not from the law, but that righteousness which comes by faith on Christ,—that righteousness which, proceeding from God, rests on the ground of faith. In the subordination of all the relations of life to the relation to the blessing of salvation revealed in Jesus Christ, the Christian spirit manifests itself as the fulfiller of the will of Christ (Matt. 10:37). The habitual personal state in which this supreme object of life remains constantly present, *piety* (εὐσέβεια), is *virtue*, since it is on the one hand the effect of the operation of God's Spirit, on the other *the fruit of one's own practice*. 1 Tim. 4:7, 8, Γύμναζε δὲ σεαυτὸν πρὸς εὐσέβειαν. But the central importance of εὐσέβεια, which is expressed in the following words, Ἡ εὐσέβεια πρὸς πάντα ὠφέλιμός ἐστιν ἐπαγγελίαν ἔχουσα ζωῆς τῆς νῦν καὶ τῆς μελλούσης, recurs also there, where piety presents itself as the immediate operation and form of manifestation, as well as the proximate object of the communication of grace. Comp. Tit. 2:11, Ἡ χάρις τοῦ Θεοῦ ... παιδεύουσα ἡμᾶς, ἵνα ... σωφρόνως καὶ δικαίως καὶ εὐσεβῶς ζήσωμεν ἐν τῷ νῦν αἰῶνι. Εὐσέβεια, as Wiesinger justly remarks on the passage, is the epitome of Christian morality, according to its fundamental relations. And the statement rises here from self-discipline, and the conformity of our actions to the will of God, to the absorption of our whole nature in the fountain of

salvation. For this very thing is the characteristic mark of Christian truth, that it leads to piety, or, as it is still better interpreted, godliness (ἡ ἀλήθεια ἡ κατ' εὐσέβειαν, Tit. 1:1). And every doctrine which is consonant with truth has therefore also the same mark of being a guide unto godliness (ἡ κατ' εὐσέβειαν διδασκαλία, 1 Tim. 6:1). For that life which is the gift of the divine power of Christ has its existence in godliness; for this power it is which gives us all things which conduce to life and godliness (ἡ πάντα ἡμῖν τὰ πρὸς ζωὴν καὶ εὐσέβειαν δεδωρημένη, 2 Pet. 1:3). This it is which embraces that great mystery which is given in Christ, and is absorbed therein (τὸ τῆς εὐσεβείας μυστήριον), which is the subject of the passage 1 Tim. 3:16. For this cause, the man who has become a man of God pursues, in his strivings after righteousness, *i.e.* conformity of his actions to the will of God, after godliness, which has its various forms of manifestation, corresponding to the nature of the blessing of salvation, in faith, love, stedfastness, meekness (1 Tim. 6:11). The exclusive conception of the word "piety," as used to express our relation to God, is not the original one. Luther distinguishes a twofold piety. The one is every human and social sense of honor. Of the other he says: "This one travels and soars far above everything that is earthly, and has nothing to do with any works. For how can it have works, since all that the body can do, and that is called work, goes forth in the other righteousness? But now it is this, where we are speaking of God's grace and forgiveness of sins, which is not an earthly but a heavenly righteousness—not of our own doing and ability, but God's work and gift."—Compare the *Sermon on the Threefold Righteousness*, in the year 1518.

§ 38. a. The Nature of True Christian Piety

The peculiarity of Christian piety, and the condition under which it can alone be acknowledged as true, lie expressed in this, that Christian piety can only be thought of as the frame of mind of a regenerate and converted man. Only where the communion of grace has actually taken place is that piety also conceivable which is able to serve unto that *edification* which is the ground and aim of all Christian activity, and therein, above all, of piety (1). And only where piety is the emanation of actual edification, and likewise desires and strives after nothing but edification in the full extent of the term (no matter whether this striving wells forth and has its quiet working from conscious intention, or unconsciously from the nature of true piety itself, and likewise no matter whether this striving has for its object the edification of self or that of others),—there alone is piety *pure*, clinging purely to the source of life in the promises of grace, to the means of grace in revelation, to the object of grace in the manifestation of Christ; there only is it a pure manifestation of that life which comes from God and embraces the whole man,—a pure, *simple* heart-devotion in reference to that experience of the heart in which, through the grace of God in Christ Jesus, we are here below translated into the kingdom of His love. Where, on the other hand, in addition to the direction towards the blessing of salvation as the supreme good of life, and in addition to the use of the divinely-appointed means of grace, there is not the actual possession of salvation, there alone Christian piety, or the piety of a true Christian, exists not in truth: there is only that of seeking and presentiment, if not that of unreal and untrue superstition (2).

(1) The essence of true piety, which naturally arises from the essence and the peculiarity of the possession of salvation, receives a further definition through its inseparable connection with the biblical idea of *edification* (οἰκοδομή). This idea, whether used as οἰκοδόμημα or as οἰκοδόμησις—whether denoting the fundamental relation upon which all Christian piety rests, or the end towards which all Christian piety strives—springs in every case from a fundamental view, in which the individual Christian as well as the Christian world in general appears to the apostles in the light of a fulfilment of that of which Israel was a foreshadowing and a type. The Christian is the habitation of God (1 Cor. 3:9), and indeed, as being in Christ, a living stone in a great temple (1 Pet. 2:5),

whose living foundation is just that Christ, who supports the single stones as well as the whole temple. To rest radically on this foundation with his whole nature, and the whole vitality of that nature, is called a being edified, being a habitation of God. And to introduce man's whole nature, and the whole vitality of his nature, into this foundation, is called to edify. But the foundation stone is in both cases not to be separated from the single stones, nor from the whole temple, *i.e.* from the fellowship of that great kingdom whose groundwork is Jesus Christ. Consequently, he who is edified, he who edifies himself, he who edifies others, is and does so only in the same measure as the character of his being and doing is this—the incorporation of the whole man, with all his faculties, in Christ and the kingdom of Christ.

When, therefore, it is a question of the pious employment of gifts and faculties received for the benefit of others, the determining rule is this: "Let all things be done unto edifying" (πάντα πρὸς οἰκοδομὴν γινέσθω, 1 Cor. 14:26). It forms the limit of Christian liberty: Πάντα ἔξεστιν, ἀλλ' οὐ πάντα οἰκοδομεῖ, 1 Cor. 10:23. It forms the aim of Christian testimony in word and work: Eph. 4:29, λόγος ... εἴ τις ἀγαθὸς πρὸς οἰκοδομήν; Rom. 14:19, διώκωμεν ... τὰ τῆς οἰκοδομῆς τῆς εἰς ἀλλήλους; 15:2, ἕκαστος ἡμῶν τῷ πλησίον ἀρεσκέτω εἰς τὸ ἀγαθὸν πρὸς οἰκοδομήν; Jude 20, ἐποικοδομοῦντες ἑαυτούς. Hence οἰκοδομή applies as much to the special activity of the Christian as to that of the teacher (Eph. 4:12). The edifying element is the same as the essential fruit of faith, namely love (1 Cor. 8:1, ἡ ἀγάπη οἰκοδομεῖ). This pious love is edifying, in as far as its effort and its operation are directed to the body of the Christian community (Eph. 4:12, οἰκοδομὴ τοῦ σώματος; comp. ver. 16). Hence the superiority of this relation to the Christian community over the mere ἑαυτὸν οἰκαδομεῖν (1 Cor. 14:4). *But this influence on the whole presupposes the fact of the individual being himself already* ἐποικοδομηθείς, namely ἐπὶ τῷ θεμελίῳ τῶν ἀποστόλων καὶ προφητῶν, ὄντος ἀκρογωνιαίου αὐτοῦ Ἰησοῦ Χριστοῦ, ἐν ᾧ πᾶσα ἡ οἰκοδομὴ συναρμολογουμένη αὔξει εἰς ναὸν ἅγιον ἐν Κυρίῳ, ἐν ᾧ καὶ ὑμεῖς συνοικοδομεῖσθε εἰς κατοικητήριον τοῦ Θεοῦ ἐν Πνεύματι, (Eph. 2:20–22). And for this very reason, in this effort of Christian piety, again coincides the operative influence of the Divine Spirit with the activity of the human soul which He has permeated. Thus edification is in like manner the work of God and of the God-redeemed man: Acts 20:32, παρατίθεμαι ὑμᾶς, ἀδελφοί, τῷ Θεῷ καὶ τῷ λόγῳ τῆς χάριτος αὐτοῦ, τῷ δυναμένῳ ἐποικοδομῆσαι, καὶ δοῦναι ὑμῖν κληρονομίαν ἐν τοῖς ἡγιασμένοις πᾶσιν. Thus edification is one with the furtherance and preservation of the whole personality in the kingdom of Christ, pointing out the end to which all pious efforts of the Christian tend for his own benefit and for that of others, since they all belong to the builders who are called on to build up the great temple. In pursuance of this end, every effort of the individual has reference to the whole body, and likewise every effort of the whole has relation to the individual, but always in such a way that the aim is directed not to this or that side of the spiritual life, but collectively to all relations of the spirit and the life. The fulness of this biblical conception is to be carefully distinguished from that one-sided limitation, in which a later phraseology has in many ways employed the words "edification" and "edifying."

(2) If it is said that only the piety of him who is already edified, and that only so far as it desires edification, can be looked upon as the true, pure, and simple piety, that is quite equivalent to the proposition that that piety alone is Christian which flows out of Christian conscientiousness. For what this means, and how there is implied herein the purity and simplicity of piety, see § 34 and the notes. As little as subjective earnestness makes piety to be Christian, so little is it Christian merely because of the object. It is of course unchristian whenever it exists without reference to the grace of God in Jesus Christ; but just as little is it Christian by putting itself in a general way in relation to the grace of God in Jesus Christ. Everything turns on the kind of this relation. And this kind is to be considered as a realization of the will of God in Jesus Christ only then, when it has become an inweaving and combining of all the relations of the spirit and life with the

collective relations of the Redeemer to His kingdom. Πᾶν ὅ τι ἂν ποιῆτε ἐν λόγῳ ἢ ἐν ἔργῳ, πάντα ἐν ὀνόματι Κυρίου Ἰησοῦ, Col. 3:17. This entrance of the whole life upon the collective relation of that standard and power of life which has been revealed "in the name of the Lord Jesus," demonstrates its pure simplicity above all in its divine object; while, in opposition to every πιστεύειν παρὰ τὸ εὐαγγέλιον, to every ἐθελοθρησκεία (Gal. 1:8; Col. 2:23), in distinct and self-conscious *knowledge* it holds as sacred the rule and limits given in the word of grace (ἐάν τις ἀγαπᾷ με, τὸν λόγον μοῦ τηρήσει, John 14:23; εἴ τις μὴ προσέρχεται ὑγιαίνουσι λόγοις τοῖς τοῦ Κυρίου ἡμῶν Ἰησοῦ Χριστοῦ, καὶ τῇ κατ' εὐσέβειαν διδασκαλίᾳ, τετύφωται, μηδὲν ἐπιστάμενος, 1 Tim. 6:3; comp. § 17). But the same pure simplicity exhibits its power also in the states of the subject, inasmuch as the latter, holding as sacred the purpose of the word not less than the word itself, is conscious that the mystery of love was revealed not merely in order to be known, but for the fulness of undivided, heartfelt, holy reciprocity of love. 1 John 5:20, Καὶ οἴδαμεν ὅτι ὁ υἱὸς τοῦ Θεοῦ ἥκει, καὶ δέδωκεν ἡμῖν διάνοιαν ἵνα γινώσκωμεν τὸν ἀληθινόν· καὶ ἐσμὲν ἐν τῷ ἀληθινῷ ἐν τῷ υἱῷ αὐτοῦ Ἰησοῦ Χριστῷ· οὗτός ἐστιν ὁ ἀληθινὸς Θεὸς, καὶ ἡ ζωὴ αἰώνιος. Πᾶς ὁ ἀγαπῶν ἐκ τοῦ Θεοῦ γεγέννηται καὶ γινώσκει τὸν Θεὸν, 1 John 4:7; εἰ δέ τις ἀγαπᾷ τὸν Θεὸν, οὗτος ἔγνωσται ὑπ' αὐτοῦ, 1 Cor. 8:3. Hence the contrast of that piety which rests upon heart-faith (καρδίᾳ πιστεύειν, Rom. 10:10) with *the semblance* of piety (μόρφωσις τῆς εὐσεβείας, 2 Tim. 3:5), with, the *mouth-work of pious acting* (Matt. 6:5), with the profession of piety from subordinate aims (νομίζειν πορισμὸν εἶναι τὴν εὐσέβειαν, 1 Tim. 6:5). Hence the believing piety of the heart is no less *joyful confidence*, παῤῥησία (Heb. 10:35; its root, Eph. 3:12; the necessity of its continuance, Heb. 3:6), in contrast with that *little faith* in corporeal and spiritual things (the type of which is given in Matt. 14:31, 8:26, comp. 6:30; 1 Pet. 5:7), and with *slavish fear*, and *the fear of the lost* (Rom. 8:15, οὐ γὰρ ἐλάβετε πνεῦμα δουλείας πάλιν εἰς φόβον; Jas. 2:19, καὶ τὰ δαιμόνια πιστεύουσι καὶ φρίσσουσι), than it is on the other side, with all its joyfulness, *holy earnestness* (1 Pet.

1:17, καὶ εἰ πατέρα ἐπικαλεῖσθε τὸν ἀπροσωπολήπτως ὑμῶν χρόνον ἀναστράφητε; Phil. 2:12, μετὰ φόβου καὶ τρόμου τὴν ἑαυτῶν σωτηρίαν κατεργάζεσθε: comp. § 16, note (1)). Hence, lastly, that simplicity of piety in which a man, with all his precision, fulness, and depth of knowledge, maintains that childlike spirit, that νήπιον εἶναι to which alone the mysteries of God are revealed (Matt. 11:25), in contrast with that immature and ambitious anticipation of future sight (νοσεῖν περὶ ζητήσεις καὶ λογομαχίας, 1 Tim. 6:4; ἃ [μὴ] ἑώρακεν ἐμβατεύων εἰκῆ, φυσιούμενος ὑπὸ τοῦ νοὸς τῆς σαρκὸς αὐτοῦ, Col. 2:18).

Where this does not exist, there can always be piety in the subjective sense of the term; for it is not the superstition but the piety of the Athenians that the apostle means, when he says to them, Κατὰ πάντα ὡς δεισιδαιμονεστέρους ὑμᾶς θεωρῶ (Acts 17:22). But that piety which does not bear the marks of regeneration and conversion remains nevertheless a piety which either has not yet, or has lost its true object; either merely seeks it, or turns itself to an untrue one. When, *e.g.*, the Stoics demand a constant speaking about God, a continual thinking of Him, in this case the form of piety is directed to an untrue and unreal God.

§ 39. *b. Christian Piety in its most Immediate Manifestation*

The immediate manifestation of Christian piety, although different in form, has its essential and characteristic feature in this, that, directed outwardly, it seeks to testify to the way in which he who is its witness and confessor recognizes the fellowship of salvation as the highest object and supreme good of his earthly life (1). And the essential characteristic of such testimony remains the same, whether the confession is made in sign, or word, or deed (2); whether it takes place in a self-chosen form, or in that of a confession, which, as *e.g.* an oath or martyrdom, is imposed by the authority of some earthly power and authority (3). In all these cases, however, this outward witness-bearing is only then a manifestation of true piety, when the object of the deed (according to which it seeks to be subservient to edification) is coincident with the right state of him who makes it, *i.e.* when the confessor is regenerate and converted, and bears his testimony in the spirit of regeneration and conversion. Only in this case it is of importance *as well* in the act as in the actor himself, that from the confession there remains shut out everything falsely selfish,—that is, everything of such a kind as that wherein the honor of God and the profit of the community are sacrificed to the interests of his own Ego.

(1) What men call *cultus externus* can, from an ethical point of view, possess its significance and truth only as the *manifestation* of a true *cultus internus*. But by this it is not meant to deny that the exercise of the *cultus internus* is not also capable of serving as a *means* for the promotion of the hidden life of the spirit. But in this adventitious element there lies neither the essence nor the truth and reality of the external testimony. Rather does this depend on the reality of the actual state, that: Ἐκ τοῦ περισσεύματος τῆς καρδίας τὸ στόμα λαλεῖ, Matt. 12:34, 35; comp. Rom. 10:10, καρδίᾳ γὰρ πιστεύεται εἰς δικαιούνην, στόματι δὲ ὁμολογεῖται εἰς σωτηρίαν. Hence also again, in the ethical determination of what is a true manifestation of Christian piety, we can set out, in the first place, only from the state of the individual. But that we cannot stop at the individual and his individual state, with reference to the fellowship of salvation, clearly follows from the position of the Christian to the kingdom of God, and comes to be spoken in discussing (§ 46, § 47) his influence on the shape of the manifested piety. But even here the foundation of true pious testimony is not the truth and the reality of the kingdom in its relations to the individual, but the truth and actuality of the membership of the individual in his relation to the totality of the fellowship of the kingdom. And in an analogous way it is not the state and the law, but the fidelity of the subjects and the loyalty of their individual sentiments, that constitute the obedience of the citizen a true obedience.

(2) The equalization of the form in relation to the essential character of the piety manifested, is not also intended to ascribe an equal importance to the different forms. Rather is the form that which corresponds to the circumstances; and according to the varying of these will the sign, or the word, or the deed, either accompany or supply the place of one another. What is essentially important, consists merely in this, to assign its importance to every form, each in its own way. One may place the word, the act, as the more significant, more precise, more comprehensive, above the sign and symbol. But again, the want of the sign and of the symbolic action may point to some defect in the word or in the deed. In truth, the sign and symbol, where it does not take the place of some involuntary defect of the immediate utterance of the spiritual life, is merely an expression for this, that the man is conscious of belonging to his highest relations of life with both body and soul—that he is given over to them not *half*, but *wholly*. In this sense, it is not a mere arbitrary result, but only natural, that the suppliant in prayer should fold his hands and bend his knee, and that he who blesses should lay on his hands. It will ever be found, that wherever the mind is alienated from the highest objects, there is shown an aversion also to indicate by any bodily act that which only as a symbolical expression of a spiritual act, or as an action of the whole undivided man, possesses any truth. Hence the importance of bowing the knee (Phil. 2:10), of lifting up the hands in prayer (1 Tim. 2:8), of laying on of hands in blessing (Matt. 19:13; 1 Tim. 5:22). To the sign, however, the word, the deed, which may pass as the most immediate manifestation of Christian piety, there is this in common, that they are *confessions*. But confession is Christian confession not as a deed of man for God, but as a deed of God by man's instrumentality—as a testimony, called forth by God according to His grace in Jesus Christ, of divine operation on earth. Only in this sense is the glorifying through His creature, as it is willed by God, so also the manifestation of His own glory in and by man. To whom God has made Himself known, that man confesses himself to Him; and whoever confesses himself to

Him, to that man also does He make Himself known. For he alone who has before become a partaker of the Holy Ghost, can in truth call Jesus Christ Lord (οὐδεὶς δύναται εἰπεῖν Κύριον Ἰησοῦν, εἰ μὴ ἐν Πνεύματι ἁγίῳ, 1 Cor. 12:3); and our confession is "the fruit of our lips, *giving thanks* to His name" (Heb. 13:15; comp. § 31). He who so confesses that Jesus Christ is the Son of God, abides in God, and God in him (1 John 4:15). In this relation of confession to the operation of God in him who confesses, and to his position towards those before whom confession is made, there results also the limitation under which the difference holds good between a voluntary confession, and that which becomes necessary by submission to a higher authority. No Christian confession is free in such a sense, that one might look upon it as an unconditional voluntary act of the individual, as a matter absolutely of his own choice and determination. Only in the ordinary relations of life is the *form* of confession in so far free, as according to the relation of the individual to God, according to his spiritual and natural endowment, and according to the relations to men and circumstances, can the same piety appear in different forms; whereas in the case of the oath and martyr's death, the form of the confession is just only that *one* imposed of necessity by higher authority. On this account, even in the usual relations of life, the freedom and truth of the Christian confession will consist in this, that the act and manifestation of piety, just as the piety itself, should be and remain something wrought in us by God, flowing forth from gratitude and love to God, and not effected by ourselves; and, so far as the confession affects others and is made before others, that it should conduce, and be intended to conduce, to the ends of true Christian edification in the sense of § 38. Hence it further follows, that the essence and truth of Christian confession depend not at all on the mere contests of the confession, and the fact of confession according to its relation to objective truth, but just as much on the state of mind of the confessor, in which the true confession is valid only in the object of the confession—namely, that honor to God, whose glory dwells on earth in the kingdom of Christ. Hence a true Christian confession is not made in order to secure the honor of a confessor before men, but in order, by self-renunciation, with the confession to serve others for the ends of the kingdom of Christ. So little is the subject-matter of the confession in itself the sign of a veritable Christian and of a Christian confession, that in Scripture the same confession which John makes known to us as being, *under given circumstances and contrasts*, a sufficient sign of a *true disciple of Jesus* (ἐν τούτῳ γινώσκετε τὸ Πνεῦμα τοῦ Θεοῦ· πᾶν πνεῦμα ὃ ὁμολογεῖ Ἰησοῦν Χριστὸν ἐν σαρκὶ ἐληλυθότα, ἐκ τοῦ Θεοῦ ἐστίν, 1 John 4:2, 3), meets us also as a confession of Christ the Lord with that appeal, "Lord, Lord," on the lips of those who, on account of their other misconduct with respect to God's will, are rejected (Matt. 7; comp. § 29, note); nay, even presents itself to us as a confession of devils, who know of the Lord only to their torment (ἐξήρχετο δὲ καὶ δαιμόνια ἀπὸ πολλῶν, κράζοντα καὶ λέγοντα· Ὅτι σὺ εἶ ὁ οὑὸς τοῦ Θεοῦ, Luke 4:41; Matt. 8:29). That confession, therefore, in itself and before others, is true only in the same measure as it flows from a living faith, and is the confession of that faith, to whose nature it belongs to be love and hope, purity and simplicity, wisdom and prudence. This appears in the confession in such a way, that instead of the blind and vain pushing forward to confession, instead of zeal without knowledge (Rom. 10:2), instead of zeal without love (Luke 9:54), the Christian waits for the *occasion* as a *divine* hint, which summons him to the confession; and he makes his confession in just as great *fear* of God as meekness towards men, without doing violence to his consciousness, that with such confession he stands in an antagonistic and condemnatory position to a world which has revolted from God in Christ. Mark 8:38, Ὃς γὰρ ἂν ἐπαισχυνθῇ με καὶ τοὺς ἐμοὺς λόγους ἐν τῇ γενεᾷ ταύτῃ τῇ μοιχαλίδι καὶ ἁμαρτωλῷ, καὶ ὁ υἱὸς τοῦ ἀνθρώπου ἐπαισχυνθήσεται αὐτόν, κ.τ.λ.; 1 Pet. 3:15, ἕτοιμοι ἀεὶ πρὸς ἀπολογίαν παντὶ τῷ αἰτοῦντι ὑμᾶς λόγον περὶ τῆς ἐν ὑμῖν ἐλπίδος, ἀλλὰ μετὰ πραΰτητος καὶ φόβου. For the special promise with which confessors under special oppression may console themselves, see Matt. 10:19, 20.

(3) The oath has, according to the word and the thing itself, its sanction generally not only from Luke 1:73, but specially also in its application to the taking an oath on the part of man for human ends (Heb. 6:16, 17). For there the human oath itself appears only as the lower analogy of a higher divine relation. The misunderstanding of the passage Matt. 5:33–37, and of its repetition in Jas. 5:12, demonstrates itself as such, not merely by its contradiction to the context of the discourse, and to the nature of the several forms of adjuration there quoted, which collectively and separately do not bear the character of a confession, *i.e.* of an appeal to the living *God*, but also by the contradiction to the posture of Jesus Christ to the Old Testament law as a whole. What the Lord the Giver of the law has *commanded* in the Old Testament, viz. that men were to swear by His name (Deut. 6:13, 10:20; Ex. 22:11), that the Lord the Fulfiller of the law cannot have *forbidden*, without destroying the law in place of fulfilling it. Rather does the fulfilment consist in this, that the law commanded, without its being possible from the position of the law rightly to fulfil it; whereas, with the gospel, that has come wherein also the command of the oath finds its true fulfilment. For this is what the prophet Jeremiah points out (Jer. 4:12) in the words, that Israel then alone, *when he turns himself to the Lord*, can truly and holily swear, "So true as the Lord liveth." What is *forbidden* in the gospel of Matthew, is the levity of the forms of swearing of ungodly-minded men. In contrast with these, the simple "yea" and "nay" serve as the expression of pure veracity. To the wisdom and love of the Christian it is left to decide where, to the simple affirmation, the further asseveration may and must be added, as the example of the apostle shows; comp. 2 Cor. 11:11, 31, Gal. 1:20, etc. But the calling God to witness, as the All-seeing, has again its justification and truth only in the pure consciousness of the invoker. Οὐ γάρ ἐσμεν, says the apostle, ὡς οἱ πολλοὶ, καπηλεύοντες τὸν λόγον τοῦ Θεοῦ· ἀλλ᾽ ὡς ἐξ εἰλικρινείας, ἀλλ᾽ ὡς ἐκ Θεοῦ, κατενώπιον τοῦ Θεοῦ, ἐν Χριστῷ

λαλοῦμεν, 2 Cor. 2:17. "When we swear, we always combine two things together, viz. that we call upon God for help and protection, and imprecate His punishments upon ourselves. It is as if we would say: According as God helps me or not: if I hold to my oath, so may He be gracious unto me: if, however, I deceive any one by it, so may He punish me. Such is a very beautiful *service of God* and invocation. For he who swears *makes confession* that he calls upon God for grace and favor, and expects from Him that He will protect and help him; and that he imprecates upon himself divine wrath and vengeance if he should deceive any one with his oath" (Luther, *Ausl. zur Genes.* ch. xxii.). "Every service of God is ungodly which is undertaken and appointed without His command. It is not forbidden, but *commanded*, to take an oath: 'As truly as the Lord lives' (Deut. 6:13). It appertains to the honor of God to call upon Him as a witness of the truth, and to be sensible that He watches what we do; and when even you do anything against your conscience, that He will judge thee on account of it." (Luth. *Aus. des Prop. Hosea.* Compare also especially what is said by him in his exposition of Matt. 5, where he speaks of the oath not merely as the obedience due to the magistrate, according to God's word, but also as of an *act of free love*, as, "When I see any one in spiritual need and danger, weak in the faith, or with a desponding conscience, or of an erring judgment, and the like, then ought I not only to comfort, but also besides to swear, to strengthen his conscience, and to say, 'As true as God lives and Christ has died, so verily is this the truth in God's word,' etc. And similarly, too, when one has to clear a neighbor's character, and to save his honor against evil and poisonous calumniators, there one may even say, 'Before the living God, injustice is done him.' For this is altogether a good use of God's name, to the honor and truth of God, and the safety and happiness of our neighbor.")

The oath itself, however, is something else than the Christian asseveration and the Christian confession in general, although, as far as concerns the general idea, it coincides with both. For in the asseveration of an oath, which is at the same time the confession of one's own faith in the omniscient Savior and Judge of the world, the confessor sets up the Supreme Judge Himself as a witness of his veracity, and lays down a solemn renunciation of God's grace in case of his untruthfulness or the non-fulfilment of his own words on the strength of his oath. From this naturally result the conditions of a right—that is, Christian and pious oath-taking, and fulfilment of an oath. The first condition is, that the oath be taken only in virtue of a due requisition. If it is due in general to the confession, that it occurs in consequence of a given occasion, how much more does the same hold good of the solemn, weighty confession of an oath! But the justification to the requirement of an oath will ever be present according to the nature and way in which there are on earth and in human society human bearers of divine power and order, who in God's stead and in God's name are called upon, as it were, in the face of God to demand a testimony of every man's hearty faith. The second condition of a Christian, *i.e.* of a morally blameless oath-taking, is, that the swearer should be in truth a confessor, *i.e.* that his oath should be the expression of a believing hope really indwelling in him. The third condition is, that the obligation he enters into by his oath of confession should be such a one as to which that God Himself can confess Himself whom the swearer confesses. To be willing for the oath's sake to fulfil ungodly obligations, is merely to carry on the wickedness *begun* to a wicked *completion*, and to the first impiety to join the second. The non-fulfilment of what has been sworn is in such cases not a breach of an oath well-pleasing to God, but the penitent revocation of a God-displeasing oath. Actual perjury, on the contrary, *i.e.* the violation of what has been sworn to of an obligation well-pleasing to God—a lie under the sworn asseveration of the truth—is therefore a sin so specifically terrible, because it is the most open, most conscious form of mockery of the communion of grace,—a renunciation of the grace of God in Jesus Christ, which one gives up by hypocritically pretending to make confession of it. "To swear, means to confess that God is a helper and protector. But if you make a false oath, then hast you therewith denied God, and provoked and called down His wrath and displeasure upon yours own head" (Luth. *On Genesis*).

To have spoken here of *vows* would, properly speaking, have been altogether unnecessary, had not a false mode of view imagined that we ought to see in them acts of a very highly exalted piety—practical manifestations of an especial devotion to God and to His honor. They would so far have belonged to the chapter on oaths, as a vow is confirmed by an oath either outwardly before men, or inwardly before God. So far, however, as vows are nothing else than solemn promises to follow a certain line of conduct as before the eye of God—an acknowledgment of certain rules of action and procedure as to whose observance we consider ourselves bound before God, and promise the same to God—it becomes necessary first of all to inquire, in order to estimate justly the value of such vows, what it is to which they refer, and in what manner we regard them as binding. Above all, it is self-evident that a Christian can vow nothing which is not acceptable to God, and which He does not wish to have recognized by Christians as bounden duty. Such obligations belong partly to the general life-calling of every Christian, and partly to those divinely ordained earthly callings of a special kind, as they present themselves not to all alike, but differently in each case. These obligations are nowhere self-devised, self-imposed, but appertain either to the nature of the general Christian vocation, or to the special callings of our earthly life. A solemn promise made before God of our resolution to perform these obligations is not in itself deserving of blame. It would become so only if we supposed that the duty of keeping these obligations is first rendered necessary by our promising, while the right promise is only a formal acknowledgment of an obligation already before existing. To such vows there applies what holds good of the oaths: "Jus jurandum non producit novam obligationem, sed confirmat antea existentem." Under what circumstances, then, may Christians undertake these solemn promises without incurring censure? I am here speaking naturally only of such solemn promises as are made by the Christian from his own individual requirements, not of such as may be imposed by virtue of the general public order in church or state—as, for example, vows at confirmation, marriage vows, and the like—without having the form of an oath. If the question does not concern these, but vows which the Christian makes for himself before God, what impels him to such? If he is a true Christian, this is done not under the supposition that he now becomes more certain in the performance of his obligation from his having formally and solemnly pledged himself, as if his promise were able to effect what the power of his faithful God can alone bring about in him. It is done not from a notion that now alone he is bound, whereas he was already bound before by the will of God with respect to him; still less as if he imagined that he was thereby doing God especial honor, or performing some service of unusual merit. But it is done in the feeling of his weakness, which urges him to promise to his God the performance of duties hitherto unfulfilled,—a promise which would again be improper if the Christian wished to regard his promise as furnishing the certain strength for its fulfilment, instead of calling upon God in his promise to give him strength to enable him to fulfil it. Thus a promise may be a rousing of one's self from weakness and sloth, and may possess in the recognition of this weakness or sloth a certain moral value; not, however, if we regard this promise as evincing a higher degree and elevation of Christian piety. For we are all, by virtue of our baptism, promised to God in Christ, and have, in our conversion to the grace of baptism, taken upon ourselves the obligation of realizing this grace, and devoted ourselves to our Lord and Savior. A renewing of this dedication may be well conceived of as a necessity for the sinful weakness of the Christian, only not in such a way as if we imagined that now for the first time by our promise we were betrothed to Christ, or betrothed at all to our promise; for long since Christ has betrothed Himself to us, and we have betrothed ourselves to Him and His power, and not to the power of our promise. For all true power for the fulfilment of the divine will comes from the Spirit of Liberty, who enters in where Christ the Lord has taken up His dwelling in the heart. And where this Spirit prevails, there is required no vow in order that we should allow ourselves to be governed by Him, but He rules us and impels us to the free performance of our duties. Only where we feel that this Spirit is threatening to depart from us, or has departed, there may we rouse ourselves, and vow to God that only in this Spirit that makes free will we seek that strength which is required to enable us to do the whole will of God.

That, however, which has had a most prejudicial influence on the conception of the nature of vows, and which has led also to a denial even of their relative propriety, was the circumstance of their being esteemed justifiable and proper in cases where no antecedent obligation to their use could be found either in the will of God with respect to the vocation of the general Christian life, or with respect to the special calling of our earthly life, but where one of his own choice devised something special, which was to receive an obligatory and unconditionally binding force in and with the vow alone, especially with the vow in the form of an oath. But the oath is precisely then to be rejected when it is wished to impose on one's self by means of it a self-enjoined obligation, at the basis of which there lies no duty confirmed by God and already existing. Rather does one thereby trespass against God, since, without being called upon by the duties of his vocation for an oath, he makes the oath a snare to impose upon himself an obligation where none exists; or renders the violation of some duty actually existing doubly fearful, by taking upon himself, wilfully and of his own free choice, the penalties of an oath,— thus loading the possible violation of the duty with the additional crime of the violation of an oath. But where special leadings of God, special individual gifts, or special individual defects in regard to such, present to the individual Christian a special behaviour, and "consilia evangelica "in the true sense of the word (see § 36) may be allowed to determine his conduct, there ought this very determining reason—the perception of this special arrangement and leading of God—to be and to continue the sole motive of the act and of this special conduct, instead of involving the obligation in a special vow which binds to nothing, as soon as the particular leadings and arrangements of Providence happen to take a turn which leads us to the conclusion that these special circumstances by God's will no longer exist with an obligatory force. Hirscher, indeed, brings the vow into connection with his moral virtuosity, and says: "Whoever has but a slight knowledge of himself, must fear that he should begin again to look about him and divide his heart. In order to make an end, accordingly, of all irresoluteness and half-decidedness,—in order by the utmost collection of their strength to seize on the ideal path,—in order beforehand to cut off for ever (?) every possible wavering and looking about,— thousands have availed themselves of an eminent means—and one, too, approved of by the church—of the *vow*" (ii. 397). But against this view (quite irrespective of the wonderful notion of cutting off for ever possible irresolution by means of such vows) there holds good for general application, that which Luther says with special reference to the so-called spiritual vows in his theses concerning vows (of the year 1522): "The evangelical liberty is of divine right and a divine gift. It brings with it, that a man does not necessarily depend on any work, place, thing, and person; but that the use of all such things, however they may have presented themselves to us, should remain free.... This it knows well, that a man must needs depend solely and alone on the word of grace. Thus no creature has a right to this liberty. Hence it follows that vows must be so shaped as not at all to militate against this liberty. The question is not what is good or better, but what ought and what ought not to be done. As no man is to spoil the good for the sake of the better, so also still less is he to do violence to what is necessary, for the sake of something which is not so. And so neither also must he destroy the best for the sake of the better, nor the better for the sake of the good. And besides, we have all bound ourselves in baptism by the most solemn vow to this liberty. For this reason we dare not certainly make this vow of no account by another, strip ourselves of this, and place other vows beside it. Otherwise one vow would stand opposed to another, and the building to the foundation. Thus the spiritual vows are absolutely at issue with baptism and the holy gospel." That all vows are null which do not keep themselves within the limits of Christian piety and the edification of one's self and one's neighbor, or wherein a man binds himself to aught that is antagonistic to the word of Christ and the spirit of regeneration, is self-understood.

Martyrdom is confined, in its significance and truth, to the same limits as confession in general, and the oath in particular. Considered in itself, martyrdom (as that in which a man testifies, by the surrender of his life, that he loves it less than the fellowship with God in Christ) is the last and highest form of confession of Christ. No form of self-renunciation upon earth transcends such confession; and in its own way, martyrdom is, in its most stamped and decided shape, the surrender of that to Christ which Christ surrendered for us. Hence δοξάζειν τοίῳ θανάτῳ τὸν Θεὸν, John 21:19 (comp. Rev. 17:6, τὸ αἷμα τῶν μαρτύρων Ἰησοῦ; and 19:1, 2, Ἀλληλούϊα, κ.τ.λ., ὅτι ἐξεδίκησε τὸ αἷμα τῶν δούλων αὐτοῦ. But as a man does not become a martyr by the penalty of death in general but by this, that he suffers death as a confessor of Jesus, so the truth and Christianity of martyrdom itself do not lie in the fact of the suffering, but in the frame of mind of the sufferer. And the true Christian frame of mind does not consist in this, in seeking absolutely, and on every occasion, to meet the suffering of death for the sake of the confession of Jesus, but in submitting to suffering for Jesus' sake, when one recognizes death as a necessity laid upon him by the Lord, from which he can only withdraw himself by a violation of the Christian conscience, of self-denial, and of the edification of himself and his neighbor. When this is not the case, then is the taking up of suffering mere selfish caprice. To suffer in self-seeking, is just as unchristian as to flee from suffering for the same cause. Martyrdom out of vanity, and flight from martyrdom from cowardice, stand on the same line as perversion, only at opposite extremities. Conversely, therefore, according to varying circumstances, out of the same spirit of self-denial, will at one time flight from martyrdom, and at another submission to it, appear to the Christian as agreeable to the will of the Lord, and conducive to the objects of His kingdom. Thus the Lord Himself withdrew from the suffering of death before His hour was come (Mark 3:7, etc.; comp. with John 17:1). And thus it comes to pass, that in the same discourse in which Jesus, in opposition to self-seeking, requires that we should not hold even our own life dearer than the Lord, in the very same place He *commands* His disciples to withdraw from the persecutions in Israel, by fleeing from city to city, because they were not appointed to perish until they had seen the coming of the Lord in His power. See Matt. 10:39; comp. with ver. 23. Even so (John 10:13) it is not flight unqualified that is set forth as the characteristic of a bad shepherd, an hireling, but flight when it takes place under circumstances similar to those in which the Lord, the good Shepherd, that type of all shepherds, found Himself. To resist, even to the surrender of one's own life, the approach of the wolf that threatens to devour the flock, is the ever-abiding task of the shepherd. As little as the approach of the enemy, under all circumstances, threatens the bodily life of the shepherd, so little, under all circumstances, is the spiritual welfare of the [Christian] community dependent on the bodily abiding of the shepherd. It is only when the flight of the shepherd bears the character that in it, by the fault of the shepherd, the spiritual life of the flock is abandoned to the enemy, that it avails to do as Christ Himself did—to give up one's own life—rather than, by seeking one's own safety, to imperil the safety of the souls entrusted to him. In its way, however, what is to be said of the shepherd holds good of every single member of the Christian community. The act and suffering of martyrdom has only so far Christian truth, as it is the deed of one who has been transplanted into the kingdom of God by regeneration and conversion, and to whom his own salvation and that of the community have become one and the same; so that all testifying and confession of his own faith is regarded by him as only then and only so far true, as in it his own salvation, and the salvation of the Christian community, have equal regard paid them.

Thus, it is here shown already, that not even *one* form, in which Christian piety has its immediate manifestation, can be perceived and exhibited according to its nature, without equal regard being paid therein to the individual and to the community, or without the recurrence in the attestation of piety of what constitutes its essence (see § 38). Attestations of piety, therefore, whose characteristic would be the desire to *confine itself* to the mere satisfaction of the individual communion with God (justifiable as it is, when this retires to its "little chamber," and calls the care for its own soul its first and highest duty), must yet, in the exclusiveness of its relation to one's own person, be pronounced unjustifiable, and a spurious piety.

§ 40. *The further Manifestation of Christian Piety as the Mother of all the Virtues*

There is a something in the very essence of Christian piety that renders it impossible for it to stop at its most immediate manifestation. This impossibility lies in and with that impulse and motive to edification which is inherent in piety. For edification demands the promotion and maintenance not only of that supreme relation which was brought about by our regeneration—namely, the fellowship of the grace of the Spirit,—but also of all those objects which in ourselves and others are designed in this earthly existence to be subordinate, and to minister to the highest aim. Hence the Christian virtue of piety has not merely the one proximate, but several remoter forms of its realization, all of which only serve the one end—the edification of the kingdom of God, in the edification of one's self and one's neighbor,—but that in every aspect in which the life of this world and human nature stand in need of an edifying, shaping energy or education for the kingdom of God (1).

(1) The distinction between direct and indirect attestation of Christian piety has its significance merely in this, that a man recognizes how that which, according to its actual manifestation, stands side by side with another and a different form, is in truth of *one* essence with it, and that they are a twofold form of one and the same spirit, and so far the complement one of the other; but not the complement in the sense, as if to piety and its proximate manifestation *something else* besides, which in its essence is not piety, must further accrue, in order first of all to make Christian piety that which it ought to be. This can only then be maintained with any meaning, when one makes piety to be the inward and outward manifestation of a relation in which man only on one side or in one aspect of his personal life had entered into communion with God, and had taken up the problem of his earthly life. But the more that Christian piety has this for its specific and characteristic feature, the resting on that regeneration which is the incorporation of the personality with all the relations of that earthly existence into a fellowship of God's kingdom, so much the more must the attestation of Christian piety bear in itself an inner necessity of being, in the form of its manifestation, not merely the expression for that personal fellowship of the spirit of the individual with God in Christ, and herein of confessing and attesting the center of the new relation, but also of bearing a testimony of the way in which from that one center the whole sphere of human existence has entered into new relations to God. As little, therefore, as the form of man's earthly existence is all comprised in this, in being spiritual fellowship with God, so little can the form of that piety which rests on the removal of all the objects of earthly existence into a divine fellowship of God's kingdom upon earth, limit itself to the proximate manifestation, in which it bears testimony directly of the regeneration of the heart, and of the individual's gracious fellowship with God. Rather will that *one* piety be *genuine* only in the measure in which to this one and proximate form other and more remote ones come to be added. For in this same measure only is that realized which is the

purpose of regeneration—the penetration of the whole periphery of life by a central vital force. Hence it is that the phraseology of the New Testament recognizes not merely a εὐσέβεια, but εὐσέβειαι. A manifold variety of practical realizations are required as manifestations of one and the same piety (ποταποὺς δεῖ ὑπάρχειν ὑμᾶς ἐν ἁγίαις ἀναστροφαῖς καὶ εὐσεβείαις, 2 Pet. 3:11). And as in faith the Christian has received the strength and the call to "good works," so is *that* piety alone the true which is θεοσέβεια δι' ἔργων ἀγαθῶν (1 Tim. 2:10). Hence to that seeming fear of God, in which a man deceives his own heart while he seeks in the external "cultus," in the observance of the proximate and direct *form* of piety, his satisfaction, and deludes himself with trusting that he is pious, this is held up in opposition, that purification from all that is not virtue, and the practical manifestation of the love for our neighbor, are the true service of God (Jas. 1:26, 27). Furthermore, from the same ground, the semblance of piety, the form which is without the power of the essence (the μόρφωσις τῆς εὐσεβείας without δύναμις), is recognized, according to the Scripture, by the want of every virtue. See 2 Tim. 3:5; compare with vers. 2, 3, 4. Hence, lastly, it is less the direct practical manifestation of Christian piety, which exercises its edifying power on the neighbor, than the multiplicity of the καλὰ ἔργα, of the indirect practical manifestation of piety, in which the Christian is to shine before others, and convince them that his heart's faith and his confession are not semblance, but power and truth. Comp. Matt. 5:16 with 1 Pet. 2:12. With regard, now, to the extent and the organic way in which the remoter manifestation of piety is accomplished, measure and order will lie just in the relation in which the Spirit of regeneration is the Fulfiller of the law, and as the Mediator of a true *love of God* is also the Founder of a true *love of self* and of *one's neighbor*. Comp. § 19.

§ 41. *a. Self-edification in its Extent and Organic Arrangement*

The remoter realization of piety, which aims at promoting the edification of the kingdom of God, must *first of all* and *immediately*, in each individual, be made good in his own person. In the united action of regenerate and converted individuals rests the whole continuance of God's kingdom on earth; and only in the measure in which the individual keeps up the receptivity for the blessings of that kingdom, does he maintain for himself the qualification for activity in this kingdom, and in his own action does he lay herein the basis for the maintenance of the kingdom (1). The universal characteristic of this self-edifying activity is, that a man seeks in his own person to solve the problem of that renewal which is at the same time implied in and with regeneration and conversion (see § 25). This self-activity must, however, appear in the form of different virtues, inasmuch as the individual in the domain of his nature and existence recognizes and distinguishes different blessings, over which he has the right and power of ownership, and in whose possession, lordship, and management he has in different ways to maintain for the Redeemer His right of ownership in the redeemed. The inner organization of the self-edifying virtues rests on the right arrangement in regard to superiority and inferiority of the different blessings and objects of life among each other, as well as in their reference to the supreme good,—a regulative sway which is the general character of virtue (see § 35). Thus the self-edifying activity manifests itself in that discipline and self-rule wherein the redeemed man recognizes the vocation of his personality in soul and body, the faculties and endowments of his nature, the possessions of his earthly position in life, as just so many blessings of which he has ever to administer the one to the service and profit of the other—all in reciprocal inter-relations; each, however, again placed above the other: the heavenly calling above the earthly; the soul above the body; the vocation of the soul, according to the different aspects of its corporeal as well as spiritual relations, above the blessing of earthly possession (2).

(1) What the impulse of selfishness suggests to the unredeemed man, viz. to place the care of himself above that of all else, this very principle reappears in the life-domain of the redeemed, but from quite different motives, and therefore in quite a different way. There also the impulse, which urges the redeemed man practically to manifest his own piety first of all in the discipline and training of his own person, is not that impulse of calculating the means and the end; just as also, in the domain of natural life, one is disposed and necessitated to acknowledge that care for his own qualification must go before influence on others, that one must first be rightly advised himself in order to be able to advise others, and more of the same kind. That indeed holds perfectly good of the Christian also; but that which urges him to make the right care for himself the foundation of all further realization of the virtues of Christian piety, is something quite distinct from an intentional self-schooling for the purpose of salutary external influence. It is rather the might of the new impulse of life vouchsafed to him in grace, according to which there is in the redeemed, ὁ καινὸς ἄνθρωπος, ὁ κατὰ Θεὸν κτισθεὶς ἐν δικαιοσύνῃ καὶ ὁσιότητι τῆς ἀληθείας, Eph. 4:24. As in that new birth to "purity" of eternal truth rests the immediate impulse to self-purification, so through revelation of the mystery of regeneration there dwells in the Christian the immediate certainty that the essential shape of the kingdom of God upon earth has its existence in the fulness of the "hidden man of the heart,"—that all else which, in the further development of the life upon earth, comes to light is merely an effort to develop that fulness which the heart of the regenerate encloses; but that all effort does but imperfectly reflect what the redeemed one has already, through the rule of the Holy Ghost, in his heart; so that all fostering of the kingdom of God, which wishes to go forth from the good already won and the root already planted, must in the individual apply itself to that which he has received in his heart through the Spirit of regeneration, in order to allow it to pervade the sphere of his own life, and from thence the whole domain of earthly existence. But this

pervading is nothing else than the unfolding of that *fulness of God's kingdom*, which in the new birth of the heart has already entered into him. Consequently, not to make the state of one's own heart the first care, and in carelessness to give it up as a prey to degeneracy, is nothing less than for the redeemed *to destroy not merely the subjective receptivity for the blessings of the kingdom of God, but the kingdom of God, itself and indeed in that very shape in which it has its fullest and richest existence here below*. BECAUSE THE KINGDOM OF GOD ON EARTH, BOTH FOR INDIVIDUALS AND AS A WHOLE, IS COMPLETELY PRESENT ONLY IN THE HIDDEN NEW MAN OF THE HEART, THEREFORE TO THE CHRISTIAN, ACCORDING TO THE NATURE OF THIS KINGDOM, CARE FOR HIMSELF IS THE FIRST AND HOLIEST CARE. For the Ego of the Christian is truly not the selfish Ego, but that Ego in which Christ lives. Every redeemed man has and possesses Christ in immediate communion of life, only so far as Christ is inborn in his own heart by word, sacrament, and Spirit. If the individual has not Christ there, then also he has Him not outside of himself; if he cherishes Him not there in his heart, then also will he not with his cherishing find Him outside. To care for himself first, means, therefore, with the Christian, to care for the existence of the kingdom of Christ first of all in that part and on that side where here below for each individual it is already concentrated, and from which also in the individual life, as well as in that of the whole body, it attains to development. In the opposite way one only comes to this, to think of the mote in his brother's eye, while he perceives not the beam in his own (Matt. 7:3–5). What, therefore, holds good for the shepherd of the community—*first of all* προσέχειν ἑαυτῷ, *then* τῷ ποιμνίῳ (Acts 20:28)—in its way is also applicable to every individual Christian.

(2) The due higher and lower ordering of the different objects of life, which spontaneously results from the position of the redeemed and the nature of the kingdom of grace, has also found in the saving word of the New Testament explanations pointing towards it. The striving after the *kingdom of heaven* is the first thing; all else—all other gain—

everything that is a condition of existence on earth, or heightens one's welfare in it—is added to this struggle by God. Ζητεῖτε πρῶτον τὴν βασιλείαν τοῦ Θεοῦ καὶ τὴν δικαιοσύνην αὐτοῦ· καὶ ταῦτα πάντα (comp. vers. 25–32) προστεθήσεται ὑμῖν (Matt. 6:33). In comparison with that which Scripture so significantly speaks of as gaining one's own *soul*, all other gain, even were the blessing the whole world, is to be regarded as loss. See Matt. 16:26. Possession and loss of the *life of the body* are to be esteemed as nothing in comparison with the possession and loss of the soul's salvation. Μὴ φοβεῖσθε ἀπὸ τῶν ἀποκτεινόντων τὸ σῶμα, τὴν δὲ ψυχὴν μὴ δυναμένων ἀποκτεῖναι· φοβήθητε δὲ μᾶλλον τὸν δυνάμενον καὶ ψυχὴν καὶ σῶμα ἀπολέσαι ἐν γεέννῃ (Matt. 10:28). Conversely, the life of the body, again, is the greater and more important in comparison with *earthly good things*, which serve for its continuance and adornment, so that from the preservation of the former by God we may also infer that of the latter. Comp. Matt. 6:25, οὐχὶ ἡ ψυχὴ πλεῖόν ἐστι τῆς τροφῆς καὶ τὸ σῶμα τοῦ ἐνδύματος, κ.τ.λ. On the other hand, in like manner is the earthly good required for bodily existence and welfare of less account than that *spiritual good* which is serviceable for the existence and the development and perfection of the spiritual life; so that the first is to be staked against the communication of the second, and given up as being the inferior. Comp. *e.g.* Rom. 15:27, εἰ γὰρ τοῖς πνευματικοῖς αὐτῶν ἐκοινώνησαν τὰ ἔθνη, ὀφείλουσι καὶ ἐν τοῖς σαρκικοῖς λειτουργῆσαι αὐτοῖς.

§ 42. a. *The Preservation of the Soul in its Heavenly Calling*

The fundamental relation of the redeemed is the communion of his soul with his Redeemer, as it commenced in his regeneration. The self-edifying activity, or the further practical manifestation of piety, has therefore naturally its first aim directed to the maintenance of this relation. Herein the regenerate man, in the strength of faith, hope, and love, accomplishes in his own soul that which is the essential task of his renewal (see § 25), and the specific kind of Christian virtue (see § 30). In the maintenance of this communion the Christian recognizes and maintains his heavenly vocation. Care for the preservation of this communion has in the case of the Christian this for its characteristic token, that it is the consequence and fruit of that confession by which man—first inwardly in the heart, and then as his testimony also outwardly and publicly—makes his acknowledgment to that God who has of His grace made Himself known to us in Christ. For first must the foundation be laid, and the Christian have entered on the fundamental act of God for his redemption with his whole heart as a confessor of Christ, before he can in a right way arrive at that which is care for the soul, not in this or that sense, but care for it in its heavenly vocation. He alone who, by virtue of this calling, has gone out from himself and entered into Christ, can so take care of his soul as to make that care fruitful. For then has he, in the full perception of the need of his soul for constant self-discipline, at the same time also the perception and assurance of the constant nearness of his heavenly Helper, and the consciousness of the way in which He will help him rightly to care for his own soul. But this self-discipline has again totally different forms from those which appear to us as direct and immediate forms of piety. And it is precisely the practical realization of all the forms of spiritual self-discipline which guards us against perverting the consciousness of the possession of grace in Christ into a false and slothful security, and guides and disposes us, in the denial of *everything* selfish, to care for the preservation of Christ's right of property in the soul, and for the maintenance thereof in all its spiritual relations and movements in exclusive obedience to Christ. The confession of the soul to Christ conditions the proper care for it; and in this true care of the soul with every means of spiritual self-discipline is realized the truth of this confession. And it is alone the union of both these elements which gives to the exercise of Christian piety in the care for one's soul its genuine Christian character.

(1) All Christian truthfulness in the care for the soul consists in this, that it is the care of a *confessor of the grace of Christ*. For then only does the first care of a Christian rest on the right basis, and then only is it a manifestation of that piety which bears in itself the means and the way for reaching the God-appointed goal. See § 38, in its connection with previous paragraphs. The reason, however, why, in the first rank, the question turns upon the soul, results from the manner and way in which the very possession of salvation, and our experience of it here below, have to do with the soul-life of the individual, are intended to be taken hold of by it, and kept unto the "saving of the soul." Salvation is salvation of the soul (σωτηρία ψυχῶν, 1 Pet. 1:9). The word is mighty to save our souls (Jas. 1:21). Through faith are souls sanctified (1 Pet. 1:22). He who is of the faith, is so for the saving of the soul (εἰς περιποίησιν ψυχῆς, Heb. 10:39). Delitzsch, on the last passage, justly observes, "The soul is the subject of life and salvation." Against this soul, when laid hold of by the power of salvation, the lusts carry on their warfare (1 Pet. 2:11). And just for this reason it behooves us to give up and to commend the soul to its faithful Creator in every species of well-doing (παρατίθεσθαι τὴν ψυχὴν αὐτοῦ ἐν ἀγαθοποιΐαις, 1 Pet. 4:19). Thus, in the care of the Christian for his soul, is that very domain preserved from the assaults of the enemy, in whose safety salvation is involved, and into whose inmost recesses, the heart, it has already entered.

No doubt can therefore be entertained, that that which forms the immediate manifestation of piety (§ 39), is likewise not only an effluence of care for one's own soul, but that herein also there is to be looked for the most essential means for the preservation of that soul in its heavenly vocation. Just as little, however, as that manifestation of piety resolves itself into care for the preservation of one's own soul, so little is hereby exhausted that which serves for the maintenance of the soul in its heavenly vocation. It is merely the central activity, from which rays of other forms of practical realization must proceed; just as, in that which I call care for one's own soul, only *one*, and indeed the first, practical realization which springs from that central source is given, which, starting from the center of the soul's awakened life, applies itself to the whole periphery of the spiritual relations, faculties, and energies of the same life. Nay, it is of the last importance to bring prominently forward this very fact, that where piety is of the true kind, precisely in its relation to the individual soul of the Christian, it does not stop at that which forms the immediate practical realization of piety, but that from this point, and borne on by the spirit of this piety, it strives after all that which is a means of self-discipline, and which may bring about furtherance of the spiritual life in whatsoever is true, whatsoever is honest, whatsoever is right, whatsoever is lovely, whatsoever is of good report, if there be any virtue, if there be any praise (Phil. 4:8). For all these are the inner καλὰ ἔργα of genuine piety, without which its immediate and direct manifestation remains unfruitful (ἄκαρπος). And also in the domain of the spiritual life of the soul, genuine Christian piety does not exercise itself in such a way, that in its care for the soul it extirpates whatever in human and creature wise appears worthy of spiritual cultivation, but that it nourishes and fosters the same by all suitable human means, and merely strives to give it and to keep it in that direction, in which also this care purely and effectively preserves its preparatory purpose for the fulfilment of its heavenly vocation. For there is a mass of spiritual aberrations, which are not always in their origin anti-spiritual, or opposed to the aims and the nature of spiritual life, but are excrescences, diseased malformations of spiritual instincts incorporated in the nature of our spirit, which we cure not by the use of the knife, but by turning them into the right paths, and by good training helping them to their natural gratification. Yet it does not do to bring the highest heavenly relations and the creaturely human ones of the soul's spiritual life into harsh discord, but by all means of spiritual discipline to restore harmony between the two. This harmony, however, is not restored if we keep alive the efforts of our soul only in the one direction, while we mortify them in the other, but by maintaining both alive in true self-discipline, not against but for each other. And they are kept alive only by affording both their appropriate nourishment, and thus observing the proper regimen in both relations. This also holds good of self-discipline with respect to the spiritual blessings and powers bestowed upon us by God's grace. They cannot operate in a proper manner, unless with respect to them man enters, towards himself and towards his new spiritual life, into a relation of self-training, of restraining and regulating conduct in regard to himself and the movements of his spirit. And this very thing is what is practically important in this knowledge: in the first place, that Christian piety, very far from abandoning itself to an intoxicated enjoyment of the blessings of grace, uses the communion of grace only for the soberest and sharpest watchfulness and regulation of one's own spirit; in like manner, secondly, that communion with God, whose possession it is the struggle of piety to maintain, even in this sphere of man's intercourse with himself, does not exclude his efforts upon his own soul, and as little excludes the employment of natural gifts and powers and modes of self-training devised by man, but merely takes them up, since this self-activity, these gifts of nature, and these human methods, are animated with the principle of the divine life, which bears in itself the force and standard of proper self-training. We cannot, however, dwell too much on the fact, that from the nature of redemption, this self-training has truth and permanence only as self-denial. This is the wholesome though bitter ingredient—the salt of the sacrifice—which prevents the blessedness of the communion of grace with God from becoming an indolent and ungodly state of spiritual debauchery. Μεστοὶ ἀγαθωσύνης may Christians consider themselves (Rom. 15:14); but only because so far as Christ lives in them, and they no longer live unto themselves. He who, in the confession of his piety, boasts of being τέκνον Θεοῦ, let him be active in his concern to show himself as τέκνον ὑπακοῆς (1 Pet. 1:14), to preserve his soul undefiled in obedience to the truth (τὰς ψυχὰς ὑμῶν ἡγνικότες ἐν τῇ ὑπακοῇ τῆς ἀληθείας, 1 Pet. 1:22), and to avoid everything which borders on self-love (φιλαυτία, comp. 2 Tim. 3:2) and pride (Jas. 4:6, 7, ὁ Θεὸς ὑπερηφάνοις ἀντιτάσσεται, ταπεινοῖς δὲ δίδωσι χάριν· ὑποτάγητε οὖν τῷ Θεῷ). This self-denying discipline of the spirit displays itself, as well in its regard and estimation of the spiritual gifts bestowed upon it, as in its watching over the tendency of one's own spirit and will. Even in the first relation it is the modest limitation to the measure of gift received, in which the gift itself is guarded as a blessing. (Μὴ ὑπερφονεῖν, παρ' ὃ δεῖ φρονεῖν, ἀλλὰ φρονεῖν εἰς τὸ σωφρονεῖν, ἑκάστῳ ὡς ὁ Θεὸς ἐμέρισε μέτρον πίστεως, Rom. 12:3.) In the second respect this self-denying discipline of the spirit displays itself not only in the contest with every selfish, ungodly thought, and every human, external influence working upon the spirit and opposed to God, but also in guarding against every false raising of any kind of wisdom or of any kind of knowledge to a level with that saving wisdom and knowledge whose foundation is laid in Jesus Christ alone. What the Apostle Paul says in reference to his own external activity, applies also to self-edification: Λογισμοὺς καθαιρεῖν, καὶ πᾶν ὕψωμα ἐπαιρόμενον κατὰ τῆς γνώσεως τοῦ Θεοῦ, καὶ αἰχμαλωτίζοντες πᾶν νόημα εἰς τὴν ὑπακοὴν τοῦ Χριστοῦ, 2 Cor. 10:5. Comp. further Col. 2:8, Βλέπετε μή τις ὑμᾶς ἔσται ὁ συλαγωγῶν διὰ τῆς φιλοσοφίας καὶ κενῆς ἀπάτης, κατὰ τὴν παράδοσιν τῶν ἀνθρώπων, κατὰ τὰ στοιχεῖα τοῦ κόσμου, καὶ οὐ κατὰ Χριστόν 1 Cor. 3:11, Θεμέλιον γὰρ ἄλλον οὐδεὶς δύναται θεῖναι παρὰ τὸν κείμενον, ὅς ἐστιν Ἰησοῦς Χριστός; 1 Cor. 2:5, Ἵνα ἡ πίστις μὴ ᾖ ἐν σοφίᾳ ἀνθρώπων. In this way alone, in this domain of life, is that task accomplished which has fallen to the lot of the redeemed as the "servant of obedience unto righteousness;" comp. Rom. 6:16. For that is the object of our heavenly vocation (τῆς ἄνω κλήσεως, Phil. 3:14), in the "Lord from heaven" to give to man the law and the will of his own spirit, and to fructify it in the heart through the Holy Ghost. This purpose of grace is only attained when, in self-denying obedience of the spirit, self-seeking is steadily subdued, and every spiritual emotion of the soul is turned into the path of its heavenly vocation. In such active piety in the soul of the individual there come to accomplishment in the spirit by a spiritual process, the purification and sanctification of the spirit (ἅγιον εἶναι τῷ πνεύματι, καθαρίζειν ἑαυτὸν ἀπὸ παντὸς μολυσμοῦ—πνεύματος, ἵνα τὸ πνεῦμα σωθῇ; comp. 1 Cor. 7:34, 2 Cor. 7:1, 1 Cor. 5:5), the care for the preservation of the soul in its heavenly calling.

§ 43. b. The Preservation of the Soul in the Earthly Calling

The earthly vocation is the divinely appointed shaping of our life's problem, as, different in gifts and direction, and conditioned as well as limited by the manifold variety of the aims of life, which can be struggled after and attained on earth and in the bosom of human society in general, as well as inside the Christian community, it traces out for man definite forms and kinds of practical realization of his gifts and powers, which correspond to the nature of that problem. This calling is the divinely appointed basis in this world, on which the redeemed soul has to tend and watch over its heavenly calling here below (1). In its relation to the heavenly calling, the earthly appears as the small over against the great, the transitory compared to the eternal, the preparation to the fulfilment, the means which subserve to the final accomplishment, the temporary diversity to the all-comprehending higher and permanent unity (2). But just in this lie the appointment and the necessity of our being equally faithful in both vocations, not with a fidelity that divides itself between two masters, but with that fidelity which the soul preserves, by subordinating and embracing the relations of the earthly calling in those of the heavenly, by recognizing in the accomplishment of the inferior vocation a test of that faithfulness, in which man has to make on earth even the objects of earthly duty conduce to the ends of his heavenly calling, and in which, in this inferior vocation, he practices that self-denial which is the characteristic trait of a Christian frame of mind. But self-denial here authenticates itself alike in the recognition of the vocation as a divine arrangement, and in the right limitation of its own activity to the ends of the vocation; and that indeed in a fulfilment of the calling, which makes itself known equally in that work which the calling demands, as in that rest in the Lord where one indeed expects no blessing without work, but where also he ascribes the blessing not to the work, but to the Lord. Only for such a self-edifying disposition does the earthly calling remain the divinely-appointed and consecrated foundation, within whose limits piety finds an ordained measure of its active manifestation, and a material to be permeated by it, which it has itself to consecrate and to hallow, in the knowledge of the will of God herein revealing itself (3).

(1) The Spirit of grace, who brings about the continuance of the kingdom of God upon earth, and prepares the members of the earthly human family for recipients of this kingdom, teaches us to distinguish a twofold special vocation of individuals, from the heavenly calling which belongs to all Christians alike; and indeed, by virtue of the distinction which exists between the divinely-appointed creaturely order of human society on earth (as it began at creation, and has continued to display itself in the historical development of the human race), the shape and order of Christ's kingdom here below, and the same kingdom in its perfection beyond time, and the future blessings of glory. From the Lord of this kingdom of glory goes forth a call of invitation for this kingdom and to it (ἡ ἄνω κλῆσις, Phil. 3:14; the κλῆσις ἐπουράνιος, Heb. 3:1), which has and which brings for all those who are invited one and the self-same hope (ἐκλήθητε ἐν μιᾷ ἐλπίδι τῆς κλήσεως ὑμῶν, Eph. 4:4; comp. touching this hope, Eph. 1:18 ff., and § 19), and is addressed to men as citizens of the earth, in order that, in the midst of their earthly calling and its fulfilment, they may become citizens of Christ's kingdom upon earth, and may prepare themselves in the vocation of a citizen of this world, as well as in that of a citizen of the kingdom, to inherit hereafter the kingdom of glory. That which the will of God the Creator has appointed as the order of things for earthly citizenship, is accomplished in the discharge of our natural earthly vocation; that which His new-creating gracious will has

laid down as the order on this side the grave for the citizen of the kingdom of Christ, is fulfilled in the discharge of the earthly spiritual (πνευματικός) calling; both forming only two phases of our earthly Christian calling, both subordinated and made subservient to the supreme object of our heavenly calling (κατὰ σκοπὸν διώκω εἰς τὸ βραβεῖον τῆς ἄνω κλήσεως τοῦ Θεοῦ ἐν Χριστῷ Ἰησοῦ, Phil. 3:14). These two phases it is which form the basis of the twofold vocation of the Christian, in a shape out of which particular individual vocations are formed in manifold ways. For both man's earthly social state and the community of Christ's kingdom are so circumstanced, that the problem which belongs to both collectively is only solved by the reciprocal service of their members, who by the diversity of their gifts and powers, of their courses and positions in life, are destined to satisfy the requirements of this present state of things in *every* aspect of the relations of human life. And again, these diverse gifts and powers do not run their course side by side, in such a way that no kind of internal connection should exist between them, so far as the one are pointed out as serviceable for the solution of the general problem of human life, and the others as conducive to the discharge of our task in the community of Christ's kingdom upon earth. For that which is called the gift of the Holy Spirit, is not in the slightest degree that operation of the Holy Ghost by which these same gifts and powers, bestowed by God creatively on the individual man, which render him adapted for the accomplishment of his general human vocation on earth, experience that sanctification, exaltation, and glorification by which their adaptation for the kingdom of God is conditioned. And however distinct may be the form of realization for the objects of the general human existence upon earth, from that of the realization for those of the kingdom of Christ upon earth, yet is the ethical significance and the ethical value of both forms of realization the same, since in both domains it is the realization of Christian *fidelity* in the use of gifts and powers, which are serviceable to the one or to the other of these vocations. For this reason the call to the kingdom of Christ upon earth should alter nothing at all in the general vocation of man on earth, whether we conceive of it as in its collective relations, or as a special vocation of individual men. Especially where the call to the fellowship of Christ's kingdom on earth by the word of grace happens at the time of a fully developed position in life, there ought the new citizen of the kingdom of God to remain in his old earthly position and calling. 1 Cor. 7:17-24, Ἕκαστος ἐν τῇ κλήσει ᾗ ἐκλήθη, ἐν ταύτῃ μενέτω.... Ἕκαστος ἐν ᾧ ἐκλήθη, ἀδελφοί, ἐν τούτῳ μενέτω παρὰ Θεῷ (compare in that passage especially the important declaration about remaining even in the state of slavery). The earthly vocation designates there, as also elsewhere, according to the common use of words, the standing which the life-problem of the individual assumes within the natural human community, and in which the individual serves the natural human ends of his own earthly existence, and of the existence of this community. The general Christian vocation alters nothing in all these vocations, and in the activities corresponding to them. For this does not create absolutely new forms of activity in the earthly life, but only brings to all the spirit of true fulfilment, and teaches us to recognize the nearer or more remote relation, in which all particular callings of individuals serve for the practical manifestation of Christian fidelity, and for its exhibition both in the relations of human existence generally in itself, and in its connection with the kingdom of Christ upon earth. But the kingdom of God also, in its continuance upon earth, has a diversity of vocations, which rests on a diversity of the gifts of nature and of grace, and contributes to the development of this kingdom upon earth. Comp. Rom. 12:4, 5, ff., καθάπερ γὰρ ἐν ἑνὶ σώματι πολλὰ μέλη ἔχομεν, τὰ δὲ μέλη πάντα οὐ τὴν αὐτὴν ἔχει πρᾶξιν· οὕτως οἱ πολλοὶ ἓν σῶμά ἐσμεν ἐν Χριστῷ, ὁ δὲ καθ' εἷς, ἀλλήλων μέλη, κ.τ.λ. Comp. 1 Cor. 12:4-7, διαιρέσεις τῶν χαρισμάτων εἰσίν ... ἑκάστῳ δὲ δίδοται ἡ φανέρωσις τοῦ Πνεύματος πρὸς τὸ συμφέρον; also Matt. 25:14 ff., the parable of the entrusted pounds, and the employment of them; 1 Pet. 4:10, ἕκαστος καθὼς ἔλαβε χάρισμα, εἰς ἑαυτοὺς αὐτὸ διακονοῦντες, ὡς καλοὶ οἰκονόμοι ποικίλης χάριτος Θεοῦ.

Here, too, all good behavior on the part of Christian piety springs from the recognition of this divinely appointed difference of vocation. But that heavenly calling, which is the same for all Christians, is something entirely different from this particular vocation of the individual. The former is the call to become in Christ the heir of eternal blessedness and glory. No particular vocation of individuals is, as contrasted with this calling, a self-aim, but they are all only means which contribute to prepare us by them for the attainment of this supreme end, and to qualify us for it. To the consciousness of this end all particular individual vocations are subordinated and adapted, as to the vital root, in which alone the fulfilment of the particular vocation has a real life, corresponding to this one supreme aim, and ministering to imperishable ends.

(2) The diversity of individual special vocations on earth, and their due activity, no matter whether we conceive of it as within the earthly human community or in Christ's kingdom upon earth, is nowhere so constituted that it should of itself exhibit or be of equal validity with that which the man or the Christian is called upon to be. Everywhere is this activity in our vocation merely a means conducing to the realization of a common problem,—there of humanity for the accomplishment of the ends of the human and creature life, here of Christianity for the fulfilment of the ends of the Christian kingdom on earth; and in all these earthly callings it comes to be manifested only as in a particularly shaped fragment, as in the decomposed colors of the one [beam of] light, what man as man, and the Christian as a Christian, or man as a man of God (ἄνθρωπος Θεοῦ), is destined to be. Therefore, all these particular vocations are also, so far as they trace out one definite and particular *form* of activity, of a transitory nature, and have their ethical importance not in this their form, but in the spirit which animates this formal activity of the vocation. Its roots never lie in the material conditions by which it comes to a formal distinction of vocation (as *e.g.* in the particular talents and course of life of individuals, in the separation of men according to race, nation, and the like); but

this spirit springs from a higher domain, in which those conditions are concentrated by which man may become newly born, not for the perfect man of an earthly vocation, but in every vocation for the complete man of God. This is the domain of those heavenly powers which are concentrated in the God-man Jesus Christ. He it is who is, has, and brings that word of life, whose spirit in every case bestows in the same manner for every special and temporal activity in our vocation that one invariable element which alone is of enduring and imperishable value. Springing from that word which passes not away though heaven and earth pass away, this spirit works in the fidelity to that high calling in Christ, which in itself again embraces heaven and earth in one, fidelity also to that transitory earthly vocation; fidelity towards the common problem of man on earth within the limits of the particular vocation of the individual; fidelity towards the common problem of the Christian community on earth within the same limits of the particular vocation of the individual; fidelity to both, as the Christian's twofold school of preparation for the gaining of eternal life. This is that fidelity which has not for its object to stamp the Christian as a perfect man for his earthly vocation, but rather to consecrate every earthly calling as a training school for the perfect man and child of God. In this aim lies the higher *unity*, which embraces all particularity of vocation, and within which the separate vocation as such, and directed to particular ends, does not come under consideration. But the sense in which, notwithstanding, the special vocation comes into consideration even from the standpoint of this unity is this, that it displays the divinely ordained *multiplicity* in which on earth the *fulness of the spiritual unity* is destined to arrive at its attestation, realization, and self-testing in Christian fidelity. That is the reason why the apostle asserts both that in Christ no difference of earthly vocation is valid, and also that he who is in Christ must keep sacred the distinction of vocations. For so it is said: Gal. 3:28, οὐκ ἔνι Ἰουδαῖος οὐδὲ Ἕλλην, οὐκ ἔνι δοῦλος οὐδὲ ἐλεύθερος, οὐκ ἔνι ἄρσεν καὶ θῆλυ· ἅπαντες γὰρ ὑμεῖς εἷς ἐστε ἐν Χριστῷ

Ἰησοῦ; 1 Cor. 12:13, καὶ γὰρ ἐν ἑνὶ Πνεύματι ἡμεῖς πάντες εἰς ἓν σῶμα ἐβαπτίσθημεν, εἴτε Ἰουδαῖοι, εἴτε Ἕλληνες, εἴτε δοῦλοι, εἴτε ἐλεύθεροι, κ.τ.λ.; Col. 3:11, ὅπου οὐκ ἔνι Ἕλλην καὶ Ἰουδαῖος, περιτομὴ καὶ ἀκροβυστία, βάρβαρος, Σκύθης, δοῦλος, ἐλεύθερος· ἀλλὰ πάντα καὶ ἐν πᾶσι Χριστός. But as little as the differences of nations, of ranks, of families, of callings, disappear from the apostle's mind before the oneness of the community of the Spirit with Christ, as decidedly does even *he* teach to regard with holy veneration the difference of natural vocation as well as of the calling in the kingdom of grace, and as certainly in general does the variety of vocations *serve* only for the revelation of the divine riches on earth. And precisely in the holding as sacred these *differences*, does the Christian, holding sacred the higher *unity*, become manifest, since we recognize and hold sacred as God's will on earth, that just the variety of the earthly conditions of vocation, according to the manifoldness both of gifts and of requirements, is the means assigned for bringing about the end of the unity of the Spirit, and, where it is attained, of preserving it. Καὶ γὰρ τὸ σῶμα οὐκ ἔστιν ἓν μέλος, ἀλλὰ πολλά, κ.τ.λ., 1 Cor. 12:14; καὶ αὐτὸς (Χριστός) ἔδωκε τοὺς μὲν ἀποστόλους, τοὺς δὲ προφήτας, κ.τ.λ., μέχρι καταντήσωμεν οἱ πάντες εἰς τὴν ἑνότητα τῆς πίστεως καὶ τῆς ἐπιγνώσεως τοῦ υἱοῦ τοῦ Θεοῦ, κ.τ.λ., Eph. 4:11–13.

(3) To recognize the *divine* relations of the vocation, and of the life of that vocation, and thereunto to move accordingly in the vocation, is to preserve the soul in the *earthly* vocation. Ἐξ αὐτοῦ (τοῦ Θεοῖ) καὶ δι' αὐτοῦ καὶ εἰς αὐτὸν τὰ πάντα, Rom. 11:36. But no one learns this from the vocation itself, but only from his fellowship with God. Therefore is the communion with God of the redeemed of Jesus Christ at the same time the spirit of the true fulfilment of our earthly vocation. On the other hand, in the vocation itself the soul is overwhelmed when the vocation is to it only an earthly destiny, and not at the same time a communion with God. But to recognize and to adhere to the fellowship with God in the vocation itself, is to perceive even *in the entering into* the vocation the ordinance of God, on

the basis of this certainty to remain within the *limits* of the vocation as in a divinely appointed limitation, without that the limits of the vocation should become a hindrance to the fellowship with God; but on the fulfilling of the limits, at once to expect the blessing from the assistance of God, and to see in the glorifying of God the end of the fulfilling of one's vocation.—The divine ordinance is recognized in the entrance upon the *special* vocation, if a man, in the relation of his natural and spiritual gifts, as well as in the form in which his life has been guided, has recognized the declared will of God, which determines the individual to this or that special vocation of life. Only the guilt of earlier evident mistaking of the divine will, or special leadings in life independent of our will, justify the exchange of the calling once undertaken. Apart from this, change of vocation is self-seeking caprice. Out of the same recognition of a divine will toward us, follows also the inward necessity of holding sacred the *limits* of a vocation. It is but natural to the Christian mind, πράσσειν τὰ ἴδια (1 Thess. 4:11) in contrast to the περίεργον (1 Tim. 5:13) and ἀλλοτριοεπίσκοπον εἶναι (1 Pet. 4:15). Especially has the over busy seeming piety which avoids the sweat of the labor of its vocation, in the proper limits and labor of its vocation, a God-determined and divinely blessed antidote (Εἴ τις οὐ θέλει ἐργάζεσθαι, μηδὲ ἐσθιέτω. Ἀκούομεν γάρ τινας περιπατοῦντας ἐν ὑμῖν ἀτάκτως, μηδὲν ἐργαζομένους, ἀλλὰ περιεργαζομένους, κ.τ.λ., 1 Thess. 4:10-12. Compare in general on the necessity and the blessedness of our labor in our vocation, Eph. 4:28, and the divine example, John 9:4, ἐμὲ δεῖ ἐργάζεσθαι ... ἕως ἡμέρα ἐστίν, κ.τ.λ.). No doubt the limits of our vocation in itself, and in exclusive limitation to them, may become restraining limits for the cultivation of the communion with God; and there is an unquiet and restless activity in one's vocation, which, in spite of all seeming vocational fulfilment, is an abandonment of the heavenly vocation, and labor without peace and without blessing. This, however, is impossible to the Christian, who brings the peace of God into the unrest and labor of the earthly vocation, and whose heart has equally the need to rest in this peace, as to realize the power of this peace in the self-renunciation of his toil and the struggle of his vocation. Moreover, whatever may be set over against toil as pleasure, has the moral significance of necessary strengthening for the vocation; as, on the other hand, this relation to the vocation, and the consciousness of it also, at the same time serve the Christian in deciding as to the mode and measure of that which, as rest from toil, he ought to seek for (comp. respecting the form of this gratification, and of its significance for the community, § 47, note (4)). But it is, above all, the Christian consciousness which, in the very midst of toil, comes to rest by this means, that it knows neither the heathenish care, nor the heathenish ambition, nor the heathenish confidence in its own labor; but expects the fruit, the glory, the blessing of labor from God's grace, and ascribes it to the power of God and His influence. Thus the soul preserves for itself and its earthly life the peace of God. In spite of the struggle even of the earthly calling, it is the life-vocation of a Christian: ἤρεμον καὶ ἡσύχιον βίον διάγειν ἐν πάσῃ εὐσεβείᾳ καὶ σεμνότητι, 1 Tim. 2:2. With trust in God, instead of heathenish care or heathenish apathy, begins the activity of our vocation. To every one indeed applies: Μὴ μεριμνᾶτε τῇ ψυχῇ ὑμῶν, τί φάγητε καὶ τί πίητε, κ.τ.λ., Matt. 6:25 ff. But to acquire every virtue and every praise is also the aim of the Christian's vocation (Phil. 4:8), only accompanied by the consciousness of being in all things an unprofitable servant, *i.e.* of having done nothing worthy of special thanks, but only of having performed the task of his Lord. (Ὅταν ποιήσητε πάντα τὰ διαταχθέντα ὑμῖν, λέγετε ὅτι δοῦλοι ἀχρεῖοί ἐσμεν· ὅτι ὃ ὠφείλομεν ποιῆσαι, πεποιήκαμεν Luke 17:10.) But the Christian rejoices in his prosperity and success, not as being his own work, but as a divine blessing: to this alone he owes the fruit of his labor. Comp. with Ps. 127:1 the universal application of the apostle's words to every kind of vocational activity: οὔτε ὁ φυτεύων ἐστί τι, οὔτε ὁ ποτίζων, ἀλλ' ὁ αὐξάνων Θεός, 1 Cor. 3:7. In the repose of this resignation to the will of God vanishes the anxiety of God-estranged earthly care and working, the unblessed desecration of the earthly vocation; and in the outward shaping also of life, there makes its appearance as a decisive element, sanctification of labor in God, and sanctification of repose in God. But the measure of holiday from outward toil stands in the very same relation to our activity in our vocation, as does the struggle of the earthly life as a preparation for the rest of the future world. The struggle is the task, the rest refreshment for that struggle. Hence labor is ever the shape of life; rest from labor comes in merely as a foretaste of the future rest, as strengthening for one's proper vocation. This is the sole significance of that seventh day which makes the end of a week of labor a day of rest. In it is stamped the type alike for the relation of labor and rest, as for the divine destination of man, to transform the curse of labor in the sweat of his brow (Gen. 3:19) into a blessing through rest in God. The Spirit of Christ brings to the earthly vocation the full measure of that blessing; and He impels also to the due fulfilment of the law, through equal sanctification of rest and labor in the Lord. In such a shape the soul also, in its earthly vocation, fulfills that wherein above all its task consists—to do all that we do in the name of Jesus (Col. 3:17), and everything to the glory of God (1 Cor. 10:31).

§ 44. c. The Preservation of the Body for the Service of the Soul

The self-renunciation of Christian piety is realized further, as in the life and movements of the spirit, so also in the life and movements of the bodily and sensuous nature. For the Christian knows that his body also is embraced in the glory of his divine vocation (1). The practical realization of piety has also on this side, just as in reference to the spirit, a twofold shape, inasmuch as in the life of the body there come to light divinely ordained natural gifts and instincts, as well as seductive lusts (2). The latter element has, besides, for the redeemed, *i.e.* for the regenerate and converted man, an especial significance, since in him the sin which has been expelled from its rule over the heart has retired principally into the corporeal and sensuous life of nature; comp. § 26. But to self-edification as respects both phases of the corporeal life this is common, that the soul, emancipated for the service of Christ, strives to rule over the body for the ends of the heavenly no less than of the earthly vocation. This rule shows itself on the one side in the care for the prosperity of the bodily existence, whose soundness is a condition (along with others) of the soundness of the spirit. On the other side this rule is a mortification of the earthly lusts, by moderation, sobriety, chastity. By both these kinds of rule the soul retains the body in the service of the earthly no less than of the heavenly vocation of the soul (3). But in this relation of service, in which the life of the body stands to the heavenly as well as to the earthly vocation of the Christian, the Christian becomes aware that the life of the body is of worth and importance not for its own sake, but only in its relation to the vocation of the soul. Hence arises the justification and courage of the Christian in surrendering his bodily life, when the preservation of it would be a violation of his fidelity either in the heavenly or the earthly vocation. This surrender of the bodily life to death is, in such a case, naturally always only an acceptance of suffering from being called to it, not from one's own choice, nor from putting forth one's hand wickedly. Both things, however—to preserve the life of the body for the calling, as well as to offer it up for the calling—lie in that lordship over the body, where one regards the soul in its calling as higher than existence and well-being in the bodily life (4).

(1) Only from the spirit of regeneration do we arrive at true sanctification of the body. The ancient and modern heathenish wisdom forms the contrast with its unwisdom in respect of the body. This does not bring it beyond what Epictetus says: Τὸ σῶμα μὲν κοινὸν πρὸς τὰ ζῶα· ὁ λόγος δὲ καὶ ἡ γνώμη κοινὸν πρὸς τοὺς Θεούς (*Diss.* i. 3, 1). But not so the Christian. For to him the body is really a sanctuary, or temple, wherein the Spirit of God dwells already here below, but which is also destined through the same Spirit to enter into the glory of the glorified body of Christ. As it is therefore one and the same divine

calling, one and the same divine impartation of the Spirit, which equally applies to body and spirit, so in the case of the Christian care for the body is not, as it were, *added* to care for the soul; but *in* and *with* care for the redeemed soul, there manifests itself also care for the body as destined for redemption and glorification. Christian self-edification of the soul is at the same time essentially self-edification of the body. This deeming holy and hallowing of the body is equally far removed from heathenish *contempt* for it, as from heathenish (modern heathenish) *idolatry* of the body and bodily objects. Τὰ σώματα ὑμῶν, μέλη Χριστοῦ ἐστιν ... τὸ σῶμα ὑμῶν, ναὸς τοῦ ἐν ὑμῖν ἁγίου Πνεύματός ἐστιν, οὗ ἔχετε ἀπὸ Θεοῦ ... Δοξάσατε δὲ τὸν Θεὸν ἐν τῷ σώματι ὑμῶν, 1 Cor. 6:15, 19, 20. Νεκρώσατε οὖν τὰ μέλη τὰ ἐπὶ τῆς γῆς, πορνείαν, ἀκαθαρσίαν, πάθος, ἐπιθυμίαν κακὴν, κ.τ.λ., Col. 3:5.

(2) The glorification of God in the body, and in the care for the body, consists in the keeping up of that dominion in which it is God's will to rule over the body by means of the soul, which has been redeemed by Him. Such government is discipline and training, not the extirpation and decimation of the subjects. To the Christian especially, who has recognized the heathenish opposition of the vileness of the body and all sensible matter, in contrast with the excellency of the spirit and of spiritual things, as a wretched error, the mastery over the body is, it is true, a mortification of the sinful lusts, but not a mortification of the body, or of its divinely ordained natural desires and impulses. For even in the domain of the bodily life does the Spirit of the regeneration of all things impel the Christian to distinguish clearly what is divinely sanctioned in the nature of the body from its later depravation by sin, and in the training of the body for the life of glorification, self-actively to co-operate in this way also, that he should mortify sin, but not God's ordinance in the life of the body. Were there not such a divine element in the life of the body, the words of holy Scripture could not in any way allow the validity of the supposition that it was natural to love the life of the body, the body of this flesh. But Scripture does so, and asserts this

supposition unconditionally. Οὐδεὶς γάρ ποτε τὴν ἑαυτοῦ σάρκα ἐμίσησεν, ἀλλ' ἐκτρέφει καὶ θάλπει αὐτήν, Eph. 5:33. And consequently, what the struggle of annihilation is directed against, is the dominion of sin in the domain of the bodily life. Μὴ οὖν βασιλευέτω ἡ ἁμαρτία ἐν τῷ θνητῷ ὑμῶν σώματι, εἰς τὸ ὑπακούειν ταῖς ἐπιθυμίαις αὐτοῦ· μηδὲ παριστάνετε τὰ μέλη ὑμῶν ὅπλα ἀδικίας τῇ ἁμαρτίᾳ, ἀλλὰ παραστήσατε ἑαυτοὺς τῷ Θεῷ, ὡς ἐκ νεκρῶν ζῶντας, καὶ τὰ μέλη ὑμῶν ὅπλα δικαιοσύνης τῷ Θεῷ, Rom. 6:12, 13, comp. ver. 19. Now, truly, sin in its nature is not yet corporeity or sensuousness, and in the corporeal and sensuous character of an impulse it is not yet in the least implied that it is therefore evil. It is rather the perverted selfish direction of the heart that brings sin into the bodily life, and purification of the soul is therefore at the same time essentially purification of the body from sin. But as primarily the nurture and discipline of the spirit likewise condition the purity of the bodily life, so secondarily there is, besides the spiritual means of this guardianship and discipline of the spirit, likewise a bodily form of guardianship and discipline of the body, which works hand in hand with the purification of the soul. And to the Christian who has actually rendered due obedience to the vocation of grace, is the observance of this of twofold importance, in consequence of the position which, by virtue of the regeneration and conversion of his heart, the seductive might of sin has assumed. There ever comes to light, accordingly, in the physical and dietetic form of treating the body, a spiritual dominion of the soul; but it manifests itself not merely as a reciprocal relation of bodily impulse and spiritual power, but as a discipline and regulating of the bodily life in its reciprocal relations to other bodies and material substances.

(3) In that moral maintenance of the bodily life which bears the form of physical dietetic treatment, and has for its aim the uprooting of sinful desires, the right course of conduct is indicated precisely in this, that the destruction of sin must also be just as much due care of the body, and due care of the body must also be just as much uprooting of sin. Wherever there is

a defect on the one or the other side, there either the pretended care of the body or the pretended annihilation of sin is a moral delusion. In different forms or in different virtues does the pious maintenance of the bodily life show itself, because the bodily life, just as the life of the spirit, has certain fundamental differences in its movements. As the life of the spirit is divided into receptive and productive activity, so also the corporeal life is divided into functions of bodily receptivity and bodily productivity,—the first serving for the preservation, the others for the propagation, of the mixed spiritual and corporeal life of man. In reference to the first, the due maintenance of life is manifested in the virtues of *temperance* and *sobriety*; and in regard to the last, in the virtue of *chastity*. But in both directions the effort at pious self-edification rests on the insight into the unchangeable reciprocal relation of spiritual and bodily states; and the design is to give to the bodily wants and enjoyments on the path of God-ordained satisfaction, as well as of abstinence, that position in which the body, free alike from apathy as from irritation, maintains also for the spiritual state that freedom from apathy and irritation in which alone the soul is enabled to preserve its right receptivity and productivity also for its earthly vocation. That, by this close reciprocal relation of body and spirit, in every act of right treatment of the body a spiritual virtue, and in every physical dietetic mistreatment of the body a spiritual perversity, come to light, is just as little a matter of doubt, as it is indubitable that the ungodly position of man towards his bodily life must be looked upon by the redeemed man not merely as a violation of the dignity and vocation of the spirit, but in the same degree a violation of the dignity and vocation of the body. The so-called cultivation of the spirit at the cost of the body is to the Christian no less an ungodly and wrong thing, than is the care of the body at the cost of the spirit.

Where abstinence and where enjoyment should occur, is dependent on circumstances, in the arrangement of which alike the absolute will of God, which is binding on all, and also His relative will, which is binding on individuals, come to light.

In all cases will this will of God be understood, by considering the individual temporal state and circumstances of the individual, and never independently of them. If, according to the words of Jesus (Matt. 6), our daily nourishment is spoken of absolutely as an object of prayer that will be heard; so, on the other side, there lies in this a testimony that even the satisfaction of the unconditional need of preservation may be accepted only then, when a man can enjoy it as a gift of God, not as a self-chosen plunder. Neither does the limitation to the so-called absolute necessaries in meat and drink make our nurture of the body a Christian virtue, nor does this nurture become a sin through the enjoyment of the so-called superfluities. Everything rather turns on this, whether the limited or the more luxurious satisfaction is actually a gift of God to the individual, and is recognized, accepted, and enjoyed as a gift. Ὅτι πᾶν κτίσμα Θεοῦ καλὸν, καὶ οὐδὲν ἀπόβλητον, μετὰ εὐχαριστίας λαμβανόμενον· ἁγιάζεται γὰρ διὰ λόγου Θεοῦ καὶ ἐντεύδεως, 1 Tim. 4:4, 5. "Before God it makes no difference whether you eat fish or flesh, drink water or wine, wear red or green, do this or that: all alike are the good creatures of God, created for this purpose, that man should use them. Only to this you must look, that you art moderate therein, and abstain as much as is needful for thee, in order to resist the works of darkness. Therefore it is impossible that a man can set down any common limit for this abstinence, for all bodies are not alike: one requires more, another less: everyone must fix his attention on himself, and govern his body" (Luther). It is not in the outward determination of the quantity and nature of the means which serve for the maintenance of life, but in the divinely appointed external life-position, and in the state of the heart towards outward good things (see § 45), that there lies the moral standard for the Christian in this course of conduct. The measure or the care for the body in bodily abstinence, as regards bodily enjoyment, forms a moral element merely as a contrast to *self-chosen* superfluities, and never has absolute, but only a relative definableness, according to the will of God prescribed to the individual in his bodily and spiritual state as an individual. There is an ungodly too little, no less than an ungodly too much, although in general it may be assumed that the predominant perverse tendency of a human kind is towards an excess of enjoyment. The right division of abstinence and observance is therefore the notion of that moderation which recurs in the case of all bodily enjoyment, and therefore in the virtues of sobriety and chastity. When and how far abstinence must take place, is to the Christian ever a matter of that consideration which he makes dependent on the knowledge of his own state, and the leadings of his own life, and their relation to the highest object of his life. There is a free rule in pleasure and love, suitable and adapted to the circumstances and to the will of God which he may learn from them—a species of that ὑπωπιάζειν τὸ σῶμα καὶ δουλαγωγεῖν of which Paul speaks at 1 Cor. 9:27. A legal appointment binding all without exception, or only all members of a particular class, by virtue of which, either for all at a certain time (*e.g.* the injunction to fast), or for individuals throughout their life (*e.g.* in the forbidding of marriage), abstinence is made a legal necessity, is, altogether irrespective of the false legality and mechanical character (*Werklichkeit*) which clings to it, to the Christian a mere chimera, in so far as it shoves into the place of the true will of God, which is to be discerned in the circumstances of individuals and the leadings of their individual life, a self-invented law, which each one imposes on himself or allows others to impose on him (comp. § 52 on Marriage). The end to which the due preservation of the body conduces, is the qualifying of the soul in its earthly vocation, in which it seeks to subserve the aims of the kingdom of God, as well as the aims of earthly society. Only this is the peculiarity of Christian virtue, that here also it has its living impulse, not in the relation of the means to the attainment of the end, but in this, that the opposite vices are to it, as it were, a desecration of that state and of that dignity of which the regenerate and converted man *has already* through grace *become partaker*. See above, 1 Cor. 6:15, 19, 20; and compare 1 Thess. 5:7, 8, Ἡμεῖς δὲ ἡμέρας ὄντες νήφωμεν, κ.τ.λ.; Rom. 13:13, ὡς ἐν ἡμέρᾳ, κ.τ.λ.

Apart, however, even from the vice of desecration of the body, the Christian knows from the observation of his state, that abstinence from bodily enjoyments makes his soul freer for service in its highest concerns; and when in the soul there springs up the need of special urgency in prayer, of increased and exalted contemplation and adoration of God's ways of grace, then is abstinence from bodily enjoyments, as being the course of acting with reference to the body corresponding to the spiritual state, only natural. It is to this that the exhortation and conduct of the apostles refer, in whose case, under circumstances where they were reminded in a special way of the highest relations of life, prayer and abstinence are together brought before us. Comp. Acts 13:3, 14:23. That this abstinence at such times refers not only to meat and drink, but to sexual pleasure, also follows from the very nature of the case, and is further confirmed by what the apostle says to married people (1 Cor. 7:5, Μὴ ἀποστερεῖτε ἀλλήλους, εἰ μή τι ἂν ἐκ συμφώνου πρὸς καιρὸν, ἵνα σχολάζητε τῇ προσευχῇ· καὶ πάλιν ἐπὶ τὸ αὐτὸ ἦτε, ἵνα μὴ πειράζῃ ὑμᾶς ὁ Σατανᾶς διὰ τὴν ἀκρασίαν ὑμῶν. But with equal clearness does it also follow from the words and examples of Scripture, that bodily abstinence is not to be thought of as a condition of the praying disposition in general, but as the suitable and necessary consequence of those special circumstances in which the soul feels itself summoned to singular elevation of spirit towards God, whether in consequence of more arduous inward or outward conflicts, or whether in preparation for important and very responsible transactions. To the apostle, who looks upon the Christian's life as an *unbroken and continuous state of prayer*, abstinence could not appear as a necessary condition of prayer; and the less so, since he also allows of *no enjoyment* being valid *which is unaccompanied by prayer and thanksgiving*. See above, 1 Tim. 4:4. Wherever, therefore, abstinence comes not as a natural consequence of special admonitions of God to our hearts (μὴ δύνανται οἱ υἱοὶ τοῦ νυμφῶνος πενθεῖν, ἐφ' ὅσον μετ' αὐτῶν ἐστιν ὁ νυμφίος; ἐλεύσονται δὲ ἡμέραι ὅταν ἀπαρθῇ ἀπ' αὐτῶν ὁ νυμφίος; ἐλεύσονται δὲ ἡμέραι ὅταν ἀπαρθῇ ἀπ' αὐτῶν ὁ νυμφίος, καὶ τότε νηστεύσουσιν, Matt. 9:15), there either it has a significance merely as a dietetic means, and is to be observed or given up, according as abstinence or gratification makes the individual fit or not for the fulfilment of his calling; or abstinence becomes, as being an outward legal work or as a piece of display, moral hypocrisy, and is, as spiritual corruption (as *e.g.* that fasting which Christ mentions), to be rejected (see Matt. 6:16–18). But it is to be rejected not only as a spiritual perversity; but when abstinence bears the character of a self-enjoined (not of a divinely appointed) violation of that fostering care which is due to the body, then is it objectionable even in this, that it is a relentlessness toward the body (ἀφειδία σώματος). This point appears as specially worthy of notice in Paul's censure of the Colossians in Col. 2:23. This alone is, as a rule, ever the general significance of corporeal abstinence, that it watches against the *dominion* of corporeal enjoyment over the soul. Wherever the end of life is sought in bodily pleasure, and all satisfaction, like that of animals, resolves itself into this (Luke 12:19; Jas. 5:5), there the body has become the idol and tyrant of the soul, instead of forming its vessel and instrument. Ὧν ὁ Θεὸς ἡ κοιλία καὶ ἡ δόξα ἐν τῇ αἰσχύνῃ αὐτῶν, οἱ τὰ ἐπίγεια φρονοῦντες, Phil. 3:19. Besides, in regard to corporeal enjoyment and corporeal abstinence, the Christian is further accompanied with the special consciousness, that here he is coming into a special conflict with worldly sentiments, so as never to be understood by the world, and to suffer under this misunderstanding. For that worldly frame of mind which loves nothing but enjoyment, but yet at the same time knows such enjoyment only as something profane, is wont either to see only in abstinence a kind of holiness, and to laugh at the truth of a holy enjoyment; or it finds in abstinence a something to laugh at, because to it corporeal enjoyment alone is of any value, and it thinks nothing of holy enjoyment in abstinence. Ἦλθε γὰρ Ἰωάννης μήτε ἐσθίων μήτε πίνων· καὶ λέγουσι· Δαιμόνιον ἔχει. Ἦλθεν ὁ υἱὸς τοῦ ἀνθρώπου ἐσθίων καὶ πίνων· καὶ λέγουσιν· Ἰδοὺ, ἄνθρωπος φάγος καὶ οἰνοπότης, τελωνῶν φίλος καὶ ἁμαρτωλῶν, Matt. 11:17, 18.

In regard to the sexual relation of the body, and the virtue of *chastity*, it is first of all merely to be repeated, that here also the virtue is not abstinence, just as if the sexual relation and sexual enjoyment were sin, but that Christian virtue appears in that moderation which—ever according to the will of God with respect to the individual, discernible in the state of the individual, in the course and leadings of his life—aims at this, holily to fulfil, only within the divinely appointed ordinance of marriage, the destination of the body, alike in abstinence and in the enjoyment of sexual delight. Comp. further remarks on marriage in § 52. Unchastity there begins, where a man does not respect the divine destination of the two sexes for each other, according as it is to be thought of, within the limits of sexual maturity and fitness of divinely ordained wedlock, and of that measure of enjoyment which preserves the fitness for the vocation of marriage—where a man does not sanctify, but overthrow in thought, word, and work, this divine destination of the two sexes for each other, and the ordinance of its fulfilment. Of the greatest importance for the right management of self, is the knowledge that all unchastity is primarily a *perverted direction of mind and heart*, which leads astray the natural impulse to objects opposed to God's will (ἐκ τῆς καρδίας ἐξέρχονται ... μοιχεῖαι, πορνεῖαι, κ.τ.λ., Matt. 15:19). Spiritual regimen secures more than bodily regimen against unchaste desires; and the potency of the bodily instinct may have long ceased, while unchastity of thought still holds the spirit in bondage. *It is not through bodily old age that a man becomes chaste, but through conversion of heart*. On the other hand, it is equally as important to observe how the strength of the natural bodily instinct becomes the substratum of the perverse direction of the heart; and this strength is conditioned not only by the acting of the spirit towards the body, but also by the physical dietetic treatment of the body. Christian piety, on this account, will practically realize the virtue of chastity no less in the right management of the body than in the right management of the spirit (τῆς σαρκὸς πρόνοιαν μὴ ποιεῖσθε εἰς ἐπιθυμίας, Rom. 13:14). The progress of aberration from thought to word and deed remains true also in reference to sexual sins. The more, however, that the spiritual foundation of bodily sexual aberration becomes clear to the Christian, so much the more carefully does he disallow himself even the name of what is shameful. Πορνεία δὲ καὶ πᾶσα ἀκαθαρσία μηδὲ ὀνομαζέσθω ἐν ὑμῖν (καθὼς πρέπειν ἁγίοις)· καὶ αἰσχρότης, κ.τ.λ., Eph. 5:3, 4. Only in such wise is the life of a Christian a νεκροῦν πορνείαν, ἀκαθαρσίαν, πάθος, ἐπιθυμίαν κακήν, Col. 3:5. In like manner, there is a distinction between the act of sin and the continuance in it: those whose life, pursuit, and practice is fornication, adultery, and other kinds of impurity, have no part in the kingdom of God (1 Cor. 6:9, 10; comp. Eph. 5:5). But even the act of fornication is, especially in reference to the life of the body, pregnant with special evil for a Christian. For this act is most properly prostitution of the body and of the bodily life in its holiest relations,—a breach of the communion between the body and Christ, the Lord and Head of the body,—a surrender of the body to the power and the corporeal and spiritual influence of the author of sin,—a surrender in those organs which have the divine destination, in a holy order and in a corporeal way, to keep up the race for God. Excess in eating and drink, on the other hand, is a prostitution of the soul, in the withdrawal of the spiritual strength and spiritual consciousness,—a putting to shame of the might and rule of the spirit. Therefore Paul says of the body, which he calls a member of Christ: ἄρας οὖν τὰ μέλη τοῦ Χριστοῦ, ποιήσω πόρνης μέλη; ... Πᾶν ἁμάρτημα, ὃ ἐὰν ποιήσῃ ἄνθρωπος, ἐκτὸς τοῦ σώματός ἐστιν· ὁ δὲ πορνεύων, εἰς τὸ ἴδιον σῶμα ἁμαρτάνει, 1 Cor. 6:15, 18. Finally, to the Christian, the doubly horrible character of self-pollution as well as of unnatural impurity, manifests itself not merely in the horror-exciting, pernicious influence on body and soul, but in the utter prostitution and defiance of the divine ordinance, as, especially in unnatural impurity, it can only gain the power over a man who is fallen headlong into the lowest depth of heathen abandonment by God. For that *has* taken place where the unnatural indulgence has become a *propensity* and *passion*—πάθος ἀτιμίας. See Rom. 1:21-27.

(4) A Christian could not be a disciple of the Lord, and an imitator of His example, if in that Christian the maintenance and care of the bodily life were to transform itself into false love of the bodily life, and into false fear of death. On the contrary, nothing makes the heart bolder to meet death, and more joyful *in loyalty to one's vocation to offer one's self to death, than the regeneration to the life of divine love*. For this expels all false love of the creature, although it is the first rightly to open up the sense and the love for the life of this body; and nowhere is death more willingly accepted, than where the eye has been opened to the full glory and significance of this earthly life. But as the climax of all offence against the body and the life of the body, and therein also against the Lord Himself, the Giver of this life, and *of the season of grace vouchsafed in this life*, suicide appears to the Christian, however definitely he of all men regards himself as the master of his life and death (πάντα ὑμῶν ἐστιν ... εἴτε ζωὴ εἴτε θάνατος, 1 Cor. 3:22). For even in this his lordship, the Christian recognizes himself as the servant of Christ (ὑμεῖς δὲ Χριστοῦ, 1 Cor. 3:23); and only where in Jesus' name he can give himself up to death, and can recognize the taking upon himself the danger of death as a divine vocation, does he dedicate himself to it. But every Christian easily recognizes his call by this, that in the final determination something else than his own wish to die decides him. Even the thought of the glory of his reunion with Christ does not allow the apostle to persevere in the expressed wish to die, without immediately recalling the wish, and submitting himself to the will of his Lord (Ἐμοὶ τὸ ζῆν Χριστός, καὶ τὸ ἀποθανεῖν κέρδος. Εἰ δὲ τὸ ζῆν ἐν σαρκὶ, τοῦτό μοι καρπὸς ἔργου· καὶ τί αἱρήσομαι οὐ γνωρίζω, Phil. 1:21, 22). The thought which can alone determine the Christian to meet death, instead of fleeing from it, is this, that on this path he desires to conquer in Christ's name, and to fulfil the will of Christ, according as this will is clearly traced out before him, not in the thoughts of his own heart, but in the shape and circumstances of his vocation, and

that fidelity to it which is required of him. Thus only, in the giving up of life for the sake of the calling and of the will of Jesus, is also the highest act of devotion—an ἀποθανεῖν τῷ Κυρίῳ, Rom. 14:8—a consummation of that which the Lord requires of them that are His, and to which His Spirit in their hearts impels them—to esteem the life in Christ, and the dying in His name and in His vocation, as higher than the life of the body (οὐκ ἠγάπησαν τὴν ψυχὴν αὐτῶν ἄχρι θανάτου, Rev. 12:11; comp. with Matt. 10:39, 16:25). Compare the beautiful description in Minuc. Felix, *Octav.* c. 39 ff., of the significance of the Christian death of martyrdom; together with the correct estimate of the surrender of life by those thirsting after honor and glory, in Tertull. *Apolog. adv. gent.* c. 50, and *Lib. de Martyr.* c. 4.

§ 45. d. The Keeping of Earthly Goods for the Service of the Soul

It is essential to Christian piety to recognize blessings of this life even in other earthly possessions besides the supreme Good. For in this recognition alone lies also the acknowledgment of God's purpose with regard to us men in their possession. Whether these possessions be of a material nature, *i.e.* do not belong to the endowments of nature, or to the personal position of an individual, or whether they consist in the endowments of the bodily or mental constitution of an individual, or in the relative position, sentiments, and testimony of others towards him personally, earthly blessing is to the Christian everything that can be thought of as the property of a Christian, and which, as such, enhances his well-being in this earthly life, without its being the necessary condition of his welfare in his heavenly vocation (1). In this last relation lies expressed already the manner and way in which Christian piety employs itself with reference to these blessings. Here also it is the character of self-denial, and of the subordination of the lower to the higher, in which the Christian desires and possesses earthly good things neither for their own sake nor for his own gratification, but gratefully accepts them as additional gifts and enhancements of his welfare in his earthly existence and vocation, without courting them or desiring them in selfish passionateness, and greedily grasping at them, while he painfully feels the want or loss of them, but still regards the possession or the loss of them as of little moment compared with the possession of the supreme good, the salvation of his soul (2).

(1) To Stoicism earthly good things are something vile, because τὸ ἐκτός. All tragedy paints the trouble of such people as falsely cleave to external things (see Epictet. *Diss.* i. 4, 26, 27, 28, 29; comp. iii. 8, iii. 11). But the notion of the Christian about earthly good, as well as his bearing towards it, is different from the bearing and view of worldly sentiment. Only in this point does he coincide therewith, that besides a supreme good he recognizes other possessions, which are to him really "good things." He does not know anything of a contempt for earthly good things, and of a denial of their goodness, in which the affectation of a perverted heathenish virtue might take delight. But he knows just as little of that wrong estimation of earthly good things, which not merely reckons as good fortune the possession of them by itself, although apart from the mode of acquiring them, and the use made of them, or the bearing and disposition of the possessor, but which also so places earthly good things on a level with the supreme good, that to the possessor the aim of his life is identical with their possession, and with the want or loss of them his life appears to him purposeless. The Christian recognizes earthly *blessings*, because the earthly existence and earthly destiny are to him not merely the scene of devilish apostasy, but also the place of revelation of the creative goodness and kind condescension of his God. Therefore to him "the good things" are really good, not *because* they bring to him enjoyment and gratification, although they do bring this to him, and *although* he does enjoy them, but because in *his* enjoyment and in *his* happiness he can rejoice at the goodness of his *God*. He is bound and must recognize that the earth also is full of the goodness of his Lord

(Ps. 35:5), and he cannot do otherwise than acknowledge this loving-kindness of his God in a multitude of "good things" (בְּכָל־טוֹב, Ps. 34:9–11). But the specific difference of ungodly joy is just this, that the Christian in his enjoyment rejoices in the good things of God, and that he rejoices in the good things only *because* and *so far as* he sees in them the gift *of God*, and receives and uses them as such. Θεὸς ὁ ζῶν ὁ παρέχων ἡμῖν πάντα πλουσίως εἰς ἀπόλαυσιν, 1 Tim. 6:17; πᾶν κτίσμα Θεοῦ καλὸν, καὶ οὐδὲν ἀπόβλητον μετὰ εὐχαριστίας λαμβανόμενον, 1 Tim. 4:4. That element, therefore, which to the Christian forms the distinction between earthly good and heavenly good, is by no means transitoriness by itself. Transitory even are also the good things and gifts of the Holy Ghost; and yet the Christian will not on that account call them earthly good things, nor subordinate them to the supreme good. Nay, even that operation of the Holy Ghost which to the Christian here below is his supreme good, viz. Christian faith, is not one permanent and unchangeable in its form. On the whole, therefore, the Christian does not know of this bad distinction of perishable and eternal, as if here below all that is everlasting did not present itself before him in a perishable form, and as though the eternal and imperishable, simply because it is such, were in itself the good and divine. Or else does the torment of the ungodly become divine on this account, because it is eternal? It is only for this reason that the perishable good things of earth are to the Christian not good things in the same sense as the blessing of salvation, because he can do without them without losing the latter, because they stand out of all direct relation to the blessing of salvation, the possession of which is perfectly conceivable, whether that which is called earthly good is possessed or not. And thus, too, in Scripture it is only where a man seeks to hold earthly good for its own sake to be a good, and in that good thing has not God, and does not rejoice in Him, that the nothingness of this good is indicated by its transitoriness, and set in contrast to the eternal will and being of God. Comp. Matt. 6:19, 20 with Jas. 5:1–3; 1 John 2:17, ὁ κόσμος παράγεται, καὶ ἡ ἐπιθυμία αὐτοῦ· ὁ δὲ ποιῶν τὸ θέλημα τοῦ

Θεοῦ, μένει εἰς τὸν αἰῶνα; and 1 Cor. 7:31, where, too, the warning against *abuse* is supported by allusion to the perishableness of these good things. Thus, because a man may have these good things without in the possession of them possessing God, and because they do not, according to their intrinsic nature, bring their possessor into communion with the eternal being of God, on this account the Christian names them *earthly* goods. It is superfluous to enumerate these manifold earthly good things; it is enough to mention their kinds. Thus the possession which enhances earthly welfare is partly riches; partly bodily strength and beauty, intellectual talents and endowment; partly honorable position in society, fame, respect; partly social, friendly, or domestic intercourse, and so forth.

(2) From this character of earthly blessings it results, that, quite irrespective of their relation to the supreme good—the blessing of salvation—under certain conditions they cease to be blessings for the Christian. This is the case when a good, regarded as the possession of an individual, is really not a gift of God, but has been purchased by transgression and guilt, or when the individual forgets in its possession the Giver, and does not hold and possess as a gift that which is really the gift of God. In another view the possession of such good things becomes a curse, and the good ceases to be *good* for its possessor, if he destroys the relation of that inferior gift of God to the supreme in a false equalizing or making superior, while all of God's earthly gifts are intended only as a friendly guidance of the heart to the eternal good. Τὸ χρηστὸν τοῦ Θεοῦ εἰς μετάνοιάν σε ἄγει, Rom. 2:4. Thus Christian piety will manifest its knowledge of the nature of these blessings in the virtue of that self-denial, where in possessing them one does not desire to have treasures for himself, but to be rich toward God (μὴ θησαυρίζων ἑαυτῷ, ἀλλὰ πλουτῶν εἰς Θεόν, Luke 12:21); where one views the gift as a gift, not as his own property and desert; where one possesses as though he possessed not, since he does not permit himself to become a slave to the possession, and does not divide his heart between two masters,

but, constantly prepared to surrender his possession, strives only to keep God the Giver of these good things in his heart, who, according to His good pleasure, may bestow on us these "adventitious and contingent" blessings, preserve or also take them from us. Matt. 6:24, Οὐδεὶς δύναται δυσὶ κυρίοις δουλεύσιν, κ.τ.λ., οὐ δύνασθε Θεῷ δουλεύειν καὶ μαμμωνᾷ; 1 Cor. 7:29 ff., Οἱ ἔχοντες γυναῖκας, ὡς μὴ ἔχοντες ὦσιν· καὶ οἱ κλαίοντες, ὡς μὴ κλαίοντες· καὶ οἱ χαίροντες, ὡς μὴ χαίροντες· καὶ οἱ ἀγοράζοντες, ὡς μὴ κατέχοντες· καὶ οἱ χρώμενοι τὸν κόσμον, ὡς μὴ καταχρώμενοι: comp. Job 1:21. Not in the arbitrary renunciation of possessions, but in the right administration of the gifts entrusted to us, does the self-denying Christian piety manifest itself. The words of Christ (Matt. 19:21) which demand of the rich young man the surrender of his wealth and the following of Jesus, were neither meant to say that a man by the renunciation of his possessions, *without* the following of Jesus, would become a perfect man; nor, in short, is it their object to require from the youth the outward act of this surrender. Rather is this demand on the man who imagines himself righteous according to the law, and perfect, only meant to disclose the hidden evil of his heart, and at the same time to proclaim for what a man must hold himself prepared in the following of Jesus. *When the Lord commands us* (not when it pleases ourselves) *to give up for His sake even the dearest good He has entrusted to us*—that is the call of Jesus upon us. And this call no man can follow who has sold his heart to mammon or any other earthly good. The heart, however, is sold as soon as a man allows himself to be enslaved by the charm of possession, or of the desire after possession, instead of calmly and patiently giving up the heart to the will of the Giver. Passionate yearning for the possession of earthly good, instead of contentedness with that which (according to our rank and calling) belongs to the condition of our earthly existence, brings corruption, whether the possession is attained or not. 1 Tim. 6:8–10: Ἔχοντες διατροφὰς καὶ σκεπάσματα, τούτοις ἀρκεσθησόμεθα. Οἱ δὲ βουλόμενοι πλουτεῖν, ἐμπίπτουσιν εἰς πειρασμὸν καὶ παγίδα, καὶ ἐπιθυμίας πολλὰς ἀνοήτους καὶ βλαβεράς, αἵτινες βυθίζουσι τοὺς ἀνθρώπους εἰς ὄλεθρον καὶ ἀπώλειαν. Ῥίζα γὰρ πάντων τῶν κακῶν ἐστιν ἡ φιλαργυρία, κ.τ.λ. Ver. 17: Τοῖς πλουσίοις ἐν τῷ νῦν αἰῶνι παράγγελλε μὴ ὑψηλοφρονεῖν, μηδὲ ἠλπικέναι ἐπὶ πλούτου ἀδηλότητι, ἀλλ᾽ ἐπὶ τῷ Θεῷ, κ.τ.λ. Comp. Ps. 62:11. And this is true of every earthly possession. There is no one of them a blessing, which, through the perverted state of the heart, may not become an evil, and of which the loss would not be better than its possession at the cost of the supreme good. Thus, of the unconditional maintenance of that which is called personal honor the Christian knows nothing, simply on the ground that he knows nothing of any honor and dignity which belongs to the person as such, but because he knows only of such as accrues to him as a possession of his heavenly Lord. If in such circumstances honor amongst men also falls to the lot of the Christian, then does he take it thankfully as an additional gift; but as for seeking after honor, or allowing himself to be enslaved by the possession or the attainment of this honor, that means for him to lose the honor which is with God. See John 5:44, 12:42, 43, οὐχ ὡμολόγουν ... ἠγάπησαν γὰρ τὴν δόξαν τῶν ἀνθρώπων μᾶλλον ἤπερ τὴν δόξαν τοῦ Θεοῦ. "In this respect no one sins so much as the most hypocritical saints, who, full of self-complacency, readily boast themselves, or love to hear their own praises, honor, and applause before the world. For this reason it is another work of the divine command, to guard against, flee from, and avoid all temporal honor and praise, and indeed not to seek the making one's self a name, or renown, or loud plaudits, so that every man should speak of us and sing our praise, which is indeed a dangerous sin, and one most prevalent, though, alas! little heeded. Every one, indeed, desires to be looked upon as of some importance, and not to be the least, however little he may be; so deeply corrupted is our nature in its own opinion of self and in its own self-confidence.... Only one holds in the world this terrible vice for the highest virtue. And thus the holy name of God is, through our cursed name—our pleasing of self and seeking for honor—taken in vain and profaned, though it alone ought to be honored, which sin before God is graver than murder and adultery. But its vileness is not so easily detected as that of murder, because of its subtlety; for it is committed not in the gross flesh, but in the spirit" (Luther, *On the Fruits of the Spirit*). How, in opposition to this, the Christian sentiment must shape itself, is shown forth in the words of the apostle: Διὰ δόξης καὶ ἀτιμίας, διὰ δυσφημίας καὶ εὐφημίας· ὡς πλάνοι, καὶ ἀληθεῖς· ὡς ἀγνοούμενοι, καὶ ἐπιγινωσκόμενοι· ὡς ἀποθνήσκοντες, καὶ ἰδοὺ ζῶμεν· ὡς παιδευόμενοι, καὶ μὴ θανατούμενοι· ὡς λυπούμενοι, ἀεὶ δὲ χαίροντες· ὡς πτωχοί, πολλοὺς δὲ πλουτίζοντες· ὡς μηδὲν ἔχοντες, καὶ πάντα κατέχοντες (2 Cor. 6:8–10; comp. 1 Cor. 7:29–31, and § 28).

The loss of earthly property is a matter of indifference only *in comparison with the possession or loss of the supreme good.* Painless it never is. The Christian knows nothing of the stoic apathy; he recognizes in the possession as well as in the loss the hand of his comforting or disciplining Father. Christ has sanctified human tears (John 11:35). His apostle bids us weep with those who weep (Rom. 12:15). Besides, the ever painful want or loss is in *another* sense nothing indifferent, if it is the righteous penalty of our own guilt. Matt. 5:11: Μακάριοί ἐστε, ὅταν ὀνειδίσωσιν ὑμᾶς καὶ διώξωσι, καὶ εἴπωσι πᾶν πονηρὸν ῥῆμα καθ' ὑμῶν, ψευδόμενοι, ἕνεκεν ἐμοῦ. 1 Pet. 4:15: Μὴ γάρ τις ὑμῶν πασχέτω ὡς φονεὺς, ἢ κλέπτης, ἢ κακοποιὸς, ἢ ὡς ἀλλοτριοεπίσκοπος· εἰ δὲ ὡς Χριστιανὸς, μὴ αἰσχυνέσθω, δοξαζέτω δὲ τὸν Θεὸν ἐν τῷ μέρει τούτῳ. But even the loss or want of an earthly blessing in righteous retribution may become a gain, as a chastisement unto repentance, unto salvation. (Compare the motive of the apostolic judgment—chastisement of the flesh for the saving of the soul, 1 Cor. 5:5; and his view of his own suffering in the body, 2 Cor. 12:7.) Only as a means for confirmation in the supreme good does the possession or loss of an earthly blessing become and remain a gain to the Christian. (Comp. also here, as a contrast, the artificial deadness of feeling of the Stoics, in Epic. *Diss.* iii. 3, 14, 16, iii. 22, 13.)

§ 46. B. Self-edification in its Reflex Influence on the Community

On the community an immediate and involuntary influence is exercised by the self-edifying activity in the reproving as well as in the encouraging power of Christian example (1). But the love which springs from the Spirit of regeneration, and is the root of Christian virtue in general, as of piety in particular (see § 38), has the full realization of its strength and freedom only then, when, in addition to the involuntary and unconscious influence, there springs up the free, self-conscious activity for the edification of one's neighbor. The characteristic feature of this operation is that godly purity and righteousness unto which the regenerate man is new created, and in which, according to the measure of the Spirit of Christ that lives in him, in the room of Christ and after the manner of Christ, in Christ's righteousness and in Christ's mercy, he practices brotherly love and universal love, even to the loving of his enemies (2). Besides, out of the concurrent action of many in this frame of mind, there are produced, according to the several aspects of the edifying activity, different common forms of life, in the preservation and furtherance of which that love makes itself known, which in itself is true love of self in the love of God and of one's neighbor.

(1) In the working of self-edifying activity, as in the way of example it exercises an external influence, the regenerate man recognizes not merely a natural and inevitable relation, but a special fulfilling as well of the revealed will of the Redeemer as of that position which Christians have to assume as imitators of their Lord; comp. 1 Pet. 2:21, Χριστὸς ἔπαθεν ὑπὲρ ἡμῶν, ὑμῖν ὑπολιμπάνων ὑπογραμμόν, ἵνα ἐπακολουθήσητε τοῖς ἴχνεσιν αὐτοῦ. In this relation of imitation is also founded that double position, by virtue of which the Christian, like Christ Himself, is to one man the instrument of salvation, to another the instrument of condemnation—to one "the savor of life unto life," to another "the savor of death unto death"—in one and the same testimony bringing forth as well awakening as reproof

and condemnation. Matt. 5:13–16: Ὑμεῖς ἐστε τὸ ἅλας τῆς γῆς, κ.τ.λ., ὑμεῖς ἐστε τὸ φῶς τοῦ κόσμου ... λαμψάτω τὸ φῶς ὑμῶν ἔμπροσθεν τῶν ἀνθρώπων, κ.τ.λ. Eph. 5:8, 11: Ἦτε γάρ ποτε σκότος, νῦν δὲ φῶς ἐν Κυρίῳ· ὡς τέκνα φωτὸς περιπατεῖτε· ... καὶ μὴ συγκοινωνεῖτε τοῖς ἔργοις τοῖς ἀκάρποις τοῦ σκότους, μᾶλλον δὲ καὶ ἐλέγχετε. Phil. 2:15, 16: Ἵνα γένησθε ἄμεμπτοι καὶ ἀκέραιοι, τέκνα Θεοῦ ἀμώμητα ἐν μέσῳ γενεᾶς σκολιᾶς καὶ διεστραμμένης· ἐν οἷς φάνεσθε ὡς φωστῆπες ἐν κόσμῳ, λόγον ζωῆς ἐπέξοντες, κ.τ.λ.; comp. 2 Cor. 2:15, 16. In this position it may come to pass that even from the Christian there proceeds an offence (σκάνδαλον, πρόσκομμα), just as Christ Himself was a stone of stumbling (λίθος προσκόμματος Matt. 21:44; Rom. 9:32 ff.). But to him who gives offence this proves a curse on all occasions, except when the offence is taken at him as a copy of his prototype Jesus. In every other case, and indeed in the proportion in which the bearing of him who gives the offence is a direct contradiction to the word and will of Jesus, that "woe" pronounced by the Lord (Matt. 18:6, 7) applies to him through whom the offence comes. For to take offence is ἁμαρτάνειν εἰς Χριστόν, by going astray with regard to Christ and His truth, by giving up Christian conscientiousness and loyalty of faith; and in this sinning against Christ he participates, who by his guilt causes offence (comp. 1 Cor. 8:12, τύπτοντες τὴν συνείδησιν ἀσθενοῦσαν, εἰς Χριστὸν ἁμαρτάνετε, κ.τ.λ., with Rom. 14:20–23). To remain free from this guilt, and in truth only as an imitator of Christ to give offence, and where in that case the offence is theirs who take offence, means, however, not merely to go forth to meet the world with Christ's word and truth, but also to take up this position also in the self-denying mind of Christ. Even with Christ's word and truth one may give a self-criminating offence to another, if he brings them forward, carries them about, bears testimony to them in selfish and self-pleasing ways, and for selfish ends (ἑαυτῷ ἀρέσκων, Rom. 15:1). Hence also here, along with the possession of the truth and the power of bearing testimony by way of example, the great necessity of watching carefully over one's own position relatively to the truth and its outward attestation.

(2) Already before, it was shown how in the God-born love of the redeemed there was implied that impulse of self-action which leads one to exert influence on, and to share what he has with, his neighbor (comp. § 18). Christian piety therefore cannot, according to its nature, allow the individual to rest merely in the care for his own salvation. Yes, it holds good from the very position of one who is redeemed and translated into the communion of the kingdom of Christ, that, as a living member of a body, he cannot in any way at all care for himself, without this same method of doing so—working at the same time the salvation of his neighbor. And thus the care for one's neighbor does not prove something additional to the care for one's self, but the one is involved in the nature of the other. The most immediate working of this relation appears in the influence of example. There is, first of all, an influence all unconscious to the individual; nay, the force of the example rests essentially in this, that a man takes up this position unconsciously and undesignedly. This, before all else, holds good of the impression of the whole character, of the whole behavior of a Christian, which is effective in the same proportions as nothing of pretension or affectation is perceived, of either the power or the desire of becoming a model. For what the apostle says of himself marks out the character of every true Christian: "Not as though I had already attained, either were already perfect; but I follow after, if that I may apprehend that for which also I am apprehended of Christ Jesus. Brethren, I count not myself to have apprehended: but this one thing I do, forgetting those things which are behind, and reaching forth unto those things which are before," etc. (Phil. 3:12–14.) The genuineness of a Christian consists in this, that he does not consider himself in the whole of the relations of his existence and conduct as an absolutely binding model. This, however, does not exclude the consciousness of his *calling* to be an example; on the contrary, it involves it. For it is just this consciousness of his calling to be a model as a copy of

Christ, which sharpens the Christian's judgment respecting himself. And only in such true self-judgment can a Christian really fulfil this calling as an example. And for this reason the apostle also, in the very passage where he has spoken of the conformity of his conduct to his self-knowledge, immediately exhorts that they and others should become his imitators, and should take heed of those who so walk as they had an example in him and them (Phil. 3:17). Hereby it is at the same time asserted, that with all this accuracy of universal self-knowledge, and the consciousness of one's own imperfection which it supplies in *particular* relations, as well as even in this self-knowledge and the conduct corresponding to it, one can not only be a model for others, but may hold himself up to them as a model, in the way of reminding them, as does the apostle also elsewhere in a series of particular instances in his own person (comp. 2 Thess. 3:7, 9; 1 Cor. 4:16). And this not because he attributes to his position as an apostle a right of setting forth an example, but because he knows that in all these particular instances he has so done what is right, that it may justly lay claim to being of importance as an example to others. For not by virtue of this or that position has any one a right to look upon himself as an example for others; but rather in particular positions a particular *duty* of setting an example to others is implied. And this in all cases where, by the divinely ordained nature of that position, others are directed to emulate and imitate those who undertake such positions,—as, for example, of parents in relation to their children, pastors of churches to their flocks (comp. 1 Pet. 5:3); whence are explained those requirements of the apostle from Timothy (1 Tim. 4:12), from Titus (Tit. 2:7), in which it is not said that they were models by virtue of their official position, but that in that office they were to set an example to the church. This is something totally different from a privilege of one's calling, to be entitled to set himself up as an example to others. Not with this or that position is the prerogative of authoritatively setting forth an example associated; but to all Christians applies the demand

and obligation of exemplary conduct, and to special positions only in a special and exalted manner.

While the fulfilling of this duty of setting forth an example demands before aught else the *practical* proof of Christian character (μήπως ἄλλοις κηρύξας, αὐτὸς ἀδόκιμος γένωμαι, 1 Cor. 9:27), and is and ought to remain the most effective means for wholesome influence on others, especially where the vocation to active exertion by means of the word (particularly in public and in ways which reach the public community) is not the vocation of particular persons, as that of women (in the case of which last class also, in their purely private conduct to their husbands, the force of a right conduct, "without the word," is enjoined upon their hearts, 1 Pet. 3:1), it is self-evident that that other testimony of the Spirit who lives in us—the word, and its influence upon others—cannot be excluded from the ways and means by which, by means of a proper self-edification, we react and have to react upon society. Steadfastness in every kind of good work and *word* the apostle implores for Christians from the Lord (2 Thess. 2:17); exemplary testimony in *word* and walk (ἐν λόγῳ, ἐν ἀναστροφῇ, 1 Tim. 4:12) he requires from his disciples. And a manifestation by word and work is intended, when Peter points out as the vocation of the whole Christian community, and of all belonging to it, to show forth (ἐξαγγέλλειν) the manifestations of power (τὰς ἀρετάς) of Him who hath called us out of darkness into His marvelous light (1 Pet. 2:9). How, then, should not those who are born of the word of truth feel themselves impelled by their word also to point out to others the fountain of life! Only that here also Christian self-knowledge listens to reason, and especially in regard to what concerns public teaching, considers it an evil omen when, without any scruple, Christians in the mass desire to become teachers (μὴ πολλοὶ διδάσκαλοι γίνεσθε, Jas. 3:1). But that which, in reference to bearing testimony by the word for all and at every time, secures, and is intended to secure, for the word the beneficial effect of its working upon others, is that holy "charmingness" of speech which the apostle calls the word seasoned with salt (ὁ λόγος ὑμῶν πάντοτε ἐν χάριτι, ἅλατι ἠρτυμένος, Col. 4:6). This same element which makes the disciples the salt of the earth, must pervade their speech; and that which in themselves conduces to purify and to preserve from sloth, must be also traceable in their external testimony.

This the apostle wishes to make rightly understood by his words, "Let all that you do be done in love" (πάντα ὑμῶν ἐν ἀγάπῃ γενέσθω, 1 Cor. 16:14). But in order rightly to understand it, we must know, like the apostle, that holy love which is born of God. And when Christ says, "All things whatsoever ye would that men should do to you, do ye even so to them; for this is the law and the prophets" (Matt. 7:12), we must first be taught by the law and the prophets that which we have a right to wish for ourselves in the acting of our fellow-men towards us, instead, it may be, of making the measure of our subjective wishes the standard for ourselves and our actions towards others. But that which the law and the prophets would have, is revealed in its fulness in Christ, the Fulfiller of the law and the prophets. And in our inward man it is incorporated in the new man, which is created after God in godly purity (ὁσιότητι) and righteousness (δικαιοσύνῃ) of the truth (Eph. 4:24). But this new nature is incorporated in us by the Holy Ghost, who corrects and disciplines just as much as He comforts us. Where, therefore, our testimony in its outward manifestation corresponds to this relation of the Holy Ghost to us, and of ourselves to Him, there it has its true salt in the union of both elements; but in such a way that both appear supported by the compassion of Christ, who has translated ourselves into the communion with the Holy Spirit. Hence, where the question turns upon the attestation of our *fundamental disposition*, there must, if it is to be of beneficial effect upon our neighbor, everywhere shine forth the tender mercy of Christ which we have experienced in our own case. This is called περιπατεῖν ἐν ἀγάπῃ, καθὼς καὶ Χριστὸς ἠγάπησεν ἡμᾶς, καὶ παρέδωκεν ἑαυτὸν ὑπὲρ ἡμῶν, Eph. 5:2; and is the fulfilment of that exhortation, γίνεσθε εἰς ἀλλήλους χρηστοί, εὔσπλαγχνοι, χαριζόμενοι ἑαυτοῖς, καθὼς καὶ ὁ Θεὸς ἐν Χριστῷ ἐχαρίσατο ὑμῖν, Eph. 4:32; comp. Col. 3:12. But as the merciful Lord displays His saving compassion also in discipline and correction, so also the compassion of His followers would be an evil compassion if it did not desire, where need demands it, to exhibit the godly purity and righteousness of its nature in discipline and correction. (Comp. on this ἔλεγχος, Eph. 5:11, 2 Tim. 4:2, ἔλεγξον, ἐπιτίμησον, παρακάλεσον ἐν πάσῃ μακροθυμίᾳ καὶ διδαχῇ; Tit. 1:9, 2:15.) Thus alone do we remain, with that which as the working of God within us serves for our own self-edification, in our outward witness-bearing the salt of the community. Comp. Luther on Matt. 5:13.

§ 47. a. *The Preservation of the Soul for its Heavenly Vocation, in its Reflex Influence on the Community*

In the influence on others is revealed the right care of one's own soul as regards that subordination in which a man keeps all proofs of a just and merciful love serviceable to the advancement of the soul's salvation as the supreme object (1). Self-denial manifests itself here in the way in which a man has regard exclusively to that which is another's, and makes himself in his method of communication dependent on the spiritual state of that other and his needs (2). Since in this way all activity aims at the restoration of a community which recognizes its bond of society in this supreme end, the right love will realize itself not positively only in the keeping up of all the forms of social piety, but also negatively in this, that it makes its aim the putting aside and suppressing of everything which (be it in the way of personal communication in general, be it in the choice of personal associates, be it in the form of sociality and of common life), as a *spiritual contradiction* to the end of the divine spiritual fellowship, might weaken the mutual confidence in a co-operation towards this supreme object.

(1) As little as does the care of one's own soul shut out the care of other objects in life, but rather involves it, just as little does Christian thoughtfulness for one's neighbor resolve itself

into a care for his soul, which would shut out other forms of carefulness and of showing one's love. On the contrary, one recognizes the false Christianity of a so-called care for the salvation of a neighbor's soul in this, when it is without an active sympathy in the other elements of its well-being. But the non-Christianity of so-called sympathy with our neighbor has in this its characteristic mark, that it either does not think of the soul's salvation at all, or only in the last place. In this lies all the curse of that so-called love which by the worldly mind is lauded as the bliss of fellowship, whereas it is in fact but the sweet poison with which men mutually murder one another spiritually. On the other hand, all hallowing of the fellowship of love, and all the prosperity of that community itself, spring only out of that subordination to the care for the salvation of the soul of all other proofs of love, and from the reference of all proofs of affection to this great end. But to the Christian such acting towards his neighbor is but a transfer and application of his own state and requirements to the state and requirements of his neighbor. That which appears to ourselves as the supreme good, and in which, above all things, we desire advancement, in that shall we also before all else strive to further our neighbor. In such a relation to one's neighbor there reappears in the case of the Christian, in his own way, that which is Christ's relation to the redeemed as ποιμὴν καὶ ἐπίσκοπος τῶν ψυχῶν (1 Pet. 2:25). In this relation every member, in his own way, takes part in that which is the predominant vocation of the life of the Shepherd of the flock, ἀγρυπνεῖν ὑπὲρ τῶν ψυχῶν (Heb. 13:17). Hence the high value which the words of the New Testament ascribe to the success of such solicitude: Jas. 5:20, ὁ ἐπιστρέψας ἁμαρτωλὸν ἐκ πλάνης ὁδοῦ αὐτοῦ, σώσει ψυχὴν ἐκ θανάτου, καὶ καλύψει πλῆθος ἁμαρτιῶν.

(2) The true mutual intercourse for the end of edification of the soul is first of all grounded on this, that we should know the nature and instruments of Christian edification from our own experience. It is not, however, the adherence to the objective nature of what tends to edification, which of itself

alone brings about the edification of our neighbor and of the community. Rather is it, again, the pious, self-denying tone of mind by which the successful influence on the soul of our neighbor is conditioned. And such serving of our neighbor is in an especial manner self-denial; and excludes not only the selfish element of the vilest egoism, vanity, hypocrisy, and the like, but even the selfishness and caprice of good intention, when one directs his eyes only on the end and means, without considering the state of him to whom these means are to be adapted in order to reach that end. The general form of self-denying love, where one does not seek his own, nor consider himself and his own concerns, but his neighbor (μηδεὶς τὸ ἑαυτοῦ ζητείτω, ἀλλὰ τὸ τοῦ ἑτέρον, 1 Cor. 10:24; μὴ τὰ ἑαυτῶν ἕκαστος σκοπείτω, ἀλλὰ καὶ τὰ ἑτέρων ἕκαστος, Phil. 2:4), becomes here a special consideration of what, according to the requirements of each case, may serve for the edification of our neighbor (a considering of the οἰκοδομὴ τῆς χρείας, Eph. 4:29; comp. Rom. 15:2). This considering of what is required, is not, however, by any means waiting to see whether perhaps, to him who requires this service for his edification, the service may be agreeable or disagreeable. The exhortation of the apostle to Timothy to be instant, whether in season or out of season (ἐπίστηθι εὐκαίρως ἀκαίρως, 2 Tim. 4:2), applies to all Christians. It is not whether it appears to the other seasonable that is to decide me in serving him; but what concerns me is to know the nature of his necessity, and to assist him according to it, instead of asking whether it may appear to that other to be seasonable or unseasonable. For the true kind of service to one's neighbor is not to be made dependent on the fitness of time, which it is not at all possible to determine, but on the easily recognized need of that neighbor, if we wish in this relation to be and to abide genuine *servers* of our neighbor. (Compare what is said about this in another relation in Matt. 20:26–28.) I can only deny him my aid where I perceive an obdurate resistance to every requirement (comp. Matt. 7:6, 10, 14; Luke 10:10, 11). Otherwise have I in all cases to beg of God that He may enlighten my eyes to the particular necessities of my neighbor, provided I wish to view the edification of a soul in the way of its salvation as a *work of God*, and herein to be God's *helper*, instead of treating it as a work and device of man, and prostituting it by self-devised rushing at it. He who will not run the risk of throwing pearls before swine (Matt. 7:6), of reproving where comfort was applicable (2 Cor. 7:8, ff.; 1 Thess. 5:14), of giving strong meat where milk was necessary (1 Cor. 3:1, 2; Heb. 5:12, 14), and conversely, must permit his spiritually solicitous impulse to communicate to be guided by an insight into the requirements of his neighbor. This is to confer upon others the work of self-edification for the profit of our neighbor and of the community, to act in the spirit of Christ, and after the example of Himself and His apostles. Comp. 1 Cor. 9:19–23, ἐλεύθερος γὰρ ὢν ἐκ πάντων, πᾶσιν ἐμαυτὸν ἐδούλωσα, ἵνα τοὺς πλείονας κερδήσω· καὶ ἐγενόμην τοῖς Ἰουδαίοις ὡς Ἰουδαῖος, ἵνα Ἰουδαίους κερδήσω· τοῖς ὑπὸ νόμον ὡς ὑπὸ νόμον (μὴ ὢν αὐτὸς ὑπὸ νόμον), ἵνα τοὺς ὑπὸ νόμον κερδήσω· τοῖς ἀνόμοις ὡς ἄνομος (μὴ ὢν ἄνομος Θεοῦ, ἀλλ᾽ ἔννομος Χριστοῦ), ἵνα κερδήσω ἀνόμους, κ.τ.λ.

(3) The consciousness, the need, the fact of a mutual connection of the Christian community for the preservation of their souls in their heavenly vocation, calls forth the forms of a social worship of God as their standing expression; and these forms, in a continually reacting influence, maintain and invigorate this social consciousness. The continued existence of these acts of the worship of God from the beginning, and the (from the beginning onwards) uniform fundamental types of the same, prove so much the more significantly the necessary connection of this form of communion with the spirit of Christianity, as no legal injunction summoned them into being (comp. Acts 2:46, 47, καθ᾽ ἡμέραν προσκαρτεροῦντες ὁμοθυμαδὸν ἐν τῷ ἱερῷ, κλῶντές τε κατ᾽ οἶκον ἄρτον ... αἰνοῦντες τὸν Θεόν, Col. 3:16, ἐν πάσῃ σοφίᾳ· διδάσκοντες καὶ νουθετοῦντες ἑαυτοὺς ψαλμοῖς, ὕμνοις, ᾠδαῖς πνευματικαῖς). The cultivation and maintenance of these forms through every kind of co-operation belongs immediately to the vital impulse of the soul really redeemed; and even when contingent

circumstances permit individuals to derive small satisfaction to their personal needs in the common devotion, yet it would be a mere selfish procedure to withdraw under this pretext from the community, whose advancement lies alone in the personal co-operation of individuals. As a rule also, it is only a bad pretext under which a certain unchristian state of the heart strives to impart an artificial quieting of the conscience. When Christ places in contrast to the hypocrites, who ostentatiously display their praying in the streets, him who in his chamber pours out his heart to God in prayer, in this case He as little enjoins on the sincere a realization of their piety only in their chamber, as He forbids their attestation of it before people. For that hypocritical piety which, under the pretence of more exalted need and of special communion with God, proudly shuts itself up in its chamber, and looks down upon the social fellowship of love, our Lord would banish from the Christian churches with similar words to those wherewith it is done in Heb. 10:25, where it was a matter of near concern lest in the forsaking of the church assembly a symptom of apostasy from the faith might be traced. But where, under the notion of special piety, a man considers the common assembly of those met together for fellowship in the service of God as impure, there Luther's words are applicable: "Know, when you see one who is ready to judge and to censure, and who will have such pure perfection in Christians, that the same is only a mere legalist, a hypocrite, and gaoler, and has no true knowledge of Christ. For as among Christians there is no longer any law, but merely love, there is and can be also nothing of judging, condemning, and finding fault; and in that wherewith one judges another, he condemns himself. And as he is without compassion, and has nothing but law before his eyes, so also has he no mercy before God: he has never felt and never tasted what the mercy of God is. As God therefore savors to him, so also does his neighbor savor: both are nothing but bitter gall and wormwood." It is only a communion where is preached a gospel contrary to the "apostle's gospel" (Gal. 1), and which in the form of its assembly acts contrary to the word of the gospel and the spirit of faith, that a redeemed man feels himself moved in conscience to avoid, and even then not in order to shun fellowship, but in order to seek the right one. "For against those who condemn and persecute the gospel the principle does not apply, that my love should feel pity and endure and be patient with false doctrine. What regards faith and doctrine, is not a matter of either love or patience: there I must resist with earnestness, and not give way even a hair's-breadth. Otherwise, where the people do not interfere with the faith, and profess it, although they may be weak in life, I ought ever to be cordial and merciful, not punish, drive, annoy; but allure, beg, entreat, supplicate, bear, and endure. For faulty life does not corrupt Christianity, but rather exercises it; but faulty doctrine and false faith corrupt everything. Therefore in this latter case neither endurance nor pity applies,—nothing save anger, opposition, and extirpation, and yet only with God's word" (*idem*). For not where the multitude is, is the church; but where two or three are gathered together in *His name* (Matt. 18:20). Separating from necessity is something distinct from the separatist principle,—the arbitrary selfish limitation to the gratification of the religious wants of individuals, with a disregard of the principle of fellowship, in which the member willingly resolves, even in case of sickness, to suffer with the body, instead of abandoning it for the sake of its own comfort. "Therefore those are to be reproved who wish so to represent and depict and judge Christianity, and the church's essence and government, as if they ought and must be everywhere free from all fault and defect; or where that is not the case, there can be neither the church of Christ nor true Christians" (Luther). Every separatist principle is, as a principle, unchristian. On the other hand, the cherishing of those forms which immediately express the union of many for the supreme common object, will be, under all circumstances, the attribute and criterion of the genuine Christian spirit, to which individual and universal salvation are a matter of heartfelt and inseparable concern.

(4) The participation in a common fellowship of adoration of the common Lord is, however, only the one immediate form in which in the Christian community that state of mind manifests itself, to which the salvation of the soul is the supreme good, and in which, with this end in view, one endeavors before all things to exercise influence on another. For as in the self-preservation of the soul unto salvation an all-sided discipline of the spirit is associated with it to direct it to this blessing of salvation (comp. § 42, notes), so also in the community the effort after mutual advancement in salvation will necessarily be accompanied by certain social virtues of *spiritual intercourse and interchange*, without which an advancement towards the supreme object of spiritual life cannot be thought of. These are in their nature nothing else than manifestations of that "purity and righteousness of the truth" to which the church of the redeemed is born again (Eph. 4:24). For the Christian their root lies not so much in claims which the person of our neighbor, his personal dignity, or whatever other name may be falsely given to it, may make upon our attestation with respect to our neighbor, as rather in those claims which the grace of God makes on him who is redeemed, in that self-purification to which he knows he is destined, and in that calling to communion with God which connects the individual with his brethren in such a manner that all their mutual rights and demands on each other have their sanction merely in their identical relation to God, and in God's identical relation to them. But in the community, the impulse which has its ultimate origin in the relation of every one who is redeemed to God, manifests itself in a form which conduces to *fashion and maintain a community*. And that fellowship-producing energy which applies to the social possession of the highest spiritual blessing, is maintained only on the ground of that general purity and righteousness of spiritual intercourse, which in the *personal* relation of the Christian to his neighbor excludes everything which militates against the *truth* and *holy love*, and thus alone offers the guarantees that the influence of the individual in the community on the common maintenance

of the supreme good contributes in a truly unselfish manner only to the supreme good, and is not a self-seeking pretext for other ends. This spirit will penetrate alike the *subjective form of communication* and the *subjective choice of fellowship*, as well as the *objective forms of common intercourse*. In everything it will be made manifest, that in the church of the redeemed we desire nothing but purity and righteousness of pure, genuine, spiritual communication; and that which prevents the perfect manifestation of this endeavor is in equal degree the sin of the individual and the sinful state of the community. But it is just this side whose perfect subjugation gives to the active realization of Christian piety in social life its earthly aim and its peculiar form on earth.—Thus the *genuine character* of this intercourse is a constant struggle against falsehood within and without us, with the antagonism between appearance and reality, between that which holds good as truth before God, and that which is held as such by men. And thus the *holy love* in our intercourse is a constant overcoming of a hostile propensity within us and without us, and it wins the shape of a peaceable disposition in long-suffering and placability, by the keeping under of anger, hate, and revengefulness in ourselves, and by bearing with the anger, hatred, and revenge of others. And thus is shaped the fundamental relation of a true spiritual interchange, as an overcoming of evil with good (μὴ νικῶ ὑπὸ τοῦ κακοῦ, ἀλλὰ νίκα ἐν τῷ ἀγαθῷ τὸ κακόν, Rom. 12:21); and only in the penetration of all mutual spiritual relations by this spirit rests the guarantee of that *reciprocal confidence*, without which social furtherance towards the possession of the supreme good is impossible. This does not mean to desire to foster this spirit, to the end that mutual confidence may exist. For it is not the result that is the motive of the conduct. But whether we excite confidence or not, *one thing* is indispensable, that we should cherish the spirit in which alone the guarantee of true confidence rests. Of this security the individual will perhaps first of all experience nothing but the personal love and honor of others, and his confidence will resolve itself into the form of a confidence in persons. In fact, however, the guarantee in such kind of spiritual reciprocity of relation lies not in personal position, but in this, that *this very thing is already the operation and manifestation of the* SPIRIT OF GOD, *whose communion embraces all the relations of the spiritual life, and realizes itself in social life just in the purity of every kind of spiritual intercourse.* For the *lie*, which works the violation of confidence, is in its nature, even in cases where it appears only a sinning against men (ψεύδεσθαι εἰς ἀλλήλους, Col. 3:9), and moves in the sphere of human conditions and relations, a denying of God and His will respecting men,—an offspring of the devil, who from the beginning is a liar and a murderer (John 8:44); and it brings to pass, in the destruction of a fellowship of mutual confidence, a destruction of the divine *basis* of society, which consists not in mutual human confidence, but in truth, in which all men ought to be united (ἀποθέμενοι τὸ ψεῦδος, λαλεῖτε τὴν ἀλήθειαν, ἕκαστος μετὰ τοῦ πλησίον αὐτοῦ· ὅτι ἐσμὲν ἀλλήλων μέλη, Eph. 4:25). To speak from this truth in the communion of God, and before the eye of God, and according to His will with respect to men, and to the things and conditions of men—this is to avoid the lie (κατενώπιον τοῦ Θεοῦ, ἐν Χριστῷ λαλεῖν, 2 Cor. 12:19). Hence also even that (in a certain sense) unconscious entering upon the lie, in repeating slanders and the like, is a result of that lying disposition, in which the heart, instead of rejoicing in *the* truth alone, on whose basis men were to be united, finds a mysterious charm and comfort in that wickedness which infests human society. Hence the designation of those who are born again of the divine truth as ἀποθέμενοι πᾶσαν κακίαν καὶ πάντα δόλον καὶ ὑποκρίσεις καὶ φθόνους καὶ πάσας καταλαλιάς (1 Pet. 2:1). For all is a lie which does not flow from that love which came into the world in and with the truth of God, where man desires for himself and his neighbor before all things the soul's salvation, and has but this one consideration for the highest and final aim of all speaking and acting. (At this stage I have formerly discussed what is called the "necessary lie." I confess that on this point I have become very doubtful, and indeed not only with respect to the nature of my previous argumentation, but with regard to the thing itself. It is well known how variously this question has been treated in the church since the attack of Augustine on Priscillian and the Priscillianists, and also how the subject of what was called the necessary lie was viewed outside the circle of that saving truth revealed by God in Christ; how they limited it to the domain of creaturely human things, relations, and conditions; how they understood the lie as an assertion of the opposite of what was known to be the real state of the case, and sought its extenuation, if not justification, in this, that they assumed a disturbance and disorder of the personal and individual or general relations of society, in consequence of which they could neither admit the right in another to hear from me the actual state of the matter; nor could they discern in my concealment or distortion of the real facts of the case a violation of the duty of love towards this other. And in support of this, they casuistically brought forward as proof a series of partly imaginary, partly actual instances, taken in part from the history of the Old, or even from that of the New Testament. On this domain of casuistry I should not now wish to enter. But antecedently there remains the almost invincible suspicion, whether then, when the question really turns in such instances upon a lie, *i.e.* on an assertion which perverts the actual state of the fact into the opposite, this does not appertain to those evil things which one may not venture to do that good may come of it? [Rom. 3:8.] I admit that there is a distinction, whether I do this sort of thing from a desire and love of lying, or under the supposition of being able only in such a way to ward off evil from others, as perhaps, *e.g.*, in the flight of the persecuted from their persecutors, murderers, hostile warriors, and the like, who desire to be informed by me as to what I know, and of the refuge of the fugitives, or the direction of their flight, and so forth. I should not be justified in such cases in putting such lies on the same footing, with respect to the greatness of their guilt, with those which proceed from a pleasure in and love of lying; but could I assert that they are absolutely not sinful, and that no kind of guilt lies upon them? Let us only examine in how many cases, with the endeavor to avert evil from others, the wish does not also coincide to secure one's self from harm by means of a lie. The above argumentation in favor of that which is called a necessary lie, has only so far something right, as there exists no universal obligation under all circumstances and to every one to declare the truth, *i.e.* the actual state of the case which I in reality happen to know. I am not bound to do so to those of whom I know that their possession of the knowledge of the true state of the matter would only serve for persecution and the attainment of ungodly ends, perilous to the safety of their own souls or those of others, and such as I am in no wise in duty bound to further. This truth cannot be subverted by the strange proposition, that it is a Christian duty under all circumstances and to every one to declare the truth which I happen to know, or the actual state of the case with which I am acquainted. For there equally exists a duty in certain circumstances to withhold it. But withholding it cannot be called lying. Lying it would be only if one desires, in a case where he really knows, and not merely thinks he knows, to assert that he does not know. But silence continues to be truth where one acknowledges that he does indeed know, but does not declare it, because he is under no obligation so to do. Hundreds of cases may be conceived where one indeed, by such a declaration, might bring down an evil threatening another on his own head. But how many cases, where the denial that one knows that which he refuses to declare consistently with his duty, admit of being proved to be justifiable or necessary for the safety of others? As a rule, one puts forward others because he desires to protect himself by a lie, or calls that necessary and morally justifiable which only springs from that prudence which, for the attainment of an end praiseworthy in itself, does not hesitate to employ unpraiseworthy means. To acknowledge this appears to me now, at all events, more dutiful than to devise a state of necessity which might allure us to regard that which in itself is not right as absolutely without guilt. But here we may repeat what we have before said, that such a denial of the truth does not stand, in the measure of its culpability, on the same footing with that lie which springs from an absolutely unchristian pleasure in and love for lying.)

Love, which unites as a bond of *personal spiritual fellowship* the individual to a collective body, has, according to the constitution of the individual as of the collective body, in its continuous and permanent need of renewal, to hold itself prepared for this, that it maintains and preserves its peculiar essence only in constant struggle against hostile powers. For just to this end the power dwells in it of endurance, faith, hope, and steadfast perseverance: Πάντα στέγει, πάντα πιστεύει, πάντα ἐλπίζει, πάντα ὑπομένει, 1 Cor. 13:7. It is not only the nature of the old man, which, as in the individual, so in the collective body, makes itself continually felt here below, but it is also the world's unconverted mind, in which in the world the purity of Christian love must prove itself. And thus the possibility of selfish personal emotion against the person of another in enmity, anger, vindictiveness, is taken for granted even in one? regenerate, but equally only under the expectation of immediate repression, let the wrong of personal offence be on the side of him who is angry because of injustice, or on that of the offender. Comp. Eph. 4:26, Matt. 5:23, with Matt. 6:14 ff., 18:21 ff. There will, moreover, in society on earth never be wanting those who persevere in their personal animosity. (Hence it is said also in Rom. 12:18, εἰ δυνατὸν, τὸ ἐξ ὑμῶν, μετὰ πάντων ἀνθρώπων εἰρηνεύοντες.) But with Christ's kingdom there enters into society, instead of hate against hate, the endeavor to win over one's enemy by kindness (Rom. 12:20); and even where the hostile feeling withdraws itself from such active proofs, there remains for earthly society that great invisible power—prayer, intercession, in short, the blessings which Christians supplicate from God for their enemies (Matt. 5:44 ff.; 1 Pet. 3:8, 9).

This last relation remains under all circumstances, even where *the dissolving of a personal relation must proceed* from the Christian; *and the holiness and purity of his love must display themselves in that chastisement in which by word and behaviour he opposes himself to that tone of mind which shows itself inimical in word and deed, not to the Christian personally, but to the business of his Lord* (compare the following paragraph). That the holy love of a Christian is at the same time, and must be, a chastising love, has already previously been recognized (see § 46); and in this very relation it is the salt which preserves earthly society from corruption. But even in the case where chastisement must take place, since this hostility is not of a personal nature, but has reference to the ordinance of God in the kingdom of nature as in that of grace, the spirit of Christian rectitude practices long-suffering, just as the Christian himself has experienced, and daily experiences, so much of the long-suffering of God. (Gal. 6:1, Ἀδελφοί, ἐὰν καὶ προληφθῇ ἄνθρωπος ἔν τινι παραπτώματι, ὑμεῖς οἱ πνευματικοὶ καταρτίζετε τὸν τοιοῦτον ἐν πνεύματι πρᾳότητος· σκοπῶν σεαυτόν, μὴ καὶ σὺ πειρασθῇς.) Severity increases within the bounds of social life just only in the same measure as in a similar case the individual himself would have cause to double the severity against himself, viz. where the question is not of an isolated fault, a single sin, but of perseverance in sin. (Comp. the increase in the degree of refractoriness and the occurrence of punishment, as Christ indicates both in Matt. 18:15–17, where, in conclusion, it is said, ἐὰν δὲ καὶ τῆς ἐκκλησίας παρακούσῃ, ἔστω σοι ὥσπερ ὁ ἐθνικὸς καὶ ὁ τελώνης.) But it would be a gross error to suppose that the Christian could satisfy himself with punishing the thing itself, and the tendency, but that under all circumstances he could preserve his external personal relations to such an one the same after as before. Rather does the blessing which the Spirit of Christ brings to society rest essentially in this, that in the *choice of personal fellowship* the consciousness of that *true oneness* which ought to unite the community is kept alive by that external *separation* in which the Christian, *so far as it depends on his own choice and is consistent with his calling,* avoids the society of those whose sentiments he has perceived to be objectionable. It is only the want of a Christian tone of mind which can explain as Christian love the seeking and fostering the fellowship of one's *own choice* in a perfectly indiscriminate manner throughout all the world. φθείρουσιν ἤθη χρηστὰ ὁμιλίαι κακαί, 1 Cor. 15:33. And even if the individual supposes that he would himself suffer no detriment, yet is it the Christian common feeling, which on a brother's account cannot endure the thought of giving, by such a choice of companionship to the ungodly tendency of his associates, a certain sanction in the eyes of others. For in the heart's choice of personal intimacy we are wont justly to see an expression of the sentiments of our own hearts. The preacher of evangelical love, the evangelist John, wishes, for example, that no one should receive as an inmate of his house a promulgator of anti-evangelical doctrine, and should treat him as a brother with the Christian brotherly greeting (εἴ τις ἔρχεται πρὸς ὑμᾶς, καὶ ταυτην τὴν διδαχὴν οὐ φέρει, μὴ λαμβάνετε αὐτὸν εἰς οἰκίαν, καὶ χαίρειν αὐτῷ μὴ λέγετε· ὁ γὰρ λέγων αὐτῷ χαίρειν, κοινωνεῖ τοῖς ἔργοις αὐτοῦ τοῖς πονηροῖς, 2 John 10 ff.; comp. 5. Hofmann, *Schriftb.* ii. 2, p. 339). A sower of divisions, who does not desist from rending asunder the unity of the Christian church by his false doctrines, shall, after repeated and fruitless warning, be treated as no longer belonging to the community (αἱρετικὸν ἄνθρωπον μετὰ μίαν καὶ δευτέραν νουθεσίαν παραιτοῦ· εἰδὼς ὅτι ἐξέστραπται ὁ τοιοῦτος, καὶ ἁμαρτάνει, ὢν αὐτοκατάκριτος, Tit. 3:10 ff.; comp. as an example, 1 Tim. 1:20, 2 Tim. 2:17). He who dishonors the name of Jesus Christ by persistent immoral conduct, ought not and cannot be regarded as a member, and all fellowship with him is to be done away with. 1 Cor. 5:11 ff., ἔγραψα ὑμῖν, μὴ συναναμίγνυσθαι, ἐάν τις ἀσελφὸς ὀνομαζόμενος ᾖ πόρνος, ἢ πλεονέκτης, κ.τ.λ., τῷ τοιούτῳ μηδὲ συνεσθίειν. And the consciousness which leads the Christian to such strictness of separation, is no other than that of the holy love which, in such exclusion, neither satisfies pharisaical self-conceit nor exercises heartless severity, but in this means alone recognizes the preservation of the community in holiness (οὐκ οἴδατε, ὅτι μικρὰ ζύμη ὅλον τὸ φύραμα ζυμοῖ; 1 Cor. 5:6), and the possible improvement of the offender (εἰ δέ τις οὐχ ὑπακούει τῷ λόγῳ ἡμῶν διὰ τῆς ἐπιστολῆς, τοῦτον σημειοῦσθε· καὶ μὴ συναναμίγνυσθε αὐτῷ, ἵνα ἐντραπῇ· καὶ μὴ ὡς ἐχθρὸν ἡγεῖσθε, ἀλλὰ νουθετεῖτε ὡς ἀδελφόν, 2 Thess. 3:14, 15). On the other hand also, this most rigid personal separation does not prevent the continuance of that fellowship in which the Christian by prayer and intercession stands even to him to whom, on account of his sin, he must keep at arm's length. For never does even the most severe judgment on our brother amount to condemnation (Matt. 7:1; 1 Cor. 4:5). And it is only the openly manifest, ripe fruit of decided apostasy from Christ, which forms the boundary line of available intercession. On this see § 29, notes.

Out of this spirit alone of holy earnestness and compassionate love, and by nothing else, will be banished from the *forms of social life*, from the words in common use, from common social customs, from common social intercourse, the evils from which society suffers in its spiritual interchange—not only the forms of open or hidden frivolity, of open or concealed grossness of spirit, but above all, the forms of that specious intellectual affluence with which society satisfies itself, while it employs the natural gifts of the Spirit without holy earnestness, and renders the soul incapable of finding pleasure in the two-edged power of divine truth.

§ 48. b. *The Preservation of the Soul in its Earthly Vocation, in its Reflex Influence on Society*

The Christian's regard for his earthly vocation exercises on the prosperity and permanence of the earthly community, first of all, this advantageous influence, that all the forms, rights, and duties in which, within the sphere of man's earthly community, the especial exercise of the individual's activity in his calling has its limits, should be recognized as a divine ordinance. But especially does Christian self-denial display itself in the unenvying higher and lower classification, with which one lovingly recognizes and promotes the aims of the divinely indicated position according to lineage and rank, in their common effort, as well as views and treats in the same light as serving God and serving one's neighbor—the ruling over his fellow-men, or rendering obedience to them. Herein is the Christian sentiment the foundation of all civil order; and in the place of a false equality, it recognizes only one equality of all men before one and the same Redeemer and Judge (1). And in reference to Him, in the social community likewise the recognition of the difference between the earthly and heavenly vocation realizes itself in a twofold manner. First in this, that we acknowledge in general a purely earthly vocation, and the means for its maintenance, answering to its nature as willed by God; and consequently hold sacred that right and law in which the natural arrangement of the earthly vocation of human society finds its external and generally received sanction; and that within the community we strive after the maintenance and promotion of that vocation in a common effort in the way of order and rectitude consistent therewith; but at the same time hold up before the legally established community of our fellow-men, as it promotes the ends of the earthly calling, the cherishing of the communion of grace with Christ as the sole means of a true sanctifying of that earthly vocation, and of a complete solution of its problem (2). Secondly, however, from this recognition of an earthly vocation for human society, in its distinction from the heavenly vocation, springs this blessing for the ordinances of this society which have reference to vocation, viz. that, just by the pure observance of the principles peculiar to both life-domains of human society, by an equally strict keeping alike to the limits on either side as to their alternate mutual relations in all that is called public right and law of human society, nothing is allowed to intrude which would be prejudicial as obedience in the one sphere to that which is obedience in the other; which would distort the true form of the higher and lower classification in reference to both domains; and which, by a false fixing of boundaries and limits, or by a mingling (unsound in principle) of the various laws and duties of life which have their exercise in both domains, might lead to a desire to give currency, as being a claim generally valid, to any requirement as a pretended duty of the heavenly vocation against fidelity in the earthly vocation, or as a pretended duty of our earthly calling against fidelity in the heavenly vocation.

(1) We are here for the present still leaving out of consideration the social community as it is established by civil law, the importance which it has for the Christian in this arrangement, the obligations which it has imposed on him, in so far as here the question does not turn upon the laying down of the ethical significance which national vocation and the positive institution of a legally governed nation has for the Christian; but only upon our statement of what precise importance and effect attach to the Christian's peculiar acknowledgment of the variety of special callings, conditioned by birth, sex, natural and spiritual gifts, as well as by the process of historical development and leadings in life (comp. § 43). For not only from without, but from within, out of the spirit of true Christianity, even the appreciation of the earthly vocation of man's natural social state shapes itself to the Christian. This Christian recognition of the divinely ordered vocation stands opposed to that corruption which springs up in social life from the pseudo-Christian as well as from the antichristian selfishness. The pseudo-Christian selfishness abuses the unity of our fraternal relation in Christ, in order to set forth the differences as they are based by the providence and the gifts of God in the natural and historical development of the human race and of human life, as opposed to Christian equality. The antichristian selfishness knows no law other than that given in the equal struggles and desires of all men; it acknowledges no order arising from God and from God's grace, but only the results of the exertions of men's own strength, whose possible attainment is open to all in the same manner. But, in fact, both these phases of sentiment are only the outbreak of that selfishness where no one is willing any more to serve, but each desires to rule and to subdue. And this selfishness is supported by the assumed notion, that all have

an equal capacity and calling for everything. To this the sentiment of Christian piety and its realization form the direct contrast. It knows, as included in the idea of dominion, the reciprocal one of serving, distinct only in form, according to the higher and lower ordering of rank and vocation. For the placing himself in an inferior rank under the divinely willed honor of others, is in every rank a matter of honor to the Christian: Phil. 2:3, τῇ ταπεινοφροσύνῃ ἀλλήλους ἡγούμενοι ὑπερέχοντας ἑαυτῶν; Rom. 12:10, τῇ τιμῇ ἀλλήλους προηγούμενοι. This unenvying recognition of the honor and claims of the position of others is only the reflex working of that knowledge, in which the individual acknowledges the honors and claims belonging to his own vocation as a divine ordinance. Hence, in the place of a yielding to the claims of others from considerations of prudence or slavish constraint, we have the observance of the common order from *conscientious motives*. Διὸ ἀνάγκη ὑποτάσσεσθαι, οὐ μόνον διὰ τὴν ὀργὴν, ἀλλὰ καὶ διὰ τὴν συνείδησιν, Rom. 13:5; ἀπόδοτε οὖν πᾶσι τὰς ὀφειλάς· τῷ τὸν φόρον, τὸν φόρον, κ.τ.λ., τῷ τὴν τιμὴν, τὴν τιμήν, 13:7. For in the various claims of honor due to rank, vocation, age, sex, it is not a personal demand, but a divine appointment, that is acknowledged. And in this alone lies the guarantee that in social life, by virtue of the tendency of the common spirit, room is given to each vocation for its due fulfilment. For this reason also, in Scripture the arbitrary prevention of the fulfilment of the divinely appointed vocation—as, for example, in the *forbidding* of marriage, the fulfilling of the vocation and proper honor of the sexes— appears as *an apostasy from the faith* on the part of Christians. Ἀποστήσονταί τινες τῆς πίστεως, προσέχοντες πνεύμασι πλάνοις, καὶ διδασκαλίαις δαιμονίων ... κωλυόντων γαμεῖν, κ.τ.λ., 1 Tim. 4:1, 3; comp. with 2:15. But, at the same time, this mutual recognition of the divine authorization of vocation— just because the Christian herein is conscious of serving only God, not men—in serving is free from a base slavish fear of man, and in ruling is free from selfish, wicked tyranny. For by virtue of the consciousness of their unity IN *Jesus Christ* (πάντες

... εἷς ἐστε ἐν Χρ. Ἰησοῦ, Gal. 3:28), and of their equality BEFORE Him as their future Judge (προσωποληψία οὐκ ἔστι παρ' αὐτῷ, Eph. 6:9), the effort of each is directed simply to fulfil in his vocation *the will of God;* and out of the relations of service there vanishes eye-service, pleasing of men (ὀφθαλμοδουλεία, ἀνθρωπάρεσκον εἶναι), and out of those of lordship and command selfish hardness and threatening (ἀπειλή) in the reasonableness of the Christian character (ἰσότης). Comp. the passages Eph. 6:5, 9, Col. 3:22–4:1, on the relation of master and slaves, and its general analogy.

(2) The further blessing which arises to the community from our regarding and fulfilling our vocation in the spirit of a Christian recognition of a divine right in that vocation, consists again in a twofold opposition to a pseudo-Christian and an antichristian view and treatment of that privilege of vocation. The first comes to regard what is said in the gospel of a Christian spirit of patient love, as opposed to the maintenance of the honor and claims of our vocation in the way of right and law; and although they do not actually emancipate themselves from this way, yet they doubt of its Christian character. The antichristian view obstructs the welfare of social life, either by destroying the privileges and honors paid to vocation through practical disrespect, or by abolishing by a selfish use of right and law that order in which right and law are intended to minister to holy love, and earthly order is to be a discipline of training for the ends of the kingdom of God. The pseudo-Christian view is wont, where it is adopted, to take its stand on a misunderstanding of such declarations as those in which Christ contrasts the selfish, vindictive, and unloving employment of right and law with the spirit of patient and anticipating love, as in the passage Matt. 5:39 ff., where it is said that when a man is smitten on the right cheek, he should turn the other also; that in a lawsuit, where one demands a coat, we should give him our cloak also; that when one asks us to accompany him on the road, we are to go two miles with him instead of one, and so forth;—all this instead of appealing to the fundamental principle of the divine law of punishment, "an

eye for an eye," and the like. Here, therefore, instead of recognizing, in accordance with the connection of the whole discourse, a testimony of our Lord against the improper and selfish application and transfer of the righteousness of the law to the relations of personal fellowship, a contrast between *pharisaical and God-pleasing sentiments*—in brief, between the *selfish nature* (considering only its *own* rights) and *love*—they saw in it a *contrast* between the *law* and the *gospel*,—an entire abrogation of the first, and its power on earth, by the entrance of the second. But then as to the reason why, notwithstanding, the father, the guardian, the judge, and so forth, could not be expected, on receiving the first blow on their cheek, to offer to the child, the ward, the appellant, their cheeks for the second—this remained under this view perfectly undetermined. One places himself as an evangelical Christian, according to the state of circumstances, under the dominion of a law (as was alleged) unconditionally abolished, and acts contrary to the alleged words of the gospel, but yet wishes still to have the reputation, in addition, of interpreting in an especially rigid and holy manner the words of the Lord! Free from such a misconception—whose stern, consistent carrying out would destroy all discipline and order, all permanence of divine justice on earth—the Christian view secures the prosperity of the collective body, by recognizing as the fundamental object of the earthly vocation the maintenance of the justice of God and of His administrative righteousness on earth; the guardianship and preservation of the rights of vocation by the power of the law; the warding off and punishing their violation in a legal way; and the not mixing up of the personal communion of grace, and its external attestation and manifestation, with that divine and legal determinativeness in which the nature of man and his earthly existence, in the individual as in the collective body, are found, and for whose free and perfect *fulfilment* the spirit of evangelical freedom and love will only qualify us, instead of *destroying* right and law under the title of freedom and love. Nay, even the apostle suffered in his person and in his civil vocation no violation of his rights, and protested against it in a legal manner (Acts 16:37, 22:25, 25:10, 16). In like manner will he have judges appointed by the Christian community for the maintenance of civil right (1 Cor. 6:1 ff.). And while the Christian thus accurately distinguishes the domains and relations of life, in which God's righteousness and God's gracious compassion, each by itself, have their complete and definite manifestation, his mode of thinking alone secures the permanence of earthly society for the ends of its existence on earth. But since he acknowledges the subordination in which the social state on earth promotes the kingdom of God, the earthly vocation promotes the heavenly one, the fulfilling of his vocation promotes the exercise of divine righteousness, *and not his personal selfishness*, he thus guards himself against the abuse of right and law, the failing in the highest aim, and the falling away into an evil state of mere legality. For only where Christian public spirit prevails, does one understand where the question turns upon personal relations, and he has to forego his rights in love; and where the question turns upon his vocation, and he has to exercise holy love in maintenance of his rights, and in the form of legal justice. Herein alone appears the complete application of those words of Christ in Matt. 22:21, ἀπόσοτε οὖν τὰ Καίσαρος Καίσαρι· καὶ τὰ τοῦ Θεοῦ τῷ Θεῷ. Then in both cases neither the object rendered, nor the form of rendering, is one and the same; but the spirit that in both cases enables us to render it rightly, is one and the same—the spirit proceeding from God. For, above all, it becomes possible for the Christian only to understand in a right and complete manner—from his insight into the specific difference of his own heavenly vocation and his human and earthly one, and into the inseparable mutual relation nevertheless subsisting between the two—that which is called man's earthly vocation with respect to the race of man, to a popular community, to the politically ordered commonwealth. It is for him a matter of absolute impossibility to confound that which belongs to Cæsar with that which belongs to God (Matt. 22:21). He cannot be brought to regard the fundamental conditions, the moving powers, and the forms of realization, the ultimate aims of the kingdom of God, as identical with those which determine the peculiar shape and task of the kingdoms of this world. The Christian knows that Christ's kingdom is not of this world (John 18:36): the kingdoms of the earth, however, are of this world, and for this world. The sphere of dominion and the means of that dominion in the kingdom of God, are essentially different from those in the kingdoms of this earth: the sovereignty and the exercise of power take place and are accomplished in the one domain by other instruments and for other aims than in the other (Matt. 20:25; Mark 10:42; Luke 22:25). That which builds up and preserves the kingdom of God consists of divinely established and divinely furnished means and powers of the grace of God in Christ; but the political ordinance is for the Christian a human creation (1 Pet. 2:13), serving men for the ends of their earthly calling, and securing their fulfilment by right and law, by the authority which right and law bestow upon them. This is the difference. And yet again, with all this difference, an analogy and connection. For that which is called man's creation, because it attains its external form by man's own energy, is for the Christian no less founded in its ultimate ground on the will of God with respect to the human race. The systematic organism which also lies at the base of political communities and their order, manifests itself in the variety of the objects of earthly vocations; and their exercise is no thing of human devising, but the result of the will of the Creator, and the creative endowment of man's race for the fulfilment of its collective vocation on earth. This natural basis of all human society on earth is nowhere the result of the coming together of men; but they find this as a pre-existing act of their divine Creator, in order from it to develop in human creation ordinances whose object is the preservation of the divine purpose of creation by right and law. For there exist no form and maintenance of earthly *social* life except in the form of right, which regulates by the obligation of law the external order and shape of social life, and the external or practical conduct of the individual with respect to the collective order.

And as in the kingdom of grace it is not the isolated vocation of single members which in itself bears the law of the whole body, but the whole body, and the conditions of its spiritual life and its spiritual health appointed by God, form the supreme law of the conduct of its individual members; so also in the political order it is not the particular privileges and the particular will, not the individual task and the individual vocation, but the collective task and the collective vocation, public and general right and law, that form the supreme rule of the conduct of its members. Nowhere, however, does it attain such form of order merely by man's pleasure; but everywhere it is a natural created gift, and a working of God's providence in the history of nations, by which alone it becomes possible for a people to estimate rightly its vocation as a people, and to create by human energy those ordinances which serve for securing its vocation. Thus, since for the Christian all that is meant by order of political communities, establishing of the earthly calling in man's social state, is traced back by him in its ultimate origin likewise to God, to the divine will, to divine bestowal, and to a divine government of the world, he has also found the point of union in which both ordinances on the domain alike of creation and of new creation exist on earth for each other, and unite together. For he knows from this source, that only when he belongs to this God, and gives to this God what belongs to Him, viz. himself and his whole being and life, can he be and render to Cæsar, *i.e.* the worldly and natural order, that which he ought to be and to give to it. In this consists the moral perfection of the *individual*, in his obedience to the rights and laws of the commonwealth. And if the fundamental law of those ordinances which serve the ends of man's natural social state rests upon the immutably ordered, creative, and yet creaturely endowments of the human race, and is established by men in forms of human right and law as a recognition of this will for the object of its maintenance, then the Christian neither rejects this as something purely human, nor does he make of this community with its rights and laws in itself an authority to legislate in the kingdom of Christ and of

His grace; but he knows, indeed, that the *spirit* of true fulfilment even in the domain of this creaturely human society comes only from the Spirit of grace, whom he has obtained as a citizen of the kingdom of Christ, and according to the vital law of this kingdom. To reverence as holy the earthly vocation of the race of man, and of the special social community, is not less an affair of the Christian, than to seek the right strength for such reverence in the communion of Christ's kingdom, in which he has his proper and permanent home, and the source of all genuine godly realization of life (comp. § 54).

(3) The blessing of this Christian public spirit fixes itself in the earthly community by penetrating the natural and historical forms of society—in the family, the nation, and the state—and here reacting against everything which might be in a position to disturb the solution of the problem of our earthly vocation, and the pure relation of our earthly calling to the heavenly one. This common spirit will regulate by common habit, common custom, and common right, the natural relation of rest and labor, and will lead back the requirements of those who command, as well as the services of those who obey, in their labors and in their rest, to the true standard, excluding alike that excessive rest which is contrary to the duties of the vocation, and that excessive labor which puts it to shame. The permanent type in this matter is that of the six working days and the one of rest in the week (comp. § 43, note (3)). The same common spirit will, in common habit, common custom, and common right, guard the relation of the earthly vocation to the heavenly from a false position with respect to each other, by keeping pure the reciprocal principles and the appropriate standard for their realization. It will permit no common custom and no common right to intrude and fix itself where we might desire to make the obedience to the master of our earthly vocation a principle of conduct in our heavenly vocation, and might perhaps desire to make the nature of our conduct towards God in our heavenly calling, the substance and attestation of our faith, dependent on the command of an earthly master and the order of things in our earthly vocation.

By virtue of the same spirit, no common custom and no common right will be able to gain a standing which should fix for the individual a degree of activity in the one vocation, which either entirely or in its true measure and proportion should do away with our energy in the other, as perchance a form of earthly obligation to our calling which should exclude the pious manifestation of care for the soul in our observance of the social worship of God either altogether or out of its true proportion, or a form and custom of devotional practice and churchly piety which should stand out of just proportion to the measure of exertion in our earthly vocation. And in place of all false forms of society in which the relations of both vocations fall into a spurious *confusion* or *independence*, out of the common spirit of Christianity there will spring forth those common forms which clearly display the *mutual adaptation* of the earthly and heavenly vocation, and render attainable a just realization of both callings as well for the individual as for society. (Compare further, § 51 ff.)

§ 49. c. *The Preservation of the Body for the Service of the Soul, in its Reflex Influence on the Community*

The view the Christian takes of the body and the bodily life is—alike in the care which is the result thereof, in the discipline and restraint belonging to it, and finally in its perception of the obligation of sacrificing the bodily life under certain circumstances—a blessing for earthly society. In one relation this becomes manifest in the setting up and maintenance of praiseworthy customs; in a second relation, in the recognition of a legal claim which the earthly and human society (as the supporter and administrator of divine right and divine righteousness) has upon the bodily and earthly existence of the individual, no matter whether it demands the surrender of the same as a self-offered sacrifice for the common good, or whether it imposes that surrender in punishment affecting the body and its life, as an atonement for very heinous transgression committed against those blessings entrusted by

God to the legal protection of the earthly community. From the care for the body, and from the restraining of the lusts thereof, there spring those forms of society and of social life, which, as common customs, partly exclude the occasions for excessive excitement of a mixed mental and bodily nature, and for a mixed mental and bodily stupefaction in feasting and banqueting; which partly also banish not only the acts of mutual sexual pollution, but also the temptation thereto in the common observance of external decency, and in the etiquette of society; and, finally, which partly also, in a positive shape, in social institutions for instruction and education, devote attention to bodily training, and thus tend to promote in the health of the body that also of the soul (1). But as a second thing, the Christian knows already—from the cheerful readiness for sacrifice in which he is prepared, for his confession of Christ and His kingdom, to give up life and limb (§ 39, note (3), towards the end), as well as in the subordination of his own individual existence to the collective aims of the earthly problem of human society, and to those privileges of law and authority entrusted (in accordance with the divine will) to this society for the securing of its common task—that he cannot make the preservation of his own individual bodily life hold good against higher and legally grounded claims to it on the part of the community (as, *e.g.*, in the case of war), nor regard his right to this bodily life, when forfeited by offences, as a possession, of which the divine right of punishment in force in the earthly society, and to be carried out by human agents called thereto, might not be entitled to deprive him. In both cases the Christian subordinates the bodily life to those higher ethical aims for whose maintenance human society on earth has a divine authorization: in the one case for the security of the earthly rights of public society when threatened by illegal violence; in the other case for satisfaction to that penal justice of which the ordained authorities of the same society are the executors (2). But as the Christian acknowledges no right in the individual as such to do violence to his own life by his own act (§ 44, note (4)), but only knows of a duty of love to sacrifice his own life to save that of others in case of need, so does he also deny the right to the individual as such, of his own arbitrary will to abandon his own life to the hazard of death through others, or to threaten that of others with destruction, except that he has, in the absence of the ordained authorities of the general vocation, or in case of the absolute impossibility of the interference of these authorities, to represent in his own person the right and power of earthly society against unjustifiable assaults on person and life, and to resist such unjustifiable acts of violence by a justifiable exertion of force in defense (3). For in these also, as in the previously mentioned cases, it is proved to be for the guard and protection of that legally established order of things which must be maintained in society, that we should recognize the fact that the higher ethical ends of the earthly community, the preservation of the bodily life of the individual both in respect to his own person and to that of others, is to be subordinated to the higher ethical ends of the earthly community; and in general, that preservation of the life of the body is not the ultimate end nor highest good of earthly existence, in the securing of which the vocation and duty of the individual to that earthly society, or the vocation and duty of society to the individual, should be wholly comprised.

(1) In every human society there exist social forms for the care of the body and the augmentation of bodily well-being, in which not only the spirit of the community is reflected, but whose existence also reacts in turn upon the form of this spirit. That which is called social enjoyment forms one side of these. Now the Christian sentiment recognizes, above all, neither in the fact that they are connected with bodily well-being, a something in itself bad; nor in this, that they are intended to contribute to the care of the spirit, anything in itself good. At least neither here nor in other relations does the Christian spirit, which sets its seal on the form of true Christian social life, start from the bad opposition between soul and body in its estimation of the value of the forms of Christian society, *i.e.* from that depreciation of what relates to the body, in

opposition to a recognition of the importance which the body has of itself as being that organization which supports the spiritual life of the soul, and here below conditions its actual state (§ 5, note (5)), and of what it signifies to the Christian as being the receptacle of the soul, which has become a partaker of fellowship of the Holy Ghost (§ 44, note (1)). For although the Christian calls that which ministers to the body, and whose aim is bodily pleasure, in so far the inferior, as the Christian, for the *ethical* quality of his will, has the power of his self-determination not in the body or bodily well-being, but in his spirit, which the Spirit of God has laid hold upon; and although, consequently, that which serves for the care of the soul must, in his view, stand in a higher position than that which tends only to the care of the welfare of the body,—yet in the care of the soul the important point is not that it has the *soul* for its *object*, but *of what character* the *care* for it really is. And again, the value of our care for the soul is not measured by the degree in which it abandons all consideration of the body, but by this, whether this care is so constituted that it does not oppose itself to the divinely appointed care of the body. When, therefore, we are engaged in determining the value of common customs of mutual intercourse, in which we may conceive them as distinct in their form, according to their relation to bodily or spiritual well-being, it is not in the formal relation by which they are distinguished that their higher or lower value or worthlessness lies, but in the quality of that which is called *care* of bodily or spiritual welfare. For the right care consists in the maintenance of those material relations on which the normal relation of body and soul to each other depends, and on whose basis not the soul or the body, *i.e.* an abstraction in this shape impossible to be thought of, but the entire mixed spiritual and bodily life, is subordinated, and ought to be subordinated, to the ends of the general-human as of Christian culture and improvement. If we apply this to the common customs and forms of social intercourse, it does not naturally follow from this, that in every single instance the form of intercourse can only then be justified when it equally directs its attention to bodily and spiritual welfare, as if perchance in any sense the meeting together for purely spiritual intercourse were inadmissible without bodily enjoyment. But this follows therefrom: that Christian sentiment puts up with no kind of social customs and forms of intercourse wherein bodily welfare should be so cared for, that it should become inimical to the preservation of the body in holiness, the care of the spirit, and the concern for the soul. If, therefore, forms of sociality exist whose shape has a preponderating relation to the bodily phase of existence, this is equally as inoffensive to the Christian sentiment as its eating and drinking, and so forth, are inoffensive; and this alone need be a matter of offence to it, if this form of sociality were that which predominated over social intercourse generally. "The saints, especially when laden with tribulation and sorrow, may well revive and delight themselves in bodily fashion, inasmuch as Scripture says (Prov. 31:6), 'Give wine unto those that be of heavy hearts;' also, 'Wine makes glad the heart of man' (Ps. 104:15). For to this end ought good cheer to be especially directed to make the heart joyful, and to revive the spirits again after trouble. For God is an enemy to sorrow; neither can the heart oppressed therewith either praise God or thank Him. For this reason let this text be well considered (Gen. 21:8) against gloomy and austere hypocrites" (Luther on Gen. 21:8). But, in general, it is not the measuring out the more and the less of those relations in which the form of sociality inclines either to the spiritual or the bodily side of our existence, but it is the specific relation of the bodily life and well-being of the body to *the service of the soul in its earthly and heavenly calling*, from which the Christian spirit penetrates the forms of social life, and gives them their true scope and measure. It will no less react against that spiritualistic mode of appreciation in which mutual intercourse is allowed to be legitimate only in so far as it serves, as they are wont to say, for the satisfaction of spiritual wants, than it will oppose itself to those socialities established under the pretext of taking care of the body for purely sensual and corporeal gratification, in which not the body, but the sinful flesh, is fostered, and by common custom both the bodily and spiritual existence are thrown into disorder. And here, moreover, it is far from being the forms of rude intemperance only in which sin against the body is effectively accomplished, but not less those forms which in a more refined and hidden manner attract the thoughts and senses to the profanation of the body, and plunge men, with respect to their earthly and heavenly calling, into a mixed spiritual and bodily sluggishness, indifference, and apathy. For according to the character of mind and susceptibility, more refined debauchery corrupts the morals of society in the same manner, and often more, than the indulgence of open and gross intemperance (κῶμοι καὶ μέθαι, Rom. 13:13; comp. Luke 21:34). And wanton attire (Prov. 7:10, in contrast with καταστολὴ κόσμιος, μετὰ αἰδοῦς καὶ σωφροσύνης, 1 Tim. 2:9), wanton gestures (Prov. 6:25)—in short, that phase of conduct which the Germans (since they no longer call things by their right name) have named coquetry (*Koketterie*), and which constitutes the soul of so many social forms—eats its way in certain circumstances, more deeply and more unobservedly into the heart, and allures the body to sinful concupiscence, than keeping company with open and complete shamelessness (those κοῖται καὶ ἀσέλγειαι, Rom. 13:13), because companionship of this latter nature repels the finer feelings; but the former nuisance more easily ensnares, by the refinement of its mode, even those of refined feelings. To such nuisances in society and general habits the Christian sentiment puts a stop, as before said, not by sending us off to the spirit and the care of the spirit, in the general sense of the word (as if in the history of nations the periods of the greatest wealth in human intellectual culture did not oft enough coincide with those of the greatest profligacy); but this [same Christian] spirit, which is a spirit of sanctification of the mind as well as of the body, will oppose in the community the right forms to the evil forms of corporeal enjoyment, since it redounds to the honor of a community, in its customs and social practices, to care in its pleasures and discipline, by the strengthening and tempering of the body, for its due excellence. In the last relation I here expressly include that which is incumbent on human society not only in the form of social enjoyment, but as established means of training and exercise for the care of bodily qualification. The error so long indulged by that spiritualistic depreciation of the body in the name of a one-sided and therefore erroneous culture of the mind, ought not to be pronounced good in the name of Christianity, nor ought we to oppose its suppression from a perverted view of Christianity. We can in reality only do so if we either place Christianity out of all connection with man's qualifications for his earthly calling, or if we are ignorant of the bodily conditions of a sound and fresh state of the mind, or if we are averse to bodily exercise because perverted forms thereof, or a perverted and exaggerated estimation of their value, exist. But who has ever rejected anything commendable in itself on account of its abuse, or because it has been wrongly lauded? Let one provide for the proper form of such exercitation, and for a just and commensurate recognition of its utility—this becomes a Christian, instead of rejecting the matter on account of its being vindicated and carried out in an improper way. In this matter the apostle's words have permanent significance, that, compared to godliness which is "profitable unto all things," bodily exercise, and especially that which has sprung from the spirit of the Greeks, "profiteth little." (And besides, that coxcombical bodily discipline and gymnastic system, carried out as it was for show, was already a subject of ridicule for antiquity itself. See Epict. *Diss.* iii. 12.) But, as opposed to the prostitution of the body, "it profiteth much;" and the Christian spirit, inasmuch as it is one which justly appreciates the value of the body, must manifest itself in the community likewise in reference to social habits of proper care of the body, and thus bring a blessing on the social body.

(2) It is, however, by no means merely the Christian consciousness of a divinely appointed care and maintenance of the bodily life which conditions and effects the welfare of earthly society. This is rather based just as much on the perception that the maintenance of bodily life must give way to the higher aims of existence. We have already treated of the

way in which this manifests itself in the Christian community of the kingdom, in the willingness to surrender even life itself for its confession thereof. The Christian, however, recognizes the same necessity also in his relations to the earthly-human and civil community, as soon as he has justly estimated its essential character (see § 48, note (2)). And this perception consists herein, that we recognize the totality of humanity organized in public communities as bearers and executors of a *divine vocation*, to whose ends the bodily and earthly existence of the individual *is subservient*, and whose nature consists in this—the upholding in its integrity in the public administration of right and justice, and in a mode equally binding on all its individual members, God's will as Creator and Ruler with respect to these communities. Here the question does not turn so much upon showing how this idea lies in the very essence of the state, as in indicating the point where the Christian moral consciousness coincides with that whose impress in the sphere of man's earthly society appears in the maintenance of right in a righteousness to which the individual has not to oppose an unconditioned right to his own existence, but to consider this even (as it is conditioned by his earthly and corporeal existence) as subordinate to the higher ethical ends, whose representative is the earthly community in its administration of right and justice. The Christian moral consciousness, however, coincides with the consciousness of mankind, touching the importance which the maintaining of order in human society possesses in that idea of divine justice. The reflex of this in the relations of man's social community is civil justice. It has for its fundamental presupposition Right, *i.e.* not a humanly devised norm and order of man's social life, but one appointed by God, laid down in creation, and historically worked out. The object of right is this external order and form of the social state, and indeed as something always to be realized and observed. The popular consciousness respecting this right establishes itself for its executive in law, as the expression of this knowledge of right in a legally formed society carrying out this right, and organized and constituted for its executive accomplishment. Justice, however, is nothing else than the inviolable maintenance of this social order, living as right in the popular consciousness, and formularized as law for its judicial execution. Its inviolability can only be established in reference to external actions, and, indeed, in an external claim which, as a means for its satisfaction, has also only external constraint. For all legal obligation has reference merely to external actions in their relation to the collective or general order of things; and the compulsory enforcement of conformity of the actions of individuals to that general order of things, such as the restraint or punishment by outward force of actions which are contrary to it, is the accidental but inseparable character of all that justice which conduces to the carrying out of right, and which maintains and confirms that right, whether in the shape of a protective or retributive power. And even in the last relation, in the manifestation of penal justice, the import of justice lies only in the re-establishment of respect for a violated system of right; and punishment in itself, as an atonement for outraged law, has no other aim than that of proving the inviolability of that law practically to the general conscience (compare with what is here said, J. Stahl, *Rechts- und Staatslehre*, vol. ii. 2d ed. book ii. p. 161 f.). So certainly, therefore, as the preservation of the life of the individual belongs to the objects of legal protection, so certainly can that individual existence, which is only a part of a whole united together in a legal system, not claim such a right to its preservation, if it has by crime forfeited the right to this protection. It does not belong to this place to determine the nature and range of those crimes by which the bodily life of individual existence appears forfeited. Thus much only may be established, that it is not contrary to Christian knowledge to recognize such a forfeiture as conceivable, and the decreeing of death-punishment as admissible. For even Christian knowledge sees in the order of man's social life on earth, and the authorities which carry it out, not only a sum and execution of purely human propositions; but it perceives in that justice which maintains inviolate the rights of earthly social order, a realization of the will of that God of righteousness who is Lord over life and death. No man, as man, has a right over the life of another, and human society just as little, if in the maintaining of its order against individuals it could only plead for its execution the collective will of men. But since this order in its ultimate ground is of divine arrangement, and the result of the divine will, it is not repugnant to the protective power of this order of things to punish the highest degrees of culpability against it with that penalty which, in the name of the God of righteousness, carries out the divine power of life and death in capital punishment. Nowhere in the New Testament do we find that abrogated which on this point was recognized as right by the Old (compare v. Hofmann, *Schriftbeweis*, 2d half, sec. ii. 2d ed. p. 436, with pp. 431–35). And I can understand in no other than the most literal sense what the apostle (Rom. 13:4) says, that the ruler bears not the sword in vain.

War also, when justifiable, bears the same character of compulsion with full right; for its justification lies in the legitimate duties of nations, which flow from the divinely ordained special vocation of public communities for their mutual relations to one another, and whose violation the organized public community has a right to punish. It is the consciousness of a divinely willed collective right belonging to the vocation of a nation which constitutes the order of the national members, and of the collective totality of the human race, whose violation no single people can perpetrate with impunity, although *de facto* the compulsory force of the right in this case has no incontestable certainty. Since the Christian recognizes his earthly vocation as an individual member of a popular community, he neither wishes nor can he withdraw himself from the obligation to punish the violation of national rights. Nay, since he also here understands not only how to stand in the service of an earthly master, but also to serve God as a warrior, to whom in the execution of His justice on earth he owes person and life, there is manifested precisely in the form of the Christian soldier the perfect spirit of purified devotion to the carrying out of the right and the righteousness of God upon earth. For to the Christian as a soldier, the courage to lose even his life in the struggle springs not from his own choice, from self-confidence, or from that which otherwise works among men a disregard of their bodily life, but from the conviction, in the special duty entrusted to him by the authorized powers of the public community on earth, and in obedience to it, that he dare not value the body and its life more highly than the honor, advantages, and rights of that community, in case of whose peril and injury he, in the name of his God, and at the command of those above him, has to draw the sword.

(3) Even from the divinely ordered relations of our own individual life to our neighbor, and to the general rule that each ought to seek not his own, but that which is his neighbor's, there arise cases where the Christian, not as executor of a public and legal duty, but as one who performs a duty of love, has by the disregard of his own life to realize in actual fact the blessing of Christian public spirit. This occurs in all instances where, in case of the life of another being threatened, he exposes his own life to the peril of destruction, in order to save the life of him who was so endangered. For this is nothing else than practically to display the conviction that man does not possess the life of the body in order only to have it for himself, but in order with its strength and energy to serve his neighbor even to the renunciation of that life. And herein appears, although in weak, earthly imitation, a complying with that example, in reference to which it is said in John, καὶ ἡμεῖς ὀφείλομεν ὑπὲρ τῶν ἀδελφῶν τὰς ψυχὰς θεῖναι (1 John 3:16).

That which, in opposition to this, is cited as a duty of self-preservation, *i.e.* the defense of our own bodily life against unlawful assaults on it, and, as a justifiable self-help even to the slaying of another, has had given to it the name of necessary self-defense, possesses, as self-help merely for the purpose of preserving one's own life, no sufficient justification. But in fact here also the real state of the case is different. For it is not the violent assault on the life of the individual as such which here comes under consideration, but the infraction, which is at the same time involved, of the divinely ordained social order of things which condemns the slaying of a human being as a crime against the public rights of the community. And that which is called self-preservation, or the preserving of one's own life, comes into consideration here not in this sense, but so as if one asked whether in such an instance the individual was in duty bound to suffer the crime against the public rights without using all possible means to prevent it. The necessity in which the individual finds himself does not usurp the place of right, but only points out the implied impossibility of claiming the legal protection of the established authorities of society in the case of unlawful assault and violence. This involuntary defect here brought into play does not exonerate the individual from the obligation, as far as in him lies, to prevent the crime against public law; but this defect only occasions the necessity that the individual in his person should vindicate the public law against violent assault with all means that serve for the prevention of crime. For this right and this duty belong to the individual not as an individual, but as a member of a public organized society, whose order every one has to maintain, against whose person an offence against public law is going to be committed. This is not demanded by a duty towards one's self, but by a duty to the public rights of the community, whose vindication becomes the privilege of every individual member thereof, when there exists an impossibility that the public authorities established by society for its protection should interfere. There only will a limit to this duty exist, where the individual is assailed by violence on account of what he is or does in that vocation, in which he has to bear testimony not to the rights of earthly society, but to the truth and nature of the kingdom of Christ, and to answer in his own person for the laws of that kingdom. For this is not a kingdom of earthly punitive justice, but one where man conquers and rules by enduring, and fulfils in patient endurance the law of Christ. In this sense I might now again refer to that which has been related as a saying of Luther's: "Needs must," said Dr. Luther. Then H. asked him "whether, if he were attacked by robbers, he would choose to defend himself." "Yes, certainly," replied the Doctor; "for then I should be *judge* and *ruler,* and would wield the sword in comfort, *because no one else would be with me who could protect me*; and would take the holy sacrament afterwards, and should have wrought a good work. But if I should be attacked as a preacher for the gospel's sake, then would I with folded hands raise my eyes to heaven, and say, 'My Lord Christ, here am I. I have confessed and preached Thee, and so forth; if it is now time, I commend my spirit into your hands, and so would I choose to die' " (*Table Talk*).

Neither is the duel to be placed on the same footing with that which is called self-defense, nor is it to be judged by the view the Christian takes of the value of his earthly life. For the unjustifiable surrender of one's own life, or the unjustifiable endangering of that of another, is here something purely accidental; and where in reality neither one nor the other ought to take place, the judgment on the unjustifiable nature of dueling is nothing affected. This unjustifiable character lies in the view taken of personal honor, and in the disregard of the means appointed by the civil community for obtaining satisfaction for our rights. The violation of that mutual respect which the Christian recognizes as a duty (τῇ τιμῇ ἀλλήλους προηγούμενοι, Rom. 12:10; τῇ ταπεινοφροσύνῃ ἀλλήλους ἡγούμενοι ὑπερέχοντας ἑαυτῶν, Phil. 2:3),—the violation, I say, of this duty is also, according to the civil social order, so far as it lies in acts, an offence for whose punishment not the individual, but the established authority of the community, is appointed, no matter whether we view this community as the whole state, or according to its organization in ranks, corporations, and the like. Suppose also that the community were deficient in appointed means for this purpose, then is the imagined injury to personal honor to be sacrificed to the good of that community. It is not in this way—if we in a self-willed manner withdraw the right of punishing the injury done to our honor from the community, and seek to right ourselves by a means which is not even a proof of the violation of our honor, but at best only a proof of personal courage—that we render the community better. Rather by the proportion in which we make over in full confidence to the community the guarantee of our own honor, will this guarantee be afforded, and the social order hereby bettered. And for the decision of this question at the present time, we may not, in the place of established social order, substitute states of previous deficiency of law and protection, of which it might perhaps be said with some show of reason, that then the protection of honor and right was confided to the strong arm of individual prowess, and that in the idea of honor connected with the ability in the use of weapons, which absorbed all other honor, it may have been possible to see in the victory of the individual in combat of arms at the same time a judgment of God. Abnormal states give no standard for our decision of that which is right. But a Christian can least of all regulate his conduct by that which is deemed honor amongst men, or perhaps nothing more than a conventional notion of honor, untrue in itself, of man's devising, but solely and alone by that which is honor with God, and with all men who know, fear, and love Him.

§ 50. d. *The Preservation of Earthly Blessings for the Service of the Soul, in its Reflex Influence on the Community*

From that trait which is characteristic of the Christian preservation of the blessings of this world, viz. self-denial, is developed that public spirit which in custom, law, and mode of action, offers the best security for all social blessings, for civil well-being, civil honor, civil and domestic happiness. In the recognition of the divine right of the inequality of possessions, the public spirit of Christianity goes hand in hand with the spirit of the civil order of society, which opposes itself in right and law to every arbitrary, selfish invasion, every encroachment, every attempt at a false equalization, which might threaten the rightful inequality of possession actually existing (1). But this public spirit of Christianity contributes to the proper use of our possessions, in distinction from self-seeking exclusiveness and selfish enjoyment, partly by the forms and customs of society, and the exercise of charity, regulated by vocation and rank; partly by the proper observance of those ordinances and laws by which, together with the security of spiritual and temporal possessions, a provision is at the same time made for spiritual and bodily destitution; partly also in the maintenance of the proper relation between the legal form of provision for need, and the exercise of that freely giving social love, by which room is afforded to this love for practically realizing the Christian spirit of subordination of earthly blessings to the higher and the highest by an equally self-denying and wisely-regulated dispensing to the genuine wants of distress (2). Finally, this spirit keeps up in social life that highest nobleness of character, namely, with all just appreciation and all lawful possession of earthly goods the liberty of self-sacrifice, when our earthly or heavenly calling, the interests of our country or of God's kingdom, admonishes us in times of oppression, for the sake of the possession and preservation of the higher blessings, in cheerful zeal to give up what is of less value (3).

(1) It may be here also premised, that the object is not to conceive of or to set forth the public spirit of Christianity as the sole factor in the right ordering of man's civil community, but to show in what way the sphere of civil rights and civil order named in the paragraph finds through the Christian spirit its recognition and its true ethical stamp and fulfilment. The first thing from which out of the Christian spirit a blessing comes to the earthly community and its well-being, is the recognition of the *varied distribution in the possession* of earthly good as of divine right and divine appointment. And this applies naturally to all that the Christian calls earthly good (comp. § 45). As the Christian does not perceive nor suppose an equality in all individuals in their mental and bodily endowments, just as little does he look for equality in their course and condition of life, and in the honors and possessions of the latter. And if God, according to the judgment of man, permits him who, according to man's judgment, is unrighteous and ungodly to prosper in

reference to earthly good and its possession, Christian feeling neither commits nor suffers any violation of this possession, except it should be the result of a notorious invasion of the rights of others to be legally punished; but it considers even the possession, the apparent good fortune and prosperity, in the light of something in which the hidden judgments of God are being prepared, which in such cases man is not justified in anticipating. In general, Christian knowledge contents itself with knowing whether the want or the possession of earthly goods may be a blessing to the individual: it honors, in the one as in the other, the ways of God's training; and as much as the want appears to it to be a demand of God for the exercise of the riches of Christian love towards him who is needy, so little does it regard as Christian love—that which is besides impracticable—the wish by its own absolute authority to abolish this inequality of possessions. "Ista temporalia bona et mala utrisque (piis et impiis) voluit (Deus) esse communia, ut nec bona cupidius appetantur, quæ mali quoque habere cernuntur, nec mala turpiter evitentur, quibus et boni plerumque afficiuntur. Interest autem plurimum, qualis sit usus vel earum rerum quæ prosperæ, vel earum quæ dicuntur adversæ. Nam bonus temporalibus nec bonis extollitur nec malis frangitur: malus autem ideo hujuscemodi infelicitate punitur, quia felicitate corrumpitur" (Aug. *Civ. D.* i. 8). Thus Christian love honors this inequality of riches—so far as it does not arise from injustice, which it has to punish as a duty of its calling—as a divine right of divine dispensation. And it concedes this honor to every kind of good—honor with men, domestic happiness, material prosperity, and the like; and it battles against every unjustifiable encroachment by slander, misleading, overreaching, deceit, thieving, and robbery, as against an offence against God in the person and the property of one's neighbor. All such encroachments, and all these spoliations of a mental and material kind, are to the Christian the result of a heathen state of mind—a state of mind which has no part in the kingdom of God (Eph. 4:28; 1 Cor. 6:10). This same spirit of Christian insight into the significance and the rights of property also recognizes no false description of love or of godliness, which, at the expense of a justly possessed wealth entrusted to its management, wishes to display itself as generous in giving; as, for example, an excess of pious, compassionate outlay on the part of the father of a family to the prejudice of the lawful property of those connected with him (ὀφείλει θησαυρίζειν ... οἱ γονεῖς τοῖς τέκνοις, 2 Cor. 12:14; εἴ τις τῶν ἰδίων καὶ μάλιστα τῶν οἰκείων οὐ προνοεῖ, τὴν πίστιν ἤρνηται, καὶ ἔστιν ἀπίστου χείρων, 1 Tim. 5:8), on the part of the guardian at the expense of his ward, and more of the same kind. No pretended right, and no pretended duty of sacrificing love, have any weight with the Christian public spirit, if in its exercise were involved the violation of a right and duty with respect to that divinely entrusted good, in whose administration Christian fidelity had to be practically realized. In this sacred respect to the varied distribution of riches, Christian public spirit stands opposed to destructive tendencies, of which the one denies in general the divine appointment and authority for that difference in possessions; but the other views the Christian virtue of self-denial in the use of earthly goods in a manner which contradicts the divine intention in the dispensation of differences in wealth. The two tendencies concur in the error of desiring to establish an equality or community of property. The first does so, inasmuch as it sees in the possession of property, and in the difference of its distribution, the result only of a perverted organization, or properly mechanism of human society, and falsely assigns to every man a right to an equal enjoyment of earthly goods, because it knows only this enjoyment as happiness, and understands nothing of a divine blessing, or of a divine means of discipline in the school of denial. The other opinion, instead of seeing in devoted and self-sacrificing love the consecration and hallowing of wealth, looks upon giving and having as two mutually antagonistic opposites; sees, instead of divine purpose and divine right in the possession of property, in the maintenance of its inequality of distribution, a deed of selfishness, of which perfect Christian virtue can only free itself by renunciation; and thus leads (since, by the entire surrender of property to those who have none, the relation would remain certainly only the same, except that those who before possessed nothing become the selfish possessors) in another manner equally to the idea of setting up a community of property. One hears this form of a community of goods frequently lauded as a perfection of the apostolic community, to whose type degenerate Christianity must be brought back. When, in proof of this, an appeal is made to the narrative in Acts 2:44 ff., and this as an apostolically founded community of goods is regarded as a primeval, universal Christian institution, a double error is thereby committed. For, in the first place, the relation of the church in Jerusalem is not a community of goods in the proper sense of the word, but a giving up of their wealth on the part of those possessing it, for the purpose of dividing it according as the distress of individuals laid claim to support (πάντες δὲ οἱ πιστεύσαντες ἐπὶ τὸ αὐτὸ εἶχον ἅπαντα κοινά, καὶ τὰ κτήματα καὶ τὰς ὑπάρξεις ἐπίπρασκον καὶ διεμέριζον αὐτὰ πᾶσιν, καθότι ἄν τις χρείαν εἶχεν). Secondly, it was not a universal apostolical church-institution, but a voluntary sacrifice of love, which the peculiar state and the peculiar distress of the church at Jerusalem rendered necessary, which is abundantly proved by the fact that the Apostle Paul, in the various churches which he counselled, in no place called into being an institution of this nature, but rather everywhere collected and enjoined the collections of alms for the poor church in Jerusalem (Rom. 15:26; 1 Cor. 16:1-3; 2 Cor. 8:9). And besides, in the narrative of Ananias and Sapphira, the right to the possession of the proceeds of the sale, and the perfect right to its free disposal, is expressly conceded to Ananias (Acts 5:4, οὐχὶ μένον, σοὶ ἔμενεν, καὶ πραθὲν, ἐν τῇ σῇ ἐξουσίᾳ ὑπῆρχεν;)—an assertion totally inconceivable if a community of goods had been the order of the first Christian community. Where, therefore, such an especial state of need occurs as existed at that time in Jerusalem, there, even at the present day, the true sentiment of a Christian society may and will so manifest itself as it did in

Jerusalem. But the so-called apostolic institution of a community of goods is founded on a palpable misunderstanding.

(2) While the self-denying public spirit of Christianity preserves property from selfish attack, the same spirit excludes those evils which arise in a community out of the selfishness of possession—out of selfish withholding (avarice of every kind), as well as out of the selfish pleasure in spending (extravagance of every kind). For unselfish possession works, from its nature, a reciprocal distribution in the community; but, at the same time, self-denial extirpates that corruption in giving, where one even in giving and bestowing seeks after his own gratification, instead of the benefit of others. The self-denying ministration will, in its mutual sharing of earthly good things, where Christian public spirit prevails, embrace all and every blessing. For none can be thought of as absolutely incommunicable; but in every one it will be manifest, that in one aspect indeed, and in one part, it will be inalienable, and belonging to its possessor only, so long as God preserves it to him, but that in another phase it is destined to be imparted for the service of the community, and that it does not exclusively minister to the enjoyment and the gratification of the possessor. Thus only is accomplished in Christian possession, and indeed in all relations of earthly good things, that εἰς Θεὸν πλουτεῖν in contrast with the θησαυρίζειν ἑαυτῷ (Luke 12:21) by which alone every possession of the individual becomes a common good and a common blessing; and even the loss of earthly prosperity, the evils and sufferings of the earthly community, must, as an occasion for fellow-feeling and active sympathy, serve to let men experience the blessing of the compassionate love of their fellow-creatures (κλαίειν μετὰ κλαιόντων, Rom. 12:15; ἀγαπᾶν ἐν ἔργῳ καὶ ἀληθείᾳ, 1 John 3:18; οἰκτίρμονα εἶναι καθὼς καὶ ὁ πατὴρ ἡμῶν οἰκτίρμων ἐστί, Luke 6:36; comp. with Matt. 25:34 ff., where Christ declares that in the sufferings of the brethren it is *He* Himself who comes before us, in order that we should show in them our active affection *for Him*). Such blessing, however, where even the bitterness of this

earthly life becomes an occasion of a joyful experience, there only falls to the lot of the earthly community where that spirit is a prevailing spirit, in which every possession is recognized and possessed as a gift of grace. For there the possession and ministration of good is not considered the having its abundance for one's self, but for mutual help with such good things in the spirit of divine grace and love (Luke 12:15, οὐκ ἐν τῷ περισσεύειν τινὶ ἡ ζωὴ αὐτοῦ ἐστιν ἐκ τῶν ὑπαρχόντων αὐτοῦ; 1 Pet. 4:10 ἕκαστος καθὼς ἔλαβε χάρισμα, εἰς ἑαυτοὺς αὐτὸ διακονοῦντες, ὡς καλοὶ οἰκονόμοι ποικίλης χάριτος). And there every individual possession of itself conduces to the common welfare, where, in accordance with the words of the Lord, greater blessedness is found in giving than in receiving (Acts 20:35), and where all that is received serves the object of giving: the bodily and spiritual endowments for communication and for the serving of one's neighbor (κοινωνεῖν τοῖς πνευματικοῖς, λειτουργεῖν ἐν τοῖς σαρκικοῖς, Rom. 15:27; μεταδιδόναι χαρίσματα πνευματικά, Rom, 1:11); the honor of one's own position in life as a means of honoring and making others happy (τῇ τιμῇ ἀλλήλους προηγούμενοι, Rom. 12:10); the prosperity of our own household for the friends and associates of that household (in the φιλοξενία and all that is analogous: 1 Pet. 4:9, Heb. 13:2; comp. 1 Tim. 5:10, 3:2, Tit. 1:8); the wealth earned by our own efforts, and the riches which have fallen to us, for the appeasing of need, and the increase of the prosperity of others (κοπιάτω, ἐργαζόμενος ταῖς χερσὶν, ἵνα ἔχῃ μεταδιδόναι τῷ χρείαν ἔχοντι, Eph. 4:28; τοῖς πλουσίοις παράγγελλε ... εὐμεταδότους εἶναι, κοινωνικούς, κ.τ.λ., 1 Tim. 6:17-19; τῆς εὐποιΐας καὶ κοινωνίας μὴ ἐπιλανθάνεσθαι, Heb. 9:13). And such dispensing love will not merely confine itself to the special and vocational intercourse of individuals with each other,—as, for example, to the position of the shepherd to his flock, of the master of the house to his dependents, and so forth, and conversely,—but will extend itself over all that social community in which a man finds himself a member of its order, *i.e.* by that lot in life which he may view and acknowledge as God's will, and in which the wants of his neighbor become known to him, which he is enabled to satisfy by the divinely ordained means in his possession. And so far as in such case the parting with his wealth does not happen to militate against the rights of possession, the duty of its possessor, and the immediate objects of the property entrusted to him, its communication [to others] is the natural manifestation of that spirit of love in which the Christian possesses all his earthly good things. But just because the object of his giving is not that his neighbor *may have*, but that the gift may *render* him *a service*, the spirit of Christian love, which is at the same time a spirit of wisdom and prudence, will under certain circumstances equally realize itself in refusal and withholding, or in that manner which appears harsh, while it is only an exercise of true, wise, and holy love. And this also pertains to that self-denying Christian love which is cognizant of other and higher aims than the mere self-satisfaction of giving and bestowing; and just on the right distribution of refusal and granting rests that blessing which the spirit of Christian love— a spirit equally of compassion as of correction and training— brings upon the earthly society.

The same spirit also determines the form and position of those permanent ordinances and institutions in which the benevolent impulse of Christian love practically realizes itself in the community. Without such forms the existence of this spirit is inconceivable. They alone are the historical testimony that this spirit has found a historical sphere for its energy within the social body, and continues to possess one, and that the community recognizes this spirit to be genuine and authorized. The expression of this are the laws and the legally established institution, whose continuance is intended to subserve the ends of generous Christian love. In them the Christian spirit will realize itself in a threefold way for the blessing of society. First, in the extent of the relations in which, by means of law and institution, the form of social life desires to conduce to the right general use of earthly blessings. There no kind of possession and no kind of necessity will remain disregarded; rather will the general care have reference to all the needs of the intellectual as well as of the material existence, and display itself as a common duty and common acknowledgment in law and institution. Secondly, this recognition will be guided by the right higher ordering of superior blessings above the lower, and the adaptation to the purposes and requirements of particular times and circumstances. The Christian spirit will at all times battle against our estimating as equal, spiritual, mental, and material wants, and against ordinances which spring or have sprung from such error. It will not favor charitable institutions at the expense of those whose object is education, or forms and laws of intellectual cultivation at the expense of a care for religion, or conversely. In short, it will not suffer any kind of preponderance or exclusiveness, in which the practical recognition of the various necessities, and of the common care for their satisfaction, becomes a violation of the relation in which earthly blessings stand to the supreme good, or earthly blessings to each other. The Christian spirit will react against every form which, disregarding the variety of divinely appointed ranks and callings, offers and bestows the same on all alike, or which, in the satisfaction of necessities which are artificially raised above the standard of rank and calling, falsely makes a display of a particular solicitude, *e.g.* in establishments for the education of all up to an equal degree of culture, in demanding and granting such culture beyond the limits or contrary to the aim of the future calling, in charitable institutions too luxurious in endowment, and the like. Not less will this spirit of the οἰκοδομὴ τῆς χρείας oppose itself to every abstract principle with which, disregarding the existing circumstances of the community, one deems it possible once for all to give practical expression to the common care for the maintenance or distribution of earthly good things in the same form and in the same measure. Rather will it be the perception of the changeful nature of the relations and requirements by which Christian public spirit will know how to shape ever new forms of its exercise. Finally, as the third blessing of this Christian public spirit, we must name the fact, that it maintains a right consciousness of the position which the legal provision of society has to assume with respect to individual efforts, as well as the individual with respect to the legally established arrangement. The more clearly the insight of the Christian perceives that the blessing of charity essentially depends on its adaptation to the special needs of the particular time; that these individual relations reveal themselves only to the affectionate individual community; and that it is not so much the external satisfaction of wants as the maintenance of the spirit of love that is rich in blessings for the community;—so much the more will the Christian community guard itself against giving to legal prescription a character or extent by which voluntary private effort is crippled or abrogated, or against assigning the carrying out of legally ordered charity to the care of instruments whose vocation and character render it difficult, if not impossible, for them to enter into the circumstances of the individual—that duty which half assumes the nature of the care of souls. Defects of this kind, which always have new defects for their result, are, *e.g.*, excessive poor-rates, handing over the care of the poor to police boards instead of the clergy, the members of the Christian community, and the like. But another danger also, which even with right organization adheres to legally established forms, is set aside by Christian public spirit,—the danger, namely, that the individual should suppose that, by his taking part in what was legally prescribed, he has accomplished all that the spirit of dispensing love requires of him. For where the right public spirit is recognized as the exercise of *voluntary* love, there the participation in what has been legally prescribed can be characterized neither as the scope nor the essence of a true common feeling. The Christian spirit recognizes in this participation rather *one* form only of the practical realization of free love, which has no Christian value, if its exercise is *only* the effect of prescription, not of free love, and totally insufficient for the true common weal, if it does not partake of the free exercise of individual love.

Moreover, the denying, correcting, punishing love of righteousness has also its forms of legal ordering and arrangement, in which the care of Christian public spirit for the protection of property and the defense against and punishment of ungodly encroachment and robbery declares itself. The Christianity of this public spirit will practically realize itself, therefore, not only in the maintenance of all these forms of retributive justice, but especially in this, that it places the forms of punishment which conduce to the preservation of the earthly welfare of society (in those cases where by them the condition and the development of the life of the individuals punished are determined by external authority) in a right relation to the ends of the educating grace of God, and that it suffers no forms of punishment which in their nature exclude the communication of blessings and training for the higher and highest ends of life. Hence within the Christian community the ardent desire for a union of instruction and intellectual cultivation with the punishment of prison discipline—that blessing of a Christian view of things, which only is converted into a curse where one thinks that the forms of retributive justice should be framed absolutely for the object of improvement, and not by the standard of righteous retribution; whereas the true relation is this, that in the case where the form of punishment, as in imprisonment, also at the same time determines the shape of the personal life-development, that common love which trains us for the community of the kingdom of Christ must be brought to bear upon the offender even within the system of retributive punishment.

(3) That guarantee for the well-being of the social life on earth, as it lies in the Christian impulse to sacrifice earthly blessings for higher ends, has its divine nobleness in this, that necessity is not the source of this disposition, but only the condition under which the instinct of self-sacrifice practically displays itself in conformity with God's will; while one thing which remains immutable in all times and under all circumstances, independent of all human power and all earthly motive, is the deep and hidden source of that enthusiasm

which manifests itself from time to time—namely, love to the Lord of its salvation, to whom fidelity in vocation and the sacrifice to its duties is rendered, and compared with whose fellowship of grace the Christian brotherhood lightly esteems all other kinds of prosperity.

§ 51. *The Fundamental Forms of Earthly, Divinely ordered Society, and their relation to the Practical Realization of Christian Virtue*

It not only belongs to Christian piety to be energetic in that multiplicity of virtues which penetrate the different relations of earthly society with the true spirit and the true character of their fulfilment, but it also recognizes certain fundamental forms of that society which the Christian finds already existing and determining his life, as of such a nature that in their very existence they are the realization of divinely appointed bonds of community, and thus in themselves have an ethical significance. For marriage, and the family that springs from it, lie at the base of all human earthly society, as a divinely ordered natural foundation of moral personal fellowship, whose bond of union is that mutually giving and receiving, guided and guiding, piety and affection,—a bond which bears, in the names of husband, wife, father, brother, and sister, the natural prototypes of that highest fellowship which in Christ is intended to bind men to God and to one another in sacred and glorious perfection on a divine basis. The relations of life and society which, on the ground of marriage and the family, further develop and mutually limit one another—so far as they in those very limits and determination keep in view moral aims, which the community has to guard and to secure from a violation of these limits—lead to that form of human society as it organizes itself in the state and its political system for the sovereignty of right, as the external guardian of the moral ends of all the relations of life and society. As the human and earthly embodiment of that divine righteousness which rules and watches over the moral purposes of the order of creation, and in opposition to the individual caprice of individual liking, as well as to the mere natural tendency which has a consciousness of moral ends, the ordinance of the state is to the Christian a human institution, which conduces not only to earthly and human, but also to divinely appointed aims, and which, in its connection with its ultimate source and origin, bears the stamp of a divine authorization. But inasmuch as the Christian has, at the same time, a consciousness of discord, in which the moral faculty and will of the individual and of the whole body stand as well to the moral aims of the natural love-fellowship of individuals, as to that fellowship of rights (resting as it does on natural determination, and historically worked out) of political order, and the legally constituted state of nations; and inasmuch as he recognizes Christ alone as the Reconciler of this discord, as being Him in whom the foundation of the all-renewing fellowship of grace is laid, which upon earth has its existence in the social kingdom of the members of Christ's body;—therefore the Christian perceives, as the perfection of all earthly forms of fellowship, a third—the church—in which the human society, which has been apprehended by the grace of God in Christ, and which revolves round the fundamental law of the kingdom of Christ, and strives after Him, has its embodiment in this world. Since the consciousness of the Christian recognizes the reciprocal relation in which these three fundamental forms of society mutually limit and interpenetrate each other in their earthly existence, it is just as remote from wishing to change, for the sake of this reciprocal relation, the essential peculiarity of the one form of society to that of the other, as it is also far, on account of its aims after moral perfection, by which these several forms are supported, from seeing in their empirical form the perfect copy of that truth which constitutes its original form, and lays down its aims. On the contrary, these forms of fellowship in marriage and family, the state, the church, remain for the Christian earthly and human realizations of a natural, individual, and personal fellowship of love; of a fellowship of rights which ministers to the existence of society, and ensures its permanence; and a fellowship of grace which serves for the purification and sanctification of both these social forms, none of which is in itself a perfect realizing of the idea which lies at their basis, or of the real divine will which conditions them: each in itself and all united also, in their most ideal form, are only preliminary stages and conditions of a future perfection of the moral world in God's kingdom of glory, and all destined, according to the fundamental law of the kingdom of Christ, and in the spirit of the regenerate and new man (shapen as he is in purity and righteousness), in perpetually renewed purification and holiness, to be carried onwards to their final goal. From this knowledge, that also which in the general domain of life—in a domestic, civil, and in a religious sense—may be named virtue, gains in the Christian community, and its relation to family, state, and church, a specific character, and a realization in a specific form (1).

(1) The Christian has in Christ not only the Lord in the kingdom of grace, but also Him by whom and for whom all things were made (Col. 1:16), who upholds all through the word of His power (Heb. 1:3), and who has directed His work of redemption on earth to the end that this complete whole—whatever is in heaven and on earth—in Him should be delivered from its dismemberment and division, and that the lost center of unity should be again recovered for the same in Christ (Eph. 1:10). Thus, at the basis of all creatively established and historically maintained creature order, lies a primitive original world-plan, which has its root in Christ, whose real power mirrors itself in continual self-testimony in every form of human society, but which is only properly recognized and followed by those who are in Christ. Herein lies for the Christian the twofold necessity and justification: on the one hand, of looking upon nothing which is an ordinance of the creature as something standing out of connection with Christ; on the other hand, however, of regarding everything which in the same sphere of arrangement is subject to human regulation and realization, as needing to be referred to its divine center of

union in Christ, and capable of such a reference, and appointed with a view to the same. Thus the Christian excludes no form of earthly and human order from a connection with the world-plan of God in Christ; but he includes them all also in their need of redintegration through Christ, since he distinguishes that which is the work and realization of man on the ground of a divinely appointed order, from that which lies at the root of all human form and strivings after the maintenance of order, as the eternal and divine idea of order. And this so much the more, because the realization of this idea has, in every form of earthly and human society, its stages of development, and its disturbance by human sinfulness; and all forms of community in this world, the church not excepted, are only preparatory and transition forms, which are to find their perfection and the accomplishment of their purpose alone in a new earth and under a new heaven in the kingdom of glory. But for this very reason, that no form of human society lies out of this relation to the aim of that future perfection of man, it is not true that to the Christian it is merely the community of grace in Christ, and the earthly form of its social attestation and realization, that are essential, and everything else unimportant. The other forms of society are to him not transitory in such a way, that they should have to resolve themselves here below into the earthly form of the community of grace; but he recognizes in all these forms stages of preparation and transition, in none the eternal and perfect form of the realization of the divine idea, none appointed to experience this perfection before the future appearing of Jesus, but for this very reason, all three being ordained, each in its separate peculiarity, to minister to that plan of training designed by God's redeeming wisdom. But if all these fundamental forms minister to one and the same idea, so, in the measure that the perception of this penetrates the race, will the separate speciality of the one form not become an isolation from the other; but there will ensue a mutual relation, in which every fundamental form of man's Christian community will partake of the other, without, however, this participation becoming an obliteration of the speciality of that other. The state of the family and of the church will participate in the right ordering of the state, and will step into a relation to the order of the social community which is not contrary to the independence and self-maintenance of the spirit of the family or that of the church. In like manner, conversely, will the spirit of family affection and the spirit of the community of grace pervade the ordering of the public community, without that public order ceasing to be distinct from the spirit of the family love and that of the community of grace. This recognition of their mutual appointment for each other it is, which, without interference or confusion, guides Christian virtue to its realization in the fundamental forms of human society.

§ 52. A. a. *Marriage, and its Relation to the Realization of Christian Virtue*

As concerning marriage, Christian virtue is realized primarily in the recognition of its peculiar and divinely ordained nature. To the Christian, marriage is the highest and most perfect form of personal fellowship on earth,—a communion entered into for all the relations and circumstances of life, resting on the natural difference of sex, which in marriage, by the union of the sexes, has found its divinely appointed end; and in this union as a mutual giving up and forgetting of one's own Ego in love and care for the other, there is in itself a moral relation, just as much as it calls for the purification from that self-seeking which clings to everything that is natural (1). In the knowledge of this, the Christian desires marriage as the divinely appointed means for the gratification of the sexual instinct; but its gratification in marriage alone, and marriage only as the highest, most unselfish personal fellowship of *two* individuals, and therefore the fellowship of the body on the ground of *mental* and corporeal attraction, and the fellowship of spirit on the ground of that *spiritual* relationship which itself, in its essence, is not merely love of man, but love of the image of God in man (2).

Thus, inasmuch as the natural love is supported by divine love, the relation finds not only its right recognition, since it is recognized as divinely ordained, though also needing its consecration through Christ (3); but it also gains from the spirit of this recognition its due and actual fulfilment. For this love, in which man loves himself in Christ, secures not only the right mutual subordination and superordination of the sexes in common submission to the ordinances of God their Creator and Redeemer (4), but also guards it against frivolity in entering upon this relation, and also against the violation of it by infidelity and ungodly divorce (5); since it excludes all selfish passion of love, which is the poison of marriage, and inwardly teaches the Christian to desire and to have a spouse merely like any other blessing, so that the love of this blessing should not weaken the love for one's heavenly vocation, or for the supreme good, or separate him from it (6).

(1) The recognition of marriage as a divine ordinance embraces for the Christian a series of conditions, in which for him marriage possesses a divine significance. The one side refers to the history of the race, and the counsels and deeds of God therein, as when, *e.g.*, the separation and destination of the sexes are recognized as the divinely ordained condition of the creature, under which the rule of the race over the earth and, after the fall, the birth of the Son of man, the Lord and Redeemer of the world, and in this birth the restoration of the true rule over the earth of the human race, were to be brought about. The other side of those divinely significant constituent elements refers to the relation of the destination of the sexes, and of its fulfilment in marriage, to the normal development of individuals in all times for the kingdom of God; and it is this side alone which is to be taken into consideration for our investigation. In the relation of the sexes, therefore, the Christian recognizes a condition of nature which to him, simply according to the express declaration of Christ, the Creator and Redeemer of human nature, must bear the character of a divine institution. The saying of Christ, in which

the words of the Old Testament are repeated, is to him an express authority on this point (ὃ ὁ Θεὸς συνέζευξεν, κ.τ.λ., Matt. 19:6; comp. with Gen. 1:27, 28, 2:18, 22). From the same passage also flows the testimony for this, that that which makes a marriage to be a marriage, and without which it is not what it should be, and wherein lies its distinguishing peculiarity from every other form of communion, is the object of sexual union (ἔσονται οἱ δύο εἰς σάρκα μίαν, Gen. 2:24; Matt. 19:5; Eph. 5:31; τῇ γυναικὶ ὁ ἀνὴρ τὴν ὀφειλὴν ἀποδιδότω· ὁμοίως δὲ καὶ ἡ γυνὴ τῷ ἀνδρί· ἡ γυνὴ τοῦ ἰδίου σώματος οὐκ ἐξουσιάζει, ἀλλ' ὁ ἀνήρ· ὁμοίως δὲ καὶ ὁ ἀνὴρ τοῦ ἰδίου σώματος οὐκ ἐξουσιάζει, ἀλλ' ἡ γυνή, 1 Cor. 7:3, 4). 'But that which distinguishes communion in marriage from the unmarital intercourse, is the consciousness that this sexual communion is only intended to be the natural basis (corresponding to the natural sexual duty of man) for a relation which is a personal and vital communion for the whole duration of life, and is entered upon for the purpose of mutual participation in all the relations of that problem of life appointed for man by God (Matt. 5:32, 19:2; Rom. 7:2, 3). Hence comes the insight, that the union of the sexes makes up in truth the peculiar essence of marriage, but that the sexual communion of a wedlock pleasing to God cannot be thought of without that reciprocal personal confidence and that spiritual esteem, which is the necessary condition of a voluntary union of the lot of life for its whole duration. For the aim of marriage does not resolve itself into its natural basis, but this is only the peculiar substratum of wedlock for a relation of communion which comprises in itself all those higher moral and personal postulates and requirements by which the God-pleasing solving of the problem of a community of life and vocation, entered into for the whole duration of life, is conditioned. Therein also is the moral significance of marriage determined. It is in itself a moral relation, not on account of that which perhaps may further be looked upon as the fruit and result of marriage. In particular, the propagation of children is not to be named as the aim of marriage union, as if marriage and the conjugal fellowship, apart from the attainment of this object, were displeasing to God. Nay, rather the Christian knows that the fruit of the marriage union is not a thing lying absolutely within his own power, but as the grant of the divine blessing (Gen. 1:28; Ps. 127:3), which God according to His grace attaches to the fulfilment of marriage—the sexual union—without its being the case that in cases where God does not give the blessing, or where the marriage fellowship is effectuated apart from the certainty of being able to beget children, that marriage fellowship should be contrary to the character of marriage. On the contrary, the word of the apostle holds good (1 Cor. 7:5), from which it fully follows that the sexual intercourse simply of itself is the fulfilment of the end of marriage (μὴ ἀποστερεῖτε ἀλλήλους, εἰ μήτι ἂν ἐκ συμφώνου πρὸς καιρὸν ἵνα σχολάσητε τῇ προσευχῇ—comp. the note (3), § 44—καὶ πάλιν ἐπὶ τὸ αὐτὸ ἦτε, ἵνα μὴ πειράζῃ ὑμᾶς ὁ σατανᾶς διὰ τὴν ἀκρασίαν ὑμῶν). If now this sexual intercourse of marriage is a divine ordinance, there must be in it simply as such a good, a divine blessing. Now this lies, apart from the granted blessing of children, and the other accidental gifts and virtues of the husband, just *in the sexual intercourse itself*, as a contrast not only to unnatural and ungodly self-gratification, but also to that self-denial which is also opposed to God and to nature, as a divinely ordained service with body and spirit in the vocation of sex, as self-forgetting and self-renouncing love, wherein one loves another as one's self, as one's own body, as one's own Ego (ἀγαπᾶν ὡς τὸ ἑαυτοῦ σῶμα, ὡς ἑαυτόν, Eph. 5:28, 33). That this love of the other is at the same time gratification of self, is just as natural as that every attainment of a God-appointed end of life is a pleasure and joy of the heart. But that the sexual intercourse of marriage possesses quite a different character from the selfish, ungodly sexual enjoyment outside of marriage, lies just in this, that a man by virtue of sexual intercourse in wedlock places himself in the service of self-denying fellowship of life and vocation, and that the satisfaction of the sexual instinct here is but the foundation of a relation in which a man, both in spirit and in body, and for all circumstances of life, actually renounces all selfish aims, and has entered into a fellowship of life, since he knows he is indissolubly bound to another, to serve that other with his body and spirit.

This blessing the divine ordinance of marriage hints at through its very form. So far as, on the way of natural inclination of heart and its divinely ordained gratification, it is possible to experience what is really a self-sacrificing communion of life, which comprises both body and soul; so far as it is possible, on the soil of this natural and earthly life, and in the form of such fellowship of life, to understand by one's own state the nature of divine love; so far, but no further, is this understanding brought nigh to us in marriage itself. For it is also only the earthly embodiment of a relation, of which the thought and eternal divine truth are not opened up by the relation itself. Marriage is the divinely appointed ordinance and form, within which the spirit of divine love can find on earth, and agreeably to nature, its most unlimited exercise, and in such operation can teach us to measure the fulness of divine love; *but marriage itself brings not nor effects this spirit of pure, divine love.* It is merely the vessel which is prepared for it: the spirit and the power of divine love come not out of the earthly copy of this divine communion of love. Rather does the Christian recognize that the ordinance of itself does not at all guard against the pollution and desecration by selfishness of every kind; that by nature the heart of every man is inclined to the abuse of the divine institution; that the fulness of protection against such abuse comes not to the heart out of the divine ordinance of wedlock, but from the grace of the new covenant; and that this grace is procured for him not through marriage, but through the word, baptism, the Lord's Supper, the repentance and the faith of the New Testament; on which account it is impossible for him to call this divine ordinance (through a misunderstanding of Eph. 5:32) a sacrament in the same sense that baptism and the Lord's Supper are so called.

(2) On the ground of such knowledge, therefore, the natural procedure of the Christian is a desire for marriage. The victory over all selfishness appears here in the subordination of the

desire to the guidance of God, which is to be discerned in the bodily endowment, the position and providential dispensation of life. Where such especial circumstances do not allow us to recognize the suppression of such a wish as the will of God, there the desire is natural and ordained of God; and, on the other hand, abstaining from wedlock is capricious and arbitrary. The nature of these circumstances may in a measure be known by their analogy to those conditions of things which the apostle had in view (1 Cor. 7), although even there he only speaks of conditions which make abstaining from marriage *advisable*, and not of such as allow us to recognize abstinence as the *absolute* will of God with regard to individuals. He calls the remaining single something good (καλόν, vers. 1, 8, 26); nay, in a certain relation, the better (κρεῖσσον ποιεῖ, ver. 28; comp. the μακαριωτέρα ἐστίν, ver. 40), although not done in depreciation of marriage, which even there is called something good (καλῶς ποιεῖ, ver. 38), but in respect to the care and affliction peculiarly belonging to this time and this world, and from a desire to be able to bestow undivided care upon that which is the Lord's (comp. vers. 26, 28, 32; and v. Hofmann, *Schriftbeweis*, ii. 2, p. 416 f.). And since the apostle places "the better" under the point of view of what is expedient for them (πρὸς τὸ ὑμῶν αὐτῶν σύμφορον, ver. 35), and of forbearance toward them (ἐγώ δὲ ὑμῶν φείδομαι), in which he desires to spare them extreme afflictions (θλίψιν τῇ σαρκί, ver. 28), it is self-evident that, in contrast to this, he cannot and does not call (vers. 28, 36) marrying or being married a sin, just as certainly (and even at the present time) as it remains true, that for undivided attention to that which belongs to the Lord celibacy is more desirable than marriage, where other circumstances do not make marriage more advisable. For in this, according to the words of the apostle, regard must be had to that which is bestowed upon each individual as his peculiar gift of grace (ἕκαστος ἴδιον ἔχει χάρισμα ἐκ Θεοῦ ὁ μὲν οὕτως, ὁ δὲ οὕτως, ver. 7). Here from the context it is difficult to conceive any other meaning than that it is given to the one class to be able to renounce marriage, in order thus, in a way undistracted by the earthly cares of marriage, and undividedly, to serve the Lord, but to others even in marriage so to undergo the earthly cares, that they should form no hindrance in their devotion to their service in the kingdom of Christ. The apostle took this view not only indefinitely and in general, but in reflection on his own person in comparison with Peter and the other apostles (1 Cor. 9:5), to whom their being married formed no obstacle to their performance of the duties of their vocation in the kingdom of Christ. Whence it should become clear to the individual, whether the strength is given him to renounce marriage; and where the opinion of possessing this gift has its limits, the apostle states immediately afterwards. It is that incapacity for abstinence which declares itself in a state of passionate desire under the influence of the sexual instinct, in which state the entering into wedlock is much better than refraining from marriage (εἰ δὲ οὐκ ἐγκρατεύονται, γαμησάτωσαν· κρεῖττον γάρ ἐστιν γαμῆσαι ἢ πυροῦσθαι, ver. 9; διὰ τὰς πορνείας ἕκαστος τὴν ἑαυτοῦ γυναῖκα ἐχέτω, καὶ ἑκάστη τὸν ἴδιον ἄνδρα ἐχέτω, ver. 2; comp. 1 Tim. 5:14). Only we would deliberately ignore the whole context of the discussion given in the Epistle to the Corinthians, and other statements of the apostle, if we wished to abuse the reference to the possible case of a lapse into unchastity, as if it were the apostle's view of the import of marriage that it should be merely a safeguard against fornication. The apostle says nothing more than what is to be considered if one, without reference to his own gift, nay, in opposition to his state, perversely renounces marriage or the use of it. That marriage, *considered in itself*, is no impediment to cases of lapse into unchastity or adultery, is proved by that declaration of Christ, in which some, with the guilt of an equally perverted ignoring of the context, have wished to find that a higher enlightenment, *by virtue of the mere consideration of the heavenly vocation of Christians*, could move a Christian to remain unmarried. For that statement, "There are some eunuchs who have made themselves eunuchs for the kingdom of heaven's sake" (Matt. 19:12), has exclusive reference to the remark of the disciples, that in such a case it would be a grievous thing to become married if a man might divorce his wife only in case of adultery (see ver. 9); and it says neither more nor less than this, that certainly it would be hard for selfish fleshly lust under such condition to take upon itself marriage as a heavy yoke, but that such Christians would understand Christ's word, to whom by Christ's grace it should be given even to make eunuchs of themselves for the kingdom of heaven's sake, *i.e.* to root out the fleshly lust for the sake of God's will (compare my treatise, die Ehescheidungsfrage, Stuttgart 1861, p. 53 ff.). Thus it remains clear from the statement, that it is only the consideration of especial circumstances, which are independent of human self-will, which make the desire of marriage and entering upon it advisable or unadvisable, but by no means either one's own caprice or the caprice of others, and that in the last case the κωλύειν γαμεῖν may be designated as unchristian in its nature (1 Tim. 4:3). Finally, we find just as little in the divine dispensation, by virtue of which marriage is dissolved by death, or a separation is brought about by divorce (see afterwards), any impediment for him on whom such loss has fallen blamelessly, to the desire or entrance into a second marriage. Marriage is not a communion which by its peculiar and exclusive character binds two individuals together for this life and the life to come. On the contrary, the peculiarity of the state of wedlock is that of a relation limited to this world (comp. Rom. 7; 1 Cor. 7:39; the passage in Matt. 22:30, ἐν γὰρ τῇ ἀναστάσει οὔτε γαμοῦσιν, οὔτε ἐκγαμίζονται, ἀλλ' ὡς ἄγγελοι τοῦ Θεοῦ ἐν οὐρανῷ εἰσι). Even so does the apostle recommend a *second* marriage to the young widows, on grounds given (1 Cor. 7:8, 9; 1 Tim. 5:14). When, therefore, the apostle in the same epistle names it as a reproach to widows, to deacons, to bishops, if men should say of them that the woman was not the wife of *one* man, the man not the husband of *one* wife (μιᾶς γυναικὸς ἀνήρ, ἑνὸς ἀνδρὸς γυνή, 1 Tim. 3:2, 13, 5:9; comp. with Tit. 1:6),—if this reproach in the first passage is placed on the same line with gluttony and covetousness, and the like, and in the four passages forms a part of the contrast to the traits of a good father of a family, of a good housewife, then the immediate context should have guarded us from understanding by the expression husband of one wife, and so forth, one that had only once been married. Still more impossible would be the view, according to which those many times married would be like husbands of several wives—would be living, therefore, in a kind of polygamy—when we compare [the passage] with the counsel given by the apostle in the same epistle to a second marriage (comp. with 1 Cor. 7), and with his distinct declarations of the perfect lawfulness of a second marriage after the loss of the first consort (Rom. 7; 1 Cor. 7). The expression, consequently, can mean nothing else than *fidelity to the marriage vow*, in opposition to every violation of it, whether in actual bigamy, or in adultery, or in arbitrary divorce and re-marriage; in all which cases a person is no longer ἑνὸς γυνή, μιᾶς ἀνήρ, and has lost the honor of a God-pleasing father of a family, or of that of a God-pleasing housewife before God and men. How much soever, therefore, especial circumstances may be conceived in which one repetition of marriage or several has in it something repugnant to the Christian or the general sentiment of mankind, so little, when these circumstances disappear, or other special circumstances justify and make such a step advisable, is second marriage against God's ordinance; but the contrary assertion binds the conscience of men with a human dogma instead of with the truth of God.

The character of the desire for wedlock will and must correspond to the essential nature of marriage. That which under special circumstances, when entering into marriage does not appear unconditionally advisable, decides for the entering upon it, namely, the sexual instinct (1 Cor. 7:9),—this same thing lies, whether we are conscious of it or no, at the root of the desire, by which a man is induced to enter into marriage as a true marriage, and for the ends of marriage. Hereby it is not asserted that the divinely ordered basis of marriage is to become predominant in the mutual attraction of the sexes, and that the desire of marriage and of entering into marriage shall only be recognized as justifiable in the proportion in which we are sensible of the sexual impulse, without before all things asking for the influence of that moral and spiritual appreciation in which the communion of our life with the other appears worthy to be desired. On the contrary, the moral and spiritual esteem of the character is the fundamental condition for the right entering into a tie which is to bind together man and wife for their earthly lifetime; and the true virginity of the entrance into marriage rests in this very thing, that it is not the idea of the natural and sexual aspect of marriage, but of the spiritual and moral value of those who love each other, which satisfies the wakeful consciousness, and forms the true germ of personal attraction. But, on the other hand, there is no greater self-deception than when one desires to make the purity of the desire dependent on the absence of the sexual instinct, or on the so-called purely spiritual affection in which one pretends to desire the state of wedlock with a person of an opposite sex. For where the attraction of two persons of different sex is purely intellectual, not of a mixed spiritual and corporeal, sexual nature, there their mutual relation revolves within the limits of that respect and esteem, from which of itself it never comes to a desire for the communion of marriage. Christian virtue preserves itself, therefore, in its entrance into wedlock, not by disregarding the sexual attraction, but by not allowing this for itself only, and as an isolated cause, to be the deciding motive for so doing, but by subordinating it to that higher moral and spiritual attraction in which alone lies the guarantee for a happy state of marriage. And this right conduct corresponds also to the nature of the communion of the sexes in wedlock, in which communion of the sexes is only the natural foundation of a moral personal communion of life and vocation for the whole duration of life, and thus becomes the highest corporeal and spiritual communion upon earth. As *this definition* of marriage excludes the impurity of desire, where the sexual impulse seeks its gratification outside of marriage, so does it also exclude this, that we should seek in marriage nothing but sexual gratification; that the personal relation before marriage and after entering on marriage should resolve itself into the sexual and corporeal aspect only; and that, by the exclusion of all personal mental and spiritual alternation of relation, or by ranking in a higher order the transitory communion of sex, which constitutes the foundation of marriage, *above* the spiritual communion, wherein the imperishable charm and the crown of the marriage relation consists, we should approximate or level the human tie of marriage to the sexual fellowship of the brutes. Nothing of this *can* occur where the spirit is alive, which sees in the communion of the sexes only the natural basis of the highest bodily and mental personal communion of life and vocation, as it is appointed for man, and in this shape also for man alone.

This spirit of itself impels us to the preservation of marriage as a *monogamy*. But where the sexual instinct arrives at an exclusive and unjustifiable ascendency, and, in place of a personal communion of love, the possession of the spouse appears the possession of a mere object and means of gratification, or where man seeks the end of the marriage communion of the sexes not in that communion itself, but in its further consequence—in the propagation of children— there is polygamy, no matter in what form, a natural result of the predominance of this perverted sentiment. This last error it was which caused, for example, the polygamies of the patriarchs of the people of Israel (Abraham and Jacob),—a relation which nowhere in the Old Testament is mentioned with approval; nay, rather, is actually set down as something abnormal, since the theocratic blessing, according to God's will, passes on to the sons of the first and lawful wife, as to Isaac, Judah, and not to the sons of the concubines or of the additional wife, as Ishmael, Joseph, etc. And it has justly been found to be significant, that this violation of the original order of things began with one of the race of Cain (Gen. 4:19). That it is a violation of that original order, is shown by the words of Christ and His apostles in the appeal to the divine creation of one wife for the first man (Gen. 1 and 2),—an original order, by the way, which continually finds renewed confirmation in the continued numerical relation of the sexes. According to these words of Christ and His apostles, the ungodliness of *adultery* consists in this, that the adulterer, by virtue of his sexual intercourse with another, is no longer the spouse of *one* other, but of more. Where more than *two* have become *one flesh*, there a violation of the original order of the communion of the sexes has taken place (comp. Matt. 19, 1 Cor. 7, 1 Tim. 3, with Eph. 5). And this relation of monogamy is then the only natural one, when communion of the sexes *coincides* with personal communion of life and vocation. There occurs, but in a more powerful manner, that exclusiveness which, for example, is the characteristic trait of personal friendship, in which it is justly called unnatural when one shows the same spiritual and confidential devotion towards all; whereas we find it only natural when one before all others, and in such a way as none other, is the beloved of the heart. In order perfectly to enter in the communion of the sexes into the highest form of the communion of personal life, the highest personal attraction and the greatest personal confidence is the natural and necessary preliminary condition; and when this is truly found, it can by its very nature thus—in this sexual, mixed bodily and spiritual, personal manner—exist only between two persons, or else there steps into the place of the highest personal devotion, as an ungodly distortion of that communion of the sexes, the exclusive dominion of lust in transitory animal gratification.

Then, further, from marriage, as the sexual and personal communion of life, Christian knowledge attains to the just understanding and right appreciation of that sort of mental attraction which conditions the prosperity and happiness of marriage. As on one side the merely spiritual attraction, without that of the sex and the person, is looked upon by it as incongruous with the aims and nature of wedlock, so also it could not permit, as a motive for entering into a personal communion for life, an inclination which is a mere appreciation of endowments of an intellectual nature, and not of the personal character, or mere approval of the personality in itself, but not of that personality in its position with reference to the kingdom of Christ. For that life-communion which we enter into in marriage, embraces all the life-relations of the personality; and if a Christian, in any personal partiality, is conscious that he will be obliged to exclude from his estimate of the other one phase of the personal life, perhaps entirely in its highest relation, then would a desire of personal union be contrary to the nature and the purpose of marriage, and contrary to the individual position of the desirer to Christ. In a Christian communion of life, the chief condition is certainly mutual confidence and mutual love, that they should look one upon the other as being "fellow-heirs of the grace of life" (1 Pet. 3:7). And thus the consciousness of a communion of mutual grace and faith must be present to the Christian, as the chief condition for a blessed entrance into wedlock. Christian insight will, however, exercise itself in its requisitions in keeping to the right limits. One will not devise these or those external tokens for the hidden man of the heart, and estimate by such exterior signs the worth of a future spouse; but will hold fast the fact that the incorporation into the kingdom of God is a work of God's grace in the heart,—the working of His word and sacrament, growing with the divine training in the earthly course and maturity of life,—and will therefore, especially where one at a youthful age wishes to enter the married state, not lay down as a condition of the Christian marriage-tie the fiction of a Christian maturity, which at such an age rarely if ever exists, and is just only attained in God's own way in the development of the earthly life. But, instead of wishing to recognize in outward behavior the presence of the grace of God, one will at once proceed in God's name to the bond of wedlock, where no actual evidence is given in word or deed, in sentiment or mode of behavior, that the object of our choice has consciously abandoned the grace of that kingdom in whose community he has been planted by the sacrament of baptism.

(3) This consciousness of the Christian, that he desires as a Christian to enter on his marriage; that he needs for the prosperity of the same the blessing of his Lord, and that purification of the heart which is His work; that he desires and

may take this step as a member of the Christian community, before its eyes and with its blessing,—this it is which makes the entrance into wedlock without the blessing of the church unnatural and impossible for the Christian, quite irrespective of the fact whether the Christian state makes the civil recognition of such marriage dependent on such blessing or not. For certainly it is not the blessing of the church of Jesus Christ which makes a marriage a true and genuine one, but rather the blessing of the church is the attestation of a true and virtual marriage-tie, which the Christian, as a member of a Christian community, must desire as necessary for the ratification of marriage, if he will be "married in the Lord" (γαμεῖν ἐν Κυρίῳ, 1 Cor. 7:39), and in taking this step wishes to present himself before Christ and His church, and has no reason in such a step to hide himself from the eyes of Christ and of His church. But just because it is only the consciousness of a Christian marriage, and one well-pleasing to Christ, which impels the Christian to desire the church's blessing, and in which he may hope to receive its blessing; and because, conversely, he knows that such a tie entered into in opposition to God does not become by the church's blessing a God-pleasing, true, and genuine bond of wedlock,—therefore does the Christian guard himself against the delusion that an invalid and surreptitious marriage, perpetrated by fraud or force, or that a blessing dispensed unconscientiously by the servants of the church, can render a marriage in opposition to God's will a valid one, even if the civil code of laws should permit the mischief of allowing such marriages entered into in an unhallowed way, or blessed in an unhallowed way, to be regarded and treated in a civil light as virtual and valid marriages.

(4) Marriage itself, entered into in Christ, and cherished in the spirit of Christ, preserves for the married the blessing of its natural objects, by the maintenance of that distinction of the sexes appointed by God in its mutual relation, viz. in the proper dominion of the man and the true obedience of the wife. This the Christian knows to have been established at the original

creation of man and wife; not that, apart from or independent of the marriage communion, the vocation of the woman should be merely service, and that of the man sovereignty (1 Cor. 11:11, πλὴν οὔτε γυνὴ χωρὶς ἀνδρός, οὔτε ἀνὴρ χωρὶς γυναικὸς, ἐν Κυρίῳ): for, e.g., in the maternal vocation the woman's office is even for the male child to represent the training sovereignty of God with respect to her son (ὥσπερ γὰρ ἡ γυνὴ ἐκ τοῦ ἀνδρὸς, οὕτω καὶ ὁ ἀνὴρ διὰ τῆς γυναικός· τὰ δὲ πάντα ἐκ τοῦ Θεοῦ, 1 Cor. 11:12). But in the relation of marriage as man with respect to his wife, and as wife with respect to her husband, there is the man in his rule the image and glory of God, the woman in her service the glory of the man; and in this relation that reaches its fulfilment which the manner of the original creation (and, indeed, for the communion of marriage) incorporated in the nature of the two sexes (ἀνὴρ εἰκὼν καὶ δόξα Θεοῦ ὑπάρχων· γυνὴ δὲ δόξα ἀνδρός· οὐ γάρ ἐστιν ἀνὴρ ἐκ γυναικὸς, ἀλλὰ γυνὴ ἐξ ἀνδρός· καὶ γὰρ οὐκ ἐκτίσθη ἀνὴρ διὰ τὴν γυναῖκα, ἀλλὰ γυνὴ διὰ τὸν ἄνδρα, 1 Cor. 11:8, 9; comp. with 1 Tim. 2:13, Gen. 2:22). But that which, by the curse of sin, was changed in this relation to an absence of blessing (comp. 1 Tim. 2:14 with Gen. 3:16), which reached its accomplishment in the wicked, selfish tyranny on the part of the man, and the wicked throwing of herself away, the selfish surrender of the woman to the desires of the man,—that is on both sides done away with in Christian wedlock, by participation in the same grace, by membership in the same body of Christ through the spirit of Christian love, where the love of the man honors the vocation of grace of the woman, instead of enslaving the woman in selfish severity (Col. 3:19, μὴ πικραίνεσθε πρὸς αὐτάς),—where the proof of the self-forgetting love of the husband is only guided by the affectionate consideration of the natural weakness of the woman, which is to find its strength just in the ministering sovereignty of the husband (comp. Eph. 5:25-31 with 1 Pet. 3:7, οἱ ἄνδρες ... συνοικοῦντες κατὰ γνῶσιν, ὡς ἀσθενεστέρῳ σκεύει τῷ γυναικείῳ ἀπονέμοντες τιμήν, ὡς καὶ συγκληρονόμοι χάριτος ζωῆς); while the reverence of the woman for the man, and her obedience, applies not to the man as man, but to him in his godly vocation, or as to the Lord (ὑποτάσσεσθαι τῷ ἀνδρί, φοβεῖσθαι τὸν ἄνδρα ὡς τὸν Κύριον, comp. Eph. 5:33 with ver. 22; 1 Pet. 3:7 f.; ὑποτάσσεσθαι ἐν Κυρίῳ, Col. 3:18); and thus the responsive self-forgetting love maintains that *pure* gentleness which preserves the ruling will of the husband from selfish harshness, so that the love of both husband and wife only makes them mindful how they should both be mutually subject to one another in the fear of Christ (ὑποτασσόμενοι ἀλλήλοις ἐν φόβῳ Χριστοῦ, Eph. 5:21).

(5) Frivolity in entering upon marriage—which is excluded by the spirit of Christian knowledge, to which marriage is a holy vocation of life and a holy personal communion of life—consists in that unholy frame of mind, in which the choice cannot be kept within bounds by a regard to the necessary qualities of the spouse, or to the will of God in the individual course and position of life, or to the right of consent on the part of those in obedience to whom the individual as a member of a family is placed. In regard to the last point, it is the Christian insight into the nature and importance of the family which springs from wedlock which herein leads us on the right road (compare on this point the following paragraph). But since here already, where the question turns upon the right entering upon marriage, the question presses itself upon us, how far the force of the parental will may be justified in opposing limits to our own choice, this point may at once and briefly be settled in this place naturally, not in the sense of a positive legal determination, as the community of the church or state settles it, but in the light of moral justification and duty, in the way in which parents have to lay down a standard, and children to recognize the regulative wishes of their parents. What Paul (1 Cor. 7:36, 37) says with respect to a father's will, may serve analogously to show how far it may decide the question of the marriage or non-marriage of a daughter. The apostle places this, in neither of the two cases, in such a way as if the parental decision was a matter of purely arbitrary caprice. The father must first have become convinced in his heart, and indeed in such a way that he makes the decision of his heart depend upon

the way in which he has come clearly to understand the position of the child. According to this he judges whether he is master of his own will, while he knows his own will to be free from any determining necessity (μὴ ἔχων ἀνάγκην) which may exist in the state of his child (comp. with μὴ ἔχειν ἀνάγκην, ver. 37, the consideration which in ver. 36 is claimed for the ἀσχημονεῖν ... ἐὰν ᾖ ὑπέρακμος). By analogy with this, we should be justified in saying that even there, where it was not a question of marrying or not marrying, but simply of the latter, the expression of the wish of the parents is justified, and son and daughter are bound to give it consideration. And the moral affection of children will not demand the recognition of the just right of majority and independence, but in all cases will seek for the consent of their parents as for a blessing on their marriage. The positive *command* of parents, however, to marry this or that person is, from the very nature of that unconstrained inclination which the very essence of marriage lays claim to, out of the lawful jurisdiction of parental authority. And an unconditional authority *to forbid* marriage can neither be conceded to parents, nor can a duty of unconditional obedience be imposed upon children, if the refusal of parents is tainted with injustice; and the right is conceded to son or daughter by public law to free themselves from the unjust invasion of their free independence on the part of their parents. For Christianity recognizes no right of parental authority without a moral motive; and in the case of children who have grown up to independence of resolution and decision, no duty of obedience apart from a moral feeling. Neither under the appeal to parental right may an immoral pretension be hidden; nor may such be granted or recognized under the name of filial obedience, whether this pretension assume the shape of command or prohibition. Purely arbitrary authority is excluded on both sides: on that of the parents by the moral and religious care for the child, and on that of the children by moral and religious affection towards the parents. No absolute rule on either side can be laid down: the nature of the individual instance must decide in all cases. The main point is, whether children and parents can justify and answer for their conduct, not to each other, but to the Lord. That, moreover, the future fate of marriage is essentially determined by the mode of forming the tie in the married relation, and that it is seldom possible afterwards to rectify what is done in this matter against God's ordinance, may be considered scarcely to need mention, if this sin were not one of almost constant occurrence.

To guard against any breach of marriage in our social intercourse with others of the opposite sex, is, irrespective of the earnestness in which marriage and the sanctity of marriage is held by the Christian (τίμιος ὁ γάμος ἐν πᾶσι, καὶ ἡ κοίτη ἀμίαντος· πόρνους δὲ καὶ μοιχοὺς κρινεῖ ὁ Θεός, Heb. 13:4), and of those weapons of grace which he possesses for the struggle, an easy matter for the Christian frame of mind, because the Christian recognizes the beginning of sin, and because for him even a glance of concupiscence on the wife of another is a commission of adultery in the heart (πᾶς ὁ βλέπων γυναῖκα πρὸς τὸ ἐπιθυμῆσαι αὐτὴν ἤδη ἐμοίχευσεν αὐτὴν ἐν τῇ καρδίᾳ αὐτοῦ, Matt. 5:28).

Finally, for the Christian sentiment, to which the sexual communion of marriage is an entering into an association of life and duties, which from its nature is to have a life-long permanence, two grounds alone, apart from the sundering of the tie by death, can be conceived as dissolving this bond by human culpability. The one is by the sinful violation of the substantial character of wedlock brought about by a fault on the part of one of its members, by reason of which the guilty party forfeits a right to the continuation of the tie, and hereby gives to the blameless partner a justification for dissolving the still existing marriage, or for causing its dissolution. One offence alone is mentioned in Scripture (Matt. 5:32, 19:9, and the parallel passages in the other evangelists) as a ground for a moral right to dissolve an existing marriage—that of adultery. Another reason which we may conceive for the dissolution of the married communion which is entered upon for life, consists in the sinful disruption of the tie itself, *i.e.* in the culpable deprivation of possession which one spouse inflicts upon the other, in such a manner that there can no longer be a question of the continuance of marriage. This is that culpable separation which Paul has in view (1 Cor. 7), and in which he pronounces one so deprived of possession, without blame on his part, free of the duty of considering himself still bound to the depriver (7:15, εἰ ὁ ἄπιστος χωρίζεται, χωριζέσθω· οὐ δεδούλωται ὁ ἀδελφὸς ἢ ἡ ἀδελφὴ ἐν τοῖς τοιύτοις). Neither in the one nor in the other case is it declared that the innocent party *must* there dissolve the still existing marriage or cause it to be dissolved, here look upon the dissolved and disrupted wedlock as also for him dissolved and torn asunder; but only that he has a *right* in the one case to dissolve the still existing marriage, in the other case to be allowed to consider himself in his own person free, and no longer bound to a marriage which has already ceased to exist. On the ground for so viewing the two expressions of Scripture, and on the way in which they are destined to regulate the conscientious behaviour of the Christian, and how from them are developed privileges for the community, without these declarations being of themselves of the nature of legislative rules, I may refer to a work of mine I have before mentioned—*die Ehescheidungsfrage*. The question of the *law* of marriage does not here come into consideration, but only the moral sentiment of the Christian, which prevents him from thinking of a dissolution of the marriage-tie, except in the case of ungodly crime on the part of the partner, by which such a one either forfeits his right in marriage, or has in matter of fact robbed the other party of the state of marriage. And if civil society in its sphere and by its legislation may perhaps, as in the case of Israel, admit, on account of the hardness of men's hearts, other reasons for divorce (comp. Matt. 19:8), yet will the genuine Christian in his own person never lay claim to such grounds of divorce, nor will he ever or in any form be able in the name of Jesus Christ to pronounce such divorce or such re-marriage on these grounds good. The protection possessed by the Christian against the misery and trouble of the married state by which the world is polluted and troubled, is Christian conscientiousness in entering upon and in the cherishing of marriage.

(6) The evil passion is the selfish selling of the heart to the possession and will of one's spouse, accompanied by an undervaluing of the will of God in the vocation of marriage, and in the vocation of the married with respect to the kingdom of God, as well as in the disregard of that difference in which even in the state of wedlock the common possession of inferior blessings must be subordinated to the mutual possession and mutual guardianship of those of a higher nature. Hence the fulfilling of household and other virtues of the calling not for the sake of the spouse, but for that of God and of His divine word (comp. *e.g.* Tit. 2:5); the placing in a lower rank of the relations to one's partner as compared with our relations to God (according to the analogy of 1 Cor. 7:1-6); in short, the having a wife as if one had not (1 Cor. 7:29). But in the sanctity of self-denying love alone the married relation is and remains analogous to that mystery in which the love of Christ stands to His church; and the latter also is, like the wife from her husband, flesh of His flesh, bone of His bone. See Eph. 5:21-32.

§ 53. A. b. *The Family, and its Relation to the Realization of Christian Virtue*

The distinct character which belongs to the family as the result of the tie of marriage, is that of descent or blood-relationship. By virtue of this, every individual human being finds himself in a social relation which is totally independent of his own choosing—whose natural force, as the supporter of the higher moral aims, and as a means of education for the ends of our earthly human social existence, it is the problem of Christian virtue to recognize, to regulate, and to sanctify. And wherever that family state which is the result of marriage has concentrated itself into the narrowest circle of the household, and separated itself into a community of which we allow not only the members of the family, but also other inmates of the household as helpers and servants in the family vocation, to partake, there Christian virtue manifests itself, by transferring also to all members of the household that which it has recognized as the power, right, and duty of a true family affection. That everything which is called a household should be supported by the spirit of that true family love, is the most immediate object of Christian family virtue (1). The sincerity of this family love however, as it is destined to be the soul of the household, shows itself further in this, that it maintains intact the self-denial of affection, as it is involved in the natural and mutual higher and lower rank of the members of the family and the household, *i.e.* that it equally preserves the display of family affection in the limits of that personal higher and lower rank which properly belongs to the vocation of the different members of the family and household, as it keeps the accomplishment of that higher and lower ordering in the limits not alone of the natural, but of the divinely sanctioned affection, and thus not less checks the worldly absence of love, than inordinate affection in the relations of the members of the family and household to each other (2). As, however, the maintenance of the vocation of each member in its proper limits and its proper tasks is a problem of Christian family virtue, so does the same hold good for the maintenance of those divinely appointed natural limits, in which individual family groups are comprised and separated from those of others. The more closely and intimately, through consanguinity and affinity, the moral ties of connection of piety and of higher and lower rank are already fixed in nature by divine appointment, so much the more ungodly and unnatural it is for the Christian to break this order of connection, once for all and already laid down, by a disregard of a reverential dread of the already existing family ties, in its stead to place the matrimonial bond of sexual fellowship by a wicked exercise of arbitrary power,—to traverse one order of things with another, and thus to destroy both. Herein lies the moral ground of the horror of marriage within near degrees of blood-relationship, and of the duty of the Christian family spirit to guard as holy those natural limitations which lie in this relationship against the confusion of sexual attraction, as being a divine arrangement (3). But it is, above all, the business of the Christian family spirit to keep the appreciation of the natural force of family affection itself within its just bounds, and even in it to recognize only the natural basis of higher moral relations and duties; to check the blindness and pretended despotism of purely human and natural family love; and to take heed that we do not raise up, out of the limitation to the possession of earthly and human family happiness and enjoyment, a barrier and a rampart against the coming in of the Spirit of God into the house, and against the just subordination of all family relations to the higher ends of the community of God's kingdom; nay, also, even to the higher task of the social community, which is to be placed in a higher rank than the spirit of family (4). For, superior to the private bond of family affection and family privileges stands the ordinance of the community and of public law, to which the family and its vocation only stand in the relation of a part to the great whole; which comprises the family in it, but is not comprised by it; and for which the family offers types of a real fellowship of love, without being able by their means to maintain in its due force the objective bonds of the community; while, conversely, the public community guards by right and law the existence of the family in its fundamental import for the public society as a legal institution; and while, again, that which the family offers to us as an earthly type of a natural innate love reaches only, in the fellowship of the kingdom of Christ, its perfect and holy realization in that brotherly and sisterly affection which is born of God (5).

(1) That marriage and family are as closely related to each other as foundation and superstructure, is evident of itself. But strange is the requisition which is thence derived, that we should not take into consideration the nature of the family and the spirit of the family by itself. For the communion of the sexes, as it determines the nature of marriage, does not come at all into consideration in regard to the family which springs

from marriage; so that it either must be directly excluded from the relations that bind together the members of the family, or in any case may not be named as the bond of union in which, under all circumstances, the nature of the relations of family associations lies. The existence of the family is therefore the natural and divinely blessed result of marriage. The personal communion of two individuals of different sexes enlarges itself in the family to a community of many persons in dependence on the founders of the family. The blessing which marriage confers upon those whom it has united extends itself, by means of the family state and in the family, to the human race. But as the family condition itself is by no means the free union of two persons for the fulfilment of the natural purpose of the sexes, but presupposes this, and is its natural result and consequence, therefore also the blessing which, by virtue of the family state, comes to family affection is brought about in a different way than to the married in wedlock. There are, it is true, the same elements of unselfish affection, of higher and lower ordering in personal position, in which the moral and educational importance of the family relation is shown. But, whereas with the married the spirit of a true community of the sexes supposes these moral elements by the voluntary establishment of a new relation, and finds itself with them in this self-formed relation, these same elements are found in the family apart from all reference to a communion of the sexes, by virtue of innate and natural instinct, by virtue of an innate social relation, by virtue of a personal and mutual relation founded on birth and descent, and on a spirit of good-will and affection resting on this. This is a divine dispensation of the greatest moment, that, just by virtue of the family ties (in which the existence of the race continually renews and increases itself, and which is the foundation of all future human society), the individual life of man is destined to find itself in a fellowship whose intrinsic nature and order suggest to man the sentiment and display of a self-subjecting, self-denying love, as that which is natural; only not in the sense of a natural necessity, but "naturally," as a result of instincts which are innate, of a mixed spiritual and corporeal nature, and according to the nature of that community which has surrounded man from the commencement of his existence with the charms and impulses for him peculiar to its nature. To recognize this as a blessing given by God to His creatures, and to feel as a severe affliction the destiny of being deprived of this family society, as it may occur through death or the fault of men—all this suggests itself to the Christian as readily as he, on the other hand, knows how often family impulses can become a curse to men,—how closely to all that is inborn sin and corruption cleave, from which it must first be purified in order to be a natural determination in the sense in which such is a creaturely ordinance of *God*,—and how little on this account the empirical state of the family in itself is for the Christian that moral blessing which is to be struggled for and obtained on the ground of this union and within its sphere, but only the vehicle of a divinely ordained fruitful soil, on which with due care the plants of natural human and God-pleasing affection can and are intended to germinate. As an institution established in the order of creation for the education of man, the family union has a divinely moral signification; but whether it remains what it is and should be, lies not in the magical influence of the ordinance, but depends on the moral estimation of this blessing on the part of those who stand within its sphere.

The order of the community which associates individuals more closely with each other is given in blood-relationship itself. But the outward form in which it attains a more intense effect is that of the household. So far as this is founded on marriage, it comprises those united together by the fellowship of descent. In this sphere has to be developed that which is called natural and inborn family affection. The first sign, however, that this family love is not of a selfish nature, and does not resolve itself into egotistical covetousness and selfish pleasure, must be shown in this, that it forms the atmosphere of the house in which one feels it incumbent to let all take a part who stand in nearer or more remote connection with the house, above all those who by the family have been voluntarily admitted therein in order to be helps and servants in the family vocation. This is a point which expressly characterizes the true Christian family feeling, and renders it necessary, in the definition of the family, along with the narrower and proper family circle to mention in a wider sense also the members of the household. That which, independently of the family and household circle, presents itself as a relation of mastership and servitude, has its law in the division of vocations appertaining to the human and civil community, and to that spirit of the kingdom of Christ appointed to penetrate the social community.

Since it lies in the nature of all divinely bestowed creature ordinances and endowments, that man should receive from them the impulse to seek and to find in them that which he has to recognize as the moral idea imparted to them by God, and the self-realization answering to it; therefore the blessing of that natural impulse (as it exists in the innate family order and family love) goes only so far as to lend to man natural relations and natural instincts, on whose ground the personally free conduct may develop and exercise itself in a God-pleasing form, and learn to discover and to love within the domain of the creature life the divine idea and the divine truth which God has placed within the reach of every one in the innate relations of his life on earth. But the more man is disposed not only totally to misapprehend and misappreciate the purpose of that natural impulse which has become his portion from God, but also to pervert the divine ordinance in this way, that he loses, in his love for the means of his education, the love for the divine ends of that education, and thus, in the cultivation of the natural love of family, loses sight of its pedagogical importance for the understanding and the requirements of that community of love which prevails in the kingdom of God, so much the more is shown also in the family and its divine object the spirit of the Christian sentiment as the spirit of true fulfilment of that which is ordained by nature.

(2) The blessing which the *limits of the vocation* of the individual members of the family circle, as of that of the

household in a narrower or wider sense, are designed to bring in *personal superiority and subordination*, may by selfishness be destroyed in two ways, viz. either by perverting the law of love into a false equalization of the vocation of the members, or by not fulfilling the law of the ordering of vocation and its maintenance in a spirit of love, but making it felt in a manner repugnant to love. This unnatural violation of the order of nature may, under certain circumstances, assume a pseudo-Christian appearance. Thus the weak, ape-like love of parents, the neglect of righteous severity and discipline, borrows often the name of Christian mildness and indulgence. Harshness and bitterness of training (ἐρεθίζειν, παροργίζειν τὰ τέκνα, Col. 3:21, Eph. 6:4) calls itself, on the contrary, Christian denial of natural love. Under the pretext of Christian maturity or Christian resolution, children often emancipate themselves from that paying of honor (τιμᾶν, comp. Matt. 15:4, Eph. 6:1–3) which under all circumstances, even when direct reproaches ought to reach parents, must remain the form of childlike testimony. Not less is it to transmute the relation of Christian brotherhood (under which pretext servants from of old have cherished their lusts), the divinely appointed relation between masters and servants, into a false equality; or under the name of Christian liberty, and of Christian duty of reproof, to give themselves up to disobedience and opposition in place of obedience. (Comp. the reciprocal exhortations of the Apostles Paul and Peter to the slaves: οἱ δὲ πιστοὺς ἔχοντες δεσπότας, μὴ καταφρονείτωσαν, ὅτι ἀδελφοί εἰσιν· ἀλλὰ μᾶλλον δουλευέτωσαν, ὅτι πιστοί εἰσι καὶ ἀγαπητοί, 1 Tim. 6:2. Οἱ οἰκέται, ὑποτασσόμενοι ἐν παντὶ φόβῳ τοῖς δεσπόταις, οὐ μόνον τοῖς ἀγαθοῖς καὶ ἐπιεικέσιν, ἀλλὰ καὶ τοῖς σκολιοῖς. Τοῦτο γὰρ χάρις, εἰ διὰ συνείδησιν Θεοῦ ὑποφέρει τις λύπας, πάσχων ἀδίκως, 1 Pet. 2:18 ff.) But the perverted bearing of servants is also just as often met by a perverted bearing of masters, who either think, in the abandonment of their rights as masters, to make the servant sensible of the benefit of the relation of Christian brotherhood, or who, under the mask of a Christian assertion of their rights, disguise selfish and unloving harshness. Against all self-deception and hypocrisy of this kind reacts that one spirit of Christ, by virtue of which a man transfers to the relation of family only that which he has recognized as the signification of his earthly calling, and of his earthly position in general; that is, that in the family also the fixing of limits is a divine order of things, which is not to be set aside, but maintained—maintained by the power of the Spirit of Christ, who is just as much a Spirit of righteousness as of self-denying, merciful love. For then the relation of parents to children becomes παιδείᾳ καὶ νουθεσίᾳ Κυρίου (Eph. 6:4), in the power and after the model of that training in which God the Lord trains us men, His children (comp. especially Prov. 3:11, 12, Heb. 12:5 ff., ὃν ἀγαπᾷ Κύριος, παιδεύει· μαστιγοῖ δὲ πάντα υἱὸν ὃν παραδέχεται, and Prov. 13:24, 23:13, 14, 29:15). For the end of parental care and labor is not the obedience of the child in general, but ὑπακούειν ἐν Κυρίῳ (Eph. 6:1); and if there is once that obedience in the Lord, then also it will not be wanting in the self-denying love of the child, who is far removed from being embittered by righteous chastisement (comp. Prov. 13:1), or from denying, in any way soever, pious, active love to his parents (Prov. 23:22; comp. as a contrast to hypocritical piety, Mark 7:11 ff.). And thus, through the one transference of the God-designed family relations into the relation to the will and spirit of a Christian, everywhere does the spirit of just fulfilment make itself felt without any disturbance of divinely ordered limits. For, according to the apostle, slaves render obedience to their masters "as to Christ" (Eph. 6:5); and masters cause their servile condition to be forgotten by their treatment of them as brothers (Philem. 15). In this way nothing is changed in the form (1 Cor. 7:21), but all is new through the spirit of liberty in Christ, which alone gives to every earthly form its right character, and excludes every perversion of earthly forms by selfish abuse (comp. 1 Cor. 7:22).

(3) The history of nations bears in law and morality evidence to the fact that the relation here touched upon is rooted in an *ethos* of human nature, and did not first become the object of the moral consciousness through the revelation of

Christ. This is expressly confirmed by the Apostle Paul, when he reproaches the Corinthians that they allowed a scandalous connection which does not take place even *among the heathen* (as a *res licita*), viz. that a man, in violation of blood-relationship, should have intercourse with his father's wife, *i.e.* his stepmother (1 Cor. 5:1). The tracing out of boundaries, as to how the knowledge of the ties of relationship within which marriage and the intercourse of the sexes is a sin, differently defines the forbidden degrees in right and law, belongs not to the object of our work. But only in illustration of that upon which the question turns, it may be mentioned that this "horror naturæ" holds good unconditionally of marriages between parents and children as well as between brothers and sisters, between step-parents and step-children as well as between step-brothers and step-sisters; and more conditionally between uncle and niece, aunt and nephew, and between cousins. And when we call this a "horror naturæ," it ought not to be forgotten that this horror has reference not only to the naturally existing awe and piety towards those relations of the community hereby laid down for individuals, but at the same time rests on the dread of violating that natural vocation by which the race should form and shape itself out of the family in historical succession, not as *one* family, but as one out of distinct and remote groups of families, by means of the marriage connection ever newly replenishing, extending, and diversifying itself. From a consideration of both these points, results that moral principle which lies at the root of this natural feeling of horror, and with which principle we are here only concerned. From their consideration also, we arrive at the understanding why this natural horror must necessarily follow a historical development. It could not hold good where, as in the days of the first creation, the whole race of humanity consisted of and was represented by *one* family. It must necessarily have arisen when, by the diffusion of the human race, the difference between family arid race, the vocation of the family and that of the race stood out in a light growing ever clearer, and the duty of its vocation suggested to the family that it should watch over the natural and specific basis of its special organization (established through blood-relationship and intermarriage), and the relations of piety thereby given, with just as much awe as conversely it must have become a matter of conscience to the community to keep sacred the specific basis of the family organization, and to separate it from that specific way in which, through entering into marriage connections, the members of the race not yet united by family ties, nor bound to each other by specific and moral piety, are naturally destined to enlarge and extend in new family associations the articulated organization of the whole. The horror of an obliteration and mixture of the specifically distinct natural basis of the organization of families and the race, and of the moral relations of attraction and of fellowship, which condition in a manner specifically distinct the organization of both these states,—this it is which is the inmost germ of that general conscience with respect to the different degrees of family relationship which forbid wedlock. This has also come to be expressed in the law of Moses (Lev. 18 and 20), and indeed not only in reference to the relations of the nation of Israel, however much the exceptional case of the Levirate marriage (Deut. 25:5 ff.) rests on the specific importance of the individual family descent of the Israelites. This case can only serve in general analogy to make us understand that, in the more distant degrees of family relationship which arise from affinity, the rule is not an inviolable one, but only opposes its violation becoming a practice of general morality or immorality, while in individual cases of a peculiar character a justifiable exception is not inconceivable. But the more definitely the question turns upon the family bond in its relation to the general association of race, and conversely not upon the moral advantages of the individual's private possession, but upon those of the community; so much the less can the conscience of individuals decide upon the right preservation of these advantages, but the general conscience of the community by public right and law, the observance of which then becomes a duty of Christian conscientiousness. On the development of this right, comp. *e.g.* J. Stahl, *Rechts- und Staatslehre*, 2d ed. p. 354 ff.; also some pertinent remarks in Marheinecke, *System of Theological Morals*, pp. 500–502.

(4) In the full recognition of the blessing and of the divine appointment and importance of the family and the family spirit, yet even here to assert its right limits and true liberty is essentially a power of the spirit of Christian piety. This exerts itself first of all in life within the family itself. The Christian spirit excludes here also all human slavery, and all deification of man. In an orderly way, the energy of this spirit is brought into play by the Christian deportment of parents, and the training of their children in this spirit, which is something quite distinct from mere instruction in the doctrines of the Church, discourses concerning Christianity and Christian truth—[not that], but the personal attestation of Christian truth to the child in act, power, and life. Then will the liberty in Christ be preserved to the child, by which in the years of knowledge it will be able to decide how far the divine will has been presented to him in the will of his parents, and how far not. For Christian parents do not *wish* to train their children to an unconditional subjection to *their* will. In such a spirit, then, also will brothers and sisters be guarded against an idolatrous mutual admiration, and servants from a blind surrender to every godly or ungodly act of will of their masters. But if this Christian family spirit does not take its rise from the heads of the family themselves, but makes a way for itself through the hearts of the subordinate members of the household, in that case it is the power and perception of this spirit which preserve the family from the misfortune, that the natural higher ordering of the heads of the family should become an ungodly obstacle to the influence of the Spirit of God, and the family obedience and family love should become an unholy impediment to the divinely willed attestation of the truth. For it is not family spirit and family pleasure which are the end of the ways of God upon earth, but a spirit of family which is subservient to the kingdom of God, and a family happiness that is happy in the peace of God. Therefore, even when the family

happiness and the peace of the household should apparently give way before the entrance of the truth and the peace of God into a house, this does not deceive the Christian, nor entice him in any way to a denial of the truth for the sake of the maintenance of this happiness. For that saving truth here below is taken possession of with a struggle, the Christian has already experienced in his own heart; and that peace and that happiness which give way before the blessedness of the peace in Christ, show themselves in this very circumstance to be the peace and prosperity of *ungodly self-delusion*. If, therefore, the chastising judgments of the Spirit of truth come upon the false peace of a household, the Christian is not terrified, and does not resist it, painfully as he feels and much as he sorrows under the infliction. For he remembers the prophetic declaration of his Master (Matt. 10:34–38, Μὴ νομίσητε ὅτι ἦλθον βαλεῖν εἰρήνην ἐπὶ τὴν γῆν, κ.τ.λ. Ἐχθροὶ τοῦ ἀνθρώπου, οἱ οἰκιακοὶ αὐτοῦ, κ.τ.λ. Comp. Mic. 7:6). And equally well he knows what his task is, if the love he has for his own family should become a temptation to him to renounce the love and the imitation of his Master (Luke 14:26, Εἴ τις ἔρχεται πρός με, καὶ οὐ μισεῖ τὸν πατέρα ἑαυτοῦ καὶ τὴν μητέρα, καὶ τὴν γυναῖκα καὶ τὰ τέκνα, καὶ τοὺς ἀδελφοὺς καὶ τὰς ἀδελφάς, ἔτι δὲ καὶ τὴν ἑαυτοῦ ψυχήν, οὐ δύναταί μου μαθητής εἶναι). This is the sacrifice of no slight happiness for the possession of a higher, but the sacrifice of a delusive and sin-corrupted happiness for the possession of that which is the true. And thus also is accomplished the gracious will of God not only towards the individual, but towards the family itself, when the man learns and teaches how to discriminate in his family between the family blessing and the blessing of God. For precious as is the parental blessing, in which they bless their children in accordance with God's will (comp. Eph. 6:1–4), equally valueless is it if they bless in opposition to the will of God, and equally powerless is their curse if it contravenes the blessing of God (קִלְלַת חִנָּם לֹא תָבֹא, Prov. 26:2).

(5) The Christian estimation of the family spirit and the family love preserves the divine blessing not only for the family,

but also for the public community. On the one hand, namely, the Christian understands right well, that in the manner of family affection is given the natural type for the character of the social fellowship, in the way in which it is intended to unite together the members of the human race in general; that every vocation of superior rank, by virtue, age, and profession in life—as in the case of the old man, the teacher, the master—has the honors of a father, and finds its accomplishment in the manner of a father (comp. 1 Tim. 5:1, πρεσβυτέρῳ μὴ ἐπιπλήξῃς, ἀλλὰ παρακάλει ὡς πατέρα; in reference to teachers the apostle's exemplar, 1 Cor. 4:14, 15, 1 Thess. 2:11); that the right equality in personal friendship, as in the intercourse of mutual vocations, is intended to bear the character of brotherly love, etc.; nay, that the active operation of the Spirit of Christ in His kingdom aims at training men in brotherly and sisterly communion, so that the whole conception of this community and its affection resolves itself into this, τὴν ἀδελφότητα ἀγαπᾶν (1 Pet. 2:7). On the other hand, in this very thing the Christian recognizes the fact that this form of community is the end of all earthly society, and is not the result of the natural spirit of the family, but of the Holy Ghost, and therefore cannot be obtained by the spirit of family; nor will it exist as the general form of human society, apart from the kingdom of grace and of glory. What, therefore, the Christian knows as a result of the Spirit of the grace of God in Christ, that he cannot conceive as being restored by the spirit of the family and the natural family affection in the family itself, to say nothing of its being so in human social existence. He cannot do so even in reference to that species of empirical family and social state which needs sanctification and purification by the grace of God. But he cannot do so also in consideration of the difference which exists between the aim of the mere family life and that of the collective body of the human race, as well as of the condition of individual nations. The moral idea of the family belongs to the divine plan of the world, but this plan does not resolve itself into the idea of the family. The very isolation of the family and its relations excludes the possibility of regarding its form and spirit as the spirit and form of the community. Nay, the ecumenical idea of the sovereign destiny of man over the earth cannot make itself felt as being able to be accomplished by the family and the family spirit. For a vocation which embraces the totality of all earthly life-relations, cannot attain to shape and understanding from the nature of that one relation of life which, like the family, ever determines only one isolated life-sphere of individuals. The common *ethos*, the national *ethos*, has the existence and the moral import of the family for a factor; but this one factor does not comprise all the factors which condition the existence, the moral significance, and the problem of the community, of the conditions of peoples, of the collective body of man's race. As the family, in its purely natural aspect, does not exist for itself, but bears in it the destination to be the natural root of the existence and the diffusion of the race, the species; so, conversely, is the race, the species, with its life-relations, not merely for the family, but bears in itself the universal aims of life which belong to the whole human race, which the consciousness of the social body has to embody in public law for all divisions of the community as a higher power, to which the community, in the unity and connection of all its members, is subjected as to common ends and commands which stand over all of them. Like the existence of the individual, so also that of the family, as a separate but perfect part, is an *object* of public law; but the *subject* of law is neither the individual nor the complete section consisting of the family, but the totality of human society in the organization of all its natural social ties, as supporter of the idea of law which embraces all the relations of life. As such, the community is destined for a protection and guard of the family, but not the family for a protection and guard of the community, neither on the side of its power nor on that of the idea, which lies at the source of its existence, and conditions its peculiar spirit as well as the peculiar form of its association.

From all these reasons taken together, the restoration of a universal family community appears not only like a utopian dream, but also as a misapprehension of the essence and vocation of the family, and a violation of the destination of the public community and of the problem (individualized therein) belonging to the human race and to man's social existence.

§ 54. B. *The Community of the Nation and of the State, and its Relation to the Realization of Christian Virtue*

The concrete form of the collective order of man's social state—as, with a view to the care and protection of all the moral aims of our earthly life, it exists individualized in the national community, organized by legislation and authority to secure the dominion of right—possesses for the Christian the significance of a human institution, of which a divinely ordered arrangement and a divinely arranged order form the basis. For there are moral intellectual ideas and aims of man's collective existence which, living in the common convictions of the people, and first established by them as the right of custom, and afterwards by legislation, constitute the essence of those political institutions, in whose bond of common association the Christian in his natural human existence finds himself, and which are destined to limit and regulate his actions in all that which works upon the whole body, and not merely relates to the man himself, or is embraced in his influence on the relation to other individuals (comp. § 48, 51). In this subordination of the individual to the common or national *ethos* as the common conviction concerning the *moral* aims of all the relations of life—no matter in what external form of political popular constitution a people has organized itself for the establishment of its rights—the Christian sees a moral obligation towards the actually existing community of rights; which duty is at the same time a religious one, because he recognizes the order that lies at the basis of all these human institutions as a postulate of the divine will, and as a providential arrangement in the divine government of the world (1). Since, however, the divine will and God's providential government of the world are never carried out in human society without the instrumental co-operation of man; nay, since on this very co-operation the moral significance of human society rests; and since, moreover, there constantly clings to it not only the weakness of human imperfection, but also the tendency to a disregard or perversion of the divine will,—therefore in the established legal and political community the knowledge of the Christian clearly distinguishes the imperfections of the human form from the perfection of the divine will, or that of the fundamental idea which lies at its basis from its human development; and with the recognition of the divine foundation of social order the Christian is far removed from the opinion that what is actually established is absolutely the morally reasonable, or that the human form of the institution is unconditionally an expression of what is divinely intended. On the contrary, the sense in which the Christian surrenders himself to the empirical form of the system of right which belongs to the political community, is rather this, that he sees in the fact of a social state, organized for the carrying out of law, the realization of a divinely willed and divinely purposed ethical order, whose moral significance he honors, notwithstanding all its conceivable shortcomings in detail, by conforming his conduct and actions, so far as they in their object or operation have relation to the community, to the laws of the community (2). And it is not the laws of this or that particular state which have in the eyes of the Christian, as it were like the law of God, a binding and obligatory force; but by virtue of his connection with the public community within which he lives, it becomes his duty to obey the existing ethical system as laid down in law and right, and to reverence it as a bond which he is just as little justified in disregarding or violating by a wicked exercise of arbitrary power as this very connection with his people (3). As, however, that maintenance of the moral system of life in the community which is rendered possible by public law, is, from the very nature of law, not the realization of the positive nature of the idea, but only the establishment of its external limitations, beyond which a line of action becomes a violation of the moral idea of the community, and must be tested not by positive law, but by the idea which lies at its root, whether these external limits have been justly traced;—so it is hence to be inferred, that that legal order which regulates and binds the actions of the members of a community, cannot be the rule which constrains the judgment concerning the propriety and immutability of the legal institutions; and that it cannot be deduced from the existence of a legal system in itself, that it is destined to a permanent and immutable existence. For this reason also it is not the actual shape of the laws and institutions in existence which the Christian looks upon as something immutable, but he finds the immutable element only in the most general and highest principles of positive law (the *Rechtsidee*), which, although in themselves they do not contain the framing of law, do yet contain the standard for opinion on every positive law, and a guide for its continuous development. And for this very reason, because the Christian cannot transfer the immutability of the principles to the nature of those positive legal ordinances which are formed by man in accordance with them, and which are capable of free shaping and historical modification, he cannot view the duty of the public community in framing and maintaining the laws, and the participation of individuals consistently with their vocation, as the mere maintaining of that human institution, but always at the same time also as the preservation and furtherance of the idea which lies at the root, and of the corresponding proportion of support and development of the existing state of positive law; and he can regard all this on his part as a Christian duty (4). In like manner, however, as the Christian recognizes as his guide for his service in the earthly duties of the individual the relation of the same to his service to the kingdom of Christ, and is aware that in the spirit of this kingdom alone the strength is given for a due performance of his earthly duties, so he expects also the proper fulfilment of the collective vocation and order only in the measure in which the spirit of Christ pervades the popular sentiment both of those who command and those who obey. And conversely, he recognizes no ordinance or power of the state which either can or dare determine him to act contrary to the ordinances of the kingdom of Christ, instead of battling against the contradiction between human and divine law, and, if need be, of suffering for Christ's sake for disobedience to the claims of human authority (5).

(1) What has been said in the above paragraph may directly be compared with those positive assertions respecting this question to be found in the Scriptures of the New Testament, in order by just deduction to throw a light from them on that which has in part here been given, and which in part will be afterwards discussed, touching the significance of a constituted public community, and its existence for the guidance of the Christian's conduct. It would, to me at least, appear in more than one sense doubtful to take into the circle of our consideration that which the Old Testament presents us in laws and history as the type of the public community of Israel. For, quite irrespective of the peculiar and especial vocation of Israel among the nations of the world, here all is so rigidly determined and regulated by positive law and continual divine declaration of God's will towards this people by prophetical announcement, that no question can be entertained of an immediate transfer of the origin and regulative value of the legal state of Israel to the framing and force of the laws of other popular societies; and a recourse to the law of analogy, on account of constant exceptions, has in it something ambiguous and unstable. The history of Christianity also offers sufficient warning as to what results, if we would arbitrarily strip the unique history of Israel of this character, and would make of the popular constitution of this people, both considered in itself as well as in its relation to other nations, a type or a rule whereby to estimate the shape, value, and significance of the legal institutions of other popular communities, or to frame and legitimate their legislation. So much merely to explain why in this place a reference to the Old Testament has not been accidentally but intentionally omitted.

What we find, however, in the writings of the New Testament, is limited to a few passages, whose substance bears evidence alone to the fact that, and why, the members of the newly-formed Christian societies were not to regard themselves as withdrawn from the civil ordinances of the state in whose association they found themselves, but were to consider themselves bound to obey its ordinances. As to what concerns the established order of state government, Israel in the time of Christ assumes a position analogous to that of the apostolical Christian communities. To the actual sign of their subjection under the dominion of the Roman emperor, Christ refers the Pharisees with their hypocritical question (Matt. 22:19), in order to show by the image and superscription on the money the fact that it was, and why it was, their duty to render to Cæsar, not only the tribute, but in every other matter, the things which were Cæsar's. It is the act of submitting to the government of a foreign sovereignty whose reality is undeniable, and whose actual existence binds those subjected to it to a corresponding obedience. Further than this the passage does not go, although we know also from the history of Israel how just was the dispensation in which that people, who gave not to God what belonged to God, was bowed under the yoke of a foreign master. The relation is a different one in which the apostle finds the members of the Christian community at the same time members of the Roman state. Since Paul as well as Peter exhorts the members of the Christian community to obedience, and to the fulfilment of those duties required of them by the civil order of the state, these exhortations themselves permit us to infer what importance the apostle attributed to the nature of this ordinance itself. Two things are here asserted at the same time—that this order is a human establishment and institution, and that it proceeds from God, and comprises in itself a divine substratum. Peter declares the first, when he urges the Christian to obedience to every human ordinance (πάσῃ ἀνθρωπίνῃ κτίσει, 1 Pet. 2:13) which serves ends which a king has to carry out, or governors appointed by him. But since Peter requires such obedience for the Lord's, for Christ's sake (διὰ τὸν κύριον), and includes "the giving honor to the king" (τὸν βασιλέα τιμᾶτε) in the sphere where the freedom of the servants of God is duly exercised (vers. 16, 17), there must lie in this "ordinance of man" a relation which is not of a human, but of a divine character. A human ordinance certainly is that civil community of which Peter knew his readers to be members; and a human ordinance it is (except in Israel) in all public communities, since in them all legislation is the product of human effort. But it has a divine relation, because that which the law is intended to protect is moral aims of the community, which man cannot originate in himself, but which have been engrafted by God in the human race. Touching this hereafter. Paul, on the other hand, since he declares every one, without exception, bound (πᾶσα ψυχή, Rom. 13:1) to be obedient to the existing authority, immediately declares the whole weight of the reason on which this duty depends. "For," says he, "there is no power which is not of God" (οὐ γάρ ἐστιν ἐξουσία εἰ μὴ ἀπὸ Θεοῦ); "and the powers that actually exist are ordained of God" (αἱ δὲ οὖσαι ὑπὸ τοῦ Θεοῦ τεταγμέναι εἰσίν, Rom. 13:1). For this reason he calls resistance to authority resistance to the ordinance of God (διαταγή, ver. 2), and says it is their (*i.e.* of those who resist) fault and blame when (that which they fear in the magistrate) punishment comes upon them (οἱ δὲ ἀνθεστηκότες ἑαυτοῖς κρῖμα λήψονται, ver. 2). And now in what follows there is brought forward just the moral import which teaches us to recognize the idea of authority in itself, as well as the vocation of those actually appointed to exercise it, as something proceeding from and ordained of God. For, so it is declared, he who does *evil*, and not he who does right, has to fear the ruler; he, however, who wishes not to dread the magistrate, let him do what is good, and he will have praise of him. For to the good applies the relation (εἰς τὸ ἀγαθόν) in which the magistrate is for us the servant of God. But if we do evil, then may we fear; for the magistrate bears not the sword in vain, for he is the servant of God in vengeful promptitude for wrath against him who does evil. Hence the necessity of obedience, not alone because of this wrath, but for conscience sake (vers. 3–5). And this same moral element in the idea of the magistrate—punishment of evil-doing, and praise of well-doing—is also mentioned by Peter (ἐκδίκησις κακοποιῶν, ἔπαινος δὲ ἀγαθοποιῶν, 1 Pet. 2:14). We understand from this passage the sense in which we are exhorted to obedience, to subjection to that which is called government and authority (ἀρχαῖς, ἐξουσίαις, ὑποτάσσεσθαι, πειθαρχεῖν, Tit. 3:1), and why kings and all other rulers are pointed out (βασιλεῖς καὶ πάντες ἐν τῇ ὑπεροχῇ ὄντες) as objects which have a claim on the prayers of the Christian, in order that we may lead a quiet and peaceable life in all godliness and honesty (1 Tim. 2:1, 2). It is a different object from that of the mere external order of things which the magistrate is appointed to serve. They are moral aims of the government of the world, whose maintenance forms the vocation of the magistrate. This vocation goes no further than the nature of the relation admits. The power of the magistrate extends, and is intended to extend, to the actions of men, but not to their sentiments. He is appointed to reward well-doing, to punish evildoing; to watch over that which God desires that men should do as members of human society, and that which He desires they should leave undone. Thus does authority rest upon a divine foundation; and its historical existence may be viewed as a divine institution, as the object of its existence is the maintenance of moral and divine aims, to which all human society ought to consider itself subject for the sake of God. These are the aims which are binding on men in their conscience, and not from fear of authority alone. And not to the human institution as such does the Christian feel himself bound, but to it as the divinely appointed bearer and guardian of divine and moral requirements made on human society. In what form and manner among men the power of the magistrate is to be established by them—on this point the writers of the New Testament say nothing. But that wherever men look upon its establishment as an affair merely of human choice, or for human ends alone, or where authority is regarded merely as carrying out mere human will, whether of individuals or of the whole body, there Scripture declares plainly that it is established on a false foundation. Such an ordinance is not for the satisfaction of man's *will*, but of his *consciousness*, that the ordinances he establishes for the preservation of these moral aims of the community are consistent with the divine will. Not less, however, is this the moral view of all existing ordinances of society, that every human course of action without divine direction is insufficient for the maintenance and preservation of such order. No man—no human authority—is in such a way master of the conditions of the people, that the maintenance and preservation of the powers that minister to the moral ends of human society can be thought of without the providence of the divine government of the world. Even in this point of view the authorities which exist, and which are subservient to this order, may consider themselves as appointed by God. Nowhere, indeed, for the sake of the person, but for that of their office and vocation which they exercise. This bestows on them the right to an exercise of power which is just as much the discharge of duties towards God as towards human society. In this divine authorization, however, all members of public constituted power have their share, each in his own order. For the order of this membership alone, and not an exclusive prerogative of vocational right derived from God, is intended, when the apostle places the king as exalted above the others (ὡς ὑπερέχοντα), over against the governors (ἡγεμόσιν) as sent by him (ὡς δι' αὐτοῦ πεμπομένοις, 1 Pet. 2:13, 14). Obedience for the sake of God applies to all rulers and powers whose office it is to minister to the preservation of the divinely purposed order of things in society; and the measure of respect given to them differs only according to the position occupied by each as a member of the body. And not any particular kind of organization, whether monarchical, a supreme senate, and the like, is prescribed by the Scriptures of the New Testament; but as the apostles found them, so they describe them, and, without calling them in question, merely say in what their service consists, so that we might recognize in it a service towards God, and our vocation in such service as one willed by God and proceeding from Him. This lies in that right whose nature in its ultimate ground is of divine origin; and in the execution of right alone, all power and dominion have the character of a divine mission, let them bear what name they may. Not that we might not draw, according to the naturally-organized division of the human race, a conclusion as to the kind and manner in which forms of constitution for the administration of law correspond either more or less to the natural tendencies of the human race in general, or to those of a people in itself and its historical development. But no divine rule is given for this; and if a judgment has been pronounced on this subject, it is a judgment of the human understanding, not that of a Christian bound in his conscience by a divine rule. Therefore Christian knowledge does not shut out all judgment as to the different political forms of the polity of nations, and a preference of one before others; but it destroys that political fanaticism which declares the existence of one order of things to be no order, merely because its form does not answer to this or that theory of the best form of government. In order to be obedient to any order of things, it is enough for the Christian that it exists as a legal order and for the maintenance of law, whether that order may be called monarchy, aristocracy, democracy, or by any other name.

(2) Submission to the existing order of things gains its true character by means of the other side of the knowledge, that according to the ground of its existence it is indeed divine, though as regards the means of bringing about and the form of its existence it is *human* (κτίσις ἀνθρωπίνη). It is not therefore to the Christian an incarnation of the divine will on earth, but only a human copy, with very many defects and faults; and all the different state forms constitute only so many ways of approximating to the method of God's government of the world in right and righteousness, one nearer, another more removed from the divine model, and no one ever equal to it,— a model which Christ alone will realize in the revelation of His kingdom of glory. Hence, because the Christian knows that every form of government will be accompanied, one by this, another by that defect, it would appear to him absurd to make the postulate of the *best* form the determining ground of

obedience to the *existing* order of things in which he, in spite of all defects, honors a manifestation of *God's* government of nations; and because, on the other hand, this divine order of things appears in an *earthly and human* copy, it would appear to his mind equally foolish and sinful to identify the *existing* national constitution with the law of God's divine will, and idolatrously to venerate it as the absolutely conditioning standard of life. All legal duty, moreover, only regulates that portion of the *conduct* of men which has reference to the community. In this sense alone is the individual under obligation to observe the laws; and the community organized in the magistracy for the execution of the law, to administer it. For from the external and already realized order of the state arises the legal obligation for the members of the community, and has only the maintenance of this external order for its object. The inward perfection of man is as little as the establishment of right in its true ideal a legal duty. Each is a moral obligation. Legal obligation has merely for its object, that the realized order in its regulated form should not be violated, and should be carried out by a course of action consistent with it. Hence also the result, that the fulfilling of the law is compulsory, and must be insisted on for the maintenance of order,—a relation which is totally inapplicable to the law of moral perfection. And for this reason it is least of all possible for the Christian to see in the fulfilment of legal duty the fulfilling of the law of human moral perfection. How the true moral fulfilment even of legal obligation is attained, the Christian knows out of a law of liberty and of life, which neither is a human institution, nor does it impose legal obligation; nor does it aim merely at the order of human society, but at the communion of God with man and of man with God, from which he derives the power for that doing of what is good, and for avoiding of what is evil, for which, and not against which, the order of human society also exists.

Law supposes in every case a naturally given order of things. This it does not found, but only establishes its recognition. It is not law which first forms social order, nor does it first bring it into a unity, but it presupposes the originally and naturally constituted unity of the nation, and superior to this that of the human race, as a collective and morally established existence. In the connection of the individual with this morally formed collective existence, lies the obligation to recognize its order as realized in law and discerned as common *ethos*, and to obey it. In this sense and for this reason the *existing* order of things binds the Christian also on the side of his earthly vocation to this aim, that the fulfilment of his individual vocation should correspond to the earthly collective vocation which the people, and the families of nations, the human race, have to fulfil. In like manner this order of things binds the Christian in its *existing state*, inasmuch and *so far as* the Christian, with the vocation of his earthly life, finds himself within an *existing* order of things. In such an order of things the individual is generally born. It is for him the given order to which he owes obedience, so long as he in his earthly vocation belongs to it. But if its existence comes to an end, so with it ceases the obligation of obedience which binds the Christian in his earthly calling, and no further. The existence of a present order of things can for the Christian cease to be, either in this way, that he believes that he ought on grounds of his vocation to withdraw by emigration from the people and the region in which it prevails; or in this way, that the existing order of things ceases by a destiny independent of the resolution of the individual, and gives place to another new one. In the first case the Christian character realizes itself in this, that it does not in a self-seeking arbitrary way dissolve the relation in which the Christian, through birth and by his lot in life, belongs to the order of things existing in a particular people; but only either when compelled by the individual lot in life, which never even then bears the character of caprice, or in the clear perception of a duty of his vocation, whether earthly or heavenly. For wherever the condition of a people renders the fulfilment of a man's vocation impossible, or compels him to a violation of it, he may withdraw from the grievance on account of his calling, and in that respect is in no wise prevented in justice, unless some particular legal duty or duty of his vocation binds the sufferer to the soil. The Christian sentiment forms, however, the most decided contrast to that unsteadiness of self-seeking, gain-seeking, or trouble-shirking love of adventure. Different is the state of the case under the second hypothesis, viz. that the existing order of things ceases through an event independent of the resolve of the individual. If the change is according to order, *i.e.* if there occurs in due order a change in the person of him who is invested with the exercise of power (by succession, or by a new election, etc., according to the different forms), or if there proceeds from him who is invested with the power of regulation and legislation a change in the laws consistent with the existing rights and in furtherance of good order, then the Christian will find in his vocation no hindrance to his submitting to the change as a new order of things. But if the change in the order of things comes to pass through the fortunes of nations, through the issue of a struggle entered into for the sake of the God-given vocation of a nation, in which the ordinance of a new rule is imposed upon a conquered people,—in that case there lies, neither in the violence by which the new order of things has been produced, nor in the legitimacy of that which previously existed and in the fact of having sworn to observe the same, nor in the mere fact of the abolition of the former state and the introduction of a new system, in itself a rule to determine the conscientious conduct of a Christian, *i.e.* the question whether to render obedience to the new order of things, or to refuse it. That which rather has to determine his conduct, is the question whether the law in the given case is compulsory, whether and how far the attempt at its enforcement belongs to the individual legally and in accordance with his vocation, and if and how far the nature of the new order of things is repugnant to the conscience of a Christian citizen. Now there exists in the very nature of the case, according to national right, *i.e.* for the right of one nation over against another, or of one ruler over against another, no compulsion of rights in the sense that we might hold the attempt to maintain the former possession or the former state of independence by force, as a legal duty unconditionally valid and one to be carried out. "It is a misconception," therefore, justly says Stahl (*The Existing Parties in Church and State*, Berlin 1863, p. 303), "that the principle of legitimacy, as a rigid logical doctrine in favor of an absolute unalienable nature in dynastic rights, should ignore the events of the whole history of the world, and oppose itself to all the necessities that belong to that history, and thus censure the history of the world." And it is precisely the Christian who knows of the calamitous fates of nations which by God's appointment are destined to happen either for the purpose of a righteous judgment or of wholesome chastisement; so that for the question, what conduct in such cases the people or the individual has to observe, the Christian is unable to derive any satisfaction for his conscience from any general rule, but only from an understanding of the concrete case, and from the consideration whether the compulsory character of the right is actually involved, or not. With respect, however, to the legality of the previously existing order of things, and of fidelity sworn to it, just as little can be decided therefrom, since the oath of the citizen and the subject binds him to the existing order of things, not to an order of things which, without any violation of the oath of those who have sworn it, has ceased to exist. But all that we can hence deduce is nothing more than that in such case the oath formerly taken forms no *obstacle* to our submission to the existence of a new state of things, or to our binding ourselves thereto by oath. On the contrary, we have not even in this a decisive motive given, whether a man should, on account of conscience, submit to the new order of things or not. And this so much the less, as it is not only conceivable, but a matter of historical fact, that individuals are allowed and suffered to unite themselves to a people and a state, without the requisition of the obligation of an oath to the new order of things on the part of the ruling powers. The mere fact, however, that in the place of the former legalized order of things, a new system has arisen, is just as little a motive by which to determine the conduct. For not an existing order, realized in any way, justifies us in regarding it as a real order of things; but we recognize the character of a genuine *order* of things in a social community in this, that it does not destroy, but maintains, the universal moral ends of those life-relations which are the support of human society, and those particular objects in the vocation of its members which are naturally given in a public community. Something which, under the name of a system of things, suffices to destroy the one or the other of these aims, or has such a tendency, cannot be looked upon as an order of things binding on the people or on its individual members, although that cannot be called a naturally established vocation for a people, that one nation should rule over another, or one be subjected to another, *i.e.* should discharge the duties of the calling of its national peculiarity in independence, or in dependence on another people. For this very thing is not an original and inborn system of things, but the result of a higher dispensation belonging to the history of the world. But whether in the independence or dependence of a people, *that* order of things has no claim on Christian recognition for conscience sake, which by the national *peculiarity* of the vocation and of its people militates against the universal moral ends of human society, and against the individual realization of the same. Nevertheless, nothing yet would here be said concerning the particular line of conduct in which this non-recognition for conscience sake has to realize itself. It is at least not yet given in the subjective opinion of the individual on the non-obligatory claim of a system of things; but it takes its measure and its form at the same time, according to the special vocation of the individual, and the actually existing compulsory force of the law. Herein lies the subjective and objective, the moral as well as the legal limits of our conduct. For it is one thing, the position of those who for the common weal are appointed by public law to represent and to carry out the laws of a people, for the preservation of the national vocation; and again, it is a different thing, the position of those whose duty as simple citizens is to contribute, by conforming their personal conduct to the popular order, to the maintenance of the public rights of the community. The former *are obliged* by their vocation to contend against every power which has a tendency to destroy those aims which belong to man's social state and that of nations. This the latter *can* also do, but have no vocational obligation so to act for the community's sake. The latter have only to consider if, and to what extent, the new state of things renders impossible the fulfilment of their own individual calling in its moral aims, as these are imposed upon them as members of a naturally constituted popular society, by its civil and religious relations. In the case of the one, as in that of the other, the nature of the maintenance of violated law will depend upon the measure in which this maintenance can be asserted in a legal form, *i.e.* in such a case made relatively valid. They must distinguish what social good is attainable in a legal manner for the nation as a whole, and what for the individual personally. That which, in the case of its subjugation, the people as a whole body have not succeeded in, the individual must in his own person, for the sake of the whole community, strive to rescue and to maintain. If he is convinced that he can and ought to remain in union with his native community, while the new shaping of its order of things violates his conscience, he cannot do so without protest against the obligation of such a state of things for him, and refusal of the oath of allegiance. If the authority which has subverted the legitimate constitution of the people permits such persons to remain members of the state, then any conscientious question of leaving it falls to the ground. If this is not permitted, then will the same authority compel the recusant to depart, if it does not rid itself of him in another manner. But to bring about either one or other by means of a protest, will be better than to shun the duty of protesting, and that of refusing the oath, by flight and abandonment. The latter will only then appear justifiable or not reprehensible, where the certainty previously exists, that every attempt to guard the right will, even before it is put into execution, be rendered nugatory by authority. If, however, it does not turn upon a defense against such a state of things as is in itself a subversion of the moral aims of human society and the vocation of nations, but merely upon the question of the independence or dependence of the nation; in that case at least, the justification of any resistance we may think of as founded on justice and morality, is not to be looked for in a pretended inalienability of national independence founded on divine right. For the natural separation of a people into an independent unity may be forfeited by their own fault. And the inviolability of the so-called principle of nationalities is an untruth, if it is desired to make this principle valid, in opposition to the decrees of divine justice and divine judgment in the world.

More difficult is the question when an existing order of things is assailed and overthrown *within the established* system of the community *in opposition to that order*, whether it be done by those appointed to its rule or by those subjected to their sovereignty. For in the *maintenance of order* the power of authority and the obedience of its subjects coincide; and a man cannot be called upon in the name of obedience to destroy, or to allow to be destroyed, an existing order of things in opposition to order. Where, consequently, an existing state of things is threatened by an antagonism to that order, then every Christian feels himself called upon to take part in the resistance to this order-destroying power, yet in such a manner that the form of this resistance and the individual participation in it keep themselves rigidly within the limits of the existing popular order of things and the calling of the individual, in the shape of a protest framed in accordance with the law and his own calling. Force opposed to law and order is never wielded by the Christian against revolution; nor does he advocate such a course, whether the revolution originates from above or below. He knows indeed that injustice gives birth to injustice, and violence to violence, and that in such universal disorder the judgment of God is brought about; but he is equally aware that the sin-burdened instruments of such judgments do not escape their own destruction, and that in the Christian the justice of God is thereby conqueror, that the Christian opposes justice only to injustice, and in making a stand for rights, instead of by violence, disarms the might of the aggressor by patience and perseverance. For the doctrine of the rejection of all active resistance, and of the unconditional obligation to passive obedience, contradicts equally the Christian veneration of rights, as the opinion that authority is to be obeyed merely because it is authority, while by denial and disregard of law and justice it divests itself of the claims to power which it does not possess of itself, but only on account of that right whose guardian and dispenser it is its vocation to be. I shall venture, in proof of the truth of this assertion, to quote Stahl as a testimony above suspicion, when, in reference to the doctrine of Filmer and others in the times of the Stuarts, touching "non-resistance," or the rejection of all active right of opposition, he says: "This doctrine is carried to the extreme, viz. that *an exception to the principle is never admissible, that in no possible or conceivable case resistance can be permitted*" (*Parties in Church and State*, p. 288). The *coup d'etat* which is called revolution has no sanction in the fact, that it proceeds not from below, but from above. Hence also no renunciation of the *duty* of resistance in the name of Christian obedience holds good. If, however, the resistance by means of just and constituted authority is overpowered, whether it be from above or from below, and in place of the old legitimate order of things a new one has been established, how then has the Christian to conduct himself? Even here no general rule can be laid down, but a decision must be made according to the nature of the individual case, and the position of the individual with respect to his particular vocation. For an obligatory order of things is not restored by the fact that perchance, in place of antecedent anarchy, a so-called law of order has been established. Right and rightful order are not *made* by the law, but rest on nature and history, and are something naturally and historically handed down. Law is consonant with order, if and seeing that it produces the recognition of this right; wrong does not become right by its being declared right by law. If a law establishes the principle of arbitrary tyranny or permanent revolution, since it subjects order to the mere will and caprice, whether it be of the ruler or of the people, then is such a law contrary to right, and changes order into disorder, since it constitutes, as the foundation of human order, human caprices instead of divine arrangement and guidance in nature and history. When such a law, or one similar, *i.e.* approximating to this, formally binds (which is not intended to be denied) those who are members of that community in which the law has been established, then they cannot desire so to remain members of the community, as not at the same time constantly to stand up for the right against the law which is opposed to right, and to endeavor to strive, in a way consistent with their calling and with right, to the end that right may be maintained against the law. They will not take part in any act of violence against the law, and also will not reject a law which does in effect protect legitimate order, because it has been brought about by an act of violence which they have neither sanctioned nor shared. Where, however, a law has been laid down which violates the right, there lies in the limitation to a protestation and counteracting efforts not only the exclusion of revolutionary opposition to the existing authority, but also the exclusion of that false so-called patriotic enthusiasm which, by overlooking the diversity of gifts and vocations, supposes every member of a popular community in the same way and to the same extent, according to his own discretion, appointed guardian of popular order, giving to such a perverse course of conduct the name of the virtue of political citizenship.

(4) The way in which the Christian, conformably to law and to his vocation, takes an active part in the *maintenance* of the existing *popular constitution*, has a double aspect, which is also conditioned by the Christian insight into the nature of national state systems as they exist on earth. If it is impossible for him to take part in any attempt which assumes an antagonistic position to the existing *public order of things*, there is not the least ground from this for concluding that Christian sentiment resolves itself merely into maintaining *that which actually exists*. This could only be the case when the Christian ceased

to feel convinced that in existing popular constitutions he sees ἀνθρώπινα, or if to him all which belongs thereto were an unalterable θεῖον. The more the Christian recognizes the fact that, under the name of existing order, very much that is destructive of order is to be found, so much the less can he regard as identical the conception of the maintenance of existing *order* with the maintenance of *that which exists*. If political party phraseology has placed the expressions "conservative" and "reformer" as contrasts, of which the one tendency excludes the other, there is implied, if we consider merely the abstract notion, and not the tendency which lies hidden under the name, in the Christian conviction a determination neither for the one nor for the other side, but for both at the same time, or more correctly for the one in the other, since it is impossible for Christian knowledge to conceive a maintenance of the existing order of things without a constant renewal, and the rejection of what is opposed to that order, or of a change produced in conformity with order without the maintenance of the order that exists. Only where we acknowledge in the human and legalized popular constitution either *no* divine obligatory right, or *nothing* but divinely obligatory law, there can maintenance and renewal meet each other as irreconcilable opponents—as *uncontrolled* innovation and *falsely controlled* immovability. Moreover, as well on the side of renewal as again on that of maintenance, the limitation to efforts conformable to law and vocation excludes all disturbance arising from unauthorized political meddling.

And just as little can Christian knowledge limit all share in the preservation and renovation of the popular constitution simply to those who are appointed to rule, and exclude all such as are subject to this rule. For if the *form* of the existing popular constitution completes itself in this, that some command and others obey, yet its *substance* does not resolve itself merely into the abstract relation of ruling and obeying, but has in its appointed character of a ruling exercised agreeably to its duties and to law, and obedience agreeably to its duties and to law, a plenitude of relations which makes it impossible to view the mere act of obeying and the mere act of commanding as fulfilment of the duties of our vocation. The fulfilment of a vocation is rather this, in command duly exercised according to vocation and law, and in obedience of a similar character to maintain the vocation of the individual, and that of the collective body for the welfare of the whole. That order of things which, grounded on right and acknowledged in law, is binding on all, determines the fulfilment of vocation, and makes, under certain circumstances, alike the refusal of obedience in compliance with duty, as well as the withdrawal of a command, a matter of conscience to Christian rulers and subjects. For command, like obedience, has its limits; and the same limits which exclude the self-seeking abuse of command, also exclude the self-seeking obedience as well as the self-seeking arbitrary refusal of obedience. That refusal of obedience consistently with our vocation, which in self-denial surrenders itself to every further consequence of that refusal, without on its own side leaving the ground of duty and of right, is as distant as the poles from that ἀντιτάσσεσθαι which the apostle forbids (Rom. 13:2), and which, through the connection with ver. 4, is expressly designated a πράσσειν τὸ κακόν.

But while such is the state of the case,—while command and obedience have right and law equally for their foundation as for their limit, ruler and people are equally called upon, not indeed to the execution and exercise, but to the preservation, of that right which is guarded by law,—it is in the highest degree necessary that this similar calling (which differs only in the form of its exercise) should have also in the community appointed methods of its fulfilment, by which a mutual participation in active realization is obtained; and in case of a conflict between ruler and people, justifiable resistance is released from the necessity of an arbitrary choice of means, and regulated by public order. Such is the characteristic of those political constitutions which are termed limited monarchies, because they not only keep the ruler in bounds, but also the people, to the end that both should take their part in the preservation and guardianship of the right only in efforts constitutionally regulated. Their value should least of all, in the name of Christian piety towards the sovereign, be misunderstood or denied on this account, because they, like every human institution, may be abused by dishonest intention, or in one way or the other are affected by failings or deficiencies with regard to the principle of their foundation, or to their formal shape. "I take this as my starting-point," says Stahl, "that the true unlimited monarchy is neither in itself the more perfect form of state polity, nor one more suitable to the historical relations of the German peoples; consequently that the existence of a popular representation which limits the power of the rulers under sound relations and with a sound arrangement, is a development and enrichment of the constitution—that it is, in fact, an element of German state policy." And he starts therefrom, because he has rightly recognized the fact that such a constitution is a matter of necessary requirement where the previous character of the bonds of association—one of private rights—has ceased, and into its place public right, the public import, and the political unity of all institutions and powers and rights, have entered. For there "it is a precept, that the relations of mere personal authority develop themselves into institutions and ordinances in internal conformity with law—that the magistrates rule as members of these institutions, limited by their conformity to law. It is, before all, the idea *of the state,* which the feudalistic party rejects as revolutionary or as a mere abstraction, and which signifies nothing else but just that legal order of things— that inner necessity and that ministration for the higher problems of the state—which are the limit and the precept for its rulers as well under a monarchy as in a republic." From this view results that of "political citizenship, which is the essential fellowship and the essential equality of all members of the state. There every one is immediately and of himself accounted a member of the nation and of its community" (Stahl). And on all this rests the right and the need of a popular representation. But its most essential and highest value is not that in it is given a guarantee against unjust and unlawful encroachments on the part of its rulers, and the means of regulated opposition, and such as is consistent with vocation against such attempts; but that the people, trained by living, active realization to a veneration for right and law, at the same time acquires in this very exercise, according to the manifold variety of the rank, calling, and education of the members who are its representatives, room to bring to light from the most immediate perception the problems and requirements as well as the wrongs and deficiencies of actual life of the living present, and so to contribute to that development of positive right against which only that false immovability or "reaction" sets itself, which indeed no one has so well traced out as Stahl himself: "False reaction consists in mistaking and opposing itself to those problems which are actually incumbent on the present, and which revolution has only misunderstood. The well-grounded demands for the protection of personal liberty, for the guarantee of civil rights, for political and social privileges of the higher citizenship, for an inviolate constitution and legal order,—to reject and oppose these, because the manner in which Liberalism puts them forth and struggles after them leads to commotions, and, on the other hand, to defend the arbitrary aims of the government, the ancient and exclusive privileges of the aristocracy—that is false reaction." Afterwards Stahl goes on to say: "*It is false reaction when it reacts not only against the material of disease, but also against the seeds of development, and when it desires not only to destroy and paralyze the disease, but the members which are affected with it*" (*Present Parties,* etc., pp. 334, 335).

(5) Where, in the case of the Christian, the line commences within which he feels himself independent of popular ordinances and the laws of the state, there exactly begins the domain of that Spirit by whose operation alone the Christian looks for the right fulfilment and impression of all the ordinances of the popular community. This is the domain of the spirit of the grace of Christ. Where kings and rulers no longer govern "by the grace of God," and their subjects no more render obedience "in the name of God," there will even the best

form be corroded by the deceitful spirit of selfishness; and to the ruler who says, "I am the state," will the other lying extreme follow, viz. that of the "sovereign will of the people." But there, on the contrary, will the people be wisely counselled, where ruler and people are reminded by law and justice that the object of order is to secure to the members of the community the possibility of together contributing, in the spirit of the love of Christ, to their common vocation; and where the divinely appointed vocation reminds all equally of the divine judgment (comp. *e.g.* Ps. 82), and of the gifts of grace, without which even natural qualification in the earthly calling cannot in blessing fulfil its duties (compare in reference to rulers, Prov. 20:28), so that an invisible power comes to aid the bond of law and justice which unites rulers and subjects—the spirit of prayer and intercession for each other (comp. 1 Tim. 2:2 with 1 Kings 3:6–9)—by virtue of which God Himself dwells in the government of nations.

But the order of things which secures the blessings and means of salvation is different from that which contributes to the earthly vocation of a people. And as it was not by means of the divinely purposed order of popular society that the power of redemption from their sins came to the nations, so is it even now still, after the revelation of grace has appeared, not the legitimate sovereignty of the state which *of itself, and from the divinely bestowed supreme power of its office*, is permitted to determine this relation of the members of a nation to the ordained revelation of grace, or to turn itself completely against the decisions of this kingdom of grace. The spirit of Christianity, which honors the manifold wisdom of the divine training of nations by keeping distinct their different vocations, reacts against both these things. And if the misconduct of the powers of the state ventures, in *arbitrary* determination of religious and ecclesiastical conduct, so far as to determine against the manifest and ecclesiastically acknowledged will of God in Jesus Christ, *then the Christian refuses obedience.* Πειθαρχεῖν δεῖ Θεῷ μᾶλλον ἢ ἀνθρώποις, Acts 5:29. Εἰ δίκαιόν ἐστιν ἐνώπιον τοῦ Θεοῦ, ὑμῶν ἀκούειν μᾶλλον ἢ τοῦ Θεοῦ, κρίνατε, 4:19. The Christian character of this refusal will, moreover, consist in this, that the refusal is kept within the limits of vocation and right; that petitions, representation, and complaint precede the renunciation of obedience; and that the refusal of obedience is never converted into an unlawful attack upon divinely appointed authority, but rather opposes nothing to the abuse of power but the force of justice and self-denying patience and endurance. The ground of the refusal of obedience and its divine authorization, however, is this, that the system of the earthly collective vocation ministers in subordination to the system of the heavenly collective vocation; that each, by virtue of its destination, has a peculiar law for its movement and accomplishment; that the transferring of the peculiarity of the one sphere to the domain of the other, and the false super-elevation, or indeed interference, with the one order on the ground of the power of the other, is a confusion of the divine order upon earth, to prevent which, and in every way to do battle with it, according to the position of his earthly vocation, every Christian, in his calling as a Christian, has a divine authorization.

§ 55. C. The Church, and its Relation to the Realization of Christian Virtue

How it is that the believer's consciousness of Christ is inseparable from that of a kingdom established and maintained by Christ on earth, had already to be explained (see especially § 17). The specific peculiarity of this community, and its difference from the family and the state, consist in this, that its foundation does not rest upon a natural basis; that it has no aims which concern only the present life and the human race in its limitation to itself and to the temporal purposes of its collective and nationally diverse existence; and that for the attainment of these ends it is not directed to impulses and means which are of human origin, and which consequently partake of a natural and human character. Rather is it that community which has its foundation in an act and doing of

God in Christ, which is from God and for God, having for its purpose our training for future glory and perfection, and possessing for the attainment of this purpose those means in word and sacrament which owe their existence and legitimacy to a divine operation and establishment, and as such are designed to effect the foundation, maintenance, and promotion of a communion of God with man, and of man with God. For these means cannot be separated from the person of the only Mediator between God and man, but they are the instruments of His mixed spiritual and corporeal (*geistleiblich*) presence upon earth, by which the church of Jesus Christ is founded, and by which it has unceasingly to maintain itself, to extend itself outwardly and inwardly, to confirm and promote itself. The specific peculiarity of these means of grace is alone the real basis on which rest alike the new life-relation and the new problem of the life and the vocation of the church of Jesus Christ. Both taken together—the fellowship of the Spirit and of faith, effected by word and sacrament, and the community of the Spirit and of faith, realizing itself in and by word and sacrament—form the idea of this kingdom upon earth as the church, invisible in its essence and condition as a community of the Spirit and of faith, visible in its divinely appointed means, by which it exists, and in which and through which it verifies its existence (1). But the outward existence, the empirical form of the church, does not resolve itself merely into that which it is by the internal necessity of its nature. For since the church attains to one form of man's social life, it, as such, also becomes an object of man's consciousness of rights, which embraces all that is called human society, and consequently also Christian society in its working reality, and is thereby impelled to peculiar forms of right, determined by the nature of this social life, but not identical with it. Inasmuch, namely, as the church recognizes the relation of life and society, worked out and appointed for her by God, in its organic form at the same time as a rule and order of her common life which exists as law for the community, and consistently with this creates external ordinances, by which she strives to guard the proper realization by and in the word and sacrament, and thus out of herself sets forth a system regulated according to churchly rights; therefore she is and becomes a *churchdom* as a human establishment, a legal institution, which stands in the same relation to the essence of that kingdom of the church which is brought about by the grace of God, as does the state to that natural moral order of family and popular society which is realized and determined by the will of God its Creator. And just because the revelation of the New Testament in the word lays down legislatively no positive rules of right for her existence as a churchdom, it is precisely that side of forms of churchdom which have been limited and regulated by man according to churchly rights, of which, as being facts historically given, it may be asked what course *with respect to* them it behooves Christian virtue to follow. For while the divine *source* of all Christian virtue is the word and sacrament apprehended in faith, upon which the kingdom of the church rests, the legally constituted church establishment—the churchdom—is the historically given human *object* on which Christian virtue has to realize itself conformably to faith. The recognition of this difference between church and churchdom is the first requisite for a just realization of a legally constituted church system (2). This recognition, however, with all its relative analogy with the moral appreciation of the legal ordinances which belong to the civil and social life of man, has again its specific difference. The resemblance consists in the perception that churchdom as well as state is a legal institution, a human system resting on a divine foundation, and from the nature of law, as from the accidental constitution of all that is human, neither a faultless nor a perfect realization of the positive nature of its divine foundation, consequently also subject to all the further consequences which have been previously traced (§ 54) in reference to the legal order of civil society. But an essential difference is found not only in the fact, that in the positive law of man's civil life it is only the naturally moral determination of all the relations of man's earthly life which finds expression objectively, but also in this, that by this right, and its being made valid in law, this naturally moral determination is only laid down as a power binding society and its members objectively; and hereby the social order of things, so far as it is consistently with the nature of law itself compulsory, is framed and realized in the only way which is possible for it, while the case is different with the legal shaping of what belongs to the nature of the church. For in this case there is antecedent a moral and religious community, founded on grace and the operation of grace, and called into existence by grace, *i.e.* realized and actual, and not simply resting in the idea of its divine Founder, which has the fundamental law of its existence not in a legal order of things, but in an order of salvation, which for its part rests not on a new revelation of law, but on a new revelation of grace, and which does not set forth as the definition of the community subject to it, that they are a people of the law, a legal community, but a people of grace, a community of salvation. To this its legal constitution stands in the relation of something accessory and secondary, which this community adopts, not indeed only from some imaginary or actual reference to the legally ordered civil society, but out of itself, only, however, just as a human society, subjected also to the earthly conditions of an established and common order of things, on account of which it finds it necessary, not only in respect to human weakness, caprice, and perversion, but mindful of the call to a realization of obedience to the divine law of that order of life which is peculiar to it, to establish this order, consistently with man's consciousness of law, as churchly law and legal institution, and herewith an external and subsidiary support for the attainment of the object of its existence upon earth (3). Hence it follows, that for the Christian conscience the legal ordering of the institution of the church (*Kirchenthum*) never may or can be primarily, but only secondarily and in a derived measure, a binding power; since what belongs to the church as a right never has its legitimacy in itself, or in the obligation of law as such, but in that relation in which it stands to the divinely appointed conditions of a true community of life and salvation with Christ, and in which the specific and peculiar nature of these conditions remains inviolate. Inviolate, however, it remains only if we do not make primary that which is only secondary, putting the legally ordered establishment—churchdom—in the place of the church, the community of the Spirit and of faith, which rests on the means of grace, and do not attribute to the legal institution as such that divine authority which belongs only to Christ, and to His gracious will embodied in the word and the sacrament. For as certainly as it accrues to churchdom (as to every human society) to establish legally the common obligation to that order of life, external and internal, which is acknowledged by her as a public law; so little is the doctrine prevailing in the church, and the external order of worship and office, constitution and government, derived from it, in the fact that it is clothed with the force of public law, in itself alone that external and internal churchly order which is binding on the conscience with divine authority. She is so rather only conditionally, by her agreement with Scripture, *i.e.* in the proportion in which all these institutions and functions conduce to help forward the sole dominion of Christ in His word and sacrament, and to establish the faith which makes blessed, not on propositions of law laid down in churchdom, but on Christ's word and sacrament alone (4). Herein is at the same time given the standard for a conscientious Christian decision, and the conduct answering to it, as well in reference to that form of churchdom in which a man finds himself by birth and baptism, as also in reference to the relation to each other of Christian societies ecclesiastically separated from each other. If, namely, churchdom in itself and in its legal shape were the church, as the kingdom of the communion of Christ, then could the conscience of the Christian find itself determined to nothing less than an unconditioned obedience in faith. Its judgment would be bound by nothing else than the law of this community, and we could not speak of any certain standing-point in and by God for testing it, which might be found outside of it. Just as little would it be possible to conceive of a plurality of churchly communions to which the name of church could apply. For the church, as the community of the kingdom of Christ, is at all times one and the same, has an immutable law of life always self-consistent; no means being afforded for recognizing and experiencing its nature and efficacy, excepting alone the believing apprehension of Christ, according to the presence of His will and essence in His word and sacrament. But just because such is the case—because the essence of the church cannot be resolved into a legally constituted churchdom, and it is not in the legal proposition of the latter, but in the word of the grace of Christ, upon which the essential church rests, that a standing-point is given which is derived from God, and has in God its certainty for testing every form of ecclesiastical existence—therefore has the conscience of the Christian, bound by the word of God, liberty to test, and the justification, nay, the obligation for measuring the value and the divine validity of the forms in which churchdom exists, according to the measure in which the possibility is afforded of becoming a partaker, by means of the word and sacrament, of the incarnate Son of God, and of the efficacy of His grace. Where such possibility is present, there must it be acknowledged; and the connection (hereby maintained) of the separately existing ecclesiastical organization with the essential church must not be denied on account of errors which cleave to separate forms of churchdom. Only where, as a principle, the connection with the (at all times one and the same) church of Jesus Christ, and the object of desiring to lead to the Incarnate One, and the presence of His grace in the word and sacrament, are refused and denied, must every claim to the name of a Christian church be withheld from a community. Where, however, such a denial in principle does not take place, there the name of Christian church is not to be made a matter of contention, but not in the sense of viewing them indifferently as equal, but with a testing of the distinctions and their value, according to the measure in which one or the other form of churchdom either promotes or impedes our access to the spiritual-corporeal presence of Christ, and the efficacy of His grace, in and by His word and sacrament, *i.e.* to their incorporation into the essence of the kingdom of His church. The tie of the particular church in which the individual finds himself by birth and the baptismal rite, has no right or power over his conscience, sharpened by the word of God, to prevent him separating from that church for conscience sake, whose shaping, either in principle or in actual fact, becomes an anxiety to his conscience, in respect of that relation and obligation in which a man is immediately placed to Christ and His kingdom by baptism (5). By virtue of the same association by baptism is also determined the positive behavior which the Christian has to observe towards that church in which he believes he can remain with a good conscience. Subject as he is to every external legal order of things for the sake of that order, and for the sake of love and peace, for the Christian notwithstanding this order of things is neither the law of his inner life, nor its fulfilment, as obedience to a legal obligation, the fulfilment of that obedience which, as a free and moral performance in Christ, he owes to Christ his Lord, to say nothing of the act of an obedience in which he has his justification before God. Rather does the Christian regard it as his task and duty to set the law of life in the church of Christ's kingdom above the law of right in churchdom, and regulating the last by the first, to keep all the legal ordinances of churchdom in connection with the vital law of the essential church, and to penetrate with the living spirit of the kingdom of Christ all legal forms of churchdom; and in the same spirit not only to fulfil all requisitions of churchdom which have their ground in the essence of the church, but to assist it also, according to the particular vocation of individuals in the family and the people, to ascendency in all the natural moral relations of society. For only that spirit of churchdom which is falsely limited and severed from the essence of the true church, regards as the domain of its realization the external association of churchdom alone; while the true spirit of the church of Christ and its members recognizes all the relations of human life and society, without displacing their limits or setting aside or restricting the fundamental principles peculiar to them, but rather in preserving intact and sanctifying their mutual alternate relations, as the sphere of the sovereignty of that Lord to whom also the individual Christian, from baptism onwards, is bound as a member in faith, and in whom he has to exert himself in every one of these spheres of life, to the end of preserving the original order of things, and for the renewal and setting right all that has fallen away from that order. Only where this spirit is the living impulse in an ecclesiastical society, will there be realized in churchly fellowship also, that vocation of disciples to be the salt of the earth, and to guard themselves against that slothful indifference which threatens alike a dead Christianity and a dead church.

(1) The object of the last paragraph was to show what ethical significance the natural forms of human communities have for the Christian, and in what way his realization in them shapes and has to shape itself from the spirit of regeneration. The question now is respecting that supreme community into which the Christian is transplanted just by regeneration itself,—respecting the community of the kingdom of Christ, and respecting the sense in which here below this is called the church, in its nature is specifically distinct from all natural forms of human communities, and yet in its historical and earthly form has one side in it, in which it partakes of the peculiarity of man's public life on earth, and has an earthly and human character, and thus becomes an object in which, in the Spirit of regeneration, and for the ends for which this Spirit is bestowed by God, the Christian has to realize his faith. The earthly and human churchdom is consequently here our chief object of consideration. The essence of the church is only so far to be taken into our consideration, as may serve for a just comprehension of its connection with the earthly and empirical manifestation of churchdom, and of the difference between the two sides of the real existence of the church. For the one is not related to the other as idea and manifestation: each is equally a historical reality, but the conditioning principles of their real existence are not the same on both sides.

Consequently our first question has respect to the community of Christ's kingdom, to the specific difference of this in comparison with every other natural and human community, and to the sense in which it is, and is called on earth, the church. Of this also alone do the Scriptures of the New Testament treat. That which, in a sense of the word hereafter to be investigated, is called churchdom, is the product of a later historical development, which did not exist at that time in a complete shape, and which, not in its manifestation, but only in its essential principles, is the subject of the New Testament testimony. We find the most concentrated expression for this in the Epistle of the Apostle Paul to the Ephesians. Hofmann (*Schriftbeweis*, ii. 2, 2d edition, pp. 116–142), in my opinion, has discussed the testimony in this epistle in the most comprehensive, profound, and pertinent manner. And to this exposition I would refer, since I have nothing better to say, and much that I previously remarked in my exegetical analysis of the passages of this epistle is there corrected. But that does not apply to the fundamental view that I have already taken of the substance of the declarations in the New Testament concerning the nature of the church.

I would refer, for what has been said on the idea of the essential church, to that which may be found partly in Hofling, *Grundsätze ev. luth. Kirchenverfassung*, 3d edition, 1853, pp. 8–10; partly in Harnack, *die Kirche, ihr Amt, ihr Regiment*. In a remarkable manner coincides with this also what H. Karsten says on this point in his *Symbolik für Theologen und Nichttheologen*. He starts rightly from the point, that the church in its inmost essence is a *vital relation* of the community to the *ever* present, and indeed spiritually and corporeally present, Lord Jesus Christ, What removes this community from the world, and that in which it has the beginning and end of its faith, is the belief in this presence of its Lord, who out of the fulness of His nature imparts blessings which embrace both soul and body—reconciliation and redemption, justification and sanctification—since He communicates and imparts Himself. In this His eternal presence has its work in the church;

and this present Christ is to her "the continually sufficient and sole ground and source of reconciliation and redemption." By virtue of this vital relation to Christ the church knows herself as being an organized unity, a living organization (not establishment or institution); also as the place in which the Lord carries out effectively and continuously His mixed spiritual and corporeal presence in personal intercourse between Himself and the church. For she knows her existence not as one ever becoming new in such a sense that Christ takes immediately out of the world individual souls, and transplants them into the fellowship of His salvation (perhaps as Stahl says, that "according to Protestantism the church, as it were, at every moment anew springs immediately from the word of God"); but she knows herself once founded by the divine act of her Lord as the communion of salvation, in which and through which the Lord desires to have the sphere of His presence and efficacy. This was done on the day of Pentecost, when by the outpouring of the Holy Ghost all were filled with this personal Spirit of God, and by this act the church of our Lord was formed out of individual believers. "The [Christian] community, therefore, since it is a church community, a fundamental factor of the church of Jesus Christ, has been constituted by God for this object, and is itself—not any particular class in it, and not particular establishments and institutions, but itself—furnished with specific and divine qualifications, owing to which it is appointed to have an existence of an entirely peculiar nature in the world" (Karsten). Its peculiar existence, however, which renders it in its essence and import totally distinct from any other association in the world, "in its inner nature, taken once for all out of the sphere of humanly devised and humanly maintained associations," is just this, to be and to continue the community of the Holy Ghost—so to continue by virtue of the promise of its Lord: "Lo, I am with you always, even unto the end of the world" (Matt. 28:20). And as in the days of its commencement, so for all time is the assembly destined and impelled, from the nature of this fellowship of the Holy Ghost, by an inner necessity to attest itself outwardly. For as the first act that lies at its basis was the fulfilment of a promise made by its Lord (Acts 1:5), so is the church ever and ever urged on to testify to itself as being the same which derives its true existence from the effect of that promise of its Lord, and recognizes as its appointed task to preserve and extend, by its ministry of the word and sacrament, the fellowship and the community of the Holy Ghost. Thus, from the nature of her origin as of her problem, this church is not at the commencement of her existence, as it were, an invisible body, which would only gradually become visible; but she is, as having become a church by the promise of her Lord, according to the impulse and self-testifying of her inner essence, also the visible, the invisible and visible church in one,—but always the former—the spiritual community, as the cause of the latter— the visible attestation, as the working and self-realization of its own inner essence (Karsten). And as the essence of its internality is created by God, so also the factors of its visible form are divinely created; and the order according to which the two belong to each other is a divine creation,—not, however, as an institution, but as a vital law of the organization of the community of the Holy Ghost. For the vital law of the church is this, that just as she herself has become by the word of promise of her Lord the community of the Holy Ghost, and only in a word of promise possesses the security that she will remain so, she should also in like manner let nothing pass as the essential ground of her visibility, but the visibility of those organs and means provided by God in word and sacrament, "through which Christ Himself, in His essential presence by means of the service of the church, takes up and transplants individuals from the world into His present life" (Karsten). But even the empirical churchdom does not resolve itself merely into this visibility. And here, above all, it is of importance as well rightly to estimate the difference which exists between churchdom and church, as to meet the double error, whereby one either looks upon what belongs to the churchdom as an inner essential necessity of the church, and absolutely identifies it therewith; or, because this is inadmissible, holds the ecclesiastical existence of the church in itself as nothing but a corruption of the essence of the church.

(2) As to what respects the meaning of the distinction between church and churchdom, I should like first of all to bring forward what follows. There is, above all, the *specific difference of the church from all other earthly and human communities*, which is preserved intact by rightly distinguishing what is essential from what is accessory. To churchdom belongs the idea of an institution constituted by law, legally regulated, and brought about indeed not by a divine law, and not by human confirmation of a divine law, but by human law-making and legislation. With the church it is not so. The church is one and the same with the organism of the body of Christ upon earth; but churchdom is not so. The latter has its vicissitudes of temporal and historical development and formation; the church has not. The church, as the living fellowship of the community with Christ, is always the same—has always like fundamental conditions and fundamental characteristics of its existence; for the fellowship of the Holy Ghost and of saving faith is at no time a different one in its nature and its means. Churchdom, however, as the humanly constituted and institution-shaping expression of this society which has become conscious of this vital communion, is not only subject to the temporal human conditions of its external shaping, but also to human vacillation and error. He who identifies churchdom with the church, not only makes essential that which is only adventitious, and that which is human, and in fact formal, a means of the fellowship of salvation (a means of grace), but he deprives himself of the possibility of recognizing that continuity of the nature and existence of the church which always remains consistent with itself as the sole work of her Lord and Savior. For in the place of that Christ who is always spiritually and corporeally present, and actively operating, appears the human and formally established. The temporal and earthly *working* of existing vital communion with Christ becomes the pretended *founder and mediator* of the life in Christ; and the actual historical diversity

of these institutions and forms of constitution makes it perfectly impossible to adhere to the identity of essence, so soon as we conceive of the same as an immutable institution, in place of viewing it as a permanent communion of life, brought about wherever Christ is present working through the word and sacrament, guaranteed not by institutions, but by the faithfulness in promising of a present Christ. Thus, for example, that church which is named after Luther is not without that shape which, as something constituted in an established form, is called churchdom. Not, however, that she knows herself to be the church of Christ on this account, but because and provided that she does not pass off anything which is merely formally established as the true essence of the church, nor puts it in the place of the Lord's spiritual and bodily presence, by virtue of which He alone dispenses, by means of the service of the church in the word and the sacrament, His healing efficacy.

Is it therefore the case, that for this reason the ecclesiastical form is against the true nature of the church, because the essential relation of Christ to His believing ones does not consist in their existence as a rightly composed, legally regulated and established community? We ask, on the other hand, Can we draw, from a just appreciation of the *nature* of a relation alone, the inference that its *effect*, even in its formal character, must be similar to that in which the essential peculiarity of that relation consists? Is it contrary to the essence of a Christian community, as a community of faith, that in its result it is also a community of those who are zealous of good works? Is it repugnant to the character of a human society which is born of God, that it has its life also in the form of human life and human realization? Is the essential relation of those who have been regenerated by the Spirit of God, whether it be of each particular individual or in their social relation to each other, so constituted, that it does away with the creaturely organization of individual or collective convictions of the community and their natural human expression, and puts it down as repugnant to its nature? Does the order of grace so present itself to man's consciousness, that it removes the natural and creature order for the expression of this consciousness? We have an analogy in the natural relations of human society. These rest by their nature on divinely appointed natural tendencies—not on positive right, or on the legal promulgation of this right. Is it perhaps repugnant to the nature of the thing, that the human consciousness of this natural tendency should put it in the form of positive right, and confirm it by law for the administration of this right? Positive right and law would then only be repugnant to the nature of a divinely appointed natural tendency, if by the same were denied that a divinely appointed natural tendency formed its basis. But equally would it be a contradiction to the nature of the human spirit and its creature organization, if man did not reproduce and legally confirm the divinely appointed and moral determinations of the nature of the relations of all human society in the form of positive human law. If, indeed, he supposed that law and justice, as established by him, supported and conditioned the world-system of the creature, this would indeed be a perversion repugnant to the nature of things. But it would also be a perversion of his human nature and of his human duty, to hold the opinion that he might not embody in the form of positive human law that which is in its nature a divinely given natural tendency in its effect upon his consciousness. It is not in the mode of its establishment that we can look for a contradiction to the nature of its principle. This takes place only when the substance of human law is at issue with the nature of divinely appointed and natural tendencies, or when it ignores and disowns its divine origin out of which it has sprung. Analogous to this is the state of the case with respect to the formation of law within the church, or with the establishment of churchdom. It does not belong to the essence of the divinely constituted community of grace, that it should take the shape of a churchly code of rights; but it does indeed belong to the nature of the divinely constituted organization of men and of man's social consciousness. The nature of the church on earth exists for this end, that it may possess a human world-reality in such a manner that, instead perhaps of having nothing to do with the human consciousness of right, it should apply in its operation to this also, and fill it with a new and determinate character, from which man arrives at new, *i.e.* churchly, codes of rights. For thus says A. v. Scheuerl with perfect right: "Man brings his *sense of right* into the church with him." And that relative freedom in lawmaking wherein precisely its character as human (*i.e.* not immediately proceeding from God), statute-framing, and legal appointment consists, has its ground in the nature of the church, because the essential church itself does not rest upon law. "The collective consciousness of right" (which appertains to the church) "has for its basis certain expressions of the will of her divine Founder, but is free in its development, in so far as, for the legal shaping of the relations of the churchly community, the ascertainable will of the Lord with respect to the fundamental principles of the same admits of different possibilities" (*idem*). "But this will of Christ is in itself not legislative; in the consciousness of the church alone does it become principles of right to her. The church has, by virtue of its divine foundation, just as little of a legal constitution as any particular state;" or, as I would rather say, any naturally detached popular community. "In the church, as in a popular community, the original law is the law of custom, *i.e.* law which arises immediately, without legislative effort; only subsequent to this follows statute-making by means of legislation." When the further remark is made, that this consciousness of right has developed itself in the church in opposition to false brethren, then will this have equally its historical justification, as I believe it would, out of an immanent necessity of human nature, even without this opposition, have come to the formation of a system of law. However this may be, as Scheurl justly says: "This supposition (of a churchly code of laws) is only then inconceivable if we speak of legal precepts established by Christ for the church." Of such, however, man has spoken, and still speaks. And from this source legal enactments have been framed which are false in principle, and exercise a disturbing reflex influence on the essential and vital relation of the church. This is the modern, as I might call it, *juristic* corruption of the idea of the nature of the church; while at a more ancient period a prejudice was done to the church in her essential import and peculiarity, by transferring to it the religious and legal determinativeness of the Israelitish people, ordained by God for a pedagogic purpose—the legal constituting of a special priestly race and the like, at least in part. Where, however, neither the one nor the other presents itself, there we find human legislation, as it lies at the basis of churchdom, in its due force, and not opposed to the nature of the church so long as the rightly constituted church establishment does not itself pretend to be the essence of the church, and has not in its character tendencies opposed to the true essence of the church.

(3) If a parallel were drawn between law-making in the natural human society, in the public community, and the same in the church, we dare not overlook the distinction which exists between them. These systems of law are alike in their formal character as law—unlike in their substance: alike, in respect of the historical reality of their basis, a community already existing, and not one first to be formed by means of law and legal constitution—here the public community, there the society of believers; unlike in reference to the divinely ordained root out of which these communities sprang: alike in their object and aim to fix by human law and right the divinely appointed fundamental conditions and ordinances of the one as of the other community as objects of common recognition—to give them an objective existence, and hereby to secure the common welfare against disturbance; unlike in the import, the authority, and the obligatory force of the legal enactment. For the moral idea of those relations (not of conduct) which are proper to the natural state of human society, finds in law that realization which is possible for men. This idea lies, as to its substance, in the relations themselves, but is formally set forth incorporated in words, established as law only by man's own legislative activity. This is a relation which is not far from

applying to the church also. In her case we have to do not with an idea, the laying down of an object which in latent form indwells in the existence of the church, but with an act and working of God by which she is herself called into existence and continually upheld, made public in the word, powerful in working through the word, spirit, and life in the word and the Lord of this word, which is a word of grace and not of law, and makes known, as the essence of this community, the fact of its being a community of grace. To wish to *realize* the essential peculiarity of this community, in the form of a legal community, would be an internal contradiction. It is, however, no contradiction, to desire to give an expression to the common recognition of this essential peculiarity of the society in right and law, in such a manner that it may be perceived therefrom *how* the community views this essential peculiarity, and adheres to it, as its common sanctuary, so that it is recognized as a common right and common duty to permit nothing to crop up within the community which might tend to alienation and perversion of this essential peculiarity. Then, however, it must also be the desire of this legally constituted churchdom, to be and to remain what it is, not the realization of the idea of the church, but, as Stahl has previously very justly observed (*Rechts und Staatslehre*), "purely a means of help and an external support." For the church, in its original nature, belongs purely to the domain of ethics.

(4) For justly estimating the church as a legally constituted institution, it is not less important to recognize and distinguish its constituent factors, in their proximate or more remote connection with the essentiality and the essential problem of the church,—in their immediate or only mediate determination by the divine factors of the essential church,— in their greater or less decree of control by the divine message of salvation, and the (consequent) greater or less degree of liberty for human legislation. For on this depends the dignity, the higher or lower ordering, the real placing first and last, of the several institutions which support churchdom, which is grounded in the nature of the church. The precedence is taken

by those institutions wherein that which, according to the gospel and in the same, is laid down as a condition of life and a living realization of that which is essentially the church, is given back as a legally valid expression of the social churchly consciousness. Standing next to these are those legal forms whose purpose it is to serve for the maintenance of external order within the churchly union. In the case of the first, that which, according to the gospel, is of divine right is to be distinguished as the substance from the particular form in which the same exists in churchdom as churchly valid right. This distinction finds no place in the second class; but the object here is, as in the created natural order of all human society, the consideration of that fitness and suitability which have for their criterion the negative result, that the institutions do not run counter to those conditions and practical manifestations of life belonging to the essential church, which are laid down in the gospel. To the last domain belong those external ordinances, in which the ecclesiastical community, in its constitution and government, desires only to shelter and protect the essential life-activities proper to the church, but does not aim at bringing them, as such, to a legally valid expression, according to their divine fundamental conditions. On the first domain there manifest themselves those forms, in which the ecclesiastical community lays down that which is peculiar to the inner nature of the life, and to the life-activity of the essential church,—believing and confessing (in the sense of Rom. 10:10), appropriation and offering of the means of grace, as the legally valid expression of the common consciousness,—and bestows upon confessing faith, in the form of public and valid church doctrine, and upon the receiving and offering of the means of grace, in the form of public official regulation and order of divine worship and the like, the form and significance of a legally binding order of life for the community. These last fundamental forms of the ecclesiastical community stand in essential and direct connection with the divine system of salvation, derive their existence from a divine mandate laid down in the gospel, participate in the divine authority of the dispensation of grace revealed in the gospel, but are neither this authority itself, nor the divinely appointed organs for carrying out this dispensation of grace, but are in their origin, as in their form, only a reproduction by man of an effect which, from the gracious will and the means of grace in Jesus Christ, has passed into the consciousness of the society of the faithful, and mirrors itself in the sense of right belonging to the [Christian] community. And just because it is so—because the churchly sense of right springs up in consequence of an effect which rests in the same on divinely given, divinely effective, and divinely authorized means—it cannot pretend that those forms, which have been created by the Christian consciousness of right, are in themselves divinely given, divinely effective, and divinely authorized means for the production of a consciousness of Christian faith as of Christian right. These shapes and forms of ecclesiastical law do not for the first time set forth that which in itself would have divine authority and claims; but they only express, in the form of law, that which the consciousness of the church has, on the ground of divine authority and divine agency, recognized as the principle and rule of the life-fellowship and life-activity in a Christian community ("*non imprimunt credenda, sed exprimunt credita*"). And the expression consistent with this knowledge has only to set forth the aim, the nature, and manner in which this divine system of salvation is reflected in the sense of right belonging to the Christian community; but it does not possess the right to attribute divine authority to humanly established right as such. In this authority the human shaping of rights only so far participates, as the substance of legally established public doctrine, and of the legally established public official authority (in accordance therewith), is actually in conformity with the nature of God's gracious will, and with the divinely-willed nature of the administration and the use of the divine means of grace. For churchdom is wholly a rightly organized service in the essential church, not a realization of that church itself, and has its divine legitimization not in its legally valid condition, but in the conformity of its state with the vital conditions and life-activities of the essential church. The legally established doctrine cannot be recognized as of divine force, because it is so legally established, but because and if it is the expression of a faith which has actually sprung from the Source of life, the word of salvation, whose substance it has appropriated, and before and by which word it can legitimately establish itself. The official administration is not for this reason the fulfilment of the divine mandate, because it is legally established in the church, but because and provided that the divine mandate is so executed by it as to be, in respect to the nature of the divine dispensation of grace, right in God's sight, and is able to legitimize itself before and by the divine word. Divine authority is not inherent in the system of ecclesiastical law in the *form* in which it lays down what is to have currency in the church; but divine authority is only to be attributed to its *substance* in the way of derivation, provided that and because the same contains the substance of the system of salvation inviolate, and makes this serve as its only and supreme norm. If this relation is not preserved intact, great danger is incurred of falsely binding the conscience—of attributing to churchdom what belongs only to the essential church—of assigning to the ecclesiastically valid doctrine, and to the ecclesiastically established official administration, rightly constituted conformably with this doctrine, in themselves divine authority, divine efficacy, and divine authorization, and of clothing them with those divine attributes and promises which belong indeed to God's word, but not to churchly constituted doctrine, and belong indeed to the office as administration of God's word and sacrament; not, however, to the churchly established officialism in itself, but only in proportion to the pure maintenance of the divine basis both of the doctrine and the office. This, notwithstanding, is strictly peculiar to churchly doctrine, that it neither pretends nor can be an *absolute* and exhaustive, but only a *relative* expression of that faith which is born of the word, and indeed in a twofold aspect: first, in that relation in which faith born of the word has attained through historical disposing to a common *recognition*, and as such has become the foundation of the establishment of a regularly ordered Christian community; and secondly, in the relation in which this knowledge has shaped and separated itself in opposition to a supposititious knowledge, but one antagonistic to the nature of the faith. For this reason all churchly doctrine is not an absolute, but only a relative expression of this cognition touching the nature of the faith; and if it were not so, nothing would be more contradictory than, in the place of a mere verbal repetition of the churchly doctrinal formulas, not merely to allow to prevail, but expressly to demand, individual liberty in preaching and instructing in the common faith, limited only by the substance of the divine word and the doctrinal teaching of the church. It is just the fulness of the faith and of the word which is destined to attain in the ecclesiastical community, only relatively restricted by the doctrine which is held in common to be valid, to expression, to application, and to a manifold character of attestation and efficacy; and in this way the words of Scripture are to obtain a living realization by the community. With respect, however, to the church's objective forms of doctrine, and the ordinances of the ecclesiastical community derived from them, what Harnack has justly observed holds good: "There exists no absolute form of doctrine, worship, discipline, or constitution."

Certainly not of constitution, nor of the government which conduces to its maintenance. As that in itself has for the ecclesiastical community only a secondary and not a primary import, and as we may well make the doctrine—not, however, the constitution and its form in themselves—our criterion of an ecclesiastical community constituted in accordance with the word of God; so is the form of the constitution and of the government, or the legal shaping of the external order of the ecclesiastical community, in no-ways restricted by a law of the divine will, through pretended positive rules of right derived from the Scriptures of the New Testament; since neither are the Scriptures of the New Testament a revelation of law, nor is the community of grace of the New Testament, the true church, a community of law, an institution legally regulated by external ordinances. The charismatically ordered membership of Christ's body, as it is given us by the Apostle Paul (comp. 1 Cor. 12:4–30 with Rom. 12:4–8, Eph. 4:7, 11 ff.), refers, irrespective of the peculiar nature of the endowments of the [Christian] community in that first period, and of the questionable meaning of the word κυβερνήσεις (1 Cor. 12:28), not to the relations of the external system of constitution, but to the functions of the members for promoting the inward life of the whole body; does not establish external ordinances, but only opens up in the way of promise the prospect that at no period will *persons* be wanting who shall be qualified and endowed for the due performance of the services manifold in nature in Christ's body; disperses, however, at the same time also every notion of the setting up by man of constitution and government, through which perhaps the church could be charismatically endowed with that which the Lord had reserved to Himself to bestow. Nothing can be derived from such passages but the fact that the established organization of the ecclesiastical community must not be repugnant to the nature of the organism of Christ's body; a law of external order, however, in constitution and government, an obligatory precept and ordinance of right for her formal character, least of all allows itself to be discovered in these passages. Rather with the exception of the general will of order expressed in creation, the divinely appointed moral tendencies of nature, which support all human society, and from whence also take their rise the declarations of the apostle (1 Cor. 14:34, 35; 1 Tim. 2:11, 12: comp. Wiesinger on the last passage) on the position and vocation of woman in the Christian church, nothing has validity for the external form of the ordering of the ecclesiastical community and its government, except the rule that we should *not* reckon such and such constitutions of the community and forms of government as the essence of the church, and that even in the ecclesiastical community we should not make them instead of the doctrine the center of our care, and least of all should expect from constitution and government saving efficacy, but should only estimate their value according to the measure in which they so further and maintain external order, that thereby the sole dominion of Christ in word and sacrament is in nothing injured or impeded. For there alone where He as ruler is embodied and lives in a community is the true church, the Lord's people, which in the glory and fulfilment of the New Testament bears the predicates of the people of the Old Testament,—namely, "a chosen race, a royal priesthood, a holy nation, a peculiar people" (1 Pet. 2:9). To transfer this definition to the members who belong as a matter of church right to the ecclesiastical community, and to make it the ground for the constitution and government of churchdom under the title of the universal priesthood, is the most monstrous perversion of divine truth, as well as of the principles of the Reformation,—a perversion which ought scarcely to be conceived as possible. Possible to be conceived it is only as a caricature of the truth, that there exists no order of human dominion privileged and instituted by Christ in His church. For with respect to the last point, in this way without doubt all striving after anything approaching to this—nay, all prevalence of anxiety about constitution and government as a supposed guarantee for this, that Christ abides in the government—may be taken in general as a sign that a churchly community has fallen away from the true center of its life, or threatens to do so; since, in lieu of the sufficiency of the Lord's presence in His divine means of grace, and the believing confidence in the exercise of the Lord's power in the preaching of His word, it begins to place its reliance on means of human ordering, and in a perverted manner idolizes them. "It is a matter of urgent need in a time like the present, when so many look to an arm of flesh, that the church should remain true to herself,—that she should with exhortation hold up her true form to the anxious and desponding, the unbelieving ministers of human schemes and provisions, as the incontestable guarantee that those will not be put to shame who look to the Lord alone for help. What can it profit if she preaches faith and condemns works, which are to serve to deliver hearts and souls, if nevertheless she herself places the confidence as to her existence and her development on human institutions and ordinances?" (Karsten.)

(5) With the recognition of the marks which distinguish church from churchdom, of the conditions under which the two have and maintain their proper connecting tie, instead of diverging from each other as true church and false churchdom, and in the independence, visibility, and comprehensibility of the divine foundation, on which the true church and the right churchdom are equally built and have to be built, is therefore also the basis given for the right and conscientious line of conduct in regard to all that may put forth a claim to the title of a Christian church. For this knowledge derived from God's word is in itself Christian *freedom of conscience*, and herewith a capability of *discerning the spirits*, even *the spirits of the churchly communities*; and in the due discrimination between church and churchdom at the same time, in a derivative measure, a safeguard against churchly *fanaticism* as well as churchly *indifference*.

There exists no holier palladium for the Christian than *freedom of conscience*, and there is no sanctuary which men have more profaned than the word "freedom of conscience." What freedom of conscience is to the Christian, how inseparably it is connected with the commencement of his own life in Christ, and how precisely with this beginning of life the relation of freedom of conscience to church and churchdom is supposed, will become manifest of itself from what has been said in the above paragraph. If I have here in view both the birth of the body and regeneration by baptism, that will be liable to no misapprehension. For even in the first it is determined by Divine Providence to the child of Christian parents, in what churchly communion it should find itself at the beginning of its existence. But this dispensation has not that importance which attaches to birth within this or that popular community. In the latter case is established, according to God's will, a bond of love and piety, a type of national character and belongings which we reverence as sacred, and in certain ways never can or dare deny, and which remains for us, even if one should be constrained and justified by after events in life externally to dissolve the ties of this association. That, however, which is decisive for the conscience of a Christian with respect to belonging to this or that churchly society, is not the birth after the flesh; nor can it be so. It is a dispensation carefully to be weighed, which has its root not in human consideration, that in the administration of the sacraments that relation remains intact, by virtue of which the baptized child in and by baptism is incorporated into the fellowship of the Lord Jesus Christ, the true church, not this or that particular church, this or that churchdom. If, when arrived at consciousness, he cherishes and fosters this relation in faith, and according to God's word adoringly enters into its full meaning, recognizes himself as free, as one bound alone by Christ and His word of grace, then will he also perceive what that freedom of conscience really is, which for our life in God owns no lord and master, neither human authority, nor any human ecclesiastical system; but the Lord Jesus Christ alone, the Head of His body, the Lord of the essential church, who can be found by every man in His word. Happy is he who, from a knowledge of Christ and His word, feels himself free in conscience, and enabled to remain in that churchly society in which he, through the determination of his birth in the flesh, was presented to the Lord Christ in baptism. But there exists no piety proceeding from this dispensation, which may free the Christian from the right—nay, the duty—according to his freedom in Christ, to examine (ὁ πνευματικὸς ἀνακρίνει τὰ πάντα, 1 Cor. 2:15) how that church is constituted, in which he, by an act of God in Christ, was made a member of His church. For church and churchdom are not essentially one and the same. Were it otherwise, there would exist no standing ground for the Christian, from which he, bound in Christ, might freely examine how matters may stand with that community which, not without a near approach to misconception, is called briefly by men the church. For the vital law of the church it is which binds the Christian conscience, but it is not the law of this or that ecclesiastical community.

If we call the latter without further heed or reservation the church, then there presses itself upon us from another empirical perception also the certainty that this mode of expression labors under a defect. For with our Christian conscience we stand over against a plurality of church associations, which call themselves churches. If the churchly association as such is really the church, then is a plurality of churches a *contradictio in adjecto*. For the church is, by the will and the promise of her Lord, only one, at all times one and the same, powerful, by the same means which called her into existence, also to be preserved in the same. If the several church societies are fragments of the church, more or less the church, more or less the truth, then has this very promise of the one church come to a failure. If, however, of these diverse church societies, one only is the church; and if the others are all pseudo-churches, then has "the church of the living God," destined to be the pillar and ground of the truth for the world and in the world (1 Tim. 3:15), either never existed in such a way as to be powerful to preserve the church as one and the same, or it only began to do so after the lapse of centuries when it did not exist. In the one as in the other case, the promise that the gates of hell shall not prevail against the church (Matt. 16:18) has remained unaccomplished. To all these false conclusions we are led by falsely identifying church with churchdom. He who rightly discriminates their difference is alone capable of guarding himself against confusion of conscience and judgment in reference to churchdom, whether he finds it in the world as a single or as a plurality of churchly associations. For he never and nowhere transfers the promises and attributes which hold good of the church to the churchdom. He cannot do so, for the churchdom is not the church, but only the human community regularly organized for the service of the church. All the factors which constitute churchdom as such are not the organs by which the Lord of the church has His efficacy for building up and preserving the church; but they are, or can and would be only the guides and pointers of the way to the Lord of the church and the organs of His efficacy. The constituent factors of churchdom—doctrine, church order, church constitution—are by their nature not destined to remain one and the same in their form, as in matter of fact they never have remained, but have, as human institutions, the object of continually increasing in everything which renders them appropriate for serving as guides and pointers of the way to the church and to her Lord. The Lord Himself, the manner of His agency, its divine media, word and sacrament, and the nature of the saving faith effected by them and making them its own, abide what they are, undergo no change, are unsusceptible of increase or decrease, and are the divinely-human constituents of the church. But the constituents of churchdom, the human expression for the conception of the word and faith in public doctrine (the confession), and the church order and system framed according thereto, must not only, when they are of the right kind, have a constant increase in reference to the expression and shaping of what is required for knowledge and order, but may equally well, in consequence of human weakness and sinfulness, decrease, perish, and become more or less unsuited for the service of the church. For, as being human creations, the one thing befalls them as the natural tendency of all that is human, the other as the destiny of human fallibility. Against a possibility of the last holds good and remains the promise, that the Lord of the church is mightier than all conceivable or actual corruption of churchdom, and that He builds up and preserves His church wherever in a churchdom word and sacrament remain, through which the Lord builds and preserves His church. So long as an ecclesiastical community does not deny that Jesus is the Christ, the Son of the Father, come in the flesh (1 John 2:22 ff., 4:2 ff.), efficaciously working in word and sacrament, so long has it still part in the church, still stands in connection with her, and may still call itself *churchdom*, although not the church; and has only so far to be tested, whether it permits, along with the other arrangements of its system, the way to the

Lord of the church, and His word and sacrament, certainly to be found, and consistently with the vital conditions of the church, or doubtfully and in disagreement with them. But he who wishes to prove and determine this must not only be acquainted with that scaffolding destined for the workman's service in the building of the church—churchdom: but he must know also the Builder, the building plan, and the manner of the Builder in shaping and adapting living stones, in order hereby to decide whether the scaffolding which man has erected, really more or less furthers the design of the Architect, or not at all. And this the Christian can and ought to know from God's word. If he, from this knowledge of any particular churchdom as being one of such scaffoldings, leaves it because it appears to him awry and dangerous for him to stand on, or alters and improves it, neither is such a departure in itself a departure from the church, nor the alteration and improvement in itself an altering or improving in the church; but it is a work with respect to or in churchdom, to labor our for whose just and end-answering form, in a human manner and with human means, is the continual task of the man who belongs to a churchly association. For since the Lord of the church does not wish to build His church in *such* a way as not at the same time to admit those who confess His name with all their human powers, endowments, and energies, to a trial service in His church, therefore is such a labor in the restoration of a churchdom in harmony with the church in the highest degree worthy and deserving of human solicitude and effort. Since, however, men's works and actions themselves have first to undergo a fiery ordeal (1 Cor. 3:10–15), whether the human edifice is constructed in the spirit of the church and her Lord, it can therefore be asserted of no churchdom on earth, that it is not equally capable as needful of constant testing, sifting, improving, and setting right.

This twofold perception is the antidote against that twofold *fanaticism* which clings to the mingling of church and churchdom. For the one party, since they see that those predicates of the church which are consistent with the promises are adapted to no one form of churchdom, are furious against every form thereof as being a purely human contrivance, as a distorted representation of the church, as a Babel instead of the kingdom of Christ, and would wish, the sooner the better, that all that is churchdom, and pretends to the name of church, should be extirpated. Against the pretension they have a relative right; but for the rejection of churchdom as such they have no right at all. Nay, as a just punishment, this confusion of speech is wont to overtake themselves, that, though scarcely freed from this or that form of churchdom, they impose upon themselves churchly regulations, and name their communion alone *the church*. So little do they perceive, that wherever any spirit, no matter what, has instituted a human society, the very nature of the spirit of society impels them to give a human expression to that which the united body hold as their common right, and although it should be set forth with purely negative formulas, as the positive right of the society, that they should not admit the validity of any formal maxims of right. The others, however, while they give to churchdom in itself the name of the church, and then become fully aware that they must in such a case claim for churchdom the predicates of the church, strip the ecclesiastical community to which they belong of its human character; hold the institutions in which it has its existence, collectively and separately, and without any distinction between its divine foundation and earthly form, for divine and saving creations; apply the perfectly true proposition, that we have salvation in Christ not outside of the church, but only within the church, to their form of churchdom; and thence exclude, with perfect consistency, all who do not belong also externally and by churchly right to this churchdom from salvation in Christ. In the first place, this fanaticism is to be justly condemned, from its having the blot of being historically false. For should the constituents of churchdom—doctrine, church order, church constitution—be maintained to be the constituents of the church, and that therefore also churchdom is equivalent to church, then must they also have been at all times one and the same. If forms of church communities which sprang up at an after period—such as those at the time of the Reformation—wish to refuse this test, then must they also renounce the pretension of being *the* church, but ought not in any way to grieve at not possessing such a claim. If, however, a churchly community like the Roman Catholic, which asserts its existence to have lasted from the days of the apostles to the present, stand upon the proof of the unchanging character of her doctrine, order, and constitution, such an attempt can in no wise be made without doing violence to historical truth, which does not even present a picture and proof of constant uniformity of constitution, to say nothing of doctrine, but rather to the contrary. Thus even in her case does the fanaticism of setting herself up as *the* church fall to the ground, in the same manner in which it cannot crop up in the opposite party without causing perplexity to that better knowledge, as well of the nature of the church as of the essential character and task of churchdom. And, indeed, on both sides with bad reactionary effects on the moral and religious sentiments. For although human perversity is able, even in respect to the word of salvation laid down in Scripture, or in its substance confirmed by word of mouth, merely to look upon it with the eyes, to hear it with the ears, to impress it upon the memory—without, however, letting it penetrate the heart and conscience—and thus is able to refuse to accept it in penitence and faith, yet is the divine word of salvation in its form and nature so truly an appeal to the conscience, that the sting of open variance between such word and such conduct can only remain unfelt in cases of unqualified obduracy. But in the form of that which churchdom establishes, and naturally must establish, in the intelligible expression of doctrine and formula, of legitimate order and constitution, if we hold the acceptance and observance of these forms alone and of themselves merely to be a life in the spirit of the *church* of Jesus Christ, the danger is imminent of accepting all this as a matter of the understanding, of observing them as law, and at the same time continuing devoid of all godly change of mind—orthodox from top to toe, but void of life and love—nay, often within full of arrogance, hatred, envy, bitterness, and the like; and with all this, being also of opinion that we are sure, by reason of our own incontestable orthodoxy as respects all matters of church law, of the blessedness of our churchdom as a means of salvation. Into such a soul-perilling delusion may he fall, who takes the churchdom for the church, and forgets that the church does not exist for the sake of churchdom, but churchdom only for the church, and abides in its true character only when it maintains the true and legally valid forms of its existence in constant dependence on the Spirit and the vital law of the church of Christ.

Conversely, however, it is the knowledge of the origin, vocation, and true significance of churchdom which protects us from the danger of *indifference*. We are not here speaking of that indifference of unbelief which asks with a shrug of the shoulders, with Pilate, "What is truth?" and which is unwilling to know anything at all of positively revealed religious truth. We mean rather the indifference of so-called believers. The root of this is of a twofold nature, and is connected with a false supposition both of the nature of faith and of that of churchdom. Faith is viewed as something which, more or less, has nothing to do with certain and distinct knowledge (see on this, § 18, note (4), pp. 157–162),—as a faith in which the chief point is not so much as to the "what," but as to the "how"—an excitement of feeling, a flight of enthusiasm, a general moral elevation, and the like; in short, a somehow or other conceivable, but ever a religious and moral, only not a definite and fixable, relation to Christ. But touching churchdom, the idea has been more or less entertained, that it is purely of human origin, a garment of man's weaving, that has just as little direct connection with the inner soul as a man's vesture with his heart; and that, since the possibility is not denied that the Lord is able to save some in every Christian churchdom, it is also a matter of tolerable indifference to what form of churchdom one may belong. Thus, or nearly thus, will run the ideas of all indifferentists; and if I do not venture to give what

I have just said as a definition of indifferentism, as one determined and equally applicable in every case, the reason is this, that in such opinions everything is wont to be indeterminate and impalpable. Now it lies at once in the nature of a true faith born of the word, to recognize itself very distinctly as a definite and divinely effected knowledge. But he who is acquainted with such knowledge belonging to faith, distinguishes from it its intelligible and human reproduction in the doctrine and confession of churchdom. If the latter, however, is actually such—namely, the reproduction of the nature stated—then is it also not purely human ordinance. And if, therefore, reproductions of this nature lie before us as the foundation of separate churchly existences—that is to say, various churchly confessions and doctrines; then in the points in which perhaps not only the form of the expression is distinct, but the contents of the formularies—the substance—is opposed contradictorily to the substantial contents of the others, the reason of such difference must be looked for only in an alteration of the knowledge belonging to faith on the one or the other side. There indifference of merely human modes of expression ceases, and becomes an essential difference in points of that faith and knowledge which God desires to effect by His word, not as something indifferent and conceivably different, but as essentially one and uniform in relation to the substance of its contents. Now it is perfectly true, that it is by no means so easy to ascertain in what points the difference of churchly confessions is perhaps only a difference in human modes of expression, and where an alteration of that knowledge of faith which is effected by God's word is involved,—a departure from the truth which is in Christ. But the more certain it is that the division into separate churches is not conformable to the will of Christ and the essence of the church, the more definitely it may be deduced from this, that this division is associated with sin against Christ and the church; so much the more is it absolutely impossible to hold up to the conscience of a Christian indifferentism or listlessness in respect to the difference of churchly constitution as a conscientious duty, instead of representing as his duty the keenest and most conscientious examination into the reason why he believes himself able, with a good conscience, to look upon this or that churchly confession, or better, the churchdom of this or that confession, as the place in which he can live without a conscientious burdening of that certain faith which he has derived from God's word. For it is morally contemptible to hold one's self out to be a member of a churchdom, and hereby in fact to be willing to acknowledge its authority, whose objective churchly rules he holds as either something indifferent, or as contradictory to that which he has learned from God's word to consider as the nature and essence of the church, and of the living faith and knowledge which belong to her.

At this stage some one might ask me why then I profess myself a member of that church which bears the name of Lutheran. And consistently with what lies in the context of the foregoing investigations, I will give a reply. I cannot, indeed, give as my reason, "Because the Lutheran church (Lutheran churchdom) is the one holy universal church," or "professes herself to be the one holy universal church" (as Karsten says). I can only say: For this reason, because she holds herself out as being *for* the one holy universal church, whose ever unchangeable existence she knows in faith, and on this account places this faith at the head of her confession. This she could not do, were she not cognizant of roots of her existence, which are given in the one church, and that lie at the foundation of her own particular churchdom. The one church, however, she would be obliged to declare herself, did she not know that the existence of the one church is not involved in her existence alone. Inasmuch as she is fully aware that the factors of that one holy and universal church (word and sacrament) are also the factors of her own existence as a community, she asserts her identity with this church. But she denies that its existence only dates from that of the Lutheran church. What she has called into existence as an established churchdom, gathered and gathering, she knows as the working of that Spirit who belongs to the one holy and universal church. But she denies that this her established churchdom is alone the sphere in which this Spirit manifests His activity, or that her established form is the spring and mediator of the working of this Spirit. And of her confession, which belongs to the factors of her churchdom, she knows indeed that its expression and substance are conformable to the design of leading the community for its fellowship in salvation, *i.e.* for its reconciliation and redemption, justification and sanctification, exclusively to the effective presence, spiritually and corporeally, in word and sacrament, of the Lord of that one holy and universal church. She, however, at the same time denies that only by her doctrine as such, not to speak of its intelligent adoption, the relation is rendered possible, in which the ever present Lord bestows the fruit of His saving deeds by word and sacrament as a living possession. The Lutheran churchdom knows herself in her historical existence and shape to be a fruit of the one holy universal church *already existing*, but not as the founding and exclusive focus of the one holy universal church. And for this reason simply, because she does not attribute to churchdom that which is the result of the presence of the faithful Lord, and of His efficacy in word and sacrament. This is the principle on which the Lutheran church rests. If men have wished to make of her some other thing, that does not concern me. Up till now the principle stands fast, and human devices again will be scattered like chaff. According to this principle must be measured, moreover, the relation of this "church" to other confessions. For since the Lord suffers Himself to be found only in His word and sacrament—and even errors of confessions, or the darkening of the general conviction with respect to the nature of the church, cannot become an absolute hindrance to the presence of Christ in His word and sacrament—the Lutheran church, therefore, notwithstanding of her conviction of the substantial correctness, *i.e.* of the harmony, of her confession with Scripture, does not limit the existence of the one universal Christianity to the sphere of her own creed, but believes that in all Christendom (*sparsi per totum orbem; Apol. Conf.* Art. vii. and viii.) some may be saved, whose life-giving Head is Christ, whom as members in the obedience of faith they worship. For we know well one false churchdom, which renders difficult the way of salvation,—a churchdom in which, however, so long as Christ the incarnate Son of God is confessed, it is not absolutely impossible that the power of Christ in word and sacrament should be proved. "With such convictions," I therefore cheerfully say with Karsten, "the Lutheran church feels herself equally free from that unionistic confusion of churches, as from that false and unbelieving intolerance which scarcely admits the possibility of the members of other Christian confessions being saved." And all this for this reason, because the Lutheran church does not make herself the center-point of her consciousness in her confession of faith, but faith, knowledge, and the essence of the one holy and universal church.

(6) From the foregoing investigations, we may now also conclusively deduce what may be viewed, consistently with the nature of Christian conscientiousness, as the right conduct *within* that form of churchdom to which one may belong not only externally, but inwardly by a free and conscientious conviction regulated by God's word. The spirit of a proper course of behavior springs even there not from any churchdom in itself, but from that vital relation in which man is placed from baptism onwards to Christ and His kingdom, is thereby impressed in faith, and has through this faith become powerful in that love which desires to serve in Christ, and not to enjoy that which one has for himself as a "spoil." To fulfil and vivify what belongs to churchdom in the power of faith and love, and to carry it forth into the world and into all the relations of human life and society—that is to stand in the churchly bond after the spirit of the church of Jesus Christ, and to labor for the solution of the church's problem in this world and for this world. And this spirit is just as much a spirit of true churchmanship, in contrast alike with that *subjectivism which refuses all obligations*, as well as with *external legality*, and in

contrast with that *churchmanship which limits itself only to churchdom.*

It is peculiar to the true faith, that it makes itself felt as a personal and individual possession of the freest nature, as a deliverance from human authority, freedom in Christ alone, bearing the law of its life in that Christ who rules and lives not only above and without us, but within us. But as we are incorporated with this Christ as the Head of His body, and therefore not merely in individual and personal isolation, but in the relation of membership to other members under the same head; and as out of this faith that love is born which longs after fellowship among the members, and readily yields itself to the service of the members, there is implied in the divine nature and destination of this faith, that it should know itself as a faith common to all, impelled to a common display of faith and love in brotherhood. Such is the divine foundation of the ties of churchdom. Now, as we have seen, the churchly tie in itself certainly is not the realization of the divinely purposed and divinely effected community of faith and love, and has its existence in the form of law and right,—which form can neither in itself be called that of the vital law of the Christian, nor has arisen absolutely out of relations to the essential life-conditions and life-activities of Christian fellowship,—but has reference to a series of external relations, in which the churchly community, from its world-reality and the conditions of its external existence, stands and must stand in this its earthly existence. A whole series of churchly ordinances could be named which owe their existence to the purely human and earthly phase of all social community, and possess in no wise a divinely obligatory force, except in the general sense in which all legally established ordinances of a human community are conformable to the divine order of God's will expressed in creation. But even here there holds good for the members of the churchdom, who have not ascertained its system of ordinance as being in essentials contrary to their faith grounded on the word of God, what applies to the members of a political community. It appertains not to the convictions, to say nothing of the will of the individual, to lay down the law, but to the consciousness of the whole community in common organized action. If the law has been established, the individual submits himself to its injunctions. Christian liberty in the individual does not become a charter for disorder and caprice; least of all under the pretext that a number of ordinances are purely of human origin. It would be very bad if a churchdom had nothing to show of purely human shaping. For this would only be a proof that the divine foundations and forces by which it is supported in its ultimate ground, had remained without fruit, faith without works, the working of the Divine Spirit without any reproductivity in the spirit of man. A human regulation, however, in the most objectionable sense of the word, is not that which in churchdom proceeds from man, but that which, while it is of human origin, is put forth as divine, and of divine obligation, as necessary for salvation, as a means of grace or as a divine law, on whose observance salvation, favor with God, justification before God, depend. Against such ordinances must Christian freedom in Christ oppose itself. But whatever else is an ordinance deserving of praise, we observe for the sake of order, and of love, and of peace (πάντα εὐσχημόνως καὶ κατὰ τάξιν γινέσθω, 1 Cor. 14:40).

Such observance, when it flows from the spirit of faith and love, has not then, however, in this domain of churchly ordinances (on whichever of them one may choose to think), the nature of the performance of a mere legal obligation. Here applies what was previously said (§ 54, note (2)), with reference to the state, on the meaning of law and the observance of law in comparison with the problem of moral perfection. And the more that a churchly legal system desires to rest in the service of that divine order of life and society which has for its vital rule the means and powers of Christ's kingdom of grace, so much the less is it a fulfilling of the appointed service of the legal code of churchdom, if, determined merely by the legal rule of the community, in external conformity of action with the objects of this law, and by a due legal obedience, we satisfy that which belongs to the church as her right. This mere legal correctness, which does nothing that is against these external ordinances, but which in its actions has no other aim than the observance of the outward ordinance, is, where it attains the sole ascendency, fatal to all genuine churchly life. For not only may such a conformity of conduct be exhibited without any correspondence of the mind and spirit of those legally obedient, with that spirit and faith from which the church's legal ordinances took their rise, but this mere external legality reacts in an equally pernicious way on individuals as on the churchly community. It impedes the development of that which constitutes the essence of the church, the fellowship of the Holy Ghost, from being a community of those regenerated to the liberty of the children of God in evangelical faith and love. The whole internal character of the church and her members becomes, through this mere legality of churchly observance, mere externality, a dead work, a worship of legal institutions, of legally valid form and order, of legal obedience, which, itself void of spirit and life, neither fosters nor produces spiritual life, and in place of the worship of God in spirit and in truth, but reduces it to a legal and ceremonial character. Such is the natural and unavoidable result, if the legal ordinances of churchdom, in place of being kept to their purpose of instrumental service in the church, are regarded as an end in themselves and identified with the church, if her legal forms are viewed as means of grace; and if legal obedience to these is held to be the fulfilment of their object, instead of our laboring for ourselves and others, in order that these churchly forms should find their fulfilment not in a kind of external legal observance, but in the spirit of the church of Jesus Christ, her faith and her love. Where this is not done, all merely legal churchly obedience, as an external and dead work, profits nothing.

Finally, just as little is he who sees in the legal code of churchdom and its legal observance at once the problem of the church and its members realized, and suffers it to be exhausted therein, in a position to take a just view of that relation which the highest earthly community, the church, is called upon to occupy with regard to the other forms of human society. For the legal regulations of the church serve in themselves only for marking off the sphere in which the religious community has, with a view to the preservation and securing of its common existence and duties, given an expression to the fundamental law of the order of its inner life in the shape of external laws and order. These legal rules of churchdom cannot, nor are intended to become, *the* legal rule for other human common objects: they cannot, nor are they intended to have as their object, to lay down as church law those natural moral tendencies on which, for the aims of this earthly existence, the other relations of human society depend. It is not the natural system of the relations of human society established at creation, but that communion of God with man and man with God, restored by God's redeeming act in Christ, and the aims hereby set before us of that future perfection, which form the basis of that relation of fellowship from which springs the peculiar nature of the legislation of churchdom, whose duties thereby defined are specifically distinguished from the legal duties of the relations and ordinances of other communities. Here it cannot be objected that the church also recognizes such ordinances as have for the Christian a churchly obligation of right in connection with the relations of the Christian to the naturally established associations of society. This, for example, in reference to marriage (comp. § 52, note (3)), the institution of the state, in churchly acts of benediction, churchly recognition of lawful authority and lawful order, and the like. For all this respects not the ordinance itself, but the Christian who enters into such ordinance. What takes place on the part of the church does not first establish the ordinances in their legality, but is only the church's legal expression for the Christian's obligation to recognize, partly the divine basis of such ordinances, partly their need of sanctification by the Spirit of God's grace. The particular and specific right which belongs to marriage and the married, to the state and the bearers of its order and authority, is not first established by the church, as was the doctrine of the Middle Ages. There is only laid down in the form of churchly right, the Christian's duty to verify the Christian view of such social relations resting upon a divinely ordained natural foundation, on his entering into them, by the performance of a legal churchly ordinance. By such an actual procedure, however, the inner sanctification of these relations is far from being accomplished, as the church strives to realize it; and the means of this can neither here nor in other relations be or pretend to be the legal institutions of churchdom in themselves consistently with their nature. Hence also the danger of a so-called churchly frame of mind, which falsely confines itself to the legal duties of churchdom, but not as if these forms of churchly rights had in themselves sprung from evil, but because one attributes to churchdom an import which it does not possess, and so views the same, or enjoins it to be viewed, as if the legal ordinance of churchdom in itself were the realization of the destiny of the church, and the accomplishment of these churchly obligations in itself the fulfilment of the life-problem of the members of Christ's kingdom, the essential church, in this world and for this world. Conversely, it is rather the destiny of the church of Jesus Christ and its true members to stamp all the relations of human society with the spirit of *the church*, the spirit of Christianity—to enjoin men to seek, and to assist them in seeking, moral perfection in the solution of those problems of life which are placed in these domains, and are peculiar to them, only in the spirit of Christianity; and all this in that character of free action which belongs to the moral personality of the Christian, which neither in its origin nor its form is the mere fulfilling of a legal obligation of churchdom, nor makes legal rules of churchdom the legislative principle of the forms of natural human society, but rather in all earthly relations of the communities of men brings the influence of those relations vitally to bear which flow from the spirit and the life of regeneration, and which verify their renewing, sanctifying, and glorifying power, in everything which belongs to man's earthly existence. If this object is not kept in view, and if churchliness of sentiment confines itself to churchdom, to the mere care for the public forms of the church, the legal institutions of churchdom, then arises that unwholesome separation, in which the churchly institute may indeed remain a sanctuary; but the outside world, the family, the state, the whole life of the spirit, is given and abandoned over to the profane spirit. Such a separation can only then be looked upon as natural, or consistent with the nature of the church, if in some quite inconceivable manner we regarded the church as a creation out of nothing, which, I know not how, happened to be placed alongside the spheres and life-domains of the order of nature connected with man; or if we identified the latter with that corruption of nature against which the church of Christ on earth has certainly her work,—not, however, as a destroyer of that order of nature, but as a restorer, by purification and sanctification, of the minds of those who belong to such natural ordinances. And to such ordinances of nature belong all those who are or will be Christians, and as such do not cease to belong to the household, the family, the public community, the state, in which they are by their natural human existence rooted. What the church, therefore, owes to her members in this aspect, cannot be better negatively expressed than Nitzsch has done, when he says: "She (the church, *i.e.* churchdom) may not operate either as doctrine, or as morals, or ritually, in a spirit opposed to what is citizenship, or the household, or nature" (*Prakt. Theol.*). And since the whole of man's intellectual life, in its efforts to understand the natural aims of his being, to cultivate those means which minister both to the perception and realization of these aims, and to foster a rational and moral spirit, in opposition to the blindness and crudeness of the natural instincts, goes to form a historical life of civilization, whose fruits are not, forsooth, one and all civilized corruptions (and would be such only in Rousseau's view), but blessings of that divinely-willed human development which is natural to man's spiritual organization; therefore we might even venture further to say with the same good reason, that the church may not operate in that which she establishes in her external form as churchdom in a spirit hostile to this civilization. All these are negative definitions, and in a certain sense are not at all the business of the church, as an institution, to enter upon. For vital relations and the moral or intellectual impulses of life, which have for their root creative natural tendencies and dispositions, which belong to man as such, and hence must be so left to human fostering, that this fostering can and ought to follow no other rules than those which are given in the development (belonging to the history of civilization) of those natural tendencies and dispositions—for such relations and impulses of life the church cannot pretend to create positive institutions, without taking up a ground which does not at all belong to her as such. For the church has not for her foundation that natural basis on which the social relations of man's earthly existence rest, within which the general human culture develops itself in a human, creaturely, historical manner; and she would on her part abandon her essential task, if she wished to become an institution for human culture. But it does not lie outside her task, but within it, that she should not permit anything to crop up among her members which would alienate them from the care of those duties which appertain to man's earthly life; and it behooves her members not to allow the household, the state, to stand beside the church, and without relation to it, but to sanctify and ennoble all domestic and civil virtue, all struggle and action of the human spirit, with the influence of those sentiments, of that faith and that love whose spring is not churchdom in its external form, but rather its inmost sanctuary, that Christ who works in word and sacrament, for whose service the church community is established. For this reason *churchly* sentiment consists just in this, to allow in nothing either a false separation or a false mingling of those vital ordinances to arise, in which the Christian finds himself placed by his earthly and his heavenly vocation,—either to be confused with one another, or to be torn asunder, but to be maintained for each other. This, however, will also only attain a practical accomplishment, in proportion as the churchly sentiment guards churchdom and church, the kingdom of Christ, from false blending as well as from separation, neither confounding them together nor rudely dividing them, but maintaining them for each other. Otherwise, man looks upon churchdom as the "immediate and sole reality, and divinely appointed carrying out of the kingdom of God;" whereas it is only the mountain fortress of the divine institutions of grace, from whose believing acceptance there flows forth that spirit of divine life, which has the task and the power to introduce, in sentiment, word, and deed, every domain of creaturely life into that vital power of Christ's kingdom which renews and glorifies the world.

www.ingramcontent.com/pod-product-compliance
Lightning Source LLC
Chambersburg PA
CBHW070712160426
43192CB00009B/1162